Negro League
Baseball

THE RISE AND RUIN OF A BLACK INSTITUTION

Negro League Baseball

NEIL LANCTOT

UNIVERSITY OF PENNSYLVANIA PRESS

Philadelphia

10   9   8   7   6   5   4   3

Published by
University of Pennsylvania Press
Philadelphia, Pennsylvania 19104-4011

Library of Congress Cataloging-in-Publication Data

Lanctot, Neil, 1966
    Negro league baseball : the rise and ruin of a Black institution / Neil Lanctot.
        p.   cm.
    ISBN 0-8122-3807-9 (cloth : alk. paper)
    Includes bibliographical references and index.
    1. Negro leagues—History.   2. Baseball—United States—History.   I. Title.
GV875.N35 L36   2004
796.357'64'0973—dc22   2004043547

Contents

Preface

Sunday, August 13, 1944, was a sweltering day in Chicago. The 98° heat, however, hardly deterred the 46,000-plus baseball fans at Comiskey Park who had purchased tickets not to see the struggling fifth-place White Sox but to enjoy the East-West game, an annual promotion featuring black all-star teams representing the Negro National and Negro American Leagues. While the West eventually took the contest by a 7-4 score, the outcome was less significant than the phenomenal attendance, which surpassed every major league game played that day.

On the surface, the game was an unparalleled triumph for the NNL and NAL owners, who grossed nearly $56,000 for the promotion. After a decade of nonexistent profits, black professional baseball had truly come into its own by 1944, enjoying consistently strong attendance for league games. Yet the East-West game was riddled with problems, reflecting the industry's vulnerability and instability even at its healthiest period. Satchel Paige, black baseball's most marketable commodity, failed to participate after a dispute involving allocation of the game's profits. A threatened strike nearly resulted in the game's cancellation until the owners yielded to the players' demands for increased wages. Finally, in the aftermath of the game, two all-stars bolted their teams to join an outlaw promoter and were eventually followed by several other league performers.[1]

The key figure behind the strike and player jumps was Gus Greenlee, an African American entrepreneur from Pittsburgh who was involved in a number of enterprises, both legitimate and illegitimate. As Greenlee sat in his box seat that August afternoon at Comiskey Park, he likely experienced a mixture of pride and dismay. The promotion he had helped establish eleven years earlier and the institution he had simultaneously helped preserve had evolved into substantial money-making propositions. Yet despite his crucial involvement, Greenlee now found himself shunned by his fellow owners and unable to reclaim his position in black professional baseball. Hoping to reemerge as a force in the industry, Greenlee engineered a desperate series of moves that weekend in Chicago designed to undermine the established leagues.

Buoyed by wartime profits, most owners remained confident of their ability to withstand the threat of Greenlee or any other rival promoter. Few realized, however, that their segregation-driven monopoly on black talent and fans would come to an abrupt end in only fourteen months with the signing of Jackie Robinson by the Brooklyn Dodgers. Within four years, the leagues would be struggling to survive and within ten, the East-West game and the industry itself would be virtually irrelevant.

◆ ◆ ◆

The rise and fall of black professional baseball provides a window into several major themes in modern African American history, illustrating the initial response to segregation, the subsequent struggle to establish successful separate enterprises, and the later movement toward integration. Unofficially banned from the white major and minor leagues in the late nineteenth century, blacks responded by establishing their own professional organizations and ultimately succeeded in creating, in the words of writer Gerald Early, a "more elaborate and enduring institutional relationship with baseball than with any other sport."[2] Providing entertainment for thousands of fans throughout the country, baseball functioned as a critical component of the separate economy catering to black consumers in the urban centers of the north and south. While most black businesses struggled to survive from year to year, professional teams and leagues operated for several decades, representing a major achievement in black enterprise and institution building.

Few would disagree that baseball occupied an undeniably important social and economic role in black communities. Yet Negro League baseball, unlike other major black institutions such as the press, churches, colleges, insurance companies, and protest groups, remains poorly understood by both serious historians and the general public. Although well intentioned, too many accounts of black baseball have been marred by reductive analyses, an appalling number of inaccuracies, and a tendency to categorize the principal administrative figures (both white and black) into a simplistic hero/villain dichotomy. Moreover, like a good deal of baseball history in general, the literature has often focused on the exploits of individual players and teams without attention to historical context or the actual administration of the leagues themselves.[3]

My motivation in writing this book was to transcend earlier accounts and provide a much-needed scholarly non-nostalgic look at the inner workings of the eastern-based Negro National League (1933–1948) and the black baseball industry in general during three crucial periods of its growth: the Depression, World War II, and the beginnings of the Civil Rights era. Yet achieving this goal proved more difficult than I anticipated. The principal league figures are long deceased, and only a modest amount of documents, interviews, and correspondence have survived.

Facing these barriers, I initially turned to the weekly black press which remains perhaps the most valuable source of information on the African American experience during the first half of the twentieth century. Rather than relying exclusively on the *Pittsburgh Courier* and *Chicago Defender*, as many other historians have done, I attempted to read virtually *every* sports page of every black newspaper located in a league city. As I read multiple accounts of various developments and events, I was slowly able to piece together the outline of a still-fragmented story. I was also able to reconstruct, to a limited extent, the lives of the entrepreneurs who operated these leagues, although detailed accounts of their backgrounds generally remain elusive to historians.

With a basic understanding of the industry and its leaders in place, I then moved on to other primary sources. I interviewed several former players, scrutinized existing financial records and correspondence, and unearthed material from court and federal records. By the time my research was complete, I had a greater appreciation of the complexities and nuances of black baseball that previously have been largely overlooked.

This book traces the national development of the black baseball business from its lowest ebb in the worst days of the Depression to its extinction during the early years of the Civil Rights movement. The eleven chapters are primarily structured chronologically, tracing the three distinct phases of the industry's growth: failure (1933–1940), success (1941–1946), and irrelevance (1947–1960s), with close attention to larger contextual developments shaping each period. (By "industry," I refer to the organized structure of professional black baseball consisting of both the Negro American and Negro National Leagues, although the focus here is on the more profitable NNL.) Chapters 6 and 7, however, depart from the chronology to treat two vital issues thematically: the experiences of players, owners, fans, and writers and the relationship between Major League Baseball and the Negro Leagues.

How did this industry evolve from near bankruptcy to become a short-lived "million dollar empire"?[4] The answer is complex and related to a number of unique internal and external factors during each developmental phase.

As noted, black baseball was one of a number of "race" institutions and enterprises created in response to segregation. During the 1920s, the combined forces of discrimination and urbanization created a conducive environment for the development of separate enterprises such as professional baseball. Yet the mass unemployment of the Depression destroyed most of the earlier economic gains. Struggling to keep the enterprise alive, entrepreneurs such as Greenlee coped with a number of difficulties during the 1930s, including weak administration, individualistic owners, inade-

quate financing, and uneven support. The industry also contended with a
press and public less tolerant of flawed black institutions, player defections
to foreign countries, and the growing appeal of boxer Joe Louis, whose
triumphs in a largely interracial setting occasionally overshadowed the exploits of black baseball teams in a segregated environment.

In the early 1940s, however, the seemingly stagnant industry revived.
After years of decline, the economic status of blacks suddenly improved,
thanks to wartime developments. Black unemployment dropped considerably in league cities, enabling several teams to attract unprecedented
crowds of fans flush with discretionary income. Not surprisingly, the increased profits generated increasing anxiety over the involvement of white
promoters. Changing racial ideologies during the war raised additional
concerns, as the growing advocacy of integration in all facets of American
life suggested that the current prosperity of this "shadow" institution
might be short-lived.

As anticipated, the foundation for the segregation-driven monopoly
proved shaky, increasingly weakened by the movement for the reintegration of Organized Baseball. Yet as this movement gained momentum in
the early 1940s, the role of black professional baseball drew increasing
scrutiny. While some officials favored integration, black baseball, like
other race businesses, undoubtedly had much to gain by the maintenance
of segregation. Moreover, the fate of black franchises had become increasingly intertwined with Organized Baseball, whose parks allowed black
teams to draw larger crowds, gain greater publicity, and achieve a new
level of legitimacy. Not surprisingly, black baseball failed to develop a
coherent plan to prepare adequately for the looming prospect of integration and was caught off guard by Branch Rickey's 1945 signing of Jackie
Robinson of the Kansas City Monarchs, a triumph for the nation's African
Americans but an embarrassment for industry officials.

The decline of black baseball in the post-Robinson era was inevitable.
As African Americans made gradual yet perceptible progress into the
American mainstream in the late 1940s and early 1950s, the value and
purpose of all-black organizations, hospitals, and other once-cherished
separate institutions came under scrutiny. Black teams could not hope to
compete with the enormous symbolic appeal of Jackie Robinson and the
handful of other black players now appearing in the major leagues, although the actual integration of Organized Baseball initially remained
minimal. Moreover, African Americans grew increasingly impervious to
racial pleas touting the continued utility of black teams, instead gravitat-
ing to major league baseball, an enterprise not only far superior in organization, publicity, and financing but now increasingly available through
radio and television. Player sales to Organized Baseball and dates in the

segregated south enabled several clubs to operate into the early 1950s, but the industry had clearly outlived its usefulness for black athletes who found better opportunities with white teams. The virtual extinction of black professional baseball by 1960 ultimately concerned few African Americans, many of whom viewed the institution as an unfortunate reminder of a segregated past. Yet regardless of their flaws, the Negro Leagues and other aspects of black institutional life performed an indisputable service by providing African Americans with otherwise unavailable training and experience, facilitating eventual gains made during desegregation.

This summary highlights the major themes explored in this study; the chapters that follow also attempt to present the evolving responses and attitudes of fans, players, journalists, and owners toward black baseball, demonstrating the gradual philosophical change among African Americans toward the development and necessity of separate institutions. Wherever possible, I have intentionally allowed the historical actors to speak in their own voices, employing quotes culled from a close examination of a wide range of archival sources, newspaper accounts, and interviews. This technique hopefully will not only add vibrancy to the narrative but provide a more evocative portrait of an industry and a people.

A number of individuals have assisted me in bringing this manuscript to publication. I particularly wish to thank Professors Raymond Wolters of the University of Delaware, Jules Tygiel of San Francisco State University, Rob Ruck of the University of Pittsburgh, and David Wiggins of George Mason University, all of whom read earlier drafts and offered invaluable criticisms and suggestions. Robert Lockhart, the history editor at the University of Pennsylvania Press, provided immeasurable assistance during the prepublication phase of this project. Finally, I would like to thank Dr. Larry Hogan of Union County College, Dr. Robert Weems of the University of Missouri, Larry Lester, Dick Clark, and John Holway, all of whom graciously lent me photographs or provided other materials used in this book.

PART I
SEPARATE BUT EQUAL?

1

A Fragile Industry and a Struggling Community

This is the year of the depression, and baseball will again
have a lean and hungry look at the end of the coming season.
—Black sportswriter Rollo Wilson, January 1933

The unfortunate position of black professional baseball by 1933 reflected
the disturbing decline of a once promising enterprise. The effects of the
Depression threatened to destroy an industry whose stability and future
success had appeared secure only a decade earlier. Yet from its beginnings,
black baseball had faced a number of difficulties, and the transformation
from amateur sport to commercial force had been gradual, fitful, and often
rocky.

Professional baseball in the United States arose in the late nineteenth
century largely through the intertwined processes of urbanism and indus-
trialism. Evolving from other bat-and-ball games such as rounders and
cricket, baseball became professionalized by 1870, as factories increasingly began to dot the urban landscape of the north and midwest, and
thousands of workers streamed into the cities to man the new machines.
Enduring long hours of tedious and often monotonous labor, urban industrial laborers eagerly sought cheap amusements during their limited leisure
time, and professional baseball emerged to help fill the void. By 1900,
professional franchises represented nearly every major city in the United
States. Continued economic and industrial growth coupled with a rising
standard of living and shorter working hours enabled white professional
baseball, along with other commercialized amusements, to enjoy unparalleled growth during the first quarter of the twentieth century.[1]

Baseball among African Americans developed concurrently, although
the relatively modest urban black population in the north prior to World
War I hindered the professional game's evolution. Philadelphia, already
home to 22,000 African Americans by 1860, was a key location in the

early years of black baseball. Facing discrimination and segregation, local blacks organized their own teams, most notably the amateur Pythian Club in the late 1860s. The Pythians, however, were subsequently barred from membership in two amateur organizations: the National Association of Base Ball Players and the Pennsylvania state association, foreshadowing the eventual de facto exclusion of African Americans from white professional baseball later in the century. In response, African Americans in Philadelphia and elsewhere embraced the self-help strategy advocated by Booker T. Washington in the late nineteenth century. Rather than actively agitate for participation in Organized Baseball (defined as the major and minor leagues), blacks began to build separate institutions of their own, forming their own amateur and later professional teams by the mid-1880s. Unable to survive solely through the support of the black community, black teams earned the bulk of their income playing white independent "semipro" clubs outside Organized Baseball, a near constant practice during much of the existence of black professional baseball.

Black baseball and other enterprises, however, benefited from a substantial increase in the urban black population after 1900. As economic and social conditions declined for southern blacks in the late 1890s, a steady stream migrated to northern industrial cities, resulting in the development of sizable African American communities in Chicago (44,000), New York (92,000), and Philadelphia (85,000) by 1910. The burgeoning black "metropolises" of the northeast and midwest facilitated the establishment of separate hospitals, banks, self-help organizations, publications, and businesses, most notably the continued expansion and development of black baseball. From about 1890 to 1916, a number of professional teams emerged, generally in the larger black communities in the east, mid-Atlantic, and midwest, but also in upper south cities such as St. Louis and later Baltimore. Typically, a team's extensive travel, nearly constant schedule of games, and payment of players determined its professional status. Yet black professional teams remained unorganized, lacking league affiliation and the formal contracts employed in white Organized Baseball, which bound players to individual clubs.

Black professional teams also contended with limited financial backing, and like other African American institutions, seldom operated without direct or indirect white assistance. Few black entrepreneurs possessed the necessary capital, and even those with adequate resources were unenthusiastic about investing in something as uncertain as a professional baseball team. Moreover, because of rampant prejudice, blacks at least initially needed whites to lease playing fields and arrange games with white opponents, and white booking agents, controlling parks and schedules, soon became a permanent yet controversial fixture in black baseball.

Despite the encroachment of whites, black entrepreneurs such as Andrew "Rube" Foster in Chicago and C. I. Taylor in Indianapolis gradually began to make a greater impact prior to World War I. In the east, the formation of the black-owned Hilldale Club of Darby, Pennsylvania, in 1910 marked the beginning of a new era. Organized as a local amateur boys' team in the Philadelphia suburbs, the club eventually rose to professional prominence under the management of a postal employee, Edward W. Bolden.

Bolden, Foster, and other black baseball entrepreneurs capitalized on the effect of the Great Migration of 1916–1919, when 500,000 blacks, responding to northern industrial demands and deteriorating social and economic conditions, left the south for the urban north. The black population in Philadelphia rose to 134,000 by 1920, and urban centers such as New York, Chicago, Cleveland, and Detroit recorded similar increases, spurring unparalleled growth and development of black enterprises. Bolden's Hilldale, for instance, enjoyed remarkable success from World War I through the mid-1920s, thanks to an expanding fan base, as well as a convenient and central location that allowed easy travel to New York, Baltimore, and Atlantic City for profitable games. The growth of Hilldale occurred as part of a national trend of remarkable profits for professional black teams, leading to the formation of the first permanent professional black leagues: Foster's midwest-based Negro National League (NNL) in February 1920, followed by a Bolden-headed eastern organization, the Eastern Colored League, in December 1922.

Yet as the economic fortunes of African Americans began to deteriorate in the mid-1920s, the leagues experienced a concurrent decline. In the west, sportswriter A. D. Williams warned of a "downward trend of interest in Negro baseball" by 1930, citing a disturbing attendance drop in Chicago, once the most profitable venue in the NNL. Within a year, the city's American Giants, organized by Foster two decades earlier, had dropped out of the league and temporarily ceased to be a relevant factor in the midwest. The abrupt loss of the American Giants disturbed veteran western observer Frank "Fay" Young, who questioned how "a great big city like Chicago" could be without a top black team.

Philadelphia, the strongest city in the Eastern Colored League, experienced similar difficulties. A local industrial recession after 1925 crippled the black community, as numerous blacks, typically the last hired and first fired, found themselves unemployed even prior to the onset of the Great Depression. As unemployment mounted, attendance began to drop at Hilldale Park, falling from an average of 1,844 per holiday/Saturday game in 1926 to 1,371 three years later.

The Depression only intensified the difficulties of Hilldale and black

professional baseball, and Ed Bolden, seemingly aware of the increasingly
fragile economic situation, attempted to dissolve the Hilldale corporation
in 1930. While Bolden was blocked by other corporation members and
subsequently ousted from the organization, Hilldale, like other black enterprises, struggled to survive in the harsh environment. Black patronage,
tenuous under even the most favorable conditions, declined to an insubstantial level, as black urban unemployment reached well over 50 percent
nationally by 1932. Not surprisingly, Hilldale was forced to disband in
July 1932, after drawing a total of only 295 fans for its last two Saturday
home games, revealing the startling descent of a once prosperous black
baseball industry.[2]

◆ ◆ ◆

The plight of Hilldale, a major organization with a payroll and investment
far beyond the scope of most black enterprises in Philadelphia, was an
inevitable consequence of the Depression, whose effects destabilized numerous white and black businesses. The large urban black communities
of the north, long the pillars of the industry, found themselves contending
with a discouraging set of social and economic forces likely to deter even
the hardiest of promoters.

Black employment opportunities, limited even under the most ideal conditions by discrimination, fell to a new low during the 1930s. Unskilled
labor opportunities that had once provided the bulk of black employment
began to disappear, prompting a YMCA official to complain in 1933 that
"numerous jobs used to be considered our positions [but] as jobs became
more scarce . . . our workers in high and lowly positions were replaced by
whites." Reflecting the shockingly fragile status of African Americans in
some cities, only 13 percent of black Philadelphians were employed full-
time from late 1929 through 1935. By 1935, roughly half of all northern
black families were receiving relief, while in southern cities such as Atlanta, a startling 65 percent of black workers required public assistance.[3]

In such an environment, the potential for building a separate, self-sustaining black economy became increasingly bleak. During the 1920s, the
expanding black urban population had facilitated the establishment and
expansion of separate race-owned and supported enterprises, intended to
provide increased economic opportunity, independence, and employment
for African Americans. Yet many black businesses had struggled to survive
even during the relatively stable financial climate of the post-World War I
era. Catering exclusively to black trade, lacking capital and access to
credit, and often competing with better financed white businesses, black

enterprises continually encountered nearly insurmountable barriers that would only worsen during the Depression.

Typically, the most successful businesses were small service-oriented establishments such as barbershops, beauty parlors, cemeteries, and funeral parlors, all of which served blacks in ways that whites would not. Yet black support of these and other "race" enterprises remained problematic, as black entrepreneurs could seldom anticipate the wholehearted and unquestioned backing of the entire community. An informal survey conducted in 1937 of whether "members of the Race [were] ever justified in not trading at Race Stores" revealed the diverse set of factors determining patronage. While one respondent asserted that "we are justified in helping because that's the only way the merchant is able to compete against other stores," others refused to be swayed by racial appeals, contending that support of black stores should be contingent upon "price, service and quality." Yet another respondent argued that trading exclusively at black stores was "an endorsement of segregation."[4]

As the possibility of establishing profitable businesses grew remote during the 1930s, several organizations increasingly shifted their emphasis from encouraging economic self-development to securing employment in white-owned businesses located in black neighborhoods. Utilizing a more militant picketing and boycott strategy, "Don't Buy Where You Can't Work" campaigns emerged in Chicago, Philadelphia, and New York. Yet some African Americans rejected the use of pressure tactics, such as journalist Samuel Reading, who felt it "silly for people who have no proprietary interests in a given establishment to try and blackjack people into hiring folks they don't need or want," and instead touted "sensible people . . . going right ahead establishing business of their own."

Reading's comments reflected the views of a segment of the African American community still supportive of the philosophy of building strong separate institutions, offering hope for a potential revival of black professional baseball. As one woman observed, since African Americans had successfully established their own churches, they should be able to develop "flourishing enterprises such as department stores, factories, etc. ice cream firms, bakeries . . . any industry that is a profit to the other races could be a profit to our race." Moreover, the continued prevalence of segregation and discrimination in many theaters, hotels, cafes, and other places of amusement seemingly provided opportunities to establish facilities catering exclusively to the black trade. White entrepreneurs, however, controlled many of the major recreation centers in the largest black population centers. As early as 1929, Roy Wilkins noted that not one dance hall in the jazz mecca of Kansas City was owned by blacks. The majority of cabarets, clubs, and cafes in Philadelphia catering to blacks were also white-owned, a phenomenon similarly apparent in New York, where whites controlled the popular Savoy Ballroom and Apollo Theater in the late 1930s.[5]

Sports, however, offered another area of commercialized amusement still ripe for exploitation by black entrepreneurs. With the exception of a handful of blacks in the National Football League (NFL) during the early 1930s, the major professional sports organizations remained all-white during the decade. The stance suited the average white fan, including one northerner who insisted in 1934 that blacks "should be kept from playing in National and American League Parks. To permit them to play lowers standards and creates race rivalry." Contending with such attitudes, African Americans had little choice but to continue to organize and develop their own sporting activities at the professional and semiprofessional level.

The profitability of each sport differed considerably. Notably, football never attracted a tremendous amount of support, although Lincoln University's annual Thanksgiving Day game with Howard University was a popular social event, as were other black college games. The lack of suitable playing grounds, meager financial returns, and the cost of equipment hindered the development of black football teams at both the professional and amateur levels. Meanwhile, the exploits of Jesse Owens at the 1936 Olympic games sparked greater interest in track and field, although the potential earnings for black track stars were insignificant. Black professional basketball teams, with the exception of the Harlem Globetrotters and the legendary Renaissance 5 of New York, also remained marginal, never able to develop an organization anywhere near that of the Negro Leagues. Reflecting the limited financial opportunities, the strongest black basketball teams in New York reportedly earned only $50 to $75 per game in 1937.[6]

Boxing, however, assumed the greatest symbolic role in the sporting lives of African Americans during the 1930s, mainly due to the rise of Detroit heavyweight Joe Louis, who became world champion in 1937. As Louis neared the heavyweight title, his interracial fights engendered profound reactions among blacks, who anxiously awaited the outcome while "crowding around either automobile radios or in doorways of stores." Yet, with the exception of a handful of outstanding black fighters such as Louis and Henry Armstrong, the profits from professional boxing were modest. Moreover, despite the rising influence of black managers such as John Roxborough and Gus Greenlee, white promoters such as Mike Jacobs retained tight control of the industry.[7]

As a business enterprise, professional baseball continued to offer the greatest potential for black entrepreneurs seeking to invest in sports during the 1930s, due to the expense of football, modest interest in basketball, and white control of boxing. Yet the successful promotion of sports enterprises, white and black, became increasingly difficult as the Depression worsened; as historian Charles Alexander has observed, the decade was a "bleak period for baseball entrepreneurs or anybody else trying to make money in professional sports."[8]

Reflecting the dire state of the industry, several minor leagues in Organized Baseball suspended operation during 1932, while others reduced salaries, player rosters, and ticket prices in an attempt to remain solvent. Black professional baseball teams similarly suffered, not only from the effect on black patronage but also from the concurrent loss of lucrative games with white semipro teams, many of whom were forced to disband. Meanwhile, the Depression destroyed whatever fragmented structure existed among black teams nationally. The Negro National League, in decline since founder Rube Foster's institutionalization in 1926, collapsed after the 1931 season, while the East-West League, an ambitious attempt spearheaded by Homestead Grays owner Cumberland ("Cum") Posey, disbanded halfway through its first season a year later. By late 1932, black professional baseball in the east and midwest had virtually returned to its pre-1920 status of a handful of unaffiliated professional teams scheduling exhibition games on little more than an ad hoc basis.[9]

In the punishing Depression environment, the black baseball owner as a legitimate entrepreneur, exemplified in the 1920s by Bolden in Philadelphia, Foster in Chicago, and Posey in the Pittsburgh region, found it increasingly difficult to operate alone. Lacking adequate financial resources, they began to look for additional backing from two sources: white booking agents and black underworld figures involved in profitable, yet illegal enterprises such as the numbers lottery.

With the decline in black patronage, the already considerable influence of booking agents grew even larger. More than ever, survival for black teams depended on a steady diet of dates provided by promoters such as Nat Strong in New York and Eddie Gottlieb in Philadelphia. Receiving a booking fee of 5 to 10 percent, Strong and Gottlieb controlled most of the parks as well as the schedules of the strong white semipro teams in the east. Although disliking Strong's occasionally frankly exploitive tactics and policies, even Posey was forced to admit that in 1932 "no club in the East could have finished without the help of Strong" and felt that the promoter was "due much credit for the help he gave colored baseball in 1932."[10]

Simultaneously, black underworld figures, long a part of the industry and seemingly impervious to Depression conditions, would provide a necessary influx of capital into the moribund enterprise. The most spectacular example occurred in Pittsburgh, where William Augustus "Gus" Greenlee made a sudden entrance into professional black baseball in the early 1930s as the owner of the Crawfords. Born in 1895 in North Carolina, Greenlee was the son of a masonry contractor. His mother was half-white, the illegitimate offspring of a well-known local white man. After spending his early years in the south, Greenlee migrated to Pittsburgh prior to World War I, working as a taxi driver and then serving in the 367th Infantry Regiment/153rd Depot Brigade during the war. Returning to Pittsburgh in 1919, Greenlee soon became involved in bootlegging. Along with Latrobe Brewery owner Joe Tito, his white partner, Greenlee eventually profited heavily through the illegal numbers lottery (discussed more fully in Chapter 2). By 1933, Greenlee's financial empire included two hotels, a restaurant (the Crawford Grille), and several other enterprises in Pittsburgh.

Greenlee, like other numbers operators, enjoyed considerable support from urban blacks and also cultivated close ties with the local Republican party. Judy Johnson, who jumped Hilldale to join the Crawfords in 1932, recalled that Greenlee, despite his sometimes questionable activities, was "no killer" and "sincerely cared about the community . . . stayed away from stuff that really hurt people . . . like protection, dope and loan sharking." Greenlee also won local approval through his contributions to the National Association for the Advancement of Colored People (NAACP) and the "thousands of dollars' worth of turkeys and good eats" he gave away every Christmas.[11]

To further build community support, Greenlee also began in 1931 to finance the Pittsburgh Crawfords, a young sandlot team organized during the 1920s and named for a municipal recreation center located near his restaurant. By 1932, Greenlee had escalated his involvement by incorporating the team, signing professional players for the Crawfords and subsequently providing at least half of the financing for a ballpark in the heart of the heavily black populated "Hill" district of Pittsburgh. While not entirely financed by black capital, Greenlee Field, completed in 1932 during the midst of the Depression, represented a substantial, albeit flawed accomplishment and a nearly $100,000 investment. The construction of Greenlee Field, coupled with Greenlee's ownership of the Crawfords, not only solidified his community ties but simultaneously provided a convenient means of laundering profits from his numbers business.

The ascension of Greenlee's Crawfords, however, posed a serious threat to Cum Posey's western Pennsylvania-based Homestead Grays, who had long enjoyed nearly unquestioned dominance in the coal region. Despite a shared interest in baseball and the community, a clash between the two men was inevitable. As veteran player Dick Seay later observed, Greenlee "looked like the racketeer that he was. Dressed neat, big expensive hats, always a big crowd around him." In contrast, future Grays star first baseman Buck Leonard recalled that Posey "was an educated fellow, liked refined things."[12] Born in 1891 in Homestead, Posey was the son of Cum-

Figure 1. Gus Greenlee and friends, 1936.
Photo by Charles "Teenie" Harris. Courtesy
Carnegie Museum of Art, Pittsburgh.

berland Willis Posey, who had prospered in steamboat construction and
the coal business and later provided financial assistance to the fledgling
Pittsburgh Courier. Between 1909 and 1918, the younger Posey attended
Penn State, the University of Pittsburgh, and Duquesne, studying chemistry and pharmacy but achieving far greater success in sports than scholas-
tics. For two decades, Posey enjoyed a remarkable career, initially as a
basketball player and later as manager and promoter of the Grays. In
addition, Posey actively participated in local politics and had been elected
to the Homestead school board in 1931.[13]

Figure 2. Cum Posey (far left) with his Homestead Grays, 1931. Courtesy Baseball Hall of Fame Library.

As anticipated, Posey and Greenlee increasingly struggled over territory, players, and patronage, sending shock waves throughout the already beleaguered industry during 1932. Not surprisingly, Posey viewed the newly constructed Greenlee Field as a threat to the continued local success of the Grays, as its location was far more accessible than Forbes Field, the home of the major league's Pittsburgh Pirates, often rented by the Grays for home games. To counter Greenlee, Posey intentionally excluded the Crawfords when organizing the ill-fated East-West League, hoping to isolate them from the major black professional teams. After the Grays and the East-West League suffered severe financial setbacks by mid-season, however, Posey reconsidered and began to schedule games with the Crawfords. While the Grays won the season series against the Crawfords, Posey found himself unable to match Greenlee's superior financial resources. The Grays lost numerous star players to the Pittsburgh promoter, including Oscar Charleston and Josh Gibson, and as Jimmy Crutchfield of the Crawfords later recalled, the Grays "just seemed to disintegrate—just like that" in 1932. Notably, as Hilldale's fortunes similarly waned, several players also defected to the Crawfords, reportedly the only team to continue paying salaries in 1932.

Although Greenlee established his presence in the industry and drew a surprising 69,229 baseball fans to his park during 1932, his success came at a substantial cost. Despite his interest, business acumen, and relatively stable finances, the Crawfords reportedly lost at least $15,000 during the season. The Grays were hit equally hard, suffering their worst year financially in over two decades of operation. Virtually no black teams profited, and one club was reduced to paying opposing teams with IOUs. After almost 50 years of fitful development, black baseball as a business enterprise had reached its nadir by the end of 1932, perhaps best epitomized by the absence of a strong professional league. As veteran player, manager, and umpire Ben Taylor lamented, "our baseball has been going back for several years," and there seemed little to be done to stop the decline as the 1933 season approached.[14]

◆ ◆ ◆

The status of the industry was nearly uniformly bleak throughout the country. Historically, black professional baseball had developed predominantly around the major centers of African American population in the mid-Atlantic, midwest, and upper south. During the 1920s, franchises emerged in a number of cities, including Philadelphia, New York, Atlantic City, Harrisburg, Wilmington, and Newark in the east; Baltimore, Washington, and St. Louis in the upper south; Chicago, Cincinnati, Cleveland, Columbus, Dayton, Detroit, Indianapolis, Kansas City, Milwaukee, Pittsburgh, and Toledo in the midwest; and Memphis, Birmingham, and Nashville in the south. Yet even during the more economically stable decade, only a handful of cities had proved capable of supporting black baseball on a semi-regular basis. By 1933, the unfavorable economic conditions had only intensified the unique pre-existing difficulties inherent in each region, and even the strongest cities, regardless of their populations (see Table 1.1), seemed ill-fitted or unwilling to support franchises.

In the upper south region, the Baltimore Black Sox had enjoyed success during the 1920s as members of the eastern-based professional leagues, despite difficulties with white ownership under George Rossiter and inferior home grounds at Maryland Park. As the team's economic fortunes began to wane during 1932, Rossiter abandoned Maryland Park, which eventually became a junk lot, and turned his club over to Joe Cambria, a local white laundry owner who also promoted minor league and semiprofessional baseball. After drawing poorly at its new home, the Cambria-owned Bugle Field, the team took to the road by mid-summer. Sensing that the team's future was in doubt, several Black Sox players drifted to other organizations after the season. Adding to the team's woes, a rival

Table 1.1. Black population of selected cities, 1930

City	Population	National rank
New York	327,706	1
Chicago	233,903	2
Philadelphia	219,599	3
Baltimore	142,106	4
Detroit	120,066	7
Birmingham	99,077	8
Memphis	96,550	9
Cleveland	71,899	12
Pittsburgh	54,983	14
Indianapolis	43,967	19
Nashville	42,836	21
Kansas City	38,574	26

group sued over ownership of the team's name, and the franchise, now known as the Baltimore Sox, entered 1933 in a severely weakened state.[15]

In the midwest, the Chicago American Giants and Kansas City Monarchs had been the cornerstones of Rube Foster's defunct Negro National League. As noted, the once proud American Giants had been beset by increasing instability since the late 1920s. The return of black ownership in 1932 temporarily encouraged fans, as Robert A. Cole, a former Pullman porter and livery service operator, assumed control of the struggling team. Born in 1882, Cole had previously managed a gambling club for Daniel Jackson, a prosperous black Chicago funeral parlor owner also involved in illegal enterprises, and eventually purchased Jackson's Metropolitan Funeral System Association in 1927. Although the ascension of Cole, a capable entrepreneur and "professional" gambler who would preside over the successful Metropolitan company for 29 years, seemed to indicate a potential return to the glory days of the Foster era, park difficulties soon plagued the franchise. Formerly the home of the Chicago White Sox, the American Giants park at 39th and Wentworth Streets had been leased by the team's owners since 1911 and was conveniently located in the heart of the black belt. Yet prior to the start of the 1933 season, Cole surrendered his lease on the park to white promoters who planned to build a dog track on the site, leaving the American Giants without suitable home grounds and destroying their connection to black Chicagoans.

Unlike the American Giants, the Kansas City Monarchs had continued to benefit from strong and stable ownership. Organized in late 1919 as a charter member of the Negro National League, the team's white owner,

J. L. Wilkinson, had won nearly universal praise from black players, owners, and sportswriters as a fair and generous individual. Yet even Wilkinson had been forced to cut expenses, as the Monarchs played only
abbreviated seasons in 1931 and 1932, delaying their initial appearances
until July.[16]

In eastern cities, the status of black baseball paralleled the steady deterioration in Philadelphia since 1930. In New York, home of one of the
nation's largest black communities, fans had once supported the white-
owned Lincoln Giants, who had operated from 1911 until disbanding after
the 1930 season. The team's would-be successor, the New York Black
Yankees (originally the Harlem Stars), had been initially financed in 1931
by two white men: John Powers and Marty Forkins, the manager of black
entertainer Bill Robinson (whose own involvement with the team was minimal). The new team planned to rent Yankee Stadium and the Polo
Grounds for home games and was even equipped with old Yankee uniforms.

After Forkins and Powers soon abandoned the investment following financial setbacks, M. E. Goodson, a black cabaret owner and barber, and
his associate James Semler assumed control and operated the team
through 1932. Costly park rentals, however, limited the home appearances
of the Black Yankees, and by September 1932, Romeo Dougherty of the
New York Amsterdam News observed there was "not a game by Negroes
worth speaking of in the section." By 1933, Goodson had exhausted his
finances, leaving the Black Yankees on the verge of collapse and desperate
for fresh capital. The economically vulnerable team subsequently came
under the virtual full control of the always controversial promoter Nat
Strong. While the move disappointed some fans, Semler explained that
"we needed cash and couldn't get it from any colored business men so we
borrowed it from Strong."[17]

Despite seemingly poor prospects, New York and other eastern cities still
offered more promise than the south. While home to the majority of African Americans, the south had generally proven to be an unprofitable area
for black professional teams, remaining more valuable as a training
ground for young players. During the 1920s, Foster had attempted to include southern franchises, yet the considerable travel distance to other
league cities presented a constant obstacle. Moreover, southern clubs, isolated from lucrative interracial games because of segregation laws, typically could not compete financially with other teams. Since 1920, a series
of lower-level southern organizations had developed, and the most recent
attempt, the Negro Southern League, was the only circuit still operating at
the end of the 1932 season. Yet the affiliation of the Pittsburgh Crawfords
and Chicago American Giants with the league had been marred by the

same travel problems. Most observers agreed that the revival of black baseball seemed unlikely to emanate from the south. As one Chicago columnist explained, northern fans felt the region "comprises minor league territory, and you cannot make 'em see it differently."[18]

In such an unstable atmosphere for promoters and owners, the players themselves predictably found it increasingly difficult to eke out an existence. Team payrolls had peaked during the 1920s, when the most affluent professional black clubs such as Hilldale, the Chicago American Giants and the Baltimore Black Sox paid nearly $4,000 monthly in salaries, ranging from $150 to $450 per player. Yet salaries dropped precipitously during the early 1930s, and by June 1932, veteran umpire Bert Gholston reported that "some of the players haven't received a full month's pay since the season opened."

Numerous teams not only cut wages but took their players off fixed salaries altogether, instead turning to the "co-op" or "co-plan," where the management received 25 to 30 percent of the net profits of a game and the remainder was allotted to the players. With the co-plan, player income became increasingly unstable, as unfavorable weather and the inability to obtain steady bookings often prevented a consistent source of income for most teams. Under the most favorable circumstances, players on co-plan teams might earn $100–$125 per month, although they were also responsible for their own room and board while traveling. The system's inherent difficulties were illustrated by Hilldale's attempt at co-plan baseball during the team's final days. Between June 26 and June 30, 1932, the team appeared at five different local parks, receiving only $50 to $80.87 per date. After transportation and booking fees were deducted, the players' total share was typically less than $40, leaving each man lucky to earn $2 to $4 per promotion.

Owners, responsible only for travel costs, sometimes found the co-plan attractive for its reduced financial risks. Homestead's Cum Posey, however, questioned "whether this 'Utopian' idea will succeed" and wondered how owners "could be made to believe that ball players who have been making $250 a month will be satisfied to 'go along' and split each games [sic] profit equally with players who have been making $150 a month." Not surprisingly, co-plan teams experienced particular difficulties in preventing players from leaving to seek more profitable situations, and as John Clark, a former journalist and later publicity man for the Pittsburgh Crawfords, observed, "men who are financially responsible shy away from club ownership under the present setup."[19]

The overwhelmingly discouraging environment throughout the country seemingly offered little prospects for black entrepreneurs hoping to establish a new business, let alone one in the volatile world of professional sports. Yet the Crawfords' Gus Greenlee, still profiting from his numbers lottery and one of the few owners who could "take a financial loss without wincing," emerged as the one figure both capable and motivated enough to transcend the current difficulties and potentially revive the industry. Perhaps hoping to ensure a steady stream of popular attractions to his park, Greenlee in late 1932 began to explore the possibility of organizing a new league, ideally placing franchises in several of the cities of Foster's old NNL. Concurrently, his publicity agent, John Clark, attempted to build support for such a scheme, issuing press releases suggesting that "one-man rule should benefit Negro baseball."[20]

In early 1933, Greenlee announced plans for an organizational meeting of a new league, subsequently held in Chicago on January 10. With Greenlee as temporary chairman, six teams agreed to join the new Negro National Association of Baseball clubs (later commonly referred to as the Negro National League, NNL): the Pittsburgh Crawfords, Homestead Grays, Chicago American Giants, Nashville Elite Giants, Indianapolis ABCs, and a planned new franchise in Cleveland that failed to materialize after park problems. At the second meeting, Greenlee was unanimously elected league chairman (or president) and two additional teams joined: the Detroit Stars and Columbus Blue Birds. Wary of the fragile economic situation, the new organization drafted a constitution that called for limits of 16 players per team until June 1 and 14 afterward, a $1,600 monthly salary cap, no minimum guarantee for visiting teams, and, in an allusion to a failed East-West League experiment of 1932, "no extravagant policy of every-day league baseball." The league teams also agreed to cut admission prices to a range of 25 to 35 cents in "keeping with the times."[21]

Although some observers felt that Greenlee's league would be a catalyst in the rebirth of professional black baseball, others felt the new organization had no real chance of success. Even during the more prosperous 1920s, the long jumps involved in travel throughout the midwest had hampered Rube Foster's Negro National League, resulting in, as one sportswriter lamented, "a nightmare for everybody but the railroads." The new NNL would face the same problems of heavy travel, although the railroads had now been abandoned for more economical transportation by bus and automobile.

Perhaps more critical, Greenlee faced the additional dilemma of an oppressive economic environment, certain to wreak havoc on his attempt to bring together a handful of barely functioning franchises. While journalist Al Monroe of the *Chicago Defender* claimed the league had stronger financial backing, without the past "fly-by-night promoters, whose funds barely exceeded the price of a railroad ticket to the meeting," more cynical observers such as Bill Gibson of the *Afro* suggested that the organization was "just the old independent ball under a new name, with little money put on the line to guarantee the carrying out of agreements and contracts." For others, the league seemed a dubious proposition during a period of such economic insecurity. The Kansas City Monarchs, for example, chose to barnstorm and play independent baseball rather than to be saddled with a potentially expensive and unprofitable league schedule to follow. John Drew, a wealthy black politician and successful bus line operator who owned Hilldale during its final two seasons, also remained pessimistic, remarking that "baseball is a luxury and not a necessity, and the people don't have too much money for luxuries during these times."[22]

As 1933 loomed, the position of black professional baseball appeared tenuous, despite the heightened involvement of Greenlee, a relative new-comer to the industry. Described by one player as a "a big man, a great big man," Greenlee had emerged as a larger-than-life figure possessing a considerable bankroll and an abundance of street-smarts, toughness, and bluntness. To Detroit sportswriter Russ Cowans, the "rough and ready" Greenlee loomed as "the Moses for Negro baseball . . . attempting to lead the owners out of the wilderness of depression." Yet whether he could successfully organize a league and develop black professional baseball into a paying enterprise remained uncertain.

Greenlee and other promoters also faced the difficult task of recapturing the patronage of urban blacks, now impoverished by the Depression. Recognizing the considerable risks ahead for all black baseball entrepreneurs, Rollo Wilson observed that "Negro baseball is at a low ebb and both owners and players must make sacrifices and more sacrifices to maintain it until such a time as the fans are again in funds and able to storm the ballyard ramparts as they were wont to do in the yesteryears." Whether sacrifices alone would be enough to resuscitate the industry in the current economic climate remained to be seen.[23]

◆ ◆ ◆

The early months of 1933 hardly offered encouragement to Greenlee and his fellow NNL owners. By March, following "the most harrowing four months of the depression," according to historian William Leuchtenberg, the economy of the United States had virtually hit rock bottom, shaken by numerous bank failures and massive unemployment. Not surprisingly, most observers viewed the future of black professional baseball and other African American enterprises with pessimism, and as sportswriter Bill Gibson remarked, "the fullest co-operation of every member of the group is paramount and even then, the odds against a financial success are great."[24]

Owners, however, had seldom demonstrated even the slightest trace of cooperation in the past. Well-intentioned pre-season promises of sacrifice and unity typically dissipated by summer, as officials reverted to increasingly individualistic behavior, often observing league schedules and regulations only when convenient. The problem was apparent to Dick Lundy, manager of the newly formed Philadelphia Stars, who contended that too many owners exhibited an "opposition to organization," and were "in the game for the little notoriety they derive from it, with no thought whatever of the game's advancement." Umpire Bert Gholston similarly questioned the commitment of the typical owner, noting that most failed to recognize that the "secret of a successful organization is co-operation, and . . . never will as long as [they are] engaged in the numbers and gambling racket, or any other business outside, which will interfere with baseball."

Yet the unanimous election of Greenlee as league president appeared to usher in a new era of harmony. Perhaps responding to the current economic climate, owners had set aside their usual disagreements to band together to form a new organization under the control of Greenlee, whose successful involvement in the numbers lottery had demonstrated his ability to build prosperous, albeit illegal, businesses. Notably, even his former adversary, the Grays' Cum Posey, claimed to be "enthusiastically" supportive of Greenlee as chairman. The strong backing of the owners and Greenlee's own considerable finances, however, would prove insufficient, as the new president soon encountered an almost continuous series of difficulties, both economic and administrative, that would threaten the existence of the organization in its first year.[25]

The chronic problem of obtaining suitable home grounds proved a major stumbling block for the NNL in 1933. With the exception of the Crawfords' Greenlee Field, no league team had unlimited access to its own home park, instead turning to facilities used by white Organized Baseball teams. In Nashville, Tom Wilson's Elite Giants planned to use Sulphur Dell, a Southern Association park, while the Indianapolis ABCs rented Perry Stadium, the home of the local American Association franchise. Meanwhile, the Columbus Blue Birds leased Neil Park, formerly used by the American Association, although team official Arthur Peebles promised that a new park was under construction and would be ready the following season. The Homestead Grays, however, temporarily abandoned Forbes Field in favor of occasional home games at Greenlee Field, a decision necessitated by fans "antagonistic" to the Grays renting a white major league park instead of a largely black-sponsored local enterprise.[26]

The situation in Chicago and Detroit, two of the key cities in the early days of Foster's NNL, was particularly disheartening. The now homeless American Giants were unable to secure a replacement park in Chicago and faced the possibility of becoming a road team as the start of the season dawned. Prospects in Detroit were equally discouraging, as Hamtramck Stadium, built in 1930 and the major venue for black teams, not only was inconvenient for black fans because of its Hamtramck location but was also controlled by John Roesink, an unpopular white promoter and pants store owner. Moreover, Roesink's occasional derogatory remarks about African Americans during his past involvement with black baseball had alienated fans, leading John Clark to lament that "the present park ownership is a hindrance to Negro patronage."[27] The volatile park situation predictably discouraged black sponsorship of a league team in Detroit, as the franchise's original owners withdrew financing prior to the start of the season. Meanwhile, John "Tenny" Blount, a black numbers banker who had operated the Detroit Stars from 1919 through 1924, briefly considered investing in the team before rejecting the idea.

To keep the league intact, a bizarre series of franchise shifts occurred soon after the outset of the season in May. After playing a single poorly attended home game in Indianapolis, the ABCs moved to Detroit, where they would play at Hamtramck Stadium as the Detroit Stars. The league, however, maintained a presence in Indianapolis, as the American Giants subsequently relocated their home games to the vacated city, leaving black Chicago without regular league baseball. Finally, in a surprising move, Joe Cambria's weakened and geographically distant Baltimore Sox were admitted to the NNL in late May as a seventh franchise.[28]

With the league lineup now complete, Greenlee and the other owners envisioned each team scheduling three to four league games per week (Saturday through Monday), augmented by exhibitions with independent white semiprofessional teams. The NNL was to receive 10 percent of the receipts of each league game (5 percent per team) and planned to issue regular standings, statistics, and pertinent information to maintain and encourage the interest of fans and players. Yet league publicity, never an industry strength, was predictably sporadic and inconsistent at best. While John Clark bombarded both black and white newspapers with abundant copy about the Crawfords, other officials took a more casual attitude toward publicizing and reporting their team's games. As Clark observed, many owners spared no expense on equipment and transportation, "but the majority will not pay 60c or one dollar for a scorebook. Nor will they pay to have records kept and transmitted of the game played. . . . Their general conduct is more like first-year sandlot promoters than big league owners." The compilation of accurate standings and statistics was nearly impossible, minimizing fan interest, and the league, as Cum Posey remarked, was almost "forgotten" by mid-season. Clark, who became league secretary during the season, warned that publicity would ultimately decide the league's fate, noting that "the only way to put Negro baseball on a par with what we call major leagues, is to keep records of performances, relay the same information to the public and play fair with the press."[29]

As expected, the NNL struggled financially during 1933. Except for Sunday doubleheaders, attendance was negligible for most games, and according to Posey, "league cities, with Chicago not playing at home, and three or four games a week being played at Greenlee Field, were not sufficient to pay players' salaries and look after incidental expenses." Posey soon became disenchanted with the organization, objecting not only to the preferential position of the Crawfords but also to the dual involvement of John Clark as a league and Crawford official. By late June, the league expelled Homestead for refusing to return two Detroit players who had jumped their contracts, hardly disturbing Posey, who claimed that "the League was no help to the Grays," citing the team's more profitable opportunities playing white independents in Ohio and western Pennsylvania. Clark, however, offered a different perspective, claiming that Posey had "always been opposed to organized baseball," and alluded to the impact of his ongoing financial difficulties.[30]

While Greenlee attempted to stabilize the league after the departure of the Grays, the organization spiraled into mounting chaos. A team of Cubans and African Americans owned by white promoter Syd Pollock declined an invitation to replace the Grays, and soon filed a suit against a league club for failing to honor a $200 guarantee for a doubleheader. Greenlee subsequently organized a replacement team based in Akron, Ohio, but inadequate financing forced a merger with the remnants of the ill-fated Columbus Blue Birds. Although the combination provided the nucleus for another new team, the Cleveland Giants, the NNL's third attempt to develop a stable Ohio-based club proved no more successful than earlier efforts. Meanwhile, the Baltimore Sox virtually abandoned the league after two costly and unprofitable western trips, while poor attendance prompted the Detroit Stars to cancel their remaining home games by late July. The league's continued operation appeared increasingly questionable, and by August, Baltimore sportswriter Bill Gibson noted that "only about three clubs [the American Giants, Crawfords, and Elite Giants] are being bothered by a schedule."[31]

To some observers, the NNL had achieved little and had been a disastrous failure for Gus Greenlee, whose support from his fellow owners had deteriorated as the season progressed. Like Posey, nearly every league official chafed under Greenlee's virtual one-man control of the organization, secretary, and strongest franchise, creating a situation aptly described by one sportswriter as "unfortunate and possibly embarrassing at times." Elite Giants owner Tom Wilson, for example, accused Greenlee of abusing "the laws which the body with him helped to make" and advocated that the league be "governed by a commissioner and executive committee. The head or commissioner should not be attached to any club whatsoever, his sole commission being to deal with fairness to all concerned." Yet regardless of Greenlee's shortcomings, his fellow owners did little to alleviate the league's difficulties during 1933, a fact recognized by a sympathetic John Clark, who subsequently criticized officials "guilty of childish pouting and the outrageous belief that they were members of a prejudiced and unfair group. . . . Herculean demands were expected from the association, but invariably, the owners regarded their own obligations to the league as a most flexible object."[32]

In reality, only through the efforts of Greenlee had the NNL survived the 1933 season. While admitting that "the Big Fellow from Pittsburgh has done some things which were not to the advantage of the league," sportswriter Russ Cowans reminded doubters that "without his assistance this year organized baseball would have been a greater flop than it is." Despite losing another $6,000 on the Crawfords, Greenlee reportedly lent money to other owners to keep the league afloat, and even Posey admitted that the NNL president had "done as much as could be expected or as much as anyone could have done in his position." Yet Greenlee's most remarkable achievement in 1933 was his role in the promotion of what would soon became an annual event in black professional baseball, the East-West game, played at Comiskey Park, the home of the major league Chicago White Sox, on September 10. Featuring the finest players in black baseball selected through the votes of fans, the game would quickly increase in prestige, and within four years, Bill Nunn of the *Pittsburgh Courier* would identify the game as "our connecting link with organized baseball. It's our big opportunity to show . . . under perfect conditions . . . just what we are capable of producing through the years."[33]

The East-West game was somewhat of an outgrowth of the major league All-Star game which had also successfully debuted two months earlier through the efforts of Arch Ward, sports editor of the *Chicago Tribune*, who had proposed a "dream game" in conjunction with the Chicago World's Fair. While the exact origins of the idea for the East-West game remain obscure, several individuals appear particularly significant in its genesis as a major African American sporting event. Several accounts suggest that Roy Sparrow, a black journalist with the *Pittsburgh Sun-Telegraph* and associate of Greenlee, may have been the driving force behind the game; others cite the role of Dave Hawkins, a well-known black sportswriter and promoter who had staged a successful game in July 1933 between the Chicago American Giants and Pittsburgh Crawfords at League Park, the weekday home of the Cleveland Indians. Regardless of who truly originated the idea, the role of Greenlee in the execution of the game was particularly crucial. Although Greenlee, Tom Wilson, and Robert Cole shared equally in the promotional expenses, it was reportedly Greenlee who took the greatest risk by paying $2,500 in advance for the exorbitant rental of Comiskey Park.

To ensure a financial return, the promoters hired Sparrow to coordinate the game's publicity. Sparrow not only barraged 55 black weeklies with news of the upcoming game, but also contacted 90 white daily newspapers. Yet several black sportswriters were initially unenthusiastic about the promotion. In a soon to be common complaint, Randy Dixon of the *Philadelphia Tribune* questioned the veracity of the vote tabulation as well as the game's financing. Meanwhile, Fay Young criticized the composition of the two selected teams, particularly the disproportionate number of American Giants on the "western" team and the corresponding lack of Kansas City Monarch players.[34]

Regardless of its flaws, the promotion (won by the West by an 11-7 score) emerged as the sole positive development in an otherwise dreadful 1933 season for Greenlee and the NNL. While rainy weather somewhat limited attendance, the crowd of about 12,000 fans represented a remarkable achievement during the heart of the Depression. The three promoters reportedly realized a small amount or broke even, but as Greenlee himself noted, the "profit angle . . . was secondary." The East-West game, more than any other prior promotion during the fifty-year history of black baseball, exposed black ballplayers to a larger audience, as daily newspapers, particularly in Chicago, provided generous coverage. As Greenlee later observed, the game had caught the daily press "off guard" and "had the effect of arousing interest among colored players and made a decided hit with sports writers." Equally remarkable was Sparrow's feat of arranging for two players, Oscar Charleston and Willie Foster, to be interviewed on two local radio stations. From its humble beginnings in 1933, the East-West game would not only evolve into a superior money-making proposition for league teams and a showcase for black talent to white America, but also demonstrate the potential financial capability of the industry.[35]

◆ ◆ ◆

While players from several of the non-league eastern teams participated in the East-West game, the NNL (like Rube Foster's league of the 1920s) operated in 1933 without the active involvement of clubs located in New York and Philadelphia. Boasting large black populations and thriving semiprofessional baseball scenes, both cities had long enjoyed a reputation as the most profitable eastern venues. Yet, with the exception of the Baltimore Sox, the east remained non-affiliated, as Greenlee had abandoned a tentative plan for a separate eastern league after encountering resistance and a general lack of enthusiasm. The absence of an eastern league in 1933 disappointed veteran sportswriter Rollo Wilson, who claimed "certain factors do not want league baseball down here." To Wilson, perhaps the most significant barrier was the still substantial role of Nat Strong and other booking agents, who "frankly . . . are opposed to league baseball by colored teams. It cuts their percentages, and that is something to yell about."

For more than thirty years, the involvement of Nat Strong in black baseball had particularly frustrated sportswriters and owners. Born in 1874 in New York City, he had been involved in booking and promoting since the late 1890s and eventually controlled a number of white semipro parks in the metropolitan New York area. Black clubs looking for profitable games with white semiprofessional teams in New York had little choice but to deal with Strong, who like other booking agents charged a 5 to 10 percent fee for his services. Strong's openly exploitive tactics and seemingly mercenary attitude toward black baseball drew steady criticism, particularly his co-ownership (with Max Rosner) of Dexter Park, home of the Brooklyn Bushwicks, one of the finest semiprofessional teams in the country. Although regularly booking black teams for lucrative Sunday games at the site, Strong offered only a flat guarantee of $500 to $600 and refused to offer visiting clubs the common option of receiving a percentage of the profits. However unfair, the guarantee remained attractive enough to continue to entice black teams to Dexter Park. Ed Bolden's break with the Negro National League in 1922 to form the Eastern Colored League, for example, had been partially driven by the prospect of profitable Sunday dates at Dexter Park and other sites in New York, particularly crucial with Pennsylvania's blue laws banning commercialized sports still in effect.[36]

Ironically, Strong heavily depended on black teams as attractions at his parks. Promoter Syd Pollock recognized the reliance, observing that Strong's "business . . . would fall away to nothing" without black opponents. Yet black teams had largely failed to exploit their appeal, and Strong had continued to hold the upper hand in his dealings with African American promoters in the east. Meanwhile, Strong, as Cum Posey quipped, had long remained a pet "aversion" for black owners, prompting entrepreneurs such as Hilldale's John Drew to remain idle rather than to use his booking services. New York journalist Romeo Dougherty, however, felt that Strong was merely a convenient scapegoat and advocated self-help rather than criticism and blame:

the only menace we have had in Negro baseball is our own selves. Nat C. Strong runs a business down on Park Row and is entitled to every dime he has earned booking Negro teams. We should stop shouting about what Strong has done to us and see if we can't do something for ourselves. . . . When Negroes decide to take the risks the other fellow takes in supporting amusement ventures they will be in a position to criticize intelligently, but if others must pay the piper it is foolish to expect that we can call the tune.[37]

If not an actual "menace" to black baseball, there is little doubt that Strong was primarily driven by profit and had little interest in developing the industry into a stable institution. His enthusiasm for league baseball had been tepid at best, reflected by his half-hearted participation in the Eastern Colored League from 1923 through 1927 as owner of the Brooklyn Royal Giants. By the early 1930s, Strong was openly hostile to any organization that might potentially cut his bookings by weaning black teams away from their reliance on independent games with white semipros. Nevertheless, Greenlee recognized Strong's vital role in keeping black teams afloat in 1932 and subsequently met with him in early 1933 to discuss possible involvement in the new league. Strong, however, had little interest, explaining to Greenlee that his "investment of money and energy over a period of almost forty years could not afford the sacrifice which our organization would demand," although Strong promised to reconsider if the league or any other group of owners could "build up attractions to draw crowds in large numbers." Greenlee did succeed in negotiating an agreement with Strong and Philadelphia promoter Eddie Gottlieb to arrange games for league teams with white semipros in the area east of Pittsburgh, yet Strong's Black Yankees remained outside the NNL in 1933, as did the majority of other eastern teams. With no eastern organization in 1933, Rollo Wilson predicted "a grand scramble for choice dates with the white semi-pros and I see some clubs being booked into parks at figures below what others will demand."

Wilson's speculation proved remarkably apt, particularly in Philadelphia, where teams such as Ed Bolden's newly established Philadelphia Stars aggressively competed for bookings. Despite the declining status of local semipro ball, the city had continued to be the lifeblood of eastern teams. At times during 1932, one of the most dismal financial years in black baseball history, as many as four top black teams *simultaneously* appeared in Philadelphia to take on white opponents. Recognizing the city's still considerable potential, the venerable Bolden had recently organized the veteran-packed Stars, hoping to match his earlier success enjoyed with Hilldale in the 1920s. Seeking to give his new team every advantage in the fierce quest for paying dates, Bolden worked closely with Eddie Gottlieb, who provided the team with regular games throughout the 1933 season. Yet the team's reliance on white teams for income troubled local observers such as Randy Dixon, who complained that "what we all want to know is how they rate with the Black Yanks, the Crawfords, or the Homestead Grays." By late June, the Stars had only played two black clubs, the Bacharach Giants (a Philadelphia-based team named for the earlier Atlantic City-based professional black team of 1916–1929) and the Pittsburgh Crawfords, and spent the bulk of their time competing against local white squads.[38]

Despite disappointing black fans, the preference for white competition appeared a sensible response to the current economic status of African American communities. With the potential for black attendance marginal at best, Bolden was understandably reluctant to commit to regular home games. The cautious approach enabled the Stars to survive the season without collapse, a distinct advance after the debacle of Hilldale's final season. The Stars' emergence offered hope for a revival of Philadelphia as a profitable venue, but the team's financial status bore little resemblance to the prosperity enjoyed by Hilldale a decade earlier. Like virtually all black businesses, the Stars and all black professional teams struggled to remain solvent in 1933 in the still withering Depression environment, and as Randy Dixon remarked, the "diamond pastime showed little profit to the owners." The fate of the industry in eastern and midwestern cities remained shaky entering into the new year, and further changes seemed necessary for continued survival.[39]

◆ ◆ ◆

After the decidedly mixed results of the NNL's inaugural season, Gus Greenlee recognized the need to streamline the operation of the organization. Greenlee's proposed solution involved reorganizing the league around its three strongest franchises (Pittsburgh Crawfords, Chicago American Giants, and Nashville Elite Giants), eliminating unprofitable midwestern cities such as Detroit and Indianapolis, and shifting the league's composition by incorporating major eastern teams, including Bolden's Philadelphia Stars. Several clubs not only expressed interest in the plan but appeared more prepared for full league participation than in 1933. Robert Cole's American Giants, for example, had regained control of their home field in Chicago after dog racing failed to be legalized in Illinois. The league also received encouraging news from the Baltimore Sox, which had reacquired the use of their original "Black Sox" name after a court battle and subsequently announced plans for regular home games at Bugle Field. Moreover, team owner Joe Cambria, now confident that league teams "should be all through losing money," supported Greenlee's proposal, provided that "the League can be organized to get everybody going along together."[40]

For Harry Passon, the owner of the Bacharach Giants, a "compact, well-balanced league" with salaried players was the only salvation for black baseball. Passon was particularly eager to dispense with coop baseball after difficulties in 1933:

It's bad business for me, co-plan baseball. . . . I'll never own such a team again. I will put the man on salary if I go into baseball . . . and they will be paid that and nothing more. The fellows took advantage of me last summer. They came into my sports goods store, got radios, clothing and other articles and never paid for them. Not all of the men did this, understand, but some of them did, and I am stuck for plenty. I have had my experience in that line and I am through.

Despite the enthusiasm of Passon and other eastern owners for organization, the same logistical problems remained in place. Traveling continued to be a major deterrent, particularly the nearly 500 mile "jump" from Pittsburgh to Chicago. The always astute Cum Posey also questioned whether it would be "a paying proposition for an Eastern club to stay in the West from two to three weeks," noting that "practical baseball men like Bolden and Strong will do this but once." Meanwhile, independent teams such as the Kansas City Monarchs and New York Black Yankees had kept busy in 1933, scheduling 148 and 156 games respectively, and had little desire to tamper with their success by participating in a potentially unprofitable league. As Black Yankees owner James Semler asserted, "it will be a long time before a colored league will stand its ground. Finances will stop them dead. . . . If there are eight teams in the league maybe two of them will be able to meet the pay roll for three months without waiting for games to play." Semler predictably preferred to maintain his close relationship with Nat Strong, who could "keep the team working and I know the league can not."[41]

With the failure of Hilldale and the problems of eastern league baseball in the 1920s still fresh in his mind, Ed Bolden himself was reluctant to place his Philadelphia Stars in the NNL and was more interested in a simple working agreement among teams to respect player contracts. As Bolden warily recalled, "Hilldale . . . made all of its money playing independent baseball and then went into a league [and] started losing money." Moreover, the NNL's financial performance in 1933 hardly encouraged participation, leading sportswriter Bill Gibson to anticipate that Bolden would not "go through with the new combine. Bolden has more practical experience than any of the men engaged in the business today and . . . [is] not interested in joining the organization for the sake of his health alone."

Yet the modest improvement in the nation's economic and unemployment situation by the spring of 1934 after the relentless hardships of the prior two years could not help but encourage Bolden and other African American entrepreneurs. White New York sportswriter Rud Rennie recognized the positive impact on consumer behavior, marveling at the "crowds of people . . . enjoying themselves. They may not be rolling in wealth, but evidently they have a few 'bucks' to spend on amusements. That's something they did not have last year."

Other developments pointed to a more profitable season in 1934, particularly the November 1933 repeal by statewide referendum of Pennsylvania's archaic blue laws forbidding commercialized Sunday sports. Although most eastern and midwestern states had abandoned the legislation years before, the strong rural presence in the Pennsylvania legislature had continuously blocked repeal despite heavy resistance among both urban blacks and whites. Unable to schedule local games on Sunday without fear of possible prosecution, black and white entrepreneurs found themselves at a distinct financial disadvantage, losing the most profitable day of the week for baseball. Although some religious leaders, both black and white, favored continuation of the Sunday ban on commercial sport, the *Philadelphia Tribune* epitomized the local African American attitude, citing the hypocrisy of "religious fanatics" who "object to Sunday baseball but their mouths are tighter than a clam's shell while their black brothers and sisters are segregated and discriminated against. . . . Their religion makes them oppose Sunday sports but it does not cause them to become interested in human rights."[42]

Most promoters predicted the legalization of commercialized Sunday sports in Pennsylvania would provide a much-needed stimulus to Depression gate receipts in the east. Philadelphia Athletics manager and part-owner Connie Mack, who had failed to overturn the ban in the past, felt that Sunday baseball would be "a big boon . . . but I want to say that it also means joy and recreation for thousands of players and followers of semi-pro teams." Booking agent Eddie Gottlieb welcomed the "great news" and anticipated that "independent baseball is sure to take a big boom." Gottlieb enthused, "think what Sunday baseball will do for the unemployment situation in Philadelphia . . . it will mean that at least 1500 persons will be earning money—and money they will spend, too." Yet former Hilldale owner John Drew offered a more pessimistic assessment, warning of possible negative ramifications for black teams:

Sunday baseball won't help conditions until business gets better. . . . In cities where Sunday baseball is in vogue I feel that it has hurt the game generally. Most of these cities . . . offer the public double-headers on Sundays and by the time the fans have sat through 18 innings of baseball . . . they are fed up. They don't want to see any baseball as a rule until the following Sunday. This means that baseball during the week suffers.[43]

If the benefits of Sunday games ultimately failed to materialize, Bolden and other promoters were also poised to capitalize on the increasing availability of night baseball by 1934. After lighting arrangements had been perfected in the early 1930s, numerous semiprofessional and minor league ballpark owners began to install lights in an attempt to revive sagging Depression gates, while other teams, such as the Kansas City Monarchs, utilized a portable lighting system while barnstorming. Although twilight games in Philadelphia and other cities had attracted solid support in the 1920s, the greater convenience of night baseball for working fans dramatically increased the potential for profitable weekday promotions.[44]

With the Pennsylvania blue laws repealed, night baseball in place, and a more encouraging economic outlook, Bolden looked optimistically toward 1934 and began to reconsider his original opposition to affiliation with Greenlee's league. Yet several issues still needed to be resolved, particularly the franchise security deposit, a fee the cash-strapped Bolden was reluctant to post. Perhaps of greater concern was the potential membership of a second Philadelphia team, Harry Passon's Bacharach Giants, a proposition viewed negatively by Bolden, who argued that two league franchises could not be successful locally. Other owners, such as Cum Posey, disagreed, suggesting that "there is room in Philadelphia for Bacharachs and Philadelphia Stars if the clubs do not play home games on the same date." Although Passon subsequently withdrew his team's application, the Bacharachs eventually joined the league for the second half but returned to independent baseball in 1935 after faring poorly in their only league season.

Bolden's long experience with the economically sensitive local black population and familiarity with the often cutthroat world of black professional baseball shaped his seemingly inflexible attitude toward the Bacharach Giants. Determined to remain solvent and maintain every advantage for the Stars, he also began to seek additional financial backing, despite limited options. While the Grays' Posey, under increasing financial stress, had recently secured fresh capital from thirty-four-year-old Rufus "Sonnyman" Jackson, a Homestead-based black numbers banker and jukebox entrepreneur, Bolden preferred to continue his policy of avoiding such direct associations with black underworld figures. Yet John Drew's heavy losses with Hilldale in 1931 and 1932 deterred most local legitimate black entrepreneurs from investing, leaving Bolden little choice but to seek white financing. Although some black promoters may have rejected such an arrangement, Bolden had never shied away from working with whites. Though racially conscious, Bolden had always been a businessman first and a "race man" second, insisting earlier in his career that "close analysis will prove that only where the color-line fades and co-operation instituted are our business advances gratified. Segregation in any form, including self-imposed is not the solution."[45]

Bolden subsequently decided to bring in well-known promoter Eddie Gottlieb as a partner. As a child, the Russian-born Gottlieb moved with his family to New York and then Philadelphia, where he soon took an interest in sports, particularly basketball and baseball. After a stint with the South Philadelphia High School basketball squad, Gottlieb and several other players organized a new team in 1918, named for its sponsor, the South Philadelphia Hebrew Association. While the SPHAs lost their sponsorship within a few years, the name remained, and, under Gottlieb's management, the team developed into a major force in the early days of professional basketball from the 1920s through the 1940s. Gottlieb also became part-owner of a sporting goods store with SPHA teammates Hughie Black and Harry Passon (future head of the Bacharach Giants) and briefly taught physical education, yet achieved greater success in sports promotion, particularly as a booking agent for baseball. Described by famed sportswriter Red Smith as "a wonderful little guy about the size and shape of a half-keg of beer," the thirty-five-year-old Gottlieb by 1934 had nearly exclusive control over baseball bookings in the lucrative Philadelphia and mid-Atlantic market and had strong ties with the equally successful Nat Strong in New York. Within a few years, Gottlieb not only would play a substantial role in the affairs of the Stars but would also become a major power in the NNL.[46]

Upon cursory examination, the alignment with Gottlieb seemed logical, as Bolden, like other black entrepreneurs in other fields, notably the film industry, simply found it expedient to obtain white assistance during the Depression. For the fifty-three-year-old Bolden, earning a comfortable yet unspectacular salary as a special clerk at the Philadelphia Post Office and unable to advance despite thirty years experience, the financial risk of owning a black team was clearly overwhelming by 1934 and the profit margin comparatively small. In contrast, Gottlieb had a relatively stable financial situation and also offered the prospect of continuous bookings. Under the new arrangement, Gottlieb would receive a 50 percent share in the team in return for providing most of the team's financial backing. Bolden, however, would continue to handle the bulk of the administrative tasks of the Stars yet would now split the profits (if any) with Gottlieb, a relationship that would endure through the remainder of the Stars' existence.[47]

Figure 3. Promoter Eddie Gottlieb (far left), with Philadelphia A's part-owner and manager Connie Mack, Louis Schwartz (sponsor of Sunday sports bill), and Philadelphia Phillies president Gerry Nugent, 1933. Courtesy Baseball Hall of Fame Library.

The involvement of a white promoter in a black baseball team and league, however, was not without its risks. Despite Bolden's alliances and amicable relationships with whites, the Hilldale club had always been touted as a "race institution," entirely owned and controlled by blacks. The arrival of Gottlieb threatened to violate the trust that black fans had placed in Bolden as an entrepreneur and seemed to foreshadow yet another takeover of a black enterprise by whites. For decades, African Americans had debated the issue of white involvement in black professional baseball and other enterprises. Some advocated all-black ownership at all costs. Veteran player Ben Taylor, for example, asserted that "as long as we look for the white man to come to our rescue, just so long will we stay on the bottom." Others, like sportswriter Rollo Wilson, disagreed, noting that "white men, with nerve and money, took the chances to bring it [professional black baseball] along thus far, and their money, combined with the money of far-visaged Negroes who can afford to INVEST in baseball, and who are not SPECULATING ON A SHOE STRING, will benefit it more and more as the years pass." Moreover, white owners such as J. L. Wilkinson of the Kansas City Monarchs had earned nearly unanimous praise from black players and officials such as Bolden, who considered him "the most fair-minded square shooting white man I have ever met who is interested in Negro baseball."[48]

Although controversial, white ownership was generally viewed as less objectionable than the continual role of whites as booking agents. As noted, black teams often found themselves dependent on the whims of booking agents such as Gottlieb in Philadelphia and Strong in New York, who provided profitable dates to certain favored clubs while virtually ignoring others. Moreover, booking agents, though often affiliated with black professional baseball in the past, seldom allowed league interests to take precedence over their own concerns, and Gottlieb would prove to be no exception. Sportswriter Randy Dixon aptly explained the influential yet troubling position of Gottlieb:

Gottie's word is law and he can play you or slay you. Now Gottie is a fine fellow and has done much to keep Negro baseball together, but first, last and always he is a booking agent and has to protect his own business. Hence schedules are drawn to suit the purposes of his business and if it doesn't jell with the Negro National League, the league can go to any place that rhymes with jell.

Others, however, argued that white entrepreneurs such as Gottlieb had simply filled a void that blacks had been unable and in some cases unwilling to fill. Cum Posey, who objected to the sometimes exploitive methods of the booking agents and believed in minimizing their use, nevertheless asserted that "where clubs are booked continuously for months by agents, and make no effort to book themselves they are lucky to have men in position to do this for them and should pay accordingly."[49]

Finally, the Jewish background of Gottlieb also posed difficulties. In Philadelphia, Chicago, and other cities, the continued Jewish control of much of the black housing, stores, theaters, and places of amusement engendered increasing hostility during the 1930s. In August 1934, a major riot occurred in North Philadelphia when Edward Morton, a "Hebrew merchant," reportedly kicked Lucille Suber, an eighteen-year-old pregnant African American woman, during an argument in his store. When Morton was subsequently released by police but Suber held in custody, violence erupted. Blacks unleashed long-suppressed hostility toward Jews, hurling bricks through the windows of 42 white Jewish establishments. While the riot eventually subsided, tension between blacks and Jews remained present in North Philadelphia and throughout the city.⁵⁰ Perhaps intentionally, Gottlieb's investment in the Stars would be muted in the local black press during the mid-1930s, only gradually surfacing as the decade closed.⁵¹

◆ ◆ ◆

Armed with additional capital, Bolden finally agreed to return to league baseball, and in February 1934, Philadelphia joined the reorganized NNL along with the Chicago American Giants, Nashville Elite Giants, Pittsburgh Crawfords, Cleveland Red Sox, and Newark Dodgers, the latter owned by a group headed by Greenlee's wartime friend Charles Tyler. The organization also included several clubs, including the Bacharach Giants and Homestead Grays, as associate members, a vague status allowing games with the league and protection against potential raids by league teams in return for 50 percent of the franchise fee.⁵²

Despite the involvement of the once-influential Bolden and influx of several new franchises, the NNL remained largely under the control of Gus Greenlee, who was reelected league chairman. Yet in response to the criticisms of bias in the operation of the league during 1933, the revamped organization took the progressive step of naming a salaried commissioner, W. Rollo Wilson, to arbitrate league disputes. Born in Franklin, Pennsylvania, Wilson had received a bachelor's degree from Temple University in Philadelphia and subsequently graduated from the University of Pittsburgh School of Pharmacy in 1914. Despite his pharmaceutical training, Wilson eventually became a well-respected sportswriter with several black newspapers, most consistently with the *Pittsburgh Courier*, despite residing in Philadelphia, and had served as deputy athletic commissioner for Pennsylvania. By 1934, Wilson not only doubled as a columnist with the *Courier* and editor of the *Philadelphia Independent* but was also in the midst of an unsuccessful campaign as a Republican candidate for the state assembly.

Although non-affiliated league presidents had been appointed in the late 1920s in the waning days of the Eastern Colored League and first Negro National League, neither Isaac Nutter, an Atlantic City attorney, nor William Hueston, a Gary, Indiana, judge, had sufficient authority to function as independently as the commissioner of major league baseball, Judge Kenesaw Mountain Landis. Whether Wilson could transcend this difficulty remained uncertain, yet few observers doubted his abilities. Wilson not only was a long-time astute observer of the difficulties of black baseball but also offered practical experience as a former secretary of the American Negro League in 1929. To Al Monroe of the *Defender*, Wilson's most im-

Figure 4. Early portrait of W. Rollo Wilson
(1890–1956), distinguished sportswriter and first
NNL commissioner. Courtesy Venango County
Historical Society.

portant asset was his impartiality, and "certainly no better candidate could
have been placed in the running than the man elected." The *Courier* also
welcomed the selection, observing that "what we need now are dictators
for our restaurant, barber shop, drugstore and other businessmen."[53]

After assuming office, Wilson attempted to address several of the industry's chronic difficulties, including the problem of scheduling. Although
daily baseball remained economically impossible, NNL teams planned
three league games per week during the 1934 season, divided into two
halves, with the winner of each to meet for the championship. The lure
of lucrative dates with white semipro teams, however, soon undermined
adherence to the schedule, and Wilson himself recognized "the necessity
of providing . . . certain booking to help carry the owners' overhead." The

influence of booking agents thus remained relatively undiminished in 1934, although Greenlee managed to temper Nat Strong's hostility to the league, even convincing him to book several NNL teams, including the Crawfords, for dates at Dexter Park. Yet as Greenlee noted, Strong continued to resist organized black baseball, believing it would "destroy his institution which had taken a lifetime to build." Meanwhile, as anticipated, the increasing influence of Eddie Gottlieb as team official and league booking agent antagonized several league owners, including Charles Tyler of the Newark Dodgers. After openly objecting to Gottlieb's presence at a league meeting, Tyler subsequently found his team cut off from profitable dates.[54]

Weak financing and negligible attendance in several league cities also mitigated against an equitable schedule and created other unforeseen administrative problems during 1934. As Fay Young observed, a balanced schedule was nearly impossible to achieve "unless Negro business men . . . come together and underwrite the expense of a club, thus helping the club owner out of a rut." The problem was apparent in Baltimore, where a new edition of the Black Sox, now controlled by Jack Farrell, a black Chester, Pennsylvania, sportsman, hotel owner, and former boxing promoter, joined the NNL in the second half. The club, however, played only a handful of home games, as several league teams avoided scheduled dates, believing Baltimore was no longer profitable. Similar circumstances resulted in several cancellations in Cleveland, and by late August the local franchise had abandoned the league to play independent baseball. Meanwhile, the considerable traveling distance to Nashville forced the Elite Giants to largely desert their home in the second half, leading Cum Posey to advise a move "to a Northern city or else join the South League." Despite the schedule's obvious deficiencies, a league press release nevertheless defended the arrangement as "the best which could be developed under the conditions confronting the organization."[55]

Although chaotic scheduling and shaky franchises hindered the NNL's development, some teams enjoyed modest success. The Philadelphia Stars, now under an interracial partnership, prospered in 1934 after acquiring permanent home grounds at Passon Field at 48th and Spruce, a convenient location for black fans whose modest seating capacity was its only disadvantage. Although the Bacharach Giants also rented the park, the Stars proved a superior drawing card. The team's strong home attendance for weekend games soon made it the backbone for NNL teams, prompting Posey's observation that "Bolden should not be away from his park over four Sundays in the season."[56]

Despite strong competition from the Crawfords and Robert Cole's American Giants, the Stars soon emerged as a major power in the league. In late June, the team moved into second place shortly after sweeping successive doubleheaders at Passon Field on June 23 and 24, winning three of the games by shutouts. Although the Chicago American Giants won the first-half flag, the Stars eventually captured the second-half title with a record of 11-4, earning a berth in the best of seven championship series.

The championship series between the American Giants and the Stars loomed as a potentially crucial event, one that not only would demonstrate the legitimacy of the league to still undecided black sportswriters and fans but might also illustrate the playing strength of black players to interested white onlookers. An organized, well-attended, and exciting series of games would also culminate the season on a positive note and ideally overshadow some of the league's ongoing administrative problems. Yet championship series staged between the winners of the Eastern Colored League and Negro National League from 1924 through 1927 had attracted only modest attendance, failing to maintain the interest of fans over a prolonged period. Unless all conditions, particularly weather, were ideal, a similar series during the height of the Depression seemed questionable at best.

Initially, the decision to hold a championship series appeared to be a master stroke for the league. The first four games were well played and generally free of argument and problems. But the remainder of the series featured several embarrassing episodes and questionable decisions which epitomized the industry's chronic administrative weaknesses. The fifth game, for example, was inexplicably delayed for ten days, dissipating whatever fan and press interest had been established. In the interim, the Stars barnstormed, playing a meaningless doubleheader in Philadelphia on Sunday, September 23, against the New York Black Yankees.[57]

Game six further damaged the league's credibility. The outcome, a 4-1 victory for Philadelphia that tied the series at three games apiece, was overshadowed by a series of unfortunate incidents revealing the league's shaky authority, weak umpiring, and inability and unwillingness to discipline rowdy players. The major controversy occurred early in the contest, when the always pugnacious Jud "Boojum" Wilson of the Stars was seemingly ejected after striking Umpire Bert Gholston, but "to the amazement of the spectators . . . was allowed to stay in the game." Although Chicago manager Dave Malarcher complained, Gholston explained that because he was unaware of which player had struck him, he had not ejected Wilson. A similar incident occurred later in the game, when catcher Ameal Brooks of the Stars pushed Umpire Craig but received no apparent punishment.

Not surprisingly, Malarcher promptly filed a protest with Commissioner Rollo Wilson, arguing that Jud Wilson should have been ejected from the game and suspended for the remainder of the series. Prior to game seven on Monday, October 1, representatives from both teams met with the commissioner at the Douglass Hotel in Philadelphia. At the meeting, Gholston disclosed that he had actually intended to eject Jud Wilson but had reversed his decision because of a threatened attack by the player after the game. Gholston's disclosure had no effect on Ed Bolden, who allowed his overriding loyalty to his players to transcend his usual advocacy of "clean playing," warning that if Wilson were suspended, the Stars would not play "if 50 or 50,000 people were in the park." Although favoring punishment, the commissioner ultimately weakened under pressure from Bolden and Gottlieb and allowed Wilson to participate in the remaining series games.

With Wilson in the lineup of the Stars, the series, now tied at three games apiece, resumed on Monday evening, October 1, at Passon Field. An estimated crowd of 5,000 fans watched the two teams battle to a 4-4 tie before a local curfew halted play. The series finally ended on Tuesday, October 2, at Passon Field, where Slim Jones culminated a brilliant season by shutting out Chicago 2-0, winning the league championship for the Stars. Yet the final two games were similarly marred by arguments and violence, as Umpire Gholston was again struck by a player, this time Mule Suttles of the American Giants. Adding to the league's woes, both teams protested the final game: Chicago objected to an umpire's decision and Philadelphia complained of the use of an ineligible player by the American Giants.[58]

Not surprisingly, most sportswriters and fans focused less on the outcome of the series and more on the questionable administration of the promotion. Rollo Wilson, who had performed competently in his first year of commissioner, bore the brunt of the ensuing criticism for his handling of the Jud Wilson affair. The commissioner subsequently offered a somewhat vague explanation, admitting that, while the "conduct of the umpires in the game was unjustifiable," he "had no authority to overrule them on that particular game. Any action to punish the arbiters for indefensible conduct must be in the future on the basis of their efficiency or lack of it shown in the past." Wilson's reasoning failed to mollify Dave Malarcher, who asked, "now what sort of commissioner is that? . . . if he cannot allow a protest under this condition, when, and under what condition will he allow a protest?" To Malarcher, the entire affair suggested that Wilson was "afraid of Philadelphia or partial to the Stars, or just simply inefficient and not qualified to act as commissioner." *Philadelphia Tribune* sportswriter Ed Harris, however, blamed the umpires, who "set unfortunate precedents, the evil of which will react only upon themselves. If but for no other reason than their self-respect they should have put the men out."[59]

The championship series thus provided an unsatisfactory and disappointing conclusion to a season that had offered several positive developments for black teams, most notably the potential for profit for the first

time since 1931. As the worst conditions of the Depression eased somewhat, black fans began to patronize baseball more consistently, confirmed
by Nashville manager Jim Taylor who noted a 25 percent increase in attendance during 1934. Notably, Philadelphia returned to the forefront as a
major venue, prompting league secretary John Clark to assess the city as
"constantly good—more so, than any other . . . in the circuit." Heartened
by the improved financial climate in 1934, Cum Posey assessed the season
as "one of the best, as a whole, ever experienced by colored baseball."
Rollo Wilson, however, offered a more realistic view, admitting that "few,
if any, clubs made any money," although financial losses were "surprisingly small."[60]

Perhaps the most encouraging development during 1934 was the staging of three remarkably successful promotions at major league parks. The
second annual East-West game, once again at Comiskey Park, drew over
25,000 fans, reportedly the largest crowd for a black sporting event to
date. Equally impressive were two four-team doubleheaders in September
at Yankee Stadium, both attracting over 20,000 fans. The Yankee Stadium
promotions featured mound duels between Slim Jones and the increasingly
legendary Satchel Paige of the Crawfords, including a memorable 1-1 tie
on September 9 and a 3-1 win by Paige three weeks later. Ironically, the
New York dates (one of which was deceptively promoted as the "Colored
World Series Classic") clearly overshadowed the playoff series, which was
suspended to allow Philadelphia and Chicago to participate in the more
profitable four-team doubleheader at Yankee Stadium on Sunday, September 30.[61]

Once more, the financial role of Gus Greenlee was paramount. While
again sharing the promotional expenses of the East-West game with Cole
and Tom Wilson, Greenlee provided the bulk of the financing for the Yankee Stadium games, and even Posey admitted their success was "due almost entirely" to Greenlee. Perhaps more than any other owner, Greenlee
realized the importance of presenting black baseball in a major league
venue, transcending the usual white perception of black baseball as semiprofessional in caliber. As Greenlee noted, "in staging these games, we not
only made a profit but forced baseball into a most favorable picture—the
daily newspapers, radio, and a mixed patronage." Similarly, Rollo Wilson
remarked that "thousands of fans who had never seen baseball played by
high-class colored teams have been converted."[62]

While Greenlee and other owners had demonstrated the financial potential in individual promotions, the league itself still appeared far from a
functional and reliable institution. The too often disorganized state of the
NNL compared to white Organized Baseball continued to disappoint fans
and sportswriters. Others criticized the unbalanced nature of the league,

citing the weakness of half of the eight franchises, particularly Cleveland, Newark, Baltimore, and the Bacharach Giants, and the lack of accurate statistics and standings. Sportswriter Dan Burley provided a typical pessimistic assessment:

Ask any Chicago fan at random what he thinks about the league. His reply is usually a question itself as to "what league?" . . . We would far rather see the building of strong home teams in various key cities for a season or two and then the molding of a real league . . . than a makeshift affair in which the gentry above "green" in ample pockets while they tell the folks glibly about some kind of "half" or a "pennant."

Yet other journalists embraced a more sympathetic outlook. While recognizing the league's weaknesses, Romeo Dougherty cited the NNL's perceptible progress in 1934, "a distinct improvement over performances of 1933." Meanwhile, Ed Harris urged patience, noting "half a league was better than no league" and the "league is only a baby and not yet one year old."

Revitalized by improved financial stability in 1934, black professional baseball appeared poised to make further gains in 1935, and as commissioner Rollo Wilson remarked, the league "should feel encouraged on its work this year." Yet Gus Greenlee, who had sunk a considerable amount of money into the industry in the past several years, recognized the still fragile status of an enterprise relying on black income during the Depression. Assuming a more guarded attitude, Greenlee presciently warned that "in spite of the success of last year, we have not arrived."[63]

2

External Threats and Internal Dissension

Surely, we have a good product in our baseball, as it is played today. But as yet, we have not created a uniform demand for it. Until the demand exists, somebody will—every owner should—make sacrifices.

—Gus Greenlee, 1935

As the 1935 season approached, black professional baseball appeared considerably more viable as an enterprise than only a year earlier. Yet as Gus Greenlee predicted, the Negro National League still had a long way to go, and a number of pressing issues would emerge in the mid-1930s threatening the fragile status of the new organization. Within the league itself, lack of cooperation among owners persisted, while from the outside, the emergence of star athletes from other sports, the founding of the Negro American League, and player defections to foreign leagues would soon present new challenges. Meanwhile, the Depression would continue to severely limit the profit potential for any business.

Nevertheless, the NNL looked toward the new season with optimism. Greenlee's reorganization of the NNL in 1934 to include eastern franchises had been largely successful, evidenced by the strong attendance in Philadelphia and in New York at the two Yankee Stadium promotions. Like prior league organizers, Greenlee began to recognize that the east offered a more conducive environment for the industry than the midwest, which could not match the sizable black population crammed along the relatively compact 250-mile corridor between Washington and New York.

Looking to continue its development and expansion into the region, the league targeted New York as the ideal home of a potential NNL franchise. Though potentially lucrative, the area was fraught with difficulties, particularly a black population predominantly unemployed or on relief and a local black press with a seemingly tepid interest in baseball. The major barrier, however, remained the promoter Nat Strong, whose continued dominance had thwarted recent local attempts at league baseball, forcing both Cum Posey's ill-fated East-West League of 1932 and Greenlee's reorganized NNL of 1934 to instead place franchises in Newark. With the exception of sporadic home games by the Black Yankees and NNL promotions at Yankee Stadium and Ebbets Field, New Yorkers had had virtually no opportunity to see black professional baseball on a regular basis since 1930. Moreover, as in other cities, suitable home grounds were unavailable, too small, or, in the case of the accessible major league parks such as Yankee Stadium and the Polo Grounds, too expensive to rent consistently.[1]

Yet the Yankee Stadium promotions of 1934 had demonstrated that New York, if properly developed, could once more become a profitable city for black baseball. In a risky move designed both to counter Strong's power and to make inroads in the New York market, the NNL voted in November 1934 to add a new team, the Brooklyn Eagles. Owned by Abraham Manley and his wife Effa, the franchise planned to use Ebbets Field in Brooklyn for home dates, thus competing directly with games booked by Strong at Dexter Park and other venues.

The admission of the Brooklyn Eagles not only provided the NNL with a much-needed New York outlet but also introduced a remarkable yet soon to be controversial couple into the professional black baseball scene. Abe Manley, a Hertford, North Carolina, native, had established successful businesses in Camden and New York, yet like Gus Greenlee he had profited most by the illegal numbers lottery, particularly in New Jersey. Like Greenlee, Manley was a rabid baseball fan, avidly supporting Hilldale and even establishing his own semipro team, the Camden Leafs, in 1929. While attending a World Series game at Yankee Stadium in 1932, Manley met his future wife, Effa Brooks, who would subsequently play a major role in the administration of the Eagles. Born in 1900 in Philadelphia, Effa Manley represented a cultural anomaly for the times, raised in an interracial environment by a white mother of German/Native American descent and a black stepfather. Manley's biological father was white, but she viewed herself as an African American throughout much of her life (her marriage license listed her as "colored") and, in a rare reversal, "passed" as black rather than white.[2]

With the establishment of the Eagles in Brooklyn, most observers predicted a difficult season ahead contending with the still firmly entrenched Nat Strong. But the anticipated battle failed to materialize, as Strong died in January 1935 at age sixty-one after suffering a heart attack. The death of Strong represented the end of an era in black professional baseball, climaxing a career of nearly four decades at the head of a booking empire that remained an undeniable yet often obstructive force to black entrepreneurs. Fittingly, his death facilitated the NNL's ongoing penetration into

Figure 5. Abe and Effa Manley. Courtesy Negro
Leagues Baseball Museum, Kansas City.

the previously untapped New York market, as Cuban promoter Alejandro
"Alex" Pompez, thwarted by Strong in the past, finally succeeded in placing a second league team in New York: the New York Cubans.

The return of the forty-four-year-old Pompez to organized black baseball seemed a particularly fortuitous development. Unlike Manley, the bi-
lingual Pompez (who claimed to be a native of Key West, Florida, but may
have actually been born in Havana) had years of experience as a baseball
promoter as owner of the eastern-based Cuban Stars from at least 1916
through 1929. Organized by Pompez, the Cuban Stars were one of several
independent teams of predominantly dark-skinned Cubans that barnstormed the United States during the baseball season and then returned to
their homeland for the winter. An enthusiastic advocate of organization,
Pompez had placed his team in the eastern leagues of the 1920s, yet the
lack of home grounds had been a continuous handicap, forcing the club to
travel extensively.

By 1930, as the future of black baseball appeared dismal, Pompez abandoned baseball promotion and the operation of his cigar store on Lenox Avenue in Harlem to devote himself to one of the few businesses offering profit for black entrepreneurs during the Depression: the illegal numbers. Armed with family connections, Pompez soon established a remarkably successful enterprise in Harlem and by 1931 was reportedly earning $7,000 to $8,000 daily. Yet Pompez and other black numbers bankers in New York eventually surrendered control to famed white gangster Dutch Schultz, and the Cuban promoter was eager to return to baseball by 1935. Flush with cash, Pompez acquired home grounds at Dyckman Oval at 204th Street and Nagle Avenue in Harlem and invested thousands to remodel the conveniently located park, considered too small for league baseball in the past.[3]

The entrance of two New York-based clubs dramatically transformed the composition of the league. Several franchises were dropped, including the Baltimore Black Sox, Bacharach Giants, and Cleveland Red Sox, one of the league's least profitable teams. Meanwhile, the Homestead Grays, which despite entreaties had remained an associate member during 1934, accepted full membership for the 1935 season. Although it strengthened the organization, the seemingly cavalier shuffle of league franchises disgusted observers such as Cleveland sportswriter Bill Finger, who felt that the discarded teams had been unfairly made the "goats of the League," at the expense of stronger franchises in Chicago, Philadelphia, and Pittsburgh. Yet the always individualistic owners had little sympathy for less profitable clubs, as Bacharach owner Harry Passon discovered when he attempted to sell his franchise to the league for $400, the total advanced to his players. Reflecting the ruthless attitude common throughout the industry, one official simply urged the owners to forgo the expenditure and "just go on and sign them up anyway." Not surprisingly, the unfortunate Passon permanently withdrew from the NNL, returning to his sporting goods store and sandlot sports promotion in Philadelphia until an apparently self-inflicted gunshot wound ended his life in 1954.[4]

Nevertheless, the league's new lineup, featuring eight relatively stable franchises, at least half financed by numbers money, seemed to encourage greater cooperation and confidence. Beneath the seemingly calm facade, however, serious cracks remained in the league's administrative structure, particularly the tenuous status of Rollo Wilson. The commissioner's handling of the playoff debacle of 1934 had alienated several owners, most notably Robert Cole of the American Giants, whose position as league treasurer allowed him to retaliate by delaying payment of the balance of Wilson's salary. Moreover, Wilson had recently accepted a civil service position in Philadelphia that appeared likely to reduce his time available for league duties. Finally, a deteriorating power base sealed Wilson's fate.

Figure 6. Early portrait of Ferdinand Quintin
Morton, NNL commissioner, 1935–1937.
Courtesy Schomburg Center for Research in Black
Culture, New York Public Library.

While Wilson had enjoyed the support of Greenlee, Passon, and the Philadelphia Stars' Ed Bolden in 1934, Passon's departure and the addition of
two New York teams had dramatically altered the league's balance of
power. The subsequent alignment of Manley and Pompez with Cole and
Grays co-owner Cum Posey, the commissioner's two most ardent critics,
resulted in the ousting of Wilson in March 1935.[5]

The selection of New York-based Ferdinand Quintin Morton as Wilson's
replacement further demonstrated the power of the new owners, prompting a disheartened Bolden to denounce the league's "filthy politics." Yet
Morton's distinguished background seemed to offer promise. Born in 1881
in Macon, Mississippi, to former slaves, Morton subsequently moved to
Washington, D.C., where his father obtained a position with the Treasury
Department. Morton received educational opportunities typically unavail-

able to African Americans at the turn of the century, graduating from prestigious Phillips Exeter Academy in 1902 and attending Harvard University from 1902 through 1905. After developing an interest in law, Morton moved to New York in 1908 and passed the state bar exam in 1910. Under the sponsorship of Tammany leader Charles Murphy, Morton became involved in black Democratic politics in New York, eventually as head of the United Colored Democracy. Morton's Tammany connections facilitated his political rise, culminating in a 1922 appointment as the first black to serve on the New York Municipal Civil Service Commission, a position he would continue to hold while commissioner. By the late 1920s, Morton was an influential black liaison to local political power and influence, and, as black Communist William L. Patterson later recalled, functioned as "a leading Negro spokesman and fixer in Tammany."[6]

Racially conscious, Morton was nevertheless ardently pro-integration (except with regard to his own United Colored Democracy) and had articulated his views in a recent column in the NAACP *Crisis*. Dissenting from W. E. B. Du Bois's increasing advocacy of a separate, self-sustaining, economically cooperative black community, Morton insisted that

the Negro always . . . should resist segregation in every form. . . . He should never voluntarily accept and institutionalize the status resulting from segregation except where sheer necessity compels him to do so—and then only under continued protest. . . . Every separate institution . . . undeniably tends to perpetuate our present status. . . . The only separate minor institutions or organizations which we should build, or maintain and support, are those that serve our daily needs and those that are designed for the achievement of our major objective—demolishing of all racial barriers.[7]

Thus Morton apparently perceived the NNL and other black institutions not as permanent concessions to discrimination but as temporary yet dynamic forces contributing to the end of segregation. Notably, Morton favored the integration of white Organized Baseball, although he pursued only modest measures (discussed in Chapter 7) to achieve the goal during his term in office.[8]

Morton's baseball background, however, was virtually nonexistent except as an interested fan, and sportswriters such as Ed Harris questioned his selection, predicting that he would last "one season and then the junk pile." As Harris observed, the owners had replaced Wilson not for inefficiency but because he had "ruled wisely, but too well." Yet others felt that Morton, who reportedly would receive no salary, would be less susceptible to the influences of other league owners. Morton's actual authority, however, remained questionable, particularly because Gus Greenlee remained entrenched as league president. The new commissioner appeared likely to face the same problems as Wilson, who cited an impossible working environment, noting that he had been "under the impression that he had been elected to arbitrate between and among club owners, but soon found out that his authority was not given the strength to which it should have been entitled."

Despite the controversial ousting of Wilson and the shifting of several franchises, the NNL appeared to have achieved a new level of legitimacy as the 1935 season approached. Even the most cynical observer could not help but delight in the promise of Morton "to see to it that the players get a good break and that the umpires live up to the Constitution and by-laws and that umpiring is of an unimpeachable quality." Financially, the league seemed more secure, as all eight clubs posted a $500 forfeit prior to the planned 72-game split season. The continued progress of the organization appeared assured, prompting Ed Harris to quip that "with Nat Strong dead and Cum Posey in . . . the National Association will have no one to blame their troubles on." Greenlee, however, warned owners to remain focused and disciplined, as "the public will not be willing to overlook our weakness this year or in the future."[9]

Encouraged by the circuit's bolstered stability, fans and sportswriters eagerly awaited the new season. Yet the league lurched backward in 1935 following a series of unexpected developments affecting the success of the organization. Initially hailed as a master stroke, the NNL expansion to eight franchises proved more expensive and problematic than anticipated. Notably, the new franchise alignment, now including four east coast (Newark, Brooklyn, New York, Philadelphia) and two western Pennsylvania (Pittsburgh, Homestead) teams, resulted in increasing difficulties for the two most geographically distant clubs, based in Nashville and Chicago. Hoping to reduce travel, the Nashville Elite Giants relocated to Detroit before the start of the season, planning to lease John Roesink's Hamtramck Stadium for home games. Yet as in 1933, park problems thwarted the establishment of a Detroit franchise, as Roesink experienced tax troubles and lost control of the property. After Greenlee's efforts to regain the use of Hamtramck Stadium failed, the Elites moved to Columbus, Ohio, a city whose location and modest black population (32,774 in 1930) offered little appeal to eastern clubs.

Chicago, though historically the most profitable midwestern city, proved equally burdensome. During 1934, midwestern sportswriters such as Dan Burley complained that eastern teams rarely journeyed west. Yet the 750-plus mile trip remained a continued deterrent. The situation in Chicago deteriorated further during 1935, as owner Robert Cole's numerous other enterprises and increasing disenchantment with Greenlee diverted his full

Figure 7. Robert Cole. A key figure in the early days of the NNL, Cole eventually became disillusioned with the league and Gus Greenlee. Courtesy Robert E. Weems, Jr., and Robert A. Cole, Jr.

attention from the administration of the franchise. The New York Cubans, for example, arrived in Chicago in May for a three-game series with the American Giants, only to find the park in unplayable condition, forcing a cancellation of the first game. The two teams managed to relocate the second game to a neutral site, but the third game was rained out. The unprofitable experience of the Cubans was hardly atypical, and by the season's end most observers recognized the obvious mismatch of a Chicago franchise with an increasingly eastern-based league.

The difficulties in Chicago and Columbus were partially offset by the enthusiastic participation of new owner Alex Pompez in New York. Sparing no expense, the Cuban promoter not only refurbished Dyckman Oval and installed an excellent lighting system, but also assembled a strong franchise featuring Cuban along with several American players. In a further treat for fans, Pompez even succeeded in hiring the recently retired Babe Ruth for an exhibition game in September. Meanwhile, Pompez functioned as a key figure in the league's battle for New York following the death of Nat Strong, raiding the weakened Black Yankees and signing several players. Along with Greenlee, Pompez also attempted to break the power of Strong's agency, now headed by his assistant William Leuschner, by establishing his own booking organization in New York and lining up several white clubs. While only partially successful, the effort finally convinced Max Rosner to offer black teams percentages rather than a flat guarantee at Dexter Park, a long-sought concession.

Despite Pompez's considerable investment and commitment, the anticipated profits in New York failed to materialize in 1935. The Cubans, for example, were burdened by a heavy payroll and surprisingly ambivalent local interest. Meanwhile, the Brooklyn Eagles reportedly lost $30,000 in their first year of operation, hindered by Abe Manley's inexperienced ownership, the inaccessibility of Ebbets Field to the densely settled Harlem community, and competing independent games in New York.[10]

The league's financial woes were hardly limited to Brooklyn. As sportswriter Chester Washington noted, in two or three cities, "the best clubs in the league barely draw enough customers to pay the visiting club's expenses." Perhaps most alarming was the situation in Pittsburgh, a city which, unlike Philadelphia, New York, and Chicago, had never been a consistently profitable venue for black professional baseball, perhaps due to its smaller black population (54,983 in 1930). While the construction of Greenlee Field had revitalized black baseball locally, the lack of a roof at the park became an increasingly significant liability. As Washington observed in July, "even after the absence of the league-leading hometown club for more than three weeks, a Sunday doubleheader hardly drew 'flies' to Greenlee Field." Meanwhile, Greenlee's financial empire had begun to crumble, as the Crawfords' team bus was seized for nonpayment, and by August the team was reportedly a month behind in payroll. Moreover, Greenlee had also become increasingly sidetracked by other interests, notably boxing, after assuming the management of John Henry Lewis in May 1935. After Lewis became light heavyweight champion in October, Greenlee's attention to baseball matters noticeably began to wane, foreshadowing the behavior of other black fans whose growing interest in top black boxers during the 1930s would adversely affect the appeal of baseball.

The inherent financial instability of the league in 1935 seemed to confirm Ed Bolden's initial fear that league baseball was not feasible in the Depression environment. Moreover, his Philadelphia Stars failed to draw as well in their second league season, despite shifting the majority of their home games from Passon Field to the larger Pennsylvania Railroad YMCA Field (nicknamed the "Bolden Bowl") at the southwest corner of 44th and Parkside. Disillusioned by the setbacks, a Stars spokesman issued a statement in late August, warning that unless the NNL made changes, the team would leave the organization and return to independent baseball. From Bolden's perspective, the Stars had not only gained little from the league, but also been crippled by long, unprofitable road trips to western cities such as Pittsburgh and Chicago, where the important dates with white semipro teams needed to meet expenses were difficult to secure. In contrast, despite a drop in attendance, league teams continued to rely heavily on Philadelphia, and as sportswriter Randy Dixon noted, "were it not for Philly, the big Negro clubs would be lost in the financial fog."

As the NNL's problems mounted in Philadelphia and other cities during 1935, fans, players, and owners turned to newly elected Commissioner Ferdinand Morton for answers. But Morton remained largely silent, and by June one wag suggested that the commissioner "wishes that he had never heard of baseball. To be unkind, there are those who say he hasn't." Yet as the Grays' Cum Posey explained, Morton's only authority lay in his role as a "one-man board of arbitration" or "a safeguard," and the true power, as anticipated, remained in the hands of league president Gus Greenlee. Greenlee, however, had become increasingly disenchanted with his position, which he noted "carries only responsibility with limited and always questioned authority" yet was "a target for the most vicious criticism."[11]

To his credit, Greenlee attempted to address the concerns of Philadelphia and other franchises who began to look longingly to a return to independent baseball. To Greenlee, the current widespread "dissatisfaction" in the NNL could be attributed to several causes, including "unfavorable weather," but more notably a "failure to develop interest among fans in a majority of the franchise cities." The blame lay in owners who wanted "immediate results and substantial profits" yet sought the "most trivial excuse to evade fulfilling obligations." Several, for instance, had failed to allocate 5 percent of gate receipts for league expenses and avoided contributing other funds necessary to the NNL's operation. In contrast, Greenlee felt that the players seemed more committed to the organization, doubting "if twenty . . . would choose independent clubs over league baseball."

Despite ongoing problems, Greenlee remained steadfast in his belief that a league remained the best hope for black baseball, insisting that "there might be ever so many faults, but I believe the idea is a good one, and only those owners who can't see beyond a wart on their noses will disagree." Like Bolden, Greenlee recognized that the Crawfords and other league teams could probably earn more playing independent baseball. Yet Greenlee argued that the long-term financial potential for the NNL was more substantial, citing the promotions staged at major league parks in 1934, which had earned "the kind of money unknown to independent baseball."

Determined to protect the young organization, Greenlee warned dissident owners that, while he had been a "congenial fellow" to date, the rumored withdrawals from the league would result in a "fighting Greenlee, equipped with everything needed to win."[12]

Regardless of Greenlee's bravado, few were unaware of the increasingly shaky status of the NNL. With the exception of the third annual East-West game at Comiskey Park and several four-team doubleheaders at Ebbets Field and Yankee Stadium, there had been few positive developments in black professional baseball during 1935. Meanwhile, the league failed to meet following the completion of the season, despite the clamoring of several owners for the return of their $500 forfeits posted earlier in the year, and several umpires remained unpaid. Reflecting on the current chaos, former commissioner Rollo Wilson observed that fans "do not know what to think and are thinking the worst." Posey, however, offered a more sanguine view, asserting that the league was "not tottering," yet admitted that a meeting should be convened immediately.

After a league meeting organized by Commissioner Morton at the behest of the two New York franchise owners failed to materialize in January 1936, the NNL seemed near collapse. Perhaps most concerning was Greenlee's increasing ambivalence, demonstrated by his unwillingness to attend the gathering because of a John Henry Lewis bout in St. Louis. A rebellion against Greenlee's rule now appeared certain, and as Wilson remarked, "certain individuals have privately expressed the opinion that if the president's pugilistic contacts interfere with the conduct of league business . . . he should be relieved of his baseball responsibilities." Unbeknownst to Wilson, Greenlee, preferring to focus more on his growing stable of boxers, had already decided to resign, although he presided at the league meeting held on January 25–26 in Philadelphia. With Greenlee's interest and authority waning, franchises in disarray and others contemplating withdrawal, the meeting would be the most significant since the NNL's formation three years earlier.[13]

After the league's weak financial performance in 1935, the fate of several clubs lay undecided. As Posey noted, the league was "stretched out a little too far geographically," and an obvious solution involved jettisoning franchises west of Pittsburgh. The Chicago American Giants had become an increasing liability to the organization, and by August 1935 owner Robert Cole had turned the team over to his associate Horace Greeley Hall, an official at Cole's Metropolitan Mutual insurance company. Recognizing the incompatibility of a Chicago franchise in an eastern-based league, Hall withdrew from membership at the Philadelphia meeting and instead proposed the development of a midwestern league, which failed to emerge until months later and without the involvement or approval of the NNL.

The NNL lost a second club during the Philadelphia meeting, the Newark Dodgers, who ended their league involvement after contending with a modest-sized black population (38,880 in 1930) and weak financing for two seasons. The franchise reverted to Brooklyn Eagles owner Abe Manley, who had loaned $500 to Dodgers owner Charles Tyler during 1935. After combining the two clubs, Manley abandoned Brooklyn, where the team had drawn poorly, and shifted his franchise to Newark. Meanwhile, after a year in Columbus, Tom Wilson's Elite Giants relocated once again, this time to Griffith Stadium in Washington, D.C., an undeveloped yet potentially fertile area because of its growing African American community, the fifth largest in the country.[14]

From its midwestern beginnings, Greenlee's NNL had now evolved into an eastern organization similar in composition to the Eastern Colored and American Negro leagues of the 1920s. Nearly all the major eastern cities and teams were fully integrated into the organization, with the exception of New York, where the troublesome Black Yankees continued to operate independently, often functioning as a "haven for dissatisfied ball players," according to one observer. James Semler had operated the Black Yankees during 1935 after the death of Nat Strong. Born in Texas, Semler served in the army in the Quartermaster Corps from 1913 to 1920, reportedly receiving the nickname "Soldier Boy" while baking bread for troops during World War I. After discharge, Semler eventually relocated to New York, where he became involved in the numbers, baseball promotion, and later a farm on Long Island. Semler's success in the numbers, however, failed to match that of Greenlee, Pompez, Manley, and Grays co-owner Rufus Jackson, as revealed by the chronically underfinanced state of the Black Yankees during their existence. Alluding to Black Yankees' limited financial backing, Posey grumbled that Semler's ascendancy to ownership occurred "without spending a penny of his own or anyone else's money."

Weakened by raids, the Black Yankees had attempted to affiliate with the NNL in 1935 despite opposition from the league's Newark and New York franchises, who objected to additional local competition. At the Philadelphia meeting, the Black Yankees' request for full membership privileges was again deferred and eventually rejected over the protests of Greenlee, who preferred to have the team under league control. Greenlee's view proved prescient, as the renegade club remained an annoyance during the early months of the 1936 season, particularly after a dispute over several players prompted Semler to file lawsuits against the New York Cubans and Newark Eagles. By June, the league reconsidered its initial stance, admitting the Black Yankees as a full member for the second half after Semler and booking agent William Leuschner withdrew their legal actions against league teams.

The Philadelphia meeting resulted in the reconfiguring of the NNL, but the status of the league government remained undecided. Greenlee had yet to resign officially, yet after his relatively quick exit from the gathering to fly to Denver for another John Henry Lewis promotion, a shakeup in league officers was likely. For Posey, a constant opponent of Greenlee and his associate John Clark, the change was necessary, as "every player in the League and every loyal League fan knows the affairs of the League have been handled in a loose manner for two years." On March 8, Greenlee formally stepped down as president at a league meeting in New York. In a surprising move, Posey nominated Ed Bolden as replacement, seconded by Greenlee. Although initially expressing concern over presiding over an organization so splintered by factions, Bolden eventually accepted the nomination and was elected after running unopposed. Bolden's election represented a stunning comeback for a man whose career had appeared finished six years earlier. The enviable position of Philadelphia as the strongest league city, coupled with Bolden's nearly 26 years in professional black baseball (rivaled only by Posey, who did not want the job) undoubtedly facilitated his elevation to president.[15]

Despite his unanimous selection, Bolden now headed an organization in which cooperation had deteriorated to a dangerously low level. The earlier debate over the admission of the Black Yankees revealed the prevalent attitude, as startled journalists overheard Tom Wilson loudly proclaim his intention to play the New York club, saying, "I don't give a damn what you do." Perhaps most concerning was the animosity between Greenlee and Posey, which exploded once again in a series of disagreements ultimately counterproductive to the league. Angered by the continued presence of Crawford official John Clark in the league government, Posey stormed out of a meeting after failing to remove him as NNL secretary. In a more ominous development for the league, Posey and Greenlee then clashed over the Grays' decision to abandon Greenlee Field for a return to Forbes Field. Noting that "rains and burning sun" had severely limited attendance at Greenlee Field in 1935, Posey argued that the Grays "reserve the right to play our home games where we think they will draw." Greenlee interpreted the maneuver as but "one number on a long program aimed directly at me," noting that Posey had constantly undermined his position through "correspondence with club owners, creating a condition of dissatisfaction, and used his newspaper column as an official medium for right and wrong in colored baseball." Yet Greenlee was forced to acknowledge the difficulties at Greenlee Field, particularly "the disadvantage of being without a top. But even so, it represents an investment of close to $100,000 of cash money, one half of which came out of my pockets." Unwilling or unable to compromise, the Grays and Crawfords not only refused to schedule each other in the first half but even planned competing games in Pittsburgh.[16]

Bolden and other league officials eventually managed to amend the schedule to suit both teams, but the new president also had to attend to the affairs of his own club, which revived in 1936 and found itself contending with the Washington Elite Giants in a heated duel for the first-half race scheduled to end in the first week of July. A major dispute arose involving a league ruling that each team must play other league clubs at least five times per half. If prevented by postponements, the games had to be rescheduled if they would affect the final standings. Hoping to overtake the Stars late in the half, the Elites had invoked the ruling to arrange a makeup of two postponed games with Philadelphia. But following the Stars' slide to second place, the Elites refused to play the makeup games, leaving Washington first in the final first-half standings with a 14-10 record and Philadelphia second at 15-12.

Called upon to resolve the dilemma, the normally inactive Commissioner Ferdinand Morton ordered the two games to be replayed. On July 30, the Stars defeated the Elites by a 7-1 score in the first of the rescheduled games. The game was disallowed, however, after Tom Wilson claimed that the Elites had been unable to field a representative team, and the two games were rescheduled for September. A second attempt on September 17 resulted in a Philadelphia defeat, rendering the second game superfluous and giving the Elites the first-half flag with a 15-10 record, edging the Stars' 15-13 mark. Meanwhile, the games and Morton's authority had already been made irrelevant by Greenlee's pre-series announcement that the Crawfords would not play the Stars for the league championship regardless of the outcome.[17]

The convoluted controversy and its unsatisfactory conclusion drew widespread criticism from observers such as Rollo Wilson, who labeled the "disgusting riddle about who won the first-half pennant" as "the biggest farce the game has known." The dispute also raised more troubling questions about the league's stability and administration, particularly the role of Ferdinand Morton. While Bolden felt that Morton was "honorable, just and fair-minded," others criticized the commissioner's lack of authority and failure to act quickly to resolve the situation. Meanwhile, the discord over the first-half pennant had undermined Bolden's own effectiveness as president, rendering him largely unable to act decisively in the best interests of the league. With a stake in the outcome, Bolden realized that any decision made, however well intentioned, would face harsh criticism, yet insisted that "had two other League clubs been involved . . . I would have ordered them to play the two postponed games."

The contested first-half championship was but one of a number of frustrations for Bolden in 1936. Like his predecessor Greenlee, Bolden was hindered constantly by increasingly uncooperative owners, whose individualism, difficult to check in even favorable circumstances, proved nearly impossible to contain. While Wilson and other observers recognized that the owners desperately needed "the thing they have never learned . . . TEAMWORK!" the prevailing attitude, as Posey quipped, remained "try to be all for one and please let me be that one."[18]

The handling of several NNL promotions revealed the deep divisions and lack of cooperation within the organization. The league, for example, had originally planned to send an all-star team to the *Denver Post* tournament. The "Negro National League All-Stars" subsequently captured the August tournament and $5,093 in prize money, but the team was privately sponsored by only three franchises (Grays, Elites, and Crawfords), who willingly sent the cream of their own teams to participate. To the disgust of fans, the severely weakened teams continued in league competition without their star players. Although Posey later admitted that the "worst mistake of all was the breaking up of clubs in August to send star players to barnstorming," the potential profit proved too much to resist.

The promotion of the popular East-West game was similarly flawed, as the game was staged in 1936 by two NNL officials (Greenlee, Tom Wilson) and two independent team owners (Horace Hall of the American Giants and J. L. Wilkinson of the Kansas City Monarchs) without the involvement or participation of other NNL teams. Objecting to a recent ruling limiting individual promotions, Greenlee reasserted his right to promote the game, noting that "when no one had any faith in the idea, it was perfectly all right for us to gamble with our money. But after its success had been assured, we were sorta shunted out of the picture." Yet the subsequent game, featuring players from only four teams, lacked the all-star quality of previous years.

A disastrous playoff between the Elites and the Crawfords provided a fitting end to a catastrophic season and seemingly revealed the organization as a league in name only. To the dismay of fans, several star players from both teams failed to appear at the opening game scheduled on September 21 in Philadelphia, preferring to barnstorm together after being taken off salary at the close of the regular season. After the abrupt cancellation of the series after only one game, Bolden cited the league's continued woes at the box office, noting that "it is not mandatory that two champion teams complete a World Series if it does not pay financially." Although several league officials subsequently suggested that the series be resumed in the spring, other observers denounced the idea as ridiculous.[19]

Marred by the first-half controversy, an aborted playoff, uncooperative owners, and continued financial reverses, the NNL again appeared on the verge of collapse at the close of the 1936 season. Philadelphia columnist Ed Harris aptly expressed the disappointment of most black fans:

The league as a league is a flop. It seems that some of the teams in the group are in it the way some people are married—simply because it sounds nice. . . . They will have to decide which field they will emphasize, sand-lot semi-pro playing or league playing. They can't have both as lots of them are trying to have now.

Equally discouraged by the sluggish progress of the NNL, Bolden observed that "if good results won't obtain from the League then it would be better to have an association until the time arrives we can get at least six substantial clubs to maintain a real League." Posey agreed, citing the difficulties of an organization with "three pulling one way and four pulling opposite." Fast losing support from sportswriters and fans, black professional baseball appeared largely incapable of growth and an increasingly questionable investment as the Depression continued.[20]

◆ ◆ ◆

For decades, baseball had a virtually uncontested claim to the loyalties of sports-loving African Americans, reinforced by generous coverage in the black media. With the possible exception of Jack Johnson's reign as heavyweight champion between 1908 and 1915, few black athletic accomplishments generated the ongoing community attention and support enjoyed by baseball. Now, during the mid-1930s, two black athletes emerged whose startling success in interracial competition elicited a profound reaction among African Americans, a response shaped by the considerable barriers facing minorities in American society. As St. Claire Drake and Horace Cayton, authors of the landmark *Black Metropolis*, subsequently explained, "unable to compete freely *as individuals*, the Negro masses take intense vicarious pleasure in watching Race Heroes vindicate them in the eyes of the white world." Sons of Alabama sharecroppers who migrated north, track star Jesse Owens and boxer Joe Louis not only provided a refreshing antidote to the troubled state of black professional baseball in 1936 but ushered in a new era of black athletic celebrity.

Jesse Owens was first thrust into the national spotlight in May 1935 after a record-breaking performance at a Big 10 championship meet in Ann Arbor, Michigan. A year later, Owens skyrocketed to fame at the summer Olympics in Berlin, where he captured four gold medals. The brilliant effort coupled with Adolph Hitler's slight of American black athletes earned Owens plaudits and sympathy from both the white mainstream and black media, transforming the young track star into a national celebrity.

While remarkable, Owens's success was ultimately overshadowed by the unprecedented rise of Joe Louis, who in June 1937 became the first black heavyweight champion since Jack Johnson. During the 1930s, Louis's amazing streak of triumphs over a series of predominantly white opponents not only won him the adulation of the black community but also earned him the respect and admiration of numerous whites. Like Owens's track feats at the Berlin Olympics, Louis's defeat of German heavyweight Max Schmeling in 1938 functioned for all Americans as a vicarious victory over German fascism and its claims of Aryan supremacy. Less threatening to whites than the controversial Johnson, Louis became an American icon during his long reign as champion.[21]

No black sporting event, with the possible exception of the East-West game, could compare in importance to a Joe Louis fight. Black men and women from all socioeconomic levels thrilled in his victories, which offered not only the prospect of recognition and the grudging respect of white America but also immediate and constant gratification. The astonishing exploits of Louis, like those Jackie Robinson would accomplish in 1947, achieved what black baseball largely failed to do: create new fans and attract previously uninterested parties into the attendance mix. One new fan was editor E. Washington Rhodes of the *Philadelphia Tribune*. Previously indifferent to sports, Rhodes revealed his newfound passion after witnessing a Joe Louis bout: "Call it the savage in me or anything you like—I was thrilled, my blood tingled. I was joyously happy."[22]

Not surprisingly, the rise of Joe Louis sometimes relegated black baseball to an inferior status. As early as June 1935, the Philadelphia Stars management broadcast results of Louis's battle with Primo Carnera, subsequently repeating the practice during any of his fights coinciding with an NNL game. Meanwhile, black sports pages lavished column after column on the young boxer, and important NNL games were sometimes "pushed to the background by the hysterics encircling Joe Louis and his activities." By 1938, the exhaustive coverage prompted one fan to request "more baseball news. . . . Joe Louis is all right. But so are Paige, and Bell, and all the others. Besides, most of us get fed up on too much of anything."

Yet black (and white) sportswriters typically reflected rather than shaped the interests of their readers. The majority of African Americans craved news of Louis, who received more front-page mention and headlines in the *Chicago Defender* between 1933 and 1938 than any other individual. Meanwhile, the heavy exposure of Louis reportedly boosted the *Pittsburgh Courier*'s circulation considerably during the mid-1930s. With the abundant news of Louis and other boxers, the often spotty black baseball coverage and publicity was inevitably displaced on occasion. (As later discussed, the integration of major league baseball in the late 1940s would result in a similar reduction in coverage of black baseball.)

While the impact of the rise of Louis and boxing remained unclear, several observers warned of a problem that would only grow in the future: the declining interest in baseball among black youths. Randy Dixon, for instance, claimed in 1938 that "the kids just ain't going in for baseball with the same enthusiasm these days. Their heroes are the Joe Louis', the Henry Armstrongs et al." Black sociologist Charles S. Johnson similarly cited the appeal of Louis, Armstrong, and Owens among young black males, noting "this racial superiority in the field of athletics has contributed more to race pride than any other single factor in recent years." Black baseball stars were conspicuously absent from Johnson's discussion, hardly surprising to sportswriter Leon Hardwick, who suggested that "the average boy thumbs his nose" at the sport which "holds nothing for him."[23]

Ironically, Louis himself aspired to baseball stardom as a child and remained a passionate fan of the Detroit Tigers. Recognizing Louis's fondness for the sport, celebrity status, and increasing wealth, NNL officials attempted to interest his managers, John Roxborough and Julian Black, in financing a Detroit-based league team in 1936 and 1938. Louis reportedly was enthusiastic, but Roxborough vetoed the venture, citing cost and time constraints.

The individual athletic feats of Joe Louis and Jesse Owens succeeded in transcending the usual limited sphere of white recognition of black accomplishment during the mid-1930s. Moreover, their tangible achievements stood in stark contrast to black professional baseball, whose unsatisfying operation continued to bewilder and frustrate even its most dedicated followers. A black Brooklyn fan, for example, contrasted Satchel Paige's non-appearance for a scheduled New York promotion in 1935 with Joe Louis's "level-headed and superior judgment. What would the white race think of Joe if he was in Chicago fighting a ham, and failed to show up the night he was scheduled to meet Max Baer?" While black baseball, despite its flaws, maintained a firm grip on the attention of African Americans, the veneration of Louis and Owens during the 1930s suggested that black fans could easily derive racial pride from individual achievement in interracial competition and could be weaned from imperfect black enterprises.[24]

◆ ◆ ◆

After four fitful years of operation, the NNL stood at a crossroads after the 1936 season. Despite several franchise shifts and sporadic changes in league government, the organization had progressed only marginally since 1934. The stalled growth was confirmed by league secretary John Clark, who lamented that "the financial results are just about the same." While offering the encouraging news that "several clubs showed a paper profit for the season," Clark admitted it was "not a drop in the bucket to offset losses sustained in the three previous years." Yet Cum Posey, whose Grays reportedly profited in 1936, asserted that the NNL was "not in bad financial straits but is in better financial condition than any former Negro league."

Posey's appraisal was somewhat optimistic in light of the continued turmoil surrounding the league's operation. As Posey admitted, "not one member is satisfied with the way the league was operated in 1936," and a shakeup in the NNL's leadership seemed likely. While Posey believed that "Bolden has the League more at heart than any of the . . . officers," the numerous controversies and unsatisfactory conclusion of the prior season had jeopardized his position. Moreover, Bolden had struggled to govern the seriously divided circuit, and as Rollo Wilson insightfully noted, "did not show the enthusiasm for the office" he had exhibited in the 1920s.

To the surprise of few, Bolden was deposed as president in January 1937 after only a single year in office. Several candidates emerged as potential replacements, most notably several nonaffiliated individuals, including Ira Lewis, a former sportswriter and current editor of the *Pittsburgh Courier*. In a peculiar move likely engineered by Greenlee, the league eventually selected Leonard "Big Bill" Williams, an obscure Pittsburgh underworld figure, who subsequently declined the position. At the behest of Greenlee, the league then considered Lemuel Williams, a Cleveland promoter and former official in Rube Foster's NNL of the 1920s, before ultimately returning Greenlee to the office. Although owners continued to occupy other NNL positions, the league did select a nonaffiliated league secretary, William Nunn of the *Courier*, to replace John Clark, who had stepped aside amid continued criticism of his dual role with the Crawfords. Meanwhile, the genial yet generally powerless Ferdinand Morton was retained as commissioner for a third year.[25]

Though increasingly committed to John Henry Lewis and his other boxers, Greenlee appeared reinvigorated after resuming his position as league president. Attempting to alter the balance of power with white promoters, Greenlee announced that "former arrangements would be discarded." Rather than continue the current practice of individual clubs competing for dates with several booking agents, Greenlee and other league officials advocated employing a single individual to arrange all independent games for league teams. The league subsequently hired the Stars' Eddie Gottlieb to book all independent games east of Altoona, Pennsylvania. Although

Gottlieb would receive his usual 10 percent booking fee, a quarter of his share would be returned to the league treasury as a commission, a departure from past practices. While the Nat Strong agency predictably resisted, William Leuschner eventually agreed to the new terms and later became the league's agent for metropolitan New York games. Now assimilated into the league structure, the two major eastern booking agents would ideally work in tandem, rather than in opposition to organized black baseball.

Although the new collaborative relationship with booking agents neutralized a potential threat, the NNL faced a new source of competition with the sudden existence of a rival organization, the Negro American League (NAL). Organized in December 1936, the NAL featured an alignment of midwestern and southern franchises strikingly similar to Foster's NNL of 1920–1931, including the Chicago American Giants, Kansas City Monarchs, Detroit Stars, Cincinnati Tigers, St. Louis Stars, Indianapolis Athletics, Birmingham Black Barons, and Memphis Red Sox. The new circuit was headed by Major Robert R. Jackson, a former postal employee active in Republican politics in Chicago who had served in the Illinois legislature for three terms and as an alderman since 1918. A veteran of the Spanish-American War, Jackson had prior experience in black baseball as an official with the Chicago-based Columbia Giants, the Leland Giants, and more recently as part-owner of the American Giants.

With the formation of the NAL, black fans could look forward to enjoying the operation of two fully functioning upper-level black professional leagues for the first time since 1929. The relationship between the eastern and midwestern leagues of the 1920s had been contentious at times, exacerbated by the generally stronger economic status of eastern teams less handicapped by traveling distances. Geographically distant from the east, NAL franchises posed no real threat to the NNL, as recognized by Posey, who observed that "the greater number of good players prefer to play in the east." Yet disputes over six players who had reportedly jumped to eastern teams in 1936 but returned to the midwest in 1937 prevented an immediate agreement. With continued struggles over players likely, St. Louis Stars owner Henry Moore asserted that "a working agreement . . . is needed at almost any cost." The two leagues cooperated little in 1937, however, and failed to reach an accord.[26]

The NAL soon became a secondary concern after a series of devastating financial crises within the NNL, beginning with the sudden loss of Alex Pompez's New York Cubans. Though Pompez was reportedly no longer involved in the numbers by the mid-1930s, his earlier successes and association with Dutch Schultz had made him one of the targets of New York special prosecutor Thomas Dewey's crackdown on the policy racket and its influential Tammany liaison James Hines. After his indictment in May

1936, Pompez left for France along with his partner Joe Ison, hoping to avoid increasing local pressure. While the two men eventually returned to the United States, Ison's arrest in January 1937 forced Pompez to flee to Mexico by private plane. Apprehended by Mexican authorities in late March, Pompez vowed to fight extradition to the United States, noting that "if they get me before that Dewey grand jury I'm licked before I start. They ain't got nothing on me but gambling and that ain't a crime here in Mexico. I'm a good guy and I got lots of friends in Mexico." Insisting that he had been inactive in the numbers for two years, Pompez claimed his "only interest now is baseball." Promised leniency in return for testimony, Pompez finally returned to New York in October 1937, where he was placed under police protection.[27]

With Pompez now unavailable, the NNL shrank to six franchises in 1937. Perhaps more important, the highly publicized Pompez situation raised larger issues of whether the involvement and investment of numbers bankers was ultimately counterproductive. As we have seen, numbers money had played a vital role in black baseball during the Depression, filling a void by providing much of the necessary cash to sustain a struggling organization (nicknamed the "Bankers' League" by one newspaper). Moreover, as historian Juliet Walker has noted, without the venture capital generated from the numbers and other illegal businesses, the "picture of black enterprise in the first half of the twentieth century would be even more dismal than the historical record shows."[28] Yet the involvement of numbers bankers also undermined the legitimacy of an enterprise struggling to win recognition from blacks and whites, leading sportswriter Sam Lacy to warn that organized black baseball needed to be "more discriminating in . . . [its] membership requirements." In a further condemnation of the industry's leaders, journalist Dave Hawkins privately denounced Gus Greenlee as a "crook" who "had no respect for anything that was honest and straight."[29] Others were equally uncomfortable with the enterprise, denounced by one observer as the "biggest, most vicious racket in America," one that preyed on "the superstitions of the gullible, the hopes of the poor."[30]

Cum Posey, however, defended both Pompez and the continued operation of the illegal numbers lottery. Posey argued that Pompez had been a "bigger benefactor in the life of Harlem than he has been a nuisance," and that "lotteries of any kind should not be put in the same illegal category as burglary and other major crimes." Dixie Davis, a lawyer linked to Dutch Schultz, similarly insisted that "the policy bankers were not mobsters. They were merely gamblers running an illegal business, on a very peaceful, non-violent basis. There is a distinction, very real, between ordinary law violators and the public enemies of the organized underworld."[31]

Even conservative editor E. Washington Rhodes asserted that "the numbers business should be legalized and taxed. Since the government can't stop the number[s] business, it should get the revenue." One advocate offered the familiar argument that the numbers, when operated and controlled by blacks, offered financial opportunities largely unavailable in white America: "A man with $20 worth of numbers daily was able to support a family and pay bills. He didn't have to commit crimes that would send him back to jail. Since the colored man had less than others, money gained from numbers did him the most good." The distinguished black writer J. Saunders Redding, however, dismissed the supposed positive benefits of the numbers bankers and the "notion . . . that they are the benefactors of their people." Redding noted, "it is not a game in which the bankers can lose," and so it ultimately resulted in "helping a poor people grow poorer."[32]

Regardless of its merits or flaws, the numbers lottery represented a dangerously volatile enterprise that offered entrepreneurs the potential of substantial profits but also equally enormous losses. Pompez, for example, reported losing $60,000 after the commonly played number "527" hit in November 1931. Moreover, the risk of prosecution always loomed, depending on the current relationship with local political leaders and law enforcement. Like Pompez, Gus Greenlee (who had dodged a conviction in 1934) found himself under increasing pressure by 1937, reportedly resulting from a crackdown by local authorities, and his once profitable business in Pittsburgh began to fade.

Desperately needing money, Greenlee began to auction off his superstar players to other teams. In March 1937, he sent Josh Gibson and Judy Johnson to the Grays for Henry Spearman, Lloyd "Pepper" Bassett, and $2,500, reportedly the largest sum involved in a player deal in black baseball to date. Continuing his salary dump, Greenlee sold Harry Kincannon to the New York Black Yankees for $1,000 and traded Jimmy Crutchfield and Dick Seay to the Newark Eagles for Harry Williams and Thad Christopher. The trades failed to alleviate Greenlee's financial distress, however, leaving the Crawfords increasingly vulnerable to outside offers, not only from other league teams but from newly established professional leagues in Latin America.[33]

Capitalizing on the collapse of the New York Cubans along with Greenlee's financial woes, the Dominican Republic suddenly emerged as a major threat to the NNL, thanks to the efforts of President Rafael Leonidas Trujillo Molina. Born on October 24, 1891, in San Cristobal, Trujillo had been a sugar estate policeman and then advanced in the Dominican army through the sponsorship of the United States Marines, who occupied the country from 1916 through 1924. Trujillo eventually became a brigadier general and chief of staff, and a subsequent coup placed him at the head of the troubled nation in 1930. For the next thirty-one years, until his assassination in 1961, Trujillo maintained dictatorial control of the Dominican Republic, ruling, as one observer noted, "as a baronial fief with an absolutism seldom rivaled in modern history."[34]

The country's tremendous interest in baseball since its introduction to the region in 1891 would thrust Trujillo into sudden involvement with the sport in 1937. Increasingly fierce competition among Dominican teams had resulted in their affiliation with influential business and government leaders by the mid-1930s. Seeking to counter strong clubs sponsored by his opponents and to bolster his already enviable political position (a motive rejected by some sources), Trujillo began to assemble the finest baseball team in the Dominican summer league. Unable to offer the salary or lifestyle to attract the best white professionals, Trujillo instead began to recruit black American and Cuban players for his Ciudad Trujillo ("Trujillo City," the new name for Santo Domingo) team with the assistance of Martin Dihigo and Lazaro Salazar, two players from Alex Pompez's now disbanded New York Cubans.

With Greenlee's finances increasingly shaky, the Crawfords were particularly receptive to Dominican offers. After accepting $2,500 in April, Satchel Paige left the Crawfords training camp in New Orleans to board a plane headed for the Dominican Republic. Paige was soon joined by several of his teammates, including catcher Bill Perkins and outfielders Sam Bankhead and James "Cool Papa" Bell. By late June, reportedly 18 players, 9 of them Crawfords, had bolted the league after receiving $800 to $2,200 and traveling expenses to play with either Ciudad Trujillo or the other two league teams, Estrellas Orientales (backed by an opponent of Trujillo) and Aguilas Cibaenas.[35]

The decision to leave the United States to play abroad reflected the minimal appeal the league held for most players in the late 1930s. Offered an alternative, black players eagerly embraced opportunities to better their incomes and working conditions. As Satchel Paige explained, "the opportunities of a colored baseball player on these islands are the same or almost the same as those enjoyed by the white major league players in the States. That's something to think about, you know." Paige meanwhile expressed his contempt for the league, asserting his willingness to "go to South America and live in the jungles rather than go back to the league and play ball like I did for ten years." Yet the continuous specter of the ruthless dictator Trujillo created a less than idyllic environment in the Dominican Republic, viewed by one contemporary observer as "one of the most frightful tyrannies in the history of the Americas or of the world." Posey, for example, claimed that the players "were almost prisoners when not prac-

Figure 8. Ciudad Trujillo 1937 team. At least nine of those pictured had played in the NNL in 1936, including Satchel Paige (second row, far right) and Josh Gibson (rear, far left). Courtesy Baseball Hall of Fame Library.

ticing or playing. They were not permitted to buy a glass of beer in a saloon. They were not permitted out of the hotel after dark on any night except Sunday and Monday nights." Paige himself largely confirmed Posey's charges, later admitting that "I wasn't down there very long until I wished I wasn't."

The country's potential drawbacks, however, failed to offset Greenlee's tottering financial status, leading Posey to suggest that "perhaps the Crawford players were more willing to talk business than players of other clubs." Paige himself later noted that "Gus was feeling a money pinch . . . and the checks from him weren't what they used to be." James Bell similarly recalled that Greenlee was "losing money . . . matter of fact, the whole league was going bad at that time."[36]

The stunned NNL staggered to recover from the sudden loss of the equivalent of a team's worth of players, including several star performers. As a first step, Greenlee threatened suspension for any player who failed to report by May 15, warning that "the men who have sacrificed their time and money to develop baseball, will not allow any one player or any group of players to wreck the league. These men must realize that the league is far larger and more powerful than they are." Meanwhile, Greenlee and Rufus Jackson of the Grays facilitated the May 8 arrest of two Dominican representatives for tampering with league players in Pittsburgh, although the case was eventually dismissed.[37]

The league then attempted to involve the federal government in the dispute. In a May 25 telegram to Democratic Senator Robert Wagner of New York, NNL commissioner Ferdinand Morton explained the difficulties of the league and black players, who remained "shamelessly discriminated against by organized baseball." As Morton noted, while the league had made "steady progress," there were few "highly skilled colored ball players," as the "economic inducements are not sufficient to attract intelligent young men." The recent raids from the Dominican Republic thus posed a serious threat, and "all the work which we have done to secure for the colored ball player a decent wage will go for naught unless we are able to prevent further inroads." While recognizing the possibility of pursuing legal action, Morton suggested that an appeal to the State Department to order the return of the players was warranted. Morton subsequently retained New York attorney David Ticktin to discuss the case with State Department officials, who were already aware of the controversy through an earlier letter from Ira Hurwick, a white Pittsburgh lawyer representing the Crawfords. At a meeting at the State Department on June 21, Ticktin reiterated the league's difficulties and suspicions of the direct involvement of the Dominican government, but was informed that the "case did not appear to contravene the general principles of international law or our own treaty rights with the Dominican Republic."[38]

The State Department agreed to grant a more formal hearing to the league eight days later. Accompanied by Hurwick, several officials including Greenlee, Bolden, Elite Giants official Vernon Green, Effa Manley, and the NAL's Major Jackson traveled to Washington to discuss the situation with Division of American Republics head Laurence Duggan, who was later implicated as a spy for the Soviet Union and apparently committed suicide shortly after being questioned by the FBI in 1948. Hurwick described the league's dilemma, explaining that the Dominican government appeared unlikely to intervene and had already dismissed the matter as "a private one of no concern to the Dominican authorities." Legal proceedings were also unlikely to bring relief, as Hurwick acknowledged that ballplayers were "not liable in law for damages for breaking a contract." A potential solution, however, might be possible if the Dominican and black baseball seasons were arranged to avoid overlap in the future. Although Duggan supported Hurwick's suggestion, Major Jackson pushed for a more aggressive stance, recommending a "kind diplomatic note" to the Dominican Republic requesting that the government abstain from recruiting American players. Moreover, Greenlee and Effa Manley offered to furnish a doubtful Duggan with "ample proof of the direct concern of the Dominican Government" in the raids, which would warrant a more thorough State Department investigation.

Wary of a legal struggle and believing that an "amicable arrangement would be the best," the league ultimately agreed that Duggan would speak to Dominican minister Andres Pastoriza about adjusting the baseball season to avoid future conflicts. Meanwhile, Hurwick would gather evidence of the involvement of the Dominican government and also attempt to meet with Pastoriza.[39] The unspectacular outcome of the three-hour meeting, however, could not help but disappoint black baseball officials hoping for a speedy return of their players. Greenlee blamed Morton, cryptically claiming that the commissioner had "made certain moves without consulting me" (perhaps the telegram to Wagner and hiring of Ticktin), placing the league "in an embarrassing situation when we went to Washington." Fortunately, the intervention of the State Department would prove unnecessary, as the Dominican league subsequently scaled down its salaries and ceased to be a threat after 1937.

Frustrated in attempts to recover their men, the league then turned to deciding appropriate punishments upon the players' anticipated return following the 36-game Dominican season. While initially imposing a two-year suspension and a fine, the NNL later modified the penalty to a fine of one month's salary, recognizing that a lengthy ban of several players would wreak havoc on several teams. Most observers expected a weakening of will, citing the failure of black baseball to enforce five-year suspensions for jumping contracts in the late 1920s. Several players had also escaped serious punishment in recent years despite jumping league teams to play for a white semiprofessional club in Bismarck, North Dakota. Long familiar with the weak authority in the industry, Randy Dixon expected the owners to "do an about-face and forgive and forget. They're funny that way." Satchel Paige remained equally confident, noting that "I am pretty sure when I get to America I will not be a stranger to the N.N.L."[40]

Yet league officials initially showed surprising unity, refusing to reinstate the jumpers after their return to the United States in late July, with the temporary exception of catcher Josh Gibson, who had reportedly received permission from the Homestead Grays to play abroad. Blocked from appearing with league teams or in parks in which league teams appeared, blacklisted players faced the possibility of lost income during the summer months. Not surprisingly, Cum Posey had little sympathy for the plight of jumping players such as Paige, who had been "treated royally" by Greenlee and had "gotten more out of Negro baseball than anyone ever connected with Negro baseball. Negro baseball does not owe him anything.

He owes Negro baseball plenty." Meanwhile, Crawfords official John Clark denounced the players who had "cast their lot with foreigners—and forgot the men who had met payrolls with empty parks."

To the chagrin of the NNL, the jumpers easily circumvented the intended punishment by organizing their own team and establishing contact with major midwestern promoter Ray Doan. Doan, who had handled barnstorming tours of the Dean brothers of the St. Louis Cardinals and had also booked the bearded House of David team, promptly provided dates for the "Santo Domingo All-Stars" throughout the west. The team of jumpers even entered and won the *Denver Post* tournament, the second consecutive year the feat had been accomplished by a black club.[41]

The jumpers' relative ease in evading league regulations led some observers to question whether the intended punishments had exacerbated rather than ameliorated an already unfortunate situation. To Posey, the ruling had ultimately done little but weaken the league's already tenuous grip on the players, offering them "tacit encouragement by allowing them to perform for a man who is not and never has been in sympathy with organized Negro baseball." Meanwhile, the situation took an increasingly bizarre turn when rumors began to surface that league president Greenlee, despite his outward opposition, had actually encouraged the jumpers' alignment with Doan. Though Greenlee initially denied the charge, his promotion of a series of games involving the Santo Domingo All Stars against league players seemed to validate the accusations. Greenlee subsequently offered the weak rationalization that the games had been scheduled after the completion of the league season and that the blacklisted players had agreed to pay their fines, but the explanation failed to placate observers such as Randy Dixon, who lamented that "it reveals just what kind of organization they have. It proves that their rules mean nothing. . . . It proves that the public doesn't give a happy damn about the joke league they have imposed on us folks for the past two years."[42]

After five years of operation, the Negro National League appeared unable to advance beyond the financial and organizational promise of 1934. With profits and salaries negligible due to the Depression, the majority of league owners and players had understandably pursued a self-centered path, resulting in stalled progress during the mid-1930s. The continued lack of cooperation further crippled an already precarious industry, now increasingly vulnerable to raids from foreign interests, a problem that would only recur in the future. Moreover, the meteoric rise of athletes such as Joe Louis who excelled within in a white sporting milieu had provided African Americans with an alternative to the chaotic state of black professional baseball. Marred by squabbling owners, jumping players, and disheartened fans, the enterprise of black professional baseball stood in desperate need of reform at the end of 1937.[43]

3

Growing Pains

The owners . . . can only go so far with their midget minds.
They have too many complexes, too many petty scruples, too
many false ambitions, with not even a child's sense of cooperation or gratitude.

—John Clark, 1937

By 1938, numerous African American sportswriters, owners, players, and
fans had begun to doubt whether professional black baseball could ever
fulfill its potential as a profitable enterprise. The meager financial returns
and fragmented organization discouraged most potential investors, and
little improvement seemed forthcoming as the Depression continued to
cripple the black communities of league cities. Yet the industry's ability to
function during the 1930s, when numerous black businesses either collapsed or fell into the hands of whites (such as the motion picture and
record industries), attested to the surprising resiliency of the institution
despite its numerous flaws and fostered hopes of future profits with the
return of a more stable economy.[1]

No obvious solution, however, existed to ameliorate the current troubled
financial state of black baseball. League officials such as New York Black
Yankee owner James Semler linked the difficulties to declining patronage
and increasing expenses such as player salaries, equipment, lodging, and
park rentals. Semler claimed that each team needed to gross at least
$27,000 to turn a profit for the five-month season from May to September,
an increasingly formidable feat during the Depression. Outlining the discouraging conditions affecting his club's stability, Semler noted that "in
New York there are over 300,000 colored people but the best we can hope
for at any time is about 5,000 customers—and with an admission prices
of 55c or 30c for a doubleheader! At night games, with the same prices
they draw even less than that." Like other black entrepreneurs, Semler
also cited the problem of white competition, complaining that "every time
the Yankees or Giants play, you can find at least 5,000 of our people in
the stands, paying twice as much and more."[2]

Long familiar with the midwestern black baseball scene, veteran columnist Fay Young shed additional light on the limited black attendance:

Many who own automobiles go to the country. The radio keeps many at home. But out of 250,000 of our group in Chicago, it is a sad state of affairs when such a club as the Monarchs can draw but 5,000 on a Sunday—and at a double header at that.

While league officials conveniently blamed the lack of fan support for the industry's woes, other observers felt that flimsy business practices and general lack of acumen had been equally detrimental. Although sportswriter Leon Hardwick and others believed that "colored baseball is a business proposition and should be treated as such," umpire Bert Gholston lamented that "very few business men engaged in baseball understand the fundamental principles of the game as a business asset." Few, if any, of the owners had substantial experience in legitimate business activities, and as writer Chappy Gardner asserted, "as fine as these owners are, personally, they lack business training. Running a baseball league is big business. These men have not had 'little business' training even."[3]

The major attempts to stimulate league attendance were modest at best, including occasional "Ladies' Days" and free Saturday admission to boys under sixteen at Greenlee Field, season passes sold in 1936 by the Crawfords and the Chicago American Giants, and an automobile giveaway at Dyckman Oval in 1935. Newark Eagles owner Abe Manley cited financial constraints to launching more ambitious promotions, explaining that black baseball "like all big business . . . requires big capital. Many things which it seems we should do simply cannot be done because of cost. But more widespread support of colored teams would elevate standards all around."

Most observers agreed that the league's weak finances needed to be strengthened. The problem was obvious to the accomplished black poet and scholar Sterling Brown, who concluded in a memorandum for the landmark Carnegie-Myrdal study of black American life that "Negro professional baseball is in need of much more capital, much more centralized organization instead of individualistic entrepreneurs." Veteran player and manager Dick Lundy similarly felt the league needed to "get some men in the game with some money and who don't have to pull a lot of funny moves to cover up every little loss. It's foolish to expect to make any headway when the money is being put up by people who don't stand to lose a penny."

Yet the difficulties in finding adequate financial backing from whites or blacks were paramount. Distinguished former Hilldale hurler Phil Cockrell provided a particularly blunt appraisal in 1936:

Our house of colored baseball has been built on stilts, the foundation has been utterly neglected. We talk contracts, training camps, holdouts and other tomfoolery aping of the Big leagues when the best of our colored players barely eke out an existence. . . . Our baseball has advanced only in the proficiency of playing ability, the material returns are even worse than they were 20 years ago.

Sportswriter Ed Harris, meanwhile, felt the owners needed to scale down the league's expectations:

It would be sensible for them to come down out of the clouds and stop trying to be the American League, which has been operating for many, many years or the National Loop which has been running longer. We all have our ambitions, boys, but right now your loop is composed of eight clubs, none of whom are really rich, catering to small crowds and paying small salaries. Pattern your league after your requirements and you will get along better.

Harris was but one of a group of younger and increasingly more militant black journalists who were less tolerant of the difficulties inherent in baseball and other black enterprises and unwilling to accept proffered excuses. In the past, many African Americans had preferred to praise rather than criticize black institutions and chose to minimize the league's flaws while reminding doubters that the league was only in its infancy. Yet by the Depression, long-time observers took a less sanguine view, and as sportswriter Randy Dixon griped, "twenty years ago the hue and cry was the same. If that baby has not attained maturity by now when in the hell is it ever gonna grow up?" Moreover, Dixon felt that in the punishing Depression environment, blacks no longer felt the urgency to support race institutions unhesitatingly. As Dixon observed, "I see no reason why anyone should patronize anything just because it is a Negro proposition unless the proposition has enough merit to stand on its own feet." Journalist Marcus Cooke offered a similar view, noting that "many point out that Negroes are no longer buying race pride when they pay their 75c to see a ball game; they want a ball game."[4]

Black entrepreneurs, however, had often focused more on winning customers through an emphasis of "race pride" and less on the actual improvement of their product or services. Yet as the respected black poet and former NAACP secretary James Weldon Johnson warned, the concept was "a mighty shaky business foundation. . . . A Negro American in business must give as excellent quality, as low a price, and as prompt and courteous service as any competitor, otherwise he runs a tremendous risk in counting on the patronage even of members of his own race." R. S. Simmons, a future official with the Chicago American Giants, agreed, acknowledging that "a business can't depend on race pride—it must produce."

To Randy Dixon, the success of black professional baseball ultimately remained in the hands of the owners, who needed to improve their product, "give the fans something worthy of the price of admission and lay off the appeal via racial sentiment." Yet the industry's ability to progress remained doubtful to Wendell Smith, a young sportswriter with the *Pittsburgh Courier*, who argued that the league had "refused to do anything constructive . . . and until it reforms, it should be kicked and kicked and kicked." Even the venerable Cum Posey, often at odds with black sportswriters, admitted that the current social and economic climate warranted changes in black baseball:

The days of the rooters who want their home boys to win at any cost, is rapidly passing; the days when Negro fans will support Negro athletic enterprises merely because they are Negro enterprises, is past. All who are connected with Negro enterprises must deliver if we wish to "cash in" . . . [and] give them the same brand of football and baseball as Joe Louis does in fighting—that is, a comfortable place to sit, very much action, and very little talk.

Yet despite ongoing criticism, African Americans recognized that the operation of professional black baseball during the Depression represented a significant achievement in black enterprise. By late in the decade, several commentators proudly acknowledged the NNL's "$300,000 business structure" and even the usually skeptical Dixon considered black professional baseball a $100,000 business at the least. Offering further proof of the industry's financial magnitude, John Clark cited the considerable amounts invested by Greenlee and Pompez in park construction and renovation.[5]

Despite limited cooperation and often short-sighted attitudes, the owners also realized the value of league baseball. Cum Posey felt it remained the "salvation of Negro baseball" and warned that "any one or two club owners who have the wild idea that they can prosper . . . without the help of the Negro National or Negro American leagues will wake up older but wiser men." To Posey, there was little question that black baseball deserved support, explaining that the leagues' existence helped to pump money into "Negro neighborhoods with Negro Restaurants, Hotels, Theaters. Negro Baseball gives the public a high class of entertainment. You are not asked to give something for nothing, but in supporting Negro Baseball you are supporting a well established Negro Enterprise."

Despite witnessing the failures of earlier leagues, Philadelphia official Ed Bolden also endorsed organized baseball. Recognizing Bolden's keen commitment, Posey confided to Effa Manley in 1939 that "every club except Philly Stars are in the League just to get a good schedule." Explaining his support of the league, Bolden contended that "every owner should receive protection for his investment. I think the fans, every ball player and everyone else involved should get an even break, and, if possible, a chance for advancement through experience and contact." The potential of future profits also shaped the attitudes of Bolden, who confidently predicted that "before I retire and shuffle off this mortal coil I expect to see a real snappy Colored League operating along the Atlantic Seaboard, for this region is where the money is to be obtained for successful operations." Yet whether Bolden, Posey, or any other entrepreneur could ever harness the true financial potential of black baseball remained uncertain by 1938, as did the continued existence of both major black professional leagues in the current economic climate.[6]

◆ ◆ ◆

As the start of the 1938 season approached, organized black baseball stood desperately in need of financial and administrative reform. Several observers suggested that new leadership was needed, particularly in the NNL, where Gus Greenlee had presided for four of the five years of the league's existence. Posey, opposed to Greenlee even during more favorable periods, now aggressively called for his ouster after the Dominican Republic debacle of 1937. Citing Greenlee's heavy involvement with his boxers, Posey claimed that the president "does not have the time, is not sufficiently interested in the league welfare and above all is not personally closely enough acquainted with baseball . . . to continue." Despite Posey's attempts to unseat him, the embattled Greenlee announced that he was "in organized baseball to stay" and would remain in office. Acutely aware of the league's severe difficulties, Greenlee warned that the organization "owes plenty of bills right now," but blamed "unwarranted and unauthorized interference" that had hampered his leadership, particularly from Posey and the increasingly aggressive Manleys.

Although Greenlee's position remained secure for the present, a change in league administration somewhat reduced his authority. At the suggestion of Bolden, the NNL in January 1938 designated a three-person board of governors (Greenlee, Abe Manley, and Elite Giants owner Tom Wilson), headed by Greenlee, to oversee league matters and settle disputes. Under the new government, if a controversy involved any board member, then alternate owners would serve. The new league administration left no role for Commissioner Ferdinand Morton, whose three unspectacular years in office had won him little support. Posey and other owners had touted Morton as "one of the finest men our race has produced," but the affable civil servant had been unable to establish a power base within the league and became easily dispensable. The departure of Morton hardly troubled Greenlee, who believed the new administration would ensure that all teams would be given "an equal break" with less partiality than in the past.[7]

League officials turned to drastic cost-cutting measures after the financial disaster of 1937. To reduce expenses, the NNL trimmed its umpiring crew from six to three and merged the offices of secretary and treasurer. Moreover, team rosters would now consist of only 16 players plus two first-year men, and salaries would be cut. The owners rationalized the decision in a statement claiming that, while they had "done all they can to make it [baseball] pay and increased salaries from year to year," the industry had operated at a loss for seven years. Meanwhile, league officials explained that salaries were simply a reflection of attendance, noting that, while "Colored Baseball players are not paid as much as white players of the same ability . . . when a comparison is made of salaries paid white players with the crowds they put in the parks at high prices, and the salaries paid Colored players for the number of fans they draw, it will be found the Colored players receive more pay according to the gates than white players receive."

As a further move to reverse financial losses within the league, the Elite Giants once again relocated, this time to Baltimore, which had lacked a strong professional club for several years. The move was inevitable, as the team had drawn only modestly in Washington in 1937 and owner Tom Wilson believed "Baltimore far superior . . . as a baseball town." Obtaining home grounds, however, remained a problem. While Wilson and his associate Vernon Green considered leasing Oriole Park, the home of the local International League affiliate, the complaints of local white residents prevented regular use in 1938, and the Elite Giants instead turned to Bugle Field, a 6,000-seat wooden park owned by former Black Sox owner Joe Cambria located in East Baltimore in an area somewhat inaccessible to black fans. Ultimately, Wilson's decision to move the Elites to Baltimore proved to be one of the more fortuitous acts by the NNL in 1938, as the franchise soon gained favor locally and remained for the next thirteen years.[8]

Although Wilson, like several previous owners, had been unable to tap Washington's vast potential as a black baseball market, the NNL remained unwilling to abandon the territory entirely. In March 1938, the league granted a franchise to local interests headed by Earl McDonald and Roy Sparrow, who planned to lease the local major league park, Griffith Stadium, for home games for their new team, the Black Senators. Yet with the league increasingly shaky, the decision to add a new franchise made little economic sense. Meanwhile, McDonald's numbers involvement revealed the league's continued inability to secure financial banking from legitimate sources, and according to Washington sportswriter and team publicist Sam Lacy, would ultimately hinder the success of the new franchise.[9]

With the league lineup set at seven franchises, owners turned their attention to their most pressing issue: the fate of the players who had jumped to the Dominican Republic in 1937. After consideration, league officials decided to lift the suspension and reinstate the players upon payment of their fines of reportedly a month's salary. While some observers questioned the leniency of the league's decision, Abe Manley explained that "heavy penalties would be all right in this case if only two or three players were involved. . . . But here you have enough so called outlaws to form a rather formidable outlaw team. Such a development would do the league no good."

To the chagrin of the owners, several of the jumpers, including ringleader Satchel Paige, balked at paying the fine, which according to Cum Posey was actually "a nominal sum" of probably a week's salary. Paige not only refused to pay but threatened to organize his own team with other blacklisted players. For Paige, the league's low salaries fully justified his jump to the Dominican Republic: "if we got the kind of dough that we deserve, we wouldn't want to run out on anybody." As Paige explained to one reporter, "say you are getting a salary of $600 a month and someone comes along and offers you three times that amount. Wouldn't you take it?" Claiming no ill will toward the NNL, Paige remarked that "the League is all right. All the owners are all right with me. . . . I would rather play in the League if they want me. If they don't I got to look out for myself."

The attitude hardly placated owners such as Abe Manley, who advised that if Paige organized an outlaw team, the club should be "blackballed by the league. If that is done, there is no way they can make the money they have been accustomed to." Greenlee similarly warned Paige and other jumpers that "if they do not feel that they owe the organization anything in the way of apology, or consider the depressed times, and refuse to sign under the conditions proposed, they can go right on back to Santo Domingo."

In the past, Greenlee had overlooked Paige's sometimes troublesome behavior, insisting that he had "no regrets for a single dollar I have spent on Satchel Paige. He is worth it." By 1938, after Paige had bolted the Crawfords twice in three seasons and was threatening once again, Greenlee's patience had finally been exhausted, and he began to consider selling his biggest box office attraction. The potential loss of Paige hardly troubled

Crawfords manager Oscar Charleston, who preferred that the team retain pitcher Johnny Taylor and dispense with Paige, considered by some to be a "grade-A prima donna." Other observers, such as Posey, recognized Paige's popularity but worried how outside observers viewed him, noting that Paige "played when he wishes, disappointed fans at leisure by his failure to show up when advertised, and was still put before the baseball public as an achievement accomplished by Negro baseball."

Greenlee subsequently sold Paige's contract to the Newark Eagles for a reported $5,000 ($3,200 according to Paige), but the deal was contingent upon Paige's agreeing to report to his new club. Paige, however, had little interest in playing for the Eagles and instead began dickering once again with foreign interests, this time from Venezuela. The specter of Paige leading yet another mass exodus of marquee players abroad stirred the normally dormant league machinery into action. In late April 1938, the Eagles obtained a restraining order from the New York State Supreme Court, temporarily preventing Paige from leaving the country. Nevertheless, Paige refused to report to Newark, forcing the league to ban Paige "for life" and bar all league clubs from playing any team featuring Paige or scheduling games at any park where he had been allowed to appear.

With Latin America now an option for black players, however, league officials began to weaken in their previous hardline attitude toward the punishment of other Dominican jumpers. Fearful of pushing the suspended players into the arms of foreign interests, including Mexico, which had already signed three of the jumpers, the league decided to delay the fines until after June 1938. By October, Posey reported that the fines were "not paid and never will be paid." While the ban of Paige remained in effect, Posey viewed the ruling as "all hooey. Satchel will come back when he feels like it, and the League members will be glad to have him."[10]

From beginning to end, the league's entire handling of the Dominican Republic affair was a public relations nightmare, appalling long-time fans and sportswriters and illustrating the unwillingness of black professional baseball to impose discipline when faced with the potential loss of star players. Journalist Leon Hardwick offered a common response to the controversy, arguing that the players should have been punished and "not eased back in with soft soaping 'penalties' and jelly fish 'explanations.'" To Ed Harris, the league's policies reflected a chronic shortsightedness, observing that "if the Negro ball club owner would take a lesson from their older and more experienced brothers in the big leagues, they would learn that regardless of how painful and unpleasant discipline in the form of a sound league administration may be, in the end it pays. The big leagues do not employ presidents and commissioners to give [Ford] Frick and [Will] Harridge and Landis work or because they are in love with them."

Yet the weak control over players was the inevitable consequence of a league whose administration and authority fell to a new low during 1938. The revamped league government seemed even less able to stimulate cooperation among owners, who continued to pursue their usual individualistic paths. The Black Yankees, for example, canceled a scheduled game on June 26 with Newark to appear instead at Yankee Stadium, leaving the Eagles idle and their owners livid. By July, Posey blamed the league's failures on the "owners themselves," warning that only the Philadelphia Stars, Newark Eagles, and his own Homestead Grays were fulfilling league obligations. An increasingly cynical Hardwick agreed, noting that "the majority of my good club owning friends just don't seem to know or give a damn what happens—as long as a few shekels can be hustled up spasmodically in a haphazardly handled schedule of exhibition and 'league' games."

The remarkably shoddy administration only exacerbated the league's ongoing financial difficulties wrought by the Depression. After signs of improvement during the mid-1930s, the economy had once again faltered during 1937–1938, dealing a serious blow to African Americans. By 1937, black unemployment in the north more than doubled that of whites, creating a predictable impact on the NNL. The Newark Eagles reportedly lost $10,000 in the first two months of the season due to poor attendance and limited bookings, and by August began cutting salaries up to 15 percent for some players. Commenting on the reduction of the already modest league wages, Ed Harris quipped that "with some of the salaries paid the best players . . . the Association would be better named the WPA League." The Elite Giants also suffered financial setbacks, faring only modestly in their first season in Baltimore, while in Philadelphia, the usually profitable Memorial Day home game featured "many pews in the stands unfilled."

Not surprisingly, the league's newest club, the Washington Black Senators, failed miserably. Since 1920, newly established black professional teams had encountered increasing difficulty in developing functional franchises, largely due to their inability to secure the services of the best players, who remained bound to other clubs. Typically, the new team, unable to compete immediately with league clubs, soon lost the support of local black fans, who were unwilling to expend their already limited discretionary income on a weak outfit, and the Black Senators proved to be no exception to the pattern. Although the team received players from each league franchise, manager Ben Taylor warned that it was "impossible to get a club overnight strong enough to compete with other older and established clubs in the Negro National League." Defeats by the non-league

Bacharach Giants soon exposed the team's considerable deficiencies, and by early August the Black Senators abandoned Washington and Griffith Stadium, planning to play independent baseball in the Philadelphia area. After experiencing difficulties paying a hotel bill in New York, the team disbanded, sold its bus for $800, and distributed the proceeds to the disheartened players.[11]

The failure of the Black Senators and yet another incomplete playoff series climaxed a nightmarish season for black professional baseball. Even Posey, whose Homestead Grays had reportedly profited, admitted that the institution was "in bad shape" and at its "lowest ebb since December, 1932," before the formation of the NNL. Perhaps more worrisome, frustrated journalists and fans had become increasingly intolerant of black baseball's perceived deficiencies. Leon Hardwick, for example, felt that "colored baseball as it's conducted today is a gigantic joke," little more than a "loosely run bunch of ball teams banding together, calling themselves a league." A Maryland fan agreed, noting that "there is a baseball league of a fashion, but it does not do justice to its many supporters who would give their right eye to see some real baseball." Other fans such as Robert Davis of New York had grown tired of the chronic administrative problems, noting that league officials "are always copying some rule for organized baseball, but never stick to it. . . . The owners have such little regard for the paying public that they seem to consider them just a bunch of halfwits, but are ready to complain when the public doesn't come out to see the games."

The ongoing attacks on the industry provoked a predictably defensive posture from most league officials, who objected to the "chronic, pessimistic criticism" and "unfair articles" emanating from the black weekly press. NNL press releases quickly pointed out that exceptionally bad weather during 1938 had wreaked havoc on already modest attendance, yet "the owners did not throw up the sponge and place . . . employees out of a job, when they were barely able to play one game a week, at times." Moreover, officials reminded readers that black professional baseball, unlike the white majors, had "no millionaire owners . . . but there are men who put their life earnings into the game, some through hope of financial reward, some for love of the game."

Most observers recognized and were genuinely sympathetic to the financial difficulties facing the owners. Fay Young of the *Defender*, for example, acknowledged that "baseball games are NOT being supported by our group. The depression may have had something to do with it. The recession may have something to do with it now." Yet others such as Hardwick offered the sensible (and soon to be familiar) argument that, regardless of the current economic situation, the league's administration and publicity could be improved, leading to greater profits in the future. As Hardwick observed, "it doesn't take a million dollars to organize a publicity set-up for the league." Despite his criticism, Hardwick remained hopeful, insisting that "there's money to be made in this thing. Plenty. Like everything else, colored baseball is not so dead it can't be revived to equal—yes, even surpass—the halcyon days of [Rube] Foster and [C. I.] Taylor." Any potential rebuilding task and revival, however, remained dependent upon greater cooperation and financial commitment among league officials, still unlikely to occur in the current environment.[12]

◆ ◆ ◆

As the troubled Depression decade entered its final year, black professional baseball appeared to be in a state of flux. While the current operation of a dozen professional teams in two separate and largely unprofitable leagues clearly needed reform, no obvious answer existed. Posey, however, felt that the "successful solution for the ills of organized Negro baseball" was to develop one league composed of the strongest eastern and midwestern franchises, a suggestion he would often revive in subsequent years. The Negro American League was understandably reluctant, since several of its teams, particularly its southern-based franchises, would revert to associate status, and the product of the merged leagues would most likely be dominated by the east. Fearful of losing their autonomy as appendages of the NNL, NAL franchises eventually rejected Posey's suggestion.

Rebuffed by the NAL, the NNL would soon contend with a more serious internal dilemma, the status of Gus Greenlee. Immediately after the 1938 season concluded, rumors surfaced that Greenlee would step down as league president, relinquish control of the Crawfords, and devote his full time to John Henry Lewis and his other boxers. Several critics such as Wendell Smith had long recognized that Greenlee "has his heart in baseball, no doubt. But his main interests lie elsewhere. The business of handling . . . Lewis is a full-time job, and anything else that steps in the way is bound to suffer." Along with his commitment to boxing, Greenlee had also clearly tired of the industry difficulties after eight years and could not help but be disillusioned after several of his players, so "petted and pampered" in the past, had abandoned the Crawfords for foreign offers in 1937.

Greenlee's shaky financial situation ultimately became the major factor in his decision. He had struggled to pay salaries for several years, and players such as Gene Benson, who spent a brief period with the Crawfords in 1938, soon discovered that Greenlee "wasn't payin' off." Moreover, the increasingly unprofitable Greenlee Field, once expected to be the salvation of black baseball in Pittsburgh, contributed to his woes. Aware that the lack of a grandstand roof was a continued liability, Greenlee had attempted in recent years to raise needed cash through season ticket sales and a common stock offering without success. By 1938, Posey observed that "fans apparently will not support games played at Greenlee Field," and the Grays avoided the facility whenever possible. In December 1938, Greenlee finally gave up, selling the park for a mere $38,000, and the location subsequently became the site of a housing project.

Greenlee Field represented a grand failure, one of only a handful of attempts by a black entrepreneur to construct and control a sports facility. The park's shortcomings, combined with a weak economy and a local black population considerably smaller than those of other black baseball centers, resulted in its inevitable abandonment by the Crawfords. The park also failed to fulfill its promise as a fully race-controlled institution, as the involvement of whites at Greenlee Field proved more pronounced than anticipated. Because Greenlee had received white financial assistance to construct the facility, whites ultimately dominated park employment.

The sale of the park was the first of a series of personal and professional setbacks for Greenlee. On January 24, 1939, Greenlee's brother Marcus, a 1937 graduate of Howard University Medical School, died in an automobile accident. Meanwhile, an attempt to transform John Henry Lewis from a light heavyweight to a heavyweight failed, culminating in a first round knockout by Joe Louis on the day following Marcus's death. The bout did succeed in generating a considerable purse for Lewis, whose days as a professional boxer were nevertheless numbered. Five months later, Lewis's career abruptly ended when the National Boxing Association stripped him of his light heavyweight crown after an examination revealed partial blindness.

Despite his anticipated withdrawal from the NNL, Greenlee remained undecided and briefly considered operating a franchise in New York at Ebbets Field or in Ohio, but his financial problems proved too difficult to overcome.[13] By April 1939, Philadelphia Stars co-owner Eddie Gottlieb contacted the other league officials to explain that Greenlee "has exhausted every possible means trying to formulate plans which would enable him to operate the Crawfords," and the "only alternative" would be financial assistance from other league members. Recognizing the "value of the Pittsburgh Crawfords as an attraction and debt of gratitude which we owe Gus Greenlee for his efforts in organizing the League," Gottlieb suggested that each owner advance Greenlee $200 for the upcoming season. Greenlee, however, eventually decided to disband the Crawfords, although Gottlieb promised that should he establish another team, "we would cooperate in every possible way, and that we would keep an opening for him which he could avail himself at any time."

Unfortunately, the subsequent relationship of Greenlee and the NNL would be marked by increasing tension and distrust. Before his departure, Greenlee bitterly denounced his fellow owners, claiming they had "violated their pledges in respect to players. It is safe to say that 95 per cent of my roster has been approached with offers." Yet Greenlee himself had raided other teams in the early days of the Crawfords, and as Ed Harris wryly noted, "the only reason Greenlee did not indulge in as much robber-baroning as the other moguls was . . . that he had practically all the best colored players in the East on his roster." Meanwhile, league officials claimed that Greenlee had left behind bounced checks and numerous unpaid debts, particularly from a September 25, 1938, promotion at the Polo Grounds, and subsequently stripped him of his position as honorary league president.[14]

With Greenlee gone, a vacuum existed in the league power structure, and changes were soon forthcoming. After discarding the three-person advisory board employed in 1938, the NNL returned to its previous administrative structure of a president, vice president, treasurer, and secretary, augmented by a three-owner arbitration committee. The league also selected a new leader, turning to the familiar figure of Tom Wilson, the only owner to participate as a full member for six years. Born in 1889 in Atlanta, Wilson relocated to Nashville with his parents, who had both attended Meharry Medical College and later became noted physicians. Wilson became interested in baseball as a young man, and began promoting black sandlot teams, including the Nashville Standard Giants. By the early 1920s, the team had taken a new name, the Elite Giants, and achieved professional status, participating initially in lower-level southern organizations but later in Rube Foster's NNL. Simultaneously, Wilson became a leader in the Nashville black community and grew wealthy through numerous investments in real estate, a farm, night clubs, and later the Paradise Ballroom. Like several other black baseball entrepreneurs, Wilson is believed to have derived at least some of his income from illegal enterprises, including a gambling casino and perhaps the numbers lottery.

The new president was undoubtedly a popular figure, aptly characterized by Cum Posey as a "rough and ready fellow, who probably controls more votes than any Negro in America . . . probably the best liked man in baseball by players, owners and the public." To some observers, however, Wilson seemed a somewhat puzzling choice. Sam Lacy cited the age-old problem of impartiality, noting "the presence of a club-owner in a position often calling for judgment . . . on matters vitally important to himself is certainly bad medicine." Effa Manley later recalled that Wilson was "on

Figure 9. Tom Wilson, Baltimore Elite Giants
owner and NNL president, 1939–1946. Courtesy
Larry Lester/NoirTech, Inc.

the playboy side; he liked to have a little drink and have a little fun.
Baseball wasn't that serious to him." Yet NNL owners, typically leery of
any strong authority, remained satisfied with Wilson's unaggressive and
largely hands-off administrative style, maintaining him as president for
the next eight years.[15]

Wilson's first challenge was to find a replacement franchise for Greenlee's departed Pittsburgh Crawfords. In April, with the start of the season
only a month away, the league dispatched Posey to Toledo, Ohio, to negotiate with a group of white entrepreneurs who already owned a minor league
team in Lima, Ohio, in the class D Ohio State League. After receiving
assurances that they would be granted the rights to all former Pittsburgh
players, the group (which reportedly included one black man) agreed to
finance a new franchise, the Toledo Crawfords, based at Swayne Field,
home of the local American Association affiliate. With the addition of Toledo, the NNL managed to outflank the still embittered Greenlee, who

according to Posey "tried to block this . . . proposition by sending a man to these fellows offering half interest in a Semi Pro club with Satchel Paige as the attraction."[16]

The league received another encouraging sign by the surprising return of Alex Pompez after a two-year odyssey involving a flight to Mexico and a subsequent return to New York. Pompez, under police protection since late 1937, had agreed to testify for the state in the August 1938 policy trial of James Hines, the powerful Tammany leader of the 11th Assembly district. His lengthy testimony, describing his involvement in the numbers lottery, and its subsequent appropriation by Dutch Schultz, impressed on-lookers such as a *New York Times* reporter who considered Pompez "the most compelling as a personality" of the early trial witnesses. While Judge Ferdinand Pecora eventually declared a mistrial, the second trial in early 1939 culminated in a guilty conviction for Hines, a triumph for district attorney Thomas Dewey. In return for their testimony, Pompez and former partner Joe Ison received suspended sentences and probation. The earlier death of Schultz in 1935 probably influenced Pompez's willingness to tes-tify and his avoidance of subsequent reprisal, and, as historian Mary Stol-berg has noted, "without Schultz's backing, Hines posed much less of a threat to potential witnesses." The relieved Pompez subsequently prom-ised reporters that he would abandon the rackets and devote his full time to baseball: "There may not be as much money in it . . . but it's safer."

Now free to return to professional baseball, Pompez eagerly planned to place his New York Cubans back on the field for the first time since 1936. The return of Pompez pleased observers such as Al Monroe who noted, "even . . . when his other businesses were most discussed, his heart and soul were in baseball." Newark Eagles owners Abe and Effa Manley, how-ever, were less enthusiastic, fearing competition in a seemingly already glutted New York City/northern New Jersey market. Moreover, the Man-leys quickly noted that the Cubans no longer had home grounds, since Dyckman Oval, on which Pompez had lavished thousands of dollars for refurbishing in 1935, had been demolished. The loss of Dyckman Oval particularly disappointed Pompez, who later claimed that he "would have made a million dollars. But outside developments made me close the park." Ironically, Dyckman Oval and Greenlee Field, the two most sub-stantial investments in black baseball during the Depression, both failed to survive beyond 1938.

Initially deciding to defer full membership until able to acquire home grounds, Pompez ultimately recognized that the lack of a park hardly de-terred other league teams. Only at Parkside Field in Philadelphia and Bugle Field in Baltimore did league franchises enjoy anything near full control of home grounds, relying instead on rentals of white Organized

Figure 10. Alexander Pompez (center) departs from a
New York courtroom after testifying at the Jimmy Hines
trial, August 19, 1938. Courtesy AP/Wide World Photos.

Baseball parks in Pittsburgh, Newark, New York, and Toledo. After promising to attempt to lease Yankee Stadium for home games, Pompez rejoined the league as a full member in April, along with the new Toledo franchise. The addition of the two franchises delighted Posey, who confided to Effa Manley that "there is no doubt that the Toledo club will draw. Also the Cubans will draw."[17]

Despite Posey's optimism, the expansion of the league to seven franchises in 1939 proved less successful than anticipated. The new Toledo team predictably encountered major difficulties in securing the services of the former Crawford players, several of whom had already accepted advance money and signed with other NNL teams. Moreover, a potential interleague war loomed after NAL owners also attempted to sign several of the disbanded Crawfords, prompting Effa Manley to warn NAL president R. R. Jackson that "most of the players want to be in the East, and I am sure your League would suffer a great deal more than ours if we engaged in a war over ball players."

Although Toledo official Hank Rigney blamed Posey, Gottlieb, and Tom Wilson for the entire dilemma, Gus Greenlee's intentionally disruptive handling of the dissolution of his team had clearly played a significant role. Jackson, for example, claimed that Greenlee had not only "failed to pay his ball players at the end of the 1938 season" but had even advised them they were free to play with any team. Abe Manley similarly placed the "root of all the trouble on the door steps of Greenlee," citing his delay in informing the league of his plans for 1939. Fearing the loss of "these valuable men to some outside interest," NNL owners had little choice but to sign the players as almost a defensive posture before the deal with Toledo had been finalized, and were now unwilling to part with players to whom they had already advanced salary.

By early May, Rigney claimed that his franchise had only received three of the promised Pittsburgh men. Bewildered by the league's failure to fulfill its agreement, Rigney noted "why we should have to beg . . . is something I cannot understand." Despite eventually acquiring several of the disputed players, Toledo became expendable after the readmission of the Cubans, and by mid-June the team had reportedly played only five league games before unimpressive crowds. To the relief of both parties, the Toledo franchise subsequently transferred to the NAL at a joint meeting on June 20, 1939, reducing the NNL back to six teams. With the exception of the brief involvement of the St. Louis-Harrisburg Stars in 1943, the six-franchise lineup remained intact for the balance of the NNL's existence.

The unfortunate incident with Toledo not only symbolized the industry's frighteningly tenuous control over its players but also demonstrated the need for greater harmony between the NAL and NNL to prevent further unrestricted player movement between the two organizations. Developments at the June joint session offered some encouragement, as the two leagues reached an agreement whereby no player could sign with a team in the opposing league until all clubs in his current circuit had waived on his services. Attempting to rectify a chronic problem with salary advances, the new ruling also mandated that owners had to collect all debts incurred by a player from his last owner or return the player to his previous team. Meanwhile, officials who tampered with players under contract to other organizations would now be subject to $50 and $100 fines, and those who intentionally used a player owned by a another league team faced suspension from professional black baseball.[18]

Although well intended, the new agreement did little to ameliorate the difficulties between the two organizations. Despite switching leagues, the

Toledo Crawfords remained in the center of controversy, as Hank Rigney continued to blame the NNL for problems with players such as Napoleon Hairston, who had been advanced $45 but had failed to report. Gottlieb, however, felt the charges were groundless and privately considered Rigney "damn lucky we allowed him to take any players like Carter, Harvey, Clarkson, etc., out of our league. I am positively convinced something is wrong with the man." The already shaky interleague relationship deteriorated further after a dispute between the Homestead Grays and Toledo over money advanced to a player resulted in the Grays' decision to withhold a portion of the Crawfords' gate receipts. When a Toledo player protested, Rigney reported that Homestead owner Rufus "Sonnyman" Jackson "promptly laid a sucker punch in his face." Toledo's subsequent unauthorized use of Homestead outfielder Jerry Benjamin under the assumed name "Christopher" almost ensured that the wobbly agreement would not last beyond 1939, and as Posey's brother Seward ("See") ominously warned, "if the West does not want to keep their agreement, I am ready to take some of their men."[19]

Despite ongoing difficulties with the NAL, the NNL achieved a surprising degree of administrative progress in 1939, perhaps a response to the heavy criticism of recent years. The departure of Greenlee had removed one of the major points of division among the league owners, contributing to increased cooperation under the relaxed leadership of Tom Wilson. The improved compliance manifested itself in the adoption of a new plan requiring all results of league games to be wired to Gottlieb or Manley, and all scoresheets to be sent to Posey for statistical compilation. Some owners continued to be lax in reporting statistics and scores, but black newspapers received league information more consistently in 1939 than they had in several years. Moreover, in contrast to prior years of aborted playoffs, the Grays and Stars actually completed their post-season series, and, according to Ed Harris, the games generally had been run "cleanly and decisively."

The NNL also made modest financial gains in 1939, largely fueled by several profitable promotions at major league venues. The East-West game, now in its seventh year, drew 33,489 fans, the largest crowd to date, and grossed over $33,000 for the two leagues. The league also benefited through more extensive use of Yankee Stadium after general manager Ed Barrow leased the park to the NNL for five doubleheaders and donated the Ruppert Memorial Cup (named for late Yankees owner Jacob Ruppert) to be awarded to the league's strongest team. While Greenlee and the NNL had rented Yankee Stadium several times since 1934, the exorbitant fee of at least $2,500 per date had prevented more extensive use of the park. Yet in the aftermath of the avalanche of bad publicity following the racist utterings of Yankee outfielder Jake Powell in July 1938 (discussed in Chapter 7), Barrow offered the league a more favorable deal in 1939, charging only $1,000 per rental. While some fans dismissed the use of the park as an inadequate substitute for actual integration and "a sort of capitulation on the part of the Negro owners—who no doubt would lose considerable if their stars were taken over by a major league team," Yankee Stadium's easy access to Harlem's 458,000 citizens offered unprecedented financial opportunities. The five doubleheaders at Yankee Stadium not only drew a total of 60,000 fans but also gained valuable exposure in the white press, including the *New York Times*.

Although few, if any, owners profited in 1939, black professional baseball, particularly in the east, had seemingly finally transcended the crippling losses of the mid-1930s. The NNL proudly announced that not only did the league have a balance in its treasury for the first time, but all umpires had been fully paid. Meanwhile, Al Monroe enthused that "the attendance at all parks has been good," although a less optimistic Vic Harris still insisted that "our crowds are not what they should be now."[20]

In general, the moderate gains enjoyed in black professional baseball paralleled concurrent developments in American sports in the late 1930s, facilitated by the stabilization of the economy after the recession of 1937–1938. Although 9.4 million Americans remained unemployed, consumer spending on minor, major, and semiprofessional baseball reached a pre–World War II high of $21.5 million in 1939. Minor league baseball set a new attendance record, and professional football also enjoyed greater prosperity late in the decade, experiencing attendance increases in 1938 and 1939.

The improved attendance in 1939 provided much needed encouragement to officials and fans who had long believed that black professional baseball, if properly exploited, could potentially become a profitable African American enterprise. Yet Posey's insistence in early 1940 that "organized Negro baseball, as white organized ball, has become big business" still appeared premature. The fallacy of such a view was acknowledged by Fay Young, who sensibly observed that "few business men will invest in our ball clubs." Despite limited progress in 1939, both leagues still possessed a myriad of seemingly unsolvable problems and as Young warned, "the public is losing confidence—and once it is lost it is never restored."[21]

◆ ◆ ◆

Recognizing the still fragile status of black professional baseball, several officials, particularly Effa Manley of the Newark Eagles, looked toward further reform of the enterprise as the new decade loomed. After entering the NNL in 1935, Abe Manley had gradually delegated an increasing amount of authority to his wife whose involvement in league affairs also expanded. By 1937, Cum Posey observed that Effa Manley was "rapidly learning the business end of the baseball game" and subsequently praised her role in protecting the NNL's share of the 1937 East-West game. Others, such as Greenlee, objected to her growing responsibilities, and, according to Rollo Wilson, believed that "the proper place for women is by the fireside not functioning in positions to which their husbands have been elected."

Yet Effa Manley's background as an energetic and active civic leader in the Harlem community had anticipated her increased league participation, particularly her work in the 1934–1935 "Don't Buy Where You Can't Work" campaign and her commitment to the NAACP. Refusing to be intimidated by the virtually all-male environment in black baseball, Manley proved to be a formidable league force. At a 1938 league meeting, sportswriter Randy Dixon reported "the sonorous tones of Mrs. Abe Manley often drifted out from the meeting room. The lady seemed to have what it took to get over points." While praising Manley as "a woman of unusual appeal and charm and a worthy foe in debate," Dixon also noted her toughness, recounting how "the charming one took 'Your Man' Dixon aside and administered the worst tongue lashing I have received." Over time, the presence of a woman at league meetings barely raised an eyebrow and by 1946, Manley noted that "at first they may have thought it funny, but now they don't even consider I'm there as a woman. Even during stormy sessions the gentlemen have always been nice."

Manley's handling of the business end of the Newark Eagles generally engendered respect from players such as Monte Irvin who complimented her as "unique and effervescent and knowledgeable." Rollo Wilson also offered praise, observing that "like her or not, one must concede that Mrs. Abe is forthright in her opinions and most of the time . . . correct in her conclusions." Yet others, such as former Eagles first baseman George Giles, tired of her constant heavily publicized battles with the press and other officials, later comparing her to flamboyant major league owners such as "Charlie Finley or George Steinbrenner. They're not good for baseball. You're supposed to have some kind of class, dignity, when you get to the big leagues." Moreover, Eagles outfielder Johnny Davis questioned her baseball knowledge, noting that "she knew about baseball like I knew about shooting a rocket up in the air. And Abe didn't either."[22]

Yet Effa Manley provided a necessary stimulant to the often torpid and stagnant world of black professional baseball. While sometimes self-serving, Manley's suggestions and innovations often forced the sluggish league administrations to confront vital issues that they might otherwise have ignored. Manley, for example, became a driving force following the 1939 season in a revived movement to streamline the administration of the industry through the selection of a commissioner to oversee both leagues. Although the NAL had named Major Robert R. Jackson as commissioner, most eastern clubs remained wary of his involvement with the Chicago American Giants and refused to accept his authority. The NAL was similarly leery of any NNL- sponsored candidate, and, as Al Monroe explained, "either section would frown on a plan to have a 'Landis' [commissioner] rule their loop who was doing business as a part of another section's planning board."

Recognizing the dilemma, Effa Manley searched for an impartial figure to preside over the two organizations, eventually settling on William Hastie, dean of the Howard University Law School and a key figure in a number of NAACP legal fights (which would include the Texas "white primary" case in 1944). The thirty-five-year-old Hastie possessed impeccable legal credentials, graduating from Harvard Law School in 1930, serving as assistant solicitor in the Department of the Interior from 1933 to 1937, and then serving in the Virgin Islands from 1937 to 1939 as the first black federal judge in American history. After Hastie expressed a willingness to accept the position, the Manleys contacted owners from both leagues to build support for their distinguished candidate. While not making an open commitment to Hastie, Jacksonville Red Caps official J. B. Greer offered encouragement, noting that "colored baseball should have a commissioner without any inside affiliation . . . the nomination of Major R.R. Jackson to this position is absurd and I will never vote for same because I do not think him capable or qualified." In the NNL, Eddie Gottlieb voiced cautious enthusiasm, noting that Hastie "sounds interesting and might be very interesting if he understands baseball. A whole lot depends on what the cost would be."[23]

Despite Effa Manley's appearance at the NAL's meeting in December 1939, the western league eventually deferred judgment on Hastie, and, as Fay Young observed, "wasn't ready to have a hand-picked candidate jammed down their throat." Meanwhile, Hastie himself became increasingly ambivalent about the position. By February 1940, he confided to Manley that with his numerous commitments such as chairman of National Legal Committee of the NAACP, it would be "doubtful whether I can have time to do the job you contemplate . . . If it were just a case of hearing club disputes or player disputes and making rulings on particular controversies, I would probably handle the job. But I know that in your mind there is a larger job of guidance, direction and publicity which will take more time than I am going to have in the months ahead."[24]

Thwarted in their attempts to place Hastie at the head of both leagues, the Manleys then turned their attention to their own organization. Despite the improved administration and first-ever league balance, the Manleys looked to replace NNL president Tom Wilson, and soon found support from the two New York franchises, which resented Wilson's seeming tacit approval of the role of Eddie Gottlieb in the Yankee Stadium promotions. At the league's February 2, 1940, meeting in Philadelphia, the Manleys nominated C. B. Powell, publisher of the *New York Amsterdam News*, for president. Born in 1894 in Virginia, Powell attended Howard University Medical School and subsequently relocated to New York, where he became one of the first black physicians to build a practice specializing in x-rays. Powell had also become involved in business, helping found the Victory Mutual Life Insurance Company in 1922, and later purchasing the *Amsterdam News* in 1936 with his partner Dr. P. M. H. Savory.

While the Manleys touted Powell's business accomplishments, non-league affiliation, and willingness to serve without pay, the opposing faction of Philadelphia, Baltimore, and Homestead had little interest in a change in leadership and questioned the impartiality of an inexperienced New York-based official sponsored by local interests. Believing that there was "none more practical" than the current president, Cum Posey promptly renominated Wilson to oppose Powell. Not surprisingly, a subsequent vote of the owners resulted in a 3-3 deadlock, predictably divided along factional lines.

The major issue driving the nominations of both Powell and Wilson concerned the further exploitation of the New York market and the profitable Yankee Stadium promotions. The Newark ownership particularly objected to the 10 percent received by Eddie Gottlieb for handling the Yankee Stadium dates in 1939, whereas the Black Yankees felt they warranted an opportunity to promote games at a park located in their own territory. Meanwhile, Alex Pompez wanted to break into the New York market by leasing Ebbets Field for the Cubans, but encountered resistance from booking agent William Leuschner and the Dexter Park interests, who feared potential competition. At the Philadelphia meeting, a terrific battle over Gottlieb's role evolved into a larger argument over white involvement, led by Effa Manley, who claimed that "we are fighting for something bigger than a little money! We are fighting for a Race issue" (an ironic statement considering Manley's own "race"). When Posey disagreed, she denounced him as a "handkerchief head," leading him to threaten to boycott future meetings until Manley returned to "where she belongs—in the kitchen." The officials eventually adjourned the meeting without selecting a president, planning to resume the battle at a later date.[25]

The Philadelphia meeting, one of the most tumultuous in the league's history, splintered whatever marginal harmony existed among the league owners. The usually low key Tom Wilson was infuriated by the "secretive manner" in which "a few of the members attempted to oust me without a notice" and according to the *Defender*, nearly "broke into tears" when James Semler of the Black Yankees voted against him for president. Interestingly, several owners defended Gottlieb, noting that at the beginning of the 1939 season the NNL (except Newark) had voted to allot 10 percent of net receipts to whoever coordinated league promotions, equivalent to Gus Greenlee's share in the past. Moreover, Gottlieb had negotiated a better deal with Yankee officials and had also saved the league money on liability insurance. Posey reminded critics that "the promoter took all the headaches . . . league clubs walked into the Stadium, and twenty minutes after the game was over, walked out with their shares."[26]

Not surprisingly, Effa Manley's attempt to inject race into the dispute won her little support from officials such as Posey and Bolden, who had long worked amicably with white promoters. For Posey, Manley's behavior toward the "the sole white member, who had helped organize the league in 1934 . . . was a disgusting exhibition for a lady. It was embarrassing . . . as we looked for a certain amount of courtesy had we been the lone colored member of a white meeting." Even black sportswriters normally critical toward white promoters did not rise to the defense of Manley. Fay Young, for example, felt that she had erred by raising the "race question. This is no time for that." Others such as Art Carter questioned her actual race consciousness, noting that "at the same time that she says she desires to see more of the dough reach the coffers of her racial brethren she hires a $50-a-week white publicity agent." To Carter, the league owners were ultimately to blame for their current troubles. As Carter explained, if Gottlieb's "percentage is too high, it is the fault of the league. Not Gottlieb's or Wilson's. Gottlieb as a wise businessman, is expected to get as much as he can."

With the league presidency still undecided, the NNL met in Chicago on February 23, 1940, prior to a joint session with the NAL. The New York faction not only continued to support Powell for president, but also nominated Al Monroe, veteran sportswriter and manager of the New York office of the *Chicago Defender*, to oppose Posey for league secretary, and unsuccessfully proposed Rufus Jackson of the Grays for vice president. The two factions remained at an impasse, however, and eventually Alex Pompez helped negotiate a compromise whereby all current officers (President Wilson, Vice President Bolden, and Secretary Posey) who received three or more votes would be retained for 1940. In an apparent sop to the New York interests, Abe Manley became the league's new treasurer at a salary of $250 per year. The league also agreed that, while Gottlieb would continue to handle most of the Yankee Stadium promotions, the Black Yankees would be allowed to promote a doubleheader of their own at the stadium on May 19. The statesmanlike intervention of Pompez won praise and as Cum Posey observed, his "opinions are honestly given . . . heart and soul with the Negro National League."[27]

The compromise only partially placated the fiery Effa Manley, who remained opposed to Tom Wilson's presidency. Manley, however, professed no ill will toward her fellow owners, claiming "there is only a difference of opinion on policy. . . . We are all friends." As she explained to Posey, her stance at the meeting was "not done to cast any reflection on Mr. Wilson as a man. We all have a friendly feeling and personal regard for him, but we are not satisfied with his policies." Similarly, Manley asserted that the Gottlieb controversy was not racially motivated, as "some white owners are the best of men. I even admire Gottlieb's business ability. He would be all right if the chairman [Wilson] could handle him. He needs to be whipped into line." Yet criticism of the role of Gottlieb and other white promoters, muted somewhat during the Depression, would soon become more prominent coinciding with the increased profits in black baseball after the onset of World War II.[28]

◆ ◆ ◆

The heated arguments and disunity exhibited in early 1940 were soon overshadowed by the threat of yet another major assault on black professional baseball by foreign interests. Despite weathering raids from the Dominican Republic, Venezuela, and Mexico in the late 1930s, the leagues had taken no real step to standardize and enforce the contracts and agreements between owner and player which were often easily broken at the convenience of either party. Yet during 1939, the lack of airtight contracts had become an increasing liability, as the leagues had little recourse to prevent an increasing number of jumpings and/or players remaining in South America after the winter baseball season. Aware of the potential for disaster during 1940, the two league presidents (J. B. Martin and Tom Wilson) agreed that any player jumping to a foreign locale would be suspended for three years, and all league clubs would be barred from playing independent teams using or competing against the suspended player. Both leagues also planned to contact the State Department in the hope of revoking the passports of jumping players.

The league's threats deterred few players, and by April 1940, numerous star performers had jumped to Venezuela or Mexico. As Josh Gibson, perhaps the best hitter in black baseball, explained to a sportswriter, the incentives were considerable, including "twice as much salary, my room and board and transportation expenses," despite a lighter schedule. In response to critics who objected to the contract breaking, Gibson echoed the earlier sentiments of Satchel Paige, asking, "what would you do if a company offered you twice as much money for doing just half as much work?" Offering a further endorsement, Specs Roberts, a native Philadelphian and former Homestead Gray playing in Mexico, enthused that he had "never been treated better or lived amid more hospitable surroundings any-where." Posey, however, claimed that Venezuelan officials were paying players with "a dollar amounting to 64 cents, and are the players yelling murder!"

Mindful of the league's modest financial resources, several black sports-writers sympathized with the jumping players, revealing an increasing preference to encourage individual athletes, rather than support a flawed black enterprise. Ed Harris of the *Philadelphia Tribune*, for example, viewed the jumps as inevitable, as some players were not even "getting the wages he would on WPA." Offering a similar argument, the *Courier's* Wendell Smith questioned the league's attempts to reclaim their men, con-sidering the move "a bit communistic, trying to prevent a player from going where he can better himself financially." Other journalists such as Chester Washington cited the cruel irony that players such as Gibson had to leave their own country to earn a salary remotely commensurate with their skills.[29]

The loss of several star players dealt a severe blow to the NNL, which had finally appeared to be progressing financially and administratively in 1939. Relations with the NAL created additional difficulties, as the rela-tionship between the two leagues remained tempestuous during 1940 de-spite the shared loss of numerous players to foreign interests. To the surprise of no one, the prior agreement reached between the two organiza-tions failed to prevent continued disputes over ballplayers, leading to a major controversy over the status of the always controversial Satchel Paige. Sold to the Eagles in 1938, Paige had failed to report, instead jump-ing to Latin America. Subsequent arm problems, however, had placed Paige's career in jeopardy, and he had spent much of 1939 appearing in the west with an independent team booked by Kansas City Monarch owner J. L. Wilkinson's brother Lee, attempting to regain his form and attracting little notice from professional teams, including the Eagles.[30]

By spring 1940, Paige's stellar pitching skills had returned, prompting Effa Manley to renew her attempts to bring him into the Newark fold after displaying only tepid interest in 1939. Realizing Newark's eagerness to gain his services, Paige toyed with Manley, expressing a willingness to play, provided she "became his secret girl friend." Manley, who was known to engage in extramarital affairs with her players, nevertheless rejected Paige, and as she recalled years later, "I didn't know what to tell him. He was a married man you know." Yet Paige continued to dicker with the Eagles and even agreed to meet in Richmond in early June with Manley and other Eagles officials. The meeting achieved little, however, and enraged Effa Manley, who increasingly sensed the involvement of J. L. Wilkinson, despite his denials, in Paige's ongoing barnstorming activities as part of a team featuring several former Monarchs.

For the second time in 1940, Manley found herself in the center of controversy. Always publicity conscious, she quickly apprised writers of the current situation, insisting that "Paige is my property and I'll get him or the league will be looking for one and perhaps three new members." In a concurrent letter of protest to both league presidents, Manley expressed her disgust at "Negroes who have invested so heavily in this business, and the honest white man [sic] connected with it, standing for this sort of thing." Arguing that Paige should be returned to the Eagles, Manley asserted that "if organized baseball is not strong enough to do this, it is not strong enough to call itself organized and anything may happen." She warned both men that black professional baseball was "probably at the crossroads, and its future may depend upon your handling of this present situation."

It was the involvement of the Eagles in yet another player controversy, rather than the intervention of the league presidents, that ultimately resolved the Paige dilemma. The Eagles' mid-June purchase of infielder Bus Clarkson and pitcher Ernie Carter from the Crawfords (now based in Indianapolis) prompted the NAL to protest that players could not be traded out of their league unless all teams in their current organization had waived on their services. At a subsequent meeting, the leagues managed to settle both player disputes; the Eagles agreed to relinquish all claims to Paige but were allowed to retain Clarkson and Carter.[31] To western officials such as B. B. Martin of the Memphis Red Sox, the Eagles and other NNL teams deserved the greatest blame for the latest crisis. A disgusted Martin reportedly related that he was "damn sick and tired of the East trying to break up organized Negro baseball and wasn't going to stand for it." Meanwhile, the interleague struggle only exacerbated the divisions among the still fractious owners of the NNL. According to Fay Young, the non-New York teams would have willingly accepted Newark's threatened withdrawal, and "the consensus is that as long as she [Effa Manley] can talk and have things her own way—there isn't going to be any peace in the East."

Following the meeting, Paige officially became NAL property and as anticipated, joined the Kansas City Monarchs organization, where he began a new phase of his remarkable career. The suddenly elevated status of Paige during 1940 initially bewildered several observers, including

Young, who questioned the "excitement about one long-legged pitcher." Similarly, Hazel Wigden, a New York fan, wrote to Effa Manley, scornfully asking, "so who is Satchel Paige that you should desire him as tho he were God Himself? Aren't there other pitchers in this whole wide United States of America." Yet Paige's pitching renaissance combined with his colorful personality transformed him into a national celebrity in 1940, earning him profiles in *Time* and *Saturday Evening Post*. While Paige's fame continued to skyrocket, the focus on his individual achievements at the expense of publicizing the institution of black professional baseball would begin in 1940 and only increase in the future.[32]

◆ ◆ ◆

The negative publicity of the Paige controversy and foreign jumpings dealt a heavy blow to an industry struggling with a concurrent decline in gate receipts at most cities during 1940. In Philadelphia, local fans, perhaps spoiled by the phenomenal success of Hilldale in the 1920s, became increasingly less tolerant of the Stars' failings and failure to eclipse the Homestead Grays. Randy Dixon, never a fan of Bolden, claimed not only that the "majority" of fans rooted against the Stars but that "Philly fandom has long been sour on Ed Bolden. They accept him now for just what he is." Journalist Charles Campbell similarly admitted that "the fans are tired of supporting a losing ball team. . . . The steady supporters are the loudest talkers against the local club in the National League." Not surprisingly, attendance continued to drop, as Ed Harris noted "half-filled parks since the beginning of the season," and by late July Eddie Gottlieb confided to Effa Manley that "we are not drawing so good at home."[33]

The dismal status of professional black baseball in Philadelphia mirrored the equally miserable situation in Chicago. During the 1920s, a combination of a large black population, a strong team, and available home grounds enabled Philadelphia and Chicago to reign as the most consistently profitable venues in their regions, yet both cities failed in the 1930s and 1940s to equal their earlier success. In Chicago, the situation reached its nadir in 1940, as the American Giants ownership headed by Horace G. Hall struggled with debts, unpaid players, and the increasingly problematic condition of the team's aging ballpark at 39th and Wentworth. Veteran columnist Fay Young disgustedly lamented, "Chicago baseball fans deserve better than what they are getting," citing the team's park, "which we would expect to find in some small town in Mississippi," and warned that local fans, who now could "go to too many places on Sunday," were increasingly unwilling to patronize the games. To culminate a dreadful year, a fire destroyed the grandstand in December 1940, and the park was permanently abandoned.[34]

Conditions in other league cities in both the NNL and the NAL were nearly universally unfavorable. By August, Ed Harris noted that "the League is taking it on the chin as it has not in many, many years," and suggested that baseball had ceased to be "the money-making proposition it used to be years ago." Attendance at Newark, for instance, had dropped so precipitously that Effa Manley reduced the salary of press agent Jerry Kessler, explaining that she "must cut down on expenses if I am going to continue to operate the Ball Club . . . it is very evident that the publicity alone cannot attract people to the Park." After a yet another year of substantial financial loss, most observers expected the Manleys to sell the club, despite their denials. Ultimately, the Eagles remained in the league, but only after receiving additional financial backing from Percy Simon of Norfolk, Virginia.[35]

Not surprisingly, the New York Black Yankees, the perennial doormat of the NNL, also continued to struggle under the ownership of chronically cash-strapped James Semler. In a thinly veiled swipe at Semler, Cum Posey denounced an unnamed NNL owner who "signs a player to a year's contract, then takes the player off salary after six weeks and puts him on Co-Plan." Outfielder Charles Biot, who appeared with the Black Yankees in 1939 and 1940, recalled his unhappy experience with Semler, who "wouldn't pay me my money. I got $160 per month, so Jim took me in the back room and talked me into him paying me $80 every two weeks. Then he started cutting me each time, $50, $45, he was underpaying me." By 1941, increasingly concerned NNL officials considered granting free agent status to all Semler's players, but finally decided to grant him another chance.[36]

Perhaps the only fortuitous development in 1940 was the Homestead Grays' decision to divide their home games between Pittsburgh and Washington. With the exception of the early years of Greenlee Field, Pittsburgh had never been a consistently profitable venue, marred by its relatively small black population and dispersed settlement. By 1940 Wendell Smith observed that "baseball has been on the dump pile here for the past five years." In contrast, Washington's large black population continually intrigued promoters, as did the potential use of the major league's Griffith Stadium in the heart of the city's black community. Despite the failure of the Black Senators, several NNL and independent clubs had leased Griffith Stadium during 1938 and 1939, encouraged by a July 1938 doubleheader drawing 10,971 fans, a new record for black attendance in Washington. Journalist Eddie Gant doubted that Homestead or any "other out-of-town baseball outfit will ever gain but so much popularity in Washington," but the Grays gradually built a strong local following and within a few years had shifted the majority of their home games away from Pittsburgh (although they retained "Homestead" in their name).[37]

Despite the move to Washington, Cum Posey admitted that the season was "not a success, financially or otherwise." In general, black professional baseball in 1940 still seemed economically fragile, stuck in a holding pattern, and unable to build upon previous success. While Ed Bolden was "determined to see why the machinery won't click to the financial advantage of the league treasury and individual club owners," no single explanation was apparent to explain the inconsistent financial performance of black baseball from year to year. During the late 1930s, the cooperation of league owners remained problematic, finances shaky, and the threats from foreign owners had presented yet another unresolvable problem. Ed Harris, however, recognized the major cause: despite the lessening of the Depression's worst effects, "the average [black] spectator does not have the money to go to baseball games continually." Seemingly, no amount of thoughtful reflection and change in regulations by league owners could transcend this difficulty, and it would take a major global conflict to transform black baseball's status in the early 1940s.[38]

4

A New Beginning

The fact that three sepia baseball games—in three successive Sundays—drew nearly 100,000 cash customers . . . clearly shows the possibilities of the colorful tan-tinted version of the great American pastime. It shows what can be done and what could be done if the owners would see the light of a new day for Negro baseball on the horizon and have vision enough to invest something to perpetuate its future success.
                                    —Chester Washington, August 1941

The United States preparation for and eventual participation in World War II significantly transformed the social and economic experience of African Americans. The conversion to a wartime economy not only lifted the country out of the Depression but eventually created unprecedented job opportunities for blacks. Simultaneously, the war against foreign fascism helped to galvanize increased attention to the oppression of blacks in the United States, resulting in important strides in the fight for integration and an increasing ambivalence toward all-black institutions. Ultimately, the dual effects of economic and social progress during the war had dramatic ramifications upon all black enterprises, including professional baseball.

Most blacks initially saw little indication that the war would substantially affect their lives. As the prospect of the draft loomed in 1940, factory worker Paul Dunn remarked that "conscription will be all right for everybody except the Negro. You can rest assured he will get all the $21-a-month jobs." Dunn's pessimism appeared justified, particularly after army officials rejected African Americans attempting to enlist after the Japanese attack on Pearl Harbor, claiming that the black units were already fully staffed. While subsequent policy changes allowing black marine enlistments and expanded navy opportunities provided some encouragement, individuals such as housewife Rebecca Lee still believed that "they really have not given us anything, because segregation is going to still be very prominent. When the difference in races has been overcome and our boys have been permitted to train with white sailors, then I think something will have been accomplished."[1]

Economically, the prospect of war seemed to offer marginal change for African Americans. While lucrative war contracts created thousands of new jobs, most firms continued their policy of discrimination. The minimal black employment in war industries during late 1940 and early 1941, however, eventually prompted black leaders to action. In January 1941, A. Philip Randolph, president of the black Brotherhood of Sleeping Car Porters, organized the March on Washington movement, a plan for thousands of blacks to march to the Capitol on July 1 to protest discrimination in the defense industries. As support for the mass direct-action protest grew, the Roosevelt administration became increasingly wary of the movement's potential as propaganda easily exploited by the Axis powers and the possibility of a race riot. Randolph ultimately called off the march, after Roosevelt agreed on June 25, 1941, to issue Executive Order 8802, outlawing discrimination in defense industries and the government. Simultaneously, the order established the Committee on Fair Employment Practices (later reorganized in May 1943 as the Fair Employment Practices Committee or FEPC) to investigate discrimination complaints.

Although welcomed by the black community and providing an outlet for grievances, the FEPC hardly ended employment discrimination. Largely underfunded and understaffed, FEPC branches lacked the authority to compel employers to hire blacks, and many firms, fearful of antagonizing white workers, initially were reluctant to change existing employment patterns. Although the largely unskilled nature of the black population also presented a barrier to employment in defense industries, highly qualified black men often found themselves unable to obtain work. In 1941, for example, a black applicant to Cramp's Shipyard in Philadelphia with a degree in chemistry and prior graduate work at the University of Pennsylvania received an interview invitation, yet the company's interest soon waned after learning his race.[2]

Ultimately, the tremendous labor demand during the war, more than the creation of the FEPC, accelerated black employment. By 1945, blacks had made noticeable gains in defense work, as thousands found jobs in aircraft industries and shipyards for the first time. Meanwhile, the number of blacks employed in manufacturing rose 135 percent between April 1940 and January 1946. Not surprisingly, the increased employment in war production centers in the north and west stimulated yet another heavy migration of blacks from the south, approaching half a million.[3]

With black migrants pouring into the cities and earning unparalleled wages, black entrepreneurs found themselves in an ideal climate to launch or expand successful businesses, including professional baseball. Despite numerous organizational weaknesses and shaky financing, the leagues had weathered one of the most dismal economic periods in African American history and could now look toward operating in a less oppressive environment. Moreover, league officials could not help but be encouraged by the earlier example of World War I, which had provided a major stimulus to black baseball by expanding the attendance base and economically stabilizing the black population. Finally, the leagues still faced no direct competition for the black entertainment dollar, as white Organized Baseball seemingly had no intention of relaxing the color bar in the near future.

Yet during the war, black enterprises would begin to encounter gradually shifting attitudes toward integration and separate black institutions. Discouraged by the failure of numerous businesses during the Depression, younger black leaders began to doubt whether black business could ever provide the economic opportunities once anticipated. Scholar and future Nobel Peace Prize winner Ralph Bunche, for instance, questioned whether the continued growth of black business would appreciably improve conditions for black workers. By the early 1940s, Bunche denounced black business as a "parasitical growth on the Negro society, in that it exploits the 'race problem.' It demands for itself special privilege and parades under the chauvinistic protection of 'race loyalty,' thus further exploiting an already downtrodden group. It represents the welfare only of the pitifully small Negro middle-class group, though demanding support for its ideology from the race conscious Negro masses."

John F. Perdue, a black leader in Philadelphia whose protest group picketed several white-owned chain stores during the late 1930s hoping to force black employment, also reflected the newer philosophy, insisting that "the economic salvation of our group is not in the idea of a separate, independent 'black economy' but . . . in the integration of the Negro into the business and industrial pattern of America." While some observers continued to tout the utility of black enterprise, integration seemed to offer the prospect of greater benefits in the future.[4]

Concurrently, increased economic prosperity, America's fight against fascism abroad, and the presence of the FEPC encouraged increasingly assertive attitudes among African Americans, who would no longer accept discrimination and segregation without resistance. Claude Barnett, the founder and director of the Associated Negro Press, acknowledged the change, noting the "prevailing widespread opposition by Negroes in all walks of life to segregation. . . . The Negro as a group 25 years ago fought for equality but would have been satisfied to take it separately; today he fights not only for equality but wants integration." Editor E. Washington Rhodes linked the change to the war's economic impact which had allowed blacks to shift their concerns from basic survival issues to larger matters of their full rights as American citizens. By 1943, the *Philadelphia Tribune* increasingly advocated "the slow but much more American and democratic policy of integration," warning against "the quicker but much less self-respecting attitude of suggesting and submitting to segregation."

Segregation attempts, once tolerated and even praised in the past, engendered considerable resistance during the early 1940s in urban centers such as Philadelphia. Local leaders, for instance, rejected suggestions for a separate pool for blacks in North Philadelphia. Similarly, blacks initially welcomed Sun Shipyard's 1942 plan to expand and upgrade its black workforce until the company disclosed that the majority of new hires would be consigned to an all-black work area. The NAACP opposed the policy, as did the *Tribune*, which denounced the arrangement as "unnecessary, undemocratic, and will not in the long run help either America or colored people." Sun, however, maintained its hiring program, eventually employing a black workforce variously estimated at 9,000 to 18,000 at its peak, the majority in a segregated yard that closed in March 1945.[5]

The issue of recreational establishments for black servicemen in Philadelphia also provoked controversy and reflected the increasing movement for integration. Hoping to avoid separate facilities, local activist Arthur Huff Fauset nevertheless anticipated a "battle of wits, with many whites and some Negroes endeavoring to achieve the usual kind of set-up, as against other Negroes and some whites who are eager for a really democratic situation." Blacks were admitted to the USO Labor Plaza at Reyburn Plaza near City Hall and the Stage Door Canteen at the Academy of Music, but the *Philadelphia Independent* noted that "intermixing of the races is the exception rather than the rule. No one keeps a colored serviceman from dancing with a white hostess but then no one encourages him either." Despite protests from Fauset and others, the establishment of both a USO center and a second Stage Door Canteen in the 500 block of South Broad Street within South Philadelphia's black community eventually precluded greater interracial interaction.

The nascent struggles against segregated work and recreation facilities revealed a segment within northern black communities that was increasingly ambivalent about black institutions. The question began to arise whether separate institutions in some way precluded integration, exemplified by an almost apologetic 1943 *Tribune* editorial admitting that "it may be necessary for years to come to have our own churches and other types of private social organizations, but from now on our fight must be for full and complete integration and acceptance as American citizens." By the end of World War II, integration, while remote, appeared less elusive than before, raising concerns whether its growing immediacy would adversely affect the support of professional black baseball.⁶

◆ ◆ ◆

After a disastrous 1940 season, black professional teams had little reason for optimism. The preparations for war had begun to provide employment opportunities for whites, yet African American unemployment initially remained at Depression levels. While league presidents Tom Wilson and J. B. Martin predicted that increased factory and defense work would ultimately boost attendance in 1941, several NNL officials were less confident. The Manleys considered disbanding the Newark Eagles, and rumors surfaced that the Philadelphia Stars would withdraw, relocate to Hilldale Park, and play independent baseball. Increasingly disenchanted with the league's administration, Ed Bolden claimed that there was "a skunk in the woodpile" and suggested an investigation of black baseball. An equally disheartened Cum Posey confided to Abe Manley that he could "see little hope for success in 1941 unless many drastic changes are made" and admitted that his partner, Rufus Jackson, was "very doubtful about what he will do in 1941."⁷

Hoping to resolve current uncertainties, the NNL met at the York Hotel in Baltimore on January 3–4, 1941. In contrast to the heated battle the previous February, the meeting was surprisingly harmonious. With relatively little fanfare, the owners reelected Tom Wilson president and Bolden vice president and installed Posey as secretary-treasurer. Although the volatile Yankee Stadium issue once again surfaced, the matter was largely defused after Eddie Gottlieb agreed to turn over 20 percent of his net share to the league treasury. The league also planned expanded interleague competition with the NAL, although the Stars remained leery of unprofitable western trips.

Despite the productive session, the major issue still facing all black professional teams was Mexico. Both leagues not only had to decide the fate of the players who had jumped in 1940 but also faced the threat of a second round of raids in 1941. As early as December 1940, Posey lamented that "more players will be in Mexico next year than before," noting that several star players were a threat to bolt.⁸

As usual, the always aggressive Effa Manley proposed several solutions to prevent further damage. Claiming that she did "not blame the ballplayers from going away where they can get more money," Manley nevertheless felt it was "positively stupid for us to sit idly by and not make an effort to protect ourselves." Noting the wealth of most foreign owners, Manley suggested that there be "an effort made to contact these men and

Figure 11. League officials at the York Hotel in Baltimore, January 3, 1941. Left to right. Back row, standing, Rufus Jackson (Homestead Grays), Art Carter (*Baltimore Afro-American*), James Semler (New York Black Yankees), Jock Waters (New York Black Yankees). Back row, seated, Charles Brown, Edward Witherspoon, Alex Pompez (New York Cubans), Thomas Wilson (Baltimore Elite Giants), Effa Manley, Abe Manley (Newark Eagles), Cum Posey (Homestead Grays), J. B. Martin (Chicago American Giants/president of NAL). Front row, seated, William Leuschner (booking agent), Eddie Gottlieb (Philadelphia Stars/booking agent), Seward ("See") Posey (Homestead Grays), Frank Forbes, Eary Brown, Douglass Smith (Baltimore Elite Giants). Courtesy Larry Lester/Noir Tech, Inc.

see if they would not willingly pay us . . . I should think they would welcome an opportunity to have us operating as high class farms for them. That is all we really are. There is so much harm being done, so much destruction being wrought, that it is very possible if these men were informed of the true state of affairs they would be glad to cooperate on a sensible practical program, whereby we could develop players for them, and no one would be hurt." Manley even consulted with Robert Hartgrove, a black New Jersey attorney, who recommended that the league utilize airtight contracts comparable to agreements between boxers and their managers.[9]

Although the league predictably failed to act on Effa Manley's suggestions, Posey agreed that some action was necessary. Posey advocated reinstating the jumping players, as "otherwise our League is too weak to charge the prices we charge, especially where white Semi Pro clubs beat us consistently." Attempting to deflect criticism from his stance and build sympathy for the players, Posey noted that "we cannot blame anyone for attempting to make their future financially safe." Posey's attitude, seemingly contradicting his past views on jumping players, was hardly unbiased; it was strongly influenced by a desire to recover the services of his star catcher, Josh Gibson. Despite the reticence of the Manleys and the majority of NAL franchises, the two leagues eventually agreed in February 1941 to provide a temporary grace period for the jumpers, allowing them until May 1 to return to their teams and pay a $100 fine or face an additional three-year suspension. As anticipated, Posey promptly announced the signing of Josh Gibson to a $3,000 contract, reportedly the highest salary to date in black baseball, leading Ed Harris to observe that "the moguls ought to be wise to the fact by now that POSEY tells them to do one thing and does something else himself."[10]

Unbeknownst to Posey, Gibson apparently had no intention of remaining in the United States in 1941. On March 11, Gibson left Pittsburgh for Mexico after agreeing to a $6,000 offer. While Effa Manley and Eddie Gottlieb expressed disbelief, Posey initially was ambivalent, privately admitting that he "hated to see him go but personally I was not in favor of paying him the high salary we were to give him." Grays officials eventually initiated legal proceedings against Gibson for breach of contract, seeking $10,400 in damages for potential loss of profit and advertising costs. Ordered to appear for an April 7 court date but still in Mexico, Gibson told his wife Hattie to secure legal representation. Nevertheless, on April 19, Judge Thomas Marshall of the Court of Common Pleas of Allegheny County handed down a $10,000 verdict in favor of the Grays, citing Gibson's failure to appear in court.

Jacob Frank, Gibson's attorney, then sought to open the judgment and grant Gibson an extension to allow for his return to the United States. Although Gibson later gave a deposition to a U.S. consul in Mexico claiming that Rufus Jackson had granted him permission to go to Mexico, Marshall noted that "the testimony was not convincing, or at least sufficiently convincing, to make the Court believe that the ball club had surrendered rights to a valuable player so easily." Judge Marshall also rejected Frank's suggestion that Gibson's contract was "unilateral," citing the legal example of the famous Napoleon Lajoie case forty years earlier and thus seemingly validating the legitimacy of black baseball's contracts, if exercised properly. The Grays later relinquished their claim, after Gibson, faced with the potential loss of his property, returned in October 1941 and agreed to a two-year contract.[11]

The entire Gibson affair disheartened veteran observers such as Sam

Lacy, who was disturbed that his "ex-favorite" player apparently regarded a "contract with a colored business enterprise" as "no more nor less than 'a scrap of paper.'" To Lacy, such episodes served only to weaken an already shaky institution and undermine any hopes for integration. As Lacy observed, "so-called organized colored baseball—with its questionable integrity, lackadaisical administration and frequent indifferent performance—has enough handicaps as it is. I can well do without the player who shows an utter disregard for the advancement of the institution." Meanwhile, whether legal proceedings and suspension threats actually deterred players remained questionable. Although several players returned from Mexico, stars such as Willie Wells and Ray Dandridge of the Newark Eagles, Johnny Taylor of the New York Cubans, Bill Wright of the Baltimore Elites, and Sam Bankhead of Homestead remained south of the border.[12]

The continued loss of marquee players dismayed Vic Harris of the Grays, who warned, "we can't ignore the fact that all the good ball players are playing on foreign soil." Yet the past failure of the industry to enforce penalties for jumping players coupled with the strong appeal of Mexico guaranteed continued defections. The Mexican League not only offered better salaries but often improved working conditions. After speaking with several of the jumpers, *Philadelphia Tribune* columnist Eustace Gay related that the players traveled by rail and received decent housing and medical care during the season. Gay also noted that the players valued participating in a "real" league, where each team had its own park and with "no double-headers with one game a league game, and the other a 7-inning exhibition tilt with neither the players nor the fans able to keep track of the standing of the teams, their batting averages etc."[13]

Not surprisingly, Mexico remained an ongoing industry problem during the early 1940s. Although draft classifications subsequently kept several players in the United States, such as Bill Wright who returned to the Baltimore Elite Giants in 1942 after two seasons in Mexico, players unfettered by draft status remained receptive to Mexican offers. While the NNL continued to impose suspensions and fines on jumping players, several officials began to pursue more aggressive tactics during 1942. Hoping to delay or prevent the loss of Monte Irvin and Lenny Pearson, Effa Manley notified the Essex County, New Jersey, draft board of the players' plan to leave the country to play in Mexico. Manley also subsequently retained black attorney Robert Hartgrove, whose suggestions the league had ignored a year earlier, to address the matter of jumping players with Mexican authorities. In an uncharacteristic show of unity, both leagues rallied behind Manley and agreed to divide the fee for Hartgrove's services among the twelve franchises.[14]

In July 1942, Hartgrove presented black baseball's case to Mexican official Juan Richer. Deemphasizing the shaky nature of the league contracts, Hartgrove instead questioned the legality of the players' passports, arguing that "it is patent that these ball players breaching their contracts are not going to Mexico as tourists on a two-weeks' trip or are they going to Mexico for occupational pursuits by reason of a lack of occupational opportunities in this country. . . . There can be no argument as to the illegality of procuring these passports, both as to the false pretenses under which they are obtained and the extensions of stay which undoubtedly are procured by the baseball players when once they are able to go to Mexico." Receiving little response, Hartgrove then met with a State Department official, who expressed sympathy but offered no solution to the leagues' dilemma. Hartgrove, however, anticipated that "some definite action will be taken by which both Negro Leagues will be greatly benefitted." In a final attempt to advance the leagues' cause, Hartgrove approached Senator William Smathers, a New Jersey Democrat, noting that "the very life and security of organized Negro Professional Baseball Clubs are at stake . . . the thousands of dollars which Negroes of this country have invested have been placed in jeopardy." Smathers promised to investigate the matter with the Chief of the Passport Division, but Hartgrove's efforts ultimately proved fruitless, underscoring the lack of influence in Washington of the leagues (and of all black businesses), a problem that was soon to be crucial.[15]

With Hartgrove's failure, black baseball remained frighteningly vulnerable to foreign threats. Despite several years of player defections, the industry still possessed no effective mechanism to retain control of its players from season to season or legal recourse to prevent contract jumping. Continued jumpings appeared likely, and the NNL and NAL appeared no closer to solving the problem.

◆ ◆ ◆

Fortunately, a substantial attendance boost in 1941 allowed the NNL to weather the continued threat of Mexico. Despite only modest initial gains in war industries, African American employment began to rise as the United States drew closer to war. Black fans, flush with discretionary income for the first time in more than a decade, flocked to baseball games in numbers approaching and even exceeding the peak of two decades earlier, and the once seemingly moribund enterprise appeared increasingly reinvigorated as the season progressed.

The continued spectacular rise of Satchel Paige reflected black baseball's new vitality. While the industry typically attracted only sporadic coverage from the white media, Paige became a national celebrity after his outstanding pitching, various eccentricities, and uncertain age attracted the attention of white journalists. As his fame grew, Paige became an increasingly important commodity, noticeably boosting the already growing attendance in both leagues. To maximize his earning potential, Paige began pitching only 2 to 3 innings per game, which meant that he could be promoted for several appearances per week at a variety of league and non-league venues. Recognizing his importance as a drawing card, the Kansas City Monarchs reportedly signed the often wayward Paige to an "ironbound" contract, hoping to prevent the jumping episodes of earlier seasons.[16]

Paige's unique position, however, engendered occasional difficulties among players and league owners. While Cum Posey viewed him as "a likable big so and so" without "an enemy in the world," Paige himself admitted that "the players make it hard for me because of the publicity I get and because of my salary." Several owners also worried that the individual promotion of Paige often occurred at the expense of publicizing black professional baseball as an enterprise.

During 1941, NNL owners grappled with the dilemma of whether to exploit the growing Paige phenomenon. Hoping to increase the gate of the Black Yankees home opener at Yankee Stadium on May 11, owner James Semler hired Paige to hurl the first game of the doubleheader against the Philadelphia Stars. When Effa Manley, still indignant over Paige's earlier failure to play for Newark, objected, Eddie Gottlieb explained that Semler hoped Paige "would help pull a big crowd and enable him to make some money which would get his team and himself a good start, and assist in getting out of debt. . . . We may get quite a few fans who have never seen the Negro National League teams play and if we impress them, as we should, they may become regular patrons." Gottlieb's confidence proved correct, as the doubleheader drew over 20,000 fans, including a photographer from *Life* magazine, which published pictures of the game along with a feature on Paige in its June 2 issue. The use of Paige, however, required that the regularly scheduled league game be designated as an exhibition, much to the chagrin of Posey.

Some fans hoped that Paige would remain in the east, but the NAL claimed that Paige was still Monarchs property and that his appearance with an NNL team violated the interleague agreement. President Tom Wilson's promise to suspend any NNL franchise employing NAL players subsequently placated the midwestern owners, and eventually Monarchs co-owner Tom Baird agreed to lend Paige to the NNL for exhibition games. Eager for another profitable payday at Yankee Stadium, Gottlieb promptly booked a second doubleheader featuring Paige. The July 20 promotion, involving Paige's Monarchs and three NNL teams, eventually netted over

Figure 12. Satchel Paige's appearance with
the New York Black Yankees at Yankee
Stadium on May 11, 1941 was profitable to
the NNL, but it angered the NAL. Courtesy
Baseball Hall of Fame Library.

$6,000, shared equally among all six NNL clubs after adding the profits
from other league and exhibition games played that day. While Gottlieb
considered Paige's $300 fee "very cheap, as he was largely responsible for
the crowd, and helped all of us to make money," Effa Manley balked at
paying her share, complaining that the "Kansas City-Satchel mess makes
me ill." Yet other NNL clubs, such as Philadelphia, willingly scheduled
exhibition contests with the Monarchs during their eastern swing, hoping
to profit from Paige's box office impact. Notably, advance publicity announcing that Paige "will definitely hurl part of the game" helped to draw

Figure 13. The increasingly popular Satchel Paige surrounded by a group of admirers at Gus Greenlee's establishment in Pittsburgh, 1944. Photo by Charles "Teenie" Harris. Courtesy Carnegie Museum of Art, Pittsburgh.

a large crowd at Parkside Field in Philadelphia on July 17, despite rainy weather.[17]

Black professional baseball eventually accepted and embraced Satchel Paige's unique position as its most marketable commodity. As sportswriter Dan Burley enthused, "I might be wrong, but I believe Satchel Paige is the biggest colored drawing card we have. . . . By that I mean Satchel draws more Negroes to his games than any other individual we have today. . . . Yep, even more than Joe Louis . . . any of our orchestra leaders; our singers, etc."[18] Yet the rise of another publicity phenomenon during 1941, the Ethiopian Clowns, engendered considerably more ambivalence. The Clowns emerged from the milieu of the Depression, when numerous white and black promoters employed various gimmicks hoping to boost attendance. The Philadelphia Stars, for example, participated in bizarre attractions, including a 1934 date at Phillies Park featuring the bearded House of David, celebrated female athlete Babe Didrikson, and a "donkey baseball" game with players and fielders mounted on donkeys. A number of traveling teams offered similar blends of entertainment and athletic prowess, including the Detroit Clowns, the Jewish Clowns, Jim Thorpe's Indians, the goateed Kentucky Colonels (clad in overalls and straw hats), and the similarly dressed Hillbillies, all of whom appeared in the east during the 1930s.[19]

Among black teams, several semiprofessional clubs returned to the world of comedy, a once prevalent aspect in black baseball's early days that had become nearly extinct by the 1920s. Inspired by the success of white novelty teams, black promoter Charlie Henry organized the Zulu Cannibal Giants in the mid-1930s, featuring players clad in grass skirts, headdresses, and war paint. Pandering to white America's worst attitudes and most stereotypical views of blacks, the players entertained fans between games with various "comedy" acts including staged fights with spears and shields along with a crap game featuring loaded dice and players brandishing razors.[20]

Like the Zulu Cannibal Giants, the Ethiopian Clowns emphasized humor over athletic ability. While the exact origins of the team are unclear, several accounts suggest that the club began in Miami in 1935 or 1936 and eventually came under the management of Hunter Campbell and Johnny Pierce, a black bootlegger. With Syd Pollock—a white Tarrytown, New York, theater owner formerly involved in black baseball with the Havana Red Sox, Cuban House of David, and a version of the Cuban Stars—handling bookings and exerting increasing control, the team (now called the Ethiopian Clowns) became a popular midwestern attraction by the late 1930s.[21]

Despite the success of the Clowns, the club appeared unlikely to become part of the black professional baseball establishment. While fans valued "color" in both black and white players, the comedy stylings of the Clowns not only appeared out of place in an organization striving to parallel white Organized Baseball but also seemed to cater to the expectations and stereotypes of white America. Wendell Smith, for example, considered the Clowns' antics little better than "minstrel shows,"[22] and believed that most blacks found them offensive. New York Cubans owner Alex Pompez was equally hostile, claiming that no foreign-born player would participate in such humiliating activity.[23] Meanwhile, Cum Posey considered Pollock a "swell person" but believed the use of the word "Ethiopian" in the team name was an insult to African Americans, "capitalizing on the downfall of the only empire which really belonged to the Negro race." Pollock, however, claimed that the "title was originated and used with the full consent

Figure 14. Ethiopian Clowns with faces painted. Courtesy Baseball Hall of Fame Library.

of the late Ethiopian Government officials" with "not the slightest indication . . . to hold anyone up to ridicule."[24]

Although the Clowns continued their face painting, comedy routines, and assumed names (such as "Wahoo" and "Tarzan"), the team's financial success attracted competent players including several defectors from the two leagues. In 1940, both leagues jointly agreed to ban competition with the Clowns yet NAL teams such as the Chicago American Giants and Kansas City Monarchs soon succumbed to the prospect of profitable exhibition contests. A second joint attempt in March 1941 to squelch the Clowns hardly daunted Syd Pollock, who confidently confided to Effa Manley that "we've been banned before and will be banned again . . . and what the league clubs lose by not playing us someone else will gain by."

Pollock's prediction proved correct, as the Clowns, like other black teams, experienced a substantial attendance increase in 1941. By June, the NAL agreed to book the Clowns, provided they carried no ineligible players on their roster. After witnessing the Clowns draw an unanticipated crowd of 12,000 fans on June 8 at Crosley Field, home of the Cincinnati Reds, Fay Young admitted that "whether some of us like the white chalk put on the players' faces or not, the Clowns prove, from the crowds they draw, that they have something the public wants." In a further triumph, the team captured the *Denver Post* tournament, and by September Wendell Smith acknowledged that the Clowns, along with Satchel Paige's Kansas City Monarchs, were the best drawing cards in black baseball.

Despite their significant value to the industry, however, the Clowns and Paige ultimately contributed little to strengthen the operation of the two leagues in 1941. The Clowns remained independent, and Paige's popularity prompted growing use of the celebrated hurler in meaningless interleague exhibition games in subsequent years. Yet as long as exhibition contests remained profitable, NNL and NAL teams willingly sacrificed the scheduling of official games, stalling the administrative progress of the two leagues in years to come.[25]

◆ ◆ ◆

The rise of Paige and the Clowns was only one facet of a dramatic attendance surge in several league cities during 1941. After nearly disbanding following a miserable 1940 season, the Newark Eagles grossed nearly $61,000 in 1941 (more than the class B minor league Wilmington Blue Rocks), with attendance averaging 4,293 for their eight Sunday dates at Ruppert Stadium, including 11,674 for their home opener on May 11. In Baltimore, the Elites enjoyed strong attendance for night games at Bugle Field, while in New York, eight Yankee Stadium promotions reportedly averaged 20,000 fans by September. Meanwhile, the East-West game, now in its ninth year, set a new attendance record, drawing 47,865 fans to Comiskey Park on July 27.[26]

Even more remarkable was black professional baseball's success in previously less developed markets. Detroit, swelling with thousands of new migrants, suddenly became an attractive venue after years of irrelevance. With the assistance of promoter Joe Coles, the Homestead Grays leased Briggs Stadium, home of the Detroit Tigers and long unavailable to black teams, for a doubleheader with the Elite Giants on Sunday, August 3. The promotion drew a tremendous crowd of nearly 28,000 fans, and, according to Grays business manager Seward ("See") Posey, resulted in "the largest gate any two colored clubs ever received." While the doubleheader demonstrated that league games alone could attract crowds without resorting to gimmicks such as the Clowns or over-publicizing Satchel Paige, Paige continued to be a magnet for fans. A second date at Briggs on September 14, featuring Paige hurling for the Monarchs against the Chicago American Giants, drew 34,784, and a similar matchup at Sportsman's Park in St. Louis, also rarely leased to black teams, drew 19,178 on July

4. By the season's end, Cum Posey claimed that the Monarchs, fueled by the popularity of Paige, had grossed nearly $100,000.

Posey himself recognized black baseball's transformation during 1941 into "one of our largest business enterprises," noting that the two leagues now invested more than $400,000 per season on salaries and incidental expenses, excluding park rentals and booking fees. An equally enthusiastic Effa Manley predicted that "the baseball business . . . is just beginning to grow. It will not only supply many jobs, but is something the colored group can feel proud of." Yet black professional baseball's increased vitality in 1941 coincided with renewed fears over white involvement and potential control of the enterprise. Although the virtually nonexistent profits during the past decade had discouraged sustained discussion of white entrepreneurs, the new economic climate resulted in an increasingly critical reexamination of their roles as booking agents, team owners, promoters, and park proprietors.[27]

Despite the formation of several organizations since 1920, black professional teams had continued to earn a substantial portion of their income from non-league games against white teams before white audiences. Historically, black teams had depended on these dates, though they resented and sometimes resisted the role of white booking agents who often controlled many of the most lucrative games. The severe drop in black attendance during the worst years of the Depression had resulted in increased reliance on booking agents, whose efforts were crucial in keeping black baseball alive. According to Cum Posey, the Black Yankees and Crawfords both "came to the front through the aid of Nat Strong's office. They could not have survived otherwise." Conversely, John Drew's reluctance to work with booking agents contributed to the final collapse of Hilldale in 1932. Even as late as 1937, Posey acknowledged the significance of white competition, noting that the NNL needed "as many white independent clubs as are capable of operating ball parks. . . . In the course of a season more white fans attend our games than do fans of our race."

While some observers hoped for less reliance on white teams and promoters, the NNL eventually chose to integrate the booking agents into the league structure. In 1937, the NNL designated Ed Gottlieb to book all independent games for league teams on the east coast; he was later joined by William Leuschner of the Nat Strong agency. Although the booking agents received 10 percent of the gross from these games, a quarter of their fees reverted to the league treasury. While league teams could still book games outside the two agencies, the majority of the most profitable east coast venues remained under their control.[28]

To Posey, often a critic of booking agents in the past, the arrangement was generally satisfactory, as both offices were "experienced and fair."

According to Posey, Gottlieb and Leuschner never earned more than $2,400 from the league per season during the 1930s despite considerable overhead, as "to keep six clubs booked every day each office must have someone present every day, and most of the night. There is also the expense of running an office and using telephones." In 1939, for instance, Gottlieb and Leuschner earned $2,267.21 in booking fees from league teams, 25 percent ($566.80) of which reverted to the NNL, leaving the two agencies with a total of only $1,700.41. Moreover, Posey claimed that booking agents provided a necessary safety net for inexperienced officials, who would be in an "awful fix" without their services, and ultimately rejected racially based criticisms, considering it a "low blow to always refer to these men . . . as WHITE BOOKING AGENTS. There is no segregation in Negro baseball."

Yet Posey also recognized that the self-centeredness often displayed by the league owners was equally prevalent among the booking agents, and noted that, despite their investment in the league, "they have been known to keep league clubs idle, or send them to bad spots, and place outside clubs . . . in the larger and more profitable parks." Meanwhile, several observers questioned whether booking agents could truly have a vested interest in an institution whose success could ultimately render their own services unnecessary. Effa Manley, for example, suspected that Eddie Gottlieb "does not want the league to get too strong because he may not have as much booking if we get to the place we can draw without playing at semi-pro Parks."[29]

As black teams regained stability by 1941, several officials once again turned a critical eye toward booking agents. In the NNL, Manley objected to Gottlieb's unique position as team owner and booking agent, which freed the Philadelphia Stars from most of the fees incurred by other clubs. Manley also quarreled with Bill Leuschner, particularly after the New York promoter undermined her attempt to book the Eagles in Stamford, Connecticut. In a subsequent letter to Leuschner, Manley complained that "it is a known fact that some teams receive all your choice booking . . . if a team can get itself some choice spots, I think you are showing a very selfish attitude to hurt them, in order to benefit yourself." Manley found support from the Grays' See Posey, who was "disgusted with the booking in the East" and complained of "really pitiful" financial returns. Yet as sportswriter Art Carter noted, "the booking agents get away with a great deal in baseball, largely because owners have either been too weak-kneed or too shortsighted to see the far-reaching outcome of many strange propositions."[30]

Perhaps more troublesome during 1941 was the growing influence of midwestern booking agent and promoter Abe Saperstein. Born in London

Figure 15. Abe Saperstein (1903–1966) became
a powerful but controversial force in black baseball during the 1940s. Courtesy Urban Archives,
Temple University, Philadelphia.

in 1903, Saperstein migrated to the United States as a child and grew up
in Chicago. Like Gottlieb, Saperstein became involved in basketball as a
young man, playing on the Lake View High School team, despite a slight
stature and rotund build. Saperstein achieved greater success as a promoter, however, beginning in 1926 when he began to book the black
Savoy Big Five basketball team. The nucleus of the Savoy Big Five soon
became part of a new team under Saperstein's management, later known
as the Harlem Globetrotters. During the Depression, the Globetrotters
began to challenge the New York Renaissance as the best known and most
profitable black basketball team in the country. Yet the team's white own-

ership and increasing use of comedy to maximize its entertainment appeal to whites stood in stark contrast to the proud tradition of the Rens, who remained in the capable hands of Bob Douglas, a West Indies native who deplored clowning.

During the early 1930s, Saperstein also became involved in baseball and eventually became the leading booking agent in the midwest. By late in the decade, Saperstein not only booked the non-league Ethiopian Clowns but also handled most of the independent games for NAL teams, as well as arranging dates for the Sir Oliver Bibbs orchestra and the Brown Bombers football team. Simultaneously, Saperstein's close contacts with the white daily press in Chicago enabled him to play an increasingly influential role in publicizing the East-West game at Comiskey Park. By 1939, Saperstein received 5 percent of the gate receipts. The arrangement disturbed several NNL owners, particularly Cum Posey, who denounced Saperstein's involvement with the Clowns and his seemingly exploitive tactics toward black teams. Posey cited Saperstein's 35 percent share plus booking fees for an NAL promotion at Crosley Field in Cincinnati in 1941, warning "there should be no place in Negro or any kind of baseball for a man like this." Even Fay Young, a more objective observer, began to question the involvement of Saperstein, who was "making his living off Negro activities. The future of them is not his concern—it is the present and what he can get out of it."[31]

White promotion and ownership in black professional baseball also came under increasing scrutiny. In the NNL, Gottlieb's control over the lucrative Yankee Stadium dates continued to irritate several teams, particularly the Grays and Eagles. In an attempt to counteract Gottlieb during 1941, the two teams independently secured the Polo Grounds on September 14, which See Posey hoped would "show the bookies we don't have to have them to promote games." Moreover, Effa Manley told Posey that Gottlieb had unsuccessfully attempted to discourage the Eagles from participating, telling her that "it wasn't right for us to go in the Polo Grounds, when the League has a contract with Yankee Stadium. Isn't that rich? This is the first time I knew the contract for the Stadium was for the League. I still think it is Gottlieb's contract." Meanwhile, Cum Posey privately conveyed to Manley his fear that "Ed is getting too big. He has all the money belonging to the N.N.L. . . . . He figures if he can keep you and I fighting that we will forget about him."

To some observers, the rise of Saperstein and Pollock in the west and the continued influence of Gottlieb and Leuschner in the east seemed to foreshadow eventual complete white appropriation of the fast-growing business. Increasingly wary of white exploitation, Effa Manley urged racial solidarity, warning that "we are playing right in the hands of these *smart* men who see the possibility our baseball offers, and who are trying hard to set it up. If they are not stopped now, there won't be any stopping them . . . they are taking advantage of a lot of inexperienced business men and are hitting from all sides." Even usually inactive NNL president Tom Wilson began to worry that black entrepreneurs might lose their stake in the enterprise. As journalist E. B. Rea lamented, "it's useless and foolhardy to kid ourselves into not believing that this very thing is being attempted, and the same way in which outstanding name bands, theatrical and night club ventures opened their eyes and found themselves the pawn of white promoters."[32]

During the early 1940s, the scattered criticism of white promoters became more strident (exemplified by See Posey's comment that "white are for white colored are dogs in some of the estimations. where money is concerned"), perhaps a product of the heightened race consciousness of the war years. Yet the backlash against whites occasionally transcended racial awareness and bordered on anti-Semitism, expressed toward the powerful Jewish promoters (Ed Gottlieb, Abe Saperstein, William Leuschner) in black baseball. Manley, for example, promised in 1941 that "these Jews would be stopped in their tracks" if she or her husband were made league chairman, while sportswriter Lem Graves, Jr. of the *Norfolk Journal and Guide* complained that "Jews have taken over" after Abe Saperstein handled publicity for the 1941 East-West game. Notably, the late Nat Strong had prompted similar responses from the black press, who had termed him the "Hebrew menace in colored baseball" years earlier.[33]

The intolerant attitudes of Manley, Graves, and others were hardly atypical and coincided with the often hostile response to the continued heavy Jewish ownership of housing, stores, and entertainment centers in urban black neighborhoods during the early 1940s. In Philadelphia, local black leader Arthur Huff Fauset, whose mother was Jewish, cited the alarming trend by 1943, noting the "increasing anti-Semitism which has developed among certain types of Negroes." A year later, Fauset lamented the "destruction and pillaging of shops, chiefly Jewish, in North Philadelphia" following the Philadelphia Transportation Company strike of 1944 and criticized blacks who used "the Jewish issue as a means of venting their spleen for all the evils which the majority group perpetrate against Negroes."[34]

Regardless of their sometimes unwelcome presence, Jews functioned as an undeniably important promotional force in black sports. The trend was apparent not only in baseball but in basketball, with Saperstein's Globetrotters, and in boxing, where Mike Jacobs handled Joe Louis's New York fights and controlled most of the major bouts during the 1930s and 1940s. The rise of Jacobs was hardly surprising, and, as historian Steven Riess has noted, the involvement of Jews in boxing paralleled their similar participation in "aspects of the entertainment business that were shunned by the more established ethnic groups." Notably, Jews also invested in the black motion picture industry and controlled several black theaters, particularly in Harlem, where Frank Schiffman operated the Apollo for decades. Other major Jewish entrepreneurs included Moe Gale, the owner of the Savoy Ballroom and booking agent for numerous major black acts, and Joe Glaser, an equally influential promoter who also served as Louis Armstrong's personal manager. The success of Jewish promoters in black entertainment, however, understandably troubled African Americans whose attempts to establish comparable enterprises or agencies often faced nearly insurmountable barriers.[35]

Despite the increasing distrust of white involvement and calls for race consciousness, most black officials and players ultimately were racial pragmatists, leery of exploitation but willing to work with or for whoever could offer the greatest benefit. Moreover, there was little doubt that despite difficulties, several whites had contributed to the development of black baseball, and as Cum Posey observed, "put their money into Negro Baseball when it was at its lowest ebb." The white-controlled Kansas City Monarchs, now co-owned by Tom Baird, a sports promoter and bowling alley proprietor, and J. L. Wilkinson, had not only remained one of the strongest and best-financed franchises but earned high regard for its treatment of players. Satchel Paige, for example, considered Wilkinson "as good a boss as you could ask for" and credited his superior management, which allowed Paige to avoid the financial woes that plagued other black athletic icons of the era such as Joe Louis and Jesse Owens.

Other white promoters also drew support. Players such as Sug Cornelius touted Abe Saperstein's publicity and administrative skills, while veteran Ted Radcliffe considered him to be one of the greatest figures in black baseball.[36] Meanwhile, the Manleys admitted that Eddie Gottlieb was "truly honest where financial matters are concerned," and slugger Buck Leonard of the Homestead Grays recalled Gottlieb's readiness to advance money to black teams: "if you need 400 or 500 dollars go down there to Ed Gottlieb on Broad Street, bam, he'd give it to ya." Similarly, sportswriter Joe Bostic acknowledged that "in all fairness . . . Ed Gottlieb . . . has helped the individual members of the League over many a monetary shoal and has helped the league in other ways. Not that he hasn't been well paid, mind you, but he still has helped."[37]

White involvement in a predominantly black enterprise remained but one of a number of unsolved issues facing black professional baseball as World War II loomed. While the prospect of war offered the potential of greater black employment and profits, it would also unleash anxieties over who would control the rapidly transforming business of black baseball and whether the expanded scale of the enterprise would ultimately encourage or inhibit greater cooperation. Meanwhile, gradually shifting black attitudes toward separate institutions would begin to pose a threat by the end of the war. Nevertheless, at the close of the 1941 season, league officials could look confidently toward a seemingly bright future, as the positive economic forecast appeared likely to produce a sustained positive impact on the industry.

An Industry Transformed

It is indeed tragic that Negro baseball must continue to operate on the slip-shod basis it has existed on for so long. It has
grown to the point where it is now a two or three million
dollar business. It is one of the largest businesses operated
by Negroes in this country and is a means of livelihood, directly and indirectly, for at least two thousand people. . . . It
is a major business and I'm afraid that some day, it is going
to be killed by the very people who are thriving off it now.
—Wendell Smith, 1944

After a generally prosperous 1941 season, the NNL and NAL had every
reason to anticipate continued success in the future. But the Japanese attack on Pearl Harbor in December and America's entry into World War II
abruptly altered the position of professional baseball and other sports,
whose fate now apparently lay in the hands of the federal government.
Attempting to determine baseball's status for the upcoming season, major
league commissioner Kenesaw Mountain Landis contacted President
Franklin Roosevelt in January 1942. Roosevelt sanctioned continued operation, explaining, "I honestly feel that it would be best for the country to
keep baseball going. There will be fewer people unemployed and everyone
will work longer hours and harder than ever before. And that means that
they ought to have a chance for recreation and for taking their minds off
their work more than before." The news encouraged baseball officials, but
it offered no promise of special treatment, and white and black teams
could expect wartime policies to interfere with normal operation.

Black professional teams soon had to contend with several war-related
issues. Rumors of a ban on night baseball to conserve electricity for defense
work alarmed observers such as sportswriter Art Carter, who felt such a
policy would "virtually wreck the colored clubs. A good 50 percent of their
games are nocturnal affairs." While Roosevelt himself expressed a desire
that "night games . . . be extended because it gives the opportunity to
the day shift to see a game occasionally," subsequent "dimout" orders

threatened continued night baseball at semipro, minor, and major league parks located in coastal cities. Fearful that park lighting would benefit enemy pilots, government officials ultimately suspended night games for part of the war in several cities, including Newark and New York, the home of three NNL franchises, although the new policy exempted Philadelphia's Shibe Park, a soon-to-be-important venue for black baseball.

The impact of the draft, enlistments, and war work also undermined the stability of nearly every professional sports organization. Black professional baseball would lose more than 50 players to military service during the war, and at least one, Ralph "Botts" Johnson, who played briefly with the Philadelphia Stars in 1941, was killed in action. Numerous players obtained employment in war industries, providing them not only a previously unavailable lucrative alternative to baseball, but additional leverage in salary negotiations. Several players threatened to forsake baseball for their defense jobs, including Francis Matthews, who informed Eagles officials in early 1942 that "I have a very good job and while I'd much rather play ball, I'm only wondering if it would be worth while to quit. . . . My heart is in baseball but I'm getting no younger and must look out for myself."[1]

Virtually every black professional team encountered unexpected obstacles in the early days of the war. Players participating in the Puerto Rican winter league found themselves temporarily unable to return to the United States because of feared submarine attacks. Similarly, travel problems limited the ability of Alex Pompez to provide passage from Cuba for several of his players. Yet the financial success of 1941 fueled by rising black employment allowed Pompez and other owners to weather inconveniences that might have been destructive in the past. The NNL in particular seemed poised to achieve even greater success in 1942, and as one enthusiastic observer noted, "if business as usual is permitted, the league should break all attendance records as every city in which the regular league games are played is booming with war workers, anxious to find some form of pleasurable relaxation."[2]

◆ ◆ ◆

As the 1942 season dawned, the NNL appeared financially stable for the first time in its existence, encouraged by strong attendance in 1941, a solvent league treasury, greater discretionary income among black fans, and the federal government's seemingly tolerant policy toward professional sports during the war. Even the league's weakest franchise, the New York Black Yankees, looked optimistically toward the new season after owner James Semler merged his team with the St. Louis Stars of the NAL.

Perhaps most important for the NNL, the perennially impoverished Semler received additional financial backing from St. Louis owner Allen Johnson, a wealthy strawberry farmer and night club proprietor from Mounds, Illinois, who had left the NAL because of scheduling inequities and booking fees.[3]

The NNL still had several problematic issues to consider before the opening of the league's tenth season, in particular, the surprising return of the organization's founder, Gus Greenlee. Absent from professional black baseball since early 1939, Greenlee had seemingly overcome his financial woes and was now ready to reinvest his time, money, and energy in an institution entering a more favorable period of development. Greenlee's effort seemed certain to draw strong support from black sportswriters such as Ed Harris, who felt that Greenlee was the only owner with the "vision and the willingness to try something new." Several owners also seemed in favor of Greenlee's readmission, including Effa Manley and Ed Bolden, who considered Greenlee "one of my stanchest baseball friends. If some of his policies were carried out in the Negro National League baseball business would be better for everyone concerned." Even Cum Posey admitted his preference for Greenlee "with all his former faults—and any new ones—to the . . . hypocritical crowd who are bowing and scraping to the Sapersteins and Pollocks of today."

Other league officials, however, were more ambivalent. Tom Wilson doubted the stability of Greenlee's finances and, according to Posey, was "not anxious for Gus to come back into the league. He says he would want him back if Gus had a chance to make some money . . . but he is afraid the gates will be attached where ever Gus plays." Moreover, Greenlee had yet to secure home grounds and planned to build his new team around former Crawford players, who were now the property of other league teams. The NNL eventually considered placing Greenlee's new team on a "probation period," leading to associate membership. Greenlee, however, rejected the offer, as it would give him "no voice in the affairs of the League," and confided to Abe Manley that he considered "the whole proceeding a gross insult. They must have forgotten that I once operated the Negro National League, that my own cash money was used for operations, and that many of the clubs received help in different ways from me." Spurned by the league he had helped to create, the embittered Greenlee threatened to raid league teams but eventually remained inactive in baseball in 1942, only to resurface again in the future.[4]

Along with Greenlee's application, the league also wrestled with the Manleys' continued disenchantment over the passive presidency of Tom Wilson. Effa Manley, still unhappy over Gottlieb's role in the Yankee Stadium promotions, considered Wilson "Gottlieb's stooge" and urged See

Posey to "*please* get Tom out of there this year. It is really tragic to have a business as big as this being run by someone like Tom." For the second time in three years, Manley advocated an outside candidate, touting Joseph Rainey, a Philadelphia magistrate unsuccessfully nominated by Bolden for commissioner four years earlier. Painting a bleak picture of the current league administration, Manley related to Rainey that "we need you now worst [*sic*] than ever. We have never played the same number of games, our admission prices are all different, our umpire situation is pitiful, our contracts are not anything." League support for Rainey was lukewarm, however. While hopeful that Bolden would once again nominate Rainey, Manley expected that Gottlieb's influence would shape his decision. Meanwhile, Cum Posey was reportedly opposed to any official who was "going to be strict" and he felt Rainey had not "proved consistent in Politics or Athletics, nor do I think he is in a position as a nationally known Negro to really be of benefit to us where we need it most."[5]

Posey's resistance, along with league officials' almost reflexive rejection of any Effa Manley-sponsored motion, doomed Rainey's candidacy. Moreover, observers such as Gus Greenlee recognized that "there are too many alibis against an outsider." The subsequent reelection of Tom Wilson and other incumbents on February 15 was the final straw for the Manleys, who stormed out of the meeting, despite the entreaties of Bolden and Pompez. Frustrated once again in their attempt to shape league policy, the Newark owners not only planned to withdraw from the NNL but began to seek a buyer for the Eagles. Surprisingly, Greenlee declined an offer to purchase the franchise, explaining that he "would rather not be a member if you are going to withdraw." Seemingly aware of the Manleys' ambivalence over continued league participation, Greenlee advised the Newark owners to attend the next meeting.

Rejected by Greenlee, the Manleys then pursued other options, including a startling offer to join the Clowns, once again blacklisted by both leagues, in an affiliation with promoter Abe Saperstein. While the potential union of Effa Manley, a strident opponent of exploitive white interests, and Saperstein, the most criticized white promoter in black baseball, seemed hypocritical, Clowns official Syd Pollock offered the pragmatic argument that it would enable Newark to "eliminate many headaches, squabbles at league meetings, and make . . . just as much money." Touting the promotional skills of Saperstein who could "set up a real program for your club," Pollock advised the Manleys to leave organized black baseball until the "leagues learn what cooperation means and get a set of officials not looking out for their own private interests and no one else." After meeting with Pollock in Newark on February 27, the Manleys eventually decided to stay in the NNL, although their supposed race consciousness played little part in their decision. The risk was simply too great, as the duo feared that the lack of league attractions would hurt attendance and worried that Cum Posey might seize control of Ruppert Stadium. The prospect of wartime profits also contributed to the decision, and as Effa Manley related to sportswriter Art Carter, "Abe felt that things should be pretty good this year, and if he can get back any of the money he has invested he wants to try. If it had been left to me we would be through."[6]

With the Eagles back in the fold and the Greenlee situation temporarily resolved, NNL officials breathed a collective sigh of relief, yet soon needed to address its tenuous relationship with the NAL. Not surprisingly, the NAL challenged Allen Johnson's plan to merge his St. Louis Stars franchise with the New York Black Yankees, claiming that his players still belonged to the western circuit. After the NNL ignored the protest, NAL officials imposed a ban on interleague play with the Black Yankees, eventually lifted at mid-season. The two leagues also quarreled over the continued role of Saperstein in the affairs of black baseball. The NNL led a successful effort to wrest the lucrative position of publicity agent for the East-West game away from the controversial Saperstein, but the NAL was soon again employing his booking services, despite his involvement in the rival (short-lived) Negro Major Baseball League. In a further example of the leagues' counterproductive relationship, Fay Young claimed that one eastern team offered a position to Jim Taylor, the manager of the Chicago American Giants, provided he bring along six to seven NAL players to the NNL.

The underlying cause of disharmony, however, was the unequal financial strength of the two organizations. Historically, eastern leagues had benefited not only from the closer proximity of franchise cities but from a larger aggregate black population. Four of the nation's five most populous African American communities (New York, Philadelphia, Baltimore, and Washington, according to the 1940 census—see Table 5.1) were part of the NNL, while the NAL was represented only by Chicago. Moreover, two of the NAL cities, Birmingham and Memphis, were located in the south, an area historically less appealing to black teams because of its substantial distance from other league venues, lack of profitable interracial exhibition games, and segregated conditions. With profits and player salaries generally higher in the NNL, eastern teams often viewed the NAL in a disdainful manner. Ed Gottlieb, for example, related to Effa Manley that "our League is the Major League and the Negro American League should fall in line with whatever we want them to." The sometimes overbearing attitude of the NNL annoyed midwestern observers such as Fay Young, who felt that "the eastern circuit club owners are trying to run their own league and the Negro American League."[7]

Table 5.1. Black Population of Selected Cities, 1940

City	Population	National rank
New York (NNL)	458,444	1
Chicago (NAL)	277,731	2
Philadelphia (NNL)	250,880	3
Washington (NNL)	187,266	4
Baltimore (NNL)	165,843	5
Detroit (no league team)	149,119	6
Memphis (NAL)	121,498	8
Birmingham (NAL)	108,938	9
Cleveland (NAL)	84,504	13
Pittsburgh (NNL)	62,216	15
Cincinnati (NAL)	55,593	18
Indianapolis (NAL)	51,142	19
Newark (NNL)	45,760	24
Kansas City (NAL)	41,574	26

Despite occasional condescension, most NNL owners recognized the importance of maintaining cordial relations with the NAL. Not only did the NAL feature Satchel Paige and the Kansas City Monarchs, perhaps the greatest drawing card in black baseball, but the midwestern league was also the home of the annual East-West game, the most profitable black sporting event. With both leagues sharing in the event's profits, the game had become increasingly important, as by 1942, each NNL team received $1,904.92 from the promotion. Perhaps more significant, the practice of allocating 10 percent of the net to the two league presidents, Tom Wilson and J. B. Martin, in lieu of a salary ensured that the interleague agreement would remain intact; neither official apparently wished to jeopardize his compensation, which amounted to $1,462 apiece in 1942 and nearly $1,550 a year later.[8]

The growing influence of Martin disturbed NNL officials such as Posey, who distrusted the NAL president and privately denounced him as the "biggest fourflusher and liar I have met in all my years of baseball." Yet by the early 1940s, Martin had risen to a position of political and financial success achieved by relatively few African Americans. Born in northwest Mississippi, the son of a black landowner and farmer, Martin relocated to Memphis at age twelve and later attended LeMoyne High School and Walton University at Nashville. After earning a degree in pharmacy from Meharry Medical College in 1910, Martin borrowed $250 to open a drugstore on Florida Street in Memphis and subsequently became active in politics under the auspices of Robert Church, Jr., a black Republican leader and the son of one of the South's first black millionaires. By 1928, Martin and his brother W. S., a physician who operated Collins Chapel Hospital in Memphis, became involved in baseball promotion, eventually purchasing control of the Memphis Red Sox and their park in 1929.

Under the management of the two Martins (later joined by a third brother, B. B., a dentist), the Red Sox maintained their ongoing involvement in Rube Foster's Negro National League until weak attendance and a remote location from other clubs forced the team to depart in 1931. The Martins subsequently participated in several lower-level southern organizations before joining the NAL as charter members in 1936. While Major R. R. Jackson served as president in the early years of the league, the Martins, especially J. B., began to exert greater influence, perhaps due to their substantial wealth. After Jackson vacated the presidency in December 1939 to become NAL commissioner, Martin was elected president, a position he would occupy for the next two decades. Although Martin soon became a major force in league affairs, Jackson's role declined during his two years as a nonsalaried commissioner. Fay Young accurately described Jackson's title as "honorary . . . if one could even call it that."[9]

A personal crisis in 1940 abruptly interrupted Martin's rising fortunes. An attempt by Martin and Robert Church to challenge the political influence of their former ally, Memphis Democratic boss Ed Crump, resulted in severe repercussions. After spearheading local backing of Republican presidential candidate Wendell Willkie, Martin was ordered to terminate all political activities or face retribution. The light-skinned Martin and his wife had also offended Memphis commissioner of public safety Joseph Boyle by breaching racial etiquette and sitting in the white section at a local circus. Under orders from Crump, the Memphis police department initiated an ongoing campaign of intimidation, searching all customers of Martin's drugstore while claiming that the establishment was a center for illegal narcotics and stolen goods. Between late October and early December, law enforcement officials subjected patrons to a variety of indignities, forcing them to empty their pockets and remove articles of clothing. Simultaneously, the Crump machine also planned to prosecute Martin for operating as a bail bondsman without a license, a transgression previously overlooked by local authorities. Despite support from the Memphis daily press, Martin eventually left the city to relocate in Chicago, leaving his drugstore in the hands of relatives.

Martin's move to Chicago, however, proved to be fortuitous, as he soon matched and even surpassed his earlier achievements. Earning a substantial income from investments in a life insurance company, real estate, and an undertaking establishment, Martin became one of the richest blacks in

gure 16. J. B. Martin (center) with a group of NAL owners, 1946. Courtesy
homburg Center for Research in Black Culture, New York Public Library.

the country, reportedly worth more than $250,000 by 1949. Meanwhile,
with the Chicago American Giants in increasing disarray following the loss
of their park in December 1940, Martin became part of a group of investors (including Tom Baird of the Monarchs) who assumed control of the
battered franchise during 1941 and eventually obtained controlling interest from former owner Horace Hall. Simultaneously, Martin advanced
within the Republican party in Chicago, receiving nominations for local
offices in 1942 and 1944 despite eventual defeats. In 1946, Martin finally
succeeded, becoming the first black to be elected to the nine-member Sani-
tary District Trustee Board of Chicago, a lucrative position reportedly paying $10,000 annually for a six-year term.[10]

Although Martin's enviable success in politics and business seemed to
make him the ideal candidate to lead the NAL in a more productive direction, his performance as team owner and league president was less than
spectacular. Martin did little to resolve the problematic park situation in
Chicago, instead renting Comiskey Park for home games for the American

Giants. But Comiskey Park, like other Organized Baseball facilities, offered only limited availability, and the Giants could schedule only a handful of dates during the 1941 season. To the dismay of local fans, Martin
had reportedly rejected an offer by local businessmen to build a new park
in Chicago after the group also requested a league franchise. Meanwhile,
critics wondered how Martin could remain impartial as president while he
held one franchise and while two of his brothers owned another. Perhaps
of greater concern, Martin also initially retained a partial interest in Memphis, to the chagrin of Fay Young, who questioned "how any organization
can have at its head a man who is interested in two clubs." Although
Martin eventually sold his share, Young claimed that B. B. Martin's influence remained significant, later noting that "nothing goes unless Martin's
brother . . . puts his okay on it."

Probably one of the wealthiest African Americans to invest in black
baseball, J. B. Martin was a dedicated, yet ultimately unexceptional figure
whose tenure as owner and league president produced relatively little of
lasting value. Described by Cum Posey as a man who "likes the front row
at all times," Martin's involvement in black baseball seemingly complemented his political aspirations. Yet like his eastern counterpart Tom Wilson, Martin often seemed unwilling to confront the current difficulties in
black baseball, content to keep the leagues running in their imperfect state
and to collect his annual salary at the East-West game. Notably, Wilson
and Martin made no attempt to divest themselves of their holdings in their
league teams while serving as president during the war, another neglected
problem that would resurface in the future.[11]

Fortunately, the limited administrative capabilities of Wilson and Martin
had little adverse effect on the industry in 1942. The war's effect on black
employment had dramatically strengthened the enterprise. As Satchel
Paige later explained, "everybody had money and everybody was looking
around for entertainment and they found plenty in Negro baseball."

As during the previous two seasons, Paige, more than any other player,
helped to fuel the increased gate receipts. Three years after his career
seemed finished, Paige had emerged as the greatest drawing card in black
baseball history, commanding a minimum of $500 or 10 to 15 percent of
the net for each appearance. The phenomenon increasingly drew the attention of white Organized Baseball officials, many of whom willingly rented
their parks to black teams during 1942, hoping to capitalize on Paige's
appeal. Long closed to black baseball, Wrigley Field drew a phenomenal
29,775 fans for a May 24 Abe Saperstein promotion that pitted Paige's
Monarchs against a white team led by former major league pitcher Dizzy

Dean, featuring several other professionals now in military service. A week later, 22,234 fans jammed Griffith Stadium in Washington for a similar matchup, this time featuring Paige hurling for the Homestead Grays. A third date scheduled for June 7 in Indianapolis, however, was canceled after a controversy arose surrounding the supposedly misleading nature of the promotions. Advance publicity for the Wrigley Field game had reported that Bob Feller of the Cleveland Indians, now in the Navy, would pitch and donate his $1,000 fee to the Navy Relief fund, but Feller was denied permission from military officials. Commissioner Kenesaw Mountain Landis subsequently denounced games "allegedly played 'for relief' but actually as commercial enterprises," and army authorities curbed the participation of former ballplayers in similar exhibitions.

For many black fans and sportswriters, Landis's objections were mere smoke screens to mask his dismay at the sudden drawing power of black baseball, reflected by the Paige game at Wrigley, which had outdrawn all but one of eight major league promotions scheduled that day. As Fay Young observed, the war had cut into major league baseball's attendance, and "when a colored team, playing against an aggregation of old all-stars, can draw over 50,000 fans on successive Sundays, the judge must be disturbed." Others related the ruling to Landis's dislike of interracial competition at the professional level.

Yet Landis and other white organized baseball officials could hardly overlook the impressive attendance totals for black teams appearing at major league parks during 1942. Now playing home games in Cincinnati, the Ethiopian Clowns continued their phenomenal success, drawing 12,500 for a May date at Crosley Field, a local attendance record for black teams. In Detroit, Briggs Stadium continued to be a lucrative venue, as 16,497 fans witnessed a June 14 date between the New York Cubans and Baltimore Elite Giants. Seven weeks later a Yankee Stadium promotion featuring Paige's Monarchs and three NNL teams drew one of the largest black baseball crowds in New York, estimated at 36,000 by one observer. Meanwhile, despite inadequate security and ticket handling, the East-West game at Comiskey Park on August 16 attracted a still enviable crowd of 44,897.

Perhaps the most remarkable development occurred at Griffith Stadium, where the Homestead Grays finally succeeded in exploiting the full potential of the Washington market after drawing generally unexceptional crowds in 1940 and 1941. Capitalizing on the return of Josh Gibson and a doubling of the black federal workforce between 1938 and 1942, the Grays converted the once doubtful Washington into one of the NNL's best paying cities, at times even outdrawing the major league Senators. According to Art Carter, over 125,000 fans attended Grays games at Griffith Stadium in 1942, compared to only 403,493 for the more frequently scheduled Senators. Not surprisingly, the Kansas City Monarchs proved to be the best drawing cards, attracting crowds of 22,129 on September 15, 20,084 on August 14, and 26,113 on June 18, reportedly the first game played by black teams under major league lights, and the largest crowd at Griffith Stadium since the 1925 World Series.[12]

In a relatively short period of time, the war had transformed black professional baseball from a barely solvent business to a robust and financially thriving institution. An enthusiastic Cum Posey assessed the recent campaign as the "best financial season ever enjoyed by Negro baseball as a whole," noting that the industry had done "over a million dollars cash business" in 1942. While the Monarchs, Grays, and Clowns had done particularly well, virtually every team in both leagues reportedly profited during the season. The increased financial returns, however, were not accompanied by the institution of much-needed administrative reforms, leaving both leagues still vulnerable to unfavorable developments in the future.

Rather than confront the considerable administrative deficiencies within black baseball, league officials seemingly preferred to enjoy the current prosperity while it lasted. Moreover, if conditions remained unchanged, continued industry success seemed assured for 1943. Yet the war, a boon to black baseball to date, suddenly threatened the operation of the two leagues as the new season approached. Federal gasoline rationing, for example, had only modestly affected black teams in 1942, as the policy had only included the East Coast and was not fully in force until late July. In December 1942, however, the policy was extended to the entire country and along with the concurrent rationing of tires posed a serious challenge to an enterprise reliant on bus travel.

The imposition of other travel restrictions also appeared likely to disrupt the operation of black baseball and virtually all sports teams. With military travel requirements now paramount in importance, the Office of Defense Transportation (ODT) asked all college, high school, and professional football teams to reduce travel and barred all special trains and bus service to games. Subsequently, ODT director Joseph Eastman requested that major league baseball curtail mileage for the upcoming season, a suggestion readily accepted by Commissioner Landis who promised the leagues "will do what we can to keep from being parasites and drones in this emergency." To comply, major league teams scheduled spring training closer to home and one less trip around the league circuit during the regular season.[13]

As John Clark, the former Crawfords publicity man now with Homestead, noted, the ODT's new policies seriously jeopardized black baseball teams, all of whom needed "sufficient gasoline, oil and tires to operate successfully." Aware of the dilemma, J. B. Martin attempted in December to determine the likelihood of securing gas and tires for the upcoming season, only to be informed by an ODT official that the mileage reduction "requests which were made on the other baseball leagues are also addressed to you and to your league." In another discouraging development, a subsequent ban on pleasure driving on the East Coast lasting throughout the summer of 1943 threatened attendance for exhibition games scheduled in less centrally located smaller towns.

Although prospects for the new season appeared bleak, the ODT ultimately granted gas rations for bus travel to all NNL teams, reportedly 40 percent of the total consumed by the league in 1942. While owners recognized that travel limitations and reductions in gas would prevent normal league functioning, most breathed a sigh of relief over the government's decision to allow the continued operation of professional sports. Marty Weintraub, an associate of Eddie Gottlieb, confided to Effa Manley that the Philadelphia Stars owners were preparing for the new season as usual, and that Bolden had "already received his certificate from ODT authorizing the obtaining of gas. I believe that the amount is not too great, but will be sufficient to get by fairly well, by eliminating unnecessary and useless trips."

After the leagues had seemingly weathered the threat, Cum Posey expected no further problem with the ODT, noting that the gas and rubber used by black professional baseball amounted to a "drop in the bucket." Yet on March 1, Posey and other officials were stunned by Eastman's general order ODT 10-A, banning the use of all privately owned buses used by baseball teams, orchestras, night clubs, apartment houses, race tracks, and other facilities as of March 15, 1943. Initially hopeful that the policy applied only to semiprofessional teams, the leagues soon realized the larger implications of the order. Without bus travel, a number of teams, particularly the widely dispersed NAL franchises, had little hope of operation, and as Syd Pollock noted, "unless immediate action is taken, Negro baseball has been dealt a death blow."[14]

Facing a common threat, the two usually fractious leagues joined together to present their case to Washington. Washington Senators owner Clark Griffith, seemingly fearful of losing black baseball's lucrative rentals of his park and politically connected through his association with Franklin Roosevelt, quickly arranged a meeting of Posey and J. B. Martin with Eastman and other ODT officials on March 6. With Griffith in attendance, Martin and Posey explained that because black professional teams played in several different parks per week and seldom stayed in one location for more than a night, bus travel was the only feasible means of transportation. Moreover, in certain regions of the country, hotel accommodations were difficult, if not impossible, to obtain. Posey and Martin also noted that the two leagues not only provided entertainment for black war workers throughout the country but also offered competition for army teams. While Eastman was sympathetic, Posey noted that Guy A. Richardson, director of the Division of Local Transport, was "very opposed to any privately owned Busses to operate except for Clinics and Hospitals," citing military and industrial needs. Eastman, however, deferred making a final decision, requesting information on bus mileage and condition of tires. The two league officials offered full cooperation, promising to halve travel in 1943 and use trains whenever possible. As Posey related, "WE AGREED TO EVERYTHING."[15]

In the days following the meeting, the NNL and NAL frantically collected the information required by Eastman. Although eleven of the twelve buses were in running condition, seven of them had traveled over 75,000 miles, and three over 100,000. Meanwhile, the difficulty of obtaining new tires presented another potential problem, although some teams were adequately prepared. Ed Bolden, for example, explained to Posey that the Stars "policy has always been to keep the tires and the bus in the best possible condition at all times, with the result that I feel sure we will not require new tires or retreads for several seasons." Bolden also promised that the Stars would reduce mileage, "only travel by bus when absolutely necessary," and "pledge ourselves to use train transportation whenever we can during the course of the season."[16]

After receiving similar letters from other owners, Posey presented a written summary to the ODT of the NNL plan to cooperate. To cut mileage, the teams would follow the major leagues' example and schedule spring training close to home. During the season the NNL planned to keep "the opposing clubs in the same league city for two and three days instead of one and by using day coaches between the cities of New York, Newark, Philadelphia, Baltimore, Washington, D.C., except on Saturday and Sundays when railroad traffic is so great." Finally, league owners even agreed to turn their buses over to the ODT during the off-season. Posey once again emphasized the essential nature of bus travel, particularly for exhibition games, which were often "close to our league cities but railroad and hotel accommodations are not available after our games, mostly night games, even though in some cases the games are but fifteen miles from our hotels." Touting the importance of the enterprise, Posey claimed that "we are now recognized as the Major league of Negro baseball by the public, both colored and white" and "we have built our league through 25 years of steady work."[17]

Hoping to increase the league's chance of a favorable response from the ODT, Posey also addressed a letter to ODT official H. F. McCarthy, further

Figure 17. Tom Baird (left) and J. L. Wilkinson (right), the owners of the Kansas City Monarchs, and *Kansas City Call* editor C. A. Franklin (center) launched an unsuccessful petition drive in spring 1943, hoping to change ODT policies on bus use. Courtesy Thomas Baird Collection, Kansas Collection, University of Kansas Libraries.

articulating the industry's position. While insisting that "we are all in accord with any thing which will help the war effort," Posey argued that the black teams warranted an exemption, as "we can not be placed in the same class as small minor leagues. They can get accommodations over night in any city or town." Pursuing another line of argument, Posey reminded McCarthy of the already low morale of blacks certain to worsen "if we must discontinue Baseball . . . while white Baseball is still being played." Appealing to the innate fears of many federal officials, Posey warned of explosive consequences, noting that "the first thing every Negro, every Negro paper, and those who are not interested in the Negro Race, but take issues of this kind to incite the Negro, will say, 'They don't allow Negros in white Organized Baseball, now they make it impossible for them to play Baseball.' "[18]

The ODT, however, ultimately remained unswayed by the arguments and refused to grant an exemption to black baseball. A Kansas City-based petition drive and the involvement of several politicians, including Senators Arthur Capper of Kansas and Harry Truman of Missouri, also failed to alter the agency's stance. As Eastman explained, the buses were needed for war workers, particularly since the War Production Board had limited the construction of new vehicles, and instead recommended the use of trains, public transportation, or automobiles. Yet the ODT suggested that black teams could still function by using rail service along with the supplemental gas rations (360–470 miles per month) allotted to athletes whose "occupation" as a professional player required travel by automobile.

The more compact NNL was capable of functioning within these limitations, but the ODT decision dealt a severe blow to the NAL. President J. B. Martin gloomily predicted that it was now "practically impossible for our league to go on. . . . Our traveling problems are necessarily complicated because we play a lot of games in smaller towns where we just can't get railroad accommodations." Moreover, Martin also complained that Southern railroad routes (such as between Memphis and Birmingham) offered insufficient accommodations for black travelers, a contention the ODT was unable to confirm. Automobile travel also appeared unfeasible for the NAL, as the 470 mile monthly allowance would not even cover a round trip from Birmingham to Memphis.[19]

Although Eastman asserted that special buses had been "denied uniformly to all athletic teams," some observers felt that the development disproportionately affected African Americans. As C. A. Franklin, editor and publisher of the *Kansas City Call*, explained to Eastman, "you do not see how your regulations intended to deal with all alike, have a peculiar effect on us. . . . Please don't add to our burden by taking away any part of what we have." Franklin emphasized the importance of baseball for the black community, noting that "there is practically no summer amusement in Kansas City for Negroes but baseball. We are segregated at white baseball games. . . . We cannot afford to let our one sport be taken from us when organized baseball (white) is permitted to continue." Notably, the ban also limited black musical groups, which already were contending with the earlier ODT elimination of charter buses for bands and orchestras. Fay Young, however, noted that the heavy use of bus transportation by black entertainers would probably preclude any exemptions for baseball, as "local ODT officials point out that to give the Negro club owners the right to use their buses would be setting a precedent and that all buses owned by such orchestras as Duke Ellington, Count Basie, Father [Earl] Hines and other organizations would have to be put to use."[20]

The two leagues ultimately decided to operate in 1943, while hoping for a change in the ODT's policy. For the first time since the late 1920s, black teams turned to train travel, an often unsatisfactory arrangement for owners and players. As Effa Manley explained to James Semler, it was "not so hot traveling on the trains. It is almost impossible to get trains out of the city when you want them to the next place you are going, then you have to worry with the bats etc. In addition to this it is really very expensive." League officials also soon recognized that transporting players on the already overcrowded trains was unlikely to alleviate military and civilian travel problems. Cum Posey, for example, considered it "ridiculous to have thirty or forty players crowd into a day coach when these same men could travel in space made buses" and claimed that the Grays "paid more money for taxi fares after getting off the trains than it would have cost to make the whole trip in their bus."

Although the new regulations dealt a heavy financial blow to every league team, the effect on the Grays was undeniably considerable. Hoping for a change in policy, Posey continued to act as NNL liaison in Washington, even enlisting the assistance of two Democratic congressmen: William Dawson, a black Illinois representative, and Samuel Weiss of western Pennsylvania, a former NFL referee and proponent of the wartime continuation of spectator sports. In May, Posey again outlined the industry's problems to Eastman, explaining that his own club had been "compelled to call off games in the small industrial towns and coal mining towns. . . . Because we cannot get out of these places after the game and rooming conditions are so overcrowded that we cannot stay there overnight." Meanwhile, a round trip to Ohio had proved nightmarish for the Grays, costing $300 to transport 17 players by train, far exceeding the $40 of gas normally needed to make the journey by bus. To Posey, the ODT's stance was ultimately hindering, rather than helping the war effort. He insisted that league teams "will do more to ease the transportation problem . . . by transporting their own players instead of moving them in overcrowded day coaches and public busses." Moreover, the league's buses, specifically designed to transport ballplayers and equipment, were hardly ideal for defense workers. In a final desperate attempt to force the ODT to reconsider, Posey even made the exalted claim that league teams "will not be able to play our usual benefit games for the Army and Navy Relief Organizations, as the additional expenses of operating has forced us to conserve every penny of income. . . . We had contemplated on raising $100,000 . . . for the armed forces."[21]

Although Eastman sympathized with the industry's plight, the ODT appeared unlikely to reverse its policy. In late May, a federal official informed Posey that "the gasoline situation is so much more acute at the present moment that there is hardly a possibility of relaxing General Order ODT 10A in the immediate future." Yet within a month, the ODT reconsidered, swayed by the segregated conditions that particularly confronted the NAL.

While suggesting that "professional teams are finding it possible to continue operations by using public transportation in spite of the inconveniences," Eastman acknowledged to J. B. Martin that "the most serious difficulty your teams have in using public transportation is in the southern states. . . . It should be possible for me to give you some relief from this hardship and yet not be discriminating in favor of one particular group." Eastman subsequently authorized the use of buses for 2,000 miles per month, restricted to the south and to "the gateway cities nearest to the northerly boundaries of these states."

The new policy initially excluded the NNL, whose franchises seldom traveled in the deep south. The ODT quickly rejected a request from Alex Pompez for the use of his bus in the south, explaining that the NNL, "entirely located in the northern states in an area where railroad service is available," hardly warranted such an exemption. Meanwhile, another attempt by Cum Posey to meet with ODT and Office of Price Administration officials in early July produced little, except a promise that "we could get prior consideration when gas shortage ceased to exist." Despite Posey's ongoing efforts, the NNL would not receive relief until February 1944 when the ODT accepted the league's somewhat dubious claim that it also operated in the south. For the remainder of the war, both leagues were granted identical privileges: 2,000 miles per month limited to the southern states.[22]

The provision of special permits to NNL and NAL teams represented a triumph for the industry. The rulings suggested that the ODT recognized the two leagues' legitimacy not only as "long-established businesses" but also as the preeminent black professional sports organizations in the United States. Yet the positive development was intentionally under-publicized, probably because of the favoritism shown to black teams. The ODT, for example, denied similar permits to white minor leagues such as the Virginia-based Piedmont League. As Eastman's successor J. Monroe Johnson explained to Virginia Senator Harry Byrd, the "only exception" had been "negro professional major league baseball teams and they have been limited to operation in certain southern states where the difficulties confronted by a traveling negro group were really extreme." By 1945, Posey admitted that the ODT "has been severely criticized by Colored and White for allowing the N.N.L. and N.A.L. to be the only baseball clubs to travel by Bus" and had asked league teams to keep their buses "from public inspection as much as possible, especially in Cities where minor leagues formerly existed."[23]

The concern with keeping bus use discreet also related to ongoing violations of the ODT's policy. While both leagues were instructed to submit schedules and mileage in advance to ensure compliance, it is likely that many teams continued to use their buses predominantly in the north where black baseball remained most profitable. The use of buses by Kansas City and Memphis to reach a date in Chicago, for example, prompted an inquiry by the ODT in 1944 and a reminder to J. B. Martin that the permits were only granted for travel in the South. Martin, informed that the buses had been parked outside of Wrigley Field, subsequently warned NAL clubs about the open "use of busses in cities to transport players to and from ball parks."

A second incident in early 1945 further threatened the industry's fragile relationship with the ODT. Hoping to obtain gasoline for an upcoming tour of a Central American Baseball All Star team, midwestern promoter Ray Doan contacted Representative Thomas Martin (R-Iowa) and cited the NAL's current exemption. But Doan also intimated that the NAL had violated the ODT policy of South-only travel, noting that "the peculiar thing about it is that none [sic] of these clubs belong below the Mason and Dixon Line." Martin subsequently raised the issue with J. Monroe Johnson, citing "several cases wherein these buses have traveled outside the Jim Crow states." Fortunately for the NAL, the ODT had no means of closely monitoring actual bus use. Moreover, Johnson remained unimpressed with Martin's charges, insisting that "the Negro teams are strictly limited to 2,000 miles per month of bus travel and I would be surprised if they had violated their pledge to this office to comply with our regulations."[24]

Through a combination of negotiation and manipulation, the industry successfully withstood and adapted to a potentially destructive policy. Yet other wartime developments increasingly affected black baseball and all sports during 1943. Following a new federal order in February, draft-eligible men, regardless of dependents, increasingly found themselves channeled into essential war work or military service, sharply cutting into the operation of professional teams. In white Organized Baseball, only 10 minor league teams opened the 1943 season, 21 fewer than the prior season. Equally affected by the manpower shortage, the National Football League allowed the Pittsburgh Steelers and Philadelphia Eagles to merge to form a single team, the "Steagles." NNL franchises were hardly immune, and by early 1943, the Newark Eagles had lost Clarence Israel, Max Manning, Charles Parks, and Charles Thomason to military service. In general, however, black professional baseball was less affected by the draft than its white counterpart, as the Selective Service Department maintained a 10 percent and later 5 percent quota on black draftees.

The lure of defense employment, both for its lucrative pay and as a barrier against the draft, also wreaked havoc on personnel. In 1943, several of the Grays players maintained steady employment in war industries and were only available on a part-time basis. Similarly, Johnny Taylor worked for United Aircraft in Connecticut during the week, pitching for the New York Cubans only on Sundays, while Ed Stone of the Newark Eagles was also limited to weekend play. Reportedly, even several major leaguers held defense jobs, appearing only on weekends and evenings.[25]

The shortage of available players coupled with transportation difficulties nearly destroyed the fragile alliance between the two leagues during 1943. The NAL, increasingly vulnerable in the initial weeks following the ODT order, seemed to offer a potential answer to the scarcity of players in the NNL. Cum Posey in particular had always found the interleague agreement burdensome, and according to Effa Manley his "solution to the shortage of ballplayers is to raid the western league. That is no solution." As expected, Posey began to look toward NAL franchises, targeting the Memphis Red Sox, owned by J. B. Martin's brothers W. S. and B. B., but operating on a shoestring budget and reportedly unable to meet payroll on occasion. Ted Radcliffe, the team's manager for several seasons in the late 1930s and early 1940s, later characterized the Red Sox as "one of the worst outfits. . . . They didn't pay their ballplayers anything. When I went down there, they had ballplayers making $75 a month, which was a disgrace. . . . When I raised them to $150, the owner got mad with me."

Not surprisingly, the veteran Cool Papa Bell had little interest in playing with Memphis in 1943. Sent to Memphis from Chicago in a trade for Radcliffe and Lloyd Davenport, Bell failed to receive transportation expenses as promised but was told that B. B. Martin would provide dental care. As Bell later explained, "I didn't have a toothache and I wasn't about to pay a man to fix what didn't need fixing." Bell instead signed with the Grays, soon joined by Ralph Wyatt, Ollie West, and Charlie Shields of the American Giants, beginning an exodus of NAL players to the NNL.

The usually low-profile Philadelphia Stars also found themselves involved in the controversy. After an encouraging showing in 1942, the team suddenly faced the loss of several key players to military service by the end of 1943. While Ed Bolden admitted it would be "almost humanly impossible" to find equivalent replacements, manager Goose Curry, a Memphis resident during the winter months, recognized the financially shaky local NAL franchise as a potential gold mine. With the probable tacit blessing of the Stars' ownership, Curry met with several Memphis players, eventually signing pitchers Steve Keyes, Willie Burns, and Verdell Mathis after reportedly offering a $25 per month raise, train fare to Philadelphia, and $100 upon arrival.[26]

After several more Memphis players left to join NNL teams, a war between the two organizations seemed imminent. Left with only 11 men, an incensed B. B. Martin denounced the raids as "a simple case of out-and-out stealing" and threatened to quit and "confine myself to my practice as a dentist." Curry, however, denied enticing the players and claimed that Mathis, an outstanding left-handed pitcher, had come to Philadelphia of his own volition to obtain war employment. As Curry explained, Mathis was now employed by Sun Shipyard, and the Stars hoped to use him during his stay in the Philadelphia area. Meanwhile, the Grays offered the rationalization that Bell rightfully belonged to the NNL and had been secured by the NAL illegally in 1942, while other league officials cited the NAL's previous violations of the joint agreement, including games against the blacklisted Ethiopian Clowns. Yet outside observers such as sportswriter Art Carter felt the whole controversy again revealed the need for a commissioner, one ideally capable of preventing the matter from reaching "the silly stage that it has, what with officials of both leagues tossing personal brickbats . . . through the public press."[27]

With no commissioner to arbitrate, the NAL resorted to its major weapon, a threatened boycott of the now phenomenally lucrative East-West game. Recognizing the importance of the promotion, B. B. Martin questioned whether "the East will sacrifice at least $12,000 or $14,000—usually their share from the East-West game—for a few outlaw players." Moreover, both league presidents faced the possibility of losing their 5 percent share in the promotion if canceled, a daunting prospect forcing both executives to seek a peaceful solution.

On June 1, 1943, representatives from the two leagues met in Philadelphia. Prior to the joint session, the usually "sphinx-like" Tom Wilson advised NNL officials that it was "necessary under existing conditions for everybody to do some sacrificing to help keep baseball going and avoid fights between the two leagues." Wilson and Martin subsequently affirmed their commitment to the joint agreement, and after a grueling five-hour meeting, the two leagues agreed to the return of seven players to Memphis, two to Chicago, and one NAL player (pitcher Theolic Smith of the Cleveland Buckeyes) back to the NNL. A relieved Wilson praised the ruling as in "the best interest of the game and players themselves," and the now harmonious league presidents issued a subsequent statement warning that "we are not going to allow any one team to be bigger than the two leagues. . . . All teams must respect rules and regulations."

Leery of a costly interleague conflict and eager to maintain the current economic stability, the majority of owners had temporarily set aside their usual unchecked individualism to reach an accord. Surprisingly, only two franchises (Cleveland and Homestead) voted against the return of the players. The administration of black baseball seemed finally to have taken a step toward maturity, and as J. B. Martin observed, "it is time we all realized that our leagues do not mean anything . . . unless we model ourselves after the major leagues. We can't go around taking each other's players and expect to maintain the respect of the public." Moreover, the suddenly statesmanlike league presidents even took the unprecedented step of inviting a black sportswriter, Wendell Smith of the *Pittsburgh Courier*, to attend the meeting, providing the press with a rare behind-the-scenes look at the inner workings of the industry.[28]

Although the two leagues managed to avoid a possible devastating war over players, other issues arose in 1943 to disrupt the delicate interleague relationship, most notably the outlaw Ethiopian Clowns. Despite the reservations of some officials, the Clowns joined the NAL as a Cincinnati representative (replacing the Buckeyes, who relocated to Cleveland) and then established a second home in Indianapolis in 1944. As Buck Leonard of the Homestead Grays explained, "our players didn't like it so much. . . . We didn't want the Clowns in the league, but they were such a good draw, everyone else wanted them." Although J. B. Martin claimed that the Clowns would drop "Ethiopian" from their name, "play under their real names instead of the burlesque names adopted by the players; stop painting their faces and play straight baseball," but the team changed few of its practices and by mid-1943, the NNL complained that the Clowns were still using the name Ethiopian Clowns. Moreover, despite employing several capable ballplayers, the Clowns continued to emphasize comedy during their appearances, featuring performers including Richard King ("King Tut") and later a juggler and a midget. Bowing to the lure of increased gate receipts, eastern officials ultimately overcame their misgivings and willingly booked the Clowns for dates at NNL parks for years to come.[29]

Unlike the NAL's successful addition of the Clowns, the NNL's expansion to seven franchises in 1943 proceeded less smoothly. After terminating his partnership with James Semler after only a year, Allen Johnson reclaimed his former St. Louis Stars players and was granted his own NNL franchise. Uncertain where to locate, Johnson and his associate George Mitchell eventually chose Harrisburg, Pennsylvania, where the team became known as the "St. Louis-Harrisburg Stars." While Harrisburg had been the home of an Eastern Colored League franchise from 1924 through 1927 and was a convenient rail destination, observers such as Gus Greenlee scoffed at the choice, noting that "the town is too small. You've got to get in big towns to make any money in baseball these days." Greenlee's misgivings proved correct, as Harrisburg spent only half a season in the league before receiving permission to withdraw to barnstorm in the midwest with Pittsburgh Pirate great Honus Wagner's Victory Stars on a war bond tour. After booking an unsanctioned game in NNL territory in August, the St. Louis Stars were suspended, and all players became league property. The failure of Harrisburg represented the final attempt to introduce a new club into the eastern league, once again underscoring the formidable barriers involved in establishing and maintaining a black professional team (as the ill-fated Negro Major Baseball League had already discovered a year earlier), particularly in an ultra-competitive wartime environment affected by player shortages, gasoline rationing, and defense employment.[30]

◆ ◆ ◆

Despite occasional inconveniences, the war continued to drive attendance to unprecedented levels in 1943. With discretionary income at a new high and gas rationing in force, black professional baseball became a focal point for entertainment throughout the United States. In Washington, the Grays matched their 1942 Griffith Stadium attendance by July, earning record-setting profits for the season. Attendance in Philadelphia was also strong, bolstered by Eddie Gottlieb's successful rental of Shibe Park, owned by the Athletics and also used by the Phillies but rarely available to black teams since its opening in 1909. After an initial September 1942 date featuring the Monarchs and Grays in an unofficial championship game drew an impressive 14,029 fans on a cold weeknight, Athletics' officials granted three dates to the Stars for 1943. Determined to maximize attendance, Gottlieb booked Satchel Paige and the Monarchs for each game, eventually drawing a total of 48,139 fans, including an astounding crowd of 24,165 on June 21, probably the largest crowd ever for a black baseball promotion in Philadelphia. Not surprisingly, the Stars would soon make Shibe Park their second home, enabling the team to maximize profits by accommodating the growing crowds too large for Parkside Field.

In the west, J. B. Martin disclosed that NAL teams "all made more money this last year than they ever made in the history of baseball," including the Monarchs, who grossed more than $115,000 (probably including Baird and Wilkinson's booking income) and finished the season with a startling $53,000 profit. Meanwhile, to the delight of both league presidents, the East-West game on August 1 drew 51,723 fans (46,471 paid), the largest crowd ever to attend a black baseball game. After noting that nearly every club cleared a minimum of $5,000 and at least three made more than $15,000 in 1943, Wendell Smith asserted that "there is no doubt about it, Negro baseball has now attained the 'big business' classification. It has passed the stage of being merely a sport or a hobby."

The financial triumph of 1942 and 1943, however, led several observers to refocus attention on the two leagues' still glaring administrative deficiencies. Despite budgets increasingly comparable to upper-level teams in white Organized Baseball, the leagues still lacked balanced schedules, impartial league officers, and strong contracts. Sportswriters such as Dan

Burley complained that the two leagues "can't even match the organization of the lowliest minor league club," while the *Independent*'s Roscoe Coleman claimed black baseball's administration was "a huge joke among those who discuss the game."[31]

As usual, the always vocal Cum Posey, now the most prosperous owner in the NNL, continued to advocate a single league of the eight strongest franchises currently in black baseball, ideally five from the east and three from the west. To Posey, "a free-for-all, survival of the fittest" between the two leagues would purge the "weak links" and finally allow black baseball to go "big time." Otherwise, black baseball seemed destined to "continue to shuffle along from year to year, making money one year and losing it the next two years." Moreover, Posey insisted that "one Negro major league, aided by two or more Negro minor leagues, would soon be universally recognized as the third major league of baseball" and lead to regular statistics, "every-day [league] baseball," and improved administration. J. B. Martin and other NAL officials, however, continued to resist any suggestions of amalgamation that would be likely to reduce their own power, and the two leagues remained separate.[32]

Both leagues, however, would undertake positive steps during 1944 to correct a chronic weakness in black baseball: the lack of accurate player statistics. Unlike the comprehensive records available from Organized Baseball, black leagues had never succeeded in generating accurate records, robbing the industry of an obvious source of publicity and depriving fans of an integral part of baseball's appeal. The lack of an official scorer presented the greatest obstacle, as leagues instead relied on team-submitted box scores to compile statistics, resulting in predictably erratic compliance.[33]

This ineffective yet cost-efficient system remained in place throughout the formative years of the NNL, sporadically generating incomplete and ultimately meaningless statistical information that satisfied few fans. To publicist Dave Hawkins, the irrelevance of the league's records was obvious, noting that "if you will bring me just twenty colored, yes I mean Colored fans, who can tell you how many games Satchel Paige won or what Oscar Charleston batted last year I will go bring you the whistle off the Titanic." Yet the NNL, barely solvent and struggling with a multitude of other issues, predictably lacked the collective will to institute reforms. By the late 1930s, league data sunk to a new low, as the appearance of even the most basic of baseball statistics—standings—became increasingly rare.

In 1939, NNL officials took tentative steps to address the problem. To ensure current standings and accurate statistics, the winner of each league game was requested to phone or wire the results to Ed Gottlieb or Abe

Manley, and both clubs were to submit their score sheets to league secretary Cum Posey. While this system was an improvement over recent seasons, it was undermined by the usual bickering among league members. In late May, Effa Manley informed the *Courier* that the standings were "all wrong this week," blaming the Grays' failure to comply with the new method and questioning whether Posey preferred to "have the results handled by him in case the race is close and he might be able to do a little juggling." Meanwhile, Posey complained to Manley in June that her team was "positively holding back League batting and fielding averages. I can't understand it when I have but one score sheet from you for the season."

Despite their obvious limitations, the NNL reforms did succeed in improving the dissemination of league data in the early 1940s. Standings and game results began to appear more consistently, although individual player statistics were seldom forthcoming. Posey, for example, was unable to issue final averages in 1940, explaining that several clubs had failed to submit all their score sheets. While the league subsequently ordered $10 and later $25 fines for noncompliance, Posey continued to struggle to receive game information and by 1942 considered it "a shame that Newark and Phila. should send in box scores and the other clubs will not do the same." Nevertheless, league officials continued to compile and publish occasional statistics based on what little data they had available, often resulting in criticism from skeptical writers. Analyzing the NNL's final averages in 1943, Rollo Wilson noted the list included only 47 players, omitted the Stars' Goose Curry, and claimed Josh Gibson batted an eye-popping yet unlikely .542.[34]

The war-driven prosperity facilitated a greater willingness to address the industry's statistical shortcomings. Not surprisingly, black sportswriters, long craving the information to supply to their readers, spearheaded the effort. In December 1943, the *Courier*'s Wendell Smith submitted a proposal to the NNL and NAL, offering to perform the service for a fee of $3,000 for one league or $5,000 for both leagues. The always aggressive Effa Manley quickly embraced the idea, "the thing I have been begging for ever since we went in the business. . . . Imagine the interest if they knew the shortstop on a certain team, had a better fielding average than some one in the White Major League." Manley warned, however, of potential resistance from "the teams that do not want honest averages released, because they may not have any men in leading positions, and from others who do not want us organized for fear we might grow too big, and interfere with their plans."[35]

Despite Manley's apprehension, most franchises genuinely favored employing a statistician, although Smith's bid was viewed as too expensive. Moreover, NNL acceptance was unlikely, as Smith had alienated the powerful Cum Posey several times in the past. The NNL instead selected the Elias Bureau, a well-established white firm employed by the National League and several other leagues in Organized Baseball. According to Posey, Elias offered a substantially lower bid of $425 per season, which included stationery and mailing costs to 30 black newspapers and 50 white dailies. Meanwhile, at the behest of an increasingly ambivalent Smith, the NAL chose the American League's statistical firm, the Howe News Bureau, at an even lower rate of $300 per season. League president J. B. Martin rationalized the decision by claiming "the colored press had nothing to offer so we had to take a white firm."

The perceived rejection of Smith in favor of two white businesses over-shadowed the positive aspect of finally securing a statistical service. The cost-effective yet hardly racially conscious decision predictably drew harsh criticism from the press, faithful supporters of black baseball since its inception. As Dan Burley noted, the NNL had missed "the biggest opportunity . . . to play ball with the Negro Press. . . . Each season Negro Baseball gets thousands of dollars in free space on sports pages . . . as Negro sports writers try to keep faith with the ideal of colored enterprises." Yet according to Burley, "the owners . . . consistently refuse to put advertising in the papers which befriend them" and "go out of their way to hire white booking agents, white printers, white this, and white that." The selection of white statistical firms, however, was consistent with the racial pragmatism inherent in black professional baseball since its beginnings, and few promoters, not even the legendary Rube Foster, allowed racial concerns to interfere with practical business decisions.[36]

Despite the hiring of the Howe and Elias bureaus, the two leagues' statistical woes never entirely disappeared. The absence of official scorers remained the fundamental obstacle to accurate averages, forcing the two agencies to rely on data submitted by occasionally indifferent league teams. Recognizing the uneven compliance throughout the NAL, Tom Baird viewed the use of the Howe agency as a mistake, predicting "how incorrect it would be [on] account of [the] way we have of scoring our games." In the NNL, the Homestead Grays entrusted a player to keep score, yet as Buck Leonard explained, "maybe he didn't know how. . . . Or in the middle of the game, he'd have to go in . . . and some other player would have to finish the box score." By 1946, the ongoing problems were apparent to Effa Manley, who informed the Elias Bureau that their statistics were "still not perfect," although she admitted that "the mistakes are due to the team owners, and not your office."[37]

Rejected by the two leagues as a potential statistical service, Wendell Smith and the black press would nevertheless be instrumental during 1944 in another long-sought reform: the arrangement of an official World Series between the two leagues. While major league baseball's annual World Series represented one of the nation's major sports events, the NNL and NAL were slow to develop a comparable promotion, likely deterred by the unspectacular financial returns of four interleague series arranged in the 1920s. The concern for immediate profit, however, resulted in a missed opportunity for the two leagues to demonstrate their legitimacy, gain much-needed exposure, and provide an incentive for players. The Grays' See Posey reflected the leagues' usual short-sighted attitude toward post-season promotions, noting in 1941 that he would not "let any playoffs stop me from making money."

In the absence of championship games between the NNL and NAL, black fans suffered through sporadic "unofficial" world series between 1937 and 1943, promoted by the two clubs and marred by squabbles over the use of outside players. With the games increasingly perceived as a "glorified exhibition series" or a "three-ring baseball circus,"[38] league officials, prodded by Wendell Smith, finally recognized the necessity of assuming greater responsibility for the promotion in 1944. In August, Smith helped develop a new arrangement enabling the two leagues to oversee an official championship series, and along with sportswriters Fay Young and Sam Lacy, was selected to serve on a three-person "Arbitration Commission" to rule on any disputes arising during the games. The commission also drafted a "World Series Agreement" to be signed by both teams, requiring each to provide a list of eligible players and post a $1,000 guarantee to finish the series. The new regulations seemed certain to resolve the problems of recent playoffs, leading J. B. Martin to hail the development as "the finest thing that has happened in Negro baseball. . . . It is the first time we've had a Series in which the fans, leagues and clubs could look toward it with confidence and pride."

Despite a late season dispute over the winner of the NNL's second half, the world series between Homestead and the Birmingham Black Barons proceeded as planned, although the games generated unexceptional financial returns. Fortunately for the industry, the games were relatively free of the controversies that had marred recent attempts at championship games, validating Tom Wilson's claim that "every fan in the country can now feel sure that Negro baseball has grown up and is going places." Yet despite improved administration, the black world series remained distinct from its white counterpart, continuing to feature shifting sites, occasional exhibitions between official games to help defray costs, and other unorthodox scheduling practices. In 1945, for example, the deciding game of the series was promoted as a three-team doubleheader at Shibe Park, featuring the Philadelphia Stars as the opposing team in the second contest, prompting a complaint from local fan Leonard Garrett, who argued that "if a team of the caliber displayed by Cleveland and the Grays cannot stand upon its own merits and draw a crowd, then Negro baseball is not progressing."[39]

Nevertheless, black professional baseball's adoption of a statistical service and world series sponsorship in 1944 suggested that the enterprise was finally taking fitful steps toward improved organization. Yet the leagues were still not strong enough to prevent the jumping of players to the increasingly aggressive Mexican baseball teams. Despite negotiations with Washington officials in 1942, the exodus had continued during 1943, affecting nearly every team in the NNL. Frantic over the loss of Willie Wells and Ray Dandridge of the Newark Eagles, Effa Manley investigated whether war circumstances could compel the players to remain in the United States. A Selective Service official, however, cited the players' deferments through marriage and children, noting "no action which can be taken up under the present law to make them stay in essential industry." Leery of criticisms of racial bias, the agency also claimed that, since white organized baseball had been allowed to continue, "any attempt to prevent these persons from playing ball in Mexico might be definitely misconstrued, particularly because of their color."

With federal intervention doubtful, the Grays owners took a more direct approach to the problem after they discovered a Mexican representative, A. J. Guina, openly recruiting Homestead players during a game at Forbes Field on July 10, offering $100 a week and transportation expenses. An enraged Rufus Jackson ordered Guina thrown out of the park, and according to Cum Posey, gave him a strong "cussing out." Hardly deterred, Mexican officials approached Barney Brown and Goose Curry of the Philadelphia Stars eight days later with similar deals, ultimately rejected, to the relief of Bolden and Gottlieb.

As 1944 loomed and the player shortage was still serious, the Mexican situation appeared to be reaching a crisis. The Pasquel brothers' nationalistic efforts to place Mexican baseball at a level comparable to American professional leagues had driven salary offers to unprecedented levels. Yet for the first time, several black teams were now financially secure enough to compete with Mexican salaries. The Homestead Grays, for example, managed to retain Josh Gibson and Buck Leonard after offering each more than $1,000 per month for the 1944 season. Meanwhile, Thomas "Pee Wee" Butts and Roy Campanella returned to the Baltimore Elite Giants from Mexico, as did Ray Dandridge to the Newark Eagles. While Cum Posey confidently asserted that "the players naturally prefer to play in the States if the salaries are almost equal to those paid in Mexico," nonfinancial factors would continue to entice players such as Willie Wells south of the border. In the spring of 1944, Wells related to Wendell Smith that

Mexico offered him a "better future . . . than in the States. . . . We live in the best hotels, we eat in the best restaurants, and can go any place we care to. . . . We don't enjoy such privileges in the U.S. . . . I've found freedom and democracy here, something I never found in the United States." Unable to offer a cogent counter-argument, black baseball teams instead unsuccessfully continued to seek relief from ambivalent federal authorities reluctant to upset the "Good Neighbor" policy during the war.[40]

The NNL had greater success dealing with internal threats during 1944. After the tumult of 1943, the league maintained a cordial relationship with the NAL, despite disputes over the fate of the suspended St. Louis-Harrisburg franchise, now operating in the west as an independent team. Hoping to avoid future interleague conflicts, Cum Posey, Alex Pompez, and Eddie Gottlieb drafted a new joint agreement with the NAL in March 1944. The central part of the document, composed with the assistance of Gottlieb, attempted to address exploitive booking practices at minor and major league parks, particularly in the midwest. The new agreement required promoters to receive no more than 10 percent of the net receipts and to pay each participating league team a minimum of 30 percent of the gross.

Although no names were mentioned, the conditions clearly targeted Abe Saperstein, whose involvement in black baseball had now spread to part-ownership of the Birmingham Black Barons with black Memphis undertaker Tom Hayes. According to Cum Posey, Saperstein offered black teams only 25 percent of the gross in parks in cities such as Indianapolis and Columbus despite earning substantial promotional fees. Increasingly fearful of Saperstein's growing influence, the NNL in June 1944 subsequently voted to boycott any promotions arranged by Saperstein and required league franchises to book their own games while touring the midwest. Simultaneously, Tom Wilson instructed J. B. Martin that Saperstein be removed from any involvement in the publicizing of the East-West game.[41]

Despite the almost unanimous hostility toward Saperstein among eastern owners, other observers remained surprisingly ambivalent toward the midwestern promoter. J. B. Martin, for example, had no misgivings about working with Saperstein, confiding to Effa Manley that his agreement was "very satisfactory . . . [and] he carries it out to the letter," although fellow NAL official Tom Baird remained wary of Saperstein's unstated but suspected desire to "control Negro baseball with headquarters in his office and all bookings and promotion controlled by his office." Denouncing Posey's "national program of vilification," sportswriter Dan Burley also rose to Saperstein's defense, claiming that he had "yet to find a player who says a bad word about Saperstein." Similarly, Wendell Smith opposed

Saperstein's removal from the East-West game, praising him as "without a doubt, one of the sports world's most liberal men, and a square shooter from head to foot." Burley and Smith's positive attitudes toward Saperstein, juxtaposed with their usual criticism of Eddie Gottlieb, suggest that black press attitudes toward white promoters were complex, unpredictable, and could be shaped by factors other than race alone, including access to financial incentives sometimes provided to sports journalists. Notably, Posey claimed that Saperstein had at least a few black sportswriters on his payroll.

The NNL's strong stand against Saperstein led some observers to predict that he would join forces in 1944 with another rejected figure—Gus Greenlee. Rebuffed by the NNL in 1942, Greenlee had slowly worked his way back into baseball with involvement in the war bond tour of the Harrisburg-St. Louis Stars, followed by the revival of the Pittsburgh Crawfords in 1944 as an independent team. In June, Greenlee applied for associate membership in the NNL, hoping to lease Forbes Field in Pittsburgh, but encountered resistance from the Homestead Grays, who still used the park for occasional home dates when not in Washington. The NNL subsequently offered Greenlee an associate membership, but he declined, refusing to accept the provision that the Crawfords play their home games outside league territory. Greenlee's attempt to secure associate membership in the NAL met with similar failure.[42]

To sportswriters such as Rollo Wilson, the NNL's protective stance was justifiable, as territory represented one of the few tangible assets black teams possessed. A disgruntled Greenlee, however, announced his plans to "rid Negro baseball of the clique which has gained a stranglehold on the game," suggesting that a future confrontation was inevitable. Yet an anonymous New York team official confidently dismissed Greenlee's threats, noting that "conditions are different now from what they were back in 1933 when Gus got into the game . . . Then baseball in the east was begging for someone to save it and the league in the west was out of existence. Today we are too strongly entrenched to fear the attacks of an outside party. We have virtual control of the major league parks and Gus will . . . have two strikes on him any time he wants to make a fight for any our territory. And his bankroll is not as thick as it was ten years ago, either."

Greenlee would soon prove to be a more formidable opponent than anticipated. In August, Greenlee launched a dual attack on both leagues during the weekend of the East-West game, the promotion he had helped to pioneer eleven years earlier. In a startling move, Greenlee announced the signing of nearly a dozen players from both leagues, including Lloyd Davenport and Gready McKinnis of the Chicago American Giants, both members of the NAL's East-West team. Simultaneously, Greenlee secretly met with the two all-star teams and encouraged a strike for a greater share of the game's profits. Fearful of losing the most lucrative date of the season, the two league presidents were forced to accede to the players' demands to ensure the playing of the game.

Although Greenlee had seemingly executed a stunning victory over the NNL and NAL, the results proved to be less dramatic than originally perceived. Several of the supposed jumpers never reported to the Crawfords or spent only a brief period with the team before returning to their original clubs. Yet the raids demonstrated that Greenlee was once again a viable force in black professional baseball and could no longer be ignored. Operating independently, the revived Crawfords managed to schedule 137 games during 1944, and, as anticipated, cultivated a relationship with the similarly spurned Abe Saperstein. Marshaling forces for a more substantial confrontation, Greenlee subsequently revealed his plans to organize a rival league in 1945. The announcement sent shock waves throughout the industry, and as sportswriter Russ Cowans noted, "paves the way for one of the biggest baseball wars of recent years." Journalist Joe Bostic, however, suggested that a new league might be Greenlee's last chance, warning that if the organization "fizzles, Gus can give up the baseball ghost for keeps because his enemies will never change their position."[43]

◆　◆　◆

For the fourth consecutive year, attendance for black baseball games remained at an exceptional level, fueled by the continued economic progress of African Americans. Between 1940 and 1944, the number of black unemployed had dropped from 937,562 to about 151,000, while the percentage in war industries more than doubled, from less than 3 percent to 8.3 percent. By September 1944, about 1.5 million blacks were employed in war industries, concentrated heavily in league cities including Newark, Philadelphia, Baltimore, Cleveland, and Chicago. The heavy war employment also stimulated a continued heavy migration to major urban centers, providing both leagues with thousands of new customers eager for entertainment. According to sportswriter Alvin Moses, all teams had a "banner year financially" in 1944, including the Newark Eagles who finally became solvent after prior years of deficits. The Kansas City Monarchs did particularly well, again topping $100,000 in gate receipts and turning a profit of $56,281.87. While the Grays also continued their success, a higher payroll curtailed their profits in 1944. Yet the Grays, like other clubs, had also evolved into a more substantial enterprise, now employing a full-time business manager, publicity director, and other personnel. Franchise values correspondingly increased, as Ernest Wright reportedly declined a $50,000 offer for the Cleveland Buckeyes.[44]

Perhaps the most positive development occurred in New York, an always lucrative city whose fans had long suffered with James Semler's Black Yankees, the problem child of the NNL. Semler's limited financial resources had doomed the franchise to second-rate status since its admission in 1936, and by early 1941 the club seemed unlikely to survive. Although Bob Douglas, owner of basketball's New York Renaissance and one of the most successful black sports entrepreneurs, had reportedly expressed interest in backing a team, the franchise remained controlled by Semler, bolstered by his alliance with booking agent William Leuschner. Additional backing from various sources including Allen Johnson in 1942, Harlem taproom proprietor William Garrett in 1943, and Atlanta gas station and Black Crackers baseball team owner John Harden in 1944 kept the franchise afloat but failed to alter the fortunes of the team, which remained the league's weakest attraction. By 1944, the team hit rock-bottom, losing 30 of 34 league games, leading Rollo Wilson to denounce the "Semler stooges" as a "disgrace to the Negro National League."[45]

Yet during 1944 Alex Pompez's New York Cubans would provide a welcome alternative for Harlem's baseball-hungry fans. Without a park since their return to the NNL in 1939, the Cubans had scheduled their rare home games at Yankee Stadium, sharing the park with the Black Yankees. Eager to secure a park of his own, Pompez had attempted to lease Ebbets Field in Brooklyn, but had encountered opposition from Dexter Park officials, who profited from lucrative games between the Brooklyn Bushwicks and black teams. According to Effa Manley, "Dexter Park does not want our League baseball in Ebbets Field . . . everyone concerned knows the League attraction would be greater than the League team playing a semi-pro team in Dexter Park." Moreover, the Polo Grounds, home of the New York Giants, had also remained largely off-limits, a situation Eddie Gottlieb and Yankee Stadium officials seemed uninterested in changing. In 1944, however, Pompez succeeded in leasing the park for several dates without the involvement of Gottlieb, achieving such success that the Cubans would soon gain permanent residency, scheduling more than 20 dates at the Polo Grounds in 1945. The Cubans' long-sought acquisition of a home park not only challenged Gottlieb's dominance at Yankee Stadium but also stimulated interest on the Lower East Side among Spanish-speaking residents attracted to Pompez's cosmopolitan mixture of African American, Cuban, and Panamanian players.[46]

Pompez's successful movement into the Polo Grounds during 1944, coupled with the Philadelphia Stars' continued use of Shibe Park, reflected the sudden mutuality of interests between white and black professional baseball officials, directly attributable to the war. Grappling with declining wartime major league attendance in 1942 and 1943 and numerous disbanded minor leagues, Organized Baseball had willingly opened its parks to black baseball teams eager to capitalize on their newfound drawing power (see Table 5.2). Along with Yankee Stadium, Comiskey Park, Griffith Stadium, and Ruppert Stadium in Newark, facilities such as Rickwood Field in Birmingham (used by the white and black Barons), League Park in Cleveland (shared by the major league Indians and the NAL Buckeyes), and Ruppert Stadium (later renamed Blues Stadium) in Kansas City became increasingly profitable for both white and black teams. Meanwhile, four black baseball dates at Briggs Stadium drew nearly 85,000 fans, nearly a tenth of Detroit's total major league attendance for the season, while Abe Saperstein claimed that 108,000 fans attended games in Cincinnati, where the Reds drew only 431,000 in 1944.

Ironically, as black baseball reached its financial peak, it remained firmly bound to the whims of whites. Most league officials recognized this fact, including J. B. Martin, who acknowledged that it was "impossible for the clubs to operate unless they play in the big league parks." Yet the dependence troubled sportswriter Sam Lacy, who warned that "the very bottom would drop out of what is today the race's biggest sports enterprise if, for one reason or another, the white major league operators decide to deny us use of their parks."[47]

Some observers justifiably believed that black professional teams would never truly operate on a scale comparable to white minor and major league baseball unless all franchises owned and controlled their own parks. Rentals ultimately remained an imperfect solution, limited not only by their expense but also by their irregular availability. In Philadelphia, for example, the dual use of Shibe Park by the A's and Phillies restricted the Stars to week-night appearances, often on Monday, traditionally one of the worst days for attendance, although the team still managed to draw 70,025 fans for six dates in 1944. While financing and property costs undermined the feasibility of any future park construction venture, owners such as Gus Greenlee, Alex Pompez, and John Drew had managed to build or refurbish facilities during a less favorable economic period. As recently as 1941, Allen Johnson had offered to buy and restore the American Giants park in Chicago, only to be rejected by the team's current owners. Although wartime restrictions on building materials rendered discussions irrelevant at present, the issue seemed certain to receive greater consideration in the future.

By the end of 1944, an increasing number of individuals hoped that park construction, along with several other key administrative reforms, would be included within a general postwar agenda designed to ensure the

Table 5.2. Home Parks, 1944

Team	Park	Organized Baseball tenant
NNL		
Philadelphia Stars	Parkside Field	-
	Shibe Park	Philadelphia Athletics, Philadelphia Phillies
Baltimore Elite Giants	Bugle Field	-
Homestead Grays	Forbes Field	Pittsburgh Pirates
	Griffith Stadium	Washington Senators
New York Cubans	Polo Grounds	New York Giants
New York Black Yankees	Yankee Stadium	New York Yankees
Newark Eagles	Ruppert Stadium	Newark Bears (International League)
NAL		
Chicago American Giants	Comiskey Park	Chicago White Sox
Kansas City Monarchs	Ruppert Stadium	Kansas City Blues (American Association)
Birmingham Black Barons	Rickwood Field	Birmingham Barons (Southern Association)
Memphis Red Sox	Martin Stadium	-
Cleveland Buckeyes	League Park	Cleveland Indians
	Municipal Stadium[1]	Cleveland Indians
Cincinnati-Indianapolis Clowns	Victory Field	Indianapolis (American Association)
	Crosley Field	Cincinnati Reds

[1]The Buckeyes rarely rented Municipal Stadium in 1944; heavier use began in 1945 and 1946.

continued growth and stability of the institution of black baseball. Yet any sweeping changes in operation seemed unlikely to occur through the current league governments. Beholden to other owners for their positions, the two league presidents exercised their already limited power conservatively, generally content to protect the current interests of themselves and their supporters. The often inactive Tom Wilson, for example, was legendary in his failure to respond to correspondence, and by 1942 Cum Posey claimed he would only answer letters concerning the East-West game. Following the controversy over the second-half winner in 1944, Rollo Wilson contended that the president "has outlived his usefulness as president of the Negro National league, if indeed he was ever of real service to any save himself and a favored few." J. B. Martin's presidency received similar criticism in the west, related to his supposed favoritism toward his brother's Memphis Red Sox.[48]

For several years, officials had discussed the selection of impartial league presidents or a strong commissioner to oversee all black baseball and aggressively promote its interests. While the leagues were now able to offer a competitive salary, other logistical problems remained, particularly the still unchecked individualism among franchise owners. As Wendell Smith lamented, the owners were "skeptical of each other and afraid of the man they might select." Clowns owner Syd Pollock, for example, favored a commissioner but questioned whether "it may be worse with some 'outsider' who is apt to show partiality." Moreover, several officials were ambivalent about electing a neutral figure with potentially little or no baseball experience. Assessing the situation, Posey quipped, "there are bigger obstacles in trying to elect a commissioner of Negro baseball than the Germans encountered at Stalingrad."

To Posey, any suitable candidate needed to possess several vital qualifications. With the continuing problems of transportation and jumpings to foreign locales during the war, Posey felt that black baseball needed to "pick a man who has the ear of Washington Government Officials." The crucial importance of establishing a Washington connection was recognized by another NNL official, who noted that "if we just had the right person to make the right contact for us in Washington, a lot of our problems would disappear." In addition, to ensure the continuation of park rentals, an individual with Organized Baseball contacts, ideally with a legal background, was desirable. Yet as Posey asserted, the leagues could no longer wait to decide, warning that "if a commissioner is not selected now, when all clubs are earning profits, Negro baseball will have harder roads to travel when the economic slump comes along."[49]

Relatively secure in their operation after four consecutive prosperous seasons, the two leagues seemed more willing to suppress their usual self-centered behavior, and activity toward electing a commissioner was anticipated at the December 1944 joint session. Addressing the two leagues, *Pittsburgh Courier* managing editor William Nunn praised black baseball's recent financial triumphs but denigrated its administration, insisting that "you can't run a $2,000,000 business as you would a country grocery store," and advised the selection of a commissioner "to prove to the world that you can operate big business as big business should be operated." Although no immediate action was taken, the two leagues subsequently named a four-person committee to investigate possible candidates for commissioner, a modest step that represented an advance from prior futile efforts.

The prospect of a commissioner in 1945 raised hopes that black professional baseball's administrative development would finally match its recent economic strides. While unique wartime conditions had enabled the industry to achieve unprecedented prosperity in the early 1940s, the postwar years ahead appeared likely to be fraught with a number of domestic and foreign challenges, necessitating far greater cooperation and leadership than currently apparent. More important, stronger organization would enable the leagues to deal with another impending dilemma: the increasing push toward the integration of major league baseball (discussed in Chapter 7). As Wendell Smith observed in 1943,

perhaps they can't see it, but the fact remains that their teams, and especially their players, are potential markets for the big leagues. No one knows when the majors will drop the color barrier and decide to admit Negro players. Perhaps this will never come to pass, but it is more than likely it will happen in the not so-distant future. . . . Consequently, it seems to me, it would be wise for owners of teams in the Negro American and National leagues to stabilize themselves to the extent that they will be able to realize a financial profit if they are forced to give up some of their players.

Recognizing the dangers ahead, Smith ominously warned that "if Negro baseball doesn't soon elect a commissioner and clean up its filthy house, it will kill the goose that laid the golden egg."[50]

Meanwhile, the players, the primary occupants of the "filthy house," remained largely isolated from the growing challenges facing officials. Few could deny, however, that the financial prosperity of the war years had also affected their lifestyles and experiences. From players to fans to owners, the entire industry had dramatically changed in a short period of time, yet in many respects, both the NNL and NAL still had a considerable way to go.

6

Life Inside a Changing Industry

> Twenty years ago colored ball players had to sleep on their
> suitcases, go hungry and play in little splinter parks for $125
> a month. Now they travel good as anybody, eat the best, play
> in Comiskey Park and the Polo Grounds and get $500 to
> $700 a month and expenses.
>
> —Satchel Paige, 1944

Between 1933 and 1944, black professional baseball had evolved from a struggling business to a profitable enterprise generating thousands of dollars for its investors. Once perceived by some as little better than "high class sand-lot ball," the NNL and NAL now enjoyed an unprecedented degree of financial stability and acceptance among black players and fans. As early as 1938, the usually critical Wendell Smith recognized the fitful progress made, noting that "gone are the days when the teams appeared before the public dressed like scarecrows and reminded us of the lost legion." Josh Gibson perceived a similar improvement over the first eight years of his career, admitting that "it is better now. We have a league now which we consider well-organized. I feel as though I have something to play for now, besides just making a pay day." Yet the unique circumstances within the industry ensured that black baseball, even at its most prosperous, would remain worlds apart from its white counterpart.[1]

Despite the success of the war years, the lifestyle of black players continued to be vastly different from that of white major and upper-level minor leaguers. Heavy travel remained an unpleasant yet unavoidable component of nearly every team's season. Unable to rely solely on promotions in league cities, teams scheduled additional games in smaller towns, occasionally at a considerable distance; as Homestead official See Posey explained, "the players must understand that we must play every game we can get and will have a few long jumps." By the 1930s, buses were the preferred mode of travel, although some observers perceived their use as a deterioration, rather than an improvement, in the living conditions of play-

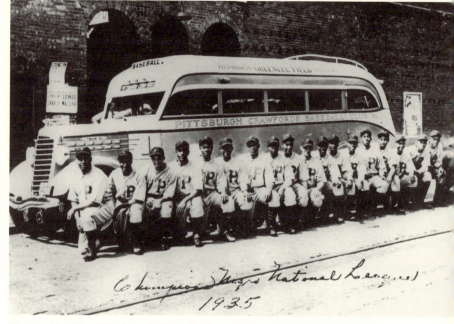

Figure 18. The Pittsburgh Crawfords and their bus, typical of those used in the Negro Leagues in 1935. Note poster advertising John Henry Lewis bout, Gus Greenlee's other major interest in the 1930s. Courtesy Larry Hogan.

ers. Dave Malarcher, an active player throughout much of the 1920s, insisted that "the standards were being lowered" in later years, as "they drove all night, didn't eat, didn't sleep at all." Similarly, former player Jimmy Fuller contrasted the life of the Depression-era player "yanked . . . around the country in buses," with the "Pullman service, decent food and good salaries" commonly enjoyed during the previous decade. Even Cum Posey, an advocate of bus travel, admitted that the "long, tedious . . . rides from city to city takes [*sic*] its toll as the season wanes."

To their credit, some owners attempted to provide for their players' comfort. In 1936, the Philadelphia Stars' bus featured reclining seats and a radio with two speakers, while the Pittsburgh Crawfords provided similar amenities. Yet the condition of most vehicles remained far from desirable, resulting in common mechanical failures and prompting journalist Ed Harris's assertion that "every team in the league seems to have a bus that never fails to break down ten miles outside of city limits." During 1940, the New York Black Yankees' bus failed several times, forcing the team to take taxis to Parkside Field on one occasion. Ten years later, the Birmingham Black Barons' bus caught on fire in the middle of the Holland

Tunnel, resulting in the loss of the team's uniforms and equipment. Although the relative affluence of the war years would have allowed clubs to acquire more reliable buses, government restrictions all but eliminated the possibility of upgrades until the cessation of hostilities in 1945.[2]

While bus breakdowns annoyed players and impatient fans, accidents and the very real potential for serious injury presented a more worrisome issue. In 1940, the Baltimore Elite Giants experienced a near catastrophe when the brakes on the team's bus malfunctioned on a steep road near York, Pennsylvania. The worst bus accident in black baseball, however, occurred in September 1942, resulting in the death of two Cleveland Buckeyes.

If occasionally hazardous, buses nevertheless offered teams a cheap means to travel considerable distances for games while reducing the need for hotel stays. Players had little choice but to adapt to long bus rides, although conditions varied depending on a particular team's scheduling practices. During the Depression, the need to maximize income forced a number of clubs to undertake lengthy, sometimes disorganized barnstorming trips far from their home territory. In September 1932, the Crawfords covered an amazing 1,200 miles in only 41 hours, leaving Pittsburgh on Tuesday evening and arriving in Monroe, Louisiana, on Thursday afternoon. Grueling travel remained common for league teams even into the 1940s. In the NNL, the Homestead Grays were notorious for a relentless schedule, exacerbated by the team's dual-city home base of Pittsburgh and Washington. A four-game series in 1946 incorporating successive games in Chicago, Cleveland, Fairmont, West Virginia, and Newark exemplified the Grays' exhausting lifestyle, confirming pitcher Terris McDuffie's belief that "they stay on the road too much." Meanwhile, NAL clubs faced even heavier travel, operating in a less geographically compact organization and often journeying to eastern cities for interleague games.[3]

In contrast, the Philadelphia Stars enjoyed perhaps the lightest travel of any league team. Like Hilldale, the club benefited from a convenient location within 150 miles of most of the important league venues, allowing the bulk of their games (both league and non-league) to be played along the Washington-New York corridor. As Stars catcher Stanley Glenn later explained, the club was "probably the most sheltered team in black baseball," at least until the late 1940s, when league conditions abruptly changed. Teammate Wilmer Harris cited the role of always watchful Stars official Eddie Gottlieb, who "made the schedules up . . . and in doing so, he was both thrifty and . . . you wouldn't travel any more than was just absolutely necessary. Because he had to pay for it." Gottlieb's firm control over an especially thriving semipro scene in the metropolitan Philadelphia area also lessened travel requirements, as a number of strong white clubs, particularly members of the Gottlieb-headed Philadelphia League, offered profitable competition for the Stars and other league teams during the 1930s.[4]

As a team that rarely traveled south of Virginia until the late 1940s, the Stars were also spared the difficulties involved in securing lodging in an age of segregation. In cities with a large African American population, the problem was less acute, as numerous establishments catering to black travelers were readily available. Teams playing in New York or Newark, for example, typically stayed at the white-controlled Hotel Theresa or the Woodside Hotel, owned by black entrepreneurs Love B. Woods and his brother Dan, who enthusiastically solicited league trade, explaining "our doors are always open to baseball teams because the Boys' deportment in our hotel has always been very good." In Baltimore, the York Hotel offered similar services, while in Philadelphia, black teams turned to the Attucks or Douglass hotels. In smaller towns, however, finding accommodations or even accessible restaurants proved far more difficult, particularly in the south. Mahlon Duckett recalled that in "Mississippi, Texas, down there they didn't have any black hotels. So what we would have to do, a lot of people would say, 'well, we can take two or three ballplayers and put you up for the night.' . . . that's how we had to sleep and then most of the time, we slept on the bus." Northern communities were sometimes no more welcoming. A black team journeying to Atco, New Jersey, in 1934 was shocked to discover "about the worst conditions this side of the Dixie Line. The stores actually had signs on the door warning the public that they didn't solicit colored trade."

Segregation thus remained an unavoidable part of each black professional team's existence. Years would pass before African Americans would enjoy anything near full access to accommodations and restaurants, forcing black players to contend with living conditions less favorable than did most white minor leaguers. Yet Effa Manley later defended the lodging provided to league teams, noting that they "weren't elaborate, magnificent, but to me they were clean, decent, honest-to-goodness." Frazier Robinson, active with the Baltimore Elite Giants and other league teams during the 1940s, agreed, explaining that "we had the best that they had to offer in the way of rooms and food and stuff like that. They said second rate, third rate. They can say whatever they want to say, but the owners did the best they could for us."[5]

While segregation exerted a powerful force on black teams, modest finances played an equally decisive role in shaping many of the distinct practices affecting player lifestyles. Cost concerns, for example, limited team rosters to 15 to 18 players, comparable to lower to mid-level minor league clubs but considerably fewer than the 23 (and later 25) men carried in the major leagues. Veteran manager Jim Taylor viewed the issue as one of the major differences between white and black baseball, noting that "I think that we have as many good players in our league as they have in the big leagues. The one big advantage they have is that they have more men on their teams. . . . As a result, our pitchers are overworked and if our men get hurt they still have to play." With relatively few backups available, league teams prized versatile men able to play several positions, such as Curtis "Popeye" Harris, who appeared as a catcher, infielder, and out-fielder during his stint with the Philadelphia Stars from 1937 through 1940.[6]

Financial limitations similarly prevented black players from enjoying the luxury of extensive pre-season preparation. While many clubs followed the major league example of journeying south for spring training, black teams almost immediately began scheduling games to help defray costs, and as the Grays' Buck Leonard later explained, "no sooner did you pull on your uniform and crack a sweat than you were in a game before paying customers." The financial returns for pre-season games, however, remained marginal, particularly during the Depression years. By 1936, the Crawfords decided to forgo training in the deep south after several seasons of losses, a policy adopted by Philadelphia three years later, following a disastrous spring in Texas and Tennessee in 1938 marked by cold weather and rain. Most teams, however, resumed spring training in the south during the early 1940s unless prevented by wartime travel restrictions.[7]

An equally cost-conscious approach characterized the leagues' handling of young players. While most major league clubs employed full-time scouts to discover promising players throughout the United States, black teams typically relied on less formal methods. Sandlot managers, hoping for a probable commission, often made the initial recommendation of a young-ster, usually prompting a subsequent contact from the team. In 1941, Mc-Kinley "Bunny" Downs, a former Hilldale player now managing the Mobile Black Shippers, attempted to interest the Stars' Ed Bolden in sev-eral prospects, noting that "the ones . . . most suitable for organized base ball I will get you in touch with and I will bet you will be satisfied." At the suggestion of Downs, Bolden subsequently wrote to Norwood "Whizzer" White, explaining that "I would like to give you a tryout. . . . Let me hear from [you] and I will send you a contract so that you will become a mem-ber of the Philadelphia Stars." Current players also provided talent leads; for example, Ches Buchanan, stationed in San Francisco in 1944, advised the *Independent* to "tell Ed (Chief) Bolden there is one of the greatest young pitchers out here I have ever seen and if he will talk cold turkey I'll sign him up."

Many black teams and newspapers also received unsolicited correspondence from youngsters eager to display their abilities in professional baseball. A 1951 letter from an eighteen-year-old Jacksonville youth offers a typical example of the genre and includes the common assertion that "I am a very good ballplayer and I would like for you to see me." Lacking the financial resources to investigate the skills of every potential player, particularly those residing in distant parts of the south, league teams realistically had only two options: either offer the player a tryout at his own expense or ignore the letters entirely. In some cases, however, teams willingly gambled on youngsters based on somewhat questionable evaluations. After receiving a letter in 1941 from E. E. Forbes touting a North Carolina prospect who "could beat Satchel Paige," Bolden attempted to arrange a tryout without success. A year later, Bolden again contacted Forbes, reminding him of his promise to bring the prospect to Philadelphia. Recognizing the Stars' keen interest, Forbes claimed that the player was "going better this season than last. . . . I feel he will be a real find for you, He is the best I have ever seen." Bolden subsequently offered to "pay expenses for you and the boy," but there is no record that the young phenom or his benefactor ever arrived in Philadelphia for a tryout.[8]

After formalizing his relationship with the club, a young player was almost immediately tested in a game situation. In some instances, the process was handled deliberately, occasionally by phasing the youngster into non-league games against weaker opponents. Wilmer Fields, for example, recalled that, as a rookie pitcher with the Homestead in 1939, the Grays "picked their spots for me to pitch . . . never threw me to the wolves or disgraced me in any fashion." Most players, however, did not enjoy the luxury of a prolonged trial and were expected to make an immediate contribution or face release. A number of observers viewed the leagues' often rushed approach to player development as unsuitable. Roscoe Coleman suggested that "a few of the good ones should be selected and prepped. Such a procedure should take longer than a week or pre-season tryout under very adverse conditions and unfavorable weather."[9]

Players deemed not quite ready for league ball presented a particular dilemma, as black baseball lacked a farm system where promising prospects could be sent for additional training and seasoning. Instead, league teams occasionally established informal "working agreements" with lower-level black clubs or leagues. The Philadelphia Stars, for instance, sent several players to the independent Bacharach Giants in the late 1930s, while the Newark Eagles developed relationships with teams in Winston-Salem and Asheville, North Carolina. With the affluence of the war years, the NNL made a greater attempt to develop an actual farm system through an affiliation with the newly organized Southern League in 1945. The arrangement was less than successful, however, as players often refused to remain with the minor league club. Southern League teams in turn were reluctant to part with promising players for the meager $300 draft price offered by the NNL.

Although the establishment of a successful farm system was beyond the financial scope of black baseball entrepreneurs, there was also little real incentive to pursue the project seriously. It was simply easier and cheaper for league clubs to raid smaller teams, stripping them of their best men without compensation. The NNL's treatment of the ill-fated Eastern Seaboard League in 1937 reflected the prevalent attitude. Organized with the involvement of several experienced officials including Rollo Wilson, Lloyd Thompson, and Otto Briggs, the ESL featured eight top semiprofessional teams based in metropolitan Philadelphia and hoped to function as a minor league for the NNL. Competing at a surprisingly high level, several teams managed to hold their own against professional clubs, but they soon found themselves victimized by their own success. Reeling from the Dominican raids of 1937, the Pittsburgh Crawfords and other NNL teams soon dipped into the ESL for replacements. By early June, the Nicetown Giants (Roy Campanella's former club) were forced to forfeit a game after "most of their team had been snatched," and the league itself collapsed by July.[10]

The experience of the Eastern Seaboard League was hardly atypical, as major black teams often cultivated an antagonistic rather than complementary relationship with smaller clubs. Struggling for their own existence, NNL franchises had few qualms about their sometimes ruthless dealings with lower-level teams, whom they viewed as competition. Hoping to work with the NNL in 1939, manager Ben Taylor of the semipro Washington Royal Giants sent the organization a list of open dates, only to discover league teams attempting to appropriate them for themselves. The same year, Newark's Abe Manley privately instructed a representative to "go and get me a Ball Player who is playing with the Norfolk Black Tars. . . . Do not let Brady Johnson [team official] know you are trying to get this boy, as he might try to stand in your way." The Philadelphia Stars followed a similar pattern, grabbing numerous players from the Philadelphia Black Meteors and Daisies in the early 1940s. By the end of the 1943 season, Rollo Wilson cited the "constant looting" of the Daisies, while lamenting the plight of black semipro officials who "will spend long hours and their scant finances in developing youngsters who can be lured away by the league owners."[11]

Despite the less than optimal player development arrangement, a number of capable rookies continued to make their way into the NNL each season. Yet the few young players fortunate enough to earn a roster spot encountered nearly insurmountable hurdles, sometimes placed by their own teammates. Veterans, fearing the loss of their jobs, often strongly resisted the younger men. Ed Bolden, for example, complained in 1935 of "an inner clique that does nothing to help along the rookies," while Gene Benson, who subsequently joined the Stars, later recalled that "it was very, very hard because the old fellows didn't want you there." Mahlon Duckett, a seventeen-year-old rookie in 1940, offered an explanation for the attitudes of older players, observing that "those fellows were men. They were all married. Not all of them but most of them were married. They had families. That was their livelihood. They only carried x amount of ballplayers on the team anyway. . . . So they played rough."[12]

If a youngster was able to withstand the occasionally hostile reception to his presence, he then had to adapt to an exceptionally competitive league. Struggling young players, however, often had no place to turn for additional instruction or assistance. Nonplaying coaches simply did not fit into the budget of most teams, forcing most rookies to fend for themselves or seek assistance from an already overburdened manager. As Wilmer Harris explained, "managers at that time had a tough time," as "they were the hitting instructors, they had the job to see if we did something wrong," while also handling financial matters. Although the veteran Roy Partlow befriended Harris and offered him valuable pitching tips, other rookies found older players less than forthcoming with advice; as Gene Benson later noted, "they wouldn't show you anything . . . and you had to learn everything on your own." Recognizing that the success rate of young prospects might improve with better coaching, a number of observers advocated employing retired players in an instructional capacity.

Careful coaching ultimately remained a luxury for black players, who typically lagged behind their white counterparts in following proper technique on the playing field. Notably, former Birmingham Black Baron Piper Davis suggested that "in Negro baseball, the players advance purely on natural talent and not much more. Their basic shortcoming is that they do not learn the fundamentals of the game." Davis, like others, insisted that more coaches were needed, noting in 1951 that "I have learned more in two years in white baseball than I learned all my years in the colored leagues." Larry Doby offered a similar view, admitting in 1947 that "I learned more in the few months I was with Cleveland than I picked up in a couple of seasons with Newark."[13]

Yet the less conventional and sometimes more exciting style of play simultaneously enhanced the appeal of black baseball. Moreover, the personality or "color" perceived as an important player attribute by both white and black fans was more evident in the Negro Leagues than in white baseball. After watching two NNL teams at Briggs Stadium in 1941, white sportswriter H. G. Salsinger of the *Detroit News* cited the "whole-hearted enthusiasm" of the teams who "play baseball with a verve and flair lacking in the big leagues." Five years later, John Lardner of *Newsweek* noted the "ironic style to which players in Negro baseball sometimes give way and which makes much better entertainment than the jeeps, bands, and gyrationists lined up by Bill Veeck and L. S. MacPhail."[14]

The stylistic flourishes, however, contributed to a perception among some observers that black baseball players were somehow less "serious" than their white counterparts. The attitude was hardly surprising, as Drake and Cayton similarly cited white Americans' "tendency to view the separate Negro institutional life with a certain amount of amused condescension and patronizing curiosity." Moreover, the mass media had long programmed whites into perceiving blacks as little more than buffoons. Although unfamiliar with the NNL, many individuals were readily aware of the supposedly "comical actions" of blacks on the playing field, confirming Sam Lacy's belief that "public opinion has the black ball player labeled as a clown." Yet occasional sloppiness on the field and the absence of the "stronger disciplinary presence" present in the major leagues also resulted in a downgrading of black baseball talent. Players occasionally smoked in the dugouts during a game, prompting a formal complaint to the NAL by Wendell Smith in 1944. Meanwhile, Ed Harris criticized the failure of games to start on time, particularly the second game of a double-header, blaming the difficulties involved in "rounding up 18 different men scattered in a crowd, making dates, eating and gossiping."[15]

An indifferent strain also occasionally crept into both non-league games against white semipro opponents and "unofficial" league contests. As early as 1936, Cum Posey warned that "it has become a bad habit among the league players to claim they did not care whether they won certain games or not because they were not league games." Nine years later, an NNL official confided to Effa Manley that in non-league games, the manager typically used "a lot of subs and saves his pitchers." The less than full effort annoyed black fans such as Hazel Wigden, who watched league teams play the Bushwicks and other top white semipros in the New York area. Like Posey, Wigden suggested that "the only time the colored teams seem to care whether they win or lose is when they play a League game," citing the "lackadaisical way they slouch out to their places on the diamond, as tho if they had to step once more they would flop." While recognizing the effect of travel on the players, Wigden nevertheless reminded officials that the fans were equally tired: "we have been working all day, have to travel miles to see these games, go dinnerless, sit in the chilly dew without moving . . . have to again catch buses and travel miles in stuffy subways—most of all we have to pay, and what do we get?"[16]

Despite Wigden's complaints, the caliber of black professional baseball was generally very high, at least for meaningful official league games. Most observers assessed the level of play as comparable to the high minor leagues, not quite matching the majors because of the widely varying quality of competition encountered on a day-to-day basis. As Alex Pompez later explained, "we used to play one hard game and coast for three or four days before another tough one came up." Moreover, the discouraging lifestyle within the industry undoubtedly affected the caliber of play, although Wigden and other fans were sometimes less than sympathetic. Philadelphia official George Lyle aptly summarized the numerous negative factors inhibiting performance, citing "long trips by bus, arriving at the point of play sometimes just a few scant hours before game time," "hurried meals off hot dogs and cokes," and the inability to obtain adequate rest. The players, however, still managed to function at a high level, yet as Lyle observed, "think of how much better they would be if they had some of the advantages which their white brethren enjoy."[17]

Although the superior lifestyle of white professional baseball remained elusive even during the war years, black players did benefit from a noticeable increase in league salaries. Payrolls had initially peaked during the 1920s, enabling top eastern and midwestern players to earn roughly between $100 and $400 monthly. In 1929, for example, each Hilldale player received a minimum of $125 per month and seven earned $250 or more, including Martin Dihigo at $400 and Oscar Charleston at $375. Yet the steadily worsening economic status of African Americans beginning as early as the mid-1920s and the corresponding effect on gate receipts resulted in increasing industry-wide attempts to reduce player salaries. In January 1926, Bolden's Eastern Colored League and Foster's NNL imposed a $3,000 monthly salary cap, lowered to $2,700 (slightly more than class C minor league salary limits) a year later. The subsequent onset of the Depression further deflated salaries and by early 1932, Hilldale officials slashed the monthly payroll to $2,200 while other clubs in the newly formed East-West League pursued a similar strategy.[18]

During the worst years of the Depression even a modest monthly salary scale was no longer practical for most owners, with the exception of the then affluent Gus Greenlee. As noted in Chapter 1, a growing number of teams replaced salaries with the "co-op" or "co-plan," where management and players divided the gate receipts from each game. Although several clubs employed the co-op plan in 1933, the subsequent modest economic improvement allowed most professional teams to reinstitute salaries by 1934. Moreover, the formation of the NNL in 1933 had provided another impetus, as the co-op plan was simply not conducive to league play, undermining the owners' already limited control over players.

League salaries, however, largely failed to match the higher payrolls of the 1920s, as revealed by a comparison of monthly salary caps. A decade after both existing leagues enforced a $3,000 limit, the NNL adopted a $2,600 monthly cap in 1936 while the NAL implemented a $2,200 maximum a year later, slightly more than class B minor leagues, whose salaries also dropped during the Depression. With most teams carrying fewer than 18 players, the average player between 1936 and 1941 thus received roughly $100 to $150 per month for a four-and-a-half-month season, although inexperienced youngsters earned as little as $50 to $60 (comparable to class D minor leagues). Meanwhile, black baseball's highest paid players, Satchel Paige and Josh Gibson, probably never made more than $500 monthly with a league team before 1941. In contrast, top black musicians could earn as much as $100 per week working for Duke Ellington and Cab Calloway in the late 1930s.[19]

The unspectacular pay scale of the period required most players to seek additional employment opportunities in the off-season months, and as Wilmer Fields later observed, "it was ridiculous for a ballplayer to think that he could survive the winter months in the States without a job. A Negro League ballplayer couldn't save anything from his summer employment." To pitcher Roosevelt Davis, the chronic problem of off season employment should have been "tackled and solved long ago. Baseball players have to eat and sleep and see the laundry man in December as well as June." Winter baseball provided an important source of supplemental income, as a number of players joined professional clubs in Puerto Rico, Cuba, and Venezuela, although the racial climate differed in each country. In Cuba, black players often encountered less than hospitable treatment, and by 1942 Terris McDuffie complained that "Negroes are segregated at the decent eating places and in the hotels because so many American white people are taking over." In contrast, McDuffie asserted that Puerto Rico was "everything Cuba is not," and other players viewed Venezuela in a similarly positive light.[20]

While profitable, winter ball opportunities were generally limited to a select few, forcing other players to seek non-baseball related employment, a particularly difficult task during the Depression. Recognizing the dilemma, a *Chicago Defender* columnist questioned in 1938 whether players had to "go on WPA and relief in order to live through the winter months?" Unable to play winter baseball, one player spent the off season as a dishwasher. Roy Parnell worked as a longshoreman during the winter, while other players found higher-paying employment selling insurance (Jimmy Starks) or operating a filling station (Henry Kimbro). Ted Page even worked for Gus Greenlee's numbers business one winter, earning $15 weekly.

Recognizing the lack of future security in a baseball career, some players viewed outside employment as their primary concern. Obie Lackey of the Philadelphia Stars, for example, refused to quit his job after joining the team in 1936, while Pat Patterson typically reported late and departed early to fulfill his teaching and coaching chores at Wiley College in Marshall, Texas. While the Stars willingly accommodated Patterson, an above-average player, the club was often less tolerant of employment-related absences of less established performers such as Darius Bea, whose reluctance to give up his job contributed to his dismissal from the team in 1940. Other league teams experienced comparable difficulties, as several Grays abandoned the league altogether in the 1930s, preferring the security of a steady mill job to the modest wages offered in black baseball. *Afro* columnist Bill Gibson believed such decisions were often economically justifiable: "some of these players have good jobs and naturally wouldn't think of leaving them in order to play ball on a co-plan or what-have-you." Moreover, employed players such as Lackey could still supplement their income performing with top semipro teams such as the Bacharach Giants, which traveled less extensively and allowed players to maintain their current jobs.

The refusal to forsake more mundane employment opportunities for the more glamorous, yet sometimes less lucrative world of professional baseball was hardly confined to the Negro Leagues. During the Depression, white players occasionally rejected minor league offers, instead choosing to maintain their jobs while performing on strong company-sponsored semiprofessional teams. Yet the inability of black professional baseball to offer more attractive wages troubled a number of observers, including Gus Greenlee, who agreed that "at best, colored players are underpaid." The veteran Ben Taylor, however, argued that league players were adequately compensated in view of the generally lackluster overall attendance of the late 1930s.[21]

Examined within the context of black employment opportunities and wages during the Depression, league salaries appear less dismal. In New York, the median income for non-broken black families was only $980 in the mid-1930s, while in Chicago, more than two-thirds of black families earned less than $1,000 annually and more than 30 percent less than $500. The situation was even bleaker in the south, where family incomes seldom exceeded $600 annually during the 1930s. Thus, even during its least profitable decade, black baseball still offered considerable economic incentives to young men, and as veteran umpire Bert Gholston explained in 1934, "with the possibilities of better pay as a baseball player than he could earn in the present set-up in the industrial and professional world, it is no wonder that the young colored athlete strives to be a star player. He knows that there may be a chance for him to sign up with one of the big teams and at least not have to carry baggage, bell-hop, wait table or fill such positions as are not in hard keeping with the education for which he has worked so hard."[22]

With the war-fueled prosperity of the early 1940s, wages in black baseball finally began to rise, eventually surpassing the previous high reached two decades earlier. According to Cum Posey, the NNL in 1942 paid salaries comparable to the class A-1 level Southern Association, citing the Grays' $25,000 payroll, and by the end of the war, Josh Gibson and Buck Leonard both topped a surprising $1,000 per month. While few NNL players drew comparable figures, established performers such as Lenny Pearson and Leon Day of the Newark Eagles enjoyed increases of $75 to $90 per month in the early 1940s, reaching $250 and $300 respectively in 1943. The rise in salaries was hardly limited to the east, as by early 1944, J. B. Martin disclosed that "players on the Chicago American Giants Club whom we paid $200 last year are wanting $300 and $400 for this year."[23]

By the end of the war, the salary structure in black baseball had dramatically changed. In the NNL, the monthly salary cap continued to rise, ultimately reaching $8,000 by 1947 (roughly equivalent to the Southern Association or Texas League; see Table 6.1) and enabling teams to pay star players $500 to $800 monthly. Meal money provided to players also increased, raised from the 50 or 60 cents daily during the 1930s to between $2 and $3 by the late 1940s, comparable to the class B Inter-State League. The always frugal owners, however, remained worried of the effect of escalating salaries on the prosperity of individual teams. According to Fay Young, the Homestead Grays' current payroll required the team to draw sizable crowds on the weekends simply to break even. Meanwhile, a nervous Effa Manley confided to Brooklyn Dodger official John Collins in 1946 that "we must make money to pay the salaries we are paying this year."[24]

Not surprisingly, most owners typically bestowed pay raises begrudgingly and only after a considerable fight. Wilmer Fields later recalled that "contract dealings with the Grays were not very pleasant. My contracts were never discussed with the Grays, and certainly never negotiated. They would send me a contract, saying in effect: 'Take it or leave it.' " The art of negotiation, however, was perhaps more important than Fields suggests, as extant records of the Newark Eagles contain numerous letters from players attempting to wrest a few dollars more out of the Manleys. Lincoln University-educated Max Manning, for example, provided a particularly powerful argument in an attempt to earn a $20 increase in 1941, explaining that "a Negro baseball player's life is a hard one. He has to make money while he is still young and spend it wisely. Likewise he must obtain his salary however and wherever he can. This is an old story but it becomes more ominous each new year of Negro baseball." Perhaps recognizing

Table 6.1. Monthly Salary Caps (dollars)

	1926	1933	1936	1946
ECL or NNL	3,000	1,600	2,600	8,000
Class AA/AAA	*	*	*	*
Class A-1	—	—	4,600	7,000
Class A	4,500–6,500**	4,250	4,250	4,250
Class B	3,200	2,000	2,000	3,000
Class C	2,650	1,800	1,800	2,200
Class D	2,400	1,000	1,000	1,800

*The three top minor leagues (Pacific Coast League, American Association, International League) generally were not subject to salary caps. The American Association imposed a $6,500 monthly salary limit in 1933.
**Figure represents range of salary limits for all Class A leagues between 1925 and 1927.
Sources: *SOMP*, 1350–88; *PT*, January 16, 1926; *BAA*, May 13, 1933; *PC*, March 26, 1936; *SN*, October 20, 1948.

Manning's logic, the Manleys ultimately acceded to his request of $170 monthly.[25]

Regardless of the occasional raise, players still contended with a less than enviable lifestyle in black baseball. Despite larger gate receipts by the early 1940s, certain chronic problems remained immutable, including extensive travel, segregated accommodations, and a lack of adequate coaching. Even at the pinnacle of its growth, black professional baseball was unable to provide its players with a quality of life comparable to even lower-level minor leagues, the majority of which were relatively compact and involved travel to only eight different cities.

Although progress appeared frustratingly limited, the lifestyle in black baseball had clearly changed in one important respect: the introduction of more generous pay during the war years that allowed black players, like the African American population as a whole, to better themselves economically. Once employed by an industry unable to pay regular salaries at times, a number of black players received wages comparable to top minor leaguers by 1946, an unthinkable development only a decade earlier. Few realized, however, that the higher salaries would prove a short-lived aberration, as earnings and living conditions in black baseball would deteriorate in the 1950s, ultimately reverting to an almost Depression-era quality.

◆　◆　◆

Like player lifestyles, the ballpark experience for black fans appeared to have changed little upon initial scrutiny. As before, baseball remained a major source of entertainment for blacks and by far the most popular sport, although boxing's appeal had dramatically increased following the rise of Joe Louis. Commenting on the modest allure of other sports, Dan Burley observed in 1941 that "segments, much, much smaller, follow football, tennis, basketball, track, golf, etc., but to the great colored public, these sports are Greek." Cleveland sportswriter Bill Finger agreed, contending that "we have among us still a majority to whom 'sports' is baseball." To Finger, the phenomenon was attributable to African Americans' strong roots in the South, an area "where baseball was the one sport universally entered into by athletes and followers alike."

With interest and knowledge of baseball unusually high among African Americans, black professional teams continued to be able to draw upon a broad cross-section of the population for their attendance. Yet an affinity for baseball had never been the only factor determining patronage. Like the annual Penn Relays in Philadelphia and the Howard/Lincoln football "classic" each Thanksgiving, weekly baseball games also traditionally functioned as a social event, a place where one could meet with family and friends in a communal setting. Not surprisingly, many fans arrived at the games dressed in their best outfits, often donned earlier in the day for Sunday services. As Stanley Glenn recalled, women typically wore "high-heeled shoes and silk stockings. Hats on their heads and long-sleeved gloves. And the men came to the ballpark dressed in suits and shirts and ties." Thus, the baseball park, like church, fulfilled a secondary function: a chance to be seen in public looking one's best.[26]

The quasi-formal game atmosphere continued to attract the black elite, always a prominent presence at any major community gathering. After attending a Yankee Stadium promotion in April 1944, journalist Nell Dodson Russell marveled at the glittering cast of entertainers, "social floy-floy and professional leaders" in the crowd, along with the "housewives, defense workers," and usual "dyed-in-the-wool fans." Recognizing that the attendance of prominent race leaders reinforced the industry's legitimacy, league officials eagerly cultivated the patronage and support of the black bourgeoisie. In Philadelphia, for example, Ed Bolden provided passes to representatives of all the major local black institutions and recruited an "outstanding race man" or woman to throw out the ceremonial first ball of the season.[27]

Despite the common presence of dignitaries, the game atmosphere was hardly restrained, and according to Wendell Smith, the typical black fan was "more vocal, more appreciative, and more responsive" than his or her white counterpart. Yet a number of whites had always supported black baseball, often watching league clubs compete at white parks against top semiprofessional teams. Josh Gibson, for example, cited several locales

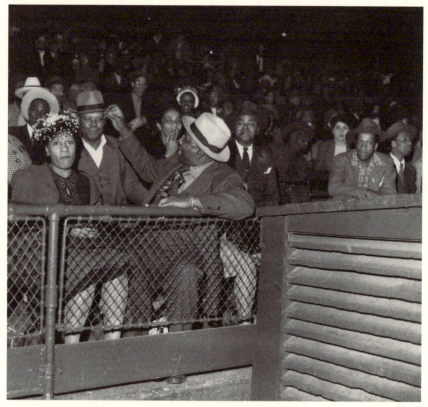

Figure 19. Well-dressed crowd at a Negro League game at Forbes Field, Pittsburgh, 1945. Photo by Charles "Teenie" Harris. Courtesy Carnegie Museum of Art, Pittsburgh.

where white fans were particularly appreciative, including New York, New Jersey, and Philadelphia. Fewer attended all-black games, however, although league teams in New York, the Philadelphia metropolitan area (Darby), Baltimore, Kansas City, and other cities attracted some whites during the 1920s.

While the subsequent level of white attendance at league games is impossible to determine, impressionistic evidence suggests the number of white fans probably increased during the 1940s after an earlier slump. During the Depression years, the presence of whites seldom elicited comment, although Rollo Wilson claimed in 1934 that "in Philadelphia you will find hundreds of white fans who will tell you that they prefer seeing colored league games to going out to watch either the A's or Phils." Meanwhile, a July 4, 1934, promotion at Greenlee Field in Pittsburgh reportedly

Figure 20. Interracial crowd at Forbes Field, 1945. Photo by Charles "Teenie" Harris. Courtesy Carnegie Museum of Art, Pittsburgh.

attracted "plenty of ofays . . . and lots of them brought their women," and the well-publicized East-West games in Chicago consistently drew a number of whites. Yet Effa Manley, who aggressively attempted to boost white attendance at Ruppert Stadium, later claimed that there were "just a few" white fans, "not enough to speak of. At that time the races just didn't mix much." Similarly, Eddie Gottlieb suggested that "in those days, the percentage of white patrons at Negro games was very small," particularly in contrast to Hilldale's stronger white attendance in the 1920s.[28]

White fans' growing willingness to patronize all-black boxing matches, increasing familiarity with Satchel Paige and Josh Gibson, and the greater number of promotions staged at major league parks likely stimulated patronage during the 1940s. Whites reportedly comprised nearly a quarter of the 20,000 fans attending a May 11, 1941, Yankee Stadium doubleheader featuring Paige, prompting Dan Burley's subsequent assertion that "the Negro league owners are at last seeing their dream of white attendance in big cities fulfilled." Noticing a similar trend in Chicago by 1943, a black fan cited the "freer social atmosphere and the sense of being all together in the war effort" creating "less inhibition on the part of the whites to come out to the Negro parks." Although scattered contemporary accounts suggested that the number of white fans still remained generally slim in league cities, it appears likely that the crowds were far more interracial than in the past. In 1944, Paige himself alluded to the greater white attendance at black games.[29]

If the greater presence of whites represented one change in the black fan experience by the mid-1940s, the move to larger and more comfortable venues reflected another break with the past. During the 1920s, the majority of fans typically watched black professional baseball at either minor league parks or modest-sized, predominantly wooden facilities such as Hilldale Park in Darby, Maryland Park in Baltimore, Catholic Protectory Oval in New York, Schorling Park in Chicago, and Mack Park in Detroit. With the growing prosperity of the war years, however, regular rentals of major league parks became not only possible but desirable in several larger urban centers where conveniently located or adequate-sized facilities were unavailable. By 1944, fans in New York, Chicago, Cleveland, Detroit, Pittsburgh, and Washington witnessed NNL or NAL games exclusively at local major league parks.

While major league facilities often provided a more enjoyable ballpark experience, their use also prompted increasing concerns about the behavior of black fans. For decades, black sportswriters had lamented the conduct of a small minority of patrons, characterized by journalist Al Moses as "irresponsible louts who give the [Westbrook] Peglers and the [Theodore] Bilbos much needed material for their smear campaigns." Most of the behavioral problems stemmed from the heavy alcohol consumption of a segment of fans who either arrived at the game with a whiskey bottle in their pocket or found illicit alcohol readily available at parks such as Crosley Field, where Fay Young witnessed fans doing a thriving business selling whiskey and gin in paper cups. Not surprisingly, the increasingly intoxicated patrons grew more unruly as the game progressed, creating an unpleasant atmosphere for other spectators. A Cleveland fan voiced a typical complaint, noting that "it is really embarrassing to see how our folks carry on. First, they seem more interested in eating hot dogs and drinking beer than they are in seeing the game. . . . They arrive at the park, half intoxicated. . . . They roam all over the park, disturbing those few who wish to see the game." Eustace Gay of the *Philadelphia Tribune* similarly criticized black fans "who think that it is impossible to enjoy a baseball game unless they are swilling liquor simultaneously. They make nuisances of themselves, annoy those fans who want to see the game minus the spirits, and give the group in general a black eye."[30]

To the disgust of some observers, female fans could be equally disruptive at the ballpark, and, as Moses observed, "were not averse to making spectacles of themselves." Dan Burley, for example, lamented instances of black women fighting "like cats and dogs over the affections of some slick-headed playboy" and wondered whether such unsavory episodes drove away whites. Burley noted that white fans "never can tell when a woman sitting next to them or behind them will rise up and start pounding her man over the head with her purse, lurid, vulgar curses pouring . . . from her lips." Fay Young also reported instances of objectionable female behavior, citing the presence at Comiskey Park of a "grandma . . . full of her hootch" who "had been smoking reefers."

Rowdy fan behavior, however, was hardly limited to African Americans, as Organized Baseball contended with more than its share of drunken and disorderly male and female patrons. In Philadelphia, for example, the Phillies were forced to forfeit the second game of an August 21, 1949, doubleheader after an angry Shibe Park crowd pelted umpires with bottles. Yet the issue was more serious for black baseball, as a number of observers justifiably feared that fan behavior problems might limit future opportunities to use parks, and several major and minor league teams, already ambivalent about opening their facilities to black clubs, conveniently used the issue to terminate rental agreements. The Baltimore Elite Giants lost the use of Oriole Park in 1942 after supposed concerns over rowdy fans, while three years later, an incident involving a gun nearly cost league teams access to Red Bird Stadium in Columbus, Ohio. In Detroit, fighting and drinking episodes marred games at Briggs Stadium, and by 1946 the venue was once again closed to black teams. Columnist Russ Cowans linked the policy change to unruly behavior, citing fans who "broke the plumbing in the men's wash room, left more than 100 whiskey bottles beneath the grandstand, and did so much damage to the concession stand that the owner threatened suit against Briggs."[31]

There is little doubt that the sometimes disorderly atmosphere jeopardized rentals and occasionally discouraged patronage. Fay Young, for instance, not only argued that the "rowdy element . . . drives away the decent and peaceful Negro fan" but also alluded to its negative impact on the integration fight, noting that "no major league park wants its patronage routed to make room for the once-a-week (on Sunday) fan who insists on seeing his ball game with the help of the whiskey or gin bottle." In Kansas City, Johnny Johnson noted that many fans "sit in constant dread," anticipating the antisocial behavior of "crowd-clowns . . . spitting up vulgar words, pulling switchblades and otherwise acting like idiots." Meanwhile, NAACP executive secretary Walter White stopped attending league games in New York after tiring of the "drinking and loud-mouthed profanity, vulgarity and fighting of some colored fans." By 1947, new NNL president John Johnson admitted that the NNL had lost the support of some "family groups," and announced plans to emphasize better behavior at league parks.

While undoubtedly well founded, the concerns of White and others over fan behavior also reflected class divisions within the black community. At the baseball park and elsewhere, the black bourgeoisie persistently sought to steer the conduct of the working class toward white middle-class norms, arguing that poor behavior undermined potential racial advancement. Disturbed by the actions of some New York fans in 1943, Morgan-educated Joe Bostic noted that "it's so godawful that any anti-race propagandist sitting in would have himself a field day." Yet Bostic admitted that "it isn't fair that the best of us are judged by the worst." The controversy over behavior also underscored the differences between urban and rural blacks, as the New York-based Dan Burley, who resided in the then-exclusive Sugar Hill section, was embarrassed by "old fashioned people who bring their dinners to the ball park" and the conduct of southern migrants, many of whom had "not had a chance to learn how to act in public, certainly not at a baseball game."[32]

The supposed behavioral transgressions of rural southerners were of less concern to the industry than the very real existence of a small element of fans whose conduct not only annoyed other patrons but spilled into serious violence. Fearing that fighting or even a fatality might result in a loss of park privileges, a number of observers urged officials in both leagues to crack down on troublesome behavior more aggressively. Yet as renters rather than owners, black teams had little control over park security and often contended with white policemen unwilling to intervene, fearful that a strong show of force might provoke a race riot.

While remaining a major concern into the mid-1940s, park rowdyism failed to deter the vast number of faithful black fans who continued to attend the games without incident. Despite his disdain for the "obnoxious" fans who "gave all Negroes a bad name," Walter White believed the "overwhelming majority" behaved appropriately. Meanwhile, Effa Manley admitted that the behavior of some fans prompted "others to stay away from the park," yet nevertheless noted that "baseball is about the only healthy outdoor sport the Negro can enjoy without fear of segregation, and most of them really appreciate it."[33]

◆ ◆ ◆

Rising player salaries, larger crowds, and the increasing movement into major league facilities represented distinct advancements for black professional baseball from the Depression years. The encouraging gains, however, were more than offset by the alarming deficiencies still present in several areas integral to the successful operation of any professional league, most notably umpiring.

Poor umpiring had remained a chronic problem in the Negro Leagues since the formation of Rube Foster's original NNL in 1920. Emerging from a semiprofessional and sandlot milieu, black leagues were unable to fully discard the much maligned home umpire system, a practice in which the home team supplied the officiating crew for each game. The system predictably led to numerous abuses, as umpires, subject to the whims of individual owners, almost always favored the home team. During the 1920s, Bolden had strongly supported placing officials under league control as in Organized Baseball, and ultimately instituted a "rotating" umpire system in 1925 in the Eastern Colored League. Cost constraints, however, contributed to the experiment's abandonment after a single season, and a later attempt by the East-West League of 1932 failed for similar reasons.[34]

Forced to adapt to Depression conditions, Greenlee's newly formed NNL appeared resigned to the use of the unsuitable yet economical home umpire system. The ascension of Rollo Wilson to commissioner in 1934 and improving gate receipts, however, prompted subsequent modifications, including plans to employ at least one league-employed umpire in all games involving NNL teams. Following the aftermath of the 1934 playoff debacle, the NNL imposed more sweeping changes designed to "do away with any so-called homers," as eight umpires were hired at league expense to handle all games. Yet meager profits soon forced league officials to reconsider the policy, as Cum Posey complained of the $4,000 cost along with transportation expenses. By 1936, the NNL returned to a modified home umpire system, retaining three traveling league umps to handle behind-the-plate duties while allowing local officials to work the bases. With the exception of 1937, when six umpires were hired, the system remained in place for most of the next decade, as the league typically employed a skeleton crew of two to three salaried umpires augmented by additional arbiters supplied by the home team.[35]

While unable to maintain a full-time umpiring crew, the NNL did succeed in reducing black baseball's earlier reliance on white officials. During the 1920s, neither the eastern nor the western league had fully committed itself to black umpires, citing the lack of experienced African American arbiters and the belief that whites were more capable of enforcing discipline on the playing field. Increasingly race-conscious black fans, however, became less tolerant of the presence of white officials. In the subsequent Depression environment, most league owners were careful not to offend the racial and economic sensibilities of African Americans by employing whites. Not surprisingly, one fan viewed such a hiring policy as unjustifiable "when so many of ours are out of work." Moreover, keen-eyed observers such as Rollo Wilson recognized that white umpires were usually no better than black, noting that "many in both groups are mediocre." While urging the hiring of black officials, Wilson nevertheless advised the owners to "get men who are competent. Don't use them just because they are colored."

League patrons overwhelmingly preferred black umpires, regardless of their caliber. Yet white umpires never entirely disappeared from black baseball, typically officiating in interracial contests, non-league games played in smaller towns, and occasionally more important promotions. The East-West game, for example, employed several white umpires during the 1930s, while as late as 1947, a white official worked home plate during an NNL/NAL World Series game in Cleveland. Meanwhile, the Manleys often used a mixed umpiring crew at Ruppert Stadium, pairing Peter Strauch with a black league official.[36]

Regardless of racial identity, the umpiring in black baseball remained generally subpar. With whites dominating many of the officiating positions in earlier years, both the NNL and NAL found it difficult to find men with the necessary background to handle umpiring duties in a professional organization. As manager Jim Taylor explained in 1936, "our men start with little or no experience in the principles of umpiring. They read the rules but no one tells him how to apply them." Too often, the inexperienced arbiters missed obvious calls, earning for some the moniker of "dumpire" from Crawfords publicist John Clark. At Parkside Field in Philadelphia, for example, umpires were often out of position to make accurate judgments, while one official, Roland Rhodes, was notorious for mistakenly reversing the signals for out and safe to the confusion of fans and players. The employment of a number of former players including Phil Cockrell, Crush Holloway, and Frank Forbes failed to solve the problem, as Clark glumly noted that "it does not necessarily follow that a good ball player will develop into a good umpire."

Besides lacking proper training, officials were handicapped by the tenuous status of their position. Without an impartial president to oversee officials as in Organized Baseball, an umpire's continued employment hinged upon his ability to maintain cordial relations with individual owners, and as Jim Taylor quipped, "our umpires are afraid of one club owner today and another the next day." Not surprisingly, umpires often strongly favored the home team or faced the prospect of contending with an angry owner and potential dismissal. George Lyle, for example, noted that umpires leaned "noticeably, toward the hand which fed them," citing games in Newark and Trenton "where the Manley interests were protected at all costs." Meanwhile, Buck Leonard recalled that Homestead often "expected a favor" from umpire Moe Harris, an ex-Gray and brother of manager Vic Harris.[37]

Lacking independence from owners, umpires predictably possessed only marginal authority on the playing field, a fact quickly recognized by league players and managers always seeking an additional competitive edge. The decision of the umpire in a crucial situation was seldom accepted without dispute, often forcing fans and sportswriters to suffer through tedious arguments lasting 15 to 30 minutes. By 1936, Ed Harris complained that "delays, needless squabbles and other hindrances make the greater number of the games sad affairs and very boring," while Cum Posey agreed that umpires allowed games "to drag along entirely too long." Two years later, Fay Young claimed that J. L. Wilkinson had to pay an extra $20 for park rentals at night, as "it takes our ball clubs on an average of 17 minutes more to play a game than it does white ball clubs."

The general failure of umpires to maintain control contributed to the persistence of violent episodes on the playing field, a serious, yet chronic problem in black baseball. Umpire assaults had marred the earlier leagues of the 1920s, as neither western nor eastern officials had been consistently able to enforce penalties even remotely comparable to the fines and suspensions mandated in Organized Baseball. Fearful of losing their best drawing cards, owners often obstructed disciplinary attempts, allowing players to escape serious punishment.[38]

Greenlee's NNL would soon face the same difficulties with curbing on-field violence. To his credit, Rollo Wilson made a genuine attempt to address the issue during his only year as commissioner in 1934, issuing a pre-season statement to players warning that "the fans are going out to see you play baseball; when they want to see fights, they know where to go." Moreover, Wilson slapped $10 fines and three-game suspensions on several players who struck umpires, including the always volatile Jud Wilson. Yet Wilson's highly publicized assault of umpire Gholston during the playoffs and lack of subsequent punishment revealed the still glaring weaknesses in the NNL's policies.

Although the league subsequently toughened its penalties by imposing a $25 fine and ten-day suspension, violence toward umpires continued to plague black baseball. Tired of Jud Wilson's endless stream of altercations with officials, a disgusted fan in July 1936 asked "why don't they fine him or do something about that sort of bad acting?" Two weeks later, Ed Harris warned that "the incidents that have been happening behind the stands between players and umpires have gotta stop before somebody lands in the hoosegow." Yet the absence of strong league administration capable of providing adequate support of its officials ensured that violence would remain an all-too-common occurrence. As NAL umpire Virgil

Blueitt explained, "if the club owners would order their managers and players to abide by the umpires' rulings, much of this trouble could be avoided. . . . League officials will have to stand by the umpires, just as is done in white leagues, and then the players won't try a lot of things that they now can get by with."[39]

The plight of league umpires reached a disturbing nadir in the late 1930s. Unable to prevent its players from jumping to foreign locales, the league proved equally unsuccessful in maintaining discipline on the field. In 1937, the NNL was rocked by an almost unbelievable series of violent episodes involving umpires and players. After a June 5 game in Philadelphia, members of the New York Black Yankees attacked Frank Forbes, who would be involved in another brawl with Newark manager Tex Burnett several days later. In July, Forbes and umpire Jasper "Jap" Washington encountered the wrath of several angry Elite Giants, who broke into the umpires' dressing room at Parkside Field, prompting Washington's subsequent resignation.

As usual, the always sluggish league administration was slow to respond, although Cum Posey admitted that "the umpires of the league are working for an honest living and do not deserve the abuse they are getting from all concerned without the least bit of help from the league owners." Greenlee, however, issued a toughly worded statement in June announcing that six players and managers had been fined $10 to $25, while insisting that "rowdyism in the Negro National League will not be tolerated any longer. . . . If patrons want to see fist fights, they'll go to prizefights. But I believe patrons . . . want to see baseball, and that is what they will see, if I have to fine every player in the league." By late July, the league finally promised full support of the demoralized umpires and also planned sanctions against stalling, profanity, and other player misbehavior.

Despite the apparent shift in policy, several league owners continued to undermine the authority of umpires, particularly when it threatened the status of their own players. In 1938, Elite Giants outfielder Bill Wright was suspended by the league after pushing an umpire. After the Elites ignored the ruling and continued to play Wright, umpire James Crump forfeited a subsequent game to the team's opponent. The move elicited a typical response, as the unfortunate Crump was assaulted by manager George Scales, "severely mussed up" by players, and then summarily released as a league umpire, either at the behest of Elites owner Tom Wilson or Gus Greenlee. While the Crump incident once again demonstrated the crying need for an impartial independent administration, the league took only tentative steps, ruling in February 1939 that no umpire could be fired without a hearing or the votes of four of the six franchises, and that owners and other team officials involved in confrontations with umpires would now be subject to fines.[40]

The new policy had little effect on players, who continued to exert their will with little real fear of repercussion. In July 1939, for example, owner Hank Rigney of the Toledo Crawfords reported an incident involving the Grays, particularly Josh Gibson, who "called the umpire the vilest kind of names and refused to leave the field even when police ordered him out. The fans were even on the field. Finally the police sent in a riot call. . . . It was the worst trouble we ever experienced here." In the midwest, Fay Young identified equally bad behavior in the NAL in 1939, even witnessing a player's attempt to hit an umpire with the ball. With the major league integration fight intensifying, Young also worried about the effect of such conduct on the campaign, noting that "now since there is a demand, we have got to put a halter on some of these bad actors."

The "bad actors" common in the 1930s were hardly limited to black baseball, as the minor and major leagues contended with more than their share of problematic conduct. White and black leagues both employed a number of men whose impoverished backgrounds and limited educational opportunities often shaped their on- and off-field behavior. Meanwhile, the presence of college-educated players became increasingly less frequent in black baseball after the financially driven decision of most black colleges to drop the sport after the onset of the Depression. Instead, a rough and tough quality characterized many players, the majority of whom emerged from either the harsh surroundings of northern ghettos or the poorest parts of the segregated south, and perhaps not surprisingly, the behavior of black teams (and their fans) did not always conform to middle-class norms. By 1940, Dan Burley complained that the players "over the years . . . haven't behaved with any too much gentle decorum," citing "angry players chasing umpires with bats; spitting at the fans in the stands; cursing opposing players; reporting to practice and to play under the influence of liquor and a number of other incidents that haven't done Negro baseball a bit of good."[41]

Burley's bleak description, however, failed to acknowledge the presence of a considerable segment of quieter and more gentlemanly players who seldom created problems for owners, fans, umpires, or opponents. Frazier Robinson, for example, disapproved of Ted Radcliffe and Willie Wells, who "carried on in public, talked bad about women, and didn't act like gentlemen." On the Philadelphia Stars, Eddie Gottlieb touted Webster McDonald, a manager who disliked profanity among his players, as a "very distinct type and easy to get along with," although Gottlieb confided to Effa Manley that McDonald "surely is the exception rather than the rule." Monte Irvin praised Buck Leonard as "an intelligent and compassionate guy," yet similarly recognized that such a player was "rare in those days." Notably, despite Leonard's presence on the Grays, Cum Posey lamented that "regardless of how much money is paid a player, or how good he is treated, he still 'breaks loose' practically every night."

Yet Posey and other owners were hardly in a strong position to preach good conduct to their players on or off the playing field. As noted earlier, several league officials had profited through illegal enterprises, prompting Wendell Smith's cruel but not entirely inaccurate observation that "few . . . respect baseball laws, or any other kind of law." Others, while not involved in criminal activities, were hardly paragons of sportsmanship. Posey, for example, was a notorious umpire-baiter, and a number of owners enjoyed betting, despite objections to the wagering habits of their own players. Even Bolden, who had earned a reputation for "fair dealing and clean playing" and preferred that his Hilldale players be "gentlemen," largely turned a blind eye to the umpire-terrorizing antics of two of his managers, Jud Wilson and Goose Curry.[42]

Although most officials recognized that continued rowdyism antagonized fans and the press, the always prevalent individualism in the league's administrative structure undermined any decisive attempt to curb player misconduct. Seemingly ambivalent about any policy that might adversely affect their own franchise, NNL owners instead clung to an ineffectual system of fines ranging by 1940 from $10 for an ejection to $25 and a three-game suspension for striking an umpire. The policy, however, deterred few players, as the money, if actually collected, was deducted from the team's share of game receipts. Following a June 1940 fistfight at Parkside Field involving Pee Wee Butts of the Elite Giants and umpire Phil Cockrell, the NNL attempted to strengthen its penalties, ruling that players involved in a second attack on an umpire would face a $50 fine/ten-day suspension and a third incident would result in a yearlong ban from league baseball. Yet, like the league's seemingly stern rulings on contract jumpers, the actual enforcement remained minimal, hindered by justifiable fears that chastised marquee players would simply take their skills to Mexico or other foreign leagues.

As the black baseball industry grew more profitable during the war years, the problem of disciplining wayward players became an increasingly pressing issue. Now relying heavily on major and minor league parks to maximize profits, owners not only fretted over the conduct of fans but worried about a potentially damaging incident on the field. Fortunately for league officials, violent episodes initially appeared to level off somewhat, a development recognized by umpire Johnny Craig, who marveled at the improved behavior of NNL teams during 1942.[43]

Players in both leagues, however, would relapse during 1943, a year marked by several ugly brawls at Organized Baseball parks. In early June, Effa Manley disclosed to Tom Wilson that during a game at Ruppert Stadium, a Black Yankee player "beat an umpire up so badly the umpire had to have two stitches taken in his face." While deducting $25 from the team's share, Manley admitted that "this is really not enough punishment for a thing of this kind" and noted that white newspapers had publicized the story. Three weeks later, Fay Young reported that Alex Radcliffe of the American Giants took "exactly 11 pokes at the umpire" during a game at Comiskey Park, eventually requiring the intervention of four policemen. While Cum Posey subsequently warned NNL owners of the growing "tendency of players to pull and shove umpires," particularly in interleague games, neither league made any special attempt to address the matter, other than by the usual fines.[44]

By mid-1945, the authority of umpires had fallen to a dangerously low level in both leagues. Despite fines and promises of support from league owners, the unfortunate arbiters remained as vulnerable as ever to assaults from angry players, demonstrated by a flurry of damaging incidents at major league parks that summer. In New York, umpire Bert Gholston barely "escaped with his life" at the Polo Grounds after narrowly avoiding a bat-wielding Louis Louden of the New York Cubans on May 30. Umpire Jimmy Thompson was less fortunate, suffering a broken nose at the hands of Piper Davis of the Birmingham Black Barons before a startled crowd of 12,733 fans at Cleveland's Municipal Stadium on July 16. Unlike Gholston, Thompson subsequently pursued legal action, a sensible response to the multiple unpunished assaults on umpires in the past, although J. B. Martin did slap Davis with an indefinite suspension and a fine of $50 (later raised to $250). While Thompson ultimately won the case against Davis, who was forced to pay $230 in court costs and damages, some observers viewed the penalty as inadequate. Cleveland sportswriter Bob Williams, for example, complained that Thompson had been "jived into withdrawing the assault and battery charges," and reported that the suspension of Davis had remained in force only while the case was awaiting trial.

Perhaps the worst incident occurred on June 17 at Wrigley Field, a venue only recently opened to black teams. Following a disputed decision, Jim Ford of the Memphis Red Sox struck umpire Roy Young and then grabbed a bat, leading fans to anticipate further violence. Other Memphis players joined the fray, including one player later accused of brandishing a knife, and manager Larry Brown, who threatened to pull his team off the field until dissuaded by the prospect of a permanent ban from ballparks. Despite the presence of NAL president J. B. Martin, order was not restored until policemen hauled Ford away, finally allowing the game to resume.

Figure 21. White umpire Peter Strauch endures the wrath of Philadelphia Stars mana
Goose Curry after a disputed call in Newark, May 5, 1946. Several policemen eventua
escorted Curry from the field. Courtesy Schomburg Center for Research in Black Cultu
New York Public Library.

The aftermath of the incident confirmed the worst fears of league owners. Cubs officials, long reluctant to open the park to black baseball and
leery of a potential lawsuit, promptly raised the minimum rental fee to a
prohibitive $5,000, effectively shutting league teams out for the remainder
of the season and the foreseeable future. The decision was entirely justifiable, for, as Fay Young noted, the promotions at Wrigley Field, a venue
relatively distant from Chicago's black community, were hardly profitable
enough to offset the risks involved in dealing with leagues seemingly unable to control their players. As one anonymous major league official explained, "when teams walk off the field and players hit umpires in our
parks we are just as responsible as anyone else. . . . It is difficult to understand why the presidents of the two leagues fail to realize the seriousness
of the situation." While admitting the failure of the NAL's current disci-

plinary measures and recognizing that continued violence "will kill our baseball," J. B. Martin appeared unable to address the situation beyond announcing the usual plans for fines and suspensions.[45]

The action of the Cubs drew little criticism, as most fans and sportswriters had tired of the perpetual cycle of violence on the playing field. As a disgusted Chicagoan observed, "is there any wonder that the big leagues bar these fellows? They want to be a Joe Louis, DiMaggio, and Hitler—all in one. Let's stop the fight for Negroes in the big leagues long enough to straighten ourselves out." Yet some observers also wondered whether the Wrigley episode might prompt other Organized Baseball teams to enact similar policies in response to continued rowdyism. After witnessing shortstop Frank Austin let his bat fly toward the pitcher following a knockdown pitch in August 1945, Rollo Wilson worried about the effect on future Shibe Park appearances, noting that "Ed Bolden and Ed Gottlieb have been selling Connie Mack on the proposition that colored teams are good tenants and that their followers are just like other group[s] of fans." Fortunately for the Stars, Austin's ejection, suspension, and fine apparently placated Shibe officials, along with the continued profitability of NNL rentals.[46]

Despite the potential loss of additional venues, neither league succeeded in eliminating on-field violence, although heftier penalties ($100/10-day suspension in the NNL by 1946) and the potential negative effect on a player's future opportunities in Organized Baseball probably helped deter subsequent incidents. Nevertheless, the life of an umpire remained dangerous, prompting some to carry knives or guns for protection, and a modest pay scale further discouraged entrance into the hazardous profession. During the Depression years, wages in both leagues remained low, failing to match the $7 to $8 per game received by umpires in the late 1920s at Hilldale Park. As late as 1939, for example, the NNL's two full-time officials earned only $130 per month, while home plate umpires collected $5 for a single game and $7.50 for a doubleheader.[47]

With the prosperity of the early 1940s, umpires increasingly pressed for higher salaries yet as Fred McCrary complained, "we . . . never get anything or any consideration from the League: we only go on and work on a basis of 'dog take what we give you.'" Hoping to win better pay and working conditions, McCrary and several other eastern officials joined together in 1944 to form the Negro Professional Umpires' Association. Rather than use the opportunity to demonstrate their support, the NNL reacted defensively, as Cum Posey demanded to know who had granted them permission to organize and then publicly condemned the caliber of officiating. After league officials refused to accede to their salary demands for 1945, the umpires responded by sitting out the early games of the season. The owners, however, simply found replacements, although fans responded negatively to the presence of white officials at a league double-header at the Polo Grounds on April 29.

Recognizing their increasingly fragile status, the umpires began to waver, and by May 10 a nervous McCrary wrote to Effa Manley, ostensibly attempting to reclaim his full-time salaried position in the NNL. Claiming "Dictator Cum Posey's ideas" had resulted in his current separation from the league, McCrary explained that he had participated in the walkout because of pressure from other umpires who had called him a "heel" and suggested that he "didn't want them to better themselves because I was on salary and was satisfied." Moreover, McCrary claimed that he had advised his fellow umpires that their demands were too high but "I was in the chair and they voted unanimously for the Prices." Within two days, Mc-Crary was back with the NNL and the remaining resistance collapsed.

Despite the failure of the walkout, the salary scale for umpires did improve during the war years. By July 1945, team-selected home plate umpires earned $10 for an individual game and $15 per doubleheader, double the rates of six years earlier. Meanwhile, McCrary and other full-time officials enjoyed similar increases, reaching $300 per month by 1946. The authority of umpires, however, still remained weak, an inevitable result of the chronically weak administration within black baseball. As long as self-interested owners remained in full control of league affairs and lacked the collective will to enforce discipline, violence remained more likely to occur than in Organized Baseball, although the minor leagues in particular had more than their share of problems. Ultimately, the NNL and NAL created a nearly impossible environment for umpires, who remained dependent on the owners for their continued employment yet carried minimal authority on the playing field. The consistently mediocre quality of the officiating in the Negro Leagues is hardly surprising, as even an experienced and well-trained umpire would have found it difficult to perform effectively.[48]

◆ ◆ ◆

The minimal authority on the field was matched by an equally weak legal hold over players, as already seen in the numerous defections to foreign countries in the late 1930s and early 1940s. For decades, white Organized Baseball had employed contracts featuring the almost airtight reserve clause, leaving player movement solely to the discretion of the clubs, which retained continual control over a player's services. While the Eastern Colored League and NNL of the 1920s had instituted a crude form of the reserve clause to curb contract jumping, neither league succeeded in matching the firm control over players enjoyed by major and minor league teams. Leery of potential financial and legal obligations, black teams generally continued to prefer less formal agreements that contained no language reserving a player beyond the current season. Such contracts were common in independent/semiprofessional leagues whose administrative practices the Negro Leagues often closely followed, yet would prove increasingly unsuitable as the industry developed by the 1940s.

Perhaps even more problematic was the questionable decision of some clubs to avoid the use of contracts altogether. Roy Campanella, who spent his entire NNL career with Tom Wilson's Elite Giants, claimed that he never signed a contract and doubted that "half of the players in the league" were bound by a formal agreement. As late as 1945, the generally well-run Kansas City Monarchs declined to tender Jackie Robinson a contract, informing him that correspondence from co-owner Tom Baird was "all the contract I needed." The rationale behind such a practice was clearly financial, as Robinson later explained that "they didn't know whether or not I would make good, so they didn't want to have trouble getting rid of me."[49]

Such makeshift agreements between players and teams resulted in numerous predictable abuses, but even written contracts lacked legal force. As Ed Harris noted in 1941, the leagues persisted in using contracts "not witnessed by notaries. Very easy to break those kind." The files of the Newark Eagles, for example, contain dozens of player contracts from the early 1940s, yet not one appears to be notarized or approved by a neutral third party. Not surprisingly, players consistently exploited the numerous contract loopholes, although the Grays' triumph in the 1941 Josh Gibson case revealed the legal force of more detailed agreements. The shortsighted yet cost-efficient preference for flimsy contracts left black teams constantly vulnerable, leading Dan Burley to assert that "the owners . . . are at the mercies of the player who might jump or not even between games if enough money is waved at all."

The weak agreements, however, appealed to the owners by minimizing their own obligations and responsibilities to their employees. Major league contracts, for example, stipulated that players who suffered game-related disabilities were still entitled to their full season's pay, yet black teams seldom hesitated to discharge men who were injured and unable to perform. During 1940, the Homestead Grays released Josh Johnson because of injury, while the Newark Eagles dropped Daltie Cooper after the veteran pitcher fractured his foot while running to first base. Refusing to accept the usual fate of the incapacitated NNL player, Cooper took his case to the Workmen's Compensation Bureau of the New Jersey Department of Labor. Surprisingly, a referee not only ruled that the Eagles were liable but forced the Manleys to admit that their players were not covered by disability insurance, as required by law.[50]

Cooper's victory, however, prompted few reforms in black baseball's contractual agreements. Until the shock of Organized Baseball integration in the mid-1940s, the owners remained content to function within an unsatisfactory system that offered little protection but occasionally allowed considerable leeway with players. Not surprisingly, the haphazard approach to contracts resulted in phenomena largely unique to black baseball, including the questionable practice of "lending" players for a single game (often an exhibition) or longer. The Philadelphia Stars, for example, reportedly received Henry Spearman from the Baltimore Elite Giants under such a long-term arrangement and later lent the services of Roy Partlow to the Homestead Grays in 1943, prompting an incredulous Rollo Wilson to comment "how come we never heard THAT ONE before."

The lending of players, like all player transactions in black baseball, ultimately depended upon an individual's willingness to report to another club. Lacking the legal force to control player movement as in Organized Baseball, owners exercised particular caution attempting to bolster their rosters. Effa Manley, for example, contacted Leon Ruffin prior to initiating a trade in 1939, noting that she would not pursue a deal "unless I am sure you will play for me after I do. If I give up a man for you and then you dont [sic] report I will be left short a man."

In reality, only the informal "gentleman's agreements" among league owners, not the contracts themselves, prevented more serious difficulties with unrestricted player movement, although such arrangements provided teams with no protection from outside forces, including foreign leagues and subsequently Organized Baseball. Moreover, as already seen, tampering among league teams was relatively prevalent, particularly during the less structured decade of the 1930s, prompting Cum Posey's 1937 suggestion that "if a league club feels that the only way to strengthen their club is to deal with players, then this club should get out of the league and dicker with whom they please." Yet two years later, the Grays apparently encouraged the accomplished pitcher Raymond Brown to offer his services to other NNL franchises, earning a sharp rebuke from Abe Manley, who considered it "ridiculous to refer him to some other Club, as we are all in one Organization, and should try to strengthen the Organization."

Weak or absent contracts undoubtedly represented a serious flaw in black baseball's operations during the 1930s and 1940s, not only costing teams players but larger credibility among fans. Although several officials and sportswriters consistently advocated stronger contracts, more budget-conscious owners stymied attempts at reform and continued to maintain only the flimsiest of agreements with their players. Without an outside mandate, both leagues lacked the will to rectify the system's obvious deficiencies, a decision that would prove costly in the future.[51]

◆   ◆   ◆

Lagging far behind Organized Baseball in the caliber of its umpires and player contracts, the NNL and NAL also contended with glaring weaknesses in other areas essential to the smooth running of a successful professional organization, particularly scheduling. In contrast to major league clubs which played 154 official games each season divided evenly among their seven opponents, black teams seldom played more than 70 to 80 league games and filled out the rest of their schedules with exhibitions. Between April 25 and September 22, 1936, for example, the Crawfords participated in 132 games, fewer than half of them league contests, while five years later, 60 of Baltimore's 127 games involved non-league teams.

Two major factors contributed to the chronic scheduling difficulties in black baseball. First, the limited financial resources of African Americans permanently mitigated against daily league baseball, as black fans were simply unable to support league games on more than a once or twice weekly basis, usually attending a night game during the week along with a Saturday or Sunday promotion. Perhaps more importantly, the majority of league teams had virtually no control over their home park and could only secure the grounds when not in use by a major or minor league club. Left with a limited number of open dates, both the NNL and NAL annually faced the nightmarish task of attempting to arrange an equitable schedule that employed minimal travel yet simultaneously allowed teams the flexibility to participate in non-league games.

Not surprisingly, the NNL pursued numerous strategies to supplement the few dates available, occasionally leasing neutral parks in nearby cities such as Paterson, Trenton, Chester, and Wilmington for additional games. Beginning in 1934, the league also increasingly utilized a practice largely unique to black baseball, scheduling doubleheaders involving three or four teams at major or minor league parks. While the promotions were generally successful and ensured that at least half the league clubs were not idle, several observers questioned their ultimate value, suggesting that fans who grew accustomed to seeing doubleheaders at a regular admission price would not support a single game. Meanwhile, Cum Posey suggested the four-team features epitomized the often fragile economic status of black baseball, observing that "clubs admit their shallow drawing power by having four clubs play the same date in one park and split the net receipts four ways." Finally, the multi-team doubleheaders did little to spread fan interest throughout the NNL, occasionally limiting league baseball to only two cities on a given date. The problem became particularly acute in 1944, when all six NNL teams appeared simultaneously in New York on Sunday, May 21 at the Polo Grounds and Ebbets Field, prompting Wendell Smith to term the situation "one of the worst in baseball history. Who ever heard of every single team in a league playing in the same city on the same day?"[52]

Unfortunately, such occurrences were common in black baseball schedules, which fell far short of the ideal Organized Baseball standard. The NNL, for example, typically strove to arrange schedules to allow each team 10 games against each league opponent, only to be undermined by unforeseen circumstances, including weather-related postponements that could not be rescheduled. Moreover, financial considerations affected the playing of scheduled games, as league teams often declined to participate in potentially unprofitable promotions. The Black Yankees' occasionally cavalier attitude toward league games prompted Effa Manley to complain to Black Yankees owner James Semler in 1938 that "you have cancelled so many in the past." Marginal gate receipts similarly dissuaded eastern clubs from traveling to Pittsburgh in the late 1930s, eliciting criticism from Cum Posey and Wendell Smith. Yet Posey's Grays were equally willing to forsake league play, reportedly contemplating a ten-day "leave" in 1939 to barnstorm in the Northwest, while four years later, Alex Pompez's New York Cubans cancelled games with Newark for a similar western jaunt.

To one sportswriter, the occasionally ambivalent attitude toward league competition was a serious problem and "one of the reasons why the National Association is no stronger than it is." Black teams, however, had little choice but to maximize their income whenever and wherever possible during the five- to six-month season, and, as Dan Burley explained, "have to play more outside ball than they do the league variety to earn enough money to keep going." Despite the growing profitability of league ball in the 1940s, games with white semipros remained an unavoidable part of each team's schedule. As Effa Manley noted in 1941, "the problem that confronts us is, we can get a guarantee to go to a park and play a semipro club, where we are gambling when we go to a strange park to play each other." As late as July 1943, Rollo Wilson reported that during a recent holiday, only four NNL teams participated in league games, as the Grays scheduled a doubleheader with the white Brooklyn Bushwicks while the Black Yankees were either idle or involved in non-league competition.[53]

Although accepting the necessity of occasional non-league interracial competition, black fans and sportswriters were less tolerant of the phenomena of meaningless exhibition games scheduled between NNL teams during the regular season. In contrast to Organized Baseball, where every game counted in the final standings, the NNL was forced to designate a sizable number of contests unofficial to prevent teams from manipulating an already unbalanced schedule. Reflecting the view of a number of observers, sportswriter Art Carter hoped the league would discard its "silly exhibitions," yet as Cum Posey explained, any attempt to transcend the current system "positively will not work . . . it will give one of the pennant contenders a chance to play the weakest club in the league 10 or more consecutive games . . . and walk off with a pennant." Instead, the NNL typically permitted a maximum of 10 to 12 games against each league opponent and labeled additional contests exhibitions.

In reality, the system created as many problems as it was designed to rectify. Too often, the distinction between league and exhibition games was unclear, reportedly prompting some players to question fans as to the status of a contest. Moreover, the decision to designate a game unofficial often appeared arbitrary. Grays owner Rufus Jackson, for example, complained that a scheduled league game at Yankee Stadium between the Stars and Elites in 1943 became an exhibition contest simply by a joint agreement of the two managers to make the switch. Finally, as noted, exhibition games simply did not always offer fans the best caliber league ball. To future NNL president Reverend John H. Johnson, the exhibitions were little more than "circuses with a lot of drinking and with no competitive element," noting that black fans were "paying good money to see a game. You don't go to see Joe Louis box an exhibition bout . . . it's not fair competition."

Interleague games were similarly marred by their unofficial status. Inexplicably, the NNL and NAL appeared reluctant to devise a system to allow the contests to count in the standings, although league officials may have believed that the NNL had an unfair advantage in interleague competition, as most games were scheduled at eastern venues. Despite the policy, appearances by the Kansas City Monarchs and other NAL clubs were popular in eastern cities after 1940, as the relative novelty of the clubs transcended the meaninglessness of the games. In addition, more than a few of the fans were probably unaware of the unofficial nature of the contests, as was the press at times. Rollo Wilson, for example, noted in 1944 that "writers on the daily papers look at you in surprise when you say to them at Shibe Park: 'these are not league games.' "[54]

Despite the increasing use and availability of Organized Baseball parks during the early 1940s, the scheduling woes in black baseball remained largely intact. In 1942, the entire NNL played only 98 official league games, ranging from 22 for the New York Cubans to 41 for the Philadelphia Stars, whereas in the NAL Fay Young reported that the Cleveland Buckeyes failed to make a single appearance in Chicago all season. Although the NNL subsequently improved slightly, averaging 113 league contests over the next three years, not one club participated in more than 50 official league games per season. As long as the bulk of black teams rented rather than owned parks, a balanced schedule comparable to even the lowest white minor league was impossible to achieve, although considerable room for improvement existed. To some observers, however, black baseball's ability to function at all within such disadvantageous circumstances represented an achievement of sorts and as journalist Harold Winston noted in 1952, "mister, it took real organization to make a league like that operate."[55]

Perhaps the industry's greatest organizational feat was not the schedule but the annual East-West promotion at Comiskey Park. Unlike the often expensive, prolonged, and unprofitable playoffs, the East-West game perfectly suited the economics of black baseball, offering a single summer promotion on a Sunday, the best day for attendance, and in Chicago, home of the nation's second largest African American community. Attracting sizable crowds even during the Depression years, the game reached an unprecedented level of success in the early 1940s, demonstrating to Wendell Smith that "baseball is the No. 1 sports attraction in so far as Negroes are concerned. No even Joe Louis—as great as he is—has ever been able to attract 50,000 Negroes at any of his great fights."

Not surprisingly, the sheer enormity of the event prompted the always thrifty owners to keep a particularly close watch over the division of the gate receipts. Initially, the three original promoters (Greenlee, Cole, and Wilson) received the bulk of the profits, although the league treasury began to receive a portion of the proceeds by the mid-1930s. After the departure of Greenlee and Cole from the NNL and the formation of the NAL, both leagues eventually devised an agreement allowing each club an equal portion of the net. In 1942, for instance, the game grossed $48,916.10. After deduction of taxes, park rental fees, and other costs, 10 percent of the balance was allocated to the two presidents and the remainder divided between the two leagues. Receiving $13,162.37 as its share, the NNL then earmarked a portion for player and other miscellaneous expenses, another 5 percent to the league treasury, and the rest to the six franchises. Each club ultimately collected nearly $2,000, providing a fresh influx of cash for financially borderline teams and confirming James Semler's subsequent assertion that "the game is played to keep us owners from taking a loss for the season's play."[56]

For two leagues often unable or unwilling to cooperate on the most basic of issues, the seemingly equitable disbursement of gate receipts among 12 teams represented a substantial achievement. Yet the allocation of East-West profits remained far from perfect, as a number of observers questioned the 10 percent granted to the league presidents in lieu of a fixed annual salary. Moreover, both men received additional shares as team owners, while Martin also profited through his involvement in the sale of souvenir programs.

Despite the rapidly increasing East-West earnings of Martin, Wilson, and other league officials by the early 1940s, the players' share of the game grew more slowly. During the early years of the promotion, the players struggled to receive any form of financial consideration for their participation, contending with the attitude of one owner who noted that "they are on salary anyhow, and we don't need to give them anything." As Randy Dixon quipped, the typical player during the Depression years was given "a sombrero . . . a package of fig newtons and a bonus amounting to the price of two Mexican hot weiners, chili sauce added free." By 1939, however, each player was paid $25, a substantial improvement from the $5 grudgingly granted four years earlier.

With the game consistently drawing over 40,000 fans in the early 1940s, the players began to clamor aggressively for a larger share of the profits. In 1942, the NNL representatives successfully wrested an additional $25 from the owners, while western players also won concessions. A year later, NAL officials yielded to Satchel Paige's demand for $800, annoying some players who received far less for their participation and setting the stage for a future clash. Attempting to boost his fee further in 1944, Paige encountered stiffer resistance, prompting a public announcement that he would boycott the game unless his demands were met. Moreover, Paige insisted that he would donate his entire share to Army/Navy charity and urged the leagues to follow suit, arguing that "colored baseball has grown up. It's big time. But they're not thinkin'. They're greedy for money."

Despite Paige's claim that the sight of wounded soldiers had inspired his altruistic attitude, a number of observers suggested that the rejection of his fee had been the actual motivation. Fay Young, for example, wondered "when did he suddenly become so patriotic" and questioned why Paige had done little charitable work to date. While the publicity surrounding the episode proved somewhat embarrassing and raised issues about the black baseball's wartime charity commitment, the leagues refused to succumb, and, as J. B. Martin noted, "Paige is not running Negro baseball. If he wants to stay out of the game it is alright with us."[57]

The resolution of the Paige controversy, however, hardly ended the owners' difficulties with player compensation in 1944. Reportedly encouraged by the exiled Gus Greenlee, the NNL team threatened to sit out the game unless their pay was hiked to $200 per man, while NAL players demanded a $75 raise to $100. The issue of Paige's $800 fee in 1943 likely factored into the dispute, as one player complained that "we're sick of being exploited for the sake of a select few." Not surprisingly, the players hardly hesitated to employ similar tactics in the future. Two years later, NAL players insisted on an extra $50 for participation in an eastern promotion in Washington, prompting a dismayed Alex Pompez to protest that "this sort of thing every time we have an all-star game has got to stop. You're doing nothing but sending your own baseball to ruin."[58]

The disputes over player compensation revealed that the East-West game, black baseball's most successful feature, was hardly immune to the administrative deficiencies common throughout the industry. As late as 1942, Art Carter felt the game was "still promoted on a ten-cent basis," citing players clad in dirty uniforms, while Fay Young criticized problems with ticket availability. Meanwhile, the occasional attempts to mirror the major league all-star game by allowing fans to select players through voting proved largely unsuccessful, as leagues already unable to compile accurate statistics were hardly in a position to tabulate thousands of ballots. Nevertheless, black newspapers dutifully published the supposed results of the voting, although Rollo Wilson noted that "I know several baseball bugs here and there but I never yet have talked with one who had sent in a list of his favorite players." Ed Harris was equally dubious, suggesting in 1941 that "now everyone who has his ear cocked to the windward knows that Cum Posey sits in his den and makes up all these statistics." Harris's assessment proved largely correct, as Posey later privately admitted to "juggling votes so we could get three men off a team and have the public think they were picking them." By 1943, Wilson advised the two leagues to "abandon the childish publicity about the fans selecting the members. . . . Nobody is being fooled and it serves no good purpose."[59]

Despite intermittent difficulties, the East-West game was generally promoted at a far higher level than the typical black baseball attraction, contributing to its enviable success. Nevertheless, too many league owners remained oblivious to importance of effective publicity and other promotional devices to build attendance during the regular season, apparently secure that black fans, lacking a real alternative, would continue to patronize their games. As in the past, most teams relied upon relatively cost-efficient means to attract fans, inserting an occasional advertisement or press release in the local black newspaper or employing men such as Frank Forbes in New York, who helped drum up community interest by making "personal contacts, visiting barber shops, beauty parlors and scores of other places." Posters and sound wagons were also employed to announce an upcoming game, although Dan Burley dismissed their impact, scorning the "spectacle of a horse wagon parading through the streets with garish signs painted all over it" and suggesting that fans "don't pay attention to window cards hidden in dingy store windows or stuck up on a wall overlooking a vacant lot."

To boost attendance, several observers urged more extensive development of "knot hole gangs" to stimulate interest among youngsters. The issue appeared crucial to Jim Taylor, who contended that by 1935, the majority of black fans were over thirty, while Burley subsequently suggested that "our kids grow up not knowing a single Negro ball player by name or sight." Despite the need to create future fans, the leagues never launched a sustained attempt to build attendance among children, although the Eagles and Crawfords sometimes admitted youngsters for free. The Kansas City Monarchs, however, not only helped subsidize a local sandlot club but invited its members to a league game at Blues Stadium in 1946. Perhaps more than any other club, the Monarchs recognized the importance of cultivating a close relationship with local black residents and the business community. Not surprisingly, the team's well-organized and active Booster's club was the envy of both leagues, enabling the Monarchs' attendance to remain strong despite the city's relatively modest black population.[60]

While Cum Posey suggested that "it would be a wonderful thing to have Boosters' Associations in every league city," most teams lacked a comparable organization to help generate interest and support of the local franchise. Moreover, few publicity outlets were accessible, as black baseball had virtually no radio exposure (except on rare occasions) or coverage in nationally distributed periodicals such as the *Sporting News*. Instead, the sports pages of the black press remained the primary source available to dispense the latest baseball news and maintain the interest of fans throughout the year. Although some teams employed local weeklies effectively, too many clubs failed to exploit the press to its full advantage. The quality and quantity of material provided by league officials often frustrated sports editors such as Johnny Johnson of the *Kansas City Call* who remarked that "Negro baseball is probably the only going concern that has never seen the wisdom of utilizing qualified publicity agents. Just anybody can write their . . . copy and judging from the kind of releases that are usually received, just anybody does."[61]

Lacking the resources to cover teams on a daily basis, black newspapers were forced to rely heavily on club-issued press releases that typically focused more on upcoming promotions than on recent games. Although journalist Lem Graves advised one NNL owner that "our readers are interested in the results of games much more so than . . . advance publicity," sports editors continued to struggle to receive box scores and accounts of contests scheduled away from home. Information on losses was particularly difficult to obtain, reflecting black teams' roots in semiprofessional baseball, where clubs were equally reticent to publicize adverse outcomes, fearing the impact on future bookings.[62]

If publicity during the regular season was generally mediocre, coverage of league teams during the fall and winter months was almost nonexistent. In contrast to the abundant news of major league trades, contracts, and the annual winter meetings in December, black teams had little to offer the press during the off season. The paucity of information frustrated not only sportswriters but also league officials such as Cum Posey, who wrote Effa Manley in March 1939 requesting that she "send me some thing concerning your club for the papers. No club sends me any thing and I do not wish to send out articles . . . with nothing but Grays activities." Two months later, the Eagles were still unaware of the composition of the Baltimore Elite Giants, forcing Abe Manley to contact Tom Wilson for player names and uniform numbers.

While financial constraints contributed to at least some of the difficulties in keeping fans, writers, and owners adequately informed, the administrative lethargy throughout the industry was equally to blame. Regardless of income, most teams were capable of exerting considerably more time and effort into publicity. Providing basic biographical data on players, for instance, was hardly a difficult or expensive task, yet examples such as the four page "Elite Giants' News" in 1940 and press guides issued by the Buckeyes and Cubans in 1948 remained a rarity. With the exception of Satchel Paige and Josh Gibson, most league players were underpublicized by owners, a ploy that, according to Joe Bostic, was a conscious decision to keep potential salary demands in check.[63]

The unsolved issue of inadequate league information and statistics remained a major source of contention between owners and journalists. Earl Barnes expressed the prevailing press attitude, remarking that "this so-called league has placed every sepia sports writer in the land in an embarrassing position" by failing to provide consistently accurate data. Yet a number of other factors shaped black baseball's complex yet tempestuous dealings with the press, a relationship too often marked by mutual dissatisfaction.

To most league officials, the basic function of the black press was to support the industry wholeheartedly and refrain from more probing analyses. The failure of black journalists to accept such a docile role annoyed Cum Posey (himself a weekly *Pittsburgh Courier* sports columnist), who in 1936 contrasted the "continued line of criticism toward league baseball" with the loyal press backing enjoyed by white professional teams. Wary of the impact of negative publicity, Posey and other officials occasionally pursued strategies to silence or intimidate reporters perceived as unsupportive. In 1939, a strongly worded column by Wendell Smith compelled Rufus Jackson of the Grays to complain to the managing editor of the *Courier*, who reportedly "bawled . . . out" the young writer, while Randy Dixon subsequently received a similar scolding from Tom Wilson. Meanwhile, Fay Young's negative statements in the 1940s angered NAL owners to such a degree that one official suggested an investigation.

In such a suspicious atmosphere, journalists found it difficult to approach league officials with recommendations or ideas for reforms. Already perceiving journalists as meddlesome and overly critical, owners often bristled at even the most sincere of suggestions. Young, for instance, warned NAL officials of the potential repercussions arising from park misbehavior, only to be informed that the owners did not need a newsman to solve their problems. After encountering similar attitudes from NNL owners, Sam Lacy commented that "the sure way to get the magnates to ignore a suggestion that looks to progress, is to have a newspaper man suggest it."[64]

Sports columnists recognized that cogent commentary, analysis, and criticism built readerships and refused to accept the widely held belief that flaws should be overlooked in race enterprises. Nevertheless, a number of owners believed that the leagues deserved preferential treatment from the press, an industry financially intertwined with black baseball. Young, for example, served in a variety of capacities for the NAL and occasionally handled publicity for the East-West game, and other newspapermen periodically worked for the NNL or individual teams. The East-West game itself further connected the two industries, as the *Courier* and *Defender* divided 5 percent of the gross after expenses were paid, presumably in exchange for column space and publicity. Despite a clear conflict of interest, such relationships were hardly atypical in the world of American sports, as white writers were known to accept similar financial favors. Although Cum Posey suggested that journalists "follow money," an occasional paid position or share of a promotion failed to muzzle the black press completely. By 1946, yet another critical article from Wendell Smith led Effa Manley to wonder "how The Courier can continue to take all that money from us at the East West game, and knock us as they did this week."[65]

For most black journalists, the issue of money was less relevant than the very real problem of cooperation from league officials and teams. As a major catalyst in the industry's success, the press believed it was entitled to greater consideration regarding disclosure of pertinent developments and other items of interest. Access to league meetings, for example, remained a hotly debated topic, as sportswriters, eager to provide their readers with inside news, chafed under the restrictions imposed by owners. Although some officials supported the admission of journalists, most remained leery of the presence of the press at official league gatherings, likely fearful of the potential disclosure of sensitive information.

For many journalists, the restricted access to meetings exemplified black baseball's general tendency to treat the press with a less than respectful attitude. Several sportswriters, for instance, complained of being forced to pay taxes or "service charges" to gain admission to major promotions such as the East-West game and Yankee Stadium doubleheaders. Others cited slights from individual owners, particularly the Manleys, whom Joe Bostic felt "should modernize their attitude and treatment of the Negro press. The patronizing attitude is strictly passe, my friends." According to Rollo Wilson, the Newark owners refused to acknowledge the press credentials of a *Philadelphia Tribune* staffer and Philadelphia Stars scorekeeper, while Rick Hurt of the *People's Voice* noted that Effa Manley only provided information to writers she perceived as "friends."[66]

Far worse were the owners who openly scorned black newspapers, including an anonymous NAL official who announced during a meeting that "the colored press ain't worth a . . . ." To the dismay of black journalists, the disregard was sometimes accompanied by active attempts to receive publicity in white periodicals. Generally, however, white newspapers never covered black baseball on more than a peripheral basis, and as Ed Harris explained, "there is too much going on in the white sports world, for the dailies to devote any space to anything other than a routine report of previous games, (meaning of course those papers that carry even that)." The Stars, for example, usually received a brief written account and a box score in Philadelphia papers, comparable to the coverage granted the strongest white independent teams locally. Similarly, the *New York Times* provided a few paragraphs on the East-West game and other important promotions but offered no broader commentary on league baseball or teams. Ultimately, the isolation of black teams from white Organized Baseball provided a convenient rationale for sports editors to automatically categorize the NNL and NAL as "semiprofessional" organizations and limit their coverage accordingly.

The largely unsuccessful attempts to generate substantial white press coverage were less disturbing to black newspapermen than the hiring of white professionals. Abe Saperstein's role as the publicist for the East-West game generated ongoing controversy, as did the employment of white journalists in several league cities, including Brooklyn, New York, and Washington, during the 1930s. In Newark, Jerry Kessler served as the Eagles publicity agent for a number of years, prompting several observers to question the validity of the Manleys' supposed race consciousness. While the Eagles later retained Oliver "Butts" Brown as publicist after Kessler entered the armed forces, Effa Manley was dissatisfied with Brown, privately denouncing him as "a very poor publicity man." Following the team's decision to employ a white journalist for a New York promotion in 1942, a disenchanted Joe Bostic lamented that "Mrs. Manley has long been firmly convinced that no Negro could do an adequate job as press agent for her, and hence has consistently given capable Negro press agents the back of her neck."

Although occasionally justifiable, the use of white publicists further alienated black sportswriters, already disillusioned by a series of slights, both real and imagined. By 1946, NNL secretary Curtis Leak admitted that the league had a "very poor Negro press," yet concerted attempts to mend the damage were seldom forthcoming. While increased sensitivity, attentiveness, and financial incentives would have allowed the leagues to build a stronger relationship with journalists, owners appeared oblivious to the actual importance of the press and too often fixated on criticism instead of appreciating the efforts of a generally supportive sportswriting corps. To Effa Manley, the failure to exploit the press to its full advantage was unintentional and resulted from a lack of commercial training, a chronic problem faced by black entrepreneurs. Attempting to explain the barring of the press from a December 1944 meeting, Manley asked a dubious Sam Lacy to "try and understand this is a big business being run by inexperienced people . . . and consequently lots of mistakes will be made."[67]

Manley's argument was never fully accepted by black sportswriters, who understandably continued to contrast their own experiences with their white counterparts who enjoyed superior privileges, pay, and access to information. While covering the Cleveland Red Sox in 1934, Bill Finger discovered that "gate passes are non-existent," unlike the major league Indians "who provide every possible accommodation for sport scribes." The disadvantages tolerated by black journalists in the past became increasingly apparent following the integration of the major leagues in the late 1940s, as Fay Young was startled to find that, when dealing with Organized Baseball, "all we do is to let the public relations men on the clubs know what we want—AND WE GET IT!"

To Young, the problem reflected an overall "laxness when dealing with the Negro press," all too frequently demonstrated by black athletic organizations. Black colleges, for example, were reportedly equally deficient in handling sports publicity and often elicited complaints from frustrated newsmen. Yet without serious outside competition for the African American entertainment dollar throughout most of the 1930s and 1940s, black college and professional teams lacked the necessary incentive to reconsider their generally flawed approach to promotion.

As early as 1939, the seriousness of the problem appeared obvious to

Dan Burley, who noted that, while the average black fan was unaware of the number of teams in the NNL and NAL, "ask him practically anything you may about the white majors and he can quote you records by the dozens as glibly and as accurately as a hired publicity man." Sterling Brown alluded to a similar phenomenon in Washington, observing black fans knowledgeable about white baseball but unaware of the "standing of the teams in the Negro leagues, and some do not know the Negro national champions." The problem remained largely unsolved, however, and black baseball's failure to substantially improve its publicity to fully exploit potential interest would ultimately prove costly, accelerating the industry's decline in later decades.[68]

◆ ◆ ◆

While league officials clearly deserved a substantial share of the blame for publicity problems and other administrative weaknesses in black baseball, it is also obvious that owners often functioned in a difficult environment. Like other race businesses, black baseball relied on the support of a predominantly impoverished community sensitive to the slightest economic fluctuations. Moreover, the operation of a professional club, white or black, involved considerable expense, as novice promoters soon discovered. With the exception of a few years during the 1920s and 1940s, industry earnings generally remained modest, and, as Curtis Leak observed in 1943, black baseball was "not an extremely rich nor a highly profitable business, but an enormous struggle to keep your head above the water."

For league franchises, survival depended almost entirely on attendance, as additional revenue streams were simply not available as in Organized Baseball. The Wilmington Blue Rocks of the class B Inter-State League, for example, earned nearly $6,000 on concessions and score cards (advertising and sales) in 1942 and by 1946 collected an additional $1,000 through the sale of radio rights. Ancillary income was even greater at the major league level: the Phillies realized $149,786 in 1948 through scorecard, concessions, and radio/television revenue. Yet black teams, lacking their own parks and appealing to a narrow fan base, had virtually no opportunity to share in concessions and little hope of attracting interest from radio stations or their sponsors.

The typical club thus had to extract as much income as possible from gate receipts, yet league attendance and ticket prices varied widely by decade. In 1924, fans at Hilldale Park paid 35 cents for a bleacher seat, 55 cents for pavilion, and an additional 30 cents for a box seat. The Depression and subsequent decline in patronage forced owners to slash ticket prices, and by July 1933, the cost of a bleacher seat at Hilldale Park had fallen to a 1918 level of 25 cents. Throughout the remainder of the decade, tickets remained relatively inexpensive in Philadelphia and other league cities, with top prices seldom exceeding 85 cents. At Parkside Field, locals could secure a bleacher seat for as little as 30 cents in 1937, rising only 5 cents (plus tax) by 1940. With the increasing prosperity of the war years, fans became accustomed to paying higher prices to see NNL and NAL games, particularly at parks owned by Organized Baseball. By 1946, admission to promotions at Blues Stadium in Kansas City and League Park in Cleveland ranged from 60 cents for bleachers to $1.50 for boxes, while Philadelphians paid slightly more to attend doubleheaders at Shibe Park.[69]

Although ticket prices remained accessible to most working-class blacks, actual game attendance depended on several factors, including team performance, attractions offered, publicity, and weather. Locale also affected patronage. By the early 1940s, the spacious major league parks in the most heavily populated African American communities (New York, Chicago, Philadelphia, Washington, Detroit, Cleveland) offered the greatest potential for large crowds, although the Monarchs drew exceptionally well in Kansas City despite a smaller black population and use of a minor league facility. Moreover, the day and time of a promotion was important, as black professional baseball, like its white counterpart, typically attracted its best crowds for games scheduled at night or on weekends (particularly Sunday) and holidays.

Perhaps the most crucial determinant of attendance was the current economic status of the black community and its available discretionary income. As noted, the Depression years dealt a predictably heavy blow to attendance, although precise data are limited and newspaper crowd estimates notoriously unreliable. Hilldale Park figures, however, reveal that average Saturday and holiday attendance fell to an unprecedented low of 339.5 in 1932, and contemporary accounts suggest similar declines, although less dramatic, in several other league cities except Pittsburgh, which benefited from the newly constructed Greenlee Field. As economic conditions gradually improved for African Americans, fans began to return to the parks somewhat more regularly, although attendance likely remained below the high reached in the early 1920s. John Clark claimed that the Crawfords, one of the NNL's more popular clubs, drew an average of 1,635 fans per game in 1936 at league and non-league ballparks. Official attendance figures for the Newark Eagles offer a more detailed glimpse of the league's drawing power, as the club averaged 3,480 fans for its Sunday dates at Ruppert Stadium in 1939, rising to 4,293 by 1941 and falling slightly to 4,084 a year later. It is likely, however, that more profitable league cities with larger black populations enjoyed greater attendance increases during the war, as by 1946, crowds of 5,000 to 10,000 fans were not unusual in black baseball and increased more dramatically for particularly important promotions.

Specific league policies determined each team's share of the gate. In the NNL, visiting clubs typically received 30 to 35 percent of the gross and were assured a minimum guarantee regardless of attendance, at least through 1940. While teams had been promised $350 for weekends and $150 for weekdays in the Eastern Colored League during 1923 and 1924, guarantees had subsequently declined, falling to as low as $50 for a Saturday game at Hilldale Park in July 1932 and remaining modest throughout the Depression. As noted in Chapter 1, the NNL initially eschewed guarantees of any kind, although by the end of 1934, visiting teams were assured $75 for weekdays and $200 for Sundays with the option of receiving 35 percent of the gross. Five years later, league guarantees had only risen an aggregate $50, revealing the financial stagnation in the industry during the late 1930s. Although information on guarantees beyond 1940 is unknown, available evidence suggests that a straight percentage may have become the more common form of financial arrangement offered to teams.[70]

For non-league games with white teams, gate shares varied by individual locale. In Philadelphia, semipro parks offered $100 to $150 guarantees or a 40 to 50 percent gate option for weekday games during the early 1920s, the most profitable period for local white independent baseball. By the early 1930s, visiting teams were fortunate to receive $50 or $75, often further reduced by a 5 percent booking fee. Desperate for any source of income, league teams continued to fill out their schedules with games with white semipros in Philadelphia and other eastern cities, although the financial returns hardly matched the profits of the 1920s. By 1939, Philadelphia-area semipro games averaged fewer than 250 fans and receipts less than $100, a decline linked by Eddie Gottlieb to the impact of major league radio broadcasts.

As black teams grew more prosperous in the early 1940s, the largely insubstantial gate receipts from eastern semiprofessional baseball became increasingly irrelevant. During 1941, for example, the Newark Eagles were offered guarantees of $75 to $100 for dates in New Jersey and Connecticut, while Grays officials complained of similarly slim receipts for semipro contests. A handful of white teams, however, continued to draw large crowds, particularly the Brooklyn Bushwicks, a valuable revenue source for black clubs since the 1920s. Reflecting the Bushwicks' importance, the Philadelphia Stars realized $647.48 from a Dexter Park doubleheader in May 1939, in contrast to a $363.48 share for a comparable promotion two months later with the Newark Eagles that drew a credible 2,164 fans.

Despite attempts to maximize income from league and non-league games, expenses often exceeded profits, requiring a substantial investment each season to keep the team operating. Salaries consumed a large part of revenue, comprising more than half of the operating costs of the Newark Eagles in 1936 and the Kansas City Monarchs a decade later. Equipment represented another major expense for each team, as by 1936 James Semler cited the cost of bats ($24 per dozen), baseballs ($13 per dozen), uniforms ($10 to $12 apiece), shoes ($16.50 per pair), and gloves ($7 to $10). Transportation also cut into profits, particularly the initial purchase of a bus, subsequent maintenance, and ongoing gasoline charges. Finally, owners were responsible for lodging players on the road, an expenditure that weighed more heavily on teams that traveled extensively, such as the Monarchs and Grays.[71]

Each owner's budget also included a number of non-player related expenses necessary to ensure continued profitability. Dues ($400 in the NNL by 1942) and booking fees created additional overhead for franchises, along with advertisements, posters, and the often sizable telephone and telegraph bills incurred while keeping in contact with promoters. Moreover, most league teams employed a small staff to handle administrative tasks and other duties, often including a traveling secretary responsible for collecting game shares and paying all expenses on the road.

With operating costs hardly insubstantial by the early 1940s, league teams had to gross increasing amounts of money to break even. A few years earlier, receipts totaling $25,000 to $30,000 appeared to be sufficient to cover all expenses, although several clubs had difficulty reaching this figure. In 1936, for example, the Newark Eagles grossed only $14,583.90, less than Hilldale's receipts in 1918 for an abbreviated 48-game season, and hardly enough to cover expenses totaling $23,615.50. Despite a better gate performance in 1937, the Eagles still failed to clear $25,000 and once again operated at a deficit. The status of the Black Yankees was likely no better, prompting Jim Semler's admission in March 1938 that "colored magnates take an awful beating at the end of the season . . . and we are in the red plenty."

The industry's dramatic transformation during the war years, however, resulted in increases in player salaries and other operating costs. According to Cum Posey, the Homestead Grays spent $45,000 to operate their club in 1942. Meanwhile, expenses for the Kansas City Monarchs rose from $61,474.84 in 1942 to $75,407.75 in 1945. A year later, the team's overhead totaled nearly $96,000, roughly comparable to an A level club in Organized Baseball (see Table 6.2 for income comparison). While the experience of the Monarchs, possibly the most profitable and hard-traveling club in either league, may be somewhat atypical, it appears likely that expenses of $50,000 to $60,000 were not unusual in the NNL by 1946, as several franchises spent up to $8,000 each month on salary alone. In con-

Table 6.2. Income Comparison—1946

	Income ($)	Expenses ($)	Attendance
Major league[1]			
Philadelphia Phillies	1,224,484.18	1,078,998.59	1,045,247
Chicago Cubs	1,930,823.03	1,192,284.25	1,342,970
AAA league average[2]			
Pacific Coast League	544,454.71	401,711.71	481,268
International League	359,094.71	326,838.86	315,937
American Association	286,424.00	268,688.50	247,837
AA league average[3]			
Southern Association	237,516.75	202,560.25	228,904
Texas League	234,300.86	200,926.86	188,550
A league			
Utica (Eastern)	67,642.42	89,687.43	93,802
B league			
Wilmington (Inter-State)	100,248.90	79,247.40	132,550
Terre Haute (Three-I)	58,607.41	68,475.31	84,248
Negro American League			
Kansas City Monarchs	155,921.20	95,915.84	100,000 +

[1]Expenses include net of player sales/purchases. [2]St. Paul, Sacramento, Rochester not included. [3]Dallas not included.

Sources: *SOMP*, 1630–35; "Philadelphia National League Club and Its Wholly Owned Subsidiaries—Treasurer's Report, 1946," 5–13; "Treasurer's Report, 1948," 122; Chicago National League Ball Club (Earl W. Nelson) to George F. H. Harrison, March 4, 1947, PP, boxes 4–5; TBC; Spink, *Baseball Guide and Record Book—1947*, 138; Three-I League Organizational Records, BHOFL; *KCC*, 1946.

trast, expenses in 1946 for the Citizens and Southern Bank, a major black business in Philadelphia, amounted to only $46,986, including $22,083 on salaries for 28 employees, almost certainly less than the Stars' current payroll for a five-month season.[72]

Although owners tried to keep expenditures to a bare minimum, certain expenses remained immutable, particularly park rental fees incurred during home and/or away games. Under the typical agreement, major and minor league parks received 20 to 25 percent of the gross receipts, although some facilities required guarantees ranging from $500 at Ebbets Field in 1940 to a reported $2,500 to $3,000 at Yankee Stadium late in the decade. Meanwhile, Briggs Stadium and Sportsman's Park demanded an exorbitant 40 percent of the gross by the mid-1940s, ultimately leading to a 1946 joint resolution by the NNL and NAL barring acceptance of rental fees beyond 25 percent.

Simple rent was hardly the only cost involved in securing a park. At a number of facilities, teams dealt with outside promoters such as Abe Saperstein, whose exclusive control over a park's open dates allowed him to collect as much as 30 percent of the gate on occasion. Teams were also generally responsible for covering the cost of ticket sellers, security, ushers, and other park help. Lighting for night games further cut into profits, costing from as little as $40 at Trenton in 1943 to $500 at Shibe Park in 1950. Cum Posey suggested that some parks abruptly raised their lighting and rental prices, a policy recognized by league officials as a "racket . . . but it is a case of take or don't play in that town."

Although some parks offered relatively favorable terms, the tenant status of league teams presented ongoing difficulties. The considerable overhead at major league facilities such as Yankee Stadium, for example, required consistently large turnouts to ensure profitability, a problem that would loom larger in the late 1940s. Moreover, teams had little control over occasionally unsatisfactory conditions at the parks. A Griffith Stadium fan, for example, complained that "it makes me sick to see them treat our National League teams as though they were church league people. I have never seen the stadium workmen drag the infield before a colored league game, and it makes me sick to think that the Griffith people regard us as 'nothing.' "[73]

While facilities not connected with Organized Baseball potentially provided a cheaper alternative, the few such parks available were often flawed by their modest seating capacities and rundown condition. The Philadelphia Stars, for example, leased Parkside Field, a park built in 1903 that probably held fewer than 6,000 fans. More problematic, however, was the field's proximity to a Pennsylvania Railroad roundhouse. As trains entered or departed the roundhouse, their engines generated an almost unbearable amount of thick smoke. Too often, fans found themselves contending with sporadic showers of coal dust and soot, leading an observer to quip that "if you were not visibly Negroid when you arrived, you were when you left." The wooden seats, already in less than sterling condition, also absorbed a considerable amount of the smoky atmosphere, resulting in trips to the dry cleaner for more than a few women fans.

Recognizing the site's inherent problems, the Stars began to schedule a growing number of promotions at Shibe Park during the war. While Eddie Gottlieb continued to lease Parkside, Shibe began to loom as the long-term solution to the club's park problems. Like other franchises, the Stars willingly accepted the higher overhead and limited choice of dates at major league parks (particularly at a facility already in use by two other teams) in exchange for the opportunity to earn vastly larger profits. As long as attendance remained at wartime levels, the rental of major league parks appeared financially sensible for the Stars and other teams, yet the declining number of locally controlled parks, regardless of their deficiencies, would prove counterproductive for the NNL in the future.[74]

◆ ◆ ◆

The problem with parks was only one of a number of difficulties that black baseball, despite the profits of the early 1940s, was never fully able to transcend. Marred by uneven scheduling, umpiring, and publicity, the flavor of league administration too often resembled semiprofessional baseball, although the player talent level was far superior. As Dan Burley (under his pseudonym "Don DeLeighbur") noted in 1943, "there is no need of kidding ourselves; colored baseball is but a poor shadow of the major league—the real thing." League officials, however, felt that comparisons to Organized Baseball and particularly major league teams were unfair. Dizzy Dismukes, for example, argued in 1933 that it had taken the majors several decades to reach their current exalted position, a view echoed five years later by Cum Posey, who cited the industry's attempt to copy contracts of "a Billion Dollar Corporation which it had taken fifty years to develop." Yet to others, black baseball's administrative weaknesses stemmed from needlessly low expectations and as veteran Dick Lundy observed in 1939, "for 25 years . . . I have listened to them get in their meetings and lament the fact that 'colored baseball is still in its infancy . . . we can't do this and we can't do that.' The result is that we're no further now than we were when the thought of organizing first came up."[75]

For most players, the industry's deficiencies were bothersome but tolerable and hardly enough to discourage youngsters from aspiring to a baseball career. Along with other forms of black entertainment, the leagues offered African Americans an opportunity for fame, money, and adventure otherwise unavailable in a still largely segregated country. Don Newcombe, who joined the Newark Eagles in 1944 as a teenager, later alluded to black baseball's importance, explaining that "the Negro Leagues were a beginning, a chance for a poor kid to get out of the ghetto and a chance to become famous. . . . Even in the Negro Leagues, you were famous if you were playing on a Negro League team." Not surprisingly, several players attested to the positive effect of their league experience on their lives. Mahlon Duckett felt that his years in professional ball "taught me a lot about life, playing with these guys and going around to different places and meeting people," while Stanley Glenn similarly noted that baseball allowed him "to travel and to meet all sorts of people." Meanwhile, Gene Benson noted that "we got treated very nice among our own people. We had good food and nice places to stay. We met some nice ladies that some of us married."

Few white major and upper-level minor leaguers, however, would have envied the clearly more arduous lifestyle of a black player in the 1930s and 1940s. The two entities of white and black professional baseball still remained worlds apart, mirroring the status of other African American institutions to the larger white society. Yet the wartime forces that had accelerated the slow movement of blacks into the mainstream would similarly contribute to a transformation of the relationship between white and black baseball, and the once distant major leagues would suddenly become less remote to owners and players.[76]

PART II
INTEGRATION

7

On the Outside Looking In

The Big League Baseball publicity bureau maintains a campaign from the beginning of each year to the end and broadcasts through the press, the radio and scouts . . . that baseball
is our national pastime, offering fame and fortune to any
man capable of making the grade. Even without reading between the lines, it has become as vivid as today's news that
there is no way under the sun for one to make the grade if
he is a Negro.
                                              —Chick Edwards, 1938

As black baseball continued its dramatic growth in the early 1940s, the
industry's relationship with white Organized Baseball would suddenly become an increasingly vital issue, an unlikely prospect just a decade earlier.
In the years following the virtual exclusion of African American players
from the white minor leagues in the late nineteenth century, professional
baseball among blacks and whites had proceeded along divergent paths.
While Organized Baseball had developed into a multimillion dollar industry celebrated and embraced by the dominant white culture, black professional teams and leagues had struggled to remain solvent, operating in
relative obscurity. Yet despite de facto segregation, black baseball had
never been entirely isolated from its white counterpart, and the Depression
and World War II would considerably alter the relationship between the
two entities.[1]

During the first three decades of the twentieth century, white Organized
Baseball, like numerous other major American industries, ignored or
evaded the issue of integration. Moreover, despite scattered protests from
both African Americans and whites, no sustained articulate movement
emerged to admit black players to major or minor league teams. Discouraged by white indifference and hostility, many blacks viewed economic
self-development, rather than agitation, as a more sensible and fruitful
path to follow. The establishment of the first permanent leagues during

the 1920s reflected this trend, creating opportunities for black players in a structure separate but roughly parallel to white professional organizations.

Black and white professional baseball, however, had never remained completely separate. As early as the 1900s, black teams had leased major league parks for occasional appearances and increasingly rented other Organized Baseball facilities. Moreover, since the 1880s, white major and minor league players had supplemented their income by participating in postseason exhibition games against black clubs. By the early 1920s, several black teams had defeated largely intact white professional teams in postseason series, generating positive publicity and respect from white participants and fans. Embarrassed by losses at the hands of both black professional and white independent teams, major league baseball eventually restricted postseason participation, requiring each player to secure permission from the league and commissioner and limiting barnstorming squads to no more than three players from a single team. While opportunities for interracial professional competition continued, subsequent series were scheduled less frequently and generally involved white "all-star" teams varying widely in quality.[2]

The strong showing of black teams during the 1920s, however, undermined any rationalization of the color bar based on the supposed inferiority of black athletes. Impartial white players clearly recognized the baseball ability of blacks, and, as Ben Taylor noted in 1933, "I have heard numbers of white big leaguers say: 'Do you know such and such a fellow? Boy, he is some player. If he were only white!'" The New York Yankees and Philadelphia Athletics, for example, eagerly pursued Hartford high school sensation Johnny Taylor in the early 1930s, abruptly withdrawing after discovering his racial identity. Sympathetic observers also recognized that black players performed at an extremely high level despite facing numerous handicaps, leading Josh Gibson to assert that "dozens of us would make the majors if given the opportunity to play under the same circumstances as the whites . . . regular schedules, modernized traveling facilities, with none of these 500- to 800-mile overnight bus hops, and board and lodging at the better spots."

The demonstrated athletic prowess of black teams during the early decades of the twentieth century had only marginal impact on Organized Baseball's policy of segregation. Moreover, as seen by the early 1930s, black professional baseball had fallen into disarray, discouraging those hopeful that institution building would prove a catalyst to integration. Yet the Depression's equally devastating effect on white baseball would stimulate sudden reconsideration of the color line. Relatively immune during 1930 and 1931, Organized Baseball began to experience the full brunt of the Depression in 1932 as attendance dropped, numerous leagues folded, and salaries were slashed. Chicago Cubs president William Veeck claimed that only one major league team profited during 1932, warning that "if we don't cut admission prices or make the game more attractive we certainly will be up against a further loss of patronage. . . . It looks to me like a good time to try something else besides a hope that the 'good old days' will soon be back."[3]

Journalists, fans, and baseball officials proposed various solutions to boost attendance, including interleague games and a split season. Surprisingly, the use of black players also received consideration for the first time in years. As early as 1931, the conservative journalist Westbrook Pegler, then a nationally syndicated sportswriter for the *Chicago Tribune*, attacked the color line in baseball, followed by a more substantial effort in February 1933 by a group of New York writers. Discussing the current problems in baseball, the February 1 *New York Daily News* editorialized that "another trouble with major league ball certainly would seem to be the color line drawn in the big leagues . . . good colored ballplayers aren't eligible: and so there must be a lot of possible fans in Harlem who don't step over to the Stadium or the Polo Grounds to baseball games." Four days later, Heywood Broun, a former sportswriter, occasional novelist, and left-leaning syndicated columnist with the *New York World-Telegram*, publicly advocated integration at the annual New York chapter of the Baseball Writers Association of America dinner. Admitting that his suggestion "met with no overwhelming roar of approval," Broun nevertheless insisted that he could "see no reason why Negroes should not come into the American and National Leagues. The race possesses a high talent for the game. There is no set rule for barring Negroes, it is merely a tacit agreement, or possibly custom."[4]

Sportswriter Jimmy Powers of the *New York Daily News* perceived a far different response to Broun's plea for integration. After soliciting various opinions, Powers claimed to be "amazed at the sentiment in favor of the idea," reporting that several officials and players "displayed a refreshing open-mindedness." According to Powers, only New York Giants manager John McGraw was openly resistant, puzzling African Americans who recalled McGraw's failed attempt three decades earlier to pass off Charlie Grant, a black player, as a Native American. Although Powers's findings and a subsequent informal poll conducted by the *Daily News* revealed surprisingly positive attitudes toward integration, Romeo Dougherty of the *Amsterdam News* remained dubious, warning blacks not to be "misguided by the questions and answers asked by the Daily News . . . and think that it is bringing us any nearer to the big leagues." Moreover, Dougherty recognized that major American newspapers, despite their current advocacy of baseball integration, were equally guilty of discrimination and "would be the first to hesitate at giving a Negro a chance to write sports not confined to the Jim-Crowites."⁵

Bill Gibson of the *Afro-American*, however, suggested that the efforts of Powers and Broun "will serve their purpose if they will stimulate the formulation of a consistent and unrelenting drive . . . to secure from the major league club owners a chance for some of our stars to try out." Gibson advocated that African Americans undertake a precise course of action, complaining that "too often we get worked up to a froth about a 'cause' on one day and forget all about it on the next." The *Pittsburgh Courier*, the most widely read black newspaper in the country, subsequently took the lead in addressing the issue during early 1933, soon joined by the *Chicago Defender* and other black weeklies. Pursuing a nonconfrontational investigational approach, the *Courier* followed Powers's example and attempted to gauge Organized Baseball's opinion toward integration.

Not surprisingly, several white officials denied any knowledge of segregation. Leslie O'Connor, an assistant to Commissioner Kenesaw Mountain Landis, maintained that no color bar existed and the subject of black players had never been raised for discussion. Similarly, National League president John Heydler asserted that "beyond the fundamental requirement that a Major League player must have unique ability and good character and habits, I do not recall one instance where base ball has allowed either race, creed, or color to enter into the question of the selection of its players." Others, such as Chicago White Sox president J. Louis Comiskey, engaged in evasive double-talk, claiming "the question . . . has never crossed my mind. Had some good player come along and my manager refused to sign him because he was a Negro I am sure I would have taken action or attempted to do so, although it is not up to me to change what might be the rule. I cannot say that I would have insisted on hiring the player over the protest of my manager, but at least I would have taken some steps— just what steps I cannot say for the simple reason the question has never confronted me."

The issue continued to be discussed throughout 1933, culminating in a *Defender*-sponsored letter-writing campaign to Commissioner Landis and major league owners in October. The commissioner's office refused to comment further on the matter, and a *Defender* reporter's attempt to attend major league baseball's annual winter meetings in December proved fruitless. Yet despite disappointments, the effort during 1933 had successfully raised awareness of baseball's color line, forcing previously silent Organized Baseball officials to address the subject of integration, albeit gingerly, for the first time. Moreover, the black press had demonstrated a surprisingly assertive attitude toward integration, shaped in part by the bleak prospects for a separate black economy during the Depression.

Yet as protest slackened somewhat during 1934, the institution of black baseball began to make its own contribution to the assault on the color line. The NNL's successful promotions at Comiskey Park and Yankee Stadium not only demonstrated to white Organized Baseball the existence of a sizable African American baseball audience but also showcased the skills of the finest black players in the country. Favorable coverage from several white sportswriters provided additional encouragement and seemingly reflected a new willingness to respect African American athletic abilities. Other racial setbacks in 1934, however, suggested that American athletics were unlikely to change their segregated pattern in the foreseeable future. The University of Michigan basketball team, a member of the Big Ten conference, refused to grant a tryout to a black student, while boycott threats from southern teams forced an integrated baseball club from Springfield, Massachusetts, to withdraw from an American Legion tournament in North Carolina.[6]

The Alabama Pitts episode in 1935 crystallized the lack of tangible progress in the integration fight. Sent to Sing Sing Prison in New York for his involvement in a holdup, Edwin "Alabama" Pitts had attracted considerable attention for his athletic prowess, including interest from several minor league teams. Following his release in June 1935, Pitts planned to join the International League's Albany Senators, operated by Joe Cambria, owner of Bugle Field in Baltimore and former NNL official. A controversy arose, however, after minor league head William Bramham and the National Association Executive Committee refused to allow the signing of the convicted felon. Following a substantial demonstration of public support for Pitts, Commissioner Landis approved his contract. Although Pitts proved to be a mediocre minor leaguer, he continued to receive offers, appearing briefly in the National Football League with the Philadelphia Eagles later that year. Never able to fulfill his athletic promise, he died in 1941 after a fatal stabbing.

The decision of white professional baseball and football to welcome Pitts while continuing to bar black athletes was a bitter pill for African Americans to swallow. Although baseball officials such as John Heydler had suggested that "character" was an important requirement of any major league player, a disgusted Washington sports fan observed that "it's now very plain that even a white man with a prison record . . . is better than a law-abiding colored man." Meanwhile, Robert Spicely of Philadelphia questioned the groundswell of national support for Pitts, noting that "it seems more unjust to have colored citizens, who are colorful athletes as well as perfect gentlemen, barred from the more lucrative fields of organized baseball and other sports." Sportswriter Mabe Kountze, however, expressed disappointment that the black press had failed to mount an aggressive campaign comparable to the 1933 effort, focusing instead on an upcoming fight of the "beloved but over-publicized Joe Louis." Recognizing that such one-dimensional coverage was counterproductive, Kountze warned that "the white man would much rather have us put all our dough and energy on a man like Joe than to have the same valuable assets directed in an important issue like the Scottsboro case and others of equal importance."[7]

The Alabama Pitts episode revealed Organized Baseball's still unflinchingly negative attitude toward black players, despite the protests of black and white sportswriters and the modest financial revival of black professional baseball. Even the most racially tolerant white officials continued to believe that integration would present unsolvable problems, particularly lodging and travel in the South. While only three major league cities (Washington, St. Louis, and Cincinnati) were located in the upper south, numerous minor league teams operated below the Mason-Dixon line, and spring training posed yet another potential difficulty. Moreover, southern authorities showed no signs of relaxing segregation laws even for sporting events, and black players on white northern college football teams during the 1930s often found themselves benched for southern games. Although Ed Harris of the *Philadelphia Tribune* argued that travel problems had been "solved time and again by colleges and other athletic organizations," National League president Ford Frick noted that a typical baseball series required longer stays than track meets or a football game. Pirates president William Benswanger suggested that separate facilities might offer a possible solution, citing the case of the team's black trainer, who "makes his reservations and arrangements beforehand" when the club traveled "into southern towns and other places where he might possibly be embarrassed."

The strong prevalence of Southern-born players in Organized Baseball presented an additional dilemma. Most officials doubted that white southern players would even consent to interracial competition, let alone appear alongside blacks, and feared potential race riots sparked by heated contacts on the playing field. Other observers such as black journalist F. M. Davis fretted over the potential behavior of "uneducated, passionately prejudiced southerners," warning that "there are still enough rabid Negro-haters from deep Dixie to so insult and taunt colored players in obvious ways as to make this a serious issue." Northern players seemed unlikely to display any greater tolerance, as Romeo Dougherty reminded his readers that "it must be remembered that we are not dealing with the most cultured minds in the world when we seek to engage in competition with the whites in a big way."[8]

The often hostile reaction that the few white or light-skinned Cuban players in Organized Baseball encountered led some to predict an even harsher response to blacks. Although several officials, particularly Senators president Clark Griffith, had willingly signed Cubans, their presence was not without controversy. Sportswriter Bob Ruark mentioned cultural differences as a source of friction, claiming in 1940 that the Cubans' "taste in haberdashery runs contra-clockwise to that of his Anglo-Saxon brother, and his high-pitched Latin laughter rubs the average ex-blow boy the wrong way." Racism, however, also shaped the treatment of Cuban players. While author Roberto González Echevarría has noted that nonwhite Cuban major leaguers of the 1930s and 1940s such as Roberto Estalella and Tomas de la Cruz capitalized on "the prevalent confusion about Cuban nationality and race in the United States," a 1940 account by Bob Considine alluded to the "rather widespread inability on the part of American ballplayers to differentiate between Cuban and Negro athletes." Considine reported that Estalella and other Cuban players on the Washington Senators faced a steady stream of insults and beanballs from opponents, some of whom were "almost psychopathically opposed to Roberto and his coffee-colored colleagues." Notably, Senators manager Bucky Harris considered his Cuban players "trash" and forced them to lodge apart from their American teammates.[9]

The experience of the Cubans foreshadowed the difficulties that any African American would face in Organized Baseball. The admission of black players ultimately threatened to disrupt race relations and attitudes, a daunting prospect for many Americans. Fay Young, for example, suggested that whites were unwilling to accept the notion of blacks earning major league salaries—"more than white men in any line want to pay a black worker. . . . It is too much money for the sepia ball players to be making." Black success in Organized Baseball would also undermine long-held notions of inferiority and potentially engender a new respect for African Americans. As one black New Yorker observed, "every time a Negro gets an opportunity to become a hero in the eyes of American youth . . . it makes it harder for prejudice to take hold in their minds." Yet the potentially elevated status of blacks disturbed more than a few Americans, few of whom were prepared to embrace social equality between blacks and whites, and according to Effa Manley, several white owners wanted to prevent black players from receiving "adulation and resultant approval from white women."

The perceived obstacles to integration provided abundant justification for an industry already notoriously resistant to change. Major league baseball, for example, had only tentatively embraced radio and night baseball despite their potential impact on gate receipts, and as late as 1939, only five major league parks had installed lights. As *Washington Post* sportswriter Shirley Povich observed, "it's a smug, conservative business not given to very great enterprise and the introduction of new and novel features." Most major league owners could only foresee negative consequences from integration, and according to National League president Ford Frick, remained fearful of "upsetting the status quo . . . [and] alienating the white clientele that largely supported the professional game." The inherent conservatism and racism in major league baseball, however, coincided with the attitude of much of American business, which was equally reluctant to employ blacks beyond a menial capacity. Not surprisingly, several owners were part of the big business establishment during the late 1930s, including Jacob Ruppert (brewery), Philip Wrigley (chewing gum), Walter Briggs (automobile bodies), and Powel Crosley (radio, refrigerator, and later automobile manufacturing).[10]

Despite Organized Baseball's clear opposition to integration, many African Americans viewed Commissioner Kenesaw Mountain Landis as the true cause of continued exclusion of black players. Born in 1866 in Ohio, Landis received his name (minus an "n"—then an acceptable alternate spelling) from the battle of Kennesaw Mountain, where his father, a Union surgeon, was wounded during the Civil War. Landis spent his early years in Ohio and Logansport, Indiana, leaving high school before graduating, but eventually earning a degree from Union College of Law in Chicago in 1891. Despite his Republican affiliation, Landis subsequently found himself part of Grover Cleveland's second administration as personal secretary to Secretary of State Walter Gresham, a long-time Republican and former military associate of Landis's father, who supported the Democrat Cleveland in the 1892 presidential election.

After declining a later offer to serve as minister to Venezuela, Landis returned to Chicago to practice law but soon became involved in Republican politics, directing the unsuccessful gubernatorial campaign of Frank Lowden in 1904. Landis also ardently supported President Theodore Roosevelt, who appointed him as a federal judge in Chicago in March 1905. Landis's years on the bench, however, demonstrated his penchant for theatrics and publicity rather than any clear aptitude for developing learned judicial opinions. In 1907, the forty-year-old judge achieved fame after imposing an extraordinary $29,400,000 fine on Standard Oil, one of the nation's most powerful companies, for accepting freight rebates. Yet an appeals court later overturned the verdict and Standard Oil ultimately paid nothing.

During World War I and its aftermath, Landis continued to grab headlines for imposing harsh sentences on members of radical groups, including the International Workers of the World (IWW) and the Socialist party. Some observers, such as author Henry Pringle, questioned his legal approach, noting that "few men have been as zealous in the suppression of minorities, and his charges to juries were dangerously close to patriotic addresses." (Roosevelt himself described Landis as having "the face of a fanatic—honest, fearless, well-meaning, but tense to a degree that makes me apprehensive lest it may presage a nervous breakdown.") Not surprisingly, higher courts once again reversed or commuted a number of Landis's decisions, including his twenty-year sentence of Victor Berger, a Wisconsin socialist elected to Congress in 1918.

Despite Landis's reputation as a "grandstand judge" and his often arbitrary behavior from the bench, his fame and stature continued to grow, eventually leading his career in a new direction. A devoted baseball fan, Landis had revealed himself as an industry friend after his delay in imposing a judgment in the outlaw Federal League's antitrust suit against major league baseball in 1915. In a move designed both to strengthen the administration of the business and to regain public credibility following the "Black Sox" scandal of 1919, in which several Chicago White Sox players admitted throwing the World Series, major league baseball selected Landis as its first commissioner in November 1920. Initially retaining his federal judgeship, Landis finally resigned that post in 1922 to devote his full time to the office of commissioner, which he would occupy until his death in 1944.[11]

Enjoying enviable authority to mediate disputes, interpret rules, and investigate "conduct detrimental to baseball," Landis earned praise from fans for his seeming unwillingness to kowtow to franchise owners. Moreover, as historian Harold Seymour noted, Landis functioned as "a symbol that reassured the public of baseball's honesty and integrity." Not surprisingly, some African Americans believed that Landis was "eminently fair" and might actually facilitate, rather than hinder, the integration of Organized Baseball. By the mid-1930s, Landis was clearly aware of the existence of black professional baseball. Prior to the 1934 East-West game at Comiskey Park, sportswriter Dave Hawkins, Gus Greenlee, and other officials met with Landis, who was reportedly "keenly interested" and "asked many questions about the players, their salaries, etc." J. B. Martin, a fellow Chicago Republican, also had several conferences with Landis in 1943 and 1944, discussing a variety of matters including a possible ban of all jumping players from major league parks. According to Martin, Landis advised him that "Negro baseball will never get on a firm footing until a commissioner is appointed and a sound treasury is built up. . . . He said he would help us any way he could to develop our leagues on a business basis."

Landis's reluctance to tackle the issue of integration, however, frustrated African Americans. While admitting that Landis had "done great things," sportswriter Mabe Kountze cited his failure to establish "baseball democracy." Like the major league owners, Landis was committed to a continued policy of segregation and was unwilling to disrupt the status quo. Yet Landis was hardly solely responsible for maintaining the color line and ultimately reflected, rather than shaped, the views of white officials. Future commissioner Albert "Happy" Chandler, for example, later noted that Landis "was doing what the owners wanted him to do, they wanted to keep it white and segregated and he kept it that way." Moreover, had the commissioner chosen to oppose the owners' position, it is questionable whether Landis possessed the authority to desegregate baseball. As his assistant Leslie O'Connor later explained, Landis "had no rule-making power. . . . If he had had any such power, there are certainly a dozen or more rules he would have thrown out." Notably, Landis himself claimed that he could not "do any damn thing about it . . . it's up to the club owners."[12]

The continued resistance from Landis and other Organized Baseball representatives led a number of black sportswriters, players, and officials to reject a protest strategy altogether. Future Chicago American Giants secretary R. S. Simmons pessimistically noted in 1939, "as long as we attempt to place our boys in the big leagues by trying to show that they are kept out thru segregation, discrimination and color, they will be kept out always." To some, economic factors, rather than active agitation, would provide the stimulus necessary for integration in baseball and elsewhere in American society. Journalist Ollie Stewart, for example, suggested that "the idea of being called good sports and humanitarians as their reward for throwing open the doors of lucrative jobs to colored ball players, does not appeal to them in the least. . . . Until owners of clubs are convinced that a big portion of the cash customers want to see colored players for their money—well, they'll never be home when you call. . . . Talk won't do it. It hasn't worked in politics—it couldn't frighten Amos 'n' Andy off the air."

Several observers embraced the earlier argument that black baseball needed to strengthen itself and demonstrate economic stability to achieve integration. In the midst of the 1933 campaign, Ben Taylor insisted that "it is time for us to stop ballyhooing about getting into the big leagues and start building our own big leagues up to the point where we will be recognized." Ed Harris of the *Tribune* shared Taylor's view, advising fans to "stop worrying about what the big leagues should or should not do and turn to our own leagues and see what we can do with them." Harris noted that, with the existence of a strong well-organized black baseball league, "we need not worry whether some of our players get into the big leagues. The big leagues will be contacting us."

A segment of African Americans even questioned whether integration was necessarily desirable or necessary. Simmons, for example, asked, "why keep trying to throw Negro ball players on a group which has proved it doesn't want you. Why not have some independence by building up and praising your own leagues and forget the other fellow has a league, like he forgets you have one." Journalist and promoter Dave Hawkins also favored a "thriving colored league" to the prospect of integrating the major leagues, as it would "benefit the greatest number of colored people with salaries and positions."[13]

During the mid-1930s, the existence of a strong black league or integration movement seemed remote. Yet developments in other sports, including Joe Louis's success in boxing, would soon return the issue to the forefront. The 1936 summer Olympics in Berlin would prove to be an even greater catalyst to the assault on baseball's color line, functioning as a showcase for black athletic skills and also offering an opportunity to expose the hypocrisy of American racial attitudes. While a record-setting number of African Americans appeared in the Olympics, only Jesse Owens attained national fame for his brilliant performance in track and field. The subsequent disclosure that Hitler had refused to congratulate Owens and other black medal winners unleashed a torrent of self-righteous commentary from white American journalists condemning Nazi prejudices. Yet in an insightful letter to the *New York Times*, Henry Slaughter scoffed at the "reams of inanity" in the press following the Olympics, noting that "writers who previously had never mentioned fair play and the Negro in the same columns jumped on the band-wagon" despite ignoring racial injustices for years.

The Berlin games did succeed in placing the issue of discrimination in sports in the national spotlight, forcing at least some Americans to reconsider their racial attitudes. Perhaps the most dramatic impact of the Berlin Olympics was the arrival of a new force in the integration fight: the American Communist party (CPUSA or CP), an organization that had already earned respect among some African Americans for its involvement in the celebrated Scottsboro case earlier in the decade. Beginning in 1935, the party had launched the "Popular Front," attempting to join with liberal, labor, and black groups to forge a coalition designed to counter fascist threats. Owens's performance galvanized an organization now committed to racial equality, eager to obtain black support, and violently opposed to fascism. Following the Olympics, the New York-based *Daily Worker*, the leading Communist newspaper, introduced a regular sports section and began its own aggressive campaign against segregated baseball as part of the CP's strategic assault on discrimination in sports. Attempting to publicize the skills of black athletes, the *Worker* would also make a genuine effort to cover black baseball contests and would remain an important, yet controversial part of the campaign for years to come.[14]

Responding to renewed pressure from black journalists, liberal white sportswriters, and American communists, several major league officials once again addressed the issue following the Olympics. Ford Frick continued to deny that any color ban existed, repeating verbatim the 1933 statement of his predecessor John Heydler. Yet Frick also suggested that desegregation was beyond the scope of Organized Baseball, "a 'sociological problem,' something society, not the big leagues, must solve." As Frick later explained, the "big leagues . . . cannot do anything we want to until public opinion is ready for it." Privately, Frick confided to Commissioner Landis his own concerns about sportswriter Jimmy Powers's ongoing campaign, admitting that "the whole thing can be a bit embarrassing."

The continued tepid response disappointed African Americans and demonstrated the still considerable resistance to integration. Moreover, despite support from liberal whites, other segments of the population remained firmly opposed to any change in the policy. Angry readers condemned Powers's efforts as "the silliest idea ever," offering numerous explanations for the color ban. As one correspondent observed, "they are gamblers. There'd be betting scandals which would ruin the sport." Others, such as one Queens resident, raised more blatantly racist objections, asking, "how would you like your sister to marry one?" Meanwhile, an informal poll of the nation's sportswriters by the NAACP journal *Crisis* in early 1937 confirmed the anticipated opposition from the South. Wilbur Kinley of the *Chattanooga News*, for example, claimed that "white men would never stand for it even in this time of rapid advancement of the Negro athlete" and suggested that black players would be "persecuted to death."[15]

Yet the New York news media, reflecting a more liberal local social climate, continued to express surprisingly strong support. While the efforts of the *Daily Worker* remained significant, more widely read mainstream newspapers including the *Post* and *Daily News* also provided sympathetic editorials in 1937. Brooklyn Dodger official Stephen McKeever's statement that he would sign Satchel Paige, pending manager Burleigh Grimes's approval, provided additional support that New York would be the ideal major league city to initiate integration. Grimes, however, remained reluctant, reportedly preferring to lose with whites than win with black players.

Despite the welcome support of white writers in New York and elsewhere during the late 1930s, African Americans remained at the forefront of the campaign. Moreover, the aggressive efforts of Washington sportswriter Sam Lacy would soon result in a surprising breakthrough. Born in 1905 in Connecticut, Lacy moved to Washington as a child and became interested in sports, later playing semipro baseball with several black teams. After writing occasional sports articles for a local black newspaper during the 1920s, Lacy became a full-time journalist at the *Washington Tribune* in 1934, beginning a remarkable career that spanned nearly seven decades until his death in 2003.

Ironically, Lacy was initially ambivalent toward major league integration. Wary of the potential for racial friction, Lacy wondered in 1935, "what's going to happen when the Nordic next to you or me let's [*sic*] loose with that fighting word at the colored outfielder who lets a fly-ball get lost in the sun at a crucial moment." Within two years, however, the young journalist had discarded his earlier doubts and become an active participant in the campaign. Dubious of the impact of prior pro-integration articles, "which never need be seen nor answered by the powers that be in professional baseball," Lacy decided to pursue a course that would instead allow "the magnates . . . to express themselves on the question." As an initial step, Lacy contacted Commissioner Landis in November 1937, warning of the ongoing "efforts of certain individuals . . . to intimidate organized baseball officials" into integration. Presenting a more moderate alternative, Lacy suggested that Landis recommend consideration of the issue and grant a hearing to three black journalists at the annual winter meetings in December.[16]

Receiving no response, Lacy then sent a copy of his Landis communication to Washington Senators president Clark Griffith, leading to a landmark two-and-a-half-hour meeting in December 1937. During his nearly five-decade career in the major leagues as pitcher, manager, and finally as part-owner of the Senators, the sixty-eight-year-old Missouri-born Griffith had elicited mixed reactions from blacks. While earning plaudits for his willingness to use Cuban players, the Senators official had also alienated black fans by banning interracial games at Griffith Stadium during the 1920s and maintaining an informal system of segregated seating for white games. Griffith, however, had consistently rented the park to black teams, often on more favorable terms than other major league owners. Moreover, Griffith recognized and appreciated the skills of black players, often watching their games with great interest.

Although black talent would presumably have enabled the cash-poor Senators to challenge the dominance of the wealthy New York Yankees, Griffith like other owners could only perceive of integration as detrimental to his franchise, and the strongly segregated city of Washington presented another formidable barrier. Not surprisingly, Griffith reiterated the familiar arguments against integration during his meeting with Lacy, the first black sportswriter to gain a prolonged audience with a major league official. While admitting that there were "some mighty good players in Negro baseball" and "very few big-league owners who are not aware of the fact that the time is not far off," Griffith cited the "cruel, filthy epithets" blacks would face in the major leagues. Griffith instead suggested that a strong separate black league offered a more immediate solution and might lead to recognition from Organized Baseball. Although Griffith's reasoning conveniently preserved the status quo and provided no tangible assistance, it also offered the possibility of future integration, seemingly validating what several black journalists had long contended, that only economic forces would open the doors to major league baseball.[17]

Two months after the pivotal meeting with Griffith, Pittsburgh Pirates president William Benswanger offered additional encouragement. The forty-six-year-old Benswanger, who had assumed control of the Pirates after his father-in-law Barney Dreyfuss died in 1932, related to Ches Washington of the *Courier* and Cum Posey that he would be "heartily in favor" and later promised to fight for integration if the issue were raised at a league meeting. One of only a handful of Jewish major league officials, Benswanger was familiar with black baseball through the Grays' rentals of Forbes Field and seemed genuinely intrigued by the prospect of integration. Benswanger suggested that black professional baseball could eventually be admitted to Organized Baseball as a minor league, providing a gateway to major league advancement. The idea appealed to Posey, who noted that "practically every player of the Negro National League can play well enough to belong to some League of Organized Ball." Benswanger appeared to be the most likely owner to sign a black player, particularly after he casually offered to purchase Josh Gibson in 1939. Posey, however, questioned the seriousness of the proposition, and Benswanger, as would be demonstrated later, ultimately lacked the resolve to initiate and guide any movement against the color line.

Although producing little, the meetings with Griffith and Benswanger confirmed that major league officials were very much aware of black baseball and had at least considered the possibility of integration. Moreover, African Americans had succeeded in initiating a serious dialogue with white Organized Baseball, raising hopes that more fruitful discussions would be held in the future. Yet no concrete program toward integration appeared imminent, and, as journalist Leon Hardwick observed, "colored baseball players seem to be a hot potato that all the big league magnates are afraid to touch for fear it'll burn them."[18]

During 1938, an unfortunate incident involving thirty-year-old New York Yankee outfielder Alvin "Jake" Powell would dramatically intensify the interaction between blacks and Organized Baseball. On July 29, WGN radio announcer Bob Elson interviewed Powell before a game against the Chicago White Sox at Comiskey Park. Asked by Elson how he spent his winter months, Powell replied that he worked as a policeman in Dayton, Ohio, and kept in shape using his club on "niggers." Although the station abruptly terminated the broadcast and issued apologies, African Americans would soon respond with a series of aggressive protests.[19]

Despite believing the "remark was due more to carelessness than intent," Commissioner Landis was forced to act, suspending Powell for ten days. The punishment, however, failed to appease a black population increasingly less tolerant of racial slurs. Several black communities circulated petitions, demanding a public apology from Powell. Others suggested sterner measures, including one fan who noted, "there's plenty of Negroes who help to pay his salary by going to the games but when he starts that stuff he's got to go."

Hoping to quell the growing furor, Yankee officials issued several apologies and offered explanations for the incident. General manager Ed Barrow blamed the unrehearsed radio interview, claiming it was a "slip of the tongue" that had caused Powell to "say something he did not mean at all." Barrow also alluded to Powell's Maryland background, noting that "white men can say things in the South that sound differently in the North." Finally, Barrow reminded critics that the franchise had donated money to the Harlem YMCA, employed blacks at Yankee Stadium, provided free passes to black elites, and rented the park at a lower cost to black teams. In the meantime, Powell attempted to make amends by claiming that he "would never mean to say anything offensive to the Negroes of Dayton, Chicago or anywhere else." On August 15, Powell publicly apologized to groups of blacks at several locations throughout Harlem, eventually appearing at the office of the *Amsterdam News*, where he professed his high "regard for the Negro people," his employment of blacks in his home, and his willingness to accept major league integration. Moreover, Powell denied making the original statement and, like Barrow, placed the blame on the radio station.[20]

Most blacks remained unmoved by Powell's apologies and called for his expulsion from baseball. While petitions continued to circulate, others advocated a boycott of all Yankee games and team owner Jacob Ruppert's beer. Powell, however, eventually returned to the Yankee lineup on August 16 in Washington, where black fans greeted him with a chorus of boos and a shower of pop bottles. Although Powell encountered similar black hostility in his rare subsequent appearances during the 1938 season, the Yankees made no attempt to part with the controversial outfielder. By 1939, Barrow had grown tired of responding to black inquiries regarding Powell, asking "why keep on stirring the matter up?" Barrow defended Powell's continued presence on the Yankees, asserting that "he is a good player . . . and it would hardly be right to kill his whole career for the one mistake." The scattered protests eventually faded, and Powell remained in the Yankee organization through 1940, although he committed suicide in 1948 after his arrest in Washington for bad check charges.

The Jake Powell incident, however, demonstrated the presence of an increasingly assertive black population that Organized Baseball could no longer easily ignore as in the past. As Al Monroe of the *Defender* observed, "for the first time professional baseball was forced to sit up and take notice of the Race's power. This could not and would not have happened ten years ago." Major league baseball, for example, had turned a blind eye to the numerous racial altercations involving the Georgia-born Ty Cobb between 1907 and 1919. Yet by 1938, Landis and Yankee officials recognized that some action was necessary to mollify a more vocal African American community. To Wendell Smith, the solicitous behavior of Organized Baseball reflected practical concerns and suggested that "the big league moguls realize the value of the Negro dollar. . . . And as a result, they treat us with care and caution. They give us interviews and hope in regards to the major league color question. They are careful not to let us think they don't give a hoot about us."

The Powell episode also focused attention on the plight of blacks in professional baseball and stimulated renewed interest in the integration fight among whites. The nationally syndicated Westbrook Pegler once again devoted a sympathetic column to the issue, suggesting that Organized Baseball's attitude toward blacks rivaled Hitler's treatment of the Jews. Meanwhile, a Brooklyn resident wrote to the *New York Times* urging fans to make a "sustained effort to bring about some action on this important issue. . . . Not only from the standpoint of justice but also from the viewpoint of sporting curiosity, I am eager to see the colored [Carl] Hubbells and [Joe] Medwicks given the chance to compete on an even basis against the nation's best talent."[21]

As the integration fight gained momentum, a number of observers pushed for a comprehensive effort in 1939, a year that would feature ongoing celebrations of the self-proclaimed hundredth anniversary of baseball. Dan Burley advised his fellow sportswriters to give the issue "first preference over everything, including Joe Louis' fights," and suggested that black players should present themselves at major league camps for tryouts. While a number of journalists remained actively involved in the movement during 1939, the *Courier*'s Wendell Smith became a particularly significant figure. Born in Detroit in 1914, Smith attended West Virginia State University and joined the *Courier* full-time shortly following his graduation in 1937. Smith soon began to attack baseball's color line in his weekly column, and would make the issue a personal crusade in the years to follow.

Unconvinced by the owners' alibi that players and managers would not accept integration, Smith conducted a landmark series of interviews during the summer of 1939 with members of each of the eight National League teams. Surprisingly, five of the eight managers polled expressed a willingness to sign blacks if the owners granted permission. Citing the recognized ability of black players, Pirates manager Pie Traynor asserted that "it is a known fact that there are plenty Negroes capable of playing in the big leagues." Bill McKechnie of the Cincinnati Reds offered a similar endorsement, claiming that he had seen "at least 25" black players of major league caliber. Smith also found Gabby Hartnett (Cubs), Doc Prothro (Phillies), and Leo Durocher (Dodgers) responsive to employing blacks in the major leagues.

While avoiding outright rejection, the three remaining managers voiced considerable misgivings over the prospect of integration. Ray Blades of the St. Louis Cardinals, the southernmost franchise in the National League, felt the "chances are very slim" and believed that the "social prejudice that exists right now will have to be broken down." New York Giants manager Bill Terry agreed, citing the "problem of mingling socially . . . and traveling about the country," and like Griffith suggested that the best solution lay in the formation of a single well-organized black league. Meanwhile, Casey Stengel of the Boston Braves questioned black fans' support of their own teams and hinted that the "unrest" in black baseball provided another rationale for exclusion.[22]

Smith's poll gained considerable attention from both blacks and whites, including American League president Will Harridge who claimed to be following its progress. As an outgrowth of Smith's efforts, the *Daily Worker* interviewed several American League managers, including Fred Haney of the St. Louis Browns and Del Baker of the Detroit Tigers, and received similarly favorable responses. By the end of 1939, an unprecedented number of major league players and managers had publicly acknowledged the issue, although the impact remained unclear. Like Landis, the players and managers simply shifted responsibility to the owners but were unwilling to champion the issue themselves. Fay Young questioned the value of Smith's efforts, noting that "all the interviews with the big league players don't amount to the space it takes to print them for the reason these players have nothing to do with the question." To Young, management and the public would ultimately determine if and when integration occurred.

The candor of white responses also appeared questionable. In the wake of the furor following the Jake Powell incident a year earlier, few major leaguers were willing to risk incurring the wrath of African Americans for a similar indiscretion. Questioned by Dan Burley in October 1939, Yankee pitcher Johnny Murphy refused to be quoted and suggested that Burley speak to general manager Ed Barrow. Manager Joe McCarthy was similarly evasive, explaining that he had "no money in the New York Yankee organization and I cannot discuss things over which I have no control."

Not surprisingly, the behavior of several white players during unguarded moments offset the tolerant responses elicited by Smith. Along with their segregationist manager Bill Terry, the New York Giants featured second baseman Burgess Whitehead, who was involved in two controversies during 1939, assaulting a North Carolina black woman and uttering a racial slur at a New York club. Harkening back to an earlier racist superstition, the Giants also hired a thirteen-year-old Harlem youth as a mascot, often rubbing his head for good luck. The experiences of future black journalist Art Rust, Jr., at major league games in New York in 1939 provided an additional barometer of white attitudes. Washington outfielder Taft Wright and St. Louis Cardinal pitcher Clyde Shoun responded to the twelve-year-old Rust's request for autographs with racial epithets, leading the disheartened youngster to believe that he would "never live to see black guys play major league ball."[23]

With player prejudice still intact, sustained pressure on the owners seemed more likely to produce results. Concurrent with Smith's poll, the *Daily Worker* and other Communist Party members mounted an aggressive petition drive, collecting signatures at several NNL games including a July 23 promotion at Yankee Stadium. Thirteen days later, the Young Communist League of Eastern Pennsylvania appeared at Parkside Field for a game between the Philadelphia Stars and the New York Cubans, gathering 1,200 signatures, including those of Pompez and Bolden. Believing the "opportunity is much more ripe in 1939 . . . than it has been before," an enthusiastic Bolden introduced the Communist activists to his players and noted that "no harm can be done and surely nothing can be lost by trying."

Some African Americans, however, remained ambivalent over the potentially counterproductive role of the communists in the movement. Communist involvement provided a convenient rationale for the ultraconservative Organized Baseball establishment to reject any suggestion of integration, and as black journalist Ric Roberts later lamented, "it is an old and oft-used Dixie custom to shout 'Communist' at any vigorous effort to improve the opportunities open to colored people." Clark Griffith would even later suggest that blacks had been merely a "tool" of the communists, insisting that "it wasn't anything but the Communists that wanted to get that program over . . . the nigras themselves didn't want it." Yet the communists succeeded in publicizing the issue beyond the realm of the black

Figure 22. Philadelphia Stars pitcher Webster
McDonald signs a petition circulated by the Young
Communist League, Parkside Field, August 1939.
Courtesy John Holway.

newspapers which reached relatively few white readers. Black sportswriters such as Dan Burley recognized the importance of the communist effort,
observing that "the Daily Worker, and you can't dodge the truth, took the
initiative in organizing committees, drawing up petitions and handbills,
and getting signatures."

The dual impact of the signature campaign and Smith's poll raised
hopes that the integration of Organized Baseball was imminent. Like Bolden, Cum Posey asserted that "there is no doubt that Negro baseball players are closer to entrance into the leagues of white organized baseball at
the present time than ever before." Black fans eagerly awaited the annual

major league winter meetings in December 1939, hoping the matter would be discussed. At the subsequent gathering in Cincinnati, a Communist Party official presented the two major league presidents with a petition reportedly signed by 50,000 individuals, including black labor activist A. Philip Randolph. Yet team owners once again failed to address the issue, increasingly frustrating black fans anticipating a breakthrough for the 1940 season.[24]

The disappointment of 1939 led to a general reconsideration of what direction the movement should now take. Former Hilldale player and official Lloyd Thompson disavowed the petition campaign as "futile as it is ridiculous," a position shared by Ed Harris, who continued to suggest that economic factors would force integration. As Harris noted, "petitions, agitation to the contrary, Negroes will get into baseball when their entry means money in the box-office and not before." Moreover, Harris suggested that prosperous teams such as the Yankees had little financial incentive to integrate and "even the Phillies and the A's seem content to get along without the help of the sepia brothers." Young Communist League official Earl Vann disagreed, claiming "the money angle is the wrong one, because if we waited to get enough money, the Negroes certainly would never make the grade. Why shouldn't the players apply on the basis of ability? . . . Pressure from the public is what is needed most."

After the 1939 protest effort once again culminated in failure, the issue faded somewhat during 1940 and 1941. While the Communists and labor organizations continued to organize petitions and the white and black media addressed the matter sporadically, the earlier optimism and aggressiveness had seemingly dissipated. The sudden loss of momentum concerned E. B. Rea of the *Afro*, who wondered whether "something has transpired to curtail, even blot out the determined drive." With baseball once again financially solvent by the end of the Depression, however, the motivation for reconsideration of integration was minimal, and the likelihood of any policy change in the immediate future appeared remote.[25]

◆ ◆ ◆

Although the movement toward integration stalled somewhat after 1939, white Americans were no longer unaware of the existence of talented black athletes. The success of Joe Louis and Jesse Owens in interracial competition had resulted in unprecedented media exposure of African American sports figures. While welcome, the increasing coverage of black athletes in newspapers and mass circulation magazines during the 1930s and early 1940s varied widely in quality, ranging from patronizing and misinformed to sympathetic and perceptive.

Many white writers, regardless of their attitudes toward integration, remained unable or unwilling to transcend stereotypical views of African Americans, often emphasizing their supposedly "natural" comedic traits. Although the furious fighting prowess of Louis lent itself less successfully to such glib characterizations, black baseball struggled to overcome white expectations of buffoonery reinforced by the media. In 1934, Dan Daniel of the *New York World-Telegram* explained to his readers the difference between white and black baseball, noting that "a Negro ball game is not a staid and stolid demonstration of fielding and hitting. It embodies comic relief impossible in white games because no Caucasian can play baseball with the rhythmic quality inherent in the black race."

Not surprisingly, white writers found Satchel Paige an ideal subject to profile. While Paige was perhaps the greatest pitcher of his generation, white or black, equally brilliant black players such as Josh Gibson received considerably less coverage. Paige's rural background, colorful antics, and lanky appearance jibed more comfortably with white perceptions of African Americans and offered ample opportunities to reinforce existing stereotypes. A July 1940 *Saturday Evening Post* article by Ted Shane featured Southern dialect ("No, suh," "is you," and "ah does") along with descriptions of Paige's "apelike arms" and his "Stepinfetchit accent." Moreover, Shane had little positive to say about black professional baseball, instead lapsing into typical depictions of black players who "clown a lot, go into dance steps [and] argue noisily and funnily." The article disappointed Sterling Brown, who felt the piece failed to highlight racial discrimination and instead offered the underlying subtext that "the Negro ballplayer plays good baseball on his side of the line, and is himself happy and to others amusing." The *Saturday Evening Post* refused to acknowledge the numerous errors in Shane's article cited by Rollo Wilson, and, as Ed Harris remarked, "all in all the inference was that we should be grateful for what crumbs are allowed to fall our way, especially when distributed by such an organization as the Saturday Evening Post."

Concurrent coverage of Paige's phenomenal pitching skills ultimately succeeded in offsetting the often demeaning one-dimensional portrayals by Shane and other white writers. Yet Syd Pollock's Ethiopian Clowns conformed perfectly to the view of blacks as entertainers rather than athletes. During the late 1930s and early 1940s, the Clowns received generous white press attention, attributable less to their athletic skills than to their comedy performances and face-painting. By 1942, media coverage focused on Edward Davis (also known as "Peanuts Nyasses"), a capable pitcher also known for his zany antics on the ball field. Although both black leagues featured numerous pitchers of comparable or superior ability, white periodicals such as the *Sporting News* and the *Chicago Daily*

News devoted columns to Davis, touted by Chicago sportswriter Gene Kessler as the leading candidate to integrate the major leagues.[26]

A September 1942 feature in *Liberty* magazine illustrated the appeal of
Davis and the Clowns to a larger white audience. Written by Shane, the
piece, like his Paige article two years earlier, carefully emphasizes the
"comical" attributes of black entertainers still expected and embraced by
contemporary white America. Davis, for example, is described as "invariably discovered snoozing somewhere in the stands" when summoned to
pitch, "usually broke," and possessing an "unfortunate fondness for po-
nies and African golf balls [dice]." Shane also provides an abundance of
Amos 'n' Andy-style quotes ("Ah pitched good—but Ah jes' didn't get
the laughs!") along with photographs of the Clowns in grass skirts. Not
surprisingly, the article largely ignored the increasingly discussed issue of
integration, although it briefly noted Syd Pollock's desire to "some day
convince big-league moguls there is a place . . . for a team like the
Clowns." The media recognition of Davis once again demonstrated that
mainstream whites accepted and remained relatively unthreatened by
blacks appearing as comedians. Washington sportswriter Shirley Povich
even suggested that clowning might offer an avenue to the major leagues,
but others believed that it provided yet another convenient rationale for
continued black exclusion.

The glorification of clowning ultimately diverted attention from the true
talents of black athletes. Similarly, the tendency of whites to offer pseudo-
scientific explanations for black success proved equally frustrating. In a
February 1938 *Esquire* article discussing intellectual function and athletic
skills, Herb Graffis suggested that recent black achievement in sports "is
easily explained by the doctors and fits exactly into their theory that primarily, the more brainless the athlete, the better the athlete. . . . The colored kid can act more like an animal as he is less apt; because of
environment and education, to deliberately think. The white boy is handicapped in athletic performance by having had more contact with what is
conveniently called civilization." While recognizing the increasing black
dominance in boxing, Graffis observed that "Caucasians can console
themselves with the thought that a prize fight is basically an animal show
in which a developed higher intelligence is a positive handicap." Not surprisingly, white sportswriters were more likely to attribute the phenomenal
accomplishments of Joe Louis to the " 'jungle' origins of his people" rather
than his training, preparation, and boxing skills.[27]

Major media outlet coverage of black athletes thus proved to be a mixed
blessing, generating positive attention yet reinforcing existing stereotypical
views and seldom challenging fundamental racial inequalities. Following
Shane's piece on Paige and an unflattering profile of Joe Louis in *Life*

(written by black journalist Earl Brown, a former Lincoln Giant) in 1940, a disgusted Ches Washington remarked that "these articles about our sports heroes in the big national magazines do almost as much damage as they do good." As late as 1942, Cum Posey continued to hope for an accurate portrayal of black baseball in a major periodical, noting the "fantastic" nature of past efforts.

Although the white media often appeared incapable and unwilling to profile black athletic figures and sports with sensitivity and intelligence, a handful of writers did display surprising objectivity. A 1938 *Esquire* piece by author-historian Alvin Harlow, entitled "Unrecognized Stars," not only avoided many of the typical stereotypes but provided relatively reliable information. Harlow delineated the often arduous conditions in black professional baseball, yet assessed the caliber of play as comparable to upper-level white minor leagues. Perhaps more importantly, Harlow refrained from convenient generalizations, recognizing the colorful play of some black players but observing that "others are as nonchalant and machine-like as any major leaguer."[28]

Three years later, *Esquire* published a more comprehensive article, reflecting an increasing awareness of racial discrimination following the recent creation of the Fair Employment Practices Committee. In "May the Best White Man Win," journalist Curt Riess offered a thoughtful analysis of the color line in American sports. While blacks had achieved remarkable success in boxing, track, and other sports, Riess cited the continued "humiliations for the Negro athletes," who remained largely barred from white college basketball teams and could play college football only in northern locales. Riess also addressed white baseball's policy of exclusion, remarking that "as far as the Major Leagues are concerned, they don't exist. Nowhere is the color line drawn so sharply." Riess argued that "the color line is doubly unfair because it doesn't really exist . . . nowhere is the color line written into rules or conditions of admission. Probably, if it were, that would be considered unconstitutional by the courts, for it would be depriving American citizens of their rights."

Unlike earlier articles, Riess provided encouragement for the future. Recent events, including the unwillingness of Harvard and the Amateur Athletic Union (AAU) to conform fully to Southern racial practices, suggested the potential birth of a new era in sports. Moreover, Riess's assertion that "all of the best sports journalists" favored equal rights for black athletes, offered hope that the white media's efforts in subsequent years would bolster rather than hinder the movement toward integration.[29]

The modest exposure granted to black athletes in *Esquire* and other national periodicals, however, represented only a fraction of the white media's relentless sports coverage that permeated the consciousness of African Americans each day. Despite steady growth, the weekly black press could only supplement, rather than entirely replace, the omnipresent white newspapers, magazines, radio stations, and newsreels. Even the most race-conscious African American found it difficult to remain entirely isolated from the dominant white culture, and many would develop an active interest in white sporting activities along with black.

Subject to heavy publicity from the major leagues, most African American baseball fans were keenly aware of white players and teams. The Yankees, for example, enjoyed strong black patronage, and, according to one commentator, one-fifth of the 30,000 fans at Yankee Stadium for the second game of the 1932 World Series were black. Not surprisingly, Babe Ruth was extremely popular among black fans, and following his signing to a Yankee contract in 1933, a reporter claimed that "Harlem is breathing easier." Black interest was hardly limited to New York, as a journalist in 1936 described the "the groups of colored 'baseball radio fans' who gather before loud speakers in front of stores in every city in the land giving vent to opinions with more depth than the baseball experts."[30]

Most black fans who followed the progress of white teams continued to support black professional baseball. A sizable segment, however, ignored black baseball altogether, internalizing the media view that white professional players represented the nation's best. Since the formation of the first black professional leagues in the 1920s, team owners, players, and journalists had bitterly criticized African Americans who chose to patronize white games rather than their own. The problem had failed to dissipate in the 1930s, leading black journalist Walter St. Clair to complain that "it has been said, and his actions where organized baseball is concerned bear out the statement, that the American Negro has less race pride and self-respect than any other individual in civilization." Philadelphia fan Charles Carrington offered a similar assessment, questioning, "why do our people allow the subject of white baseball to dominate their conversation? This particularly disgusts me. Most of these rabid fans cannot be coaxed to attend a game at 44th and Parkside. Let us go out and support our teams and thus make our own major league!"

The dilemma was particularly acute in cities that featured major league parks located in or near the black community. In New York, St. Clair Bourne of the *Amsterdam News* alluded to "regular Harlem major league fanatics" and hoped the Jake Powell incident of 1938 would encourage such fans "into giving their own boys a break." In Chicago, Fay Young noted instances in the late 1930s and early 1940s where the White Sox drew more black fans than the American Giants, citing "the young Negro who prefers to spend his money to see two all-white teams play in a major league which draws the color line." Meanwhile, Sterling Brown claimed that in Washington "during a Negro double-header, the announced scores of the white games were greeted with more applause than the game the Negro fans were watching."

White organized baseball thus victimized blacks not only through exclusion but through competition for the entertainment dollar. Virtually all black enterprises lost patronage to white competitors, and baseball was no exception. Although the caliber of play in black and white professional baseball was clearly comparable, factors other than race shaped economic decision-making, and the superior organization, financial backing, and publicity swayed some fans toward more active support of white teams. Moreover, some African Americans rejected pleas for racial consciousness and development of a black economy, and, as R. S. Simmons lamented in 1937, "you would be surprised to hear some of these conversations where Race members are busy praising the other fellow's business and downing their own." Fay Young, however, cited the negative impact of black attendance on Organized Baseball's continued segregation policy, arguing that "as long as we help to fill the ball yards—nothing will ever happen. Every time we lay down our dollar we are telling these owners that we are satisfied."[31]

◆ ◆ ◆

American involvement in World War II would prove to be a watershed for the integration fight, as it would for numerous other aspects of African American life. The need to strengthen national unity and raise the initially low morale of African Americans during the crisis resulted in greater attention to black protest than ever before. While the creation of the Fair Employment Practices Commission in 1941 helped facilitate black employment in the defense industries, breakthroughs occurred in other areas, including entertainment. In 1942, NAACP executive secretary Walter White, Wendell Willkie, and other officials met with several Hollywood studio heads, who agreed to make greater efforts to cast blacks in less stereotypical roles. Radio programs also began to modify their negative depictions of blacks. In a particularly noteworthy example, the federally sponsored national radio series *Freedom's People* aired on NBC from September 1941 to April 1942, highlighting black contributions to American life, including an episode on sports featuring Yankee outfielder Joe DiMaggio's positive comments about Satchel Paige.

The fight against foreign fascism also succeeded in creating greater awareness of discrimination. As Gunnar Myrdal observed in the 1944 landmark study *An American Dilemma*, "Negro leaders know full well that they have immense possibilities of putting pressure upon the American nation during this War for democracy." Not surprisingly, the integration movement, somewhat dormant during 1940 and 1941, received a decisive boost from the conflict, and, as journalist Julius Adams later recalled, "the war came and people everywhere began talking about ONE WORLD, the dignity of the individual, and the equality of man." Moreover, military commitments would soon drastically deplete the ranks of white Organized Baseball, bolstering arguments that capable black players should be signed as replacements and could stimulate sagging attendance.

Blacks, communists, labor unions (particularly the CIO), and white liberals escalated the campaign during early 1942, bolstered by the federal government's increasing concern with the low morale of African Americans. Citing discrimination's negative effect on the war effort, Dan Burley urged the major leagues to integrate, insisting that "if the best interests of our country are to be served, every vestige of racial and color discrimination must be destroyed at once." Several *New York Times* readers also recognized the propaganda value of wartime integration, including a Chicago man who noted that "basketball, football, track and other sports already have accepted Negro players. Let major league baseball do the same and our enemies will have one less argument to use against us and our democracy." (Japanese propaganda leaflets circulated in the Philippines during the war reportedly cited American discrimination in professional baseball.)[32]

Activists soon attempted a new strategy that reflected the growing aggressiveness of black protest during the war. On March 18, Herman Hill, Los Angeles correspondent for the *Pittsburgh Courier*, accompanied two California-based black players, infielder Jackie Robinson and pitcher Nate Moreland, to the Chicago White Sox spring training camp at Brookside Park in Pasadena, California, and requested a tryout. The twenty-three-year-old Robinson had impressed White Sox manager Jimmy Dykes in the late 1930s while playing baseball for Pasadena Junior College. Moreland had pitched in the NNL for the Baltimore Elite Giants in 1940 and then jumped to Mexico in 1941. Dykes recognized the skills of both men, but nevertheless declined to offer a tryout, repeating the familiar excuse that it was "strictly up to the club owners and Judge Landis to start the ball a-rolling." Years later, Hill presented a less favorable version of the incident, noting that Dykes, a Philadelphia native whose local bowling alleys barred blacks for years, "refused to pose for pictures with Jackie and Nate," and "several White Sox players hovered around menacingly with bats in their hands."[33]

Although the California episode was ignored or underpublicized by most white dailies, the *Daily Worker* provided enthusiastic coverage and subsequently resumed its forceful attack on baseball's color line. In May, sports editor Lester Rodney demanded action from Commissioner Landis, the "MAN RESPONSIBLE FOR KEEPING JIM CROW IN OUR NATIONAL PASTIME," whose continued silence had preserved "a relic of the slave market long repudiated in other American sports." Subsequently, the *Worker* published the commissioner's office address, urging readers and unions to contact Landis in support of integration. By late June, the 80,000-worker Ford local UAW-CIO in Detroit passed a resolution opposing the ban, while more mainstream individuals including Bishop Bernard Sheil of Chicago (founder of the Catholic Youth Organization) labeled the policy "not only a disgrace to democracy but . . . harmful to National Morale." While Landis remained silent, a meeting with a *Worker* correspondent revealed his growing awareness and discomfort with the potentially explosive issue. Asserting that "there is no man living who wants more to have the friendship of the Negro people than I," Landis nevertheless refused to comment officially on the subject. Moreover, Landis suggested that while "you fellows say I am responsible," the owners were actually to blame and should bear the brunt of public pressure.

A subsequent controversy involving Brooklyn Dodgers manager Leo Durocher provided Landis with the opportunity to publicly articulate his views. After the *Worker* reprinted earlier comments (probably from Wendell Smith's 1939 poll) revealing Durocher's professed willingness to sign black players if granted permission, Landis met with the Dodger manager, who denied the statement. Facing increasing public pressure and wary of complaints that the color bar was contributing to national disunity, Landis subsequently issued his first public comment on integration on July 16: "I have come to the conclusion that it is time for me to express myself on this important issue. Negroes are not barred from organized baseball by the commissioner and never have been during the 21 years I have served as commissioner. . . . That is the business of the managers and the club owners. The business of the commissioner is to interpret the rules of baseball and enforce them."[34]

Landis, who had confided to *PM* sportswriter Joe Cummiskey that he was "sick and tired of getting hell from various people for barring Negroes from baseball," placed the matter back into the hands of the individual franchises. Yet whether the statement would result in any tangible progress other than publicizing the issue remained to be seen. Art Carter believed that Landis failed to go far enough, observing that "all he has said, in effect is that no law keeps owners from hiring colored players. Likewise, no law prevents a colored man from being President." The always cynical Fay Young agreed, condemning the "same old worn-out statement." As Young noted, if no rule barred blacks, then "what keeps them out? That's a question that Landis ought to answer. . . . President Roosevelt has ordered no discrimination in defense work. That discrimination remains is a certainty."[35]

The response of most major league officials was predictably timorous. Ironically, several used the war to rationalize their decision, such as Ed Barrow, who dismissed integration advocates as "all wet" for "using every bad judgment in stirring up such matters at this time with the World War and many other important matters to occupy the public mind." Not surprisingly, Walter White of the NAACP bristled at the "arrogance" of Barrow's stance, which ignored an issue of "economic importance in a profession dependent upon public support, which is the essence of the professed war aims of the United Nations." Yet Barrow's view was hardly atypical throughout the industry, as Chicago Cubs general manager James Gallagher offered a similar reaction, suggesting that "everybody in this country should be doing something of more value . . . than stirring up racial hatred." Clark Griffith, profiting heavily from park rentals, also expressed opposition, asserting that "colored people should develop their own big league baseball and challenge the best of the white major leagues. . . . Why take a few stars like Satchel Paige and Josh Gibson away and put them in with the whites and ruin organized colored baseball? No, build up your leagues for the benefit of all colored ball players instead of just a few."[36]

Brooklyn Dodger president Larry MacPhail, however, provided the most candid response. Rejecting the validity of the Landis statement, MacPhail cited the "unwritten law tantamount to an agreement between major league clubs on the subject of avoiding the racial issue," and suggested that "any claim . . . that negro players have had opportunity in organized baseball is sheer hypocrisy." MacPhail instead attributed the color line to "practical baseball problems which are involved," and dismissed racism charges as "vicious propaganda circulated by professional agitators who do not know what they are talking about." The conservative, yet widely read *Sporting News* soon embraced MacPhail's stand in an August 6 editorial, "No Good from Raising Race Issue," similarly denouncing "agitators, ever ready to seize an issue that will redound to their profit or self aggrandizement, who have sought to force Negro players on the big leagues, not because it would help the game, but because it gives them a chance to thrust themselves into the limelight as great crusaders in the guise of democracy."[37]

Despite still strongly entrenched opposition to integration, the Landis statement ultimately encouraged some franchises to take halting steps toward signing a black player. By late July, Art Carter claimed that at least six major league teams had begun to scout NNL games. The Pittsburgh Pirates appeared to be the most likely candidate to integrate, thanks to their president William Benswanger, who had already expressed interest in Josh Gibson three years earlier. Emboldened by Landis's statement, Benswanger seemed finally committed to action, noting that "colored men are American citizens with American rights. I know there are many problems connected with the question, but after all, somebody has to make the first move." On July 25, the *Daily Worker* announced that the Pirates would offer a tryout on August 4 to catcher Roy Campanella and infielder Sammy Hughes of the Baltimore Elite Giants, along with pitcher Dave Barnhill of the New York Cubans. The story was soon picked up by the Associated Press and other national press outlets, raising hopes among African Americans that major league integration would soon be a reality.

The still tentative Benswanger, however, subsequently denied the *Daily Worker* account, disappointing the numerous black fans who flocked to Forbes Field on August 4 to watch the historic tryout. Eager to disassociate himself from any communist-sponsored effort, Benswanger instead designated the *Courier*, rather than the *Worker*, to select four players, warning that "there still are many problems of traveling and playing to be ironed out. . . . I am not going to hire a player only because he's colored. Any move I make will be calculated to help our team." Still convinced of Benswanger's sincerity, the *Courier*'s Wendell Smith submitted a new list featuring NNL candidates recruited from the Grays (catcher Josh Gibson and infielder-outfielder Sam Bankhead) and Eagles (pitcher Leon Day and infielder Willie Wells). Yet the continued lack of a specific date for the tryout led some observers to question Benswanger's actual commitment level. Facing increasing pressure and seemingly wary of the entire controversy, Benswanger ultimately weakened and quietly abandoned his integration plans by late August.

Although Benswanger's indecisiveness and self-doubt remained the primary reason for the disappointment, increasingly frustrated black sportswriters searched for other causes. Several journalists criticized Wendell Smith's handling of the entire affair, questioning his player selections and failure to consult other black sportswriters. Dan Burley felt that Smith had been too eager to "grab some of the spotlight" and denounced his decision to confer with Joe Cummiskey, the sports editor of the liberal New York daily *PM*, "who was called by long distance, it seems, when 'Windy's' scant knowledge of the men he purportedly follows . . . proved so meager and vague." Burley also challenged Smith's disavowal of communist support, noting that in contrast to the efforts of the *Daily Worker*, " 'Windy' has yet to show the world any handbill, petition, or evidence beyond his writings in his own paper, that he is alive on the Negro in big league question."[38]

Yet neither the involvement of the communists nor Smith's choices deserved blame for the abortive Pittsburgh tryout. Regardless of any protest strategy, major league officials remained content to pay lip service to the notion of integration but unwilling to undertake the formidable task. The Cleveland Indians, for example, epitomized the continued insincere attitude throughout Organized Baseball. After quashing rumors of a September tryout for three Cleveland Buckeyes (infielder Parnell Woods, outfielder Sam Jethroe, and pitcher Eugene Bremmer), Indians president Alva Bradley offered the excuse that the three men "just don't stack up as material for the Indians," conveniently citing their weak performance in an August 18 game.[39]

The struggling Philadelphia Phillies proved equally disappointing. Desperate for competent players and financially shaky, team president Gerry Nugent seemingly possessed little to lose and much to gain from integration. Yet Nugent proved as reactionary as other major league officials, rejecting an ideal opportunity to sign Philadelphia native Roy Campanella, who requested a tryout from Phillies officials during the summer of 1942. Despite owning a team that would win only 42 games and draw fewer than 231,000 fans that season, Nugent was unenthusiastic and dissuaded the young catcher by suggesting he would have to begin his career in the south in the Georgia-Florida League. The tryout, similar to those rumored in Cleveland and Pittsburgh, was never held. Nugent instead suggested that integration should begin in the minor leagues while offering the familiar alibi that he was "just the president" and "not responsible for the hiring of members of the team."[40]

Unbeknownst to African Americans, the Phillies would soon miss another opportunity to integrate. After the team's fifth consecutive last place finish, the National League pressured Nugent to sell the debt-ridden franchise, sparking the interest of renowned minor league promoter Bill Veeck. Following the 1942 season, Veeck and his associate Rudie Schaffer met with Nugent and began to seek financial backing for a potential purchase of the Phillies. Simultaneously, Veeck secretly investigated the possibility of signing black players for the team, contacting Fay Young of the *Defender* and midwestern promoter Abe Saperstein to discuss potential prospects. As Veeck later explained, he planned to hold tryout camps prior to the 1943 season and retain black players "if they could beat out the white players that the Phillies had, which would have given essentially a black ball club." Veeck, however, was unable to complete a deal for the franchise, which was eventually acquired by the National League and then sold to a syndicate headed by thirty-three-year-old New York lumberman William Cox in 1943. In his autobiography and interviews up to his death in 1986, Veeck blamed the failed sale on the interference of Landis, an assumption that scholars have been unable to substantiate.[41]

Despite the failed attempts in Philadelphia, Pittsburgh, and Cleveland, it remained questionable whether a tryout setting would facilitate or hinder integration efforts. To some observers, the notion that professional black players required a "tryout" was little more than a smoke screen or delaying tactic, a belief confirmed by a statement from Larry MacPhail. In a September 10 meeting with several integration advocates, MacPhail informed the gathering that "we know every Negro player who can pick up a bat or a glove." MacPhail's frankness, compared to other major league officials, seemed to offer some encouragement, as did his assertion that blacks "should have the opportunity not only to play in the leagues but should have a lot of other opportunities in employment, housing and other things!" While promising to raise the issue formally at the annual winter meetings in December, MacPhail proved as disingenuous as Bradley and Benswanger, resigning his position with the Dodgers to join the army less than two weeks after the meeting. Meanwhile, the December meetings in Chicago would ultimately prove anticlimactic. Despite threats to involve the FEPC, officials rejected an attempt by a committee representing the Chicago CIO Council to gain admission to the December 3 joint session, citing their failure to obtain prior permission from the commissioner's office.[42]

Buoyed by wartime developments, the integration movement came tantalizingly close to success during 1942. Moreover, the unprecedented prosperity of black professional baseball provided an additional financial incentive for integration and, according to Cum Posey, helped to elicit the "belated statement from Judge Landis." The general lack of collaboration between team owners and integration advocates, however, led to an increasing questioning of black professional baseball's role in the ongoing effort.

Several observers suggested that self-interest prevented black baseball officials from taking a more aggressive stance toward integration. As early as 1935, Dan Burley asserted that the owners "don't give a single yap about Negroes getting in the big leagues," citing the potential disastrous economic impact of even one black player on a major league team. Yet despite perceptions of opposition, most officials were supportive during the 1930s. Cum Posey believed it was a "positive crime" to bar Josh Gibson from major league baseball and argued that whites would pay to see black players "just the same as they will pay to see Joe Louis fight . . . or Jesse Owens run." Other supporters included Commissioner Ferdinand Morton, who publicly advocated the entrance of blacks into white Organized Baseball, and Bolden and Pompez, both of whom eagerly endorsed the 1939 signature campaign.

The considerable profits of the early 1940s, however, would generate more ambivalent attitudes toward integration. Increasingly leery of major league exploitation, Effa Manley related to Burley that she "wouldn't like to see our star players in the big leagues, unless we owners were given assurances that we wouldn't be robbed of our vested interests in the players we develop." Offering a more comprehensive argument in 1942, Cum Posey believed the integration issue should not be dropped in the hands of black baseball owners, who "have had a very hard time building up Negro baseball into a paying business." Posey emphasized the Grays would sell, not give, their players to the major leagues, insisting that "we have a business and are going to attempt to protect it the same as any other Negro or white business men." Regardless of whether integration occurred, Posey announced that "we are going to continue to build up organized Negro baseball."[43]

The Landis statement prompted widespread public discussion of the issue among officials in both leagues. While Tom Wilson predictably remained silent, NAL president J. B. Martin expressed his support of integration, noting that he could not "see where it would injure our baseball one bit and if it did I am still for it. Why, it would make Negro Baseball." J. L. Wilkinson also felt it would be a "fine thing for the game . . . although we would lose some of our stars," while James Semler believed that "nothing better could happen . . . whatever the big leagues do, our teams will profit." Cleveland Buckeyes business manager Wilbur Hayes anticipated greater interest in baseball among African Americans, predicting that "they will use our teams as builders for the majors, and you'll see a lot of Negro talent that otherwise would remain hidden." Effa Manley agreed, suggesting integration would "boom baseball among my people. . . . More and more young colored boys would take up baseball as a profession." Yet the silence of several other owners and the lack of a forceful joint policy statement from the NNL and NAL annoyed Wendell Smith, who observed that "it is no secret that some of the owners have looked upon this fight from a selfish, ungrateful angle." Equally dissatisfied with the temperate response, Dan Burley cited the "desire latent in the average club owner's bosom in which he wants to perpetuate and get rich off an institution built on a Jim Crow condition."

Statements from Larry MacPhail appeared to justify the criticisms of Smith and Burley. Attempting to rationalize the continuation of the color line, MacPhail claimed that he was familiar with the views of black baseball officials and did "not know of a single one who believes that the best interests of the negro player would be promoted by raiding their clubs and leagues of a few outstanding players." While a few men would increase their earnings, MacPhail suggested that "it might also mean that hundreds of negro players would not have any opportunity . . . to play professional baseball" and warned that integration "might wreck these leagues." Surprisingly, black sportswriter Joe Bostic, a later convert to the integration cause, echoed MacPhail's opinion, noting that the "entry of even ONE Negro player on a league team would serve completely to monopolize the attention of the Negro and white present followers of Negro baseball. . . . Organized Negro baseball is a million dollar business annually. To kill it would be criminal and that's just what entry of their players into the American and National would do."[44]

If some owners were truly resistant, their response was typical of other black entrepreneurs who recognized the long-term social benefits of integration but feared its immediate negative economic ramifications. Removed from its segregated context and stripped of its best players, black professional baseball as an enterprise appeared unlikely to achieve the same level of prosperity. Fay Young, however, noted that white minor league teams remained viable despite selling their top players and questioned why the NNL and NAL could not follow a similar pattern. Moreover, player sales to Organized Baseball might offset any loss in patronage, although several owners doubted they would receive true market value for any of their men. Effa Manley, for instance, correctly observed that "Negro baseball isn't organized to the point where we'd be protected if the big leagues suddenly decided to let in colored players. In fact, they could walk in and grab off any player they wanted for any named amount of money without the owner getting a nickel."

Affiliation with white Organized Baseball offered the only solution that might allow black professional baseball to function within an integrated setting. Black baseball would not only gain protection from potential major league raids and possible financial assistance but would also receive the same rights as other minor league organizations. A number of officials, sportswriters, and fans had proposed the idea in the past, hoping that affiliation might prove the first step toward integration. Surprisingly, the normally inactive Ferdinand Morton took the most decisive step, meeting with National League president Ford Frick in 1936 to discuss the matter. Acknowledging that "the immediate admission of colored players to the major leagues is impracticable," Morton offered a bold alternative, one that if adopted, would have changed the face of black baseball.

Morton suggested that a Negro League be created and classified as a minor league with a classification between A and B. To avoid direct competition with the white majors, franchises would ideally be located in minor league towns or in major league cities represented by only one team. While the Negro League's schedule would continue to include the usual mixture of league and exhibition games, the non-league contests would be against A and B level minor league teams, rather than semipros. Touting the potential benefits of his plan, Morton reminded Frick that, since black teams were the "chief attraction" in semiprofessional baseball, Organized Baseball could similarly profit. Moreover, the admission of an all-black league to Organized Baseball might provide a gradual, more acceptable pathway to the integration likely to occur in the future. As Morton explained, "if colored players are admitted now . . . the opposition to them will naturally be greater than if they are admitted a few years from now from the ranks of organized baseball." Although the proposal never drew serious consideration, the NNL also recognized the potential value of such a strategy and even issued a statement in 1938 explaining that "the owners have a definite object in view . . . the entrance of Negro leagues into white organized baseball and entrance of Negro players into the major leagues."

Yet the possibility of developing a formal relationship with white Organized Baseball remained bleak. Although the widespread racism of most white officials presented a substantial barrier, the irregular organization and administration in the NNL and NAL also offered an excuse for rejection. Moreover, with the exception of Morton, league officials did little to investigate or facilitate the process, fearing loss of control of the industry and the imposition of stricter organizational standards. Despite the looming specter of integration, most owners remained blinded by their wartime profits, failing to prepare for the initial shock until nearly too late.[45]

◆ ◆ ◆

Like their employers, professional black players remained largely apart from the larger integration movement surrounding them during the 1930s and early 1940s. Instead, most men pursued their baseball careers as well as possible within the segregated setting and had little time to participate in protest activities. When questioned, however, players typically expressed their desire for an opportunity to play in the white major leagues. In 1939, for example, several Philadelphia Stars publicly supported integration efforts. Stars manager Jud Wilson also backed the campaign, touting Pat Patterson and Jim West as potential major leaguers, yet remained pessimistic of the movement's imminent success. As Wilson explained, "it's too big a job for the people who are now trying to put it over. It will have to be a universal movement, and that will never be . . . because the big league game, as it is now, is over-run with Southern blood."

While most black ballplayers supported integration, a surprising number had serious reservations about its potential impact. Vic Harris of the Grays reflected the ambivalence among some black baseball officials, noting that integration "might be a good thing and then again, it might not be." Like other observers, Harris questioned whether black baseball could withstand the loss of marquee players and wondered "how could the other 75–80% survive." An unnamed player offered a similar argument, noting that "it is a known fact that if the majors would accept Negro ball players they would only take the cream of the crop. Then—what would the Negro public do for its heroes on Negro teams?"

Others worried about the potential abuse awaiting any black in Organized Baseball. In 1940, a reluctant player explained to Dan Burley that "it'd be all right to get a break in the big show, but it wouldn't last. They'd make it so hot for a Negro player that he'd have to quit rather than take all the stuff they'd try to put on him. I believe it's best for us to stay in our place and keep Negro baseball wholly Negro." Meanwhile, Felton Snow of the Baltimore Elite Giants emphasized the important yet delicate issue of temperament. As Snow observed, "I don't know if it [integration] would be a good thing, because we've got so many guys who just wouldn't act right. . . . Many of the good players are bad actors and many of the ordinary players are fine characters." Notably, sportswriter Earl Barnes believed that Satchel Paige, despite his enormous talent, was not a desirable candidate "for a host of reasons that would not look so well in print."[46]

Ironically, Paige, so often cited during the campaign as the most obvious victim of the color line, appeared somewhat uncomfortable with the prospect of integration. In early August 1942, Paige suggested that "it wouldn't appeal to me," as any major league offer would have to match his $37,000 earnings in 1941. Moreover, Paige cited the potential problems with travel and accommodation and instead advocated the admission of a single all-black team to the major leagues. The idea of admitting blacks as a unit, rather than individuals, was hardly new, proposed most recently by Joe Bostic, who believed that with "the admission of an entire Negro-owned, controlled and personneled team . . . all of the money and jobs . . . would come to us." Yet Paige's comments, in the midst of a seeming breakthrough in the integration fight, seemed to reinforce the arguments of opponents and soon drew the ire of fans and journalists such as John Fuster of the *Cleveland Call and Post*, who observed that "segregation has proved almost totally bad for Negroes. A few of us profit by it, but the wish and hope of the majority of Negroes is to be accepted as an American citizen." Facing increasing pressure, Paige explained his position to the huge crowd at the East-West game on August 16, an attempt described by Art Carter as "a three-minute pointless statement over the public address system about how he was misquoted in the press . . . a speech few people heard and fewer were interested in at the time."[47]

Paige's contention that he had been misquoted remained questionable. In a 1945 interview with Sam Lacy, Paige again discussed the possibility of placing two black teams in Organized Baseball. Paige also expressed his

Figure 23. The great Satchel Paige remained ambivalent during the 1940s about entering the major leagues. Courtesy Baseball Hall of Fame Library.

continued uneasiness with potential integration difficulties, relating to Lacy that "you writer fellows stink. You keep on blowing off about getting us players in the league without thinking about our end of it . . . without thinking how tough it's gonna be for a colored ball player to come out of the club house and have all the white guys calling him 'n＿＿＿r' and 'b＿＿k so-and-so.' . . . What I want to know is what the hell's gonna happen to good will when one of those colored players, goaded out of his senses by repeated insults, takes a bat and busts fellowship in his damned head?"

Yet Paige's misgivings were perhaps shaped by his own enviable position in black professional baseball. Now in his late thirties, Paige earned a salary comparable or superior to major league players and had achieved national fame. With integration, Lacy suggested that Paige's "star will fade more quickly than that travel-minded snowball. He knows when he's in a good spot." Moreover, Paige had already demonstrated his capability for major league baseball in numerous successful performances in postseason barnstorming games. Yet for most black players, the opportunity to earn more money, consistently compete against the best white players, and receive national publicity was understandably irresistible and outweighed the potential complications. The always confident Terris McDuffie, for example, voiced no misgivings, noting that "a lot of us could make good in the big leagues." Pitcher Bob Griffith of the Black Yankees best expressed the prevailing attitude: "I'd be tickled pink to get a chance. . . . You don't know how it is for us fellows, always on the outside looking in."[48]

◆ ◆ ◆

Despite the frustrating failure of 1942, African American activists remained optimistic that integration would soon occur. By 1943, wartime industrial demands and gradually changing racial attitudes had created new opportunities for blacks, and professional baseball seemed unlikely to escape the trend. Blacks not only offered a potential solution to the growing player shortage, but their exclusion appeared increasingly "un-American" in the midst of an ongoing war against fascism. Moreover, integration would strengthen Organized Baseball's exalted claim of its value to the war effort, epitomized by Ford Frick's contention that "the real example of genuine democracy is on the playing fields of America. It is the one place American youth meets on common ground and the real lesson of democracy can best be preached."

Hoping for a breakthrough, integration advocates continued to apply pressure on Organized Baseball officials who found it more difficult to avoid commenting on the issue. In late December 1942, Chicago Cubs owner Philip Wrigley met with the black communist activist William L. Patterson, a representative of a local integration committee, and provided yet another perspective on integration. Despite claiming that he "would like to see colored in the big leagues" and expected it to occur "soon," Wrigley offered the excuse there was not "sufficient public demand at this time." Fearful of potential riots, Wrigley asserted that the public required education to prepare for the momentous step. Wrigley also cryptically alluded to the resistance of "men in high places," while conveniently citing his own employment of blacks in his factory and willingness to rent Wrigley Field to black teams during 1942.

Wrigley's apparent endorsement of integration, however, fueled subsequent rumors that his Los Angeles Angels of the Pacific Coast League (PCL) would grant tryouts to several California-based players. West Coast journalists and fans soon applied simultaneous pressure on other PCL teams, hopeful that the scarcity of minor league players might force a change in policy, prompting Art Cohen, sports editor of the white *Oakland Tribune*, to note that "it is a side commentary on American 'tolerance' that even if the bars are lowered it will be only because of the shortage of white players." Yet PCL officials proved as insincere and hesitant as their major league counterparts and consistently dodged or shifted responsibility for granting the tryouts. While some franchises vaguely promised opportunities in the future, Oakland Oaks manager and former major leaguer Johnny Vergez openly threatened to quit baseball before he would try any black player. The rejection prompted black sportswriters Herman Hill and Halley Harding to spearhead a new tactic in the integration fight, demonstrations and pickets at Wrigley Field, the home of the Los Angeles Angels. Yet the doors of the PCL remained closed, and Wrigley instead turned his attention during 1943 to the development of the All-American Girls Softball (later Baseball) League, a novel midwestern-based women's organization.[49]

Throughout much of 1943, the movement's continued protests largely fell upon deaf ears, despite race riots in several cities, player shortages, major league attendance drop, and relocation of training camps from the South to northern locales. Late in the year, however, Sam Lacy secured a long sought concession from the major leagues: a chance for blacks to address the owners at the winter meetings. Now writing for the *Chicago Defender*, Lacy arranged a meeting on November 17 with Commissioner Landis, who surprisingly agreed to admit a delegation to discuss integration at the joint session of the two leagues in December. After Landis requested that a black organization endorse the effort, Lacy solicited the involvement of the Negro Newspaper Publishers Association (NNPA), the Urban League, the NAACP, and Representative William Dawson of Illinois. Despite Lacy's hope for a broad-based representation, only the NNPA would participate in the subsequent delegation, although Roy Wilkins of the NAACP wrote to Landis endorsing the effort.

After years of silence, the sudden receptiveness of major league baseball was puzzling. Some observers, such as *PM* sports editor Joe Cummiskey, suggested that the paucity of capable players had helped modify the usually intolerant attitudes of owners. Yet in all likelihood, Organized Baseball, like other industries, implicitly recognized by 1943 that integration would eventually occur and sought to undertake steps either to delay or control its arrival. A meeting with blacks would ideally create an impression of tolerance without actually binding owners to any particular course of action. Notably, Landis refused to commit himself prior to the meeting, explaining that "this is the first time such a question has [been] brought into the open and I don't know what might come of it. I do know that the step is a healthy one and should clear the air for all concerned . . . in my position I listen at such discussion and let the men who own the teams state their case. I can't say where I stand—one way or the other—because the owners then could come to the meeting with minds made up for or against."[50]

On Friday, December 3, 1943, forty-four major league officials, including franchise owners, general managers, league presidents, and Landis, convened at the Hotel Roosevelt in New York and granted access to blacks for the first time in baseball history. The black delegation, comprised nearly exclusively of publishers, included Ira F. Lewis of the *Pittsburgh Courier*, John Sengstacke of the *Chicago Defender*, C. B. Powell of the *New York Amsterdam News* (unsuccessfully nominated for NNL president in 1940), William O. Walker of the *Cleveland Call and Post*, and Louis Martin of the *Michigan Chronicle*. Leading sportswriters Dan Burley and Wendell Smith were also present, along with Howard Murphy, business manager of the *Afro-American* newspapers. In a peculiar development, singer and former athlete Paul Robeson accompanied the group, reportedly at the behest of Landis.

The delegation attempted to offer cogent arguments that not only supported integration but addressed the potential fears of owners. Invoking wartime patriotic rhetoric, Sengstacke cited segregation's negative impact on black morale and reminded the audience that "if any American organization establishes barriers . . . against any class of citizens, the security of all classes is placed in constant and potential jeopardy." In contrast, Robeson chronicled his own positive interracial experiences, first as a college football star at Rutgers and more recently as an actor in *Othello* on Broadway, a nearly "unthinkable" development only a few years earlier now readily accepted by theater audiences. In the most compelling speech, former sportswriter Ira Lewis argued that the "changed attitude of the sporting public," demonstrated by the success of mixed and all-black boxing matches, would result in similar profits for Organized Baseball. Moreover, Lewis openly challenged the continued "tacit understanding" or "gentleman's agreement" and appealed to the owners to "undo this wrong" and "do away with this mean precedent."

The presentation reportedly impressed several officials, including American League president Will Harridge, who praised the "clean-cut, tactful, straight-to-the-point colored gentlemen who evidently knew what they were after." Yet the aftermath of the long sought face-to-face confrontation with Organized Baseball officials ultimately proved anticlimactic. While Landis once again reiterated that "each club is entirely free to employ Negro players to any extent it pleases," no owner moved toward signing a black player and each continued to remain silent or evasive.[51]

Like the failed 1942 tryouts, the New York meeting prompted a flurry of second-guessing in the black press. Several observers objected to the composition of the committee, particularly the over-representation of non-sports journalists. Rollo Wilson suggested that more "hard-bitten sports-writers with facts and figures" would have strengthened the delegation and particularly questioned the exclusion of Sam Lacy, the driving force behind the meeting. Lacy himself viewed the group as "much too large and unschooled on the subject" and claimed their arguments "were of the flag-waving, puerile variety." Dan Burley, however, defended the meeting strategy, explaining that the delegation, confident of white officials' aware-ness of black professional baseball, had specifically omitted references to specific players and teams. Lacy also criticized the appearance of Robeson, a well-known Communist sympathizer (although never a member of the party) whose presence provided a convenient rationale to reject the propo-sition.[52]

Although Robeson's appearance was probably counterproductive, it is unlikely that a different delegation would have been any more successful in producing a change in Organized Baseball's tacit exclusion policy. De-spite years of protest, major league baseball officials remained stubbornly opposed to integration, and, as Stanley Frank of the *New York Post* noted, "privately resent that their business has been made the focal point of agita-tion for elimination of racial prejudice. They want to know why the prob-lem is not solved first in more important fields such as medicine and education. The Army and Navy and industry are not meeting the issue squarely; why should baseball?" Moreover, Frank alluded to the still con-siderable hostility to blacks throughout the industry, citing the "ugly talk" of players whose "intolerance and ignorance are frightening."

Twice in the span of less than eighteen months, the commissioner of baseball had denied the existence of any rule barring black players. Yet as Rollo Wilson observed, the concession was ultimately meaningless, compa-rable to statements asserting that "there is no law prohibiting the election of a Negro judge in Philadelphia, no laws against our enjoying many privi-leges which we do not presently have." With substantial barriers still firmly in place, integration advocates could only hope that continued pres-sure would lead to a greater measure of success in 1944. Organized Base-ball, however, appeared determined to maintain all-white leagues as long as possible, regardless of the war or ongoing black protest efforts. Despite the probable willingness of at least a few officials to consider the issue of integration, the industry had succeeded in creating an environment de-signed to discourage any promoter from bucking the current trend. Whether any owner possessed the necessary confidence, aggressiveness, and creativity to undertake the project in the face of likely strong criticism remained to be seen.[53]

◆ ◆ ◆

In the months following the meeting, several journalists hoped that black professional baseball might take an active role in the integration fight. Wilson, for example, recognized that "the proposition is more than just saying, 'Let's have Negroes in the big leagues,' and presto! . . . It is a problem which requires serious study by a varied group of sundown owners, newspapermen . . . and representatives from Organized Baseball." Like others, Wilson urged both league presidents to seek affiliation with white Organized Baseball as a potential preliminary step toward integration. Not surprisingly, Tom Wilson ignored the suggestion, while J. B. Martin was evasive, despite publicly asserting that "if the majors want any of our players, we will expect them to be purchased on the same basis and standards that are applied when minor leaguers are purchased." The chronically short-sighted and individualistic attitudes of league officials hardly surprised the former NNL commissioner, who noted that "from my own experience . . . I know that they do not want to be CONTROLLED."

To the chagrin of the black press, NNL and NAL owners also continued to dodge responsibility for advancing the cause of integration. As Martin explained, "we should not be expected to solve this problem. This is solely a major league issue. We cannot force them to admit Negroes nor will we assume that responsibility." More disturbing was the attitude displayed by an anonymous NNL owner (probably James Semler), who related to Dan Burley that "we are built on segregation. . . . If there was no segregation, we wouldn't have had colored ball clubs; we wouldn't make money, and we'd all probably be out of business."[54]

Cum Posey, never one to avoid a controversy, provided an assessment of the recent developments along the color line struggle, an appraisal predictably shaped by his position as part-owner of the NNL's most profitable franchise. Reiterating his willingness to sell his players to Organized Baseball, Posey nevertheless objected to "the way the approach was made . . . by men who do not have one penny invested in baseball," particularly the failure to consult black baseball officials. Posey questioned why the black press, which consistently "preaches to support all Negro enterprises," seemed relatively unconcerned about the fate of black baseball, a business second only to life insurance "in money handled during a year and salaries paid employees." Moreover, Posey claimed that the press had "asked for the privilege of giving away all the stars of the various Negro baseball clubs . . . stating if the white major leagues do this they will draw all the colored fans who now attend Negro games. . . . If that is not offering a whole Negro enterprise to white business men, then what is it. That would automatically put organized Negro baseball out of business." While somewhat distorting the publishers' arguments, Posey clearly grasped the potential impact of integration on all black enterprises, and correctly anticipated a different reaction from the black press if confronted with a similar exodus of talent to white daily newspapers and a corresponding loss in circulation.[55]

Yet the major factor in the reluctance of Posey and other owners to confront the integration issue was the increasing dependence on rentals of Organized Baseball parks. As early as 1942, Posey had warned that "the letters . . . sent to Judge Landis and various club owners . . . do not help to build Negro baseball and may cause the loss of some of the parks we now rent. That would set Negro baseball back 20 years." Following the Hotel Roosevelt meeting in December 1943, the NNL announced a plan to draft a resolution "to reassure major league operators of the full co-operation of the NNL and of its desire to maintain . . . friendly relations." The statement promptly drew strong criticism from black sportswriters such as Roscoe Coleman, who asserted that "with the rapid strides made by the race in other endeavors . . . there is no place for reactionaries of this type who put their own individual well being far ahead of group prog-ress."

The NNL's passivity was hardly surprising, as the fate of black fran-chises had become intertwined with that of Organized Baseball. As noted, white parks had facilitated black baseball's prosperity in the early 1940s, providing opportunities to draw larger crowds and attract greater media exposure. A July 1941 series between the Grays and New York Cubans revealed the crucial nature of Organized Baseball rentals. The two teams spent a week in Indiana and Ohio, appearing at five different parks owned by Middle Atlantic League and American Association franchises. The se-ries was hardly atypical and confirmed Posey's belief that "Negro baseball could not operate without the aid of white organized baseball. It is doubt-ful we could operate sandlot clubs and play out a season's schedule."[56]

By the early 1940s, black teams had appeared at most of the major and top minor league parks. Perhaps not surprisingly, the New York Yankees, already the most successful major league team, developed the most profit-able and comprehensive relationship with black professional baseball. After the demolition of Dyckman Oval, the easily accessible Yankee Sta-dium became the focal point for black baseball in New York, attracting thousands of fans for Sunday doubleheaders. The Yankee organization also profited through lucrative rentals of several of its minor league parks, including Ruppert Stadium to the Newark Eagles and a similarly named facility in Kansas City (later renamed Blues Stadium) to the Monarchs. Other major league clubs in New York, however, failed to capitalize on black games. Not until 1944 did the Giants regularly lease the Polo Grounds, despite its convenient location, while the Dodgers realized only minimal rental income from Ebbets Field, a facility less accessible to Harlem and contending with competition from Dexter Park, home of the popular Brooklyn Bushwicks.

In Washington, Griffith Stadium's site in the heart of the black community enabled the Senators to profit handsomely through rentals to the NNL. While team president Clark Griffith had rented the park to black teams for years, the Homestead Grays achieved unprecedented financial success in the early 1940s, even outdrawing the Senators on occasion. As Griffith's nephew Calvin, who succeeded his uncle at the helm of the Senators, later recalled, rentals to the Grays and other black teams "kept us in the game. We used to make, back in those days, thirty-five, forty thousand dollars a year maybe off of 'em." Not surprisingly, the two organizations subsequently developed a mutually beneficial relationship. Eager to maximize the Grays' already formidable drawing power, Senators officials assisted with sales and publicity and announced the Grays' upcoming schedule during Washington games. Recognizing the importance of the rental income, Griffith even helped to rearrange the Senators' schedule to allow the Grays an extra home date for the unofficial black world series in September 1943. Griffith's friendly interest and involvement with the Grays would later lead to erroneous rumors that the Washington official had purchased a share in the NNL franchise.[57]

Rarely used by black teams prior to 1942, Shibe Park in Philadelphia also became an increasingly important venue. Like other major league franchises, the Athletics recognized the increasing profitability of black baseball and sensed that park rentals might potentially offset the corresponding drop in major league gate receipts. Moreover, rentals to black baseball provided a convenient means to deflect charges of racial discrimination. Notably, Athletics manager and majority owner Connie Mack responded to an integration question by noting that "our park is open to Negro league teams in the East . . . and we do everything possible to cooperate with them." Mack, however, had little reason to reject black rentals, as ten Negro League weeknight promotions at Shibe Park drew an impressive 132,193 fans between 1942 and 1944, providing desperately needed cash flow for a franchise whose aggregate attendance totaled only 1.3 million during the same period. By 1945, occasional black college football games at Shibe provided Mack with additional income, while Bob Carpenter, owner of the Phillies, profited from appearances by the Stars and other teams at Wilmington Park, home of the Phillies' Inter-State League affiliate.[58]

Organized Baseball's considerable rental profits ultimately provided yet another rationalization for continued exclusion of blacks in the early 1940s. Although integration advocates had consistently argued that black players would boost attendance, major league franchises were already profiting from African American baseball fans and saw little reason to disrupt the current arrangement. Thus park rentals enabled Organized Baseball to exploit the largely untapped African American market, while avoiding the potential white objections to increased black attendance following integration. The apparent lack of economic incentive, coupled with the reactionary racial attitudes of most white officials and ambivalence of black owners, appeared certain to ensure the exclusion of black players from Organized Baseball for years to come.⁵⁹

◆ ◆ ◆

Comfortable with their current relationship with black baseball, major league owners continued to avoid breaching the color line. After the statements from Landis in 1942 and 1943, Organized Baseball took no further steps to acknowledge the integration issue during 1944 despite a dramatic shortage of players. Rather than consider integration, the Philadelphia Phillies instead resorted to signing several teenagers, including sixteen-year-old Ralph "Putsy" Caballero and seventeen-year-old infielder Granny Hamner. Other teams followed a similar pattern, including the Cincinnati Reds who briefly employed Joe Nuxhall, a fifteen-year-old pitcher. The apparent preference of major teams to use untried youngsters rather than experienced black players dismayed observers such as Dave "Showboat" Thomas of the New York Cubans, who noted that "if no Negroes are taken into the Big Leagues this season, then we had just as well forget all about it because they'll never take them in." The disappointing year culminated with the November death of Judge Landis at the age of seventy-eight, a development viewed ambivalently by some African Americans who hoped his successor might prove more sympathetic to integration.

Yet Landis was hardly the major cause for the failure of the integration fight between 1933 and 1944. In many ways, Organized Baseball ultimately paralleled other major American industries in its racial attitudes, resistant hiring patterns, and fear of offending white workers and/or patrons. While wartime demands, the FEPC, and union activism had compelled some businesses to increase black employment by the early 1940s, Organized Baseball remained largely unaffected by such factors. Moreover, the aggressive protests waged by blacks and whites failed to sway an essentially conservative industry notoriously fearful of change. After surviving the Depression and war years without even a token attempt at integration, Organized Baseball officials lacked any real incentive to recon-

sider its policies, and the current profitability of the NNL and NAL provided an additional convenient rationale. A series of developments in
1945, however, would finally force the industry to confront the issue,
much to the considerable discomfort of both major league and black baseball officials.[60]

8

Breakthrough and Setback

We are getting so much hell which we don't deserve, as we have built the League and did not hurt anybody while we were building it.

—Cum Posey, November 1945

Three years of war had dramatically altered the financial fortunes of black professional baseball. Catering to urban black communities enjoying unprecedented employment opportunities and eager for entertainment, NNL and NAL franchises had reaped substantial profits and confidently anticipated similar growth in the future. Simultaneously, the war had revitalized the ongoing fight to integrate Organized Baseball, thanks to a heightened awareness of domestic oppression and an increasing unwillingness of African Americans to tolerate discrimination in any form. As 1945 approached, the looming specter of integration remained a major unresolved question, and whether the two black leagues would address the issue and adequately prepare for the postwar period remained uncertain.

The more immediate concern of black and white professional baseball, however, was the war's potential effect on operation during 1945. Reflecting an increased vigilance in the wake of the bloody Battle of the Bulge and a desire to squelch domestic complacency in the waning stages of the conflict, the government took several steps that appeared to foreshadow the discontinuation of professional sports for the duration. In December 1944, James Byrnes, the head of the Office of War Mobilization and Reconversion, ordered all race tracks to close by January 3, 1945, in an attempt to alleviate transportation problems and curb defense employment absenteeism. Byrnes also recommended that the Selective Service review the cases of all professional athletes previously rejected by their draft boards, and a return to the "work or fight" policy of World War I seemed inevitable. Meanwhile, the ODT again requested that Organized Baseball reduce its travel mileage by 25 percent, resulting in limited exhibition contests and the cancellation of the annual major league all-star game.[1]

Although some observers questioned whether professional baseball could survive the loss of more players to the military or defense work, NAL president J. B. Martin remained confident, noting that "most of the players in my league are either 4-F or are working days in the defense plants or have their medical discharges. Surely, if a man has served his country, has done his utmost, and received his honorable discharge from the armed forces and can play ball, there should be no reason for him not doing so." Moreover, as the surrender of Germany became increasingly imminent in the spring, federal officials softened their stance and subsequently allowed professional players to leave essential jobs to return to baseball. In May, the reopening of race tracks further encouraged sports fans, although transportation problems remained paramount. To the dismay of numerous fans, ODT director J. Monroe Johnson subsequently warned that, unless the war with Japan ended soon, travel difficulties would probably result in shortened seasons, no bowl football games, and other cancelled promotions in 1945.

Not surprisingly, the always lucrative annual East-West game also faced cancellation, particularly after an unnamed informant disclosed to federal officials that "these Negro leagues are secretly making plans to hold this All-Star game before it comes to the attention of the ODT." Claiming that the "transportation situation today, and for some time to come, is the most critical in many years," V. T. Corbett of the Railway Transport Department asked the NNL and NAL to cancel the game. The ODT eventually relented after Martin, always eager to preserve his financial stake in the promotion, convinced officials that the game was "ninety-eight per cent a Chicago affair" and would not involve heavy travel.[2]

Despite the relaxation of federal policies, Organized Baseball still faced a severe manpower shortage, yet it remained rigidly opposed to integration. Instead, several teams found creative ways to maintain their all-white rosters during 1945. Clark Griffith's Senators not only continued to sign a number of Cubans and even tried out a part-Chinese player but also featured pitcher Bert Shepard, a former fighter pilot who had lost his leg in combat. The St. Louis Browns employed a one-armed outfielder, Pete Gray, who eventually appeared in 77 games in his only major league season, while the Phillies offered a tryout to Chet Morrissey, Jr., a nineteen-year-old player with only one hand. After years of agitation, integration still appeared remote, prompting a disgusted Rollo Wilson to observe, "a one-armed man, a one-legged man, Cubans, Chinese, Mexicans—anyone except a known colored man is welcomed into the big leagues at this time."

While the continued resistant attitudes of Organized Baseball had seemingly robbed the movement of its earlier momentum, political developments in New York prompted renewed hope in early 1945. Reflecting the increasing awareness of racial prejudice engendered by the war, the New York State Legislature in 1944 created a bipartisan commission chaired by assemblyman Irving M. Ives, Republican majority leader and future U.S. senator, to investigate discriminatory economic practices. After the commission presented its findings in early 1945, Ives and Democratic state senator Elmer Quinn introduced legislation designed to prohibit employment discrimination through the establishment of a permanent state agency similar to the FEPC. Despite fears of an exodus of business from New York, the Ives-Quinn law passed and was signed by Governor Thomas Dewey in March 1945.[3]

Although the new legislation would not take effect until July, African Americans immediately recognized its potential impact on Organized Baseball teams operating in the state of New York. If white professional clubs refused to grant tryouts to competent black players, a formal complaint could be submitted to the State Commission Against Discrimination (SCAD) for appropriate action. Ironically, Joe Bostic, whose lukewarm attitudes toward integration in 1942 had drawn criticism, spearheaded an attempt to test the law's relevance to the color line fight. Now writing for New York Representative Adam Clayton Powell's left-leaning *People's Voice* (considered by an FBI source to be a "very helpful transmission belt for the Communist Party"), Bostic began to search for players willing to present themselves for a tryout at the Brooklyn Dodgers spring training facility at Bear Mountain, New York, eventually selecting two childhood friends from Mobile, Alabama: slick-fielding first baseman Dave "Showboat" Thomas of the New York Cubans and pitcher Terris McDuffie of the Newark Eagles. The choices were somewhat puzzling, as both men were in their late thirties, providing the Dodgers with easy justification for their rejection despite major league teams' increasing reliance on older players during the war. Bostic later explained that several other players feared jeopardizing future opportunities to play winter baseball in Latin America, and "those were the only two . . . I could get who were willing to face the wrath of the man."[4]

On Friday, April 6, Bostic and two other journalists escorted Thomas and McDuffie to Bear Mountain. Startled Dodgers officials immediately refused to grant a tryout, claiming it could not be fitted into the day's activities. While team president-general manager Branch Rickey invited the group to lunch, he angrily berated Bostic for his confrontational approach but ultimately agreed to allow the pair to work out with the team on the following day. On Saturday, McDuffie and Thomas took the unprecedented step of donning major league uniforms and worked out for an hour before Rickey and manager Leo Durocher. Although McDuffie, fresh from a fine winter league season in Cuba, showed good control and speed,

Thomas was unimpressive. Moreover, Rickey cited McDuffie's age, while Durocher voiced concern for his lack of experience in "professional baseball."

Despite the unenthusiastic response to McDuffie and Thomas, Bostic had succeeded in forcing major league officials to witness black players in a tryout setting, a distinct advancement from the failed promises of 1942. Bolstered by the looming specter of the Ives-Quinn bill, Bostic placed Organized Baseball in an uncharacteristically uncomfortable position, and as Al Laney of the *New York Herald Tribune* remarked, "to catch Brother Rickey thus with his guard down and put him right behind the eight ball was an extraordinary achievement." Rickey's own description of the incident suggested his discomfort, as he confided to his associate Mel Jones that "several of them were brought up to Bear Mountain . . . and I had several bad hours, I can tell you. We gave them the tryout and I think it was handled as well as it could have been." Perhaps more important, Rickey alluded to the potential effect of the soon to be enacted state law, admitting that the legislation "has teeth in it and I don't know just what will happen."[5]

A number of black sportswriters, however, felt that, while Thomas and McDuffie were readily capable of playing major league baseball, both lacked the impeccable background required of any suitable integration candidate. According to Sam Lacy, the controversial McDuffie was "generally regarded as a sorehead and nuisance." Moreover, Thomas, an outstanding first baseman in his prime but a weak hitter, supposedly possessed a "belligerent attitude" and would be arrested two months later in New York on larceny charges. While unhappy with "goody goodies . . . making quite a todo about the character of the Negroes to make the grade," Bostic himself admitted that Rickey spoke to both Thomas and McDuffie about the "great necessity for sterling behavior on the part of big league ball players." Yet even an individual with flawless credentials would have been unlikely to alter the outcome at Bear Mountain. Unbeknownst to Bostic, Rickey was already preparing for integration and had no intention of allowing outside pressure to disrupt his carefully designed plans.[6]

At first glance, Branch Rickey appeared to be an unlikely candidate to initiate integration, as he had shown little outward interest during his long career in baseball. Rickey's administrative and organizational skills (particularly his role in devising the major league "farm system"), however, had earned him admiration and fame during his 25 years with the St. Louis Cardinals, and his seemingly pious personal qualities had also attracted attention. An exponent of "clean living," Rickey refused to play or manage on Sunday, refrained from cursing, and had been an ardent prohibitionist in his youth. Yet a relentlessly practical and sometimes ruthless attitude toward financial matters coexisted with his exterior morality. Receiving a percentage of the Cardinals' profits along with his salary as team vice president, Rickey was notoriously frugal in his dealings with players, such as Hall of Fame outfielder Ralph Kiner, who later denounced Rickey as a "hypocrite" who used "any means to sign a ball player for as little as he could get him."[7]

Despite his strong religious convictions, Rickey had shown no indication of remarkable tolerance. Former major leaguer Bob Berman claimed that Rickey rescinded a contract offer in 1918 after discovering the Bronx high school prospect was Jewish. Moreover, except for a positive response to Jimmy Powers's 1933 poll, Rickey had remained silent during the integration fight and raised no apparent objection to the segregated seating policy of Sportsman's Park (despite later claiming opposition). Like other Organized Baseball officials, Rickey was unwilling to alienate white fans and players, particularly in an upper south city strongly opposed to integration.

Although Rickey appeared an improbable figure, several factors accounted for his apparent change of heart. The player shortage of the war years offered an initial incentive to consider blacks, and Rickey's move after the 1942 season to the Brooklyn Dodgers as president and general manager provided him with a far more liberal social climate to attempt such a revolutionary move, along with the backing of a sympathetic board of directors. Yet what ultimately separated Rickey from officials such as Pittsburgh's Bill Benswanger was his innovativeness and willingness to embrace, rather than resist, the inevitability of integration in Organized Baseball, as in other aspects of American life. Despite Rickey's intense dislike of protest and melodramatic assertion that an earlier incident of segregation involving one of his ballplayers during his college coaching career had been a major stimulus in his desire to assist blacks, it seems more likely that the greater awareness of racial discrimination in the early 1940s helped to shape his decision to begin to scout black players. Rickey, who had already proved a visionary in his establishment of the farm system, also shrewdly recognized that black players offered a similarly undeveloped yet fertile ground for cheap talent and might provide the Dodgers with a competitive edge for years to come. Perhaps Rickey best summed up his motives in a later statement: "I did not employ a Negro because he was a Negro, nor did I have in mind at all doing something for the Negro race, or even bringing up that issue. I simply wanted to win a pennant for the Brooklyn Dodgers, and I wanted the best human beings I could find to help me win it."

By the time of the April 1945 Bear Mountain incident, Rickey's scouts had already secretly begun to evaluate black players in the United States and abroad. African Americans, however, remained unaware of Rickey's plans and had little reason to judge him favorably after his seemingly curt rejection of Thomas and McDuffie. Yet Rickey's interest in black baseball would soon become apparent, puzzling some observers and encouraging others. By August, sportswriter Dan Burley viewed Rickey with cautious optimism, observing that "perhaps Rickey will prove to be the man. He seems to be of the calibre to do the right thing once he makes up his mind." Burley's assessment would prove correct, as a series of moves orchestrated by sixty-three-year-old Rickey would shock the industry by the year's end.[8]

Political pressure, which had contributed to the surprising Bear Mountain tryout, resulted in a similar breakthrough in Boston, largely through the efforts of city councilman Isadore H. Y. Muchnick. Questioning baseball's "alleged morale value" in the face of the industry's continued discrimination, Muchnick and three other council members in 1944 had unsuccessfully attempted to deny Sunday baseball licenses to the Red Sox and Braves because of their hiring policies. Facing a similar threat spearheaded by Muchnick in March 1945, the two Boston teams capitulated and agreed to offer tryouts to any player, regardless of race.

Once again, Wendell Smith and the *Courier* became actively involved in the selection of players, eventually choosing outfielder Sam Jethroe of the Cleveland Buckeyes, infielder Jackie Robinson, who had recently joined the Kansas City Monarchs, and pitcher-outfielder Dave Hoskins of the Homestead Grays. While the Buckeyes and Monarchs permitted Jethroe and Robinson to participate, Cum Posey remained dubious and asserted that no Grays would take part "unless that particular member of organized baseball requests an option on the player's services, written on the club's stationery." To replace Hoskins, Smith turned to Philadelphia Stars infielder Marvin Williams, who had spent the winter months playing baseball in Puerto Rico.[9]

On Wednesday, April 11, less than a week after the Bear Mountain incident, the three players arrived in Boston. The death of President Franklin Roosevelt the next day, however, delayed the anticipated tryout until the following Monday, April 16. With Smith and Muchnick in attendance, the trio worked out at Fenway Park along with ten white hopefuls under the supervision of Red Sox coaches Larry Woodall and Hugh Duffy. Although the three black players performed capably, Red Sox officials were hardly ready to consider integration, and, as Jackie Robinson later recalled, "not for one minute did we believe the tryout was sincere." Yet unlike the Dodgers, the Red Sox lacked a convenient excuse for rejection, since all three players were under thirty and had demonstrated obvious ability. According to Sam Jethroe, the team instead provided a familiar justification, explaining that the players "had the potential but it wasn't the right time."

Meanwhile, the three men never received the promised tryout from the Braves, who offered the fanciful excuse that they were unable to "look at" players already evaluated by the Red Sox.[10]

Twice in the span of ten days, black players had worked out under the scrutiny of major league officials, leading some African Americans to believe that integration was imminent. Yet several black sportswriters and baseball officials viewed the tryouts as insincere attempts to deflect political pressure. Cum Posey denounced the workouts at Bear Mountain and Boston as "the most humiliating experience Negro baseball has yet suffered from white organized baseball," noting that the most important aspects of player evaluation, running and throwing, had been largely ignored. Posey asserted, "any white rookie one-half as good as any of these players would have been kept for at least a week and sent to some minor league club." Meanwhile, Satchel Paige cited the highly subjective nature of any white-sponsored tryouts, explaining that "the Negro will never break into the majors like that. You see, the owners and managers will always have a way to find fault with our very best players." Fay Young agreed, recalling the undeserving failures of blacks at "so-called democratic colleges and universities."

Still leery of antagonizing major league officials, most NNL and NAL owners reacted to the tryouts with their customary silence, and Posey's widely publicized caustic comments, however justified, seemed to reinforce the perception of owner opposition to integration. Yet several less vocal officials believed integration might offer potential economic benefits. Alex Pompez, for example, had already witnessed two of his former players (Oscar Estrada and Ramon Herrera, both white Cubans) in the major leagues during the 1920s and recognized that sales to Organized Baseball would provide an additional source of revenue. Wilbur Hayes of the Cleveland Buckeyes also viewed the development positively and announced his club's willingness to "aid . . . in any program to integrate. . . . Anything we could do to help the wheels of American progress turn faster, we'll gladly do—even if it means letting some of our very best players go." Ed Bolden, however, would offer the most emphatic support in the weeks following the tryouts:

If any player of mine is considered good enough for any manager of the majors to want to sign, I am willing for him to have his opportunity to advance and I would be willing to talk terms for his contract. . . .

Contrary to what Cum Posey and some of the others think, I believe that so-called colored baseball would be improved. The players would give you their best efforts for they would know that they were in a position to make the big leagues and to get in they would have to be on their toes at all times. Our leagues, therefore, would have a better brand of baseball and there would be more youngsters coming into the game because it would have a real future.

The majors could then use our leagues as developing posts for the colored boys not quite able to stand the pace. They would get more experience and our clubs would be strengthened.

Yet by 1945, Bolden's influence in league affairs was limited, as the Grays, the most successful and financially prosperous franchise, continued to dominate the course of the NNL. Not surprisingly, the NNL's attitude toward integration and affiliation with Organized Baseball in the months ahead would largely reflect Posey's suspicions rather than Bolden's acceptance. The short-sighted stance ultimately won the league few supporters and further alienated a number of black sportswriters, already impatient with the industry's apparent reluctance to embrace integration.[11]

The black press, already actively involved in the Bear Mountain and Boston tryouts, was responsible for a third major development in the early months of 1945. Sam Lacy, who had interviewed Griffith in 1937 and succeeded in gaining black access to the winter meetings in 1943, once again initiated a dialogue with Organized Baseball officials. Now back with the *Baltimore Afro-American*, Lacy contacted each of the sixteen major league owners in early March, pursuing a more conciliatory approach. In a carefully worded letter designed to appeal to the owners' innate conservatism, Lacy cited "the problem developing from the continued pressure for inclusion" of black players. Recognizing that integration would be a "slow and tedious process" requiring "a maximum of understanding and careful planning—from both the white and colored angles," Lacy suggested that major league baseball appoint "a colored man to make a survey of Negro baseball to the end of thoroughly studying the possibilities, and finding the best way of ironing out the many ramifications." While admitting the plan represented somewhat of an "appeasement," Lacy felt it would not only represent "a step in the right direction" but show that the owners were "interested in working out a feasible plan of action."

Lacy's suggestion offered major league baseball an ideal opportunity to gain control of the race issue, deflect charges of discrimination, and pursue its own gradual program of integration. Yet Lacy received only four responses, all from franchises currently facing local political pressure, further revealing the still strongly entrenched opposition. Branch Rickey, already in the midst of his own secret integration plans, was supportive, as was Larry MacPhail, recently returned to baseball as president and part-owner of the New York Yankees. The two Boston teams also expressed mild interest but suggested the matter should be referred to the league presidents for consideration.

Figure 24. Larry MacPhail and Branch Rickey, 1943. Courtesy Baseball Hall of Fame Library.

The April tryouts, however, coupled with demonstrations at Yankee Stadium on opening day, prompted more serious attention to Lacy's proposition. At the behest of Leslie O'Connor, Landis's long-time assistant and member of the three-person advisory council overseeing major league baseball prior to the selection of next commissioner, Lacy outlined his plan to the owners at a Cleveland meeting on April 24. The owners subsequently agreed to create a committee consisting of Lacy, an American and a National League representative (Rickey and MacPhail), and a fourth individual to be selected by Lacy. The addition of Joseph Rainey, the Philadelphia magistrate and unsuccessful candidate for the presidency of the NNL, completed the committee by mid-May.[12]

Despite Lacy's hopes for a productive outcome, the committee accomplished little, largely due to the recalcitrance of Larry MacPhail. A scholastic and sandlot athlete in his youth, MacPhail eventually entered Organized Baseball in 1931 as part of a group of Columbus businessmen who rescued the financially ailing local American Association franchise. Lacking any administrative experience in professional sports, MacPhail nevertheless proved to be an astute promoter, helping to reverse the sagging fortunes of the club after engineering its sale to the St. Louis Cardinals as part of Branch Rickey's celebrated farm system. While the careers of Rickey and MacPhail remained intertwined during the next 16 years, the two men differed markedly in personality. In contrast to the pious Rickey, MacPhail was a flashy dresser who drank heavily and had a notoriously bad temper. Perhaps not unexpectedly, their working relationship in Columbus would prove brief, as Rickey fired MacPhail as team president in 1933 following a series of controversies and squabbles.

MacPhail, however, would soon develop a formidable reputation as a major league promoter, initially as vice president and general manager of the Cincinnati Reds from 1933 to 1936 and later in a similar position with the Brooklyn Dodgers from 1938 to 1942. As sportswriter Red Smith recalled, MacPhail was "way ahead of most other owners," responsible for a number of developments that eventually became standard in Organized Baseball. During MacPhail's brief tenure in Cincinnati, the Reds were the first major league team to offer a season ticket plan, use air travel, and install lights for night games. Unlike most other officials, MacPhail also recognized the value of radio broadcasting and later was involved in the first telecast of a major league game in 1939.[13]

Despite his prior innovations and willingness to break with established traditions, MacPhail was unable or unwilling to view integration in a similar light. To his credit, he had been one of the few owners not to deny the existence of the color line, and he had offered cautious support of integration in the past. Moreover, his son Lee later recalled that MacPhail raised his children "not to be prejudiced." Yet following his purchase of the Yankees in January 1945 with Del Webb and Dan Topping, MacPhail had an increasing financial stake in the maintenance of segregation. As noted, the Yankees derived thousands of dollars from rental income, representing, as MacPhail explained, "the profit I am able to pay my stockholders." Seemingly determined to postpone integration as long as possible, MacPhail dodged Lacy's requests to meet and further delayed the committee's operation by recommending the addition of a white sportswriter and a representative from black baseball.

MacPhail, like other Organized Baseball officials, was also preoccupied with issues other than integration during early 1945. Along with the usual wartime disruptions, major league owners faced the task of finding a replacement for the venerable Landis, a selection potentially crucial to the integration fight. Political influence would be the major factor determining the choice of the new commissioner, as white owners, like their black counterparts, sought an individual with the authority to deal with federal officials. Moreover, a Washington connection might allow Organized Baseball to remain protected from legal challenges to the reserve clause and prosecution as a monopoly. Although former postmaster general James Farley, Democratic governor Frank Lausche of Ohio, and Democratic National Committee chairman Robert Hannegan received strong consideration, Larry MacPhail spearheaded an alternate candidate, Albert "Happy" Chandler, a conservative Democratic senator from Kentucky who earlier had enabled a group of major league owners to meet with President Roosevelt to discuss the wartime status of baseball. At the April 24 meeting in Cleveland during which Lacy's proposed committee was first considered, the owners elected Chandler as the second commissioner in baseball history.[14]

The choice of the southern politician discouraged Lacy, who expected Chandler to "suit the purposes of bigoted major league operators," while the *Sporting News* felt that Chandler's legal skills would be invaluable in dealing with "efforts to force the Negro issue in the courts." The new commissioner, however, would prove surprisingly difficult to categorize easily, although his public record seemingly offered little to inspire hope among African Americans. Not surprisingly, the Kentucky Senator had often voted in tandem with his southern colleagues on racial issues such as the poll tax and the FEPC. Moreover, Chandler had maintained separate schools in Kentucky during his first term as governor, viewed Senator Harry Byrd of Virginia as a mentor, later supported segregationist Strom Thurmond's break with the Democratic party in 1948, and was even considered as a potential running mate for Alabama Governor George Wallace's presidential bid in 1968. Yet Chandler was never as extreme in his racial views as Byrd, Thurmond, or Wallace. While hardly a vocal advocate of integration, Chandler nevertheless showed a willingness to uphold integration laws once in place and by 1956, during his second stint as governor, suggested that "every American must come to the realization . . . that we must bring about an end of segregation."[15]

Black journalists were eager to determine whether the new commissioner would simply reiterate his predecessor's typical statements toward black players. At a May 3 press conference in Chicago, Chandler surprised African Americans by relating to a *Defender* reporter his opposition to "barring Negroes from baseball, just because they are Negroes." Moreover, Chandler claimed his record demonstrated his "tolerant attitude toward all minority groups," citing the superior "educational facilities for Negroes" in Kentucky. Chandler, however, raised some eyebrows by questioning whether a consensus existed among blacks toward integration, claiming that "Negro baseball officials and players don't know exactly what they want at present. . . . They may want to play in their own leagues and then meet the major league champion in a playoff game. . . . At present, it's too indefinite to know what the desires are of both parties." While

Chandler's subsequent suggestion of a meeting to discuss the issue promised little more than had been offered previously, his willingness to confront the race question represented a refreshing change from the
evasiveness of Landis. Notably, Bob Williams, sports editor of the *Cleveland Call and Post*, advised his readers to defer judgment on the new
commissioner, citing the example of Supreme Court justice Hugo Black,
who "changed his colors to become the most liberal jurist of all times
standing 100 per cent in the corner of the Negro. . . . How do we know
that Senator Chandler will not do likewise? . . . I propose we give Chandler
a chance."[16]

◆ ◆ ◆

Despite the election of Chandler, the Boston and Bear Mountain tryouts,
and the formation of Lacy's committee, the NNL and NAL still took no
immediate steps to prepare for the prospect of integration. Most franchise
owners instead focused on short-term goals, hoping to squeeze out another
year of war-fueled prosperity with a minimum of concessions to reform
advocates. Yet league officials would face a formidable threat in 1945:
competition from a new organization headed by their former colleague,
Gus Greenlee.

Eager to regain his former stature in black baseball, Greenlee had revived the Pittsburgh Crawfords, yet his attempts to return to the NNL in
1942 and 1944 were rebuffed. Greenlee then pursued an alternate strategy, operating his team independently in 1944, while signing league players and planning for a rival organization in the future. On December 27,
1944, nearly twelve years after the birth of the NNL, Greenlee and several
other club owners met in Pittsburgh and subsequently announced the formation of the United States Baseball League (USL). The new organization
initially featured six teams: the Crawfords, Chicago Brown Bombers, Detroit Motor City Giants, Philadelphia Daisies, St. Louis Stars, and Atlanta
Crackers. Minimizing his own role in the establishment of the USL, Greenlee claimed that the six owners "merely got together and felt that they
should organize for their own benefit." While Dan Burley suggested that
the league was a "weapon of revenge," Greenlee insisted that "we do not
consider ourselves rivals of either the Negro American or National
leagues. . . . I am a firm believer in organized baseball . . . and have never
been satisfied playing weekend baseball."[17]

Greenlee, however, had managed to assemble a group of disgruntled
owners disenchanted with their treatment from the two established organizations. Determined to retain Briggs Stadium for league promotions, the
NAL had twice rejected the application of Benjamin Linton's Detroit

Motor City Giants for associate membership. League teams had also raided Webster McDonald's Philadelphia Daisies and John Harden's Atlanta Black Crackers in the past, while George Mitchell's St. Louis Stars had bounced between the NNL and NAL without achieving financial success. Hank Rigney, who had been enmeshed in controversy during his brief tenure in the NNL in 1939, would also join the new league as part-owner of the Toledo Rays.[18]

Despite the seemingly makeshift franchise lineup, Greenlee remained confident, claiming that "booking agents, promoters and club owners will want to do business with the U.S. League before the '45 season is over." Yet the USL faced several problems, most notably its inability to match the level of play of its rivals. The NNL and NAL monopolized the country's best black talent, and as Sam Lacy noted, the USL lacked "more than four topline ball players." Obtaining suitable home grounds presented another dilemma, as Greenlee's plan to lease Organized Baseball parks was initially successful only in Toledo (Swayne Field), Pittsburgh (Forbes Field), and Chicago (Wrigley Field). After discovering Briggs Stadium was unavailable, the Motor City Giants were forced to rent DeQuindre Park, located in a less convenient section of Detroit. The Philadelphia Daisies, despite additional white backing from Irving Mazzer and Joseph Hall, were similarly thwarted in their attempts to wrest Parkside Field and Shibe Park away from the Stars, yet ultimately secured the lease to Island Park in Harrisburg. Hoping to further spark the interest of fans and promoters, the Daisies were renamed Hilldale, although the team apparently decided against leasing Hilldale Park.

The USL did succeed in accomplishing a long-sought reform in black baseball: the election of a non-affiliated league president. Despite his own heavy involvement in the league's formation, Greenlee insisted that "we want a real president . . . and will select a man whose character and reputation is above reproach; a man whom the entire public will respect." In February 1945, Cleveland attorney John Shackelford became the league's first president. While Shackelford's legal skills represented an important asset to the fledgling USL, his baseball background was equally impressive. During the 1920s, Shackelford appeared on several league teams, playing under luminaries such as Rube Foster and Oscar Charleston. Recently defeated as a candidate for NAL president, Shackelford nevertheless claimed no ill will toward the rival leagues, insisting that "Negro baseball will never attain the heights that it is due unless we cease this petty bickering among ourselves. There is room for everybody."[19]

Despite the welcome involvement of Shackelford, most observers viewed the USL's chances of success as slim. The franchises not only were widely scattered, but would also face wartime travel restrictions, prompting an

Figure 25. Joseph Hall (center), flanked by the legendary Oscar Charleston (right) and Webster McDonald (left), in a publicity shot for the Hilldale team of Gus Greenlee's United States League, February 1945. Within three months, Hall and Charleston would shift the team to Brooklyn, reportedly at the behest of Branch Rickey. Courtesy Baseball Hall of Fame Library.

effort to secure the NAACP's assistance in an attempt to gain gasoline and bus privileges comparable to those of the NNL and NAL. Moreover, the anticipated assistance from Abe Saperstein failed to materialize, as the midwestern promoter chose to maintain his lucrative booking of NAL franchises and part-ownership of the Birmingham Black Barons. While doubtful of the new league's prospects, Rollo Wilson sympathized with Greenlee's efforts, noting that "when you know the story which is Negro baseball and its recent sordid chapters, you cannot help but root for a guy like Gus." Yet Wilson warned that Greenlee "has two obsessions—that Negro baseball can be made a real business and that he was double-crossed by his former satellite and friends. . . . I repeat—don't sell Gus short."[20]

Wilson would prove correct, as Greenlee, the new league's vice president, would undertake a surprising series of moves that would propel the USL into the public eye as a more viable organization. During the early months of 1945, Greenlee and other USL officials secretly began to cultivate a relationship with Branch Rickey, probably initially through attempts to rent Ebbets Field. Rickey recognized that a black team appearing regularly at Ebbets Field might not only provide income but also prove an important part of his integration scheme, acclimating white Brooklynites to the sight of black players and perhaps eventually functioning as part of the Dodgers' minor league system as a developing ground for black talent. At the reported behest of Rickey, the Hilldale franchise was shifted to Brooklyn and renamed the Brooklyn Brown Dodgers. Joseph Hall then assumed full control of the team, separating from his partner Irving Mazzer, who would develop another Hilldale franchise for league play.

The involvement of Rickey represented a substantial accomplishment for the USL, as the unprecedented participation of a major league official in the operation of a black professional team bolstered the legitimacy of the new organization. Moreover, Rickey's subsequent public acknowledgment of his interest in the USL evolved into a public relations nightmare for the NNL and NAL. On Monday, May 7, 1945, Rickey held a press conference in the Dodgers offices announcing his involvement with the USL, the formation of the Brown Dodgers with Oscar Charleston at the helm, and his plan to lease Ebbets Field to the new team. Yet Rickey also read a prepared statement blasting the two established organizations as the "poorest excuse for the word league," citing their weak contracts and use of booking agents. As Rickey explained, the NNL and NAL were "leagues in name only and not in practice. . . . You cannot have a league . . . if you admit that the clubs in it are dependent upon outside booking agents to book them, like in Shibe Park in Philadelphia and Yankee Stadium." Effa Manley, the only NNL or NAL owner to attend the press conference, quickly challenged Rickey's newfound interest in black baseball, asking why he had failed to contact the eastern or western black leagues. Rickey shrewdly redirected the question to John Shackelford, who revealed that NNL and NAL officials had failed to take advantage of the USL's prior attempt to arrange a meeting.[21]

The heavily publicized press conference sent shock waves through the baseball world. As Rollo Wilson observed, "it was incredible—the president of a major league ball club inviting sportswriters and others to come to his office to discuss the organization of a colored league." Yet the ultimate significance of Rickey's involvement remained unclear. Some suggested that Rickey's interest in the USL might foreshadow greater major league involvement in the administration of black franchises, leading sportswriter

Roscoe Coleman to warn fans not to be "surprised to wake up one fine morning and find Negro Organized Baseball (N.O.B.) exclusively controlled by White Organized Baseball (W.O.B.)." Citing the recent tryouts, other observers perceived the move as defensive, designed to divert attention away from the integration fight. Leery of the USL's potential to perpetuate segregation, one integration advocate complained that "we don't want Rickey to start a new league for us. We want him to participate in non-jim crow baseball."

Rickey's entrance into black baseball prompted a flurry of responses from the normally passive NNL officials stung by the unfavorable publicity. Although Rollo Wilson felt that "most of his charges against Negro leagues were, unfortunately, true and have been subjects of criticism . . . for years," Rickey appeared unnecessarily insensitive to the formidable barriers black leagues had faced for decades. Eddie Gottlieb, for example, viewed the press conference as an attempt to "humiliate and hamper the work of men who have been in the game for twelve or fifteen years" and complained that Rickey failed to invite NNL officials until 11 A.M. the day of the meeting. Yet the always placid Tom Wilson appeared unconcerned, noting that "I only disagree with him that we don't have good leagues." Meanwhile, Effa Manley feared whites would now usurp black ownership, a response perceived by Sam Lacy as an overreaction to the "appearance of one dubious white competitor."[22]

Manley and other owners, however, particularly fretted over the potential effect on park rentals. With Ebbets Field, leased occasionally by the Newark Eagles and other NNL teams in 1944, now available only for USL games, owners wondered whether other Organized Baseball facilities might eventually follow suit. Yet the Yankees and other major league franchises were relatively content with their current rental arrangement and made no attempt to join Rickey. Notably, Senators owner Clark Griffith quickly defended the NNL and NAL, complaining that "Mr. Rickey is attempting to destroy two well organized leagues which have been in existence for some time and in which colored people . . . have faith and confidence." Claiming "this is not the age of dictators," Griffith urged all Organized Baseball franchises to maintain their current agreements with the NNL and NAL. Yet Griffith's profitable rentals to Posey's Grays obviously shaped his attitudes, leading Rickey to observe that "whenever some one does anything to interfere with his making of a dollar, that fellow gets all upset." The inherent irony of the Griffith-Rickey public squabble was apparent to USL secretary Russ Cowans, who suggested that "the strings are being pulled in Pittsburgh by two men of color—Gus Greenlee and Cum Posey."

With a suddenly higher profile following the Rickey press conference, the USL prepared to begin its first season, planning a 100-game schedule for each franchise. Hoping to stimulate fan interest and reflecting the probable influence of Rickey, Greenlee emphasized the USL as a pathway to integration, functioning as a "solution . . . to train the potential Negro major league player." As Greenlee explained, the league eventually hoped to establish eight franchises, each renting a major league park. Once major league fans began to attend USL games and witnessed the skills of black players, they would soon demand their presence on white teams. Moreover, Greenlee insisted that black baseball could still coexist alongside integrated major league teams, asserting that "the Negro owners would benefit because the fans would come to the United States League games to see what new Negro stars are being developed. In other words, it would not detract from the drawing power or affect the investment of the Negro owners, but provide another good source of revenue for him."

Greenlee's ambitious plans failed to materialize, however, as the actual operation of the USL proved to be anticlimactic. As anticipated, the level of play was mediocre, featuring only a few established players. Moreover, promotions in major league parks drew poorly, and league games were soon being scheduled in smaller venues. By July, the much touted yet poorly promoted Brooklyn Brown Dodgers collapsed and reorganized under Webster McDonald, who replaced the duo of Joseph Hall and Oscar Charleston. Irving Mazzer's Hilldale team was equally unimpressive, playing rarely if ever in Philadelphia, and eventually disappearing after the first half season. League publicity was also subpar; by September few African Americans were aware that only four franchises had completed the season.[23]

Although the USL's impact ultimately proved marginal, the actual degree of Branch Rickey's participation remains unclear. A number of accounts have clearly overstated his involvement, however, erroneously suggesting that Rickey was the true driving force behind the league and deemphasizing the importance of Greenlee. As noted, plans for a new organization had been under way since at least mid-1944, months before Rickey's announcement, yet Sam Lacy noted that sportswriters "seem to have fallen for the gag that Branch Rickey . . . 'organized' a new colored baseball league." Moreover, throughout its existence, most observers perceived the USL as a "Branch Rickey controlled league," an assertion unsubstantiated by existing evidence.

Although later withdrawn, Joseph Hall's 1947 lawsuit against Rickey for breach of contract provides some insight into the Brooklyn promoter's actual role. According to Hall, Rickey promised to cover Hall's salary and other operating expenses, and he could "take over openly the ownership of the team via stock holdings whenever he, Rickey, considered it advisable."[24] Rickey, however, offered a different perspective, suggesting he was never actively involved in the day-to-day operations of the league. In a memo to attorney Harry Walsh in the aftermath of the lawsuit, Rickey explained that Ebbets Field had been used "constantly" in the past by black teams (a gross exaggeration), who were "in the control of racketeers—men exploiting the colored players of the country for their own purpose." Moreover, Rickey's recommendation that the two leagues should "conform to such requirements as would permit them eligibility in organized baseball" had been rejected. After discovering that "substantial folks" were organizing a new league in 1945, Rickey met with John Shackelford, whom he considered a "very reliable person," and subsequently "assisted in the drawing of a constitution . . . and the general organization was such that the structure would, in my judgment, have been acceptable to organized baseball if various teams could carry out the balanced schedule for an entire season."

In his discussion of his financial interest in the Brown Dodgers, Rickey claimed that he simply granted the use of Ebbets Field, provided the team with uniforms, and offered general assistance, yet "would not accept part ownership and I made it very plain to the League that I did not care for any responsibility of ownership . . . that I had a park to rent and I was willing to make the rental almost nominal in order to support the organization of a league that would be legal and regular from the standpoint of organized baseball." While the Dodgers ultimately lent about $6,000 to Hall to assist the struggling club, Rickey insisted that "nobody had any understanding from me that I would under-write losses or be responsible for the continuance of the club for the season."[25]

A definitive explanation for Rickey's entrance into black baseball is equally elusive. Arthur Mann, an admirer of Rickey and later his assistant, argued that, while the USL was designed to ameliorate "inferior conditions elsewhere in Negro baseball," it also functioned "as an instrument to cloak Rickey's activity in the field of scouting Negro players." Dodger scouts could then observe black players without arousing suspicion and simply claim their intent was to discover capable recruits for the Brown Dodgers. While Mann's interpretation was widely accepted, Bill Veeck, who became part-owner of the Cleveland Indians in 1946, cited Rickey's desire to maximize park rental income, explaining that "Rickey wanted money. . . . The Yankees and the Giants split the Negro league money and Rickey wanted a third of it." Hall's lawsuit offered a third perspective, asserting that Rickey "was anxious to determine the effect of colored baseball playing in Brooklyn and the reaction therefrom on public sentiment," and so he induced the transfer of the Hilldale franchise to New York.[26]

It is not altogether inconceivable that Rickey's actual intention may have encompassed all three elements. Initially, Greenlee or some other league official probably contacted Rickey simply to lease Ebbets Field, and Rickey, unsatisfied with his scant rental income from a handful of NNL promotions in 1944, readily agreed to the request. As early as March 23, 1945, Rickey and other Dodger officials discussed ongoing negotiations with black teams and the expectation that "we will increase our income from these sources very materially." Unlike other major league officials, however, the typically far-sighted Rickey looked beyond simply park rentals, recognizing that involvement with black baseball offered other potential valuable opportunities. Realizing that a local black franchise, rather than league promotions, would stimulate rentals and attendance at Ebbets Field, Rickey willingly supported the formation of the Brown Dodgers. Already planning on integration, Rickey likely also perceived that his investment might allow him to stockpile black players in an arrangement similar to the farm system idea he had pioneered two decades earlier. Effa Manley, for example, even believed that Rickey "had in mind probably forming another league, and where he'd have access to all these great Negro players." Rickey himself later acknowledged that after his initial scouting efforts of black players in foreign locales during 1943 and 1944, he recognized that "the best negro players in the world were right here in the United States. . . . Then is the time when I became greatly interested in having an ownership or a control interest in one of the Negro Clubs in this country." Once organized, the Brown Dodgers would then provide additional benefits by acclimating local white fans to the prospect of black players, and as Mann suggested, camouflaging ongoing scouting efforts.

Perhaps the most curious aspect of the USL was the alliance of the moralistic Rickey with Greenlee, although Rickey was probably unaware of Greenlee's underworld background. While Rickey might easily have instead pursued a similar relationship with the NNL or NAL, it is unlikely that either league, distrustful of outside interference, would have been receptive to such an offer. Greenlee, however, had always been willing to take chances and embrace innovations, and his involvement with Rickey demonstrated his desire to confront, rather than avoid, the prospect of integration. Had Rickey truly contributed the substantial financial backing and administrative assistance he is often credited with, the USL might have altered the subsequent course of black professional baseball.[27]

◆ ◆ ◆

Although the operation of the USL ultimately proved disappointing, some observers hoped that its formation might motivate the two established leagues to undertake much needed reforms during 1945. The USL's selection of a non-affiliated president and ambitious plan to eventually function as a minor league for Organized Baseball stood in stark contrast to the typically conservative administrative efforts of the NNL and NAL. Moreover, the two leagues, still smarting from Branch Rickey's heavily publicized criticism, faced increasing pressure to correct or at least improve the chronic difficulties in their organizations.

The selection of a commissioner was the most obvious and seemingly easiest step for black professional baseball to take. A competent high-profile head of black baseball would not only win public favor but also partially refute the accusations of Rickey and other detractors. League officials had already created a four-person committee in December 1944 to investigate potential candidates, and the volatile early months of 1945 had only further reinforced the need for a commissioner. Although the press proposed a number of distinguished names, including Representative William Dawson of Illinois, William Hastie, and A. Philip Randolph, the owners would eventually narrow the choices to two candidates, each with strong ties to individual league officials.[28]

The NAL rallied behind Robert Church, Jr., a close associate of J. B. Martin and the son of one of the south's first black millionaires. Born in 1885 in Memphis, Church attended the Academy of Oberlin College, received subsequent business training, and eventually became actively involved in local Republican politics following his father's death in 1912. Receiving backing from middle-class blacks, Church formed the Lincoln League, an organization designed to facilitate black voter registration and payment of poll taxes. Following the unprecedented registration of 10,000 blacks in 1916 and backing of congressional and legislature candidates, Church became the most powerful Republican in Memphis and the leading black adviser to the Republican national chairman. During the 1920s, Church's control over Republican patronage allowed him to maintain local influence through an alliance with Democratic boss Edward H. Crump. But following the 1932 election of Franklin Roosevelt and the subsequent loss of Republican patronage, Church's power abruptly declined, along with his value to Crump. By 1940, an attempt by Church and Martin to break with Crump resulted in immediate reprisals, forcing both men to leave the city for Chicago, while Church's property was confiscated for the nonpayment of back taxes overlooked in the past. With his political influence now waning and baseball background virtually nonexistent, Church appeared to be a questionable choice, offering little except his Republican connections and relationship with Martin.[29]

The eastern league's candidate, William Hueston, possessed stronger credentials. The sixty-four-year-old Hueston was born in Lexington, Kentucky, and later attended the University of Chicago and the University of Kansas. After receiving his law degree from Kansas in 1904, Hueston practiced law in Kansas City before moving to Gary, Indiana, in 1920. Paralleling the pattern of most successful blacks prior to the New Deal, Hueston aligned with the Republican party, becoming a city magistrate and later obtaining a federal position as assistant solicitor for the Post Office Department in Washington. Impressed by his legal and political background, the original NNL named Hueston president in 1927, where he served until the league's collapse prior to the 1932 season. In later years, Hueston had maintained an active law practice in Washington, while simultaneously holding a major position as commissioner of education for the Elks, the largest and most influential black fraternal organization.[30]

Despite Hueston's unspectacular performance as league president years earlier, most eastern owners viewed him as a far more attractive candidate than Church. Hueston possessed not only the practical experience in professional baseball that Church lacked but also the legal training necessary to address potential domestic and foreign challenges. Cum Posey, a fellow Elk, enthusiastically supported Hueston and regarded him as the ideal candidate. As early as November 1941, Posey touted Hueston's "aggressiveness, standing, ability and previous experience" and praised him as "probably the most race conscious professional man I have met." A year later, Posey again suggested Hueston as commissioner, relating to Effa Manley that he was a "personal friend of Mr. [Paul] McNutt [head of the War Manpower Commission] and Mr. [Harold] Ickes, although he is a Republican and they are Democrats." The NNL would soon appreciate the importance of Hueston's political connections, as his efforts during early 1944 helped to alleviate the league's transportation difficulties and won the confidence of the normally frugal owners who paid him $100 for his work.

Despite Hueston's demonstrated ability to negotiate successfully with Washington officials, western owners were less enthusiastic about his candidacy. Several wondered whether Hueston's ties with Posey and his Washington residence would result in obvious favoritism to the NNL. Meanwhile, NNL owners, who had always preferred an eastern-based commissioner, were equally leery of Church's relationship with the Martins. Compensation presented another contentious issue, as Hueston expected a salary, while Church was "willing to serve as a dollar-a-year man."[31]

On June 12, 1945, franchise owners convened in Chicago for what would be one of the more important meetings in either league's history. Following NNL president Tom Wilson's appeal for a harmonious session, officials considered several current problems, including the revision of player contracts and the USL, before finally discussing the election of a commissioner. After Church and Hueston emerged as the two candidates, Eddie Gottlieb proposed the new commissioner should receive $2,400 annually, while others suggested a figure as high as $4,000. NNL and NAL owners also agreed to follow the practice of the white major leagues requiring a three-quarters majority (nine of the twelve votes) to elect a commissioner, a fateful move supposedly engineered by Cum Posey.

As expected, the subsequent secret balloting largely followed league affiliation. All six NAL franchises voted for Church, while five of the six eastern teams supported Hueston. Only the Manleys crossed league lines, casting their vote for Church, perhaps hoping to increase the actual chance of electing a commissioner. Inexplicably, league officials failed to move for a second ballot, revealing the considerable ambivalence toward the selection of any candidate. The disappointing outcome was inevitable, as neither league was willing to accept the other's handpicked selection, regardless of credentials. While impartial candidates without clear ties to either league might have fared better, the general distrust, unwillingness to compromise, and unchecked individualism among the owners presented formidable barriers to the selection of a commissioner. Although the election of Hueston and Church as league presidents might have offered a feasible alternate plan to demonstrate black baseball's credibility, neither NNL nor NAL would choose an impartial head until 1947.

During the same fateful meeting, the two leagues also failed to capitalize on an opportunity to acknowledge and address one of their major dilemmas: the imminent integration of Organized Baseball. At the behest of Larry MacPhail, Sam Lacy invited the owners to appoint a representative to participate on his committee investigating integration and its potential impact. Despite scattered support from several officials, the NNL and NAL once again failed to act, largely due to the strong opposition of Posey, who predictably objected to the unsolicited involvement of Lacy or any newspaperman in league affairs. While the presence of a league official might not have altered the course of Lacy's committee, black baseball missed an ideal chance to demonstrate its interest in integration, legitimacy as an organization, and desire to prepare for the future.[32]

Despite a pressing need for aggressive leadership, the two leagues pursued their typical passive course during the 1945 season, reinforcing rather than repudiating the criticisms of Branch Rickey. The formation of the USL along with a new lower-level Southern League created a number of problems with jumping players, prompting a disgusted Fay Young to ask "why can't Negro owners act like men? Is there any wonder that Negro club owners are charged by some major league club owners as being unprincipled?" Meanwhile, continued violence on the playing field further demonstrated the lack of strong authority in the NNL and NAL.

Yet the war-fueled prosperity allowed most owners to minimize the importance of chronic organizational problems, as both leagues continued to attract large crowds at Organized Baseball parks throughout the United States. While the Homestead Grays remained the most profitable team in the NNL, the Newark Eagles also enjoyed a prosperous season in 1945. By August, Effa Manley confided to the proprietor of the black Attucks Hotel in Philadelphia that the Eagles were "drawing so well at home, we do not travel any more than we have to." Attendance in Philadelphia also remained solid, as nine weeknight dates at Shibe Park attracted an amazing 101,818 fans, a remarkable achievement juxtaposed against the *combined* A's and Phillies season attendance of 773,020. Meanwhile, Detroit blacks, lacking their own league franchise, flocked to Briggs Stadium for a series of games booked by African American promoter John Williams, including two Satchel Paige appearances attracting a total of 41,726 fans.[33]

Following the war's end in August and subsequent subsiding of travel and manpower difficulties, the future seemed relatively bright for the industry. Moreover, after several years of war-related shortages and anxieties, both white and black Americans were ready to enjoy themselves and appeared likely to patronize all commercialized amusements as never before. Yet astute observers such as Rollo Wilson suggested that, despite its recent success, black baseball still remained vulnerable without parks or tangible property of its own. Wilson wondered whether franchise owners would finally address current deficiencies "or will most of them just continue to rent other people's ball parks and have nothing to show for that 'million dollar empire' than such names as 'Black Yankees,' 'Elite Giants,' 'Newark Eagles' and 'Homestead Grays'?" Yet with the leagues still in the same hands after the abortive attempt to elect a commissioner in June, immediate structural changes in the operation of black baseball appeared doubtful, leaving future prospects questionable.[34]

◆ ◆ ◆

The problem of integration, readily dodged by major league officials in the past, was increasingly inescapable during 1945. Reflecting the increased anxiety, Red Sox general manager Eddie Collins advised American League president Will Harridge in early April that integration was an "issue that we are going to be faced with in the future, possibly the immediate future." While equally concerned, a more optimistic Larry MacPhail subsequently related to Commissioner Chandler that "Rickey and myself think we have a possible solution along the lines of cooperating in the establishment and operation of strong Negro leagues," an assertion backed by Rickey himself, who confided to an associate that his efforts to "organize a decent, strong Negro League . . . may help to solve the problem which is becoming more and more evident."

While it is doubtful that Rickey viewed his participation in the USL as a permanent "solution" to integration, MacPhail clearly believed that the establishment of well-organized black leagues might mollify critics, enable the Yankees and other teams to maintain and perhaps increase their rental income, and allow Organized Baseball to pursue a more gradual course. Outlining his plan to a *Courier* reporter, MacPhail attempted to build support by claiming that sweeping reforms in black baseball, including improved scheduling and administration, could lead to affiliation and eventually integration at a later date. Yet MacPhail, like Rickey, discouraged aggressive protest efforts, insisting that integration "will never be accomplished by agitation or picketing."[35]

Despite his apparent enthusiasm for strengthening black baseball, Mac-Phail made no attempt to assist the established leagues or participate in the USL, remaining content to collect the nearly $100,000 in rental and concession income earned by the Yankees and their farm teams in 1945. MacPhail and other New York team owners, however, could not avoid the mounting local public and political pressure for integration. In April, Representative Vito Marcantonio of the American Labor Party announced his plan to introduce a resolution recommending an investigation of baseball's hiring practices. Meanwhile, black communist city councilman Benjamin Davis urged the involvement of SCAD, recently created by the Ives-Quinn law. By late summer, SCAD had begun a probe of the three major league teams in New York, while grass-roots organizations such as the Metropolitan Interfaith and Interracial Coordinating Council (MIICC) joined the fight.

The End Jim Crow in Baseball Committee, a controversial new protest group sponsored by the MIICC, also emerged during 1945, embracing the direct action tactics favored by the Congress of Racial Equality (CORE), a soon to be influential interracial coalition founded three years earlier. Although a CORE-influenced picketing strategy had already been employed on opening day at Yankee Stadium by another protest group, some integration supporters still preferred more traditional attempts at persuasion without the overt use of pressure. The *Courier*, for example, believed that most fans favored "the matter settled in a fair, just and diplomatic manner instead of staging an ugly fight which will do nobody any good," yet warned of the potential efforts of "extremists" should the color bar remain intact. Not surprisingly, the aggressive approach of the End Jim

Crow in Baseball Committee also concerned Branch Rickey, who believed the organization was communist-influenced.[36]

Despite resistance, the Committee grew stronger throughout the summer and made plans for mass demonstrations in and outside Ebbets Field and the Polo Grounds on Saturday, August 18. Fearful of an incident at their park, alarmed Giants officials appealed to Mayor Fiorello LaGuardia, whose interracial Committee on Unity, created to promote positive race relations in the aftermath of the Harlem race riot of 1943, had already begun a preliminary investigation into major league integration. Perhaps wary of the explosive nature of the issue and its potential effect on the candidacy of his chosen successor Newbold Morris, LaGuardia announced on August 11 the formation of a subcommittee to study the problem and submit recommendations to major league baseball. The new group supplanted Sam Lacy's inactive committee, yet again enlisted the participation of Rickey and MacPhail, along with several prominent local white citizens and two African Americans: Episcopal clergyman John H. Johnson and dancer Bill "Bojangles" Robinson. Meanwhile, LaGuardia designated Dan Dodson, executive director of the Mayor's Committee on Unity, who had also been named to the Committee on Baseball, to persuade the End Jim Crow in Baseball Committee to postpone its planned ballpark demonstrations to allow the new organization adequate opportunity to conduct its business. As LaGuardia himself explained to an End Jim Crow in Baseball Committee official, a demonstration might be counterproductive "if it provokes disorder" and would ultimately "retard the solution of the problem."[37]

LaGuardia's announcement and involvement would have been eagerly welcomed five years earlier, but the war had raised the expectations of African Americans, who could no longer be appeased by the simple creation of an investigatory committee. Dan Burley doubted the sincerity of the move, noting that LaGuardia had never shown any prior interest in the issue. As Burley explained, "the job now is to get Negroes into major league uniforms, not to keep them on the sidelines while a group of big shots . . . soaks up a lot of publicity, eats and drinks up a lot of free food and winds up with a long list of resolutions that will be promptly pigeonholed along with such resolutions . . . as the [Harlem] Riot report of 1943 and that of 1935." Rollo Wilson similarly denounced the committee as "baloney" and questioned the selection of Bill Robinson, "a baseball fan, of course, but his record shows that he has never made any effort to go 'all out' to improve the conditions of any members of his own race." The End Jim Crow in Baseball Committee was equally unhappy with the presence of Robinson, who despite his formidable dancing skills, appeared to be an increasingly outdated and largely apolitical racial symbol.[38]

The LaGuardia committee ultimately accomplished little except to contain mounting pressure, allowing Rickey additional time to complete his integration plans for the 1946 season. By contrast MacPhail, unaware of Rickey's program, continued to advocate a gradual and prolonged approach to integration, and formally articulated his position in an open statement to the committee in mid-September. With his typical frankness, MacPhail explained that "the Yankees have no intention of signing Negro players under contract or reservation to Negro clubs. . . . To give tryouts to players whom you do not intend to employ is sheer hypocrisy." MacPhail nevertheless denied the existence of discrimination, while as usual condemning "political and social-minded drum beaters" who "singled out Organized Baseball for attack because it offers a good publicity medium for propaganda." While favoring "a better deal in baseball" for African Americans, MacPhail again suggested that black leagues needed to "put their house in order—establish themselves on a sound and ethical operations basis—and conform to the standards of Organized Baseball." Following affiliation with Organized Baseball, a "limited number of Negro players, who first establish ability, character and aptitude, in their own leagues, might advance to the majors or big minors of Organized Baseball."

To buttress his plea for gradualism, MacPhail enumerated the problems certain to accompany integration. According to MacPhail, few black players were capable of playing major league baseball, citing Sam Lacy's earlier comment that "we haven't a single man in the ranks of colored baseball who could step into the major league uniform and disport himself after the fashion of a major leaguer." (MacPhail, however, conveniently omitted Lacy's subsequent explanatory statement asserting that if blacks entered Organized Baseball and received similar "handling and training" as whites, they "would develop into the same quality of player as the average white recruit.") Moreover, integration would hurt black baseball, resulting in the collapse of leagues, lost investments, and unemployment for numerous players. Despite his professed desire to protect black professional baseball, MacPhail made no offer to alleviate its current problems by reducing park rental fees. The frank admission that "Organized Baseball derives substantial revenues from operation of the Negro leagues and wants these leagues to continue and to prosper" reflected MacPhail's predominant concern: integration's potential financial impact on his own and other major league franchises.[39]

Disillusioned by MacPhail's attitude and doubtful of the success of the LaGuardia committee, black New Yorkers shifted their attention to a nonpolitical development: a postseason series between a team of NNL players and a group of major leaguers. Featuring several of the NNL's top performers, the games offered the opportunity to counter MacPhail's bleak assessment of black baseball talent. On October 7, a crowd of 10,424 watched the major leaguers sweep a doubleheader at Ebbets Field by 5-4 and 2-1 scores. In the remaining three games played in Newark and Brooklyn, the NNL team dropped 10-0 and 4-1 decisions, finally managing a 0-0 tie in the last game. Effa Manley, who co-promoted the series with Dodger officials, related the disappointing outcome to "stage fright," confiding to Baltimore Elite Giants official Vernon Green that Eagles infielder Murray Watkins, suddenly error-prone, "seemed scared to death. In fact all the colored boys did." The club was also handicapped by the absence of several key Grays players, who were appearing in a separate promotion in New Orleans. While a number of capable black players participated in the series, the NNL's failure to field a truly representative team further underscored the need for a strong outside authority.[40]

With four of the five games scheduled at Ebbets Field and several Dodgers participating, Rollo Wilson wondered whether the series might have greater significance, observing that "the shrewd Mr. Rickey never does anything without a motive." As usual, Wilson proved correct, as four of the NNL participants signed Dodger contracts in the next six months. Yet in the days immediately following the series, Rickey's intentions still remained concealed to the general public, although Rickey now faced increasing pressure from LaGuardia, who planned during his October 21 weekly radio broadcast to credit his committee for its role in the imminent signing of black players. Uncomfortable with the increasing political exploitation of the issue, Rickey persuaded LaGuardia to postpone his discussion to a later date, while simultaneously accelerating his own integration plans. On October 23, at least several weeks earlier than Rickey originally intended, baseball fans learned of the signing of Jackie Robinson to a contract with the Montreal Royals, the Dodgers affiliate in the International League.

Born in 1919 in Georgia, Robinson and his family relocated to Pasadena, California, in 1920, paralleling the increasing out-migration pattern of southern blacks during the first quarter of the twentieth century. Inspired by his brother Mack, an outstanding sprinter who competed along with Jesse Owens in the 1936 Olympic games in Berlin, Robinson became interested in athletics at an early age and excelled in baseball, basketball, football, and track while attending Pasadena Junior College and UCLA from 1937 to 1941. By the early 1940s, Robinson was a nationally known black athlete, particularly celebrated for his exploits on the football field.

Drafted in 1942, Robinson was commissioned as a lieutenant but later faced court martial proceedings following his refusal to sit in the back of a bus in Texas. Exonerated by a military court, Robinson joined the Kansas

City Monarchs in early 1945 after his discharge and participated in the abortive Boston tryout in April at the behest of Wendell Smith, who subsequently recommended Robinson to Rickey. After receiving favorable reports of Robinson's background and athletic abilities from Dodger scouts, Rickey met with Robinson in August and agreed to tender a formal contract offer by November 1, 1945. In the meantime, Robinson remained with the Monarchs, but left the club in early September, unhappy with the lifestyle of black baseball and unwilling to participate in a postseason barnstorming tour.[41]

Several observers have contended that Rickey had little basis to select Robinson, apart from his college background. Pitcher Verdell Mathis, for example, later claimed "there were 100 better players in the Negro leagues than Jackie," while Sam Lacy viewed Robinson as "not the best . . . but he was the most suitable. Oh, that's a terrible word, *suitable*. But he was *the right man*." Robinson's education and experience in interracial athletics at UCLA obviously made him an attractive candidate, but he had also shown considerable baseball potential prior to his signing, receiving favorable comment from White Sox manager Jimmy Dykes and attention from Los Angeles sportswriter Dave Farrell, who touted him as a potential major leaguer as early as 1940. During his year with the Monarchs, Robinson further demonstrated his baseball prowess, earning selection to the East-West game as the NAL's starting shortstop. Moreover, press releases for Monarchs games heavily promoted Robinson during 1945, including a June column citing him "as the one colored player of major league caliber."[42]

Although the signing of Robinson should have been a triumph for black professional baseball, the promising development degenerated into a public relations nightmare. Almost immediately, Kansas City part-owner Tom Baird complained that Rickey had made no attempt to contact the Monarchs or reimburse them for Robinson's contract. Rickey responded by reiterating his earlier criticisms that "the Negro organizations in baseball are not leagues, nor, in my opinion, do they have even organization. As at present administered they are in the nature of a racket." The failure to produce an actual signed contract for Robinson further validated Rickey's assertion, although Baird later offered the explanation that such agreements "worked to our detriment. Other players . . . became disgruntled when shown contracts calling for more money than they were being paid. Our word was our bond. Telegrams and letters exchanged with Robinson was, as far as we were concerned, a binding contract." Moreover, Baird later related that "our league constitution stipulates that a player agreeing to play by signed letter or telegram is the property of the club concerned." While perhaps financially practical, such a practice left the Monarchs frighteningly vulnerable and underscored black baseball's age-old failure to require standardized contracts of all teams and to address the issue during the war.[43]

The contract dilemma confirmed that the NNL and NAL, despite warnings for several years, had inadequately prepared for the inevitability of integration. As late as August, officials appeared convinced that major league teams would respect their shaky agreements with players, a belief reinforced by a conference with Larry MacPhail. According to J. B. Martin, who accompanied Eddie Gottlieb to the meeting, MacPhail stated that "we would be consulted on everything pertaining to colored baseball. I don't think we have anything to worry about them taking our players and not giving us all the consideration that we are entitled to." Lulled into a false sense of security, the leagues largely ignored the problem, missing an opportunity to participate in the process and establish a precedent for future transactions involving black players. Certainly, black professional baseball might have collectively chosen its own potential candidates, groomed the players for integration, and then offered them for sale to interested white teams for an agreed-upon minimum price. The NNL, for example, could have rallied behind Newark Eagles outfielder Monte Irvin, whom several officials favored as the ideal player to break the color line. Yet such an alternative scenario was virtually inconceivable without the presence of strong impartial leadership, a reform the two leagues stubbornly remained unwilling to undertake.

Struggling to regroup, the NNL and NAL faced the delicate question of how to address Robinson's uncompensated signing without appearing opposed to integration. Despite deciding against a formal protest to Commissioner Chandler, Monarchs officials continued to question Rickey's handling of the matter. Part-owner J. L. Wilkinson, a veteran of twenty-five years in black professional baseball, noted that "we have been out some expense in training players such as Robinson" and "something should be done to prevent white organized baseball from just stepping in and taking our players." The Monarchs, however, had relatively few options, as a lawsuit probably would have been costly, certain to incur considerable antagonism among blacks, and ultimately futile. Not surprisingly, Baird quickly reassured black fans that "we are glad of his advancement and hope more Negro players get the same opportunity. We are not in Negro baseball just to make money: we want to see the Negro race advance to full participation in American activities." Nevertheless, Baird continued to insist that Rickey "owes us a moral obligation. Whatever he might have offered would have been okay with us—but he has ignored our efforts to obtain something for our great shortstop which is preposterous."

Baird also later complained that Rickey "was not even gentleman enough to answer or acknowledge my many letters I wrote to him."[44]

The leagues' grievance received predictable support from Clark Griffith, who along with Larry MacPhail stood to lose the most from the weakening of black baseball. In a series of statements probably influenced by his tenant Cum Posey, Griffith criticized Rickey's signing of Robinson, noting that "contracts and players under reservation with any recognized and established baseball organization should be respected, regardless of how they are organized." Moreover, Griffith argued that "there is such a thing as an unwritten law in such cases. In no walk of life can one person take another's property unless he pays for it." Insisting that owners "can't act like outlaws," Griffith suggested black baseball should be recognized and compensated for future player signings. Rickey, however, quickly dismissed the accusations, claiming he had not "signed a player from what I regard as an organized league."

While somewhat self-serving, Griffith's suggestions were hardly unreasonable and stood in stark contrast to Rickey's unyielding refusal to consider even a token payment to the Monarchs. As Eddie Gottlieb complained, "Rickey is doing just what he always does: getting ball players without spending a dime." Yet rebukes from Gottlieb and other owners failed to tarnish the reputation of Rickey, whose stance had earned him the unanimous and virtually permanent support of African American fans and liberal whites. Dan Burley, for example, praised Rickey as a "fearless crusader," asserting that the NNL and NAL were "banking on the efforts of an unholy, reactionary, anti-Negro setup led by Clark Griffith." White sportswriter Red Smith was also critical, noting that, while Griffith was now denouncing the violation of black baseball's "property rights," he had been equally ruthless in signing players from Cuba and other Latin American countries.[45]

Unable to muster much black opposition to Rickey's actions, NNL and NAL officials quietly began to consider strategies to prevent similar occurrences in the future. Rickey's admission that he had "several other Negroes in mind" raised the prospect of a raid on black baseball rivaling the past devastating efforts of Mexican and Dominican promoters. Still hoping to resolve the Robinson matter, J. B. Martin favored an appeal to National League president Ford Frick, privately relating to Effa Manley that "I believe we will get results from him. I have talked with three or four of the major league owners and they are not in accord with Rickey to say the least . . . they think that he should have gotten Robinson through the Kansas City Monarchs owners." As Martin explained, the leagues were hoping to establish a precedent, but "there will be no price named, for we are not going to jeopardize Robinson's chance. If they say $500.00 or $5,000, all well and good, we will accept it. We won't have it said of us that we asked too much for Robinson and they will have to let him return to the Kansas City Monarchs. BUT when they get other players, if they get them, we will place a reasonable price on them and demand it."

While waiting for some response from Organized Baseball, Martin issued a nationally distributed press release praising the signing of Robinson and emphasizing that "there has never been any objection . . . of the Negro American League and the Negro National League to our players advancing into the major leagues." In a weak attempt to explain black baseball's passive approach toward integration, Martin claimed both leagues recognized it would eventually occur "yet were never able to determine how or when it would take place." Martin then addressed several of Rickey's unflattering remarks questioning the legitimacy of black professional baseball, noting that each league had bylaws, a president, and permanent office and "therefore, we feel that we have an organization." Responding to Rickey's "racket" charge, Martin claimed that "we have never gone out and signed players without giving the owners some consideration," a somewhat dubious assertion in view of black baseball teams' traditionally cutthroat attitude toward players. Finally, Martin applied subtle moral pressure, suggesting that "we feel that Mr. Rickey is too big not to compensate the Kansas City Monarchs."[46]

After Martin's attempt to extract payment from Rickey failed, the NNL and NAL planned an emergency joint session on November 9 at the Hotel Theresa in New York. Simultaneously, USL president John Shackelford prepared a similar gathering and invited the rival organizations to participate in a round-table discussion with Rickey. While Abe Saperstein and Syd Pollock expressed moderate interest, other officials remained suspicious of the USL and leery of Rickey's motives.

Rather than confront Rickey, NNL and NAL officials instead turned to the business of formulating a response to the events of recent weeks. Despite declining health, Cum Posey dominated the proceedings, arriving with a letter to be sent to Commissioner Chandler articulating the leagues' position. The letter, signed by both presidents but mostly written by Posey, reiterated that black baseball was "not protesting the signing of Negro players. . . . We are glad to see our players get the opportunity. We are protesting the way it was done." Yet as Posey explained, the leagues had received no compensation for Robinson and faced the possibility of losing additional players, including pitcher John Wright of the Homestead Grays who had reportedly been recruited by the Dodgers organization. Attempting to demonstrate black baseball's legitimacy, the letter noted that the NNL and NAL "have constitutions, keep minutes of their meetings and have player contracts." Moreover, Posey reminded Chandler that Negro league contracts had withstood an earlier test in court, citing the Grays' lawsuit against Josh Gibson in 1941. The letter concluded with the suggestion that unless the black teams received consideration in future player transactions, the fate of "Negro Organized Baseball" was uncertain.[47]

At the meeting, Posey also disclosed supportive correspondence from NNL ally Clark Griffith, who claimed he had written to Chandler insisting that the two leagues were "entitled to every consideration and fair dealing from Organized Baseball." While recognizing black baseball's contract problems, Griffith maintained that Robinson "certainly made a verbal agreement . . . that he would play ball with them for so much per month. THIS in itself constitutes a contract, for had Kansas City failed to pay him he could have gone to court and collected his salary." While Griffith predicted that the leagues would receive "relief" from the commissioner, Chandler ultimately took no specific action beyond acknowledging receipt of the letter and asking to be apprised of future signings. In a further disappointment, the major leagues failed to address the integration issue at the December winter meetings, despite the hopes of black baseball officials.

Following the New York meeting, the NNL and NAL faced a number of crucial decisions involving Organized Baseball. Yet encouraging statements from the usually silent Tom Wilson in late November suggested that the NNL might be willing to take progressive steps to ensure its future survival. Wilson applauded the signing of Jackie Robinson, claiming "it will help Negro baseball. . . . I would like to see a dozen or more signed, but believe since we get the men, develop them and spend money in doing that the Negro clubs ought to be paid something." In addition, Wilson surprised observers by disclosing his plan to step down as league president because of failing health, raising hopes that the league would finally elect a non-affiliated leader. In a further encouraging sign, the influential Posey expressed support for the change, disclosing to Wilson that "if we get the right man who knows baseball and will be fair to all whether they be white or colored, I will go down the line as is."[48]

After years of administrative inactivity, the two leagues appeared resigned to enacting a series of reforms that had long been requested by fans and sportswriters. In December, officials announced plans to draft new league constitutions and adopt standardized player contracts comparable to those of the major leagues. In subsequent months, the NNL launched other progressive steps including team roster limits, an expanded schedule, incentive bonuses, and awards to the leading pitcher, hitter, and home run hitter. Perhaps the most worthwhile achievement was the hiring of thirty-four-year-old Art Carter of the *Afro-American* newspapers to head the NNL's newly created publicity bureau at a salary of $1,000. The veteran journalist had recently demonstrated his considerable promotional skills by spearheading the publication of the *Negro Baseball Pictorial Yearbook* in 1945, a surprisingly slick 32-page magazine featuring photos, rosters, articles, and statistics. While welcomed, the reforms could easily have been instituted years before, and as Bob Williams of the *Cleveland Call and Post* lamented, "it is too bad the Jackie Robinson development was necessary to spark them into action."

The crucial issue of electing non-affiliated league presidents, however, proved less easy to rectify. Unlike Tom Wilson, J. B. Martin had no inclination to step down as president, despite the criticisms of Rickey. Moreover, several owners, including Eddie Gottlieb, were reluctant to consider new leadership until an agreement of some kind had been reached with Organized Baseball, and persuaded Wilson to rescind his earlier decision. In December, Gottlieb and Martin spearheaded an effort to authorize the two current presidents to represent black baseball at a future meeting with major league officials, circulating a formal resolution to be signed by all league members and then sent to Chandler, Ford Frick, Will Harridge, and minor league head William Bramham. While reiterating several of the arguments of Posey's November letter, the resolution employed more legalistic language, requesting that Organized Baseball refrain from approaching black players without prior permission, "respect the relations existing between players and clubs" in black baseball, and "agree at any and all times to negotiate for assignment of contracts of players of our League's clubs."[49]

Yet several NNL owners viewed the resolution unenthusiastically, particularly Cum Posey, who opposed the retention of Wilson and Martin as league representatives. Posey, not illogically, perceived the support of Wilson as financially motivated, citing Gottlieb's ongoing control of the controversial Yankee Stadium promotions during Wilson's tenure in office. While praising Gottlieb as "honest in his dealing and a good baseball man," Posey nevertheless insisted that "he must come to realize that the Negro National League was not organized for his benefit." Meanwhile, Posey suggested that Martin simply wished to preserve his own financial position within the league. In a private letter to Effa Manley, Posey further outlined his opposition to the resolution, explaining that "we were asked to get presidents who were not owners . . . before we attempted to have a meeting with the commissioner. . . . Rickey will make a fool out of those who attend this meeting unless they go in with clean shirts."

Manley, however, questioned Posey's sincerity, noting that "the fact we do not have a new Chairman now can be laid on your doorstep." Neither Posey nor his partner Rufus Jackson had attended a December joint session in Chicago, preventing the possible election of Manley's preferred candidate, Samuel Battle, a sixty-two-year-old New York parole board commissioner who had been appointed one of the city's first black patrol-men in 1911. Manley explained that "as things turned out several of the members got hold of Tom and asked him not to resign. . . . I can't under-stand how people can be so deceitful. Behind his back they all say they want some one else . . . but no one will say it to his face." Although the Eagles and Grays ultimately united behind the candidacy of Battle, the remaining four NNL franchises voted to retain Wilson as president for another season. The outcome received an icy response from journalist Wil-liam Nunn, who warned Effa Manley that "we could expect The Negro Press to jump on us with both feet" for reelecting Wilson. Yet the NAL's concurrent failure to unseat J. B. Martin revealed that regardless of in-creasingly serious threats, most officials remained unwilling to surrender control to an outsider likely to undermine the influence of current alliances and agreements.[50]

As Posey feared, Wilson and Martin represented black baseball in the anticipated conference with major league officials. On January 17, 1946, the two men met in Cincinnati with Chandler, Ford Frick, and Will Har-ridge to discuss affiliation with Organized Baseball. The commissioner of-fered encouragement, approving the newly revised league contracts and relating his personal doubt that the Jackie Robinson deal would be upheld. More important, Chandler suggested that a formal agreement was possible and advised the leagues to retain the National League's attorney to draft a petition for application to Organized Baseball. Chandler, however, also cited the need for additional reforms, particularly the construction or ac-quisition of home parks.

Chandler's subsequent public comments suggested that the commis-sioner, like Larry MacPhail, viewed a strong black organization as a poten-tial substitute for integration. Chandler believed that once the black leagues "put their own house in order" and achieved better organization, "the color problem in baseball will be solved." The commissioner also asserted that "the Negro Leagues favor keeping their own boys and with their leagues on a sound basis, with a contract like the one we use, they can expect those boys to want to stay in their own class." Anticipating adverse black reaction to Chandler's statement, J. B. Martin quickly de-nied the commissioner's comments, explaining that there had been "no mention of Negro leagues wanting to hold their players if they had a chance to advance" and the catalyst for the meeting had been to seek admission to organized baseball "in order that our players would have a greater opportunity for advancement."[51]

Long recommended by African American sportswriters and fans, the move to affiliate with Organized Baseball might have been of greater stra-tegic importance if pursued a few years earlier. It is conceivable that white officials, hoping to divert mounting protests, might have sanctioned efforts to assist black baseball, and even the loosest of agreements (parallel to the USL's relationship to the Brooklyn Dodgers) would have strengthened the position of black teams when integration occurred. The industry, for example, might have benefited from a more substantial dialogue with Ford Frick, who had informed Cum Posey in 1944 that "he and the clubs of the National League were friendly toward Organized Negro Baseball and wished to help it as much as possible."

Following the signing of Robinson, however, affiliation no longer offered any real symbolic value to Organized Baseball. Moreover, the Chandler meeting now appeared less significant to some African Americans, reflecting the increasing movement toward integration in all aspects of American life and concurrent denigration and devaluation of once cherished race institutions. An *Amsterdam News* reader, for instance, scorned the appeal to Chandler as a "farce," asserting that "we need more Jackie Robinsons instead of a segregated Negro League." A *Defender* correspondent was similarly apathetic about the fate of black baseball, insisting that the "greatest error committed by Negroes of today" was "voluntary segregation. . . . If it's freedom from discrimination that we desire, then we should cast away all types of discrimination from our programs."[52]

Several sportswriters also appeared unimpressed by the post-Robinson reforms and the meeting with Chandler. Sam Lacy questioned Chandler's sincerity, suggesting that the commissioner was simply "pulling their legs," and complained that "colored baseball has been acting after the fashion of a mongrel puppy licking at the heels of a prospective master." Meanwhile, an increasingly hostile and unsympathetic Wendell Smith claimed that despite the appeal to Chandler, "few, if any, of the owners . . . are sincerely interested in the advancement of the Negro player, or what it means with respect to the Negro race as a whole" and were only concerned with "preservation of their shaky, littered, infested segregated baseball domicile." Smith's disparaging column alarmed Effa Manley, who felt that while some of the criticisms were valid, "this seems like a bad time to give the baseball such a going over." Yet Smith, foreshadowing the future actions of other African Americans, began to shift his attention away from black baseball and by June 1946, the NNL and NAL complained of declining coverage in the *Courier*.

Other observers, while more supportive, doubted the feasibility of affiliation, citing the underworld background of several officials and additional chronic difficulties. In a January 31, 1946, editorial, "Chandler and the Negro Baseball Problem," the *Sporting News* provided a typically bleak assessment of the potential for an agreement with black baseball, explaining that, while Chandler was "sympathetic to the Negro's major league aspirations" and "would like to arrange an alliance," the multitude of problems within black baseball presented a major obstacle, as "Organized Ball cannot afford to tie up with any ally with less rigid standards." The editorial quickly rejected any suggestion that white baseball should offer relief and instead preached self-help, insisting that blacks "must build anew, from the bottom up." Chandler himself embraced a similar attitude toward affiliation, providing no tangible financial or organizational assistance, while warning that "as long as Negro baseball is operated as it is now, there isn't a chance." Yet as sportswriter Rick Hurt observed, "it is certain that the owners are not, of their own volition, going to do any drastic re-organizing. They are 'too set in their ways.' And now that the books are showing a profit, a majority sentiment among them seems to be: why change, if we're doing okay?"[53]

As the 1946 baseball season approached, the relationship between black and white professional baseball remained unresolved. Much of its ultimate significance, however, depended upon whether the signing of Robinson represented a harbinger for the future or mere tokenism. Yet Dick Lundy, a veteran of three decades in black baseball as player and manager, anticipated little change and doubted that the NNL "will ever have to worry about being raided by the majors. Jackie Robinson or no other will break into the majors not in this generation . . . he will never get cooperation from those fellows."

Lundy's prediction proved mistaken, as within ten days following the meeting with Chandler, pitcher John Wright became the second African American to sign a contract with the Dodgers. Born in 1916 in New Orleans, Wright broke into black baseball with the novelty Zulu Giants in the mid-1930s and then spent several seasons with the Newark Eagles and other black teams before joining the Homestead Grays in 1941. Enjoying success as a starting pitcher, Wright hurled in the 1943 East-West game but was drafted into the navy in 1944. Assigned to the Brooklyn Navy Yard in 1945, Wright occasionally pitched weekend games for the Grays, reportedly under an assumed name, and held the major leaguers scoreless in the weather-shortened final game of the postseason series at Ebbets Field. Thus Rickey had again selected a player whose current status in black professional baseball was ambiguous. Receiving no reimbursement, an enraged Cum Posey denounced the signing as "a damned dirty trick," noting that the Grays had treated Wright well and had paid him $250 monthly while he was in the navy. Wright, however, claimed that he was a free agent as he had never been tendered a formal contract with the Grays until late 1945 and had then refused to sign it.

While Dodger interest in Wright had been reported as early as November 1945, the actual signing of a second black player convinced any remaining doubters of Rickey's integrity. To Effa Manley, the Dodgers' acquisition of Wright, a more experienced and well-regarded player, revealed that Rickey was intent on making more than simply a half-hearted gesture. As Manley explained, Wright was "a good ballplayer . . . who will not be in the game every day, rubbing elbows with the southerners," in contrast to Robinson, who appeared certain to have "an awfully tough time" displacing any of the regulars in the talent-rich Dodger organization. Moreover, other owners seemed unlikely to allow Rickey to monopolize the African American field indefinitely, and, as one observer noted, "any time you can get players like Robinson and Wright for absolutely nothing, you are not going to continue to pass up such a fertile market."[54]

The current inactivity of other major league officials allowed Rickey to continue his pursuit of black players with virtually no competition. In early April 1946, Rickey once again dipped into the NNL, grabbing catcher Roy Campanella of the Baltimore Elite Giants and nineteen-year-old pitcher Don Newcombe of the Newark Eagles and assigning them to Nashua of the class B New England League. Despite playing in the NNL in 1945, both men claimed they were under no obligation to any team, again exposing the black baseball's glaring lack of a strong reserve clause. Campanella, for example, explained that, "although I had played with Baltimore Elite Giants, for several years, after the close of 1945 season, I didn't receive any agreement or contract regarding my services in base-ball for 1946," while Newcombe asserted that after the expiration of his 1945 contract, "I was more or less a free agent." Despite anticipating the development months earlier, Baltimore owner Tom Wilson made no attempt to block Campanella and accepted the news without complaint. A horrified Effa Manley, however, complained to her husband that "we have so many boys who are Major League material we may wake up any morning and not have a ball club, if this keeps on."[55]

After losing four outstanding players in less than six months, NNL and NAL owners recognized that the problem of Branch Rickey was not about to disappear, and his continued involvement with the fragile, yet still intact USL raised additional concern. Yet a startling proposal from the USL provided an opportunity for black baseball officials to work with Rickey rather than against him. Recognizing the USL's difficulties competing with the NNL and NAL for players and parks, league president John Shackelford suggested a merger with the established organizations. Under Shackelford's plan, the NNL would absorb the Brooklyn Brown Dodgers and Greenlee's Pittsburgh Crawfords, who would relocate to Montreal, while the NAL would incorporate USL franchises at Detroit and another midwestern city. Whether Rickey influenced Shackelford's scheme is unknown, although several Dodger officials were present at a USL meeting in November 1945. Although still interested in developing black talent for the major leagues, Rickey perhaps recognized that the USL was no longer feasible and that amalgamation might offer a chance to achieve the same goal.

NNL officials, although ambivalent toward Rickey, seemed willing to consider the prospect of expansion. Tom Wilson, for example, not only favored a meeting with Shackelford but publicly stated his belief that black baseball "owed Gus Greenlee something." Moreover, assimilation of the USL would eliminate a potentially annoying competitor whose appeal had increased following the signing of Robinson. In January 1946, a nervous Effa Manley related to Cum Posey her discovery that "one of my players has decided to play with The United States League on the strength of Rickeys [sic] promise to get in The Majors. There is no telling how many of these dumb bells will fall for that."[56]

On February 21, Shackelford and Greenlee appeared before a gathering in New York of NNL officials and J. B. Martin. Admitting the USL's difficulties during 1945, Shackelford reiterated his earlier proposal, yet explained that the deal was conditional upon the acceptance of two franchises by the NNL and NAL. When queried as to the planned ownership of the Brooklyn franchise, Shackelford shocked the meeting by announcing that Rickey was interested. While the prospect of Rickey participating in an institution he had recently vilified seemed puzzling at best and hypocritical at worst, it was consistent with his apparent determination to expand his farm system approach to black professional baseball. The league, however, was spared the difficult decision of whether to accept Rickey, as Shackelford and Greenlee subsequently admitted that they had no firm commitment from Rickey or any other promoter to purchase a Brooklyn franchise.

Following a lengthy discussion, the NNL owners decided that, while they "morally wanted to do something for Gus Greenlee," a final judgment on the USL franchises would be deferred until a later meeting in March. The outcome dissatisfied Greenlee, who noted that "such a delay would of necessity cause undue hardships . . . if we suspend activities of the United States League, and undertake the job of getting things in shape for admission to the National League, and then through unforeseen difficulties the franchises were not granted, it would mean a tremendous financial loss to all parties concerned." After a subsequent rebuff from the NAL, Greenlee attempted to marshal support from NNL members, but soon discovered lingering ambivalence toward his return. Effa Manley remained suspicious that the USL had tampered with her players, prompting Greenlee's denial and complaint that "it seems to me that you have forgotten the time [in 1934] that Abe drove to Pittsburgh and asked for the Brooklyn Club and

Franchise. I gave him my word to be in his corner and I supported him when the vote came up. . . . I did not understand him being against me at the recent meeting."[57]

Greenlee failed to convince Manley or other NNL owners, who eventually rejected his bid for a Montreal franchise, along with former St. Louis Stars owner Allen Johnson's attempt to place a club in Brooklyn or Boston. League officials cited the unappealing locations, yet claimed that if Greenlee "obtained a city that would be beneficial to the league . . . he would be given first preference for a new franchise." Despite the plausible explanation, the decision likely also stemmed from fears that the return of Greenlee, a once formidable former colleague, might undermine fragile alliances and power bases within the league setting. Moreover, the NNL owners perhaps anticipated that Greenlee's readmission could lead to the involvement and unwanted scrutiny of Rickey.

Denied a league franchise for the third time, Greenlee revived the battered USL for a second season. The reorganized circuit now included the Crawfords, Cleveland Clippers (headed by Shackelford), Boston Blues (Allen Johnson), and the revamped Brooklyn Brown Dodgers, now backed by Pittsburgh entrepreneurs George and Peter Armstrong. Meanwhile, Branch Rickey maintained his friendly yet detached interest in the USL, again leasing Ebbets Field and perhaps facilitating the Crawfords' use of the park in Montreal, the home of the Dodgers' International League affiliate. Despite ambitious plans for an expanded schedule and regular statistics, the USL continued to lag behind the NNL and NAL in player strength and was unable to attract substantial press or fan attention. A mid-season merger of the Clippers and Brown Dodgers and the addition of a new team in Milwaukee failed to arrest the steady decline, although the league managed to complete its schedule.

Several USL officials, including Allen Johnson and the Armstrong brothers, attempted one final promotion: a postseason barnstorming tour featuring Jackie Robinson and other black minor leaguers. Financial problems, however, marred the trip, as Robinson not only failed to receive his promised fee, but ultimately lost more than $2,400 resulting from bounced checks. Hoping to recover his losses, Robinson subsequently enlisted the assistance of attorney Thurgood Marshall and the NAACP, without apparent success. The disastrous barnstorming tour and overall poor financial showing doomed the USL, which quietly disbanded in late 1946.[58]

During its two years of existence, the USL never seriously threatened the operation of the two established organizations, lacking the proven performers necessary to achieve true legitimacy. Except for the presence of Greenlee and the peripheral involvement of Rickey, the league could offer little to African American players, who enjoyed higher salaries and supe-

Figure 26. Portrait of Gus Greenlee. Despite his
exemplary efforts in forming the NNL, Greenlee
was unable to match his earlier success with the
USL. Courtesy Carnegie Library of Pittsburgh.

rior living conditions in the still prosperous NNL and NAL. The USL's
fate might have been far different, however, had Rickey and the Dodgers
provided the required financial backing to allow the league to fulfill its
promise as a true alternative to the currently flawed operation of black
professional baseball.

Following the collapse of the USL, Greenlee retired from baseball promotion and resumed his business affairs in Pittsburgh. Yet a series of setbacks dogged him, including tax problems, a fire at the Crawford Grille,
and a heart attack in 1946. By August 1951, his health had seriously
declined, shocking visitors such as Fay Young, who viewed Greenlee's condition as "heartbreaking." Eleven months later, Greenlee died at the age
of fifty-six. Despite realizing marginal profits during his career, Greenlee
had played an undeniably crucial role in rebuilding black baseball's foun-

dation during the 1930s, leading to eventual financial stability in the early 1940s. The Pittsburgh promoter, however, was unable to share in the renewed prosperity, and found himself permanently isolated from the very institution he had helped preserve.[59]

◆ ◆ ◆

Despite the tumult following Rickey's signings, black teams had abundant reason to view the 1946 season with optimism. With the war over, clubs would no longer contend with gasoline rationing or tire shortages and eagerly anticipated the discharge of players from military service. Now enjoying a surplus of talent, strong interest from black fans, and relatively stable finances, both leagues had reached an unprecedented level of their development.

The first compensated signing of a black player by Organized Baseball provided additional encouragement for the industry. Perhaps reflecting Ed Bolden's and Eddie Gottlieb's keener attention to administrative detail, the Philadelphia Stars had signed pitcher Roy Partlow to a formal contract for the 1946 season. Recognizing the validity of the agreement, Branch Rickey then agreed to purchase Partlow from the Stars for $1,000 on May 14. While the sum was insubstantial by Organized Baseball standards, it represented a symbolic victory for black clubs by establishing a precedent for the recognition of contracts and payment for players. As the *Philadelphia Inquirer* observed, "no . . . howls of protests" accompanied the Partlow deal, and the Stars seemed genuinely pleased with the transaction. Notably, Bolden informed Rickey that "we are sending him to you with our best wishes, appreciating the fact that you are giving him this opportunity, and sincerely hope that he makes good."

Partlow, soon to be thirty-five, seemed to be a somewhat puzzling choice for Rickey. Yet he had enjoyed an outstanding year with the Stars in 1945, finishing with a 9-4 record and leading the league in strikeouts, and a fine performance in the postseason games at Ebbets Field further boosted his credibility. Despite undeniable pitching talent and above-average hitting skills, however, Partlow apparently lacked the temperament necessary to succeed in a less hospitable white minor league environment. Buck Leonard, for instance, viewed Partlow as "the kind that would go to pieces if the umpire called a ball that he thought was a strike, or if the shortstop made an error behind him," and his stay in Organized Baseball would prove relatively brief.[60]

Although the compensated signing of Partlow demonstrated the potential of player sales as an income source, gate receipts continued to be the major determinant of the industry's financial stability. Several NNL fran-

Table 8.1. Profit and Loss, Kansas City Monarchs, 1942–1946 (dollars)

	Receipts	Expenses	Profit
1942	104,649.44	61,474.84	43,174.60
1943	115,730.57	62,259.47	53,471.10
1944	128,356.33	72,074.46	56,281.87
1945	121,724.53	75,407.75	46,316.78
5-year total	470,460.87	271,216.52	199,244.35
1946	155,921.20	95,915.84	59,889.39 *

Original statement corrected for mathematical errors.
*1946 figure includes booking income and sale of baseballs, also $34.03 from sale of an airplane and $150.00 on bad debts; specific income sources unavailable for other years.
Source: Thomas Baird Collection.

chises again enjoyed strong patronage in 1946, as the championship-winning Newark Eagles drew 120,293 fans and netted $25,000, Yankee Stadium promotions attracted 158,155, and the Baltimore Elite Giants set a new attendance record at Bugle Park after drawing 6,729 for a May 5 game. J. B. Martin claimed that all NAL franchises also profited, including the Kansas City Monarchs, who reached the zenith of their popularity, drawing over 100,000 fans to Blues Stadium, earning $155,921.20 in gate receipts, booking fees, and other revenue, and finishing the season with a probably unparalleled profit of $59,889.39 (see Table 8.1).[61]

Black baseball teams thus maintained their wartime profitability during 1946, capitalizing on the immediate postwar period's positive effect on all commercialized amusements. As one observer explained, the "tremendous pent-up demand" resulted in a pronounced growth in attendance throughout the United States. Major league baseball drew a record-breaking 18.5 million fans, while the International League and several other minor leagues also shattered attendance marks. Other sports, including professional football, also enjoyed strong seasons, along with the motion picture industry, which broke box office records in 1946.

Despite the continued financial success of black baseball, changes in American society suggested that the NNL and NAL would soon have to coexist alongside professional and college sports teams taking small but decided steps toward integration. In March, the Los Angeles Rams of the National Football League signed Kenny Washington, Jackie Robinson's former teammate at UCLA, ending the league's twelve-year unofficial ban on black players. The rival All-American Football Conference (AAFC) also moved toward integration, as the Cleveland Browns added Marion Motley and Bill Willis. Similar gains at the collegiate level attracted the attention of the NAACP's Roy Wilkins, who marveled in November at the growing number of black players on white college football teams. The trend was apparent in other sports, as two National Basketball League teams signed black players, although the newly formed Basketball Association of America remained all-white.[62]

The most important development occurred in minor league baseball, where both black and white Americans awaited the outcome of Rickey's "experiment" involving five black players. Assigned to the Nashua, New Hampshire, club of the class B New England League, Don Newcombe and Roy Campanella enjoyed remarkable seasons, quickly demonstrating their capability. In contrast Robinson, Wright, and Partlow began the season in Montreal in the AAA level (a recently created top minor league classification) International League. After failing to make an impression, Wright and Partlow were later demoted to Three Rivers of the class C Canadian-American League, where the two pitchers combined to post a 22-9 mark. Despite their solid performance in class C ball, Dodger officials questioned their ability to withstand the verbal abuse from rival dugouts, and Rickey felt that the two southern players displayed "a terrible inferiority complex when they are facing white boys." In contrast, Robinson posted a .349 average, sparked the Royals to the International League pennant, and emerged as the most likely candidate to join the Dodgers in the near future.

The effect of Robinson and other white players on black baseball remained unclear during 1946. Neither the Canadian-American nor the New England league operated in NNL or NAL territory, although the International League featured franchises in Newark, Jersey City, and Baltimore, where the Orioles attracted unprecedented black crowds for Robinson's appearances. In Newark, Effa Manley later insisted that, despite a prosperous 1946 season, black fans "started deserting right from minor league days," claiming that some even traveled to Baltimore to watch Robinson in action. In a further reflection of Robinson's appeal, Detroit promoter John R. Williams organized a charter bus trip to a Royals game in Toronto to capitalize on black interest in the young star. Yet Robinson's impact was most noticeable in the black press, as journalists lavished columns on the Montreal rookie. The *Philadelphia Tribune*, for example, carried Robinson's spring training news on the front page, while other black papers provided extensive coverage of his International League games.[63]

Despite the warning signals in 1946, few owners fully appreciated the potential economic repercussions of an African American player in the major leagues. With attendance still strong, most officials were more concerned with obtaining protection through affiliation with Organized Baseball, a development that remained dependent upon a series of reforms. Although plans for a commissioner were largely abandoned after the failed vote of 1945, the institution of standardized contracts comparable to those used in Organized Baseball represented an important step toward an agreement. In a further positive development, the NNL improved its scheduling by arranging additional dates at sites such as Wilmington and Trenton, enabling each team to play between 48 and 63 league games, an increase from recent years. Perhaps of equal importance, the NNL provided fans with an unprecedented amount of information during 1946, disseminated through the new publicity bureau's weekly recap of league games and regular statistics compiled by the Elias Bureau. The death of Cum Posey on March 28 at the age of fifty-five, however, created a promotional void in the NNL. Despite his occasionally self-serving behavior, the league would sorely miss Posey's aggressiveness, competitiveness, and leadership qualities in the years ahead.

The NNL and NAL also briefly considered a unique and creative response to the rising call for integration in American life. Following the signing of Robinson, Dan Burley recommended that black teams sign white players, later noting that "New York fans are wondering why Negro baseball is kept just that in a city and state where the man doesn't want Jim Crow in any form." While New York league teams failed to add whites to their rosters, the NAL's Cleveland Buckeyes attempted integration during 1946. In March, the club signed twenty-seven-year-old pitcher Eddie Klep of Erie, Pennsylvania, who had compiled an impressive record in semipro competition, including an effective performance against the Buckeyes in 1945, and had prior experience on mixed teams. After joining the Buckeyes, Klep encountered problems during an April exhibition game in Birmingham, where local authorities refused to allow him to participate in the game and forced him to sit in the white section of the grandstand. But mediocre talent rather than racial mores ultimately limited Klep's stay with the Buckeyes, who released him in early June. For black teams, successful integration remained difficult to achieve, as above-average white players could easily find slots in Organized Baseball that offered a more comfortable lifestyle, if not always superior pay. Perhaps recognizing this dilemma, the Homestead Grays pursued a more likely white candidate, Max Butcher, a thirty-five-year-old major league pitcher recently released by the Pirates. Butcher, however, never signed with the Grays, accepting a semipro and then minor league offer, and neither the NNL nor the NAL would consider a white player again until 1950.[64]

Despite the signing of Klep and other innovations during 1946, several officials and sportswriters questioned whether the reforms were bringing the leagues any closer to affiliation. The always aggressive Effa Manley, disturbed by the loss of Newcombe and the failure of Branch Rickey to respond to her correspondence, confided to Eddie Gottlieb that "I think we look positively stupid sitting still and letting Rickey get away with his grand larceny." Manley supported Chandler's earlier suggestion that the leagues should retain an attorney to assist in petitioning for admission to Organized Baseball, and the NNL eventually took the constructive step of arranging a meeting on September 26 with Louis F. Carroll, a forty-one-year-old New York-based attorney for the National League who had also worked with the Yankees and Dodgers in the past. With Manley, Pompez, and Black Yankee official Curtis Leak in attendance, Carroll offered cautious encouragement toward affiliation, explaining that while territorial rights might be a problem, a "special rule for Negro baseball" recognizing their heavily black patronage might solve the problem. Carroll also promised that Organized Baseball would respect the revamped league contracts, yet advised that affiliation would require evidence that the leagues were reliably operated "along the lines of established business principles." Additional discussion with Chandler and other white officials would also be necessary.

The meetings with Carroll and Chandler during 1946 demonstrated that Organized Baseball, though supportive of the notion of affiliation, had no plans to offer any real financial or administrative assistance to the NNL or NAL. Certainly, the leagues might have benefited from the direct involvement of a major league official to devise a concrete plan for admission. Perhaps more important, major league baseball could have demonstrated its support by reducing park rental fees, allowing black teams to increase profits and strengthen their organizations. Instead, Organized Baseball placed the onus entirely on black baseball officials, whose rampant individualism precluded the wide-ranging changes necessary for admission.[65]

For major league baseball, the issue of affiliation was only one of a number of problematic issues to emerge in 1946. Owners faced raids from Mexican promoter Jorge Pasquel, the challenge of a recently organized American Baseball Guild, threats to the reserve clause in player contracts, and, of course, the potential of integration. In response to the mounting postwar challenges, officials created a six-person steering committee in July consisting of both league presidents and two owners from each league (Tom Yawkey and Larry MacPhail from the American; Sam Breadon and Philip Wrigley from the National). MacPhail was elected chairman and not surprisingly would dominate the committee's proceedings and subsequent drafting of a preliminary report.

Section E of the report, dealing with the issue of integration, revealed that MacPhail had not altered his stance during the previous year. Despite no official attribution, close examination demonstrates that MacPhail simply revived his September 1945 statement to the Mayor's Committee on Baseball, added minor revisions, and inserted it as part of the larger 25-page document dealing with contracts, unions, and other labor problems.

The revised statement briefly acknowledged recent developments, noting that "the employment of a Negro on one AAA League Club in 1946 resulted in a tremendous increase in Negro attendance. . . . The percentage of Negro attendance at some games at Newark and Baltimore was in excess of 50 percent." Moreover, the committee also raised the issue that a similar growth in black attendance at the major league level "could conceivably threaten the value of . . . franchises," and in an apparent criticism of Rickey, noted that "the individual action of any one club may exert tremendous pressures upon the whole structure of professional baseball." The remainder of the statement simply reiterated MacPhail's earlier arguments, citing the importance of rental income, the supposed ambivalence of black owners toward integration, and the inadequate ability of black players.[66]

Leery of MacPhail's references to integration and the legality of the reserve clause, the committee revised the report, expunging several portions, including the section on race, and the owners subsequently approved the edited version at an August 27 meeting at the Blackstone Hotel in Chicago. The original content of MacPhail's draft remained confidential until divulged, in a somewhat distorted fashion, by Rickey months later. On February 16, 1948, Rickey addressed a gathering at the annual football banquet at Wilberforce University and disclosed that after the signing of Jackie Robinson, his fellow owners had unanimously adopted a report suggesting that black players would jeopardize the profitability of major league baseball. Rickey also claimed that he had been unable to obtain a copy of the report, which had apparently been collected and destroyed, yet dared his colleagues to "deny they adopted such a report. . . . I'd like to see the color of the man's eyes who would deny it."

The speech unleashed a predictable furor among major league officials. Robbed of its actual context, the report seemed to suggest that owners had actively conspired to block integration, and as Ed Pollock of the *Philadelphia Evening Bulletin* observed, "by implication, Rickey gave . . . the impression that the report came up as the major business of the meeting and as a separate subject." Officials soon issued a flood of denials, including former Indians president Alva Bradley, who asserted that "major league owners would never be unwise enough to do a thing like that." Cubs owner Philip Wrigley also questioned Rickey's claim of silence during the "unanimous" approval of the report, noting that "Rickey never sat silent on any subject in his life." (Rickey subsequently admitted that "I suppose I should have protested. I was simply shocked to hear it read.")[67]

Larry MacPhail, understandably touchy as the report's primary author, issued a furious rebuttal that read more into Rickey's speech than actually existed, asserting that "Rickey was lying if and when he said the commit-

Figure 27. An angry Larry MacPhail reads a
prepared statement attacking Branch Rickey's
Wilberforce speech, February 20, 1948. Courtesy
AP/Wide World Photos.

tee recommended that Negro players be barred from major league baseball." Moreover, MacPhail explained that all 16 teams, including
Brooklyn, had approved the report, which had been destroyed not because
of the section on blacks but because of passages critical of Commissioner
Chandler. MacPhail also took the opportunity to challenge Rickey's sincerity toward blacks, noted that he "raided the Negro leagues, and took players without adequately compensating them," in contrast to his own plan
for gradualism.[68]

While unswayed by MacPhail's comments, Rickey nevertheless clarified
his statements in the days following the Wilberforce speech. He explained
that he had simply intended his comments to demonstrate the marked
change in integration attitudes, later confiding to white sportswriter Joe
Cummiskey that "a year and a half ago all clubs felt, or at least approved
the reading of what was, in fact, a one-man report, to the effect that sub-

stantial investments were hazarded by the employment of negroes, and I pointed out immediately that today many clubs in the Major Leagues are interested in signing a good negro player." Rickey admitted that most owners would have no recollection of formally approving the section on blacks, recognizing that "other people would not attribute the same importance to the subject that I did and in approval they were thinking of the over-all report." Furthermore, Rickey conceded that there were "other reasons than the so-called Negro reference for removing the report from publicity" and admitted that only one owner had protested the signing of Robinson and "several have expressed approval." Always leery of any controversy involving major league baseball, the *Sporting News* complained that Rickey had "assigned himself the role of the game's great emancipator, while casting his startled colleagues as Jim Crow antagonists." The editorial, however, admitted that "possibly some of the club owners were guilty of racial prejudice, while others were sincerely concerned about the economic implications."

Though perhaps somewhat exaggerated, Rickey's comments at Wilberforce accurately revealed the general attitude of major league owners toward integration in 1946. MacPhail's section on race in the original draft had elicited little comment or reaction from most owners simply because they still had no intention of signing black players, remained apathetic to the issue, or shared the Yankee official's viewpoint. While the section contained no specific recommendation to bar black players from major league baseball, its content demonstrated the overall disapproval among white owners, and as Red Smith noted, "perhaps some such recommendation is implicit in a prediction that the employment of Negroes would injure the baseball business."

At the close of 1946, Rickey remained the only major league owner interested in signing black players. Despite the appearance of several blacks in the minor leagues, the integration of major league baseball still seemed likely to proceed slowly, allowing the NNL and NAL additional time to continue reforms, address deficiencies, and ideally forge a profitable relationship with Organized Baseball. Few realized that integration and shifting postwar attitudes would soon abruptly alter the fortunes of black baseball and other racial enterprises, forcing a dramatic reconsideration of their necessity and viability.[69]

Integration and the
Changing Postwar World

It may be that in and around the metropolitan areas, the day
of the all-colored ball team as well as the all-white ball team,
is doomed to extinction.
—"Albert Anderson" (pseudonym for Claude Barnett),
Associated Negro Press, 1947

The integration of Organized Baseball in 1946 was only one of a series of important postwar legal and political developments facilitating the gradual yet perceptible movement of blacks into the mainstream of American life. Following aggressive challenges by the NAACP, the Supreme Court declared restrictive housing covenants unconstitutional in 1948 and prohibited segregated dining cars on interstate passenger trains two years later. Concurrently, federal officials became increasingly receptive to African American protest, recognizing not only the growing importance of the urban black vote but the potentially damaging effects of the oppression of minorities within the context of the ideological struggle of the Cold War. Reflecting the heightened awareness, President Harry Truman issued an executive order in 1948 requiring nondiscrimination in the hiring of federal employees. Perhaps more significantly, Truman subsequently ordered an end to segregation in the armed forces, which would evolve into the most racially integrated of all American organizations by 1960. Although less dramatic than the civil rights victories of later decades, the accomplishments of the immediate postwar years continued the gradual trend toward integration and raised hopes for more substantial gains in the future.[1]

For northern urban communities, the period was characterized by encouraging progress yet equally frustrating setbacks for blacks. Continued southern migration, for example, rapidly expanded the burgeoning black population of cities such as New York, Chicago, and Philadelphia, although most of the newcomers found housing available only in the already overflowing black enclaves. Moreover, the potential integration of a white neighborhood continued to generate violent opposition or a mass exodus by the current residents, and as one observer explained, "whenever a new neighborhood is 'broken,' Mr. Charlie runs as if from a plague; and both Negro and white real estate dealers play on their fears and help them run, while they reap harvests selling old homes to Negroes for much more than they are worth." Not surprisingly, residential segregation would become even more prevalent in the postwar years in several northern cities, leaving blacks even more isolated from whites than in the past.[2]

The economic position of most African Americans also remained fragile. Following the end of World War II and the cancellation of defense contracts, thousands of blacks lost their industrial positions, wiping out recent economic gains. By 1954, the continued employment problems of urban blacks prompted one observer to insist that "our first need is more and better sources of income. Of course, segregation is one of our major problems, but the employment issue dwarfs the race question by practical comparison." Employment opportunities, however, did increase from prior decades, as black protest coupled with the efforts of local agencies succeeded in creating jobs at previously all-white work sites, such as retail establishments. In Philadelphia, several strongly resistant downtown department stores were forced to take tentative steps toward fair employment in the late 1940s. While one official had once asserted that "you'll never live to see the day that colored women will be selling in this store," department stores including Gimbel's and John Wanamaker's hired black salespersons by 1949. Yet job caliber improved only slightly in the postwar years, and a 1953 report revealed the disturbing fact that Philadelphia's blacks were "still by and large to be found in the largest numbers in the most onerous and least productive jobs."[3]

The barriers in employment and housing reflected the still considerable white animosity toward African Americans. Despite limited gains, discrimination continued to define the existence of most urban blacks, and as journalist George Schuyler observed in 1949, "the Negro is still pretty much a second-class citizen all over the country, and the whole concept of civil rights continues to be largely a dream." While the more overt discrimination of the 1920s and 1930s had largely disappeared, blacks still found a number of neighborhoods, hotels, recreation centers, and playgrounds less than accommodating.[4]

The continued existence of segregation, albeit less prevalent than in the past, coupled with the expansion of the black community, seemingly offered an ideal climate for the growth of black business in the postwar years. In Philadelphia, established enterprises continued to prosper, including the Citizens and Southern Bank, which claimed $3 million in deposits by 1946, and the *Tribune*, which expanded to twice weekly. Long-operating black insurance companies such as Provident Home Beneficial and the local branch of North Carolina Mutual enjoyed similar success and by the 1950s provided local blacks with desperately needed full-time white-collar employment opportunities.

Despite the scattered successes in Philadelphia and elsewhere, however, black business remained a relatively insignificant aspect of the national economy. Insurance companies, probably the most flourishing race enterprise, could claim only about a third of black policies nationally by the late 1940s and had lost considerable business to Metropolitan Life and other white firms that often offered lower premiums. Similarly, the handful of black banks in existence by 1950 failed to approach the prosperity of even medium-sized white institutions, functioning, in the words of one observer, as an "extremely small part of the American banking industry." Lacking access to capital and credit, black businesses continued to experience difficulty competing with better financed white institutions, and as before, the greatest opportunities for black entrepreneurs remained in areas without white competition, such as undertaking and hair care.[5]

The gradual postwar trend toward integration also led to increasing questioning of the role, value, and ultimate fate of black business. Black baseball officials were hardly alone in facing what Joseph Pierce's 1947 study identified as the "dilemma of the Negro business man who as a Negro disapproves of racial segregation but as a business man has a vested interest in segregation because it creates a convenient market for his goods and services." Moreover, black entrepreneurs would soon discover that expanded employment opportunities in white establishments often dwarfed the racial appeal of black businesses. In their 1949 book, *The Negro in American Business: The Conflict Between Separatism and Integration*, Robert Kinzer and Edward Sagarin identified this phenomenon as the "antagonism between the appeal for solidarity and the aspirations of the people." To Kinzer and Sagarin, the integration of Organized Baseball exemplified this tension, as black leaders hailed the breakthrough, "although it served as a threat to the appeal of Negro professional baseball." Sociologist E. Franklin Frazier similarly argued that most blacks viewed integration as more significant than economic development, noting in 1957 that "the employment of Negroes by large corporations has overshadowed even the exaggerated achievements of Negro businessmen."[6]

In general, the development of black-controlled enterprises and institutions appeared increasingly less important than the accomplishments of individual blacks in newly integrated areas of American life in the postwar era. The trend was apparent in sports, where black fans increasingly focused their attention on African American athletes starring on previously all-white squads. Black-sponsored college football, for example, continued its long decline, as attendance for the once popular Thanksgiving Howard/ Lincoln game dipped from 13,000 in 1947 to 4,200 in 1953. Following Lincoln's decision to drop football, the annual promotion ceased after 1960. In Philadelphia, the increasing integration of high school and college teams resulted in diminishing interest in local independent and club basketball by 1954. Moreover, with the integration of the National Basketball Association (NBA) in 1950, many black fans shifted their attention to mixed professional clubs.[7]

The increasing success of individual blacks in basketball and other professional sports presented new challenges for black journalists. With their readers eager to read eyewitness accounts of black athletic performances, black sportswriters sought equal press access to integrated games at white athletic facilities yet often encountered strong resistance. In Philadelphia, the Shibe Park press box generally admitted only members of the Baseball Writers Association of America (BWAA), whose requirement of daily newspaper affiliation conveniently excluded the bulk of the black press corps. Lacking BWAA credentials, black access remained inconsistent, subject to the whims of individual white sportswriters who were often less than welcoming. Rollo Wilson, for instance, condemned the Philadelphia Sports Writers Association as "one of the most intolerant . . . of its kind in the country and that includes similar groups in the south," citing the organization's failure to honor black athletes or include black sportswriters. Notably, Wilson was unable to obtain BWAA membership in 1947, despite nearly twenty-five years of distinguished sports writing.

The situation was similar for other black sportswriters. In 1949, the Pittsburgh branch of the BWAA refused to admit Wendell Smith to the Forbes Field press box despite the efforts of white journalist Vince Johnson. Sam Lacy reported that exasperated Baltimore sportswriters "threw their hands into the air" in disgust after a white Montreal journalist submitted his name for membership to the International League Baseball Writers Association in 1947. Lacy, however, would become the first black member of the BWAA in 1948, successfully convincing the organization that the *Afro*'s multiple weekly editions qualified him for membership. Despite Lacy's breakthrough and the subsequent admission of Smith, Rollo Wilson, and other writers, black access to white venues remained incomplete. At Crosley Field, Cincinnati sportswriter Tom Swope barred Lacy from the press box, forcing him to sit alone in a separate field box. Additionally, several black journalists were unable to gain full press privileges at the 1951 World Series.[8]

For journalist A. S. "Doc" Young, the ongoing difficulties confirmed the need for a strong association of black sportswriters. While recognizing the need for "a big push toward integration in existing organizations," Young suggested that the creation of an all-black group might assist in waging the fight for access and recognition. Yet as black baseball officials discovered, the advocacy or support of any exclusively black organization in sports or any other aspect of American life would be increasingly challenged during the postwar era. A growing number of blacks viewed separate institutions of any kind as ultimately counterproductive, reflecting submission and perpetuation of unjust racial practices.

In an attempt to address the problem, several organizations including the Negro Newspaper Publishers Association, National Negro Bankers Association, and Colored Intercollegiate Athletic Association consciously eliminated "Negro" or "Colored" from their titles, hoping to suggest a more integrationist philosophy. In Philadelphia, the Bureau for Colored Children became the Bureau for Child Care, while the Home for Aged and Infirm Colored Persons changed to the Stephen Smith Home for the Aged. The name changes provided a simple cosmetic solution, but they often failed to alter the actual composition of predominantly black organizations or institutions. The fundamental question remained whether all-black organizations were either desirable or necessary; as the *Tribune* noted, "one of the difficulties in the life of the American Negro is what might be termed co-existence. How can he have institutions and agencies that give his skills and learning a chance to develop themselves without seeming to segregate himself from the mainstream of American life?"[9]

In large northern cities such as Philadelphia, the perplexing dilemma of segregation versus integration presented itself in several obvious areas, particularly education. While the school system remained far from integrated (because of residential patterns and local policy), the prospect of black students gaining access to white schools appeared less remote following the 1954 *Brown v. Board of Education* Supreme Court decision. Integration, however, seemed likely not only to threaten the job security of black teachers but to result in fewer opportunities in the future. *Tribune* editor Eustace Gay viewed the trade-off as acceptable, insisting that, despite possible short-term losses, it would create a "firmer and fairer foundation for [black] teachers." Similarly, local black educator Daniel Brooks asserted that, regardless of increased teaching positions, "we should not repeat the blunder of placing ourselves on record as asking for segregation in high schools or in elementary schools."

Yet the immediate opportunities offered by segregation sometimes were difficult to resist, and, as a *Tribune* editorial explained, "many of us . . . advocate segregation in most cases because it seems to offer a short-cut to a higher economic or political status." Doubtful of the prospect of integration in the future, some blacks continued to support the expansion of existing segregated facilities or the development of new enterprises to serve the black community. Doc Hyder, the head of the local black musicians' union, opposed a merger with the white branch, noting that it "would lessen our power as we would be far outweighed by the white musicians." As late as 1943, the *Tribune* complained of an attempt to convince city officials "to create a separate 'jim-crow' fire station for Negro firemen." Five years later, a proposal for a separate black cab company evoked a similar editorial response questioning "how some of those who are now clamoring for a 'Jim Crow' cab arrangement can square this with their former opposition to all forms of segregation."[10]

The continued existence of black hospitals reflected the postwar integration dilemma. Once a source of racial pride, black hospitals, along with other once valued race institutions, appeared increasingly less relevant following expanded opportunities in white facilities. As historian Vanessa Gamble has noted, by 1945 black medical organizations "shifted from the creation of black hospitals to the dismantlement of the 'Negro medical ghetto' of which black hospitals were a major component." In Philadelphia, blacks debated the fate of financially tenuous Mercy-Douglass Hospital, the product of a 1948 merger of the two local black medical centers. While supporters cited the institution's function as a training facility for black nurses and medical students, the hospital's modest budget affected the quality of care, and the nearly all-black staff and clientele raised additional concerns. Unwilling to support an imperfect separate institution, a growing number of blacks expressed ambivalence toward the hospital's future, and a 1949 fund-raising drive realized only a third of its goal. To scholar Elliott Rudwick, the apathy reflected a rejection of segregation among " 'modern' Negroes." Rudwick himself believed that "a Negro hospital is no longer needed . . . or wanted. I believe that it only prolongs the discrimination and forestalls the day when medical equality can be attained." Although state aid would rescue Mercy-Douglass, the hospital's purpose within the black community remained unclear, as locals questioned whether the institution should function as a black-controlled and patronized entity or attempt greater integration.

By the early 1950s, any proposition sanctioning or condoning segregation in Philadelphia could expect to encounter community resistance. A 1953 attempt by the Imperial Skating Rink to offer separate nights for blacks prompted the involvement of the NAACP and ACLU. The feasibility of maintaining separate facilities of any kind also appeared increasingly impractical. Citing "misuse of manpower," the city finally ended its segregation in the fire department in 1949. Analyzing the local medical situation, observers such as Eustace Gay asserted that "there should be no such thing as a WHITE hospital or a NEGRO hospital," noting that it was ridiculous for one "hospital to serve 300,000 human beings in six or seven widely scattered regions of a sprawling city like Philadelphia."

Traditional black institutions in Philadelphia and other urban centers of the North thus faced serious challenges in the postwar decade. While many of the same physical and environmental factors that had created separate institutions remained in place, the gradual yet perceptible trend toward integration would prompt a reexamination of the support and need for black organizations and enterprises. Despite remaining far from integrated into most aspects of American society, many blacks began to view separate institutions warily unless they fulfilled a unique need or somehow appeared to be laying the groundwork for integration. Similarly, the modest and often flawed nature of most black enterprises became less acceptable when juxtaposed against new opportunities in the integrated areas of the white business community. As an institution and business in existence since the decade following the end of Reconstruction, black professional baseball was not immune to the shifting environment and soon found itself facing its severest test vying with an "integrated" competitor for the black entertainment dollar.[11]

◆ ◆ ◆

As 1947 dawned, most owners, players, fans, and sportswriters had little reason to recognize that an era in black baseball had ended and the future of the once prosperous institution would soon be in doubt. Despite the integration of the minor leagues in 1946, attendance had remained solid for the sixth consecutive year, raising hopes that the NNL and NAL might successfully weather impending major league integration. In a move reflecting the industry's still-considerable confidence, W. S. Martin announced plans to build a new $250,000 park in Memphis for the Red Sox. Meanwhile, the NAL expanded to eight franchises in March, accepting the applications of George Mitchell's St. Louis Stars, a former member of both leagues, and the Detroit Senators, who planned to operate with the assistance of Tigers officials. The usual park problems in Detroit, however, ultimately precluded the membership of the Senators, and the league subsequently rejected St. Louis after recognizing the impracticality of a seven-team circuit.[12]

In the NNL, the strong attendance and modest administrative improvements in 1946 seemingly provided the league with a firm foundation for continued progress. Yet additional gains, including affiliation with Organized Baseball, appeared unlikely without the introduction of new leadership. Unsuccessful in several prior attempts to dislodge Tom Wilson, the Manleys once again began to marshal support for an alternate candidate.

By late 1946, several New York-based individuals, including parole board commissioner Samuel Battle, attorney John Doles, and Reverend John Howard Johnson, surfaced as potential challengers, while Tom Wilson and Eddie Gottlieb offered boxing judge Frank Forbes, a former player and umpire now involved in the Yankee Stadium promotions, as a possible compromise selection.

Despite the growing number of interested candidates, only Johnson and the incumbent Wilson would receive serious consideration. At a subsequent league meeting on January 5, 1947, Newark and Homestead, the two franchises opposing Wilson's election a year earlier, supported Johnson, this time joined by Alex Pompez. As anticipated, Baltimore and Philadelphia voted for Wilson, leaving only the vote of Black Yankees owner James Semler in doubt. Semler, whose financial difficulties and obligations to other owners usually influenced his voting pattern, nevertheless broke from his usual alliance with Wilson to cast the deciding ballot for Johnson (perhaps in exchange for an opportunity to promote exclusively at Yankee Stadium). The concurrent election of Pompez as vice president, Abe Manley as treasurer, and Black Yankees official Curtis Leak as secretary completed the league's slate of offices, revealing the suddenly formidable influence of the New York/Newark bloc in NNL affairs.[13]

The selection of Johnson, the first non-affiliated official since the largely unproductive tenure of Ferdinand Morton in the late 1930s, represented a bold stroke certain to bolster the NNL's legitimacy among both blacks and whites. Born in 1897 in Richmond, Virginia, Johnson attended Columbia University, where he played varsity basketball while earning bachelor's and master's degrees. After graduation, Johnson entered the ministry, later founding St. Martin's Episcopal Church at Lenox and 122nd Street in 1928 and serving as pastor there. By the 1930s, Johnson had become a major Harlem community leader, actively participating in the local "Don't Buy Where You Can't Work" campaign with Effa Manley and later securing an appointment from Mayor LaGuardia as police chaplain and member of the interracial Committee on Unity.

Despite impressive academic, civic, and religious credentials, Johnson had little formal experience in sports except as a college basketball player years earlier. Yet Johnson was an ardent baseball fan who had served as chairman of LaGuardia's Mayor's Committee on Baseball, where he had gained a basic familiarity with the problems facing black teams. While supporting integration, Johnson was equally concerned with the plight of the black leagues, and as early as December 1945 openly recommended affiliation with Organized Baseball. Aware of the considerable obstacles involved, Johnson acknowledged that the leagues would require "definite agreements as to players, tenure, transfers and schedules before they

Figure 28. A later portrait of the Reverend John
Howard Johnson, NNL president, 1947–1948.
Photo by Austin Hansen, used by permission of
Joyce Hansen and Schomburg Center for Research
in Black Culture, New York Public Library.

would be taken into organized baseball" and that such reforms might be
opposed by several owners.

The new president thus assumed his office aware of the difficulties involved in governing a group of fractious and highly individualistic officials,
some of whom were already suspicious of his close relationship with the
Manleys. Yet Johnson's initial statements advocating standardized contracts, balanced schedules, a revised constitution, and affiliation with Organized Baseball suggested that the new head would provide the league
with much needed direction. As Johnson explained, "the Negro National
League has a great opportunity to go forward . . . [and] can conceivably
in a short space of time set the standard which will involve the improvement of the status of the player, promote a reasonable amount of security
for the owner, and give the fans an improved quality of baseball." Moreover, Johnson's consistent support of integration throughout his career
provided the press and the public with a clear symbol of the league's com-

mitment to an increasingly prevalent trend in American life. Effa Manley, for example, noted that Johnson's election "will also give the lie to hints that we don't want Negroes to go to the major leagues because our new commissioner was one of the most forceful fighters on former Mayor La-Guardia's committee . . . we want them to go in an organized fashion and not be virtually 'kidnaped.' "[14]

While veteran observers applauded the long overdue selection of an un-affiliated leader, most remained uncertain of Johnson's chance of success. Dan Burley, for instance, wondered "how will a preacher fare as head of a rough and tumble outfit like the NNL?" and questioned whether Johnson would be "mainly a figurehead, or someone with real power." Johnson's one year term appeared likely to limit his authority, as the renewal of his position and salary (reported as $3,000 or $5,000 in different accounts) remained at the discretion of the owners. Any attempt to exercise greater administrative control seemed certain to encounter resistance, and as veteran sportswriter Russ Cowans quipped, Johnson "will be in for long hours of torture as he tries to convince the owners that he needs the power if he's to conduct his office properly."

The new president, however, initially enjoyed the support of the majority of NNL franchises, particularly the Newark Eagles. Johnson's election reflected the continued shift in the league's power structure that had begun following the death of Cum Posey in March 1946 and allowed the Manleys and their allies to exercise an increasingly influential role in NNL affairs. After successfully replacing Wilson with their own handpicked candidate, the Manleys then turned to another long-unresolved aspect of their agenda: the Yankee Stadium promotions. In early January, Effa Manley and James Semler met with Yankees president Larry MacPhail, who agreed to allow Semler, instead of Eddie Gottlieb, to handle all league dates at the stadium in 1947. Although Gottlieb's removal after several failed attempts seemed to foreshadow a renewed movement to reduce the promotional role of whites, Semler himself still remained very much dependent on white capital, as league booking agent William Leuschner had purchased part of the Black Yankees in 1945. Despite reports that Leuschner sold his share to Frank Forbes prior to the 1947 season, several observers questioned whether Leuschner had truly divested himself of his interest in the franchise.[15]

Yet for an organization typically suspicious of reform, the leadership and promotional changes represented a definite advance from the arbitrary and often inefficient practices of the past. The death of the recently deposed Tom Wilson of a heart attack on May 15 at the age of fifty-seven further symbolized the league's transition into a new era. Despite a somewhat controversial stint as president, Wilson had remained a faithful league advocate and was the only owner whose teams had participated as full members in each of the NNL's first fourteen seasons. Failing health and an occasionally lackadaisical attitude, however, limited his capacity to attend to vitally important league affairs and as Wendell Smith observed, "if he had any great faults, it was his habit of literally disappearing at times when his presence was necessary. At times he was harder to find than a snowball in the tropics." Players such as Frazier Robinson, Bill Wright, and Roy Campanella would later provide a more sympathetic appraisal, recalling Wilson as a likable figure who treated his men well.

The death of the wealthy Wilson threatened to affect the stability of the NNL, but longtime associate Vernon Green assumed control of the Elites, preserving the current league lineup. Meanwhile, during the early months of 1947, Wilson's presidential successor Johnson and other league officials prepared for what they hoped would be a prosperous season. Pursuing additional administrative steps toward affiliation with Organized Baseball, the NNL adopted a new constitution modeled after the agreement used by the International League and announced plans for better scheduling, fewer exhibitions, and a World Series staged only at the parks of the two contending teams, rather than "a circus playing from city to city." The NNL and NAL also agreed to maintain the ban on all Mexican jumpers, paralleling the current major league policy. Determined to adhere to the major league rulings, Johnson even contacted National League president Ford Frick for his opinion on the eligibility of three NNL players hoping to return from Mexico.[16]

Despite the promising outlook, a series of unanticipated developments would deal nearly a crippling blow to black baseball in 1947, rendering most of the administrative improvements superfluous. In January, Homestead Grays catcher Josh Gibson died at the age of thirty-five. Increasingly afflicted with mental and physical problems, Gibson nevertheless had remained the NNL's greatest drawing card, and his loss would prove difficult to offset. Equally devastating was the diminishing role of Satchel Paige, who had provided the foundation for black professional baseball's growth during the early 1940s. During the first half of the 1947 season, Paige inexplicably pitched only rarely with the Monarchs, instead appearing in exhibition games with non-league teams. The absence of Paige and Gibson during the season's crucial early months seriously affected the box office appeal of black baseball.

Unfavorable weather also wreaked havoc on the industry's fortunes in 1947. During May and June, unusually rainy and cold conditions resulted in numerous cancellations throughout the NNL. The Eagles' opening game was rained out, as were numerous early season league dates in New York. Although white minor leagues such as the American Association and Eastern League were similarly affected, black baseball's limited park access often made rescheduling impossible, and dozens of normally profitable dates were lost during the early months of the season.[17]

Although the poor weather and loss of marquee players hurt attendance, the rise of Jackie Robinson would prove the most damaging. After an outstanding year with Montreal, Robinson appeared likely to earn a promotion to Brooklyn in 1947. Anticipating a dramatic surge in black patronage at Dodger games, Branch Rickey met with several black leaders of Brooklyn in February and warned that inappropriate fan behavior might jeopardize Robinson's chances. The black elite subsequently launched a campaign advising black working-class fans to behave with restraint, and the movement soon spread to other cities after Robinson joined the Dodgers in April. The issue of improper public behavior soon dominated the editorial and sports columns of black newspapers, featuring stern warnings to potential transgressors. NAACP executive secretary Walter White, for example, fretted over the potential "misguided enthusiasm" of black fans, while Fay Young, a close observer of black baseball for more than forty years, insisted that "Robinson will not be on trial as much as the Negro fan . . . the 'hot potato' dodged by managers who would have taken a chance by signing a Negro player. The unruly Negro has and can set us back 25 years."[18]

The attempts of the black bourgeoisie to regulate the behavior of working-class fans actually differed little from similar ongoing efforts to "improve" the conduct and manners of rural southern migrants and poor blacks in general. Yet Earl Brown, a Harvard-educated former black player and future New York city councilman, believed that such imposed restrictions were unfair to blacks, who "are so happy whenever one of their number is accepted in a position from which all Negroes have been barred, that they naturally emote. Whites do the same thing, but no one considers it bad taste." In later decades, the concern over black fan behavior would appear largely unnecessary, leading historian Jules Tygiel to contend that the "efforts of black leaders now seem excessive and embarrassing." Yet Robinson himself emphasized the importance of restraint among black fans, noting that "they could have blown the whole bit to hell by acting belligerently." Moreover, virtually every black sportswriter had long agreed on the existence of a "small unruly minority" at black games, whose behavior not only created an unpleasant environment for other patrons but threatened the continuation of park rental agreements.[19]

The fears would ultimately prove unrealized, as the initial major league appearances of Robinson occurred without remarkable incident, at least in the stands. As anticipated, however, thousands of blacks flocked to big league parks to follow Robinson's every move. At the Ebbets Field opener, reportedly 14,000 of the 25,000 fans were black, and the phenomenon was soon replicated at other National League cities accessible to African Americans. The negative impact on black professional baseball became apparent in Chicago, where Robinson's first appearance at Wrigley Field easily outdrew a competing NAL game at Comiskey Park. In the south, blacks eagerly traveled to watch Robinson in action in St. Louis and Cincinnati, prompting the Missouri Pacific Railroad to advertise a "Jackie Robinson Special" offering transportation to St. Louis. Black baseball attendance in Missouri predictably declined, and, as Monarch pitcher Hilton Smith later explained, "all the people started to go Brooklynites. . . . Even if we were playing here in Kansas City, everybody wanted to go over to St. Louis to see Jackie." By June, Black Barons owner Tom Hayes gloomily warned of the futility of offering promotions directly competing against Robinson, explaining that it was "poor judgment and bad business to buck Brooklyn."

The monumental appeal and symbolic importance of Robinson was hardly surprising and confirmed what E. Franklin Frazier and other observers increasingly recognized in the postwar era: that blacks now valued the success of individuals within an integrated setting far more than the preservation of institutions. Moreover, separate institutions, including black baseball, seemed increasingly irrelevant once successful integration had occurred. As Cleveland sportswriter Bob Williams observed, "few people have supported a Jim-Crow baseball organization without the hope and expectation that this was merely serving as a means to an end and that its continuance would eventually spell democracy in the No. 1 American sport." While admitting that black baseball "has made certain contributions," Williams believed that "it is accepted as the best of a bad situation" and "integration . . . should not be held up because of possible disintegration of the Negro leagues."[20]

After several seasons of financial stability, the NNL and NAL suddenly found themselves in a vulnerable position and scrambled to regroup at a joint session in New York in June. In an attempt to win back desperately needed press support, the NNL took the unusual step of sponsoring a dinner function for black sportswriters at Small's Paradise, the oldest black nightclub in New York. Accustomed to uncooperative and evasive behavior from the owners, journalist Roscoe Coleman marveled that "the magnates actually let their collective hair down and openly courted members of the Press." To Coleman, the attitudinal shift was attributable to competition from Robinson and the role of John Johnson, a potential "healing influence" for the league.

Ironically, Johnson apparently had envisioned a different role for the gathering: an opportunity for the industry to publicly mend fences with

Branch Rickey. In May, Dan Dodson, executive director of the Mayor's Committee on Unity, related to Rickey that Johnson was planning an up-coming dinner in Harlem to be attended by team owners along with mem-bers of the white daily and black weekly press. During the banquet, Rickey would be presented with an award honoring his accomplishments in breaking baseball's color line. Dodson encouraged Rickey to accept the invitation, noting that Johnson "is having his problems, as I suppose any Baseball Commissioner does, but it would give you an opportunity to say some things to them which would be extremely helpful, both to Negro Baseball, and the cause in general. It would strengthen his hand as well in the extremely difficult task he has of bringing them along to the point at which he can ask Commissioner Chandler to accept the League in orga-nized Baseball." Rickey was unable to attend, however, and the leagues missed an ideal chance to score a public relations coup. In lieu of Rickey's presence, NAL president J. B. Martin addressed the dinner gathering, re-emphasizing to the press black baseball's full support for integration.[21]

With the press mollified, more favorable weather ahead, and the pros-pect of several Satchel Paige promotions in August, team owners hoped that attendance might stabilize in the second half of the season. Although blacks had turned out by the thousands to root for Jackie Robinson and the Dodgers, there seemed little reason why they could not maintain a concurrent interest in NNL and NAL clubs. The Dodgers, for example, played only 22 games each season in Cincinnati and St. Louis, hardly enough to satiate the baseball appetites of black fans in Memphis, Bir-mingham, and other areas of the south. Meanwhile, blacks living in Ameri-can League cities such as Washington and Cleveland still had no opportunity to see a black player in action and could devote their attention and discretionary income to their hometown Negro League teams. Even the three NNL franchises in metropolitan New York area might conceiv-ably rebound once the novelty of major league integration had worn off.

The appearance of additional black players in the major leagues, how-ever, would dampen any hopes of a second-half comeback. After enjoying an unchallenged monopoly on black players for nearly two years, Branch Rickey and the Brooklyn Dodgers were joined by a second major league organization, the American League's Cleveland Indians. While the club had shown only marginal interest in integration in prior years, the sale of the franchise in 1946 to a syndicate headed by Bill Veeck resulted in re-newed consideration of the issue. Despite his prior integration interest as part of a plan to purchase the Phillies in 1942, Veeck had been surpris-ingly slow to sign black players, finally acting after the successful minor league seasons of Jackie Robinson and other blacks in 1946. The club subsequently began to scout black baseball for prospects, finally settling on Newark Eagles slugger Larry Doby, who joined the Indians in July 1947 to become the second black player in the major leagues in the twentieth century.[22]

From the perspective of black professional baseball, the signing of Doby was a success. In contrast to most of Rickey's prior signings, Veeck not only negotiated directly with the Manleys for Doby's contract but ultimately paid the Eagles an unprecedented sum of $15,000. The transaction satisfied the always suspicious Effa Manley, who applauded Veeck's "liberal attitude," although after Doby became a successful major leaguer she would bitterly complain she had received less than market value. The signing of Doby, however, confirmed the permanence of major league integration, and as Veeck observed, "Robinson has proved to be a real big leaguer, so I wanted to get the best available Negro boy while the getting was good. . . . Why wait?"

Unlike Robinson, Doby entered the major leagues without any prior experience in the white minors, a precedent that worried some members of the Organized Baseball establishment. In an editorial "Once Again, That Negro Question," the *Sporting News* claimed that with the signing of Doby, "the race matter no longer is an official perplexity [and] no longer exists insofar as Organized Baseball administration is concerned." Nevertheless, the editorial claimed that numerous white players remained opposed, not simply because of prejudice but also for reasons concerning the "economic stability of the Caucasian player." An anonymous major leaguer, for example, cited Doby's quick jump to the Indians, complaining that "if we are to have Negroes in the majors, let them go through the long preparation the white player is forced to undergo. Let us not discriminate against the white player because he is white." While the editorial thought this "worthy of consideration," it failed to acknowledge that Doby's apprenticeship in the highly competitive NNL more than compensated for his lack of minor league training.[23]

Despite the presence of Doby and Robinson, the prospects of a black influx into major league baseball remained remote. Veeck, for example, claimed that "cream of the colored crop has been taken" and "fewer than six players worthy of consideration remain in the Negro leagues." Moreover, most franchises still remained reluctant to add black players to their rosters at the major or minor league level, regardless of their abilities. Yet the discernible financial impact of Robinson prompted other franchises to dip gingerly into the pool of African American players, and the St. Louis Browns, one of the weakest teams in major league baseball, would be the next club to attempt integration during 1947. On July 17, shortly after Doby joined the Indians, the Browns purchased the contracts of infielder Hank Thompson and outfielder Willard Brown from the Kansas City Monarchs. Like the Doby signing, the transaction was completed without complaint, as the Monarchs negotiated an acceptable sale price of at least $5,000, with more forthcoming should the players remain with the club beyond a month. Still smarting from Rickey's handling of the Robinson signing two years earlier, Monarchs co-owner Tom Baird praised Browns vice president Bill DeWitt, who "made it very plain from the start of our negotiations that he wanted to do business with Mr. Wilkerson [*sic*] and me, and not the players. Everything was up and above-board."

Brown and Thompson, however, would find their stay with the Browns relatively brief. Unlike Doby and Robinson, the two players were burdened by expectations that their presence would swell the gate receipts of the financially shaky Browns. Despite attendance gains at Browns road games, black patronage at St. Louis failed to increase appreciably, in part related to the team's inconsistent use of both players. On August 23, the Browns released Brown and Thompson, who returned to the Monarchs to resume their careers in black baseball. The decision to terminate, rather than demote, both players confirmed that the episode had been little more than a gimmick, yet the Browns would hardly be the last team in Organized Baseball to sign blacks to boost attendance.[24]

In contrast, Branch Rickey aggressively continued to scout and sign black players in the hopes of deriving a competitive edge. By late July, the Dodgers featured several blacks in their minor league farm clubs, including Roy Campanella at Montreal and Don Newcombe at Nashua, New Hampshire, and would soon add another black player to their major league roster: pitcher Dan Bankhead of the Memphis Red Sox. As with the Roy Partlow signing a year earlier, Rickey revealed a willingness to recognize the validity of black baseball contracts when currently exercised and compensated the Red Sox $15,000 for Bankhead. Although Bankhead, the first black pitcher in major league history, was unimpressive in a brief stint with Brooklyn in 1947, the Dodgers, unlike the Browns, retained him in their organization, sending him to the minor leagues for additional seasoning.

Along with the Dodger farmhands, a handful of other blacks appeared in Organized Baseball during the 1947 season. The Stamford (Connecticut) Bombers of the class B Colonial League signed several obscure league players, including pitchers Al Preston of the New York Black Yankees and Fred Sheppard of the Birmingham Barons, while Nate Moreland, who had accompanied Jackie Robinson to the abortive 1942 Pasadena tryout, starred for El Centro of the class C Sunset League, compiling a 20-12 record. Yet only Robinson would make a dramatic national impact in 1947. Despite facing tremendous pressure and verbal abuse from opponents, Robinson enjoyed an excellent season with the Dodgers, hitting

.297, leading the National League in stolen bases, and sparking the club to their first National League pennant since 1941. Receiving generous national media coverage including a September cover story in *Time* magazine, Robinson became one of the most famous African Americans in the nation, admired not only by blacks but by many whites as well.[25]

The phenomenal appeal of Robinson culminated with the World Series in October in New York, where black fans eager to see their hero in action willingly paid scalper's prices as high as $15 to secure standing-room tickets. With limited seating availability and a quota on black ticket sales reportedly in force, radio broadcasts provided a more viable option for most African Americans, although a few fans (predominantly in the New York, Philadelphia, and Washington areas) were able to watch the games on television for the first time. Despite the Dodgers' subsequent loss to the Yankees, the impact of the Series on African Americans was soon apparent to observers such as Dan Burley, who marveled at the "overnight conversion of at least 4,000,000 Negroes into baseball fans." Previously baseball-indifferent *Philadelphia Tribune* editor E. Washington Rhodes, for example, soon became a rabid fan, later explaining that "I might just as well let my hair down . . . I am crazy about Jackie Robinson."

The heightened black interest in baseball suggested that Robinson had accomplished in a single year what the NNL and NAL had struggled to achieve in the previous decade. In contrast to black baseball's promotional efforts, which relied heavily on media outlets operating largely on a weekly basis with limited distribution and resources, African Americans could easily follow the daily exploits of Robinson through mass circulation newspapers, national weeklies such as the *Sporting News*, or even radio if within range of a Dodger broadcast. More significantly, the successful integration of a highly popular and public aspect of American life universally resonated with African Americans, providing a symbolic victory that black baseball could not hope to match. The black film industry experienced a similar dilemma, and as historian Thomas Cripps has noted, was ultimately unable to transcend "its unfocused blackness that denied spectators the delight of seeing African Americans either in alliance or conflict with white people."[26]

Whether the NNL and NAL could somehow capitalize on the growing interest of baseball and revive their financial fortunes in the future remained unclear. Blacks had increasingly channeled their baseball interest toward major league games, but the two leagues still possessed the majority of the nation's best black talent, as only five players (Robinson, Doby, Thompson, Brown, and Bankhead) had appeared in the major leagues during 1947. In addition, a solid, albeit diminished core of loyal fans had continued to patronize league games despite major league competition.

Newark and Baltimore attracted record-breaking crowds early in the season, and 16,846 packed Blues Stadium for the Kansas City Monarchs opener. As late as July, the annual East-West game in Chicago drew 48,112 fans, the promotion's highest attendance since 1943, and a second match-up at the Polo Grounds attracted 38,402, reportedly the largest crowd ever to attend a black game in New York.

The wholesale departure of black fans so often described had yet to occur, yet the overall attendance decline in black baseball during 1947 was startling. As Frank Forbes later lamented, black fans had become major league conscious, and, "while we had expected attendance to be affected: frankly we were not prepared for what we were to experience." Despite developing a championship club, Alex Pompez claimed losses of $20,000 following a disastrous World Series with the Cleveland Buckeyes that attracted only marginal interest and press attention. At Yankee Stadium, only 63,402 fans turned out for black baseball promotions, a drop of nearly 95,000 from 1946, and attendance at Newark fell from 120,293 to 57,119. In Philadelphia, fewer than 64,000 attended the eleven scheduled dates at Shibe Park in 1947, a nearly 28,000 aggregate drop from 1946 despite two additional promotions. Meanwhile, the powerful Homestead Grays reported season losses as high as $35,000.[27]

With only three of sixteen teams employing a total of five black players in 1947, major league baseball was still far from integrated. Yet already many fans had permanently turned away from black baseball, which seemed increasingly less relevant and meaningful when juxtaposed against the enormous appeal of Jackie Robinson excelling in interracial competition. As early as April, Dan Burley noted the changing attitudes among black fans, claiming that "some of the extremists are talking loudly about never going to see the Negro league teams . . . concentrating their efforts on seeing the Dodgers wherever they play." *Pittsburgh Courier* sportswriter Ric Roberts identified a similar trend, citing the "smart-alecky disdain that some fans seem to be suddenly developing for non-white league ball."

The ultimate question remained whether black professional baseball could somehow reverse its tremendous 1947 losses and eventually recover at least some of its fan base. As a first step, operating expenses would have to be cut, and a partial return to the economizing of the 1930s seemed likely. Yet black baseball's failure to resolve its park problems during the financial heyday of the early 1940s now presented a major barrier to controlling costs. The NNL and NAL had continued to rely heavily on Organized Baseball parks, whose high rental costs required heavy attendance to remain profitable. In New York, however, attendance for league promotions at Ebbets Field (used by the Eagles as a second park) and Yankee

Stadium dropped below 3,000 several times during 1947, ensuring little or no profit. With park construction now financially impractical, black teams had virtually little recourse except to appeal to Organized Baseball officials to reduce rental costs, a dim prospect at best.[28]

The leagues also faced the challenge of reconfiguring their purpose to adapt to integration. To continue to exist and flourish, black baseball and other black institutions would increasingly have to prove their legitimacy outside of a purely segregated context. Black baseball would thus have to work with, rather than against, white professional leagues, and as journalist Cleveland Jackson warned, "open opposition to Major League owners would spell disaster to the Negro circuits. They're operating on a wish and prayer and know it. The majors hold all the aces and know it." The most obvious solution lay in emphasizing the industry's value as the most effective instrument to recruit and develop black athletic talent for possible advancement to the integrated major leagues. In addition, player sales to Organized Baseball might partially offset the decline in patronage. Recognizing the financial possibilities of player sales, Alex Pompez sent a memo to major league teams in July 1947 inviting their scouts to attend the eastern all-star game at the Polo Grounds "to get a comprehensive line on the cream of Negro talent." While a strategy emphasizing player development appeared more likely to succeed with formal assistance from Organized Baseball, affiliation remained elusive during 1947 despite the hopes of Johnson and other officials.

The 1947 season ultimately confirmed that for many blacks the benefits of integration far outweighed its possible negative effect on separate institutions. Commenting on the trend, Dan Burley observed, "with characteristic disregard of consequences, Negroes wrecked their own version of organized baseball and went crazy over the Dodgers." To Burley, however, this was "definitely excusable seeing that we haven't had much to holler about over the years and the idea seemed to hover around that some day we'll go back and get Negro Baseball and build it up. But this was Jackie Robinson's Year and anything or anybody standing in the way had to go."

The year also exposed the essential weaknesses of black business when subjected to outside competition. For years, the leagues had been slow to make necessary improvements in administration and publicity, content with the knowledge that black baseball fans would continue to patronize their games. But the enterprise's still considerable deficiencies became strikingly more apparent when facing actual competition for the black consumer dollar from a better financed and run organization that provided the regular statistics and standings long craved by black fans.

In November, Roscoe Coleman provided a thoughtful analysis of the industry's chronic difficulties, explaining that "Negro baseball, like many other enterprises conducted by the group," suffered from certain inherent limitations. As Coleman noted, "very little is put in but a great deal is taken out until it will finally collapse from anemia. Nothing tangible is done to stimulate its growth so that it can carry on despite other competing forces." The "competing forces" of integration, however, appeared likely to further destroy the industry's vitality in the future, barring a sudden attitudinal shift among African Americans and Organized Baseball.[29]

"The Golden Era Has Passed"

When you think of the mothers and fathers and youngsters
who spend most of their lives either at work or in dingy, dark
and uninviting apartments, squeezed in like sardines, having
to choose between church and saloon as the major places of
inspiration, diversion or entertainment, you see what Negro
baseball has meant over the years.

—Dan Burley, 1948

As 1948 approached, segregation still remained a powerful and essential
component of African American life throughout both the urban North and
rural South. Yet the incremental social and economic advances of recent
years, culminating in Jackie Robinson's highly publicized breakthrough in
1947, had led many blacks to reconsider the necessity, desirability, and
ultimate purpose of separate institutions, including black professional
baseball. To ensure future survival, black franchises would now need to
redefine and reinvent themselves as something more than simply a segregated version of major league baseball. The black press, for instance,
would achieve new levels of prosperity in the postwar years by continuing
to fulfill a unique role in African American communities, providing coverage and commentary unavailable in white newspapers. To compete with
the appeal of the major leagues, black baseball would similarly need to
offer a distinct brand of entertainment, yet how this might best be
achieved remained uncertain.

Continued administrative improvements appeared to be a first step
toward regaining the confidence of black fans. To coexist with major
league baseball, the NNL and NAL needed to demonstrate their ability
to operate efficiently as businesses and adopt long-deferred reforms. The
leagues, for example, could no longer rely on the mediocre publicity methods that had sufficed in a less competitive market. Despite a miserable
financial showing in 1947, most teams had retreated into their typical off-
season hibernation, providing black sportswriters with few press releases

or newsworthy items until the spring, leading sportswriter Dan Burley to observe that "you don't fill parks that way."[1]

Black baseball teams also needed to adapt to the Jackie Robinson phenomenon. During 1947, most black fans had fixated on Robinson, and even those attending NNL and NAL games seemed more interested in the activities of the Dodger rookie. During one league promotion at Yankee Stadium, officials were dismayed to learn that a sudden ovation was prompted not by an exciting play on the field but because news of a Robinson home run had been conveyed to the crowd. A similar spontaneous outburst occurred at the Polo Grounds, sparked by a Dodger rally. Rather than resist Robinson's appeal, Burley advised the leagues to accommodate fans by offering concurrent Dodger updates, as many blacks (particularly those in New York) would otherwise attend major league contests or follow Robinson's progress on radio. Notably, an enormous interest in Larry Doby had already forced the Cleveland Buckeyes to provide coverage of the Indians during local NAL games in 1947.

The still decentralized control of both leagues, however, limited the likelihood that black professional baseball would assertively address the new challenges with substantial improvement or innovation. In the west, J. B. Martin maintained his stranglehold on the NAL presidency, yet appeared more concerned with Chicago politics than with the growing crisis facing his league. Unable or unwilling to acknowledge integration's impact on the industry's fortunes, Martin insisted that "we have our regular attendance here and are hurt very little. The rest of our cities are not in the National League circuit. Likewise in the east, New York is the only town that could be hurt. I can't see where Robinson does us any harm. In fact it has helped us out west." To sportswriter A. S. "Doc" Young, such denials suggested that the selection of a new NAL president was imperative and confirmed that Martin "must be blinded by the political mist that floats around his every move." Moreover, Young complained that Martin failed to attend the black World Series games played in Cleveland in 1947 and "never answers a letter completely, especially if that letter suggests some kind of improvement or requests some information that might take a couple minutes to get."[2]

In the east, most observers acknowledged that Reverend John Johnson had performed credibly, if unspectacularly, in his first year as NNL president. The *Amsterdam News*, for instance, praised Johnson's "wise leadership" and applauded his suggestion of a benefit game for the United Negro College Fund and National Urban League. Johnson had also earned respect in 1947 for attempting to crack down on player violence, requiring NNL clubs to play a minimum of 60 league games to qualify for the playoffs, and continuing to work toward affiliation with Organized Baseball.

Figure 29. The always political J. B. Martin posing with fellow Republican
Dwight Eisenhower. Courtesy Kansas Collection, University of Kansas
Library.

Most important, Johnson appeared considerably more cognizant of the industry's fragile status than Martin. Recognizing his efforts, the league reelected Johnson in January 1948.

Yet substantial changes in the leagues' operation would ultimately depend on the franchise owners themselves, who had been slow to embrace
reforms during even the most fortuitous of circumstances, and appeared
likely to cling to established practices as a response to the mounting financial risk of operation. Most owners could fall back on additional enterprises
(both legitimate and illegal), but the majority simply could not withstand
repeated seasons of losses in the $10,000 to $20,000 range, not even the
black "sportsmen" (explained by journalist Alvin White as a black press
label for "gamblers and shady characters") so integral to team ownership
since the Depression. The chronically destitute James Semler, for instance,
had been hit especially hard in 1947, claiming that "if I had gone another
two weeks, I'd have been in the poor house." As Doc Young observed,
"baseball, more to our moguls than for the major leaguers, is a business.

It must show a profit or it can't last long. There are few angels who will sport a team just for the love of the game—they can't afford to do so."[3]

In reality, the owners had relatively few options available to improve their financial status, and the failure of most teams to acquire their own parks now loomed as a serious difficulty. The heavy use of Organized Baseball facilities, expedient during the early 1940s, became a liability for several clubs, particularly Semler's Black Yankees. According to one New York observer, the attendance drop at Yankee Stadium in 1947 "represents a danger point below which operating costs, etc. would make it impossible for Negro baseball to operate." Moreover, the reliance on outside park rentals prevented the creation of additional revenue streams, and as Monarch official Tom Baird explained, "we have to make all our money at the gate, we have no concessions of any kind."

Already handicapped by expensive rentals, the chronic dilemma of park availability provided an additional obstacle for an industry desperately needing to spark fan interest. Substantial improvements in scheduling remained elusive, as available dates at major and minor league parks continued to dictate an often chaotic arrangement of league games that satisfied few fans. In Baltimore, Sam Lacy complained that local fans seldom had an opportunity to see the Eagles and Grays during 1947, but were instead subjected to a "steady diet of New York Black Yankees and the New York Cubans, with a little of the Philadelphia Stars thrown in as an occasional entree." Although the NNL would attempt to develop an "interlocking schedule" with the NAL that would provide fans with a greater variety of attractions from both leagues, logistical problems with bus travel doomed the proposal.

Even though desperate for revenue, most teams could thus only schedule a limited number of home games, making the loss of even a single date particularly damaging. Yet between 1947 and 1949, the cancellation of league promotions became increasingly prevalent. With black patronage slipping, Organized Baseball officials became willing to replace previously scheduled league games with more profitable events including rodeos, horse shows, boxing matches, high school sports, and even a rally at the Polo Grounds that canceled the New York Cubans' 1949 opener. Epitomizing the industry's lack of park control, a potential scheduling conflict with the Kansas City Blues forced the Monarchs to decline an NAL playoff berth in 1949.[4]

For many observers, the current plight of the owners was hardly surprising. Despite the unprecedented profits in the early 1940s, league officials not only had failed to prepare for integration but had made little attempt to wean themselves from their reliance on Organized Baseball rentals. As Dan Burley had warned in 1943, "there seems to be too much of the 'crap game' philosophy mixed up in the whole thing . . . there seems to be no inclination toward long term investments, etc." Yet most owners had been understandably reluctant to reinvest their wartime profits in park construction or acquisition, preferring instead to recoup their Depression losses.

Although the future of black baseball appeared bleak, few black fans or writers openly advocated the disbanding of the two leagues. Despite the wide appeal of integration, the potential loss of a long-operating race enterprise alarmed observers such as Doc Young, who reminded his readers that "the Negro majors constitute the acme of the sport in our group. It's Negro business. It needs support from us the same as our laundries, groceries, insurance companies. . . . It's an economic factor: it pays salaries . . . to about 150 players in the American League alone and to countless officials, umpires." Similarly, a New York journalist touted the still considerable necessity of separate institutions, noting that "because the major leagues reverse age-old policy and admit two or three Negroes is no sign everything colored has to fold up and die. If such a theory was factual, how about the Negro churches? There are Negroes who join white churches, but is that a sign that there is no need for the countless Negro churches we have? Because a night club downtown admits colored patrons it's no sign all the clubs uptown should close down."

Others questioned whether the current marginal level of Organized Baseball integration warranted the abandonment and possible failure of a separate enterprise. New York fan Robert Davis noted that most major league owners were uninterested in black players, and "the sooner we realize that and go back to patronizing Negro baseball the better off we will be until such time as Negroes are integrated into organized baseball the same as other races." To Davis, it was not the black owners who were to blame but the fans, who "don't seem to understand that when they desert Negro baseball they are deserting a Negro institution whose success or failure means another success or failure of the whole Negro race." Moreover, despite gains in the postwar era, complete integration remained a remote prospect, leading Doc Young to assert that "when the day comes that you can walk into any business and get the job you're fitted for, when the day comes when the likes of the Satchel Paiges, the Willie Wellses, the Buck Leonards can play, without regard for their color, in the major leagues, then, and only then, will there be a legitimate excuse for ignoring in large numbers the efforts in Negro baseball."

Whether any race-based arguments would affect the consumer decisions of African Americans during the 1948 season remained uncertain. Black businesses had long employed similar racial pleas with only partial success, as a sizable segment of the black population patronized white enterprises regardless of the existence of black competitors. Moreover, the appeal of such reasoning had declined by the late 1940s, a time when many urban blacks could recognize limited, yet tangible, progress in integration. To reconnect with black fans more effectively, the two leagues needed to market themselves not as alternatives to integration but as a vital cog in the process. Rather than justify its existence simply as a race enterprise, black baseball would increasingly contend that its survival ensured continued opportunities for African Americans in the major leagues.

A shift in emphasis toward the development of finished players for eventual sale to the major or upper-level minor leagues might not only resonate with black fans but also offer the most feasible solution to regaining lost attendance revenues. Since 1946, player sales had bolstered the income of Philadelphia, Newark, Kansas City, and Memphis, and others appeared likely to profit similarly in the future. Roscoe Coleman noted that black baseball "should awaken to the possibility of the gold to be made in developing Negro players for major league berths," yet advised greater efforts to recruit youngsters and to retain managers and coaches capable of sound baseball instruction.[5]

Although player sales loomed as a potential windfall for struggling franchises, continued lax administrative practices prevented some owners from fully capitalizing on the sudden interest of Organized Baseball. J. B. Martin's Chicago American Giants, for example, featured promising catcher John Ritchey, who had attracted the attention of several teams, including the Chicago Cubs and the Pacific Coast League's San Diego Padres. When Ritchey eventually signed with the Padres in November 1947 and became the first African American to join a PCL club, the American Giants initially received no compensation, prompting a protest to Commissioner Chandler. An embarrassed Martin, however, was soon forced to admit that because of an "oversight," he had failed to tender a contract to Ritchey. While sympathetic, Chandler explained that he was powerless to act, particularly "when the contract itself cannot be found, and when, apparently, those responsible for obtaining the contract are uncertain whether or not they did obtain it." Fortunately for Martin, Padres officials later decided to honor his dubious claim and provided a "satisfactory sum" for Ritchey, yet to Wendell Smith the entire affair illustrated the "slipshod" manner of operation still prevalent in the industry two years after Robinson's signing.[6]

Smith and numerous observers had long recommended affiliation with Organized Baseball, and the step was now increasingly essential if the NNL and NAL were to function successfully in a player development role. While imposing more stringent business practices, a formal relationship would eliminate contract disputes during player purchases and allow black baseball to demand a fairer price comparable to minor leagues at a similar level. Moreover, affiliation would eventually allow black teams, like their minor league counterparts, to develop alliances with major league franchises through "working agreements" or even outright ownership, and a fresh influx of Organized Baseball capital could prove advantageous for an industry now entering a crucial transitional period.

The meetings with Chandler and National League attorney Louis Carroll in 1946 had raised hopes that affiliation was indeed possible, provided certain reforms were enacted. The Organized Baseball establishment, however, had offered no assistance in the process, a position supported by the *Sporting News*, which asserted in 1947 that "it is up to Negro baseball to recognize the elevation of Robinson to the majors by cleaning house, and establishing itself as a clean, well-conducted feeder of the higher company." Yet as Kansas City sportswriter John I. Johnson observed, the NNL and NAL "were left with perplexing uncertainty. What shall they do? How shall they do? And who is to determine when their house is in order?"

Despite lacking specific guidance, both leagues hoped that with continued improvements a formal agreement might be possible in 1948. Yet regardless of actions taken, the prospect of affiliation or financial assistance appeared increasingly remote. With the attendance decline in black baseball in 1947, park rental revenues had dropped, and the NNL and NAL were now attempting to negotiate with Organized Baseball from a position of decided weakness. Perhaps more significantly, Organized Baseball had little real motivation to concern itself with the fate of the black leagues. In the past, the perpetuation of black baseball had offered a bulwark against integration, provided a convenient excuse to avoid signing black players, and generated an additional source of income. But the integration of Organized Baseball was now a reality, and the concurrent creation of new black fans at minor and major league games rendered the loss of rental income less onerous. Moreover, Organized Baseball saw no compelling need to formalize its relationship with the NNL and NAL, as black players had already been acquired despite the absence of an agreement. Finally, even if the two leagues managed to gain admission into Organized Baseball, additional subsidy appeared unlikely, as mounting costs in the late 1940s would soon prompt major league franchises to reduce rather than expand their affiliations with minor league clubs.[7]

Despite unfavorable prospects, the NNL and NAL submitted a formal application for admission, which was eventually rejected by the executive committee of the National Association of Professional Baseball Leagues (NAPBL) at its December 1947 meeting in Miami meeting. In a letter to John Johnson, NAPBL president George Trautman explained that conflicting territorial rights posed the greatest barrier, as black teams scheduled most of their games in regions already controlled by major and minor league clubs, thus making it "impossible to do anything with these applications . . . other than to express a sympathy for your problems." While irrefutable, Trautman's explanation hardly provided an adequate basis for rejection, because National League attorney Louis Carroll had already suggested that, since the patrons of white and black baseball only partially overlapped, a "special rule" for black baseball might resolve any territorial problems. Additionally, the inflexible attitude toward territorial rights was far less evident a year later, when the International League considered placing the sagging Newark franchise at Dexter Park in Brooklyn, "well within the territory of all three major league clubs in New York."

The territorial excuse, however, conveniently allowed the NAPBL to dismiss black baseball without making any attempt to acknowledge or ameliorate its difficulties. NNL president John Johnson perceived the explanation as particularly unfair, noting that, while black baseball had attempted to improve scheduling, contracts, and administration, "new white leagues not better organized than ours and with players inferior to ours in skill have been accepted." To Johnson, the rejection represented a near-fatal blow, as he alluded to the fragile status of organizations with "no status, no voice, no rights, no relationship at all to the major or minor leagues." Unlike J. B. Martin, Johnson made no attempt to conceal the current plight of the industry, openly admitting that "we cannot survive in competition with Organized Baseball. We do not have the parks, nor do we have the financial resources. Although we have many magnificent athletes, we do not have the advantages and the vast machinery possessed by Organized Baseball for developing their potentialities."

Johnson's frank assessment of the future of black baseball prompted a rebuttal from the *Philadelphia Tribune*, asserting that "we know he is wrong. All these years Negro baseball has survived in competition with Organized Baseball." Yet Johnson recognized that in the changing postwar environment, affiliation offered the best opportunity to delay the inevitable collapse of segregated baseball. Incorporated within the structure of Organized Baseball, black franchises might have created renewed interest and gained much needed credibility among both black and white fans. Instead, black professional baseball was doomed to remain on the periphery of the white game as it had for decades.[8]

◆ ◆ ◆

With affiliation no longer an option, owners pursued alternative strategies to prepare for the 1948 season. In the east, NNL owners considered revamping the current franchise alignment by adding teams in Richmond and Asheville where the competition from integrated baseball was virtually nonexistent. Although the plans failed to materialize, the NNL did gain a new city, following James Semler's decision to transfer the Black Yankees from New York to Rochester, where the club would play at the local International League park. While the heavy expense of renting Yankee Stadium prompted the decision, Semler also contended that "it hasn't been a good idea at all to have two Negro teams less than a stone's throw from each other playing Sunday ball at Yankee Stadium and the Polo Grounds. Many times the fans have been confused as to who was playing where and playing who." With the departure of the Black Yankees, Alex Pompez gained a monopoly on the New York market for the first time, strengthening his position against local major league competition. Meanwhile, the absence of the cash-poor Semler hardly disappointed local observers such as Robert Davis, who noted that the "fans of New York have long ago lost faith in him."

Despite franchise shifts, the NNL and NAL were still left with the problem of somehow containing expenses in an era of declining profits. Not surprisingly, both leagues targeted player salaries as a major part of their cost-cutting strategy, and, in January 1948, owners agreed to a monthly salary limit of $6,000, a 25 percent reduction from recent years. While potentially saving each owner up to $10,000, the plan also alienated the players, the leagues' only assets. With $2,000 less available per month, nearly every player could expect a salary cut, a development likely to prompt a fresh exodus to Mexico or other Latin American countries. Although the policy appeared counterproductive for leagues desperately needing to retain their gate attractions, the monthly salary limit remained in place during 1948.

Wrestling with salary cuts, franchise shifts, and rejection from Organized Baseball, neither league had reason to be encouraged entering the 1948 season. Yet there was little doubt that a tremendous number of African Americans had become recent followers of professional baseball, providing the industry with an unprecedented pool of potential customers. While the majority had focused on the major leagues during 1947, Dan Burley believed that "the novelty is bound to wear off," facilitating renewed interest in black baseball. Even the usually critical Wendell Smith anticipated that black fans would continue to patronize NNL and NAL games regardless of integration, insisting that "Negro major league ball is much more entertaining and colorful than that played by big league clubs."[9]

Evidence of a modest groundswell of public support for black baseball provided additional hope. In New York, a businessman "devoted to the climb of all Negro enterprises" promised to organize a ticket-buying group for local black games. Meanwhile, the *Baltimore Afro-American*, with the approval and partial financial support of the NNL, sponsored an essay contest on why the league "should be supported and preserved." The winning entry, written by a Washington woman, explained that the league "gave colored players a chance to develop skill and prowess, and earn a lucrative salary when the majors had their doors barred. It has done commendably well with limited capital and material." Other encouraging journalistic efforts included the *Pittsburgh Courier*'s Talent Hunt, offering $100 for any reader who recommended a player eventually signed by a black or white professional team, and the *Chicago Defender*'s plan for a baseball school.[10]

While helpful, the various campaigns seemed unlikely to overshadow the still phenomenal popularity of Jackie Robinson. Reflecting his massive appeal, black newspapers in 1948 featured an array of advertisements for Robinson products, including photographs, books, Dodger hats, and a publication containing "Every Hit—Error—Run—Stolen Base—Homer of Jackie Robinson." Robinson also gained continuous mainstream exposure through endorsement deals and media profiles. By 1950, Robinson not only hosted a weekly radio program on ABC but starred as the subject of a new motion picture. Matching and perhaps transcending the lofty level of black sports celebrity status established by Joe Louis, Robinson became an icon in the African American community, and as one journalist observed, "his rise has been such that the average Negro youngster would have difficulty choosing between Jackie and Joe as their No. 1 guy."[11]

Not surprisingly, African Americans would continue to gravitate toward Robinson and other black players in Organized Baseball during 1948. In April, Dan Burley reported black fans comprised 42 percent of the attendance for an exhibition game at Yankee Stadium featuring the Dodgers. The subsequent stadium appearance of the Cleveland Indians and Larry Doby attracted similar interest, as all reserved seats were sold several days before the game. Although attendance for NNL and NAL openers in Kansas City, Newark, and New York was surprisingly solid, league patronage rapidly declined as the season progressed. By early June, an NAL promotion at Comiskey Park drew only 1,561 fans, while a subsequent Buckeye home date in Cleveland attracted 2,622. The startling decline accelerated in late August, as crowds ranging from 700 to 1,700 were reported in NNL cities, leading a disheartened official to comment that "this is awful. . . . If this keeps up we'll be lucky to finish out the season."

Developments in mass media contributed to black baseball's mounting woes. In the metropolitan New York area, the increasing availability of major league radio broadcasts enabled black fans to easily follow the exploits of the Dodgers, facilitating the rejection of the NNL. By 1949, Julius

Adams of the *Amsterdam News* reported that radio broadcasts featuring integrated major league teams attracted more interest than black baseball. Meanwhile, sportswriter John I. Johnson marveled that at the 1948 East-West game in Chicago, "nearly every other fan carried to the game a portable radio to keep in touch" with the progress of black major leaguers. The trend would continue in the future, as by 1950, Tom Baird suggested that a Brooklyn/St. Louis broadcast on KIMO (Independence, Missouri) had cost the Monarchs 1,000 to 2,000 fans for a competing NAL promotion at Blues Stadium.[12]

Although still in its infancy, television had already begun to affect commercialized recreation, including professional baseball. In the International League, televised major league games featuring New York teams contributed to attendance declines at Jersey City and Newark in 1948, while Inter-State League officials similarly blamed television for a drop-off of patronage in Wilmington and Trenton. While relatively few Americans owned televisions in 1948, International League president Frank Shaughnessy warned that "television encourages the fan to stay home. What's going to happen when sets run into the millions?"

With the growth of television and the expansion of radio broadcasts, the NNL found it increasingly difficult to compete with the appeal and ready access of major league baseball. A radio was a relatively common household item for black families by 1940 and while television ownership was still beyond the reach of most urban African Americans in 1948, the new technology was available at many eating and drinking establishments. As Effa Manley complained, "the Negro fan would rather watch Doby, Robinson, Campanella, and Paige than a Negro league game any time. If the Negro fan cannot see the four players, he will try to get where there is television. If no television, he will try to get a radio story about them." Not surprisingly, cost constraints largely prevented black baseball from exploiting either medium, although in Cleveland WEWS-5 televised a Buckeyes doubleheader and WSRS broadcast several games during 1948. Fearful of the impact on already dwindling attendance, the Buckeyes discontinued the experiment later in the season.[13]

Lacking radio and television exposure, league teams continued to rely on black newspapers, their only effective media outlet. Yet despite increased concern with the fate of the NNL and NAL, the press reflected rather than shaped the interests of its readers and would eventually devote the bulk of its sports coverage to African Americans participating in Organized Baseball. The trend disturbed players such as pitcher Joe Black of the Baltimore Elite Giants, who was dismayed to find a black newspaper with a "whole page on the Brooklyn Dodgers and scarcely a mention of what the Negro Leagues are doing." Yet, as veteran sportswriter Fay

Young explained in 1949, "Negro papers . . . cater to a special clientele who demand the exploits of Negro stars whether they be on white or Negro clubs. Therefore . . . fans . . . do not get the Graphic description they seek, and it is up to the Negro press to give it to them." The intense interest in Robinson, for example, prompted sportswriters Sam Lacy and Wendell Smith to cover the Dodgers' spring training for their newspapers, both of which provided abundant Organized Baseball news throughout the 1948 season. By October, the black World Series between Homestead and Birmingham attracted little attention from the press, which instead focused on black players appearing in minor and major league championship games.

A bitter Effa Manley insisted that the black press had unfairly abandoned the NNL and NAL, noting that "if the sports writers . . . will evidence the same enthusiasm toward our Negro baseball leagues . . . as they do about the . . . Negro players in the white major leagues, the future of Negro baseball will not be in jeopardy." The coverage of major league training camps particularly annoyed Manley, who noted that black teams had never been extended a similar courtesy. Yet sportswriters argued that the owners were at least partially to blame for the coverage reduction. League publicity, generally subpar even during more prosperous years, deteriorated further in the late 1940s, prompting Chris Perry of the *Philadelphia Tribune* to question why the black press should "highlight dope it would take a court order to get—and nobody is interested in anyway." In contrast, Organized Baseball news was not only plentiful but easily accessible, facilitating black sportswriters' movement away from Negro league coverage.[14]

The lack of interest was increasingly accompanied by a growing disregard of black baseball's past contributions, paralleling the rejection of other once valued race institutions in the postwar era. Perry, for instance, considered black baseball a "joke" and graded the level of play as "comparable to Class D white outfits," while a National Negro Press Association (NNPA) writer similarly suggested that "colored baseball has made little or no progress since the days before the first world war." Meanwhile, Wendell Smith offered a cruel but not entirely inaccurate assessment of black baseball, noting that "they made as high as $50,000 a year profit from their segregated baby . . . without too much effort, incidentally. They rented the big ball parks, formed makeshift leagues with irregular schedules, elected puppet presidents and put on shows at excessive prices. The best that can be said for these exhibitions is that they were interesting."

Perhaps more disturbing to league officials were the attitudes displayed by former players now in Organized Baseball. Regardless of his fate with the Dodgers, Dan Bankhead asserted that he would never return to the

Memphis Red Sox, claiming "we rode all night in those dinky buses and then they made you pitch your head off in towns like Grand Rapids." Roy Campanella provided a similarly bleak depiction of black baseball following his rookie season with Brooklyn in 1948, informing Dick Young of the *New York Daily News* that "the league itself was a laugh. . . . They'd dream up some batting averages, fielding averages, and pitchers' records, but nobody ever really knew how much he was hitting or fielding. . . . They claim that organized ball killed off colored baseball by taking some of its best players. The colored league killed itself." While Campanella subsequently denied the statements, the negative publicity from the earlier account contributed to the development of an unsavory reputation for the two leagues.[15]

It would be Jackie Robinson, the most venerated of the black major leaguers, whose criticisms would prove most damaging. After relating to a reporter in February 1948 that "Negro baseball needs a housecleaning from bottom to top," Robinson articulated his views more formally in a June article in *Ebony* entitled "What's Wrong with Negro Baseball." Drawing on his experience of a single season with the Monarchs in 1945, Robinson provided a caustic critique of the industry. Like numerous past observers, Robinson cited the obvious administrative deficiencies, including the Monarchs' failure to sign him to a formal contract, "the first of many things I found to be wrong with the game." The league governments were also inadequate, particularly the NAL, where the "president of the league was and still is also the owner of a team in the league." Robinson, however, viewed the NNL's selection of Johnson as a positive step, praising the clergyman as "a very capable man with the problems of Negro baseball very clear to him and with both owners' and players' interests at heart."

Robinson then outlined the unpleasant lifestyle in black baseball. As Robinson explained, the players received inadequate salaries, rode "uncomfortable busses," and typically secured accommodations in "dingy and dirty" hotel rooms. Not surprisingly, players were "half asleep and very tired" at game time and often unable to perform at their peak. Moreover, teams failed to monitor behavior off the field, and according to Robinson, "some of the players would not get to bed at all. They were allowed to drink whenever they pleased." To maintain a more consistent level of league play, Robinson felt the owners needed to "place more emphasis on the character and morals of the men they select" and take "more interest in their players rather than worrying so much about heavy schedules and getting in as many games as they can, regardless of the caliber of ball that is played."

Like numerous past observers, Robinson identified the problem areas of the industry, including umpires ("often untrained and favor certain teams") and the "questionable business connections" of several league owners. Finally, Robinson tackled the delicate subject of ballpark behavior, noting that "a baseball game is a place where people come out to enjoy themselves and not be disturbed by some unruly person who is either throwing away his sandwich wrapper or drinking from his whiskey bottle." Yet Robinson admitted that black fans had "showed they could act properly" during 1947 and hoped they would "continue to be loyal and respectful" in the future. As Robinson warned, "we must all remember that if we want to keep the door open in baseball, we must play and act in a manner that will bring respect to ourselves."[16]

Like Branch Rickey's criticisms three years earlier, Robinson's assessment of black baseball contained more than a grain of truth. Viewed from the comfortable perspective of the major leagues, the country's most prosperous professional sports organization, black baseball was clearly heavily flawed, or, as Robinson himself later observed, "really a miserable deal." Yet both Robinson and Rickey demonstrated little sympathy for the previous decades of struggle to establish the industry and largely failed to acknowledge the impact of inadequate financing and revenue. Like most African American businesses, black baseball had long faced the fundamental problem of catering to a limited and impoverished customer base. As sportswriter Ric Roberts had observed several years earlier, "regular big league baseball requires an economy that the colored people and their resources simply cannot meet or match. . . . As long as they must depend . . . on colored pocketbooks for continuity, just so long will they remain typical 'horse and buggy leagues.'" Evaluated in this context, black baseball had achieved a great deal despite substantial odds, a fact Robinson chose to ignore while instead emphasizing the leagues' considerable deficiencies.

The *Ebony* article soon prompted a variety of responses among black fans, owners, and sportswriters. While agreeing with the article's content, several observers including Chris Perry questioned Robinson's disparagement of an institution from which he had benefited. Perry, a harsh critic of black baseball during his brief tenure as *Tribune* sports editor in 1948 and 1949, nevertheless noted that "if there had been no second-rate hotels, grasping club owners, and sloppy umpiring, it is not altogether unlikely that Jackie Robinson would be earning his living teaching at some small college in the winter and waiting on tables in the summer. He would never have gotten out of the Los Angeles semi-pros if it had [not] been for the Negro Leagues." The *Defender*'s Fay Young similarly chided Robinson, recommending "a little more concentration on his weight problem and less on writing articles knocking Negro baseball—the very thing that helped make him." As Young subsequently observed, "practically every player who has been signed and who remains in white organized baseball owes a debt of gratitude to the owners in the Negro leagues. No one should overlook that fact."

Never one to avoid controversy, Effa Manley provided the most forceful rebuttal to Robinson's criticisms. Like Perry and Young, Manley insisted that "Robinson is where he is today because of organized colored baseball." To Manley, Robinson not only was "ungrateful," but failed to comprehend the past sacrifices made by black baseball, explaining that "up to five years ago Negro owners operated in the red and even today practically all of the gate goes into salaries, which have been raised with the climbing cost of living" and were "proportionately high for the sport." Manley also challenged Robinson's assessment of the arduous lifestyle in black baseball, asserting that her Eagles, for example, traveled in a "very comfortable" bus that had cost $12,000. Moreover, Newark and other league teams provided players with "the most comfortable hotels possible within our own limitations," alluding to the considerable financial and racial barriers present for clubs seeking accommodations. While "proud of our record," Manley felt that "an apology is due the race which nurtured him—yes, the team and league which developed him."[17]

Although Robinson's article demanded a response, Manley's fiery reply accomplished little and seemed to reinforce the perception of an adversarial relationship between the black baseball establishment and the forces of integration. A less strident statement acknowledging the leagues' weaknesses while touting their contributions might have won more sympathy, particularly if voiced by a former or current league player. Regardless of the relevance of Manley's arguments, league officials could not hope to win a public battle with Robinson, a figure of enormous stature in the African American community. Not surprisingly, a number of fans and writers soon rushed to his defense, including Maisie Browne, a Camden, New Jersey, school principal, who noted that "all he said was true for I have observed the same thing many times. . . . I have often been ashamed of the dirty uniforms, the passing of the bottle while in the dug outs. Even the spectators take their bottles with them and buy a bottle of Pepsi-Cola, pour half out and fill the rest with spirits frumentae."

The Robinson article and its aftermath dealt yet another heavy blow to black baseball, whose fortunes continued to decline in 1948, particularly in the east. By the close of the season, the NNL was near collapse, victimized by competition from Organized Baseball and a second consecutive season of poor weather. Attendance at Yankee Stadium for league promotions dipped to 48,037 in 1948, a drop of more than 110,000 in two seasons. The Newark Eagles fared no better, drawing only 35,000 fans and relatively few after the opening game, while the Homestead Grays reportedly lost another $10,000. Meanwhile, the Black Yankees remained a league liability despite their move to Rochester. Unable to gain a white following in upstate New York, the team virtually dropped out of the league by late August. In a thinly veiled swipe at the club, sportswriter Joe Bostic subsequently urged President Johnson to expel an unnamed NNL franchise, a "source of constant embarrassment," whose owner "doesn't have the financial stability to assume and meet its obligations." Bostic noted in disgust that the club "has not met a single payday in full . . . this season," prompting desertions by some players. Although Johnson took no action, the future of the Black Yankees, a team of marginal appeal even during the war years, appeared increasingly questionable.[18]

The loss of the Philadelphia Stars' home field, razed in early 1948, dealt another blow to the NNL. Although conditions at 44th and Parkside had never been satisfactory, the Stars' control of the park had ensured continued regular black professional baseball in Philadelphia, creating and preserving local interest. Long accustomed to Thursday, Saturday, and holiday games, the rabid black baseball fans of Philadelphia could now see the Stars in action only during their relatively rare weeknight Shibe Park appearances, along with other "home" dates at Lloyd Field in Chester and Wilmington Park in Delaware. Between May 9 and July 4, the club scheduled only two dates at Shibe Park along with a handful at Wilmington and Chester, prompting columnist Franklin Brower to comment that "about the only things the Stars are doing in Philadelphia this season are eating and sleeping." Ultimately, only 46,293 fans attended the eight dates at Shibe for which attendance data are available, far below the wartime average, and the remaining promotion attracted little attention. The club's prolonged absences from Philadelphia not only destroyed whatever local interest remained in black baseball but also accelerated the already pronounced movement of fans toward integrated major league baseball.[19]

With attendance continuing to fall during 1948, player sales to Organized Baseball provided the only positive financial development in either NNL or NAL. Reeling from small crowds at League Park, the Cleveland Buckeyes managed to sell outfielder Sam Jethroe, rejected by the Red Sox at the 1945 tryout, for $5,000 to the Brooklyn Dodgers, who assigned him to Montreal of the International League. The Buckeyes also parted with another outfielder, Al Smith, who joined Wilkes-Barre of the class A Eastern League after his purchase by the Cleveland Indians. In the NNL, the New York Cubans' sale of pitcher Jose Santiago and infielder Orestes "Minnie" Minoso to the Indians provided desperately needed cash flow, rescuing Alex Pompez from a $20,000 season deficit. Yet in a foreshadowing of the future, Organized Baseball also acquired several black players with no prior NNL or NAL experience, including Josh Gibson, Jr. (Youngstown, class C Middle Atlantic League), Fred Thomas (Wilkes-Barre), and Ron Teasley (Olean, class D Pony League).

The most publicized and controversial signing occurred in July, when Bill Veeck's Cleveland Indians purchased Satchel Paige from the Kansas City Monarchs. While Paige had remained black baseball's best drawing card, J. L. Wilkinson (who had sold his interest in the Monarchs to Tom Baird earlier in the year for $27,000) had increasingly employed him in a non-league role as the featured attraction of a traveling club controlled by the Wilkinson family. Unable to match his fabulous earnings of the early 1940s, Paige was no longer ambivalent about entering the major leagues and eventually agreed to a deal largely engineered by NAL booking agent Abe Saperstein. Eager for pitching help in a tight pennant race, the Indians reportedly spent $30,000 on the transaction, including $5,000 to the Monarchs (divided between Baird and Wilkinson) for Paige's contract, $15,000 to Saperstein, and a $10,000 signing bonus for Paige. While the signing of the aging hurler, thought to be at least forty-two, irked the *Sporting News* and other members of the major league baseball establishment, Paige proved to be a worthwhile investment for Cleveland, compiling a 6-1 record, completing three of his seven starts, and helping the Indians to their first championship in twenty-eight years. Meanwhile, the Indians and other American League teams also profited by Paige's still considerable box office appeal: an August 13 night game at Comiskey Park in Chicago drew an amazing 51,013 fans eager to see the "rookie" take the mound against the White Sox.[20]

While generating income for the Monarchs, the sale of Paige was somewhat counterproductive, robbing black baseball of its most well-known and marketable player. Yet both leagues still possessed a number of other bankable commodities, as the NNL and NAL, rather than Organized Baseball, controlled the majority of the nation's best black players in 1948. With interest in black players largely limited to Branch Rickey's Dodgers and Veeck's Indians, integration had proceeded slowly, barely affecting the caliber of black baseball which had similarly weathered heavy Mexican defections in the past. Despite the success of Robinson, Doby, Paige, and Campanella in 1948, the majority of major league franchises remained leery of signing blacks for even their minor league teams, preferring to pay lip service to the issue. Horace Stoneham, owner of the New York Giants, offered a typical rationalization, explaining that his team had yet to find a black player to "fit in our plans."[21]

Although the sale of Paige and others helped avoid a complete financial collapse in 1948, it remained uncertain whether black baseball could ever fully capitalize on player development. Lacking a formal agreement with Organized Baseball, league teams had no leverage in player sale negotiations and had little choice but to accept whatever price was proffered. Alex Pompez, for example, reportedly received only $5,000 apiece for Minoso and Santiago, after hoping to realize $25,000, while the Kansas City Monarchs encountered resistance attempting to sell two players for $20,000.

Perhaps of more concern was the rapidly growing role of Abe Saperstein in the acquisition of black players. Despite divesting himself of his part-ownership of the Birmingham Black Barons, Saperstein had remained a prominent force as a booking agent, owner of the recently created Harlem Globetrotters baseball team, minor stockholder in the Cleveland Indians, and associate of Bill Veeck, who hired him as a "special scout" for black talent in 1948. Saperstein's potentially profitable role as the Indians' liaison with black baseball, already confirmed through his involvement in the Paige signing, disturbed observers such as Doc Young, who feared "a complete nullification of our gains . . . if Saperstein is the door through which our stars must stop." Young recognized that "Brer Abe has grown fat on his manipulations of Negro athletes," and his reported purchase of part of the New York Cubans from Alex Pompez in mid-1948 seemingly bolstered his ability to control and profit on the path of black players to the majors.

Saperstein and the volatile issue of player sales were less worrisome as long as Organized Baseball maintained its generally apathetic attitude toward integration. Although a few black players might join major or minor league clubs each season, the NNL and NAL could still conceivably retain enough capable men to ensure continued high caliber play and future sales to Organized Baseball. Salaries, however, would have to remain competitive, an increasingly remote possibility in an era of faltering attendance. Moreover, economic and competitive factors would soon force numerous teams to reconsider their earlier policy toward African Americans, ultimately transforming the movement of black players to Organized Baseball from a trickle to a torrent.[22]

◆ ◆ ◆

After successive nightmarish seasons, morale in the NNL had sunk to an all-time low, as owners recognized that the decline in attendance and interest could no longer be perceived as a temporary aberration. The Depression years had been equally devastating, but black teams were now functioning in an era of higher expenses and relying predominantly on revenues from league games, as the once profitable dates with white semi-pros had largely disappeared. By September 1948, a desperate Rufus Jackson insisted that "something must be done. We are experiencing our worst season in years and I don't know what the solution is." Yet league officials, including President John Johnson, appeared unable to formulate alternative strategies to address the financial crisis, after the initial attempts at cost reduction and affiliation with Organized Baseball. Moreover, potential solutions such as revenue sharing or franchise mergers required strong leadership and a willingness to cooperate, attributes seldom in evidence in the organization throughout its fifteen-year existence.

Crushed by heavy losses, several league franchises resigned themselves to their fate. After an unsuccessful move to Rochester, the always shaky Black Yankees permanently disbanded in September 1948, citing the impact of integration. The Black Yankees contributed little during their NNL tenure, fielding a string of noncompetitive clubs and remaining in the league largely through strategic alliances with other owners and booking agent William Leuschner. Although the Black Yankee name would be revived in subsequent years by independent teams, owner James Semler retired from baseball promotion and died in 1955 at the age of seventy-four.[23]

While the collapse of the Black Yankees surprised few observers, the decision of the Manleys to suspend operations sent a shock wave through the industry. John Saunders, for example, noted that "with the possible exception of the Philadelphia Stars, the Newark Eagles are just about the richest team in Negro baseball . . . it looks bad, very bad." Yet after consecutive seasons of deficits in the $20,000 to $25,000 range and future prospects bleak, the couple could no longer justify the continued operation of a money-losing proposition. At a September 9 press conference at her home in Newark, Effa Manley announced that the Eagles were for sale and subsequently launched a series of final verbal missiles at the press, black fans, Organized Baseball, and Branch Rickey. She insisted, for instance, that the attention focused on four major leaguers (Robinson, Campanella, Paige, and Doby) jeopardized the future of black baseball, blaming "Negro fans . . . acting like d____ fools and the press . . . not trying to educate them." The Newark official also cited the "inferiority complex of Negroes," noting that, because "white teams have put their stamp of approval" on black players, the fans and press had deserted black baseball. Finally, Manley lashed out at Rickey, blasting "the gullibility and stupidity of Negro baseball fans . . . in believing that he has been interested in anything more than the clicking of the turnstiles."

Manley's statements, like her rebuttal to Robinson earlier in the year, did little to regain much needed press and fan support. Her tirade also failed to acknowledge additional factors that had contributed to the collapse of the Eagles, including the comparatively small black population of Newark and the team's use of Ruppert Stadium, a facility located near a dump and poorly served by public transportation. Notably, problems with

Ruppert Stadium contributed to the concurrent decline of the International League's Newark Bears. While her comments were probably driven by frustration, most observers resented the implication that black fans were entirely to blame, and as Sam Lacy remarked, Manley did not want to "admit that maybe it was something else in her town, even when you present figures showing the white Newark (Bears) team playing to crowds of 238 and 361, etc."[24]

The departure of Manley, an aggressive, outspoken, yet sometimes tactless figure, elicited a variety of responses. Wendell Smith, for example, admitted that "despite the fact that she tried to tell us how and what to write, she was always good copy." Yet like other black journalists, Smith was critical of Manley's recent statements, observing that "she blamed every one for the demise of her dream world" and "refused to recognize . . . that nothing was killing Negro baseball but Democracy." Meanwhile, Jackie Robinson suggested that several Newark players had objected to her involvement in the team and later related to Rollo Wilson that "Mrs. Manley . . . has been a great help to Negro baseball by getting out of it."

There was little doubt, however, that Manley had contributed a good deal to black baseball during her tenure. More reform-oriented than the majority of her colleagues, she had consistently advocated changes in the sometimes sluggish administration of the NNL, despite facing hostility from fellow officials such as Cum Posey, who insisted in 1940 that "Organized Negro Baseball of the present day is no place for a lady, even though she be an Adams, Nation, or Joan of Arc." Yet Manley could also be self-serving, blind to the viewpoints of other owners, and largely unsympathetic to the integration aspirations of black fans and players.[25]

With Semler and the Manleys out, options for the remaining NNL owners remained limited. Reeling from another year of deficits, the Grays also appeared likely to fold, leaving only half the league clubs (the Stars, Elite Giants, and Cubans) certain of operating in 1949. The once profitable chain of venues between New York and Washington could no longer sustain league baseball, and the continued operation of the NNL as an East Coast entity appeared increasingly unlikely despite suggestions to place new franchises in upper South cities such as Richmond or Raleigh.

The fate of the Manleys' franchise presented additional difficulties. After negotiating with several individuals, the Manleys ultimately sold their club to Dr. William Young, a Texas native currently practicing dentistry in Memphis, and his associate Hugh Cherry. The always omnipresent Martin family was also involved in the transaction, however, as fellow Memphis dentist B. B. Martin had sought to interest Young in an NAL team years earlier and was also part of the syndicate purchasing the Eagles. The new ownership group subsequently shifted the franchise to Houston, a move that not only sealed the NNL's fate but troubled Eagles players unhappy with the prospect of operation in the deep south.

To Ed Bolden and several other NNL officials, the only viable solution was to seek a merger with the NAL, a humbling prospect for an organization once confident of its superiority to the western loop. Although the move would significantly increase travel, NAL membership would ensure continued bookings and basic protection from player raids from both white and black teams. Moreover, the continued segregation in the NAL's southern outlets still offered the potential of profit for black teams, particularly Birmingham, which reportedly drew 144,375 fans to Rickwood Field in 1948. The example of the Kansas City Monarchs provided additional hope, as the venerable franchise had still managed to turn a profit of $15,353.82 despite a drop in total income from $155,921.20 in 1946 to $83,221.83 in 1948. Despite the unenthusiasm of some western officials and the noninvolvement of NNL president Johnson, the NAL agreed on November 30, 1948, to accept the Stars, Elites, New York Cubans, and the newly named Houston Eagles. Surprisingly, NAL owners managed to set aside past inter-league squabbles, earning the praise of Fay Young who noted that "no baseball group ever acted as unselfishly as these men did. Their first thought was to save the game and second was to inject some new blood into the league."[26]

While the merger extended the life of the eastern franchises, virtually every black team still faced the difficulty of competing with the phenomenal appeal of integrated major league baseball. In Cleveland, for example, the presence of Larry Doby and Satchel Paige on the Indians had devastated the once prosperous Buckeyes, whose home attendance dropped to as low as 500 during 1948. Paralleling the Eagles' transfer to Houston, the Buckeyes relocated south to Louisville for the 1949 season. To several observers, including Jackie Robinson, black baseball's gradual abandonment of the urban north appeared the most sensible strategy for survival. Effa Manley, for instance, asserted that "Organized Negro baseball has been ruined in the metropolitan area," and sportswriter Alvin White advised black teams to "turn their faces southward, where jim-crow still rules the day." Yet a complete shift to the south, whose cities had seldom supported black baseball with the same zeal as the northern and midwestern urban centers, seemed somewhat misguided, and as Dan Burley remarked, "the idea of taking Negro baseball out of northern parks and to the South . . . won't stand up. There might be some degree of profit attained but it usually hovers around the break even level and isn't sound business." Nevertheless, most clubs would soon find it necessary to book an increasing number of games in the segregated southern market to remain solvent.

Franchise shifts alone would hardly be enough to keep pace with Organized Baseball, as the NAL still needed to create interest by maintaining its high level of play and actively promoting its best players. Hoping to maximize the strength and drawing power of league teams, NAL officials began to reconsider the five-year bans on players who had jumped to Mexico, a policy adopted by both leagues in 1945. Although black baseball had been reluctant to lift the penalties while Organized Baseball's similar sanctions on jumpers remained in effect, a change in policy appeared likely following the collapse of wealthy Mexican promoter Jorge Pasquel's league in September 1948. Ironically, several black sportswriters who had criticized league officials in the past for failing to enforce penalties now urged the NAL to waive its punishments, including Sam Lacy, who insisted that "face-saving isn't important when strategic retreat can spare an empire." In November 1948, the NAL ultimately ruled that all jumpers would be allowed until March 15, 1949, to return to their teams without further punishment, warning that future defections would result in a lifetime ban. Disheartened by salary reductions in Mexico and perhaps intrigued by the possibility of increasing opportunities in Organized Baseball, a number of players accepted the offer and returned to their clubs.

The apparent dissolution of two NNL franchises provided an additional opportunity for league teams to bolster their rosters. After ruling that the players of the disbanded Grays and Black Yankees were league property, the NAL conducted a draft in February 1949, allowing each club to select up to three men from the defunct franchises. While now-retired Black Yankees owner James Semler offered no resistance to the policy, Grays officials had reconsidered their decision to cease operation and were now unwilling to surrender their players. Several months earlier, the collapse of the Grays appeared inevitable, as a seriously ill Rufus Jackson reportedly informed J. B. Martin that "he did not plan to put the team in the field in 1949." Yet the Grays' victory over the Birmingham Black Barons in the final NNL/NAL world series and the rumored interest of the Cleveland Indians in several of their players subsequently convinced Jackson and the Posey family to alter their plans. By December 1948, See Posey privately informed Art Carter that, while Cum Posey's widow and Jackson remained uncertain, he intended to place the Grays in the NAL as an associate member "to protect our players" and planned to "play in some of the large cities with the league clubs. . . . In no way are we turning Griffith Stadium loose."[27]

With his own club poised to sign highly touted Grays slugger Luke Easter, J. B. Martin predictably offered little encouragement, explaining that the NAL franchise alignment for 1949 was now complete. Meanwhile, Vernon Green of the Baltimore Elites began to investigate the possibility of scheduling some NAL games at Griffith Stadium, the Grays' longtime home. Undeterred, the Grays continued to prepare for the new season, largely under See Posey, who assumed greater control following the death of Jackson from a brain tumor in March 1949 at the age of forty-eight. Denouncing the western league as a "one-man circuit" where "there's no chance for a man getting a fair deal," Posey eventually placed his club in the Negro American Association, a lower-level organization largely operating in the upper south, dashing the NAL's hopes of completely absorbing the Grays' star players without resistance.

The NAL's failure to include the Grays, long one of the most popular clubs in black baseball, was baffling and would soon create numerous difficulties. Yet as usual, immediate goals took precedence over long-term planning. Rather than embrace the Grays as a strong drawing card capable of benefiting the entire league, Martin and other NAL officials instead seized the opportunity to strengthen their own teams. Moreover, years of inter-league bickering between the Martins and Poseys presented an additional barrier to an agreement between the Grays and the NAL. Despite the current crisis, team owners generally remained unable to set aside personal feuds or transcend their unchecked individualism, and as Dan Burley had noted after the NNL's collapse, "all seemed to figure from the angle of 'what's gonna become of ME and MY investment?'" Yet a spirit of cooperation had been sorely lacking for years, prompting observers such as Buckeyes owner Ernest Wright to concede that "there is quite a bit of selfishness in our baseball."[28]

◆ ◆ ◆

While encouraging, the reinstatement of the Mexican jumpers, franchise relocations, and the decision to combine leagues appeared unlikely to reverse the industry's current financial doldrums. Yet J. B. Martin, now president, secretary, and treasurer of the NAL, expressed relative unconcern, insisting that "there's nothing wrong with Negro baseball that higher gate receipts can't straighten out." Other owners, perhaps hoping to encourage fans, offered similar confident assessments of the season's prospects. Vernon Green, for example, predicted that 1949 would be the industry's "greatest year, exclusive of the war years," while B. B. Martin assessed prospects as "anything but gloomy."

Less optimistic were Eddie Gottlieb, who perceived the outlook for black baseball as "questionable," and Birmingham Black Barons owner Tom Hayes who admitted that "the golden era has passed. Teams that are to survive must retrench and proceed with caution." Hayes, for instance, considered limiting his team's travel to within 200 miles of Birmingham to hold down costs. Meanwhile, Hayes warned fans of the potential economic consequences resulting from the failure of black baseball, citing the "thousands of dollars we spend in Negro cafes, hotels, newspapers, and similar enterprises. . . . Don't think I am against Negro players aspiring to the major league. I am definitely for it. Still, if we are to continue to furnish these players we've got to have the support of Negro business and the public."[29]

To Hayes and other officials, strong backing from the black press was crucial to the NAL's survival. Black sportswriters would not only need to offer coverage of league games but also "educate" the public as to the NAL's vital role in training players for entry into the integrated major leagues. Although a similar strategy had largely failed to galvanize fans in 1948, sportswriters such as Fay Young continued to urge blacks to "unloosen your purse strings and patronize Negro baseball." Young explained that, "when one stops to take into consideration the thousands of white boys who try for the big show and fall by the wayside, we have to be thankful for the time and training our boys received in their own leagues." Moreover, Young, like Effa Manley several months earlier, scolded blacks for a supposed lack of race consciousness:

It is high time that we begin to get more interested in our own enterprises. Time and again we hear discussions on the merits of this or that player in the majors. Averages are quoted freely in barber shops and stores. Those doing the talking rarely ever know of any averages—although they are printed each week in the Negro press—of Negro players in the Negro league. And it is not until some major league scout has okayed him and he is signed that Brother Brown wakes up. Until then Brother Brown has been among those who see fit to ridicule everything his own race tries to do.

While it remained questionable whether "Brother Brown" and other black fans would choose to patronize the NAL in 1949, early season crowds offered encouragement to league officials. The Monarchs drew close to 30,000 fans for their first two Sundays at Blues Stadium and nearly 100,000 for the season, while in Memphis a June promotion involving the Indianapolis Clowns reportedly set a local attendance record. With the exception of Kansas City, however, interest soon dissipated in most league cities as a result of both internal and external factors. League publicity, for example, deteriorated to a new low during 1949. By mid-May, Vernon Green claimed he was unable to determine the Elites' position in the league standings and contended that "the surest and quickest way to kill fan interest in our game is to keep this essential news from them. . . . Something must be done about it if we are to continue our affiliation with this league." Although Wendell Smith provided a brief weekly recap in the *Sporting News* and the Howe Bureau continued to issue statistics, the overall quality of league publicity remained poor, puzzling observers such as Chicago-based journalist Luix Virgil Overbea, who noted that black fans "know very little about any of the players. . . . Why can't they find out the results of the games? How about a box score or two?"[30]

In contrast, fans could easily access mountains of data concerning black players in Organized Baseball. The sports columns of daily newspapers barraged readers with box scores, while the *Sporting News* provided extensive weekly reports on major and minor league teams. Meanwhile, black newspapers, regardless of their attitude toward the NAL, had little choice but to focus on Organized Baseball and offer the increasingly detailed coverage of individual athletes craved by their readers. By 1949, the *Afro-American* published "The O.B. Corner," a feature following the daily progress of black major leaguers, while the *Tribune* and other black newspapers provided commentary and weekly statistics.

Yet even improved NAL publicity would have been unlikely to reorient the mass of fans toward black baseball. Although Joe Bostic suggested that "the high point of hysteria . . . has passed" and "more and more the inclination will be to take integration in stride," the presence of Jackie Robinson and other players in Organized Baseball continued to electrify black fans. In Washington, where local interest in the Grays had declined, thousands of blacks poured into Griffith Stadium on April 14 to witness an exhibition game featuring Robinson's Dodgers and the Senators. A similar trend was evident in Chicago, where black fans reportedly comprised a third to half of the attendance at Wrigley Field during games with the Dodgers in 1949. In contrast, two successive NAL promotions at Comiskey Park in July drew an unimpressive total of 5,196 fans.[31]

For many blacks, the limited integration of Organized Baseball not only was more appealing than a separate and highly flawed institution but offered the hope of additional benefits in the future. Observers such as Doc Young increasingly questioned the relevance of black baseball in the postwar world, noting that, in Cleveland, "Bill Veeck has all but erased the need for a Negro league team by integrating Negro players on several levels of organized baseball play, hiring Negro musicians to entertain the fans, Negro ushers and vendors, and by adding [track star] Harrison Dillard, the town's hero, to the public relation's staff." Sportswriter John Fuster agreed, observing in 1950 that Cleveland's blacks "have come to accept the Indians as THEIR TEAM."

The only positive development during 1949 was the rapidly growing interest of Organized Baseball in black athletes. Responding to a combination of public pressure, evidence of Robinson's gate appeal, and competitive concerns, several previously uninterested clubs began to recruit black players for the first time. The Boston Braves, for example, began integrating their minor league clubs, signing Waldon Williams, a non-NAL player, in January 1949. In the next six months, the Giants, Yankees, Cubs, and Red Sox followed suit, albeit with varying degrees of actual commitment to major league integration. The industry attitude was often one of resignation, aptly voiced by one official who observed that "I suppose we've got to fall in line; every other club is signing them." Reflecting the still common ambivalence, Oakland Oaks president Brick Laws offered the Monarchs a mere $1000 for pitcher Gene Richardson and then informed Tom Baird that "he was going to notify the papers that he had made the offer because they had been on him to hire a Negro and he seemed peeved because I would not accept his offer."[32]

Despite continued resistance, the entrance of additional major league clubs into the market for black players provided the NAL with an ideal opportunity to profit in 1949. Yet the league's failure to retain firm control over players last active with the Black Yankees, Grays, and Newark Eagles would result in a series of embarrassing controversies involving several major league teams, including the New York Yankees. Following the 1948 season, the Yankees decided to begin integrating their farm system, mainly hoping to bolster attendance for their sagging International League affiliate at Newark. In early February 1949, the Yankees announced the signing of their first black player, Luis Marquez of the Homestead Grays, whose NAL rights were now controlled by the Baltimore Elite Giants. See Posey, however, insisted that Marquez was still rightfully the property of the Grays, arguing that, regardless of the team's current non-league status, "we have the privilege of selling our franchise or our players." Complicating the matter further, the Grays had already worked out a tentative deal with Bill Veeck's Cleveland Indians for Marquez's contract. Although Sam Lacy claimed Marquez had been willing to confirm Baltimore's claims, provided he receive a share of his $5,000 purchase price, the cash-poor Elites rejected the suggestion, and the affair would eventually be submitted to Commissioner Chandler for arbitration.

The Yankees' second attempt to acquire a black player was fraught with similar difficulties, raising serious concerns about black baseball's already less than reputable business practices. After scouting Birmingham infielder Art Wilson in Puerto Rico during the winter league season, Yankee officials offered Black Barons owner Tom Hayes the now standard price for his contract: $5,000 with an additional $5,000 forthcoming if Wilson remained with the organization beyond June 1. Although Hayes telegraphed his acceptance of the Yankees' terms on January 29, the always alert Abe Saperstein subsequently became involved, informing Hayes that the Indians could offer a superior deal. Moreover, the Indians were prepared to pay a higher salary to Wilson, who was unenthusiastic about his anticipated cut from his current $725 monthly with the Barons to the more modest International League scale of $400 to $500. On February 4, Hayes canceled the agreement with the Yankees, and Wilson signed with the Indians five days later. Not surprisingly, the Yankees quickly protested, claiming Hayes' earlier telegraphed acceptance was binding, and the fate of Wilson, like Marquez, would soon be in the hands of Chandler.[33]

Although Wilson began the 1949 season in Cleveland's farm system, the Yankees and Indians eagerly awaited a final ruling on his status from the commissioner's office. More than a few observers could not help commenting on the irony of the current situation, including Sam Lacy, who observed that "two years ago major league magnates were icicle-ing Branch Rickey for bringing Jackie Robinson into their fold . . . now two of their number are hot-rodding each other over the signing of a colored player, who at 28, certainly possesses a better past than future." Fay Young similarly marveled at the prospect of "millionaire white men . . . 'fighting over a Negro ball player.' Ever think you'd live to see this?" In May, Chandler awarded Wilson to the Yankees' organization, ruling that Hayes' telegram of January 29 was a binding agreement. Chandler, however, rejected the Yankees' claim to Marquez, and, according to Lacy, questioned the NAL's right to appropriate the Grays' players, particularly in view of their own response to Rickey's earlier "raids" on black baseball. Unfortunately for Chandler, his rulings satisfied neither the Indians nor the Yankees. Decades later, Bill Veeck denounced Chandler's "silly decision" as the "reverse of what would have been . . . logical," and Yankee farm director Lee MacPhail claimed that the loss of Marquez "soured [general manager] George Weiss on Chandler." Notably, the Yankees helped oust Chandler from office two years later.[34]

Other sale problems arose during 1949, similarly related to the NAL's inability to establish its contractual rights over players with disbanded or formerly affiliated franchises. The Homestead Grays, for example, sold Luke Easter to the Cleveland Indians, despite J. B. Martin's contention that his rights now belonged to the NAL. Once again, the involvement of Abe Saperstein was apparently paramount, as Martin complained to Chandler that the Grays had contacted "a man here in Chicago" who had facilitated the sale of Easter to Cleveland. The league also received no compensation for George Crowe, a former Black Yankee first baseman who joined the Boston Braves organization, or pitcher Roy Welmaker, who signed with the Cleveland Indians after spending recent seasons in Latin America.

Despite subsequent protests that the players were league property, black baseball's general failure to employ contracts with a strong reserve clause binding players to franchises and leagues ensured that the arguments would fall on deaf ears. Still smarting over the loss of Luke Easter and a prospective lucrative sale to the Yankees, a desperate Martin reminded Chandler that "you promised us you would protect our league. We have the only colored league as far as I know, and I do not think it is fair to us." The commissioner, however, refused to intervene, reportedly preferring that black baseball settle its own disputes. As Chandler explained to Martin, "it is perfectly true that I told you that I wanted our people to respect the contractual rights of the organized Negro leagues. It was not possible for us to foresee, however, what would happen in the case of certain clubs withdrawing from your league . . . and still expecting to maintain the rights to those players' contracts." Unwilling to interject himself into the increasingly chaotic world of the NAL, Chandler showed little interest in serving as a mediator, noting that "I cannot be in the position of deciding about the property rights of the Negro clubs."[35]

For an industry in desperate need of positive publicity, the uncompensated signings of Welmaker and Crowe along with the Easter, Marquez, and Wilson controversies were particularly damaging, contributing to a perception of black baseball as a poorly run business ill-prepared for integration. Yet another dispute involving the now inactive but always volatile Effa Manley created additional image problems for the NAL. In early January 1949, the Dodgers signed Monte Irvin, a highly touted outfielder with the now defunct Newark Eagles whose background and skills had once led many to regard him as the ideal player to break the color barrier. Receiving no payment from the Dodgers who believed the Eagles had disbanded, Manley immediately pursued legal action, retaining Jerry Kessler, a white Newark attorney who had served as a publicity agent for the Eagles in the past. After Kessler filed letters of complaint with the offices of the commissioner and National League president Ford Frick claiming that the Eagles franchise was still intact, the Dodgers released Irvin. Fortunately for Irvin, the New York Giants subsequently purchased his contract in late January for $5,000, shared among the Manleys, the Eagles' new owners, and Kessler.[36]

Despite the disheartening series of unhappy transactions with Organized Baseball, the NAL did manage to complete a number of deals without incident during 1949. The American Giants sold a pair of players, sending Jim Pendleton to the Dodgers organization and Art Pennington to the Portland Beavers of the Pacific Coast League. The Birmingham Black Barons profited through the sales of Wilson to the Yankees, Alonzo Perry to the Oakland Oaks of the Pacific Coast League, and veteran Piper Davis to the farm system of the Boston Red Sox for the 1950 season. Matching the performance of the Barons, the Philadelphia Stars also completed a trio of sales, selling Frank Austin to the Yankees for $7,500, Harry Simpson to the Indians, and Ford Smith to the New York Giants for $6,500, although the Monarchs, from whom the Stars had purchased Smith prior to the deal, received most of the sale price.

Always able to develop talent, the Monarchs themselves peddled several players, including Booker McDaniels to the Cubs organization for $7,500, Henry Thompson to the Giants for $5,000, and Earl Taborn and Bob Thurman to the New York Yankees minor league affiliate in Newark. Meanwhile, the Cleveland-Louisville Buckeyes sold Dave Hoskins and Sam Jones (who spent 1949 pitching for a white team in Minnesota) to the Cleveland Indians, and with the help of Abe Saperstein, sent Parnell Woods to Oakland.[37]

The increasing interest in black players led some observers to hope that at least some NAL franchises might function as minor league clubs for major league organizations. Alluding to the "desperate situation" of the NAL, Wendell Smith urged Branch Rickey to consider subsidizing a league team, and Tom Hayes expressed willingness for his Black Barons to serve in such a capacity for any organization. Yet only Alex Pompez would succeed in developing a relationship with a major league team, the New York Giants, from whom he rented the Polo Grounds. While the arrangement between Pompez and Giants owner Horace Stoneham was largely informal, it did parallel the "working agreements" in effect throughout Organized Baseball allowing major or high minor league teams first option on a lower level club's players in exchange for financial support. The Philadelphia Phillies, for example, paid $10,000 to Toronto of the International League in 1948 and also purchased several players from the team for an apparent fixed price of $1,000 apiece. Whether the Cubans received cash assistance is uncertain, yet Pompez did succeed in selling three players to the Giants in 1949: third baseman Ray Dandridge, pitcher Dave Barnhill, and catcher Ray Noble. Perhaps unknown to the Giants, all three players were at least thirty; a growing number of players shaved years off their ages to improve their major league chances.

Although salvaging a dismal season at the gate for several black teams, player sales remained an imperfect solution for the industry's woes. The loss of star players not only stripped teams of their best drawing cards but contributed to a gradually declining level of play, leading observers such as Luix Overbea to contend that the NAL was "selling its players up the river too fast." Moreover, the prices for black players appeared insubstantial in contrast to the sizable signing bonuses major league clubs had begun to pay untried white prospects. As Effa Manley complained years later, "they paid me $5,000 lousy dollars for Monte Irvin. If he'd been white they'd have given me $100,000." Yet with attendance marginal, Manley and other struggling owners had little choice but to decimate their teams and accept whatever crumbs were tossed in their direction from Organized Baseball, a trend that appeared unlikely to change in the future.[38]

◆ ◆ ◆

By the end of 1949, it was increasingly apparent that the NAL had little hope of successfully competing with the appeal of integrated baseball. Player sales had again helped to stave off complete disaster, but the continued overall attendance decline placed several franchises in a financially precarious situation. The American Giants, for example, reportedly lost $15,000, and the Buckeyes found Louisville no more profitable than their prior home in Cleveland, prompting several players to bolt the team over unpaid salaries. Despite a recently constructed park, the Memphis Red Sox also struggled, leading Tom Baird to condemn the facility as a "white elephant" and to suggest privately that the NAL would be "better off if Memphis got out of the league." The former NNL franchises fared no better, particularly the New York Cubans, whose financial losses at the Polo Grounds remained overwhelming. Despite rumors that the Cubans and other eastern clubs would be relocated to southern cities or dropped from the league altogether, the NAL eventually retained a ten-franchise/ two-division alignment for the 1950 season.[39]

Crippled by three years of steadily eroding fan and press support, black baseball appeared near extinction. Reflecting the postwar attitudinal shift, observers such as Wendell Smith expressed ambivalence toward the impending collapse of a once valued separate institution. While admitting that segregation had allowed some entrepreneurs to profit, Smith nevertheless asserted that "discrimination at its best is no good. People who make a livelihood from it are merely exploiting those unfortunate enough to be victimized by it. That's the way it was with Negro baseball." Others viewed the development with cold indifference, echoing a gradually growing contempt for the industry. Halley Harding, a former league player now employed as a sportswriter with the *Los Angeles Sentinel*, perceived the institution as a "joke," asserting that if Organized Baseball had indeed devastated the leagues, "all I can say is . . . HALLELUJAH—a dozen times." Meanwhile, the appearance of Harding's negative comments in the widely read *Sporting News* created additional unfavorable publicity for the NAL, only partially offset by Monarch manager Buck O'Neil's published response. As O'Neil noted, the league still employed nearly 200 players, and while the salaries were modest, "it beats hell out of loafing on Central Avenue or Beale Street or Eighteenth and Vine."

Few could challenge the essential logic of O'Neil's argument emphasizing the NAL's current economic relevance to the black community. ANP journalist Luix Virgil Overbea, for example, acknowledged that black baseball was "a Negro enterprise employing Negroes and making money for the race. As a Negro I should support it." Appreciation of the NAL's employment capabilities, however, failed to translate into mass support, particularly when an integrated alternative was now offering a growing number of opportunities to black players. Moreover, the acceleration of integration in the future appeared certain to render the NAL's contributions increasingly insignificant. Black baseball appeared doomed to failure, and as sportswriter S. W. Garlington explained, "it's A.B.C. logic that you cannot penetrate organized baseball to a large extent and still hold on to a highly successful Negro league. That is the problem that Negroes face."

Doc Young, now writing for the *Chicago Defender*, provided perhaps the most thoughtful analysis of black baseball's current status, declining reputation, and historic role in the African American community. In the context of integration, the benefits of black baseball appeared increasingly slight, and as Young noted, "many of our writers have been willing to consign it to the ash-can and to burlesque it to an extreme degree." Moreover, Young admitted that the leagues, "representative of segregated living," had been seriously flawed by financial and administrative difficulties and "a book could be written about the bad things." Yet Young insisted that "despite their shortcomings . . . they have done tremendous good. They filled a void; they provided a showcase; they satisfied the baseball hunger and the entertainment desire for many people." While recognizing that integration had rendered black baseball and other separate institution less relevant, Young argued that continued racism necessitated their continued operation, asserting that "I see no more reason for ash-canning Negro baseball than I do for shutting down all Negro newspapers, Negro insurance companies, markets, real estate dealers, and other business." Thus, to Young, there was still a place for black baseball and "for ANY kind of baseball which can legitimately sell itself to the fans."[40]

By 1950, however, black baseball could offer precious few selling points to consumers, as much of the best talent was now in the major or minor leagues. Moreover, unlike the Depression, officials had virtually no reason to anticipate future improvement in the industry's fortunes. Yet to their credit, NAL owners made no plans to disband their teams despite abundant justification. The three eastern franchises, for example, were reportedly prepared to organize a new league had they been expelled from the NAL, enlisting Richmond interests along with the currently inactive Manleys and the still active Homestead Grays. Unwilling to abandon investments that had once been profitable, most owners still hoped to somehow recoup losses of recent years. Profit, however, was hardly the sole basis for continued operation, as some officials sincerely believed that the NAL could best develop black talent for Organized Baseball, a viewpoint shared by New York fan George Farrell, who suggested that "if we are to continue to infiltrate the majors, the Negro clubs must carry on."

Just how the NAL might remain functional in the face of devastating competition was unclear. Not surprisingly, league owners pursued individual rather than collective action. Hoping to stimulate New York attendance in 1950, Alex Pompez slashed prices for box seats and general admission tickets to the Polo Grounds. In Chicago, league president J. B. Martin leased his American Giants to William Little, a Tuskegee-educated local businessman long involved with the franchise. Meanwhile, the Buckeyes abandoned their brief experiment in Louisville and moved back to Cleveland under the control of longtime business manager Wilbur Hayes, who leased the franchise from Ernie Wright.[41]

Franchise shifts and front office changes alone, however, appeared insufficient to address the obstacles ahead in 1950. Encouraged by the New York Giants' informal agreement with the Cubans during 1949, a number of observers continued to vainly hope for more extensive intervention from Organized Baseball, contending that assistance or affiliation could revitalize the NAL. Fay Young, for example, suggested that the NAL could fulfill an important role for major league teams by providing a suitable alternative for the numerous southern-based minor leagues unwilling to accept black players. Yet major league officials, already in the midst of shedding lower-level affiliations, were hardly eager to strengthen ties with black clubs and continued to display less than enlightened racial attitudes. ANP journalist Alvin White reported that an anonymous NAL owner pursued an agreement during 1950, only to be rejected by a condescending official who "constantly referred to great Negroes who formerly starred as 'good boys'" and regarded black players as "funny fellows." Although Dan Burley recommended a campaign to force Commissioner Chandler to intercede, the always nonchalant J. B. Martin took no strong steps to renew attempts to secure league affiliation, remaining content with an earlier promise from Chandler to respect Negro League contracts, provided they paralleled those used in Organized Baseball. Instead, Martin offered the dubious contention that the earlier strengthening of player contracts to comply with major league standards meant that "now we are safe. They won't take our players again without paying for them. In other words, we have a working agreement with organized baseball."[42]

The fallacy of Martin's views would soon become increasingly clear to several league officials. In June 1950, Tom Baird sent Leonard Hunt and Leroy Williams to the Paris, Illinois, club of the class D Mississippi-Ohio

Valley League, with the understanding that the Monarchs would receive $5,000 or the return of the two players at the end of the season. The agreement soon collapsed after Paris manager Von Price joined Springfield, another league team, and took Hunt and Williams along with him, prompting Baird's subsequent protest to minor league head George Trautman. Trautman, however, informed Baird that Organized Baseball had "no power to 'return' players to you," and later cited an earlier directive by Commissioner Chandler stating that "it is not the function of Baseball . . . to assist in enforcing either the rules or contracts of unaffiliated organizations," although Organized Baseball teams were requested to "refrain from knowingly interfering with the valid, existing contractual obligations of others."

Perhaps more disturbing, Trautman challenged the procedure followed in earlier sales, explaining to Baird that "your conception that you have a right to assign player contracts to clubs of the National Association is entirely erroneous, for you are not a member of the National Association." Again citing Chandler, Trautman noted that "it is not sufficient for a Major or Minor League club merely to obtain the assignment to it of the player contract held . . . even though such contract is substantially similar to the Major or Minor League Uniform Player Contract." Instead, NAL (or other non-affiliated organizations such as Mexican League) teams should first release the player (for a presumed cash consideration), who could then join an Organized Baseball team as a free agent. Unhappy with Trautman's ruling and wary of the attitudes of other governing officials in Organized Baseball, a disheartened Baird confided to J. B. Martin that "the least we have to go to them the better for us, as long as we don't have to go to them I think they will let us alone."[43]

While assistance from Organized Baseball appeared increasingly improbable, the segregated south still loomed as a potential temporary solution to the league's woes. Despite continued heavy migration to northern and western urban centers, a large segment of African Americans still lived in areas of the south untouched by Organized Baseball integration. With laws barring integrated sports in Birmingham and other locales, a southern-based NAL could evade the major league competition so destructive in New York, Chicago, Cleveland, and other northern cities. Yet cracks had already begun to appear in the south, prompted by the lucrative gate appeal of black players. In 1949, president Earl Mann of the Atlanta Crackers successfully obtained permission from local authorities to allow the Brooklyn Dodgers to appear in an exhibition series at Ponce de Leon Park. Although blacks were segregated at the park during the three-game promotion, the series was a resounding success, drawing nearly 50,000 fans without incident. After a similarly successful southern tour by the Dodgers during the following spring training, white New York sportswriter Joe King questioned how long southern minor league teams would "watch Rickey wave the Robinson wand and attract record crowds . . . without attempting to breach the color line themselves?" Meanwhile, Rickey's own prediction that every minor league would be integrated within five years dampened any hopes of the NAL to enjoy a permanent monopoly in the south.[44]

A number of observers suggested that continued attempts to function as a separate institution in the south or elsewhere were ultimately counterproductive. As early as 1947, Kansas City sportswriter John I. Johnson warned that the "appeal of strictly Negro games is beginning to weaken" and advised signing white players to "prove that the idea of F.E.P.C. works both ways." Reflecting the growing postwar attitudinal shift, others argued that the continued existence of all-black teams and leagues had no place in modern American society. New York public relations man John Silvera, for example, insisted that "any institution which can be labeled 'Negro' must either gear itself to the times or fizzle out with the new day that's coming. . . . Negro owned teams must become interracial if they are to survive." In Cleveland, sportswriter John Fuster admitted that "it would be hard to get the Negro owners to take that NEGRO prefix out of their league's name, but we hope they follow the lead of Branch Rickey and open positions . . . to men of all races."

In the postwar years, the combination of gradually changing racial attitudes and declining interest in community-level sports would prompt a number of previously resistant or uninterested organizations to pursue integration for the first time. Hoping to beef up sagging attendance at Dexter Park, the Brooklyn Bushwicks signed their first black player, Joe Hardin, in 1949. In the Philadelphia area, the Eastern Pennsylvania League, one of the strongest local white organizations, accepted its first blacks, including former Philadelphia Stars pitcher Ben Hill, who hurled for East Greenville in 1948. The Lloyd A.C., a perennial local opponent for the Stars in the past, also integrated, signing veteran NNL pitcher Bill Byrd in 1950. Meanwhile, the Black Meteors, the city's top black semipro club, introduced their first white players in 1947 and continued to retain two or three whites on the roster to maintain an "interracial flavor."[45]

The development of a truly interracial NAL, however, remained virtually an impossibility. The failed Eddie Klep experiment of 1946 had demonstrated that even the most prosperous black teams were unable to attract white players of more than mediocre talent, a trend unlikely to change with budgets and salaries now slashed to a bare minimum. Yet league president J. B. Martin appeared convinced that the novelty of integration would boost gate receipts. Although a 1949 attempt to sign two white players to the Chicago American Giants had failed to materialize,

Martin continued to advocate hiring whites and eventually overcame the resistance of NAL officials. In late June 1950, the American Giants announced the signing of Louis Clarizio and Louis Chirban, both currently active with the Armour team in the Chicago Industrial League. Although Clarizio had reportedly spent time in the class D Mississippi-Ohio Valley League, neither player was an outstanding major league prospect. Martin acknowledged the borderline talent of both players, admitting that "if the majors hadn't started signing Negro players, we might not have signed these white boys." Nevertheless, the signings prompted little adverse comment and even received support from Fay Young, who felt the move finally allowed blacks to "take the bull by the horns and 'break down the color line' which seemingly existed among ourselves." John Fuster also welcomed the development, arguing that a mixed league would not only "win support from America's black masses" but "would be one of the surest indications that we Negroes believe it when we say that we want integration into every phase of American life."

As Martin anticipated, the presence of white players bolstered the gate appeal of the American Giants and created much-needed publicity. The Comiskey Park debut of Clarizio and Chirban on July 9 drew 8,579 fans, the largest home crowd of the season, and received coverage in the *New York Times*. The novelty soon wore off, however, as only 1,537 fans (inflated to 4,567 in news accounts) attended a similar promotion a week later at Comiskey despite the addition of two more white players. As in the Klep episode four years earlier, marginal talent and southern racial mores ultimately limited the effectiveness of the strategy. The city of Birmingham, for example, maintained its steadfast opposition to integrated sports and refused to permit the participation of any of the white players in a local NAL contest on August 6, even threatening Chirban with jail. With attendance failing to reach expectations, the American Giants quietly abandoned the experiment by the end of the 1950 season.[46]

The American Giants' brief interracial interval exemplified the desperate measures that team owners were forced to pursue during 1950, a season aptly described by Wendell Smith as "probably the worst . . . in the history of Negro baseball." Nearly every club continued to struggle with dwindling interest and attendance, exacerbated by a prolonged stretch of unbelievably unfavorable weather. By mid-season, a number of teams faced financial crises, including the Buckeyes, who despite loans from other owners and reported promises of financial assistance from the Cleveland Indians had accrued a $20,000 deficit along with a miserable 3-33 record, prompting their permanent withdrawal from the NAL. Faring little better, the Houston Eagles abandoned Texas and shifted the majority of their home dates to Nashville for the second half of the season. Meanwhile, declining crowds forced the Baltimore Elite Giants to drop several high-priced players, while one official claimed that at least three teams (Birmingham, Memphis, and Houston) had suspended regular salaries, resorting to the cooperative/percentage plan seldom employed by league teams since the Depression.[47]

Heavy travel and marginal profits characterized the experience of nearly every club, as seen by the May schedule of the Philadelphia Stars, a team that had once rarely needed to venture west of Pittsburgh, north of New York, or south of Washington for profitable games. The Stars began the regular season on May 7 in Baltimore, and played a rare home game at Shibe Park on the following day. After rain canceled a pair of games in Wilmington, the players boarded the team bus, arriving in Kansas City for games with the Monarchs on May 14 and 15 that drew a total of 6,698 fans, followed by five days of barnstorming through Topeka, St. Joseph, Sedalia, Independence, and Fort Smith. On Sunday, May 21, the club lost to the Monarchs in Tulsa, Oklahoma, and then spent the week in Kansas, Nebraska, and Indiana, finally returning east on May 28 for a Yankee Stadium promotion. Eastern venues, however, now offered little, as exemplified by the Sunday feature at Yankee Stadium which drew fewer than 3,000 fans and netted the Stars only $178.20, less than the team had earned in Emporia, Kansas (!) that Monday.[48]

Continued park problems added to the NAL's mounting woes. Serious difficulties arose in Baltimore, where the Elite Giants, like the Philadelphia Stars a year earlier, faced the loss of their home grounds. Following the 1949 season, Bugle Field was razed after the sale of the property to new ownership. Although the white management of Bugle Field had already begun the construction of a new park, litigation would delay the facility's completion in time for the start of the 1950 season, forcing the Elites to negotiate with the city of Baltimore for the use of the recently built Memorial Stadium, the home of the International League's Orioles. While the Elites eventually secured several dates, local officials charged a minimum rental fee of $1000 per promotion, far less favorable terms than the Orioles who paid only 7c per ticket sold.

The eventual completion of Westport Stadium, the Elites' new home, did little to alleviate the club's misfortunes. As early as 1949, Vernon Green had warned of the park's considerable deficiencies, noting that it was "inaccessible, poorly constructed, too small and doesn't have suitable parking spaces for automobiles." Inadequate drainage and the absence of a roof also limited the suitability of the park, later assessed by team official Richard Powell as a "terrible field in every respect . . . I can't think of words to say how bad it was. It only looked like a baseball diamond." Unable to attract fans to the new facility and handicapped by exorbitant rentals at Memorial Stadium, the Elites were reportedly $18,000 in debt by August and their future operation in Baltimore appeared increasingly doubtful.[49]

The NAL's devastating problems with parks, unfavorable weather, and franchise instability only exacerbated the league's fundamental difficulty: the inability to compete with integrated major league games. Despite J. B. Martin's hopeful pre-season contention that "the fans are adjusted to Negro ball players in the major leagues now," the appeal of integrated baseball showed little sign of lessening during 1950 and began to surface in previously unaffected cities. While escaping direct major league competition at home, the Monarchs now contended with three visiting integrated American Association teams appearing in Kansas City, although the Southern Association's segregated policy spared NAL franchises in Memphis and Birmingham. Yet even southern cities suffered attendance declines, as railroads continued to offer special trains to Cincinnati or St. Louis for the numerous blacks eager to see the Dodgers, three years after Robinson's major league debut. Sportswriter John I. Johnson, however, viewed the continued response to integrated baseball as "a natural reaction and no amount of quarreling with fans will change their interest."[50]

With the league's attendance base continuing to erode, the ability to develop and sell players to Organized Baseball increasingly meant the difference between financial disaster and stability. Fortunately for the NAL, several major league clubs were now fully committed to scouting and signing blacks, prompting the *Sporting News*'s somewhat premature contention that "nobody gives a hoot what color a ball player may be. Only his skills and abilities measure his degree of desirability." Yet despite an unprecedented number of blacks in Organized Baseball (54 by July), the industry remained far from integrated, as the majority were concentrated in less than a third of the 16 major league organizations at the end of 1950.[51]

Nevertheless, Organized Baseball's interest in blacks was extensive enough to allow NAL franchises adequate opportunities to complete several player sales. Alex Pompez sold pitcher Raul Lopez to the New York Giants organization, allowing his battered New York Cubans to stay afloat for another season. The equally hard-hit Baltimore Elite Giants sent veteran Lenny Pearson to the Boston Braves' American Association farm club at Milwaukee in July and swung a subsequent deal involving the transfer of infielder Jim Gilliam along with pitchers Joe Black and Leroy Ferrell to the Brooklyn Dodgers' farm system. Other NAL clubs enjoyed similar success selling players during 1950, including the Indianapolis Clowns (Sam Hairston to the White Sox, Horace Garner to Denver of the class A Western League), Houston Eagles (Curley Williams to the White Sox, Bob Wilson and James Wilkes to the Dodgers), and Philadelphia Stars (Stanley Glenn and Bus Clarkson to the Braves organization).

Meanwhile, the Kansas City Monarchs continued to excel in player development, parting with several promising youngsters: Frank Barnes and Elston Howard, who joined the Yankees organization in July; infielder Gene Baker, purchased by the Chicago Cubs; and pitcher Gene Richardson, who spent a brief period in the Boston Braves farm system. Notably, the Monarchs' player sale revenue of $21,750 in 1950 not only offset the team's nearly $25,000 drop in gate receipts from 1949 but allowed Tom Baird to erase a $1,599.43 operating loss (see Table 10.1). With similarly declining attendance and receipts in Organized Baseball, the operating strategy of the Monarchs became increasingly prevalent, and, by 1951, former major league executive Leslie O'Connor observed that "there is practically no minor-league club . . . that is able to exist on the gate. . . . They must have the profit that results from the sale of player contracts."[52]

The most celebrated player sale of 1950 involved the Birmingham Black Barons and their talented young outfielder, Willie Mays. As early as August 1949, owner Tom Hayes had boasted that Mays would be the "best ever developed" by the Barons, and several major league teams, including the New York Giants, soon began to scout the youngster. Yet Hayes, perhaps unwilling to be locked into a potentially burdensome commitment in the league's tenuous financial environment, failed to sign Mays to a formal contract in 1950. Approached by the Giants in June, Mays informed officials of his current status, yet the club was reluctant to repeat Branch Rickey's handling of the Robinson deal five years earlier. The Giants eventually completed the signing for $15,000, allotting $5,000 to Mays and the remainder to the Barons. As Giants scout Ed Montague later explained, the team "felt it was the right thing to do" to include the Barons in the transaction.[53]

Despite a happy conclusion, the Mays sale once again demonstrated black baseball's inadequate administrative practices and marginal control over players. Five years after Robinson's signing, the environment for sales was still fraught with uncertainty, creating headaches for interested major league teams and providing others with a convenient rationale for rejection. During 1950, a major league official confided to Fay Young that disputes over players and contracts "don't set so well with us. We are a big business. . . . The Negro organization has one man who is secretary, treasurer and president and at the same time owns stock in the Chicago ball club." Dan Daniel similarly claimed that Yankee general manager George Weiss's interest in Luke Easter had waned because of the potential "involvement of Negro baseball league contracts, such as they were." Meanwhile, a controversy involving the August sale of Memphis first-base-

Figure 30. Tom Baird. Despite occasional sale
problems, Baird's Kansas City Monarchs sold a number
of prospects to the minor and major leagues in the late
1940s and early 1950s. Courtesy Kansas Collection,
University of Kansas Library.

man Bob Boyd to the Chicago White Sox further reinforced the perception
of disarray within the NAL, as W. S. Martin, currently struggling with his
brother B. B. over control of the Red Sox, filed a $35,000 lawsuit claiming
the transaction had been made without his approval. Although the case
was eventually dropped in 1951, the cumulative effect of the Boyd incident
and earlier disputes prompted most major league teams to eye the NAL
warily as a potential source of talent.[54]

Although outside assistance might have helped create a more stable and
conducive market for player sales, Organized Baseball made no attempt to
intervene, and in some cases it weakened the NAL's already shaky position. Tom Baird, for example, suggested that George Trautman's rulings
would allow NAL players to become free agents simply by joining an inde-

Table 10.1. Kansas City Monarchs Financial Performance, 1948–1950 (dollars)

	1948	1949	1950[1]
Gate receipts	74,245.95	84,903.48	60,075.92
Booking/barnstorming	6,475.88	1,930.67	977.38
Player sales[2]	2,500.00	9,250.00	21,750.00
Other	0.00	462.73	0.00
Total income	83,221.83	96,546.88	82,803.30
Expenses	67,868.01	78,791.87	62,652.73
Net profit	15,353.82	17,755.01	20,150.57

[1]Figures for Monarchs traveling team not included.
[2]Portions of player sale income allotted to former owner J. L. Wilkinson not included.
Source: Thomas Baird Collection.

pendent team for a season (a view reinforced by Larry MacPhail, who claimed that the major league's reserve clause contained a similar loophole). Recognizing the potential effect on promising league players who might pursue free agency and work out their own deals with Organized Baseball, Baird recommended suppressing the development, confiding to J. B. Martin that "the quieter we can keep this . . . the better it is for us, for I am sure we don't want to get into any law suit with organized baseball about [the] reserve clause."

The likely impact of intervention on sale prices also contributed to Organized Baseball's stance. As Dan Burley complained, major league teams had done nothing except to "sit by like a vulture and snatch off the top players," paying "bargain basement prices" of $5,000 and $10,000. Moreover, in a more disturbing development for the industry's future, major league teams had begun to bypass the NAL altogether, signing high school, college, and semipro players with the assistance of newly hired black scouts, including Elwood Parsons of the Dodgers and John Donaldson of the White Sox. The Dodgers, for example, signed three pitchers from Grambling in 1949, and the Boston Braves acquired two players from St. Augustine College in Raleigh a year later. The trend would only accelerate in the future, not only robbing the NAL of talent but depriving the league of a desperately needed income source. No longer able to monopolize black talent or fans, the industry's long-term fate appeared increasingly guarded after 1950.[55]

◆ ◆ ◆

Although the integration of Organized Baseball had dealt a heavy blow to the fortunes of black franchises by 1950, there is little doubt that the NAL had also been subject to unrelated factors and impersonal forces that were affecting all commercialized amusements in the postwar era. The once profitable world of semipro baseball, for example, fell into a prolonged slump from which it would never recover. The Brooklyn Bushwicks, perhaps the most successful eastern club, had once drawn crowds exceeding 10,000, but were "lucky to get 500-paid" by 1950 and eventually disbanded following the 1951 season. In South Philadelphia, the community-based support that had sustained Ben Cain's Black Meteors for years abruptly dissipated in the late 1940s and early 1950s, contributing to the team's collapse in 1952. Although Cain blamed the impact of Robinson, integration alone is insufficient to explain why numerous black (and white) fans deserted semipro teams. Sandlot and semiprofessional baseball had always functioned as a separate entity that had largely complemented rather than competed with the major, minor, and Negro leagues. Moreover, the appeal of the Meteors and other semipro clubs was based less on their caliber of play and more on the team's strong connection to the local community, a phenomenon theoretically undisturbed by the integration of the major leagues.[56]

A number of observers contended that the mass media were the major culprit contributing to the changes affecting baseball. By 1950, daily major league broadcasts were available not only in league cities but throughout the United States, and towns previously unexposed to major-league baseball except for the annual All-Star game and World Series could now listen to games carried by the Mutual, Liberty, and team-created radio networks. Television's rapid growth would present an additional dilemma, particularly on the east coast. As early as mid-1948, three stations were operating in Philadelphia, and by early 1950 over a third of all local households owned a television. The new technology had already begun to alter American patterns of leisure, as families were increasingly choosing to stay home for their entertainment.[57]

Not surprisingly, major league baseball capitalized on television and the opportunity to generate additional revenue. In Philadelphia, the Phillies and Athletics began telecasting home games in 1947, and within two years, nearly every big league franchise offered some form of television coverage. The increasing availability of major league telecasts would create an unforeseen crisis for minor league baseball. Following a disappointing 1949 season, Inter-State League officials blamed television for a precipitous drop in aggregate attendance from 199,586 to 120,031 for league clubs at Wilmington and Trenton, both within range of televised major league games from New York and Philadelphia. Observers similarly linked

Boston- and New York-based major league telecasts to the collapse of the class B New England League along with the failure of International League's Newark Bears. While park problems and easier travel to New York hastened the decline of Newark (and Jersey City a year later), major league observers such as Red Sox general manager Joe Cronin emphasized the impact of television, claiming that the medium had "murdered" several minor league teams in 1949.[58]

Television's effect on black leisure patterns and patronage of Negro League games is more difficult to determine. Initially a luxury item available only to middle- and upper-class consumers, television sets became increasingly available through installment buying, enabling less affluent Americans to acquire them. A 1949 study claimed that 54 percent of television sets in New York were purchased by families earning less than $3,000 a year, and other observers cited similar trends. Moreover, television advertisements in black newspapers as early as 1948 suggest that at least a segment of black consumers were capable of ownership, and those unable to afford a set could easily access television at neighborhood bars. Whether television was prevalent enough in the black community to affect patronage at NAL games at this time is unclear, yet Fay Young commented on its growing importance by 1950, noting that "one owner told us that all the Negro baseball fans in Chicago couldn't attend the [integrated] games at Wrigley Field. We agree with him but we couldn't get him to see that since many of our sport fans have television sets there is a great possibility of those not getting tickets remaining home with a cool glass of beer and seeing the game in the front parlor—or even in the bedroom."[59]

Regardless of wealth or socioeconomic status, most Americans now had regular access to major league baseball through television or radio by 1950. The development would have grave consequences for a number of minor leagues, whose appeal began to suffer. By mid-July, the class B Colonial League had collapsed and the fate of several other organizations was increasingly shaky. By the end of the 1950 season, an alarming two-thirds of the 400-plus minor league teams had reportedly lost money.

Although other factors including weather, aging park facilities, inadequate parking, increasing suburbanization, competition from other sports, and the popularity of alternative forms of recreation contributed to the growing financial woes of the minors, the impact of radio and television was difficult to ignore. Juxtaposed against readily available major league games, the appeal of community-based minor league and semipro baseball was bound to suffer.[60] Analyzing the attendance decline, a number of observers cited the "major-league frame of mind in minor-league towns," a trend with origins dating back to the development of radio in the 1920s and the appearance of nationally syndicated sportswriters in small-town newspapers. By 1950, St. Louis Browns vice president Charles DeWitt complained that "radio fans are becoming big league-conscious and are forgetting the minors." Philadelphia Phillies owner Bob Carpenter identified a similar phenomenon, supporting Eddie Gottlieb's contention that

everybody is major-league crazy . . . they want nothing but the tops in any sport. If they can get major leagues, they won't take the minor leagues. If they can get big-time fights, they won't go near the club fights. This can be traced to television, I suppose. Millions of people never saw a big-league ball player or a champion fighter or a topnotch basketball team until they saw them on television. Now everything else suffers by the comparison they make.[61]

The trend was equally apparent among black fans. As we have seen, the increasing availability of radio and television accounts of black major leaguers facilitated the movement away from the NNL and NAL, prompting George Lyle's assertion that "we have become major league conscious." As early as 1948, Doc Young noted the transformation among Cleveland black fans: "Go into a barber shop, a bar, a home, a newsstand during the season; listen to the men and women as they cheer when [Lou] Boudreau hits or makes a fancy play. . . . Then, for contrast, stand around when someone says, 'Well, the Buckeyes lost a doubleheader today!' Somebody is likely to say, 'Oh, them bums! They can't play any baseball!'" Like white minor league fans, many blacks succumbed to the lure of major league contests, whose appeal had already been considerably broadened by integration.

The less favorable environment for local and community-based sport by the early 1950s suggests that even delayed integration would not have entirely preserved the prosperity of black teams. As noted, integration had little to do with the decline of white semiprofessional baseball, an important revenue source for several league teams. Moreover, the growth of television and radio may have prompted a number of black fans to shift their interest to the major leagues, regardless of their continued segregation policies. As discussed in Chapter 7, a segment of the urban black community had always supported Organized Baseball, and, as one observer noted in 1943, a black fan would "pay to go to the National Negro League games where he can play and will also pay to witness major league contests where he can't play."

Integration, however, remained the major factor contributing to the current fate of black baseball. The monopoly on black talent that had guaranteed black patronage for years and might have allowed the leagues to withstand major league television and radio had disappeared by 1950, forcing the industry into an ultimately hopeless fight for the black consumer dollar.[62]

The End of a Business

> The Negro league is a thing of the past. It is no longer a function, it merely exists. Its president, Dr. J. B. Martin, contends that the majors must still draw the potential star from this circuit. What he has neglected to watch is the trend on the part of most rookies to avoid it.
> —Malcolm Poindexter, 1955

After four consecutive years of steady deterioration, black professional baseball clearly faced a hopeless future by 1951. Player sales, extensive barnstorming, budget cutting, and continued Southern segregation had prolonged the industry's survival, but the increasingly anachronistic all-black teams faced the almost impossible task of operating in an environment less favorable to separate enterprises and newly transformed by television. American involvement in the Korean War in June 1950 presented another problem, threatening to further deplete the league's already limited talent base through the draft and defense work. Despite the bleak outlook, however, most NAL officials decided to continue for another season, reflecting the influence of noneconomic factors, particularly a passion for the game and the yearning for a small degree of celebrity that often prompted involvement in professional baseball. The surprising commitment to the decaying business impressed Fay Young, who observed that "few men want to venture into Negro baseball. Those who have gone along through the years certainly ought to have a medal pinned on them."

Although the majority of fans had abandoned black baseball by the early 1950s, a number of observers remained uncertain that the imminent collapse of the enterprise represented a positive development. Wendell Smith, for example, worried that without the NAL the integration of Organized Baseball would slow to a standstill. Though opposed to "jim-crow baseball," Associated Negro Press journalist Luix Overbea similarly insisted "if colored men are to succeed in organized baseball the NAL must continue to operate successfully at least for a few more years." Meanwhile,

J. B. Martin reminded fans that, "although a number of Negroes are in organized baseball they have not been fully integrated, particularly in the South. The NAL still is the basic training ground for the best colored baseball players."[1]

Others were less concerned with the continued presence of blacks in Organized Baseball and instead focused their attention on evaluating the actual impact of integration. In New York, *Amsterdam News* columnist S. W. Garlington devoted an entire radio program in April 1951 to a discussion of major league integration and whether eight black players on the Dodgers and Giants compensated for the loss of a local black team. The potential economic impact on the black community also elicited comment. While recognizing the indifference of some blacks toward separate institutions, William Webster of the *Courier* noted that "others contend that Negro baseball is a Negro business and . . . it needs preserving equally as much as Negro insurance companies, groceries, and bars." Webster lamented that "another of our enterprises is about to fold. Is this progress?" Yet by the early 1950s, most African Americans viewed any movement toward complete integration as more important than the preservation and/ or development of race-based institutions, and not surprisingly, Webster's comments largely fell upon deaf ears.[2]

Seemingly lacking a truly compelling reason for continued existence, black baseball and several other separate institutions faced increasing scrutiny in the late 1940s and early 1950s. While black churches, colleges, and newspapers remained an integral part of the community, African Americans became increasingly leery of other segregated organizations that failed to offer similar tangible benefits. As *Philadelphia Tribune* editor E. Washington Rhodes noted in 1949, "Negroes are growing up in their thinking about segregation. No white man can convince them now that segregation is a good thing."[3]

The integration ethos was similarly apparent in sports, reinforced by the continued gains in professional baseball, basketball, and football during the early 1950s. A growing number of African Americans shared sportswriter John I. Johnson's belief that "there is no place in the nation for teams blocked off in racial groups." By 1951, Sam Lacy criticized Jackie Robinson for continuing to participate in postseason barnstorming with a traditional all-black unit, while Wendell Smith condemned a proposed benefit game featuring major league players on two teams divided along racial lines. Reflecting the changing attitudes, veteran sportswriter Fay Young, whose career dated back to the industry's earliest days, now objected not only to the annual East-West game as "a Jim Crow affair," but also to the continued self-conscious use of "Negro" to identify racial organizations. Young believed that recent progress in civil rights rendered such terms superfluous in baseball or elsewhere, arguing that "integration is here. Jim Crowism must go. That includes all branches of sports. There isn't any Negro Urban League. It is the Urban league. Let's put an end to Negro this and Negro that. We are Americans—nothing else."

In such an environment, black baseball had no hope of rebuilding mass support or surviving integrated competition. With African Americans making slow but steady progress into the mainstream, black separatism and the concurrent strong support of race-based enterprises had only modest appeal. As Robert E. Johnson of *Jet* later noted, during the 1950s "integration was the 'in' thing. . . . It wasn't hip to be that black and proud. It was a time to be ashamed if your white classmates caught you reading a black newspaper." Moreover, the *Brown* decision, the Montgomery bus boycott, and other stirring civil rights struggles in the south in mid-decade galvanized African Americans, prompting *Independent* sportswriter Harold Winston's observation in 1955 that "with the various fights for integration going on, the aspects of an all-Negro anything is meeting with increasing opposition from the Negro people." Not surprisingly, NAL president J. B. Martin was forced to contend with fans who asked, "why maintain a jim-crow baseball circuit?" although his own faith in the enterprise remained unshaken.[4]

Already crippled by fan indifference, black baseball also experienced the misfortune of attempting to function within a volatile entertainment industry substantially altered by postwar developments. During the early 1950s, professional baseball experienced a sudden crisis, as attendance in nearly all leagues dropped precipitously. After attracting a record 20.9 million fans in 1948, major league baseball experienced a startling attendance drop over the next five years, eventually falling to 14.4 million in 1953. Minor league baseball was hit even harder, as only 4 of the 50 minor leagues increased their attendance in 1951. The trend continued during 1952, and by the end of the season a number of minor league franchises were near collapse. The Boston Braves, for example, placed their Eastern League affiliate in Hartford for sale after the club drew only 36,281 fans in 1952, a drop of more than 100,000 in three years. The phenomenon was hardly limited to the East Coast; the Southern Association and Pacific Coast Leagues experienced similarly steep attendance declines. From a high of 59 leagues and nearly 42 million fans in 1949, minor league baseball continued its downward descent, and by 1960 only 22 minor leagues remained in existence.[5]

As seen, a complex set of factors contributed to the attendance problems in professional baseball in the early 1950s. A number of promoters, however, continued to target the phenomenal growth of television as the primary cause for the slump in gate receipts. Eddie Gottlieb offered a typical complaint in 1952:

The American public is getting lazy—or let us say rather disinterested. The sports fan who used to put on his overcoat, pull on his overshoes, brave the cold weather and drive ten miles to an arena now pulls on his bedroom slippers, gets out his pipe and watches TV.

Sure he'll shake off his inertia and go to see some outstanding team like the Harlem Globetrotters, but that's all, unless his team is in a red-hot race and even then he will not "go" for the ordinary game. We have become a country of TV sitters.

Black sportswriter John I. Johnson offered a similar view, noting that "there are fewer and fewer paying fans who feel inclined to leave their comfortable homes, their televisions, their motor cars and the hundred other beguilements to go sit in a hot park and watch their boys stumble around on the diamond."

The precise impact of television during the 1950s, while significant, is difficult to determine and varied among different sports. Television, for example, facilitated the surprising success of roller derby and wrestling and enabled professional football to achieve new levels of popularity. The heavy exposure of boxing, however, nearly destroyed the viability of smaller boxing venues, resulting in the closing of 250 of 300 fight clubs between 1952 and 1959. In addition, attendance decline of nearly 3 million in college football between 1949 and 1953 prompted the NCAA to limit telecasts. Smaller schools (including black colleges) were particularly affected, unable to compete with the allure of televised appearances of nationally ranked teams such as Notre Dame and Michigan.

In professional baseball, television may have contributed to a temporary stagnation in major league attendance but it ultimately stimulated interest and generated revenue for franchises. For lower-level clubs, however, television was a far less benign force during the 1950s. The poor financial showing of a number of leagues during the decade confirmed one industry spokesman's assertion that "when people in small towns can watch major league games on television . . . they're not going to bother to pay to see minor league ball." By 1957, Larry MacPhail contended that "the minor leagues are dead. . . . We know we are not going to find many in Kalamazoo who will pay to see the Kalamazooks in a shabby park when they can stay at home with a bottle of beer and see Detroit play the Yankees on TV."

With a number of better organized and financed leagues struggling for patronage in the early 1950s, the NAL was unlikely to escape a similar fate. Like white fans, urban working-class blacks could easily transfer their discretionary income from sporting events to television sets, now increasingly affordable with prices under $300 and payments spread over 18 to 24 months. Commenting on the attendance decline of the decade, Wendell Smith suggested in 1952 that "television has proved to be a good substitute," particularly for blacks who could now "see their heroes by simply turning on the television. . . . Baseball as far as they are concerned, is now a free commodity."[6]

Facing serious challenges from television, integration, and the major leagues in the early 1950s, NAL officials had few resources to improve their current plight. While some owners were independently wealthy, the actual investment in the league remained modest at best. Perhaps more critically, the industry appeared largely bereft of ideas and leadership, weakened in the prior decade by the departures of J. L. Wilkinson and Effa Manley and the deaths of Cum Posey, Vernon Green, and Ed Bolden, who suffered a fatal stroke following the 1950 season. The NAL remained unable or unwilling to improve its publicity despite several years of heavy losses, and as John I. Johnson noted, "the owners may be living in a new day but thinking in terms of the past. Competition has come to them and they are trying to ignore it. . . . Other than a few window cards and for-free publicity in newspapers, they are trying to do business in the same old way at the same old stand." Sportswriter Russ Cowans similarly criticized league officials for "operating with a system that was in vogue immediately following World War I."

A declining level of talent, once the industry's greatest strength, further weakened the NAL. Most of the country's best black players, including future major leaguers John Roseboro, Maury Wills, and Frank Robinson, proceeded directly from high school or college into Organized Baseball during the early 1950s, bypassing the NAL entirely. Although J. B. Martin continued to insist that the NAL offered superior pay and a better chance for advancement than lower-level minor leagues, black players in Organized Baseball such as Butch McCord threatened to quit if forced to return to the NAL. Not surprisingly, black franchises began to struggle to find capable players, and the inferior caliber of play was soon evident to most observers. By 1951, former NAL star Piper Davis considered the league "not nearly as fast as it used to be. . . . All the good players have moved up to organized baseball."

As seen in Table 11.1, the Philadelphia Stars, like other league teams, had a startling roster turnover post-integration, losing most of its top players to Organized Baseball or foreign clubs. Stars pitcher Wilmer Harris, whose career began in 1945 and extended into the early 1950s, later described the era's players as "average sandlot. . . . They'd be maybe good

Table 11.1. Roster Turnover, Philadelphia Stars, 1945–1950

Regulars from 1945–1946 Stars	Status in August 1950
Barney Brown	Mexican League
Henry Miller	Mexican League
Bill Cash	Mexican League
Joe Fillmore	Mexican League
Harry Simpson	San Diego (Pacific Coast League)
Frank Austin	Portland (Pacific Coast League)
Marvin Williams	Sacramento (Pacific Coast League)
Bus Clarkson	Milwaukee (American Association)
Stanley Glenn	Hartford (Eastern League)
Roy Partlow	Granby (Provincial League)
Bill Ricks	Status uncertain, began 1950 season with Stars; with Granby in 1951
Wilmer Harris	Stars
Henry McHenry	Indianapolis Clowns
Homer Curry	Memphis (Negro American League)
Murray Watkins	Manitoba-North Dakota League
Wesley Dennis	Indian Head Rockets (independent—Canada)
Ed Stone	Black Yankee Travelers (independent)
Mahlon Duckett	Homestead Grays
Larry Kimbrough	Status uncertain, with Homestead Grays in 1949
Henry Spearman	Retired
Jim West	Retired
Gene Benson	Retired

on the sandlot and the only time they were disadvantaged were against the ballplayers who were left over." Harris explained, "most of these guys coming up . . . wouldn't have been able to play for a ticket had they come up when we were playing, when I was playing. And that's not bragging, that's just the way it was."[7]

Territory, the final remaining asset for black teams and a once hotly contested commodity, had also become largely irrelevant by the early 1950s. Several years of devastating competition from integrated professional baseball had already destroyed franchises in some eastern and midwestern urban centers. The decline was particularly startling in the east, recognized by former NNL booking agent William Leuschner, who informed Tom Baird that "he didn't know of one town . . . where we could make expenses and so short a time ago when that is where we all made our biggest money."

The NAL's last refuge, the south, began to appear increasingly vulnerable following the gradual introduction of black players into the once staunchly resistant minor leagues below the Mason-Dixon line. During 1951, clubs in Danville (Virginia), Middlesboro (Kentucky), and Lamesa (Texas) all added blacks to their rosters, although the strongest leagues (Southern Association, Texas League, and South Atlantic or "Sally" League) remained all-white. In 1952, however, former Homestead Gray Dave Hoskins joined the Dallas Eagles of the Texas League, where he not only enjoyed an outstanding season but helped stimulate attendance throughout the circuit. Hoskins's demonstrable impact on sagging gate receipts prompted several southern promoters to drop their earlier opposition, and by the mid-1950s black players had integrated several other organizations including the Sally, Florida International, Piedmont, and Georgia State leagues.

The venerable Southern Association appeared next to succumb. By October 1952, Little Rock sportswriter Orville Henry even suggested that league owners "are privately beginning to believe they are slashing their own economic throats by closing their eyes to the examples set in most every other league in organized baseball." Yet the SA and other leagues encompassing heavily segregated areas of the deep South proved more difficult to penetrate. In 1953, the class C Cotton States League blocked its Hot Springs, Arkansas, franchise from using the Tugerson brothers, Leander and Jim, provoking an unsuccessful lawsuit. In addition, at least two Southern Association cities (Birmingham and New Orleans) maintained bans on interracial sports intermittently during the 1950s. Not surprisingly, the Atlanta Crackers' attempt to integrate in 1954 with the addition of former Clown Nat Peeples failed after a brief trial, and the SA would remain all white until its collapse after the 1961 season.

The continued segregation in several southern minor leagues provided the NAL with a limited sphere to function without direct integrated competition. Yet the prospect of operating solely within Alabama, Georgia, Mississippi, and Arkansas, for example, offered little in the way of profits or lifestyle for players and owners. Although cities such as Birmingham and Memphis had been occasionally profitable, the urban centers of the north, midwest, and upper south had always been the backbone of the industry, and any exclusively southern-based league was doomed to marginality or failure. The NAL thus found itself caught in a futile situation in the early 1950s. Burdened by a shortage of talent, finances, and profitable territory, black baseball had no realistic hope of ever rebuilding its fan base, now decimated by competing attractions and changing values. Nevertheless, a handful of hardy promoters, barely eking out a hand-to-mouth existence, kept the industry afloat throughout the decade, although the league had long ceased to be a meaningful part of the African American experience.[8]

◆ ◆ ◆

During the 1950s, only one black franchise managed to maintain anything near the financial vitality of the prior decade: Syd Pollock's Indianapolis Clowns. While the team benefited from outstanding (and relentless) promotion, the success of the Clowns (and basketball's Harlem Globetrotters) lay in their strong appeal among whites who found the blend of comedy and athleticism irresistible. Over the years, the team featured a variety of eccentric performers including "King Tut" (Richard King, a product of the Philadelphia sandlots), a midget named Spec Bebop, and "Boogie Woogie Paul, a one man jazz band." On occasion, the entourage also included jugglers, circus clowns, acrobats, and even a "comedy-trick horse, Pluto." Not surprisingly, the Clowns continued to attract unprecedented mainstream media exposure for a black team, including newsreel coverage, although hardly matching the fame of the Globetrotters, the subject of two Hollywood films in the early 1950s.

The success of both the Globetrotters and Clowns, however, remained controversial. To a number of observers, the use of comedy appeared to be pandering to white expectations of blacks and reinforcing negative stereotypes. After learning of a touring black basketball team clad in grass skirts, a disgusted Fay Young complained that "our Uncle Toms continue. What some won't do for a 'little chicken feed.'" Similarly, journalist Alvin White questioned why many blacks had objected to the *Amos 'n' Andy* radio program yet tolerated the antics of clowning teams. White believed that "clowns are a major attraction of circuses. That's where they belong and that's where they should stay. In baseball it borders on idiocy to introduce ball players as clowns and the same may be said for basketball. . . . This tendency to make colored athletes laughable has paid enormous profits, but it also has tended to keep the colored athlete in the class of an amiable imbecile in the eyes of thousands of white folk who pay to see this sort of thing."[9]

Although the Clowns had also been popular among African Americans, most sportswriters became increasingly uncomfortable with the use of comedy by the 1950s. Emory Jackson, for example, suggested the Clowns limit their "unfunny" antics to before games, while Doc Young condemned the club as a "team of circus ballplayers." Young felt that athletic buffoonery hardly encouraged racial pride, noting "how many lads do you know who aspire to join the Globetrotters or the Clowns?" Meanwhile, Sam Lacy refused to sanction the somewhat flashy style of Emmett Ashford, the first black umpire in Organized Baseball and later the first in the major leagues, viewing him as "a throwback to the era of the clown."

The views of Lacy and other writers were hardly surprising during the 1950s, a decade when blacks were making modest strides in entering the mainstream of American life. Clowning in any form appeared to undermine the grudging respect that African Americans had begun to receive in the mass media. As Joe Bostic observed in 1954, clowning "only serves to keep alive a characterization that thinking people in many other areas are trying to erase. It is hard as hell to expect the people in an audience watching a group of Negroes going into the pantomime, wide eyes, glistening teeth routine, to have any respect for them or their demand for recognition as men. . . . There's nothing funny about a kid being turned down for a job because he's a Negro and the prospective employer's estimate is based on the caricatures and propaganda he's heard—or seen." Yet for all-black teams, athletic talent was no longer enough to survive, and comedy provided an additional selling point. Notably, the Globetrotters outlasted the distinguished and non-clowning New York Renaissance team, which disbanded after the 1949 season.[10]

By 1950, the indisputable financial success of the Clowns and Globetrotters led sportswriter John I. Johnson to suggest that other teams might follow their example, noting that "there is nothing wrong with making people laugh." Similarly, Tom Baird advised Cuban promoter Oscar Rico that in 1953 "just strait [sic] baseball will not make the team, you or players money" in the United States, prompting Rico to develop a "Cuban Rhumba Show" to entertain fans during games. Comedy, however, would primarily remain the exclusive domain of the Clowns, although other NAL clubs, desperate to increase sagging attendance, would become increasingly less reluctant to experiment with other novelties, including beauty contests, daredevils, and motorcycle races. While perhaps prolonging the league's survival, the comedy of the Clowns ultimately moved black professional baseball away from its original purpose and offered little to African Americans, who instead turned to the exploits of a growing number of black major leaguers as a source of racial pride.

◆ ◆ ◆

As the 1951 season approached, a series of developments provided further evidence of the fragile financial status of black baseball. After two unprofitable years in the NAL and several years of heavy losses, Alex Pompez's New York Cubans disbanded, leaving Harlem without a black team for the first time in decades. A quiet yet dedicated official, Pompez had never enjoyed the success in New York he deserved, hampered initially by the presence of the Black Yankees and later by that of the integrated Brooklyn Dodgers. Yet Pompez would be the only black owner to make the transition to a second career in Organized Baseball. The New York Giants, who had forged a working agreement with the Cubans in recent years, hired Pompez as a scout, and the former NNL official eventually helped to sign a number of talented prospects for the team.[11]

The end of the Cubans was followed by the collapse of yet another venerable NNL team, the Homestead Grays. Despite participating in the upper south-based Negro American Association in 1949, the Grays had continued to remain a part of the black baseball establishment, occasionally barnstorming with NAL clubs and pursuing a possible league affiliation. By late July 1950, the Grays had joined the NAL as an associate member, leading some observers to predict that the club would replace the defunct Cleveland Buckeyes. Yet after reported losses of $30,000 during the previous two years and the defection of several players to Canada, See Posey announced that the Grays would not operate in 1951. Like several other owners, Posey felt he had not been fairly compensated for his men, complaining to sportswriter Ric Roberts that his players had been "snatched up by a pirate, didn't need a gun, hiding behind freedom for blacks. . . . You don't know how much it cost me to build this team." Despite tentative plans to revive the team in 1952, Posey's death in August at the age of sixty-three sealed the fate of the Grays, a franchise whose enviable history had spanned four decades.[12]

The disheartening departure of two venerable eastern teams reflected the mounting instability throughout the entire industry. In Chicago, J. B. Martin sold the forty-year-old American Giants for a reported (but unlikely) $50,000 in January 1951 to a syndicate headed by Winfield Welch, a veteran NAL manager. It soon became apparent, however, that the always omnipresent Abe Saperstein was the true owner, as Welch had worked closely with the midwestern promoter in the past and was currently the secretary for the Globetrotters. Moreover, nearly every Saperstein-backed baseball team during the prior decade had employed Welch in a managerial position.

The most fascinating aspect of the deal was not Saperstein himself but his continued close relationship with Bill Veeck, who had sold the Cleveland Indians after the 1949 season and would acquire the St. Louis Browns in July 1951 with the financial assistance of Saperstein and other investors. With Saperstein already controlling the American Giants (with the partial backing of Veeck, according to some observers), the Browns possessed a direct connection to black baseball, an association that went beyond the Cubans' earlier working agreement with the New York Giants. Not surprisingly, the Monarchs' Tom Baird suggested that Saperstein had purchased the club to "keep on the inside to recruit players for Veeck," and Saperstein's dual interest in the American Giants and Browns eventually facilitated Veeck's reacquisition of Satchel Paige (signed by Chicago earlier in the season) and the signing of veteran pitcher Theolic Smith. The modest level of talent in the NAL by 1951, however, prevented the dramatic impact that such an arrangement might have created a few years earlier.

Despite Saperstein's purchase of the American Giants, the influence of former owner J. B. Martin in league affairs remained unchanged. Prior to the transaction, NAL officials assured Martin that his position was secure, and the continued strong involvement of his brothers in two league franchises (Houston/Nashville and Memphis) ensured his reelection as president. Although the obvious nepotism and its effect on the NAL raised concerns, league politics and an apparent lukewarm attitude toward change prevented any sweeping changes in the organization. Rather than recruit a strong outside figure capable of desperately needed aggressive leadership, the league apparently preferred the less threatening alternative of Martin, a well-intentioned yet ultimately ineffectual leader largely devoid of ideas to ameliorate black baseball's sagging status.[13]

As usual, Martin presented an optimistic facade to the public, anticipating a successful season in 1951 although "not . . . as good as the plush war years." Yet Martin's recommendation for further reductions in expenses revealed his actual awareness of the industry's plight. Despite advocating cost-cutting measures, Martin refused to sanction the payment of players on a percentage basis, a drastic step that several foundering franchises had pursued during part of 1950. To his credit, Martin recognized that the termination of regular salaries, while economical, destroyed whatever minimal appeal the league held for promising players. Moreover, percentage baseball would further weaken the NAL's already flimsy control over its rosters, and as Martin noted, "a club owner can not hold his players on such a plan." The NAL ultimately ruled that owners resorting to percentage would face suspensions and the loss of their players to free agency, a sensible decision that prevented further tarnishing of the league's reputation.

With the Buckeyes and Cubans disbanded, the league began the 1951 season with eight franchises, several of which appeared precarious. After two unprofitable seasons in Houston and Nashville, the Eagles were forced

to relocate again, this time to New Orleans, and would be no more successful in their new surroundings. Meanwhile, the Elite Giants continued to
encounter serious difficulties securing adequate home grounds in Baltimore. After the disheartening experience at the poorly constructed Westport Stadium in 1950, Elites official Richard Powell had few available
options except to rent the municipally owned Memorial Stadium. The
city's Park Board, however, remained largely unsympathetic to Powell's
request for 17 dates, offering the dubious contention that "we haven't
reached the point where the Elites represent the City of Baltimore as by
custom the Orioles do." In response, Powell noted that the all-white Orioles "never represented all the people" and felt it unfair that Elites might
"have to give up our franchise because we can't play in the City Stadium."
Although the Elites succeeded in wresting seven home dates and a reduced
rental fee from city officials, it proved insufficient to save black baseball
in Baltimore. Recognizing the futility of the current local situation, the
widow of Vernon Green sold the franchise to William S. Bridgeforth, a
black Tennessee promoter, for a reported $10,000. Despite plans to relo-
cate the team to Nashville, the Elites remained in Baltimore during 1951,
although they spent their final season predominantly as a road team.[14]

The NAL's other franchises fared little better than the Eagles or Elite
Giants during 1951, as most league games attracted only tepid interest,
seldom drawing more than 5,000 fans. Black Barons owner Tom Hayes,
for example, disclosed that gate receipts were often insufficient to cover
his team's payroll and began to consider reducing travel to "give us an
opportunity to sit out the present indifference." In a further reflection of
the league's shaky financial status, three appearances of the Monarchs in
Memphis during May attracted only 1,890 fans. While the strong box office appeal of the Clowns in the South and in the hinterlands and continued local support in Kansas City and Birmingham provided modest
encouragement, league income dropped to a dangerously low level, leading
sportswriter Malcolm Poindexter to question whether the organization
would operate in 1952.

As during the prior three seasons, a handful of player sales averted more
substantial deficits, although the payments from Organized Baseball remained modest. The Dodgers, for example, paid the American Giants less
than $10,000 for Clyde McNeal and probably spent a similar sum on Nat
Peeples of the Clowns. The Kansas City Monarchs received a total of only
$6,000 for the sales of Curtis Roberts to the Denver Bears of the Western
League, Bonnie Serrell to the San Francisco Seals, and Connie Johnson to
St. Hyacinthe of the Provincial League, although the sum proved sufficient
to again offset the team's $4,000-plus operating loss for the season (see
Table 11.2). The NAL, however, would benefit from the more aggressive

Table 11.2. Kansas City Monarchs—Financial Performance, 1951 (dollars)

Gate receipts	57,082.55
Booking/barnstorming	2,082.77
Player sales	14,000.00
Total income	73,165.32
Expenses	63,213.20
Net profit	9,952.12

Source: Thomas Baird collection.

stance of teams once leery of integration, such as the Chicago White Sox, who in 1951 became the sixth team to add a black player to their major league roster. Hoping to continue their development of black talent, the White Sox eventually signed several NAL players in 1951 including Honey Lott and Leander Tugerson of the Clowns and Gene Collins of the Monarchs.[15]

Changes in the front office of major league teams resulted in a further widening of the market for player sales. Perhaps most significant was the renewed involvement of two officials instrumental in the early days of major league integration, Bill Veeck and Branch Rickey, both of whom assumed new positions in 1951. As noted, Veeck obtained control of the St. Louis Browns and soon began signing blacks for all levels of his organization. While the Browns' farm system acquired several black players from the outlaw Man-Dak League, the NAL also profited through the sales of Jehosie Heard and Curley Williams from the New Orleans Eagles and James Douglas and James Sheehan from the Chicago American Giants. Meanwhile, hiring Rickey, who left the Dodgers after the 1950 season, altered the Pittsburgh Pirates' previous policy on blacks. After failing to sign a single black player in the previous five years, the Pirates organization featured twelve by May 1952, including seven acquired from the New Orleans Eagles.

Player sales to the Pirates, Browns, and other clubs during 1951 not only provided desperately needed revenue but revealed to doubters that the NAL still had players worthy of consideration by Organized Baseball. Despite heavy competition from domestic and foreign teams, black franchises had still managed to retain or recruit talented athletes, albeit a smaller number than before, and, as Tom Baird admitted in 1951, "they all want to get into organized baseball." Yet as NAL salaries dropped and Organized Baseball interest continued to increase in the early 1950s, every key player sold became increasingly difficult to replace, and the sales that had helped to sustain the league post-integration became less common. NAL teams would be largely unable to take full advantage in Organized Baseball's growing willingness to integrate, which instead worsened the industry's current plight.[16]

◆ ◆ ◆

By 1952, the struggle for continued integration of major league baseball and the exploits of current black stars occupied the bulk of the attention of African American fans. In contrast, only the most faithful devotees of black baseball viewed the NAL as anything more than irrelevant or as an unpleasant reminder of a segregated past. Nevertheless, J. B. Martin expressed confidence that the NAL would "make a comeback in 1952," although the league's prospects, if anything, appeared even more doubtful following the departure of two more franchises. After unsuccessful trials in Houston, Nashville, and New Orleans, the Eagles finally collapsed, yet managed to sell seven players to Branch Rickey's Pittsburgh Pirates before disbanding. The Baltimore Elite Giants also discontinued operation, although owner William Bridgeforth remained in the league after purchasing controlling interest of the Birmingham Black Barons from Tom Hayes and transferring several Elites to his new franchise.

In a span of only four years, half the teams of a once viable industry had failed. From a peak of two leagues and twelve teams blanketing the mid-Atlantic, south, and midwest, black professional baseball now consisted of a motley array of six widely scattered franchises, two of which (Indianapolis and Philadelphia) played almost all their games on the road (although the Clowns began to schedule "home" games in Buffalo in 1951). While continuing to follow a schedule, the NAL increasingly functioned less as a traditional league where clubs visited each other's home parks, and more as a traveling exhibition moving from town to town hoping for a decent payday. During 1952, for example, four of the six league franchises occasionally barnstormed together, staging doubleheaders with appearances by Jesse Owens at once profitable venues such as Yankee Stadium and Griffith Stadium. Yet in New York, Washington, and other former league cities, black baseball could rely only on its novelty and relative rarity to attract fans, as the remaining teams neither offered community representation nor reflected the best available talent.

A July 26 promotion at Yankee Stadium illustrated the league's status. Although about 3,500 fans attended the doubleheader featuring the Stars, Clowns, Monarchs, and American Giants, Joe Bostic noted the inescapable reality that the "quality of play has definitely deteriorated. . . . The biggest of all the appeals of jimcrow ball promotions was the fact that you saw some rattling good ball players. You could see baseball the equivalent of that you'd see in most leagues. The customers, who knew baseball and demanded high quality performance got it. . . . That quality of play generally isn't there as of now." Moreover, Bostic suggested that while the Clowns' comedy might play well in more rural areas, their "worn out routines hardly met the approval of the majority of the New York audience." The future of the industry appeared hopeless, prompting Bostic's subsequent assertion that "Jim-crow baseball is dead in every detail save the burial."[17]

Despite black baseball's apparent inexorable decline from institution to curiosity, the NAL somehow managed to retain a handful of capable players whose talents continued to intrigue major league scouts during 1952. The New York Giants acquired several men, including twenty-one-year-old pitcher Marshall Bridges of the Memphis Red Sox, who eventually spent seven seasons in the major leagues between 1959 and 1965. As usual, the Kansas City Monarchs parted with several players, selling veterans Eddie Locke for $3,000 and Jesse Williams for $3,500 to Vancouver of the class A Western International League. Meanwhile, no fewer than nine Indianapolis Clowns reportedly earned invitations to minor and major league spring training camps, although only a few received contract offers.

The Clowns would enjoy greater success marketing an eighteen-year-old rookie infielder, Henry Aaron of Mobile, Alabama, who had attracted the attention of team officials while appearing with a local semipro club in 1951. The youngster quickly made his presence felt in the NAL, slamming two homers against the Philadelphia Stars on May 18 and continuing to hit at a torrid pace in the early months of the season. By mid-June, major league scouts had began to pursue Aaron, by then leading the NAL in several offensive categories, including hits, batting average, and home runs. The Boston Braves, an organization that had aggressively signed black players in recent years, eventually purchased Aaron for $10,000 and then optioned him to Eau Claire of the class C Northern League. Hardly fazed by minor league competition, Aaron batted .336 in 87 games in 1952 and a league-leading .362 a year later after promotion to Jacksonville of the Sally League. An illustrious twenty-three-year major league career followed, highlighted by a record-setting 755 home runs and subsequent election to the Baseball Hall of Fame in 1982.[18]

The sale of Aaron provided the NAL with a faint glimmer of hope, demonstrating that black baseball was still capable of unearthing talent not yet discovered by major league scouts. Yet for many African Americans, the league's ability to develop an occasional player hardly justified the continued existence of a separate and heavily flawed institution in the face of the increasing number of opportunities for blacks in Organized

Baseball. Nevertheless, J. B. Martin argued that because "jim crow has not left baseball alone yet, the Negro American League still is a necessity," although he claimed to be "looking forward to the day when there is no need for a colored league." Meanwhile, the invariably optimistic Martin cited several encouraging developments in 1952 that seemed to suggest that "our old fans are now going to start coming back to the Negro league." Despite competition from the newly integrated Kansas City Blues, the Monarchs reportedly turned a profit, as did the Clowns, who drew 20,618 fans for a Briggs Stadium promotion on August 10. Martin also pointed to a successful postseason southern barnstorming tour featuring Roy Campanella's All-Stars and a team of NAL players, prompting his premature assumption that "the tide is starting to turn. Negroes in the majors are common, so to speak. They've been around long enough now and played good enough to satisfy every one's curiosity."[19]

The experience of the Philadelphia Stars during 1952 provided a more accurate barometer of the industry's current status. Now the last remnant of the NNL, the team functioned much the same as in recent years, emphasizing a cost-conscious player development approach and scheduling few home games. On July 28, the Stars made their only home appearance of the season, participating in a four-team doubleheader at Shibe Park before 4,710 fans. After defeating the Clowns by a 4-3 score, the club left for a date in Washington the following day and would never again return to Philadelphia.

The marginal profitability of Philadelphia and other northern cities again forced the Stars to turn to less traditional venues. Now traveling in two station wagons, they journeyed thousands of miles for games ranging as far north as Montreal and as far south as Houston during 1952. The bulk of the schedule, however, was played below the Mason-Dixon line, where continued segregation offered black teams a better opportunity to profit or at least break even. Yet the still rigid social mores of the south often imposed considerable hardships on players, particularly those who had largely avoided the region's harsh racial environment in the past. Philadelphia-born Wilmer Harris, for example, later recalled an incident in a bus terminal in Meridian, Mississippi, prompted by the purchase of a pack of cigarettes from a vending machine. Asked by a young white woman whether he had put a quarter in the machine, Harris murmured "uh huh," only to discover that his response was unacceptable. The offended woman promptly complained to a white man that "I got a fella here who don't know how to talk to ladies." Alabama native Willie Gaines defused the potentially explosive situation, explaining that Harris was from the North and "it was just a slip." While satisfied by the explanation, the aggrieved southerner advised Gaines to "take him outside so he can learn how to talk to white people."

The unfortunate episode failed to affect the pitching of Harris, who remained the mainstay of the Stars' staff and earned a spring training invitation from the Boston Braves' Eastern League affiliate in Hartford in 1952. In his eagerness to make a positive impression, Harris developed arm problems, and the Braves returned him to the Stars, depriving the team of critical income necessary to defray the cost of operating the franchise. Yet even the sale of Harris would have been inadequate to arrest the financial decline of Philadelphia and other clubs. An occasional $5,000 or $10,000 transaction was simply not enough to offset several seasons of deficits, and team owners found it increasingly difficult to justify the operation of a consistently unprofitable enterprise.

A four-day stretch in Texas during June 1952 reflected the Stars' marginal status, as only 1,403 fans witnessed four promotions against the Monarchs in Galveston, Austin, Fort Worth, and Dallas. Recognizing the urgency of the current situation, team owners Eddie Gottlieb and Hilda Bolden met in August to discuss the future of the Stars, and the team's existence beyond the current season appeared increasingly remote. Yet the impending collapse of the Stars concerned few black Philadelphians, who were largely unaware of the team or its players and remained far more committed to the integration of the city's two major league clubs, both of which continued to be reluctant to sign black players.[20]

Viewed from a modern perspective, the rigid commitment to a "lily-white" racial policy by the Athletics, Phillies, and several other organizations in the early 1950s is difficult to comprehend. The introduction of black players had clearly exerted a tremendous impact on the pennant races in both leagues, particularly the National League, where blacks were more prevalent. Between 1947 and 1956, for example, the integrated Dodgers and Giants won eight of ten National League championships. Meanwhile, former Negro League players won the National League's Most Valuable Player award nine times between 1949 and 1959. As white sportswriter Harold Rosenthal observed in 1953, blacks were now the balance of power and functioned "as a talent factor which could bring a leveling off in the won-and-loss departments in both leagues."[21]

While significant, racial attitudes are insufficient to fully explain the opposition to integration. Economic concerns also came into play, particularly the long-feared impact on white players and patronage. The integrated Dodgers, for example, experienced increasing difficulties signing young white southerners fearful of playing alongside a black player. Moreover, some Organized Baseball officials questioned whether integration and the concurrent increase in regular black attendance was ultimately a liability that drove away more fans than it created, a view expressed by White Sox general manager Frank Lane in 1950. The fear was hardly atypical in Organized Baseball, exemplified by the Detroit Tigers' reported refusal in the early 1960s to sell their more expensive seats to black fans and the continued wariness of other major league franchises of increased black patronage.

Even franchises fully committed to integration betrayed a concern with maintaining the "proper" racial balance on the playing field and in the stands. After featuring three blacks during the 1949 season, the Brooklyn Dodgers began to worry whether the team had reached a "saturation point," and ultimately sold minor league sensation Sam Jethroe rather than contend with the prospect of four in 1950. Similarly, the Boston Braves' farm director Harry Jenkins declined to purchase Jim LaMarque of the Kansas City Monarchs in 1951, explaining that the team already had three black players at its Milwaukee affiliate, "and if we take another, I am fearful that the club would get top-heavy." For most major and upper-level minor league teams in the early 1950s, three to four black players appeared to be the maximum number allowable without potentially alienating whites. The informal quota revealed that full integration and equal opportunity was far from a reality, and, as Larry Doby later observed, black players had to be "twice as good" to earn roster spots.[22]

Despite limitations, the typical black athlete found Organized Baseball a far more attractive environment than the NAL by 1953. Although J. B. Martin continued to predict recovery, the league appeared near collapse, as the fate of at least two of the six remaining franchises remained uncertain. After purchasing the Philadelphia Warriors in 1952, Eddie Gottlieb was now far more concerned with improving the shaky financial status of his struggling basketball team rather than sinking money into a hopeless cause. Similarly, Abe Saperstein's heavy commitment to basketball as owner of the Globetrotters and stockholder in the Warriors appeared likely to affect the future of the Chicago American Giants, a team devastated by major league competition.

Gottlieb's appearance at an NAL meeting in February suggested Philadelphia would again function in 1953, but a March 14 front-page story in the *Philadelphia Tribune* announced the team's withdrawal from league play. Citing the Stars' shaky financial status, Gottlieb explained that "it's been a matter of just breaking even or going in a hole every season for the past few years . . . and even though I think Negro baseball is going to become more popular, it's too big a gamble." Following a reported public outcry, Gottlieb briefly reconsidered his decision and expressed a willingness to sell the franchise for $10,000, probably reflective of the value of the team's bus and equipment, yet still seemingly high for a team whose gates had totaled as little as $50 to $200 per game in recent years. Not surprisingly, neither Hilda Bolden nor any other individual stepped forward to rescue the Stars, and the team then disbanded. Gottlieb again emphasized the unfavorable conditions within the industry, noting that "if it were humanly possible to just meet expenses I'd run the club again. . . . This is supposed to be one of the Negro American League's best years coming up, but it can't be for us when you have to play a club on the road to make ends meet." Gottlieb, however, offered some future hope, claiming that "this does not mean we won't run next year or the year after. Everything depends on the outlook."[23]

The outlook appeared even more dismal after the Chicago American Giants, as anticipated, also folded in early 1953. With the departure of Chicago and Philadelphia, two of the major centers for black baseball for decades, the NAL was now left with four franchises: Indianapolis, Kansas City, Birmingham, and Memphis. While it appeared questionable how an organization of only four teams could properly function as a "league," J. B. Martin remained unfazed, asserting that the NAL was "very much alive." Moreover, Martin continued to emphasize the league's relevance, insisting that "until I can feel that race does not matter in organized baseball, I shall always consider the NAL a necessity."

Martin and other officials, however, clearly realized that the NAL now had only the slightest appeal to African American fans and players. Hoping to stimulate attendance in 1953, the league resorted to introducing its first female player, a gimmick that ultimately proved successful. In February, the Indianapolis Clowns announced the signing of Toni Stone, a soon-to-be twenty-two-year-old infielder who had appeared in a similar role with lower-level black teams in recent years. While Clowns owner Syd Pollock claimed that "this is no publicity stunt," Stone's reported $12,000 contract suggested that she was signed to boost attendance, rather than as a sudden commitment to gender equality. Ironically, the Harrisburg Senators of the financially precarious Inter-State League had attempted a similar strategy in June 1952, only to be blocked by National Association of Professional Leagues (NAPBL) president George Trautman.

The heavily publicized Stone soon proved to a worthy investment, as the Clowns began drawing crowds not seen since the late 1940s. In Kansas City, 17,205 fans (inflated to 18,205 in press accounts) turned out for the Monarchs' opener featuring the Clowns, while Stone's late May appearance in Birmingham drew the largest local crowd for an NAL game since 1949. Meanwhile, non-league venues largely discarded as unprofitable suddenly swelled with fans eager to see the female phenomenon. A Clowns/Monarchs promotion at Briggs Stadium attracted a surprising crowd of 20,399 on June 21, while dates at Comiskey Park on July 4

(8,792 fans) and Forbes Field on August 4 (9,317) also drew well. Delighted by the surge of interest, Pollock insisted that the attendance increase proved "what I have said all along—give the fans something they want to see and they'll come out." Not surprisingly, the Clowns soon offered tryouts to other women.[24]

Despite the clear impact on the box office, the presence of Stone and other women remained controversial. While a capable athlete, Stone lacked the ability to truly compete at a professional level and too often functioned as a novelty to amuse the fans rather than as an integral member of the Clowns. As one teammate observed, "she plays pretty good for a girl. But if you're talking about really playing ball, she ain't got it." Stone typically appeared in the first two or three innings of a game, enough to satiate the curiosity of fans eager to witness her prowess with the glove and bat. Opposing pitchers, however, cooperated by throwing her only fastballs, and to Clowns manager Buster Haywood, Stone's appearances were "mostly a show."

Reflecting prevalent masculine attitudes of the era, several observers felt that women, regardless of their appeal, did not belong in professional baseball. Veteran sportswriter Wendell Smith, for example, lamented that "Negro baseball has collapsed to the extent it must tie itself to a woman's apron strings in order to survive." While more respectful of Stone's talents, Doc Young felt that "girls should be run out of men's baseball on a softly-padded rail both for their own good and for the good of the game." Luix Virgil Overbea, however, accepted the presence of women but objected to their obvious exploitation as gate attractions, explaining, "I don't want to see women in baseball togs on the basis of curiosity. I do want to see them as excellent athletes."[25]

Despite misgivings, the Stone experiment accomplished its intended purpose, providing desperately needed financial stability to the NAL in 1953. Moreover, all four clubs succeeded in selling at least one player to Organized Baseball, including the Monarchs, who sent Ernie Banks, black baseball's last great product, directly to the Chicago Cubs, where he became the team's first black player. Yet a novelty-driven revival offered little more than a temporary solution to the industry's woes and hardly contributed to the establishment of a permanent fan base. As in recent years, the NAL remained little more than a barnstorming unit, a league in name only, dominated by the Clowns and Monarchs, who, according to Alex Pompez, left the "crumbs of the bookings" to Memphis and Birmingham. Reflecting the limited value of the NAL, the Clowns and Monarchs both reportedly considered withdrawing, yet ultimately remained in the organization for another season.

The improved attendance, however, convinced several officials that the industry might be on its way to recovery. Reflecting the more confident attitude, the NAL expanded to six franchises in 1954, adding the Louisville Clippers and the Detroit Stars, owned by Grand Rapids promoter Ted Rasberry. But the league soon discovered that the previous season had simply been an aberration, largely fueled by the short-lived appeal of female players. Despite attempts to further exploit the phenomenon through appearances of Connie Morgan and Mamie Johnson with the Clowns and Toni Stone (now with the Monarchs), gate receipts returned to their discouragingly low level of the early 1950s. The two new franchises were hit especially hard, as Rasberry reportedly lost $12,000 by mid-July while Louisville was forced to withdraw from the league after only a single season of play. Meanwhile, the usual inadequate publicity added to the NAL's woes; as one observer complained, the league was "virtually a secret organization except for the Kansas City Monarchs and Indianapolis Clowns." An Associated Negro Press reporter similarly cited the "startling factor" that there were "no big names left in the NAL—there are very few familiar names in the entire circuit."[26]

A July interview with veteran outfielder Henry Kimbro of the Birmingham Black Barons provided an apt description of the current operating difficulties in black baseball. Kimbro related to Sam Lacy that the Barons now drew crowds averaging fewer than 1,000 fans, although attendance improved on the weekends. Despite the modest patronage, player salaries remained surprisingly competitive, reportedly averaging $375 per month, although the Barons also benefited through an informal agreement with the New York Giants, who had placed two prospects, Ralph Crosby and Kelly Searcy, on the team's roster and paid their salaries. The profit margin, however, was negligible, and Kimbro disclosed that team owner William Bridgeforth "isn't making any money. If he's able to break even, he's lucky, everything considered." Moreover, Kimbro cited the increasingly rigorous travel, detailing the Barons' recent bus trip from Huntsville, Alabama, to Michigan for a series of games, culminating in a grueling journey from Saginaw on a Thursday night in time for a promotion in Birmingham on Saturday.[27]

The experience of the Barons and other clubs in 1954 revealed that league baseball was no longer viable. Even the once profitable Monarchs began to suffer, operating at a deficit of over $10,000. Recognizing the NAL's bleak future, Syd Pollock announced in January 1955 that the Clowns would withdraw and reenter the world of independent baseball. As Pollock explained, the absence of league commitments would allow the Clowns to cover more territory and make shorter jumps. Perhaps more important, the team (now part-owned by white baseball comedian Ed Hamman) would now be able to emphasize its comedy without restraint, following the lead of Abe Saperstein's still enormously popular Globetrotters. Like Saperstein, Pollock implicitly recognized that in an era of slow but noticeable gains in integration, all-black teams were unappealing and could only hope to survive by catering to white fans through exaggerated displays of showmanship. Comedy rather than competition increasingly became the focal point, leading some observers to suspect that the outcomes of Clowns' games were no longer in doubt. While the Clowns' caliber and integrity of play declined, the team continued to operate as a novelty act as late as 1984, featuring a variety of gimmicks including midgets, comedy routines, and players clad in grass skirts.[28]

The loss of the Clowns, the league's most prosperous franchise in recent years, dealt yet another punishing blow to the NAL. Yet the league bravely persevered in 1955 with four clubs: Kansas City, Detroit, Memphis, and Birmingham. Largely ignored by black fans and press, league teams struggled through another disappointing campaign, exemplified by the continued deterioration of the once enthusiastically patronized East-West game. While J. B. Martin convinced officials to keep the promotion in Chicago, the league was forced to resort to several novelties to beef up attendance, including an appearance by the ageless Satchel Paige, recently signed by the Monarchs for $250 per game or 10 percent of the gross. The league also attempted to capitalize on the current Davy Crockett craze by offering free admission to 1,000 youngsters under fourteen who arrived at the game dressed as the famous frontiersman. The game ultimately drew 11,257 fans, reflecting the drawing power of Paige and nostalgia for the event's storied past rather than appreciable interest in any of the league's largely faceless young performers.[29]

Perhaps more damaging to the stability of the NAL was the sudden shift in the fortunes of the league's most valuable property, the Kansas City Monarchs. Enviable civic backing and strong management had enabled the Monarchs to avoid many of the difficulties experienced by other established franchises, but the club faced a new challenge in 1955: the presence of local major league competition following the relocation of the Philadelphia Athletics to Kansas City. As in other cities, integrated major league baseball games soon siphoned away black fans. Following the Monarchs' opening day on May 15, Tom Baird noted the As had "cut our . . . crowd over 2/3" and predicted that the presence of the majors had "killed all baseball in this territory." Equally crippling was an abrupt increase in rental fees and other expenses following the sale of Blues Stadium to the city. Several observers viewed the move as part of a deliberate strategy by the Athletics and the city to eliminate the Monarchs as local competition. Syd Pollock of the Clowns, for example, doubted that the Monarchs could profitably stage games in Kansas City, relating to Baird that "when they

Figure 31. Tom Baird receiving National Baseball Congress Award from
J. B. Martin. Despite marginal interest and profits in the 1950s, Baird was
unable to convince Martin of the futility of continuing the NAL. Courtesy
Thomas Baird Collection, Kansas Collection, University of Kansas
Library.

charge you 10 per cent office overhead, a ground crew on Saturday which
is not needed . . . the whole thing to me is ridiculous and they're finding a
simple way of keeping you out." After only a few local promotions at the
newly rebuilt stadium, Baird largely abandoned the city, citing exorbitant
park costs and charges "for everything but the flag pole."

Suffering through the worst season in the Monarchs' long history, Baird
recognized that black baseball had no future, yet found it difficult to convince the seemingly unflappable J. B. Martin. While initially proposing
that the four league teams suspend regular salaries in the second half of the
season, Baird eventually became convinced more drastic measures were
necessary, contending that "we are chumps if we don't quit July 31st. as a

league." Perhaps motivated by political concerns in Chicago, Martin remained resistant, admitting that "if we fold it is going to be real embarrassing to me." Although the NAL managed to complete the season, Baird refused to be coaxed by Martin into operating the Monarchs for another year. As Baird explained, "the people have shown they are not interested in our kind of baseball . . . why try to force something on people who have shown they don't care for it." Moreover, Baird, like others, alluded to the chronic problem affecting non-major league baseball in the 1950s—"same old story, radio of big leagues, it seems to me they have made—EVERYBODY—big league minded." By early 1956, Baird had sold the bulk of his roster to various major and minor league organizations and the franchise itself for $3,500 to Ted Rasberry, who retained the Monarchs name but largely shifted operations to Grand Rapids except for an occasional date in Kansas City.

Despite the loss of the Clowns and the death of Kansas City as a profitable venue, the NAL remained intact throughout the decade. The league continued to feature a core of four clubs (Kansas City, Birmingham, Memphis, and Detroit), occasionally augmented by newly organized southern-based teams in Mobile, New Orleans, and Raleigh. While the herculean efforts of Rasberry, the Martin brothers, and other promoters somehow kept the NAL afloat despite losses exceeding $10,000 per club each season, black professional baseball bore little resemblance to the institution of prior decades. An occasional player sale or decent crowd failed to obscure the long apparent reality that the league lacked both the talent and the fan base to survive integrated competition. Sonny Webb, who spent a brief period with the NAL in the late 1950s, aptly summarized the final days of the organization, observing that "it really wasn't a league. They were trying to hang on . . . and guys would be with this club here this weekend, maybe with another later. . . . Basically, what they were trying to do was sell some ballplayers to major league franchises. From what I saw, there wasn't a whole lot of talent there."

By 1959, even the eternally optimistic J. B. Martin admitted that "the attendance has just been terrible. I've been doing everything I can to keep them playing but it looks hopeless." Meanwhile, last-ditch attempts to secure a subsidy from major league baseball elicited only a lukewarm response and ultimately failed to materialize. In 1963, the NAL finally collapsed, a development that concerned few African American fans, many of whom were unaware of the league's continued existence.[30]

◆ ◆ ◆

Ultimately, the extinction of black professional baseball affected relatively few fans, whose primary concern since the early 1950s remained the continued integration of the major leagues. Despite the presence of blacks on several rosters, the task of "full" integration of the major leagues was nowhere near completion. As Wendell Smith observed, "competent and ethical sports writers . . . will tell you that baseball is still sick, still suffering inwards from an acute case of Negrophobia," and a number of resistant franchises braced for the onset of new pressure campaigns.

As late as 1952, only 6 of the 16 major league teams featured a black player on their roster. A *Sport* magazine editorial cited the continuing widespread discrimination, noting that "there are plenty of teams . . . that don't show any inclination to go along with the new order" and "even more individuals . . . who make it plain that they don't like to make room for the Negro." Franchise integration remained largely dependent on the attitudes of individual owners, some of whom appeared determined to resist the move as long as possible. Industrialist Walter Briggs, for example, made no attempt to integrate the Detroit Tigers, despite a past willingness to employ blacks at his plant. General manager Billy Evans candidly explained the team's viewpoint, informing a black reporter in 1951 that "the question of hiring Negro players has never bothered us. . . . The Tigers got along many years without Negro players." The death of Briggs in January 1952 and his succession by his son, Walter, Jr. facilitated modest changes in the organization, as the club finally began to scout blacks and in August 1953, became the last team to integrate its minor league system with the signing of Claude Agee (see Table 11.3). Nevertheless, not until 1958 would the Tigers promote a black player to the majors and only after threats of local boycotts.[31]

Tom Yawkey's Boston Red Sox maintained a similarly reactionary attitude toward black players during the 1950s. After the token signing and subsequent release of Piper Davis in 1950, the team remained exclusively white at the major and upper minor league level for several years despite occasional rumors of interest in black players. Although Boston's relatively small black population allowed the Red Sox to escape the relentless public pressure present in other urban centers, the organization's racial composition prompted scattered criticism from local white writers. General manager Joe Cronin offered the familiar alibi that the team had yet to find the "right" player, asserting in 1953 that "when we sign a Negro we want him to have a chance to make the Red Sox—not spend all his time in the minors. We want a potential big leaguer." Yet Cronin, like other proponents of this view, failed to acknowledge that white prospects were typically held to far less exacting standards, receiving minor league contract offers despite only marginal chances to reach the majors. Although the club eventually reintegrated its farm system with the acquisitions of pitcher Earl Wilson and infielder Pumpsie Green, the Red Sox largely con-

Table 11.3. Signing of Black Players by Organization

Team	Month of first publicized signing
Brooklyn Dodgers	October 1945
Cleveland Indians	July 1947
St. Louis Browns	July 1947
Boston Braves	December 1948–January 1949
New York Giants	January 1949
New York Yankees	February 1949
Chicago Cubs	March 1949
Boston Red Sox	August 1949
Chicago White Sox	July 1950
Philadelphia Athletics	March 1951
Pittsburgh Pirates	March 1951[1]
Washington Senators	November 1951
Cincinnati Reds	February 1952
Philadelphia Phillies	September 1952
St. Louis Cardinals	May 1953
Detroit Tigers	August 1953

[1]Date represents first attempts to sign blacks. Actual date of minor league integration is unknown, although Roy Welmaker, who joined the Hollywood Stars in May 1951, may be the first black player in the Pirates farm system.
Sources: *PINQ*, October 24, 1945; September 18, 1952; *PI*, July 12, 1947; December 11, 1948; February 5, 1949; May 12, 1951; *NYAN*, July 26, 1947; *PT*, February 1, 5, 1949; August 5, 1950; March 13, April 14, 1951; August 29, 1953; *NYT*, January 29, 1949; *BAA*, March 5, 1949; February 23, 1952; *KCC*, April 1, 1949; *CD*, August 27, 1949; *SN*, March 7, May 16, November 28, 1951; memo of conversation between Branch Rickey and Neal of Clowns, March 20, 1951, BRP, box 22, correspondence "N" miscellaneous, 1950–51; *Negro History Bulletin* (February 1955).

tinued to disregard black players until the integration of the Tigers in June 1958 left the team as the sole holdout. Facing increasing scrutiny, the organization publicized the July signing of Larry Plenty and his subsequent appearance in a Red Sox uniform during a workout. Within a year, Boston became the sixteenth and final franchise to integrate at the major league level after the debut of Green (see Table 11.4).[32]

Bob Carpenter's Philadelphia Phillies were equally slow to initiate integration. Despite the publicized signing of Ted Washington of the NAL's Philadelphia Stars in 1952, the organization subsequently did little to improve its negative reputation among black fans and players. Reflecting the team's still reactionary attitudes, scout Jocko Collins was overheard in August 1953 complaining of "too much dark meat," a probable allusion to the Phillies' inability to overtake the integrated Dodgers and Braves.

Table 11.4. Major League Baseball Integration

Team	Month of major league integration
Brooklyn Dodgers	April 1947
Cleveland Indians	July 1947
St. Louis Browns	July 1947
New York Giants	July 1949
Boston Braves	April 1950
Chicago White Sox	May 1951
Philadelphia Athletics	September 1953
Chicago Cubs	September 1953
Pittsburgh Pirates	April 1954
St. Louis Cardinals	April 1954
Cincinnati Reds	April 1954
Washington Senators	September 1954
New York Yankees	April 1955
Philadelphia Phillies	April 1957
Detroit Tigers	June 1958
Boston Red Sox	July 1959

Source: *SN*, August 5, 1959; *PI*, May 5, 1951; "Place in the Sun," *Time*, May 14, 1951, 91–93.

Meanwhile, a team employee claimed that coach Benny Bengough admitted that "we don't want any of them on the team," a view shared by the club's farm director, according to Phillies treasurer George Harrison. Facing increasing pressure from the NAACP and other community agencies as the last National League holdout, the franchise finally yielded in 1957 with the debuts of infielder John Kennedy, a former NAL player, and shortstop Humberto "Chico" Fernandez, a light-skinned Cuban. Within two years, the organization featured 27 black players on minor and major league rosters.[33]

While the prolonged inflexible stance of the Phillies, Red Sox, and Tigers reflected the most extreme resistance to major league integration during the 1950s, several other franchises, including the Cubs, Pirates, Senators, and Athletics, had succumbed by late 1954. Meanwhile, even diehard opponents wary of alienating Southern patrons finally began to relax their policies. In Cincinnati, condemned earlier by Sam Lacy as "truly an antisocial town" and known for local fans' unfavorable treatment of black players, the Reds initiated tentative steps toward integration after front office changes in 1951. Several blacks joined the team's farm system in early 1952, followed by the major league debut of Nino Escalera of Puerto Rico two years later. A more dramatic transformation occurred in the St.

Louis Cardinals, long viewed as a bastion of segregation and openly hostile to blacks. Following the conviction of owner Fred Saigh for income tax evasion in January 1953, the Anheuser-Busch brewery acquired the franchise, resulting in an appreciable shift in racial attitudes. By the end of the 1954 season, the once lily-white Cardinals not only had introduced three different black players to the majors but featured more than two dozen in their organization.[34]

While delighting in the collapse of the color line throughout major league baseball in the early 1950s, black fans impatiently awaited the integration of the New York Yankees, the most successful and profitable franchise in professional sports. After the initial plunge into the black player market in early 1949, the Yankees had pursued a conservative path, signing an occasional prospect for their farm teams to deflect potential criticism, but appearing less than eager to integrate at the major league level. Basking in the glow of a string of five consecutive world championships between 1949 and 1953, team officials apparently viewed black players as unable to fit the Yankee mold and as a threat to violate, rather than enhance, the franchise's glorious tradition. Moreover, the Yankees seemingly had little economic incentive to integrate, as the club not only was immensely popular on the road and at home but had long drawn a devoted group of fans from Harlem.

The presence of two integrated teams in New York, however, focused increasing attention to the absence of blacks on the city's third and most prosperous major league affiliate. While some observers continued to blame general manager George Weiss and owners Del Webb and Dan Topping for the team's continued color line, several black sportswriters intimated that the attitudes of several veteran Yankees, including Joe DiMaggio, were the more likely cause. Despite receiving encouragement to renounce the rumor, DiMaggio remained silent, although his retirement after the 1951 season ultimately had little noticeable effect on Yankee policies.[35]

The Yankees' reputation among blacks continued to deteriorate during 1952, a year marked by a number of incidents embarrassing to the proud organization. The team was forced to contend with an early season picketing campaign at Yankee Stadium backed by the Bronx County American Labor Party. An additional controversy emerged following a statement by Yankee traveling secretary and former major leaguer Bill McCorry, who reportedly asserted that "I got no use for any of them [black players]. I wouldn't want any of them on a club I was with. I wouldn't arrange a berth on the train for any of them."

By late 1952, most blacks viewed the Yankee organization as racist, a belief crystallized in a comment by Jackie Robinson during his November

30 appearance on the NBC program *Youth Wants to Know*. Questioned whether he believed the Yankees to be prejudiced, Robinson responded affirmatively, although noted that "it seems to be on the part of the club executives rather than the team." The unscripted remark soon evolved into a national news story, eliciting furious denials by the Yankees and a gentle rebuke from Wendell Smith, who suggested that "everyone should be very careful in these days and times about making such charges." Smith, for example, noted that the delayed promotion of Vic Power was hardly atypical, as the Yankees had been equally slow to elevate promising white players. Robinson, however, refused to vacillate, explaining that "I have to live honestly with myself. . . . There are thousands upon thousands of people in Harlem who feel the same way."

Hoping to offset the recent torrent of negative publicity, the Yankees announced in February 1953 that Dizzy Dismukes, a former Negro League pitcher and administrator most recently employed by the Monarchs, had joined their scouting corps. While welcomed, the addition of Dismukes hardly relieved the mounting pressure on the Yankees, a high-profile organization increasingly forced to rationalize its position despite being only one of a number of major league teams without black players. Interviewed by New York sportswriter Milton Gross, George Weiss disclosed that the Yankees had signed 21 blacks since 1948 and currently had 10 in their organization. According to Weiss, the team would "hire Negro players when we find the ones who can make our team," yet would not yield to "special pressure" or profit motives. Despite Weiss's seemingly noble attitudes, Gross noted that doubters wondered how an organization "so successful in its scouting of white players" could have failed to uncover black talent capable of reaching the major leagues.

The proud, image-conscious Yankees would ultimately delay integration for another two years, finally promoting former Monarch Elston Howard in 1955, nearly a full decade after the signing of Jackie Robinson.[36]

♦ ♦ ♦

By 1961, the integration of major league baseball was largely complete, reflected by a June article in *Ebony* reporting that 77 of the 450 current major league players were black. Meanwhile, what remained of black professional baseball continued its descent into permanent irrelevance as a social and economic institution. The tradeoff was readily accepted by most black communities, as seen in Chicago. In an updated profile of "Bronzeville" sixteen years after the 1945 publication of *Black Metropolis*, St. Clair Drake and Horace Cayton observed that "the Negro masses . . . applaud the new Race heroes on the White Sox and Cubs teams without giving a thought to the effect of this 'draining away of talent' from the Negro baseball leagues." Yet the authors also cited the concurrent existence of "uneasiness . . . over certain dilemmas presented by the Era of Integration. . . . Are there values and cultural products which have developed among Negroes that will be lost if full integration ever becomes a reality?"[37]

While "full integration" remained remote, the civil rights strides of the 1940s through the 1960s clearly took an inevitable toll not only on black baseball but on other once valued separate organizations. Like the NAL and NNL, black institutions that had fulfilled a vital role during segregation found themselves functioning in a vastly transformed environment, often with predictable results. Improved access to white hospitals resulted in the decline and eventual disappearance of black facilities including Mercy-Douglass in Philadelphia, which finally closed its doors in 1973. By 1993, only eight black hospitals remained, a far cry from the 124 operating in 1944. In addition, competition from better financed and organized white enterprises typically proved devastating to black businesses, including the hotel industry, which was unable to compete with the appeal of newly accessible white accommodations. Black banks and other financial institutions have experienced similar problems; approximately 45 exist today, less than half the number of four decades ago. Even black insurance companies, historically the strongest race business, encountered difficulties by the early 1960s, as white insurers not only began to pursue the African American market aggressively but hired a growing number of black agents.

The black baseball, hotel, and insurance industries were ultimately limited by the difficulty of catering exclusively to a minority population. None could attract white customers, and once the convenient market provided by segregation disappeared, survival became increasingly difficult. Not surprisingly, Parks Sausage and Motown Records, two of the more successful enterprises developed by African Americans after 1950, both prospered by marketing to a broad interracial customer base.[38]

Nevertheless, certain black institutions have remained viable in the post-integration era by continuing to offer unique services, experiences, and culture unavailable in the white world. Black churches, for example, remained largely impervious to integration, a situation explained by black social psychologist Kenneth Clark, who noted that "the Negro has managed to salvage some personal self-esteem from his church, and until he achieves such self-esteem elsewhere he will not give up this, his last and only sanctuary." Despite increasing competition from white schools for top black faculty and students, predominantly black colleges similarly continue to thrive, providing African Americans with the opportunity to obtain an education in a racially sensitive and supportive environment.

Meanwhile, a number of radio stations, television programs, and magazines cater to black audiences often overlooked by mainstream media outlets.

The once booming black newspapers, however, have also been victimized by integration, as increasing black coverage in daily newspapers resulted in a substantial drop in readership in several cities. The aggregate circulation of the *Courier*, *Afro*, and *Defender* chains, for example, declined from 661,000 during World War II to 288,000 by 1963. Moreover, black papers found it increasingly difficult to attract and retain talented black journalists who typically sought and found better paying positions with white periodicals.[39]

Despite the negative ramifications for some black institutions, most African Americans in the 1950s and early 1960s viewed the results of integration as overwhelmingly positive, particularly the improvement in social and economic opportunities. Yet a more critical view of integration emerged by the late 1960s, sparked by the growing influence of the Black Muslims and other separatist groups, which echoed the earlier call for a self-sustaining black economy. With some of the anticipated benefits of integration still unrealized by many African Americans, the question emerged whether the destruction of black institutions had ultimately proved counterproductive. Connie Johnson, a former Kansas City Monarch who also pitched in the major leagues, expressed a common ambivalence, noting that "integration helped in many ways, but in a way it hurt. . . . Things weren't ours anymore." Similarly, Philadelphia radio personality Georgie Woods later became increasingly disillusioned with integration's impact on black businesses, contending that "we had black hotels, we had our own restaurants, our own shopping centers, our own clothing stores—and we lost it all through integration."[40]

Such a nostalgic view distorts the actual reality of the separate economy, which typically consisted of marginal, inadequately financed enterprises often controlled by whites. Moreover, few if any black businesses were ever capable of providing the mass employment desperately needed in the urban centers. Integration, however, undoubtedly dealt a heavy blow to individual middle-class black entrepreneurs. As E. Franklin Frazier explained in 1947, "it is the Negro professional, the business man, and to a less extent, the white collar worker who profit from segregation" and "enjoy certain advantages because they do not have to compete with whites." Yet for most working-class blacks, desegregation provided expanded employment opportunities that far surpassed the limited potential of the separate economy. The destruction of the Negro Leagues, for example, ultimately improved the status of black athletes. At their peak in the mid-1940s, the NNL and NAL employed roughly 200 black players, a

figure more than equaled by Organized Baseball by the mid-1950s.⁴¹ In
addition, Organized Baseball provided better living conditions and the
chance for promotion to the majors, where salaries were far superior to
those in the Negro Leagues. Front office and managerial positions, however, were virtually unavailable for years and even today remain predominantly occupied by whites, supporting historian Rob Ruck's contention
that with integration, "the black community gave up a good measure of
control over its own sporting life."

Although the economic benefits of integration appear well established,
the social impact on the black community is less easily determined. Regardless of their flaws, black baseball and other separate enterprises
helped build an irreplaceable sense of collective solidarity, identity and
self-esteem. Noted black power movement writer Amiri Baraka (LeRoi
Jones), for example, grew up a fan of the Newark Eagles and viewed black
baseball as "like a light somewhere . . . connected to laughter and self-
love." Former Philadelphia Stars pitcher Tom Johnson asserted that "the
black leagues played a major role at the social level for our people. They
provided the entertainment. They provided an activity, a wholesome activity." Although desegregation theoretically rendered black baseball and
other separate institutions superfluous, many African Americans still remain far from "integrated"; in fact, the geographical isolation and jobless-
ness of blacks in Philadelphia and other cities has remained disturbingly
high. Yet some of the moderating institutional supports that once allevi-
ated the plight of blacks have disappeared, leaving a void in the commu-
nity.⁴²

Notably, no adequate replacement has emerged to fully replace the once
prevalent professional black teams. Despite enabling individual black athletes to grow enormously wealthy, integrated Organized Baseball has never
approached the importance of the Negro Leagues in black communities.
During the 1960s, black interest in baseball began to wane, perhaps a
product of the stronger attachment of most fans to individual players
rather than to teams. A lack of recreational facilities in the inner cities
further dampened interest among blacks, many of whom turned to basketball, a game that required less equipment and playing space. Finally, the
ambivalence of Organized Baseball contributed to the disengagement of
black fans. While accepting black players, the industry had never fully
resigned itself to black patrons, and as late as 1991, several teams admitted fearing the impact of black fans on white attendance. Not surprisingly,
the percentage of black major league attendance by the late 1980s fell to
below 7 percent, and to as low as 3 percent in communities such as Chicago and Philadelphia that had once enthusiastically supported black
baseball.⁴³

Unfortunately, black America's disengagement from baseball has only worsened in recent years, reflected by a disturbing decline in the number of African Americans on major league rosters. As of July 2003, African Americans occupied only 10% of roster spots, compared to 27 percent in 1975. Only two current black major leaguers emerged from the once-flourishing black baseball hotbeds of New York, Chicago, and Philadelphia. With football and basketball both offering more opportunities for athletic scholarships and a quicker path to professional play, the trend appears unlikely to shift in the near future, and as Frank Robinson, the first black manager and the current field leader of the Montreal Expos, has observed, "baseball is now third, maybe fourth in the [inner-city] household."

Several organizations have attempted to stimulate black interest in baseball, particularly the Reviving Baseball in Inner Cities (RBI) program, established in 1989, which now operates in 170 cities. In another positive step, Major League Baseball recently announced plans to construct a $3 million youth academy in the Los Angeles area. Similar facilities are anticipated in other cities, explained by Commissioner Bud Selig, who noted that "it is our intention to bring baseball back to urban America." While the success of these ventures remains to be seen, escalating ticket prices appear likely to limit black attendance. Commenting on the lack of black fans at Veterans Stadium today, former Philadelphia Star Mahlon Duckett noted that "you take the kids to the ballpark now . . . by the time, you get done buying them hot dogs and so forth and so on, plus your ticket if you have a decent seat, you can come out spending just about $100 . . . and to a working person, especially a black working person, that's a lot of money. So that, I think has a lot to do with it too but things are a little better, I can tell you that."[44]

◆ ◆ ◆

In the relatively brief period between 1933 and 1952, black professional baseball had experienced a dizzying series of financial highs and lows. Nearly destroyed by the Depression, the industry struggled to remain afloat throughout most of the 1930s and appeared unlikely to advance in the future. The subsequent war-fueled economic transformation of the black community abruptly reversed the downward trend, facilitating unparalleled profits in the early 1940s. The revival, however, proved frustratingly brief, as the industry could not hope to maintain its prosperity in a postwar environment newly altered by integration and developments in the mass media. By the 1950s, black baseball offered little of value to African Americans, who instead thrilled in the achievements of black athletes in an interracial context that more closely reflected the integration ideology and aspirations of the era.

The somewhat erratic course of the enterprise raises the question whether black baseball might have been capable of exceeding its nominal degree of financial success. There is little doubt that black teams faced a number of fundamental obstacles difficult to transcend, including modest resources and the reliance on an economically fragile population with limited discretionary income. Moreover, black baseball, like other race businesses, could seldom count on wholehearted community support, as competition from other amusements, including the always omnipresent force of white Organized Baseball, predictably cut into patronage. Black teams also contended with the rise of alternative sources of racial pride such as Joe Louis, whose nationally publicized accomplishments often seemed to offer more than a flawed separate enterprise.

The industry, however, frequently undermined its own progress by failing to address critical deficiencies affecting the operation of the two leagues. Provided with a convenient customer base through segregation, league officials had little motivation to improve the publicity and operation of their clubs. Moreover, as seen throughout, the administration of black baseball remained remarkably weak, hampered by a clear lack of authority, poorly defined league policies, and uncooperative officials. Without the presence of an impartial leader to promote the best interests of the leagues, the industry was subject to the whims of owners always eager to strengthen their own position yet reluctant to accept desperately needed reforms that might affect their own status. Individualistic short-term goals predictably took precedence over careful collective planning, contributing to a constant vulnerability apparent to Dan Burley, who observed that "Negro baseball was so poorly organized and managed that it was an open target for any situation that might produce a threat."

Yet the problems of baseball also paralleled the inherent difficulties of other black businesses. Historian Charles Hardy, for example, has cited the often counterproductive "individualism, competitiveness and contentiousness" among black entrepreneurs. Such traits inevitably surfaced in an entertainment industry such as professional baseball which demands cooperation yet simultaneously fosters intense competition among its members. The general inability to achieve a balance between these two needs resulted in a less than optimal environment for growth and stability, aptly explained by Fay Young who cited the "jealousy which existed and favoritism which plainly showed its head" in black baseball.

The essential resilience of the industry in such a negative atmosphere, however, attests to its considerable value to African Americans. From its beginnings in the 1880s to its collapse eight decades later, black professional baseball contributed profoundly to black life. Despite numerous obstacles and flaws, the institution provided entertainment and fostered a sense of racial pride. Although black baseball ultimately disappeared, its accomplishments still resonate today. Along with other shadow institutions such as black hospitals, the industry facilitated eventual integration by providing invaluable experience and training otherwise elusive in a still highly segregated nation. Ultimately, the remarkable survival of professional black baseball provided an institutional basis for fostering the skills of black athletes and to a lesser extent, black entrepreneurs. Because of this institution-building in the black community, a pool of talented African American athletes developed who were able to take full advantage of the greater opportunities that became available with desegregation. As Tom Johnson later observed, "in the absence of the opportunity, the blacks created that opportunity, created . . . a baseball world for themselves, so they could demonstrate their abilities. And so many of them were ready when the doors were opened, so from that vantage point I felt that we were winners."[45]

Abbreviations

Newspapers/Magazines

BAA	Baltimore Afro-American
BC	Boston Chronicle
BW	Birmingham World
CCP	Cleveland Call and Post
CD	Chicago Defender
DT	Detroit Tribune
DW	Daily Worker
KCC	Kansas City Call
MC	Michigan Chronicle
NYA	New York Age
NYAN	New York Amsterdam News
NYHT	New York Herald Tribune
NYT	New York Times
PAA	Philadelphia Afro-American
PC	Pittsburgh Courier
PEB	Philadelphia Evening Bulletin
PI	Philadelphia Independent
PINQ	Philadelphia Inquirer
PR	Philadelphia Record
PT	Philadelphia Tribune
PV	People's Voice
SCD	Sports Collectors Digest
SEP	Saturday Evening Post
SN	Sporting News
WT	Washington Tribune

Manuscript Collections

ACP	Art Carter Papers, Moorland-Spingarn Research Center, Manuscript Division, Howard University, Washington, D.C.
AMP	Arthur Mann Papers, Library of Congress, Manuscript Division, Washington, D.C.
BHOFL	Baseball Hall of Fame Library, National Baseball Hall of Fame, Cooperstown, N.Y.

BRP   Branch Rickey Papers, Library of Congress, Manuscript Division, Washington, D.C.

BSIP   Black Sport in Pittsburgh Collection, University of Pittsburgh, Archives of Industrial Society, Hillman Library.

COHP   A. B. Chandler Oral History Project, University of Kentucky.

CTC   Bill Cash/Lloyd Thompson Collection, Afro-American Historical and Cultural Museum, Philadelphia, Pennsylvania.

EBP   Edward Bolden Papers, Moorland-Spingarn Research Center, Manuscript Division, Howard University, Washington, D.C.

NAACP Papers of the NAACP, University Publications of America, Frederick, Maryland.

NEP   Newark Eagles Papers, Newark Public Library, Newark, New Jersey.

PP   Philadelphia Phillies Papers, Hagley Museum and Library, Wilmington, Delaware.

RG 59   General Records of the Department of State, National Archives at College Park, College Park, Maryland.

RG 219 Records of the Office of Defense Transportation, National Archives at College Park, College Park, Maryland.

TBC   Thomas Baird Collection, Kansas Collection, Spencer Research Library, University of Kansas, Lawrence, Kansas.

Hearings

SOMP   *Study of Monopoly Power.* Hearings before Subcommittee on Study of Monopoly Power of the Committee on the Judiciary, House of Representatives, Eighty-Second Congress, First Session. Serial No. 1, Part 6—Organized Baseball. Washington, D.C.: Government Printing Office, 1952.

Notes

Preface

1. See Chapters 5 and 6 for a fuller discussion of this incident.
2. Gerald Early, "American Integration, Black Heroism, and the Meaning of Jackie Robinson," *Chronicle of Higher Education*, May 23, 1997, 97.
3. Despite the widely uneven quality of the literature, a number of works remain worth consulting. For recent scholarly accounts, see James Overmyer, *Effa Manley and the Newark Eagles* (Metuchen, N.J., 1993); Neil Lanctot, *Fair Dealing and Clean Playing: The Hilldale Club and the Development of Black Professional Baseball, 1910–1932* (Jefferson, N.C., 1994); Leslie Heaphy, "Shadowed Diamonds: The Growth and Decline of the Negro Leagues" (Ph.D. thesis, University of Toledo, 1995); Brad Snyder, *Beyond the Shadow of the Senators: The Untold Story of the Homestead Grays and the Integration of Baseball* (New York, 2003); Michael Lomax, *Black Baseball Entrepreneurs, 1860-1901: Operating by Any Means Necessary* (Syracuse, 2003). Earlier academic studies include William Donn Rogosin, "Black Baseball: The Life in the Negro Leagues" (Ph.D. thesis, University of Texas, Austin, 1981); Jules Tygiel, *Baseball's Great Experiment: Jackie Robinson and His Legacy* (New York, 1983); and Rob Ruck, *Sandlot Seasons: Sport in Black Pittsburgh* (Urbana, Ill., 1987). For accounts aimed at a more general audience, see Robert Peterson, *Only the Ball Was White* (Englewood Cliffs, N.J., 1970); John B. Holway, *Voices from the Great Black Baseball Leagues* (New York, 1975), *Blackball Stars: Negro League Pioneers* (Westport, Conn., 1988), and *Black Diamonds: Life in the Negro Leagues from the Men Who Lived It* (Westport, Conn., 1989); Janet Bruce, *The Kansas City Monarchs: Champions of Black Baseball* (Lawrence, Kan., 1985); Phil Dixon and Patrick Hannigan, *The Negro Baseball Leagues: A Photographic History* (Mattituck, N.Y., 1992); James Riley, *The Biographical Encyclopedia of the Negro Baseball Leagues* (New York, 1994); Dick Clark and Larry Lester, eds., *The Negro Leagues Book* (Cleveland, 1994); Larry Lester, *Black Baseball's National Showcase* (Lincoln, Neb., 2001).
4. *PT*, August 25, 1945.

Chapter 1. A Fragile Industry and a Struggling Community

Chapter epigraph: *PC*, January 7, 1933.
1. On the development of professional baseball as a commercialized amusement, see Harold Seymour, *Baseball: The Early Years* (New York, 1960), 76–77, 348 and Harold Seymour, *Baseball: The Golden Era* (New York, 1971), 342–66.
2. *KCC*, February 7, 1930 ("downward trend"); *PC*, August 29, 1931 ("a great big"). On Bolden and Hilldale, see Lanctot, *Fair*; EBP, box 186-1, folder 1. Of the approximately 70 black players in Organized Baseball between 1878 and 1899, only Moses Fleetwood Walker and his brother Welday played in the major leagues, appearing with Toledo in the American Association in 1884. See Leslie Heaphy, "The Growth and Decline of the Negro Leagues" (M.A. thesis, University of Toledo, 1989), 13.
3. Raymond Wolters, *Negroes and the Great Depression: The Problem of Economic

Recovery (Westport, Conn., 1970), 91; *BAA*, January 7, 1933 ("numerous"); Joe W. Trotter and Earl Lewis, eds., *African Americans in the Industrial Age: A Documentary History, 1915–1945* (Boston, 1996), 169; Charles Pete T. Banner-Haley, *To Do Good and To Do Well: Middle-Class Blacks and the Depression, Philadelphia, 1929–1941* (New York, 1993), 51–52; Gunnar Myrdal, *An American Dilemma: The Negro Problem and Modern Democracy* (New York, 1962), 197; John Hope Franklin and Alfred Moss, Jr., *From Slavery to Freedom: A History of African Americans* (New York, 1994), 384.

4. Charles Hardy, "Race and Opportunity: Black Philadelphia During the Era of the Great Migration, 1916–1930" (Ph.D. thesis, Temple University, 1989), 327–28, 368; *The Brown American* (November 1936); Myrdal, *American Dilemma*, 309–10; Eugene P. Foley, "The Negro Businessman: In Search of a Tradition," *Daedalus* (1966): 120; *CD*, July 3 (survey comments), 1937. In Chicago, the majority of black businesses were "small retail stores and service enterprises on the side streets." White-controlled businesses received most of the black trade. See St. Clair Drake and Horace R. Cayton, *Black Metropolis: A Study of Negro Life in a Northern City* (1945; rev. and enlarged ed. Chicago, 1993), 438–39.

5. Mark Naison, *Communists in Harlem During the Depression* (New York, 1984), 50–51; Vincent P. Franklin, *The Education of Black Philadelphia: The Social and Educational History of a Minority Community, 1900–1950* (Philadelphia, 1979), 118–20; *PI*, March 7, November 22, 1935; March 7, 1937; November 13, 1938; *PC*, August 25, 1928; July 5, 1930; May 14, 1938; *PT*, March 15, 1934; March 10, 1938; April 20 ("sensible"), May 25, 1939 ("silly"); January 11 ("flourishing"), 1940; *KCC*, April 5, 19, 1929; Claude McKay, *Harlem: Negro Metropolis* (1940; reprint New York, 1968), 118; *Our World* (June 1954); Jervis Anderson, *This Was Harlem: A Cultural Portrait, 1900–1950* (New York, 1982), 307; Works Progress Administration, *Ethnic Survey: The Negro in Philadelphia*, 1938–39, 1941.

6. Charles Ross, *Outside the Lines: African Americans and the Integration of the National Football League* (New York, 1999), 37–44; R. R. Hickman to President, National League, August 26, 1934 ("should be"); BHOFL, *PC*, December 17, 1932; *PT*, December 15, 1932; February 22, 1934; September 17, December 17, 1936; January 7, 1937; April 6, 1939; September 26, December 19, 1940; January 2, 1941; *PI*, April 29, 1938; Ocania Chalk, *Pioneers of Black Sport* (New York, 1975), 112; Charles T. Mitchell, Jr. to Art Carter, January 17, 1942 in ACP, box 170-6, folder 15.

7. *BAA*, September 26 ("crowding"), 1936; Earl Brown, "Joe Louis: The Champion, Idol of His Race, Sets a Good Example of Conduct," *Life*, June 17, 1940; *PC*, October 19, 1935; July 30, 1938; Gerald Astor, *". . . And a Credit to His Race": The Hard Life and Times of Joseph Louis Barrow, a.k.a. Joe Louis* (New York, 1974), 66–79.

8. Charles Alexander, *Our Game* (New York, 1991), 155.

9. *NYT*, May 13, October 9, 29, 1932; *BAA*, July 23, 1932; *PT*, March 24, 1932.

10. *BAA*, June 25, 1932; May 20, July 1, 1933; July 22, 1939; June 15, 1940; *PC*, February 11 ("no club"), April 8, August 12, 1933; February 17, June 16 ("due much"), 1934; March 2, 1935; April 22, 1939; *NYAN*, March 29, June 7, 1933; *PI*, August 18, 1935.

11. Ruck, *Sandlot Seasons*, 137–50; Military Personnel Records, William A. Greenlee file, National Personnel Records Center; John Holway, *Blackball Stars: Negro League Pioneers* (Westport, Conn., 1988), 300–308; *PC*, November 19, 1932 ("thousands"); July 29, 1933; interview with Clarence "Knowledge" Clark, August 2, 1980; interview with Charles Greenlee, June 18, 1980, BSIP; James Bankes, *The Pittsburgh Crawfords: The Lives and Times of Black Baseball's Most Exciting Team* (Dubuque, Iowa, 1991), 94 ("no killer"). The Tito family controlled the Latrobe Brewery, manu-

facturer of Rolling Rock beer, for over fifty years until selling to Labatt in the late 1980s.

12. Ruck, *Sandlot Seasons*, 18, 50–57, 152–53; Donn Rogosin, *Invisible Men: Life in Baseball's Negro Leagues* (New York, 1983), 15; Pittsburgh Crawfords articles of incorporation, February 18, 1932, Pennsylvania State Archives, Harrisburg; *PT*, August 28, 1930; April 16, 1936; *PC*, June 6, 1931; January 16, February 27, July 9, 1932; March 4, 1933; December 10, 1938; *BAA*, September 14, 1935; Holway, *Blackball Stars*, 300 (Leonard quote), 308 (Seay quote).

13. *BAA*, April 6, 1946; Ruck, *Sandlot Seasons*, 125–32; Ocania Chalk, *Black College Sport* (New York, 1976), 23–26; *PT*, April 13, 1946; *PC*, April 6, 1946; June 7, 1999 email from Alston S. Turchetta, Pennsylvania State University; June 11, 1999 email from Paul Demilio, Duquesne University; June 7, 1999, email from Debora Rougeux, University of Pittsburgh; Charles A. Simmons, *The African American Press: A History of News Coverage During National Crises, with Special Reference to Four Black Newspapers, 1827–1965* (Jefferson, N.C., 1998), 44; *Pittsburgh Sun-Telegraph*, March 29, 1946, in ACP, box 170-19, folder 19. On Posey, Sr., see *PC*, June 13, 1925.

14. *NYAN*, January 6, 20, June 22, 1932; July 26, 1933; *PT*, February 18, 25, April 28, May 26, June 2, 23, 1932; *PC*, February 6, 27, April 16, October 1, November 15, 1932; March 25 (Taylor quote), April 15, July 22, 1933; June 5, 1937; *BAA*, June 11, 18, 1932; *CD*, May 28, 1932; *KCC*, April 21, 1933; Robert Peterson interview with Jimmy Crutchfield, April 16, 1968, BHOFL.

15. *BAA*, May 18, 1923; January 11, September 5, 1925; June 4, July 23, September 3, 1932; March 4, May 13, 20, 1933; Robert V. Leffler, Jr., "Boom and Bust: The Elite Giants and Black Baseball in Baltimore, 1936–1951," *Maryland Historical Magazine* 87, 2 (Summer 1992): 171–86; Brent Kelley, *The Negro Leagues Revisited: Conversations with 66 More Baseball Heroes* (Jefferson, N.C., 2000), 84.

16. *CD*, July 9, 1932; May 6, 1933; February 9, 1935; February 5, 1938; January 4, 1941; August 7, 1948; January 30, 1954; August 13, December 10, 1955; Robert A. Cole, "How I Made a Million," *Ebony*, September 1954; *PC*, November 12, 1932; February 18, 1933, February 2, 1935; Bruce, *Kansas City Monarchs*, 52, 73–74, 154; Robert E. Weems, Jr., *Black Business in the Black Metropolis: The Chicago Metropolitan Assurance Company, 1925–1985* (Bloomington, Ind., 1996); email from Robert Weems, Jr., June 30, 2003.

17. *NYAN*, August 26, September 16, 1931; January 27, September 7 ("not a"), 1932; November 24, 1934; *PT*, April 16, 1931; *NYA*, July 18, August 1, 1931; *PC*, August 22, 1931; March 5, 1932; July 15, 1933 ("we needed"); February 9, 1935; *NYT*, October 6, 1964.

18. *PC*, November 15, December 27, 1924; March 19, August 27, December 17, 1932; *CD*, May 14, December 24 ("comprises"), 1932; *KCC*, February 10, 1933.

19. *PI*, July 25, 1937; August 27, 1939; 1929–1932 Hilldale Ledgers, CTC; *BAA*, June 25 (Gholston), 1932; January 28, March 4, May 13, July 15, 1933; *PC*, March 5 (Posey quote), March 19, August 6, December 24 (Clark quote), 1932; January 7, August 12, September 30, 1933; *PT*, May 18, 1933; *NYAN*, March 1, 1933.

20. *BAA*, July 23 ("take a"), 1932; *PC*, January 14, 1933 (Clark quote).

21. *NYAN*, February 5 ("no extravagant"/"keeping"), 1933; *PC*, January 7, 14, February 18, 25, 1933; *PT*, February 9, 23, 1933; *CD*, December 17, 1932; January 14, 21, February 25, 1933; *BAA*, May 13, 1933. In comparison, class C minor leagues in 1933 imposed a $1800 monthly salary limit and a maximum roster of 15 players. See *SOMP*, 1374.

22. *PC*, January 24, 1925 ("nightmare"); February 18, 1933; *CD*, January 21,

1933 (Monroe quote); *BAA*, January 28 (Gibson quote), February 18, 1933 (Drew quote); *KCC*, May 5, 12, July 14, 1933; *PT*, July 6, 1933.

23. Holway, *Voices*, 159 ("a big"); *DT*, May 20, 1933 (Cowans quote); *PC*, January 7, 1933 (Wilson quote).

24. William Leuchtenberg, *Franklin Roosevelt and the New Deal* (New York, 1963), 18; Robert McElvaine, *The Great Depression: America, 1929–1941* (1984; reprint New York, 1993), 134; *BAA*, July 1, 1933 (Gibson quote).

25. *BAA*, April 9 (Lundy), June 25 (Gholston), 1932; *PC*, July 29 (Posey), 1933.

26. *PC*, February 25, March 4, 1933; March 28, 1936 ("antagonistic"); *Nashville Tennessean*, April 25, 30, June 4, 1933; *PT*, February 23, 1933; Paul Debono, *The Indianapolis ABCs: History of a Premier Team in the Negro Leagues* (Jefferson, N.C., 1997), 111.

27. *PC*, October 7, 1933. On Roesink and Hamtramck Stadium, see *PT*, August 7, 28, 1930; *CD*, April 8, 1933; *PC*, June 8, 1940; Rich Bak, *Cobb Would Have Caught It: The Golden Age of Baseball in Detroit* (Detroit, 1991), 94–97; Richard Bak, *Turkey Stearnes and the Detroit Stars* (Detroit, 1994), 286; Michael Benson, *Ballparks of North America* (Jefferson, N.C., 1989), 137.

28. *CD*, April 8, 29, May 13, 20, July 22, 1933; *PC*, April 29, May 27, June 3, 1933; *PT*, April 27, 1933; May 16, 1935; *DT*, April 14, 29, May 6, 20, 1933; *NYAN*, May 10, 1933; Debono, *Indianapolis ABCs*, 111. Blount's accidental death in December 1934 ended his plans for a return to black professional baseball. See *PC*, December 15, 1934; January 5, 1935; *BAA*, December 29, 1934.

29. *BAA*, May 13, 1933; *KCC*, March 24, 1933; *PC*, July 8 ("majority"/"the only"), 1933; *NYAN*, July 26 ("forgotten"), 1933.

30. *PC*, July 1, 8 ("league cities"), 15, 22 ("always"), 29, August 5 ("no help"), 1933; *BAA*, July 1, 1933; *KCC*, July 7, 1933; *PT*, February 22, 1934.

31. *BAA*, July 1, 29, August 12 (Gibson), September 9, 1933; *CD*, July 2, August 26, 1933; *PC*, July 1, 29, August 5, 12, 19, 26, October 7, 1933; *NYAN*, September 27, 1933; *DT*, July 29, 1933.

32. *BAA*, July 29 ("unfortunate"), August 5 (Wilson), 1933; *PT*, October 5 (Clark), 1933.

33. *DT*, August 12, 1933 (Cowans); *PC*, August 5 (Posey quote), October 7, 1933; June 5, August 14 (Nunn quote), 1937.

34. *PC*, September 2, October 7, 1933; July 28, 1934; July 26, 1941; August 15, 1942; *BAA*, September 9, 1939; August 7, 1943; *CD*, December 12, 1942; *CCP*, August 18, 1934; *PT*, August 24, September 7, 21, 1933; July 19, 1934; March 11, 1944; G. Edward White, *Creating the National Pastime: Baseball Transforms Itself, 1903–1953* (Princeton, N.J., 1996), 121–22; Tygiel, *Baseball's Great Experiment*, 24; Dixon and Hannigan, *Negro Baseball Leagues*, 161. In June 1933, the *Courier* reported that promoters were considering an all-star game at the Chicago World's Fair between the best white and black players. Not surprisingly, Cum Posey offered a different interpretation of the East-West game's origin, emphasizing his own role. Posey claimed he had discussed the idea of a black all-star game at Yankee Stadium with Sparrow and Bill Nunn, who subsequently mentioned the plan to Greenlee. According to Posey, Greenlee then decided to launch a similar promotion at Comiskey Park. Dave Hawkins, meanwhile, claimed that his successful effort in Cleveland had encouraged Greenlee and Cole. See *PC*, June 17, 1933; August 15, 1942; Dave Hawkins to Effa Manley, September 28, 1938 (?), NEP.

35. *CD*, July 14, 1934; May 9, 1936 ("off guard"); August 6, 1938 ("profit"); *PC*, September 16, 1933; July 28, 1934; August 1, 1936; July 26, 1941; August 15, 1942; *PT*, July 25, 1935; *KCC*, August 3, 1934.

36. *PC*, February 25, September 16 ("frankly"), October 7 ("certain"), 1933; *BAA*, January 28, 1933; *CD*, February 25, 1933; Lanctot, *Fair Dealing*, 29–31, 62, 95–97.

37. *NYAN*, May 17 (Pollock), June 7 (Dougherty), 1933; *NYA*, July 9, 1938; *PC*, February 11 ("aversion"), 1933; February 24, 1940; Holway, *Voices*, 81–82.

38. *PC*, April 8 (Wilson), July 29, September 16, 1933; January 26, 1935 ("investment"); *PT*, May 11 (Dixon), June 29, July 6, 13, August 10, 31, 1933; *PI*, September 22, 1935; *BAA*, May 13, August 12, 1933; *PEB*, July 19, 1932.

39. *CD*, July 1, 1933; May 19, 1934; *NYAN*, June 7, 1933; *CCP*, August 18, 1934; *PT*, January 4, 1934 (Dixon). According to Rollo Wilson, only one league owner profited in 1933. See *PC*, July 14, 1934.

40. *CD*, July 22, December 16, 1933; January 20, February 10, 1934; February 9, 1935; January 4, 1941; August 7, 1948; August 13, 1955; *BAA*, December 9, 1933; January 6, 1934; *PC*, October 7, 1933; January 6, 13, 20, 1934; *KCC*, January 26, 1934; *PT*, March 1 (Cambria), 1934.

41. *PC*, July 15 ("compact"), November 11, December 9 ("it's"), 1933; February 17 (Semler), March 3 (Posey), 1934.

42. *PC*, November 25, December 30 (Bolden), 1933; *BAA*, March 3 (Gibson), 1934; Leuchtenberg, *Franklin Roosevelt*, 93–94; Rud Rennie, "Changing the Tune from Gloom to Cheer," *Literary Digest*, June 16, 1934, 34; *PEB*, November 8, 1933, cited in G. H. Fleming, *The Dizziest Season: The Gashouse Gang Chases the Pennant* (New York, 1984), 18; Bruce Kuklick, *To Every Thing a Season: Shibe Park and Urban Philadelphia, 1909–1976* (Princeton, N.J., 1991), 70–72; *PT*, May 25 ("religious"), 1933; Gladys Palmer, *The Search for Work in Philadelphia, 1932–1936* (Philadelphia, 1936), 31.

43. *PINQ*, November 8, 1933 (Mack/"great news"); *PR*, February 11, 1933 ("think"); *BAA*, February 18, 1933 (Drew).

44. *BAA*, June 7, 1941; *PT*, September 15, 1932; May 11, November 16, 1933; *PINQ*, July 10, 14, 1932; May 20, June 2, 1933; *SN*, January 24, 1935, cited in White, *Creating the National Pastime*, 175; Bruce, *Kansas City Monarchs*, 69–71; 1931 Hilldale Ledger, CTC; John A. Lucas and Ronald A. Smith, *Saga of American Sport* (Philadelphia, 1978), 320–21. The first major league night game was played at Crosley Field in Cincinnati in 1935. In Philadelphia, lights were installed in 1939 at Shibe Park, where the Athletics and Phillies drew a combined 199,237 for 14 night games, nearly 30 percent of their total attendance for the season. See *PEB*, August 24, 1939; David Pietrusza, *Lights On! The Wild Century-Long Saga of Night Baseball* (Lanham, Md., 1997), 147. The impact of night baseball on minor league baseball was profound. In 1933, Harry James O'Donnell noted that "there is no denying that it rescued minor league ball from the very brink of annihilation." See *Baseball Magazine*, October 1933, cited in Neil Sullivan, *The Minors: The Struggles and the Triumph of Baseball's Poor Relation from 1876 to the Present* (New York, 1990), 138–39.

45. *BAA*, April 11, 1925 ("close analysis"); February 17, 1934; March 19, 1949; *PC*, February 17, 24, March 3 ("there is"), April 28, 1934; January 5, 1935; *PT*, February 15, 22, July 5, August 2, 1934; *PI*, March 24, 1935; interview with Helen Jackson, July 30, 1980, BSIP. Whether black underworld financing was available in Philadelphia is uncertain, as Italians controlled the numbers by the mid-1930s. See Margaret B. Tinkcom, "Depression and War, 1929–1946," in *Philadelphia: 300-Year History*, ed. Russell F. Weigley (New York, 1982), 629.

46. Bill Ordine, "A Better Team Than Money Could Buy," *Today Magazine* (*Philadelphia Inquirer*), April 17, 1977, 33–40; *PINQ*, February 16, 1916; December 8, 1979; June 3, 2001; Edward Gottlieb File, Naismith Memorial Basketball Library; *PEB*, June 1, 1929; February 18, 1940; December 8, 1979; undated clipping in Ed-

ward Gottlieb file, BHOFL ("a wonderful"); *SN*, February 21, 1951; *PT*, March 22, 1924; *Philadelphia Public Ledger*, February 13, 1933; *PR*, September 24, 1939; Holway, *Voices*, 82–83.

47. *PINQ*, April 5, May 9, 1922; August 27, 1929; May 24, 1932; Ed Gottlieb to "Sir," March 11, 1931, CTC, box 1, folder 2; *PC*, July 29, 1933; *PT*, March 22, 1934; November 22, 1941; *PI*, February 24, 1951; *BAA*, January 19, 1935; Holway notes, courtesy of John Holway; Overmyer, *Effa Manley*, 137; Thomas Cripps, *Slow Fade to Black: The Negro in American Film, 1900–1942* (New York, 1993), 322–30. Webster McDonald suggested that Bolden and Gottlieb were already partners in 1933. Yet because there are no written references to Gottlieb as co-owner until 1934, it seems more likely that he only booked the team during 1933 and had no actual financial interest until the following season. See *PC*, December 30, 1933; Holway, *Voices*, 82–84. While some observers have questioned the actual level of Bolden's ownership, his Inventory of Property (Delaware County Courthouse, Media, Pennsylvania) clearly indicates his 50-percent share in the team at the time of his death in 1950.

48. *BAA*, March 25, 1933 (Taylor); *PC*, September 24 (Wilson), November 12, 1932; February 2, 1935; *PT*, October 15, 1936 (Bolden).

49. *PT*, July 28, 1932; September 13, 1934; January 10, 1935; *BAA*, June 25, 1932; May 20, July 1, 1933; March 2, June 15, 1940; *PC*, July 29, September 16, 1933; January 5, 1935; April 22 (Posey), September 23 (Dixon quote), 1939; *PI*, August 18, 1935; Holway, *Blackball Stars*, 321.

50. *PC*, July 8, 1933; August 18, 1934; *BAA*, August 11, 1934; April 6, 1935; *PI*, April 17, 1938; *PT*, April 20, 1933; August 9, 16, 1934; August 12, 1937; Drake and Cayton, *Black Metropolis*, 198, 432, 448. See Chapter 4 for a discussion of Jewish involvement in black baseball and entertainment.

51. As late as 1946, the Stars letterhead listed Bolden as owner with no mention of Gottlieb. See Edward Bolden to Branch Rickey, April 28, 1946, AMP, box 1, 1901 May 8–1946 December 27 folder.

52. *PT*, February 15, March 15, 1934; *PC*, March 10, 1934; *CCP*, February 17, 1934. Born in Millwood, Virginia, Charles Tyler owned a chicken farm and café in Avenel, New Jersey. The team was reportedly named after part-owner Joshua "Pop" Frazier's Dodger's Bar and Grill of Newark. See *BAA*, February 19, 1944; Overmyer, *Effa Manley*, 40.

53. *NYAN*, June 16, November 10, 1926; *PT*, April 26, 1928; March 15, April 26, May 17, 1934; November 13, 1956; Lanctot, *Fair Dealing*, 154–55, 159, 193; *CD*, April 21 (Monroe), 1934; *PC*, March 24 ("what we"), 1934.

54. *PC*, March 24, 31, April 7, 21, May 12, June 16, July 7 (Wilson), 1934; January 5, 26 ("destroy"), 1935; *PT*, March 15, 22, 1934; February 26, 1944; *NYAN*, May 12, September 22, November 3, 1934; March 9, 1935; Art Rust, Jr., *"Get That Nigger off the Field!" A Sparkling, Informal History of the Black Man in Baseball* (New York, 1976), 56.

55. *PC*, June 10, 1933; June 30, July 7, 28 ("unless"), November 7 (Posey), 1934; *PT*, June 28, July 5 ("the best"), 1934; November 22, 1955; *BAA*, August 25, 1934; *CCP*, August 11, September 8, 1934.

56. *PC*, March 3 (Posey), May 5, September 22, 1934; January 19, 1935; *CD*, March 24, 1934; *Colored Baseball & Sports Monthly* 1, 2 (October 1934): 18–19 in EBP, box 186-1, folder 21; Holway, *Voices*, 82–84; *BAA*, June 4, 1932; August 5, 1933; *PT*, May 17, July 5, 1934; *DT*, July 1, 1933.

57. *PT*, June 21, September 13, 20, 27, October 4, 1934; *PINQ*, September 17, 18, 1934; *BAA*, September 22, 1934; *CD*, September 22, 1934; *PC*, November 20, 1926; Clark and Lester, *Negro Leagues Book*, 161; Holway, *Voices*, 82–85, 243; *NYA*, Sep-

tember 22, 1934. Although the Philadelphia games of the series were reasonably well covered by the *Tribune*, the *Chicago Defender* provided remarkably scant coverage the western games. In general, the coverage was far inferior to that of the 1924 World Series between Hilldale and the Kansas City Monarchs.

58. *PT*, October 4 ("to the"), 11 ("if 50"), 1934; *PC*, October 13, 1934; *CD*, October 6, 1934; January 19, 1935; *PINQ*, October 2, 3, 1934. Rollo Wilson subsequently claimed that local fans in attendance supported the ejection of Wilson. See *NYAN*, January 26, 1935.

59. *PC*, December 1 (Wilson), 15, 1934; *CD*, January 19 (Malarcher), 1935; *PT*, October 4 (Harris), 1934.

60. *PC*, June 16, July 14, September 15 ("few"), November 17 (Posey), 1934; *CD*, June 30, 1934; *BAA*, January 19 (Clark), 1935; *PT*, October 11, 1934; February 26, 1944; *CCP*, August 18, 1934. A July 4, 1934 doubleheader at Greenlee Field between the Crawfords and Grays drew one of the larger crowds of the season, as a total of 11,608 fans (6,434 and 5,174) attended the two games.

61. *PT*, September 13, October 4, 1934; August 1, 1935; *PC*, September 1, 15, October 6, November 17, 1934; *CD*, September 1, 1934; *NYAN*, September 15, 1934; September 10, 1949; Rust, *"Get That Nigger off the Field!"* 54; W. Rollo Wilson, "They Could Make the Big Leagues," *Crisis* (October 1934): 305; *NYA*, September 15, 29, October 6, 1934. According to John Clark, Jones had defeated Paige twice earlier in 1934, reducing Paige to tears. See press release, 1942 (?) in ACP, box 170-18, folder 2.

62. *PC*, November 10 (Posey), 1934; *BAA*, January 19 ("thousands"), September 14 (Greenlee), 1935.

63. *BAA*, July 21 (Burley), 1934; January 19 (Greenlee), 1935; *NYAN*, July 14 (Dougherty), 1934; *PT*, September 13 (Harris), October 25, 1934; *PC*, September 15 (Wilson), 1934.

Chapter 2. External Threats and Internal Dissension

Epigraph; *BAA*, September 14, 1935.

1. *PC*, December 22, 1934. A 1935 study revealed that a startling 43.2 percent of 56,157 black families in Harlem were receiving relief. See E. Franklin Frazier, "Some Effects of the Depression on the Negro in Northern Cities," *Science and Society* 11, 4 (Fall 1938): 491.

2. *PC*, November 24, 1934; March 2, 1935; May 9, 1942; *BAA*, January 19, 1935; December 20, 1952; *NYAN*, October 13, 20, December 1, 1934; Overmyer, *Effa Manley*, 5–16; *PT*, September 12, 1929; Holway, *Voices*, 319; Gai Ingham Berlage, *Women in Baseball: The Forgotten Story* (Westport, Conn., 1994), 118–21; Effa Manley to Elizabeth Galbreath, April 23, 1942, NEP; Monte Irvin with James A. Riley, *Nice Guys Finish First* (New York, 1996), 43–44; William Marshall interview with Effa Manley, October 19, 1977, COHP; *Norfolk Journal and Guide*, July 26, 1941, in Manley scrapbook, BHOFL. Monte Irvin claimed that after Manley's success in the numbers, he "went legitimate and bought up a lot of real estate." By 1940, Manley owned at least five properties in Camden. See Abe Manley to City of Camden, July 30, 1940, NEP.

3. *NYT*, January 11, 1935; March 30, 1937; August 20, 1938; *PT*, May 22, 1930; December 20, 1934; January 10, 1935; November 5, 1936; May 20, 1937; *PC*, December 22, 1934; March 2, 1935; *CD*, July 29, 1944; *NYAN*, December 1, 8, 15, 1934; June 1, 1935; August 7, 1943; Roberto González Echevarría, *The Pride of Havana: A History of Cuban Baseball* (New York, 1999), 83, 140, 271; J. Richard (Dixie) Davis, "Things I Couldn't Tell till Now," *Collier's*, July 29, 1939, 37; responses to question-

naire, Alex Pompez, BHOFL; *NYA*, May 25, 1935. A 1923 arrest for policy suggests that Pompez may have been involved in illegal enterprises concurrent with his participation in the Eastern Colored League during the 1920s. See Rufus Schatzberg, *Black Organized Crime in Harlem: 1920–1930* (New York, 1993), 115.

4. *PT*, March 14, 1935; *PI*, March 24, 1935; *CD*, July 14, 1934; *PC*, November 17, 1934; *CCP*, September 8 ("goats"), 1934; *BAA*, March 16, 1935; *NYAN*, December 1, 1934; *PEB*, June 1, 1929; February 17, March 3, 1954.

5. *PI*, February 3, 24, 1935; *BAA*, January 19, March 16, 1935; *PT*, October 25, November 8, 1934; January 10, 17, 1935; Jay Sanford, "African American Baseballists and the Denver Post Tournament," *Colorado Heritage* (1995): 20–34; *PC*, November 10, 1934; *NYAN*, January 19, March 23, 30, April 6, 1935; *NYA*, February 2, 1935.

6. *PI*, April 7 ("filthy"), 1935; Harvard University Archives, File of Ferdinand Quintin Morton; *PT*, August 4, 1938; *New York Post*, August 8, 1935 in Schomburg Center Clipping File; *NYAN*, November 8, 1933; Ralph Bunche, *The Political Status of the Negro in the Age of FDR*, ed. Dewey Graham (Chicago, 1973), 601; Vanessa Northington Gamble, *Making a Place for Ourselves: The Black Hospital Movement, 1920–1945* (New York, 1995), 66; William L. Patterson, *The Man Who Cried Genocide: An Autobiography* (New York, 1971), 74 ("leading"). Black politician J. Raymond Jones later suggested that the United Colored Democracy was white-controlled and condemned Morton as "an old, handkerchief head." See Weiss, *Farewell to the Party of Lincoln*, 78.

7. Ferdinand Q. Morton, "Segregation," *Crisis* (August 1934): 244–45.

8. *Our World* (December 1946); *New York Post*, August 8, 1935, in Schomburg Center Clipping File; *BAA*, June 29, 1940.

9. *PT*, January 31 ("with Nat"), March 14 ("one season"), 28 ("ruled"), 1935; January 9, 1936; *CD*, March 23, 1935; *NYAN*, January 26 (Wilson), 1935; *BAA*, January 19 (Greenlee), 1935; *PC*, May 18 ("to see"), 1935.

10. *PT*, May 16, July 4, August 1, 29, September 5, 1935; January 30, 1936; May 20, 1937; February 24, 1938; *CD*, May 11, 18, 1935; September 3, 1938; January 4, 1941; December 25, 1943; *BAA*, July 21, 1934; February 23, June 8, July 13, August 24, 1935; May 19, 1945; *Detroit Tribune-Independent*, March 23, 1935; *PC*, November 9, 1935; January 18, 1936; Weems, *Black Business*, 64; *NYAN*, January 26, February 9, March 30, June 1, 15, July 6, August 10, 1935; *WT*, January 5, 1935; *PI*, June 9, August 4, 18, 1935; *NYA*, June 22, 29, 1935.

11. *PC*, July 13, 1935 (Washington quotes); *NYA*, July 7, 1934; *PT*, January 17, June 6 ("wishes"), July 4, August 29, 1935; *PI*, June 9 (Dixon), August 11, 1935; *CD*, November 7, 1936; *PC*, May 25, 1935; January 16 ("one-man"), 1937; *BAA*, September 14 ("target"), 1935.

12. For Greenlee's statement, see *BAA*, September 14, 1935 and *PT*, September 12, 1935.

13. *PC*, September 21, 28, 1935; January 11 ("not tottering"), 18, 1936; *PT*, August 15, September 5, 12, 1935; January 9, 30, 1936; *CD*, December 28 ("do not"), 1935; January 4 ("certain"), 18, November 7, 1936.

14. *PC*, November 23 ("stretched"), 1935; January 18, February 1, April 18, 1936; *CD*, August 3, 31, December 28, 1935; *NYAN*, December 15, 1934; May 23, 1936; *PT*, January 30, March 12, 1936; *PI*, February 2, 16, 1936; *BAA*, February 1, 1936; February 19, 1944; Holway, *Voices*, 320; Barbara J. Kukla, *Swing City: Newark Nightlife, 1925–1950* (Philadelphia, 1991), 243. Tyler was killed in 1944 by a patron at his Avenel, New Jersey, tavern, reportedly after a quarrel over the price of a drink. Despite Cole's relative failure in black baseball, he later became a millionaire through the success of his Metropolitan Mutual Assurance Company and funeral parlors. Cole died

in 1956. On Cole, see Cole, "How I Made A Million"; "Key Man at Metropolitan? Big Jovial Robert A. Cole," *Ebony*, January 1953; *CD*, December 10, 1955; Weems, *Black Business*; *Our World* (January 1952).

15. National Personnel Records Center, Military Personnel Records—James Semler. *PT*, January 30, March 12, 26, April 16, May 28, June 25 ("haven"), 1936; January 15, 1944; *PC*, March 2 ("without"), June 22, 1935; February 1, 8, March 7 ("every player"), 14, June 27, 1936; *PI*, June 30, 1935; March 15, 1936; January 27, 1951; *Our World* (June 1946); *NYA*, March 21, 1936; August 7, 1937; *CD*, June 27, 1936; *NYAN*, June 1, 15, July 6, 1935.

16. *NYA*, February 1 ("I don't"), 1936; *PC*, March 14, 21, 28 ("reserve"), April 25, July 4, 1936; *BAA*, March 28, April 18, 1936; *PT*, March 26, April 16 (Greenlee), 1936.

17. *PT*, May 7, 14, July 16, 30, August 6, 20, September 3, 17, 24, 1936; *PC*, July 4, 18, 25, August 29, September 26, 1936; *PI*, July 12, August 9, 1936; *CD*, August 15, 1936.

18. *PC*, July 4 ("try to"), 18, 25, August 8 ("disgusting"/"the thing"), 22, 29, October 17, 1936; *PT*, July 2, 23, August 20 ("honorable"/"had two"), 1936; *CD*, July 25, 1936; *PI*, July 26, 1936.

19. Sanford, "African American Baseballists," 20–34; *PC*, April 21, 1934; January 19, 1935; February 1, August 1 (Greenlee), 8, 22, October 3, 24, 31, November 7 ("worst"), 1936; *PT*, August 20, September 10, 24, October 8, 15 (Bolden), 22, 29, 1936; August 24, 1936, clipping in ACP, box 170-20, folder 1; *CD*, November 7, 1936; *PI*, September 27, October 4, 1936.

20. *PT*, July 30 (Harris), August 20 (Bolden), 1936; *PC*, August 29 (Posey), 1936.

21. Drake and Cayton, *Black Metropolis*, 391; William J. Baker, *Jesse Owens: An American Life* (New York, 1986), 51–106; David K. Wiggins, "The 1936 Olympic Games in Berlin: The Response of America's Black Press," in David Wiggins, *Glory Bound: Black Athletes in a White America* (Syracuse, N.Y., 1997), 61–79; Dominic J. Capeci and Martha Wilkerson, "Multifarious Hero: Joe Louis, American Society and Race Relations During World Crisis, 1935–1945," *Journal of Sport History* 10, 3 (Winter 1983): 5–25; *CD*, July 6, 1935; *BAA*, June 15, 29, July 13, 1935; *NYT*, August 15, 1936; *PT*, November 22, 1934; September 12, 19, 26, 1935; September 3, 17, December 17, 1936; June 24, 1937; *PC*, September 7, 1935. By 1939, Owens had declared bankruptcy and was reduced to appearing with the Toledo Crawfords, performing running exhibitions between doubleheaders. See *PC*, July 1, 1939; *PT*, May 9, 1940.

22. *PT*, October 3, 1935. While the rise of Joe Louis was welcomed enthusiastically by the majority of African Americans, some were uncomfortable with his humble background and lack of formal education. One man, for example, noted that "Joe Louis is a very ignorant man to be a champion and though I am a member of his race I can't admire him because he is so dumb." Others, however, willingly overlooked his educational deficiencies, arguing that "Joe Louis has done more for his race with the fury of his fists than all the PHD's combined—Or any of our many useless and pumped up celebrities for that matter." See *PT*, October 28, November 4, 1937.

23. *PT*, June 20, 1935; June 20, 1940; *PC*, July 30 (Dixon), 1938; October 7 ("pushed"), 1939; *BAA*, March 12 ("more baseball"), August 13 (Hardwick), 1938; Drake and Cayton, *Black Metropolis*, 403; *Our World* (March 1948); Lawrence Hogan, *A Black National News Service* (Rutherford, N.J., 1984), 161; Charles S. Johnson, *Growing Up in the Black Belt* (Washington, D.C., 1941), 246. A Philadelphia appearance by Louis for a softball game at Passon Field in 1937 attracted crowds so large

that the game was rescheduled at the more spacious Municipal Stadium. See *PINQ*, September 21–22, 1937; *PEB*, September 21, 1937.

24. Joe Louis with Edna Rust and Art Rust, Jr., *Joe Louis: My Life* (New York, 1978), 44, 65, 79; *PC*, May 21, 1938; *CD*, January 25, 1936; *NYAN*, October 12 ("level-headed"), 1935; January 4, 1936; *PT*, July 25, October 3, 1935; Ruck, *Sandlot Seasons*, 167–68; Bak, *Turkey Stearnes*, 56, 205–7; Roi Ottley, *"New World A-Comin": Inside Black America* (Boston, 1943), 189. In contrast to the positive coverage of Louis and Owens, black baseball received its most extensive white media attention in 1936 from a story by Dan Parker in the *New York Mirror* accusing the Crawfords of throwing a game against the white Brooklyn Bushwicks. While Parker later exonerated the Crawfords and apologized, several league officials were concerned about the story's possible effect on the league and the fight for integration. See *PT*, September 17, 24, October 15, 1936; *PC*, September 19, 1936; *KCC*, October 2, 1936.

25. *BAA*, April 3 (Clark), 1937; *PC*, June 28, 1930; January 2, 1932; July 18, 1933; August 29 ("Bolden has"), October 31 ("not one"), 1936; January 30, February 20 (Wilson), March 20 ("not in"), 1937; *PI*, January 24, February 14, 1937; *PT*, January 14, 21, February 17, 1937; *CD*, April 20, 1940; *NYAN*, January 16, 1937; interview with Clarence "Knowledge" Clark, August 2, 1980, BSIP; email to author from Rob Ruck, November 7, 2001.

26. *PT*, January 30, March 12, 1936; March 25 ("former"), December 23, 1937; Eddie Gottlieb to Effa Manley, September 27, 1939, William Leuschner to Effa Manley, October 25, 1939, NEP; *PC*, February 1, August 29, September 5, October 31, 1936; March 13, 20 (Posey), 27, April 24, 1937; February 24, 1940; *CD*, May 9, 1914; September 19, 26, December 19, 1936; March 27, April 3, 1937; December 10, 1938; January 30, 1954; *BAA*, December 13, 1924; April 10 (Moore), 1937; *NYAN*, December 12, 1936; Florence Murray, *The Negro Handbook 1944* (New York, 1944), 234; Harold Gosnell, *Negro Politicians: The Rise of Negro Politics in Chicago* (1935; reprint Chicago, 1969), 67–68, 75, 314; *PAA*, June 20, 1942; *KCC*, December 11, 1936; February 26, 1937; *PI*, March 28, 1937.

27. *NYT*, March 29, 30 (Pompez), 1937; August 14, 20, 1938; March 27, 1957; *PT*, May 28, 1936; April 1, 8, July 22, 29, October 14, November 4, 1937; August 25, 1938; *BAA*, February 10, 1934; March 2, 1935; *NYAN*, February 7, 1934; Mary M. Stolberg, *Fighting Organized Crime: Politics, Justice, and the Legacy of Thomas E. Dewey* (Boston, 1995), 228–31; Davis, "Things I Couldn't Tell"; Richard Norton Smith, *Thomas E. Dewey and His Times* (New York, 1982), 125; Stanley Walker, *Dewey: An American of This Century* (New York, 1944), 35–65.

28. *BAA*, May 11 ("Bankers'"), 1935; Juliet E. K. Walker, *The History of Black Business in America: Capitalism, Race, Entrepreneurship* (New York, 1998), 238. Notably, Joe Louis's managers, John Roxborough and Julian Black, were also involved in illegal enterprises, including policy and the numbers. See Astor, " . . . *And a Credit to His Race"*, 32–38; Richard W. Thomas, *Life for Us Is What We Make It: Building Black Community in Detroit, 1915–1945* (Indianapolis, 1992), 116–18; "War on Numbers Racket Kings," *Color* (June 1951): 32–34.

29. *BAA*, March 11 (Lacy), 1939; Dave Hawkins to Effa Manley, September 28, 1938 (?), NEP. Even Robert Cole, an immensely successful entrepreneur in legitimate business, was tarnished by his interest in gambling and early involvement with Dan Jackson, the "most noted of all the gambling kings" in Chicago. See Weems, *Black Business*, 10, 50; Gosnell, *Negro Politicians*, 130–31.

30. David Camelon, "The Numbers Racket," *Negro Digest* (March 1950): 46–49. In the illegal numbers lottery, individuals placed bets, as low as a penny, on any three-digit number, selected in various ways such as the last three digits of the daily transac-

tion totals on the New York Stock Exchange or race track figures. Winning players were paid off at a ratio of 500 to 600 times the original bet, although the games were often rigged. According to his brother Charles, Gus Greenlee attempted to manipulate the numbers on occasion (interview with Charles Greenlee, June 18, 1980, BSIP).

31. *PC*, April 10 (Posey), 1937; Davis, "Things I Couldn't Tell," 37. In *An American Dilemma*, Gunnar Myrdal explained the importance and appeal of the numbers in black communities. For black entrepreneurs, the game was a "sure thing," offering opportunities for substantial profits unavailable in legitimate enterprises open to blacks. Perhaps of equal importance, the numbers required a "great number of middlemen," thus providing blacks with "a considerable amount of employment at decent pay." See Myrdal, *An American Dilemma*, 330–32; *PT*, March 30, 1954; January 8, 29, 1955.

32. *PT*, April 6 (Rhodes), 1939; *BAA*, July 26 ("A man"), 1952; J. Saunders Redding, "Playing the Numbers," *North American Review* (December 1934): 533–42. Ironically, Don King, one of the most successful African American boxing promoters of recent decades, began his career in the numbers. See Jeffrey Sammons, *Beyond the Ring: The Role of Boxing in American Society* (Urbana, Ill., 1988), 220.

33. *NYT*, August 20, 1938; Holway, *Blackball Stars*, 317; *PC*, March 10, 1934; March 27, 1937; *PT*, March 25, 1937; *CD*, March 27, 1937; *NYAN*, March 27, 1937; *Brown American* (Fall/Winter 1942); Peterson, *Only the Ball Was White*, 136; Riley, *Biographical Encyclopedia*, 170. According to Buck Leonard, a costly numbers hit had provoked Greenlee's trade of Gibson. See James Riley with Buck Leonard, *Buck Leonard: The Black Lou Gehrig* (New York, 1995), 79.

34. *NYT*, June 1, 1961. On Trujillo, see Eric Paul Roorda, *The Dictator Next Door: The Good Neighbor Policy and the Trujillo Regime in the Dominican Republic, 1930–1945* (Durham, N.C., 1998), 21–22; Michael M. Oleksak and Mary Adams Oleksak, *Béisbol: Latin Americans and the Grand Old Game* (Grand Rapids, Mich., 1991), 37–39, 169; *BAA*, May 11, 1946; Alan M. Klein, *Sugarball: The American Game, the Dominican Dream* (New Haven, Conn., 1991), 12–21; John Gunther, *Inside Latin America* (New York, 1941), 440–46; Rob Ruck, *The Tropic of Baseball: Baseball in the Dominican Republic* (Lincoln, Neb., 1999), 29–32; Oswald Garrison Villard, "Issues and Men," *The Nation*, March 20, 1937, 323–24; Carleton Beals, "Caesar of the Caribbean," *Current History* (January 1938): 31–34. In 1937, Trujillo ordered the execution of 12,000 Haitian sugar cane workers who refused to return to Haiti. See *CD*, February 12, 1938.

35. *BAA*, May 1, July 24, 31, 1937; Ruck, *Sandlot Seasons*, 161–62; *PI*, May 2, 16, June 13, 1937; *PC*, May 1, June 12, 1937; *PT*, April 29, May 27, June 3, 1937; *NYA*, May 29, 1937; Klein, *Sugarball*, 12–22; Peter Bjarkman, *Baseball with a Latin Beat: A History of the Latin American Game* (Jefferson, N.C., 1994), 169; Ruck, *Tropic of Baseball*, 36–37. David Ticktin, acting attorney for the NNL, claimed the players were receiving at least $250 per month. See Conversation, June 21, 1937; Memoranda on Dominican Republic May 1935–June 1937; Memorandums Relating to Individual Countries, March 2, 1918–December 31, 1947, RG 59. The Dominican league also recruited professional players from Puerto Rico and Venezuela in 1937.

36. *BAA*, July 31 ("the opportunities"/"go to"), 1937; Beals, "Caesar of the Caribbean," 31 ("one of"); *PC*, June 5 ("perhaps"), July 31 ("were almost"), 1937; *Chicago Daily News*, March 13 ("I wasn't"), 1943 in ACP, box 170-20, folder 1; LeRoy Paige as told to David Lipman, *Maybe I'll Pitch Forever: A Great Baseball Player Tells the Hilarious Story Behind the Legend* (Lincoln, Neb., 1993), 116 ("Gus was"); Donald Honig, *Baseball When the Grass Was Real: Baseball from the Twenties to the Forties Told by the Men Who Played It* (1975; reprint Lincoln, Neb., 1993), 169 (Bell).

Years later, James Bell related to John Holway that the players "didn't know we were being used for a political reason until we got there." See Holway, *Voices*, 125.

37. Memorandum to Laurence Duggan and Sumner Welles, May 12, 1937, Memoranda on Dominican Republic May 1935–June 1937, Memorandums Relating to Individual Countries, March 2, 1918–December 31, 1947, RG 59; *PI*, May 16, June 13, 1937; *PC*, May 15, 1937; *NYAN*, May 8, 1937; *BAA*, May 1 ("the men"), 1937.

38. Conversation, June 21, 1937, Memoranda on Dominican Republic, May 1935–June 1937, Memorandums Relating to Individual Countries, March 2, 1918–December 31, 1947, RG 59 ("case did not"); *PC*, May 29, 1937 (Morton telegram).

39. Conversation, June 29, 1937, Memoranda on Dominican Republic, May 1935–June 1937, Memorandums Relating to Individual Countries, March 2, 1918–December 31, 1947, RG 59. On Duggan's involvement with the Soviet Union, see Allen Weinstein and Alexander Vassilev, *The Haunted Wood: Soviet Espionage in America—The Stalin Era* (New York, 1999), 8–21.

40. *PC*, December 28, 1935; May 15, July 31, September 18 ("made certain moves"), 1937; *PI*, June 6, 20, July 11, 1937; *CD*, July 10, 1937; *NYA*, June 26, 1937; *PT*, June 3, July 15 (Dixon), 1937; *NYAN*, May 12, December 1, 1934; Harold Seymour, *Baseball: The People's Game* (New York, 1990), 279; *BAA*, July 31 (Paige), 1937.

41. *PI*, May 12, 1935; June 13, 1937; February 19, 1939; *PC*, May 1 (Posey), July 31, August 7 (Clark), 1937; *CD*, July 31, 1937; Robert Gregory, *Diz: The Story of Dizzy Dean and Baseball During the Great Depression* (New York, 1992), 123; *PT*, July 22, August 28, 1937.

42. *PC*, July 31 (Posey), August 21, September 11, 18, 25, 1937; *PT*, August 12, 19, September 16 (Dixon), 1937; *PI*, August 15, 1937.

43. *PT*, July 15 ("these are"/Bolden), September 16 (Dixon), December 30, 1937; February 15, 1940; *PI*, November 8, 1936; May 12, 1945; *PC*, June 8, 1940.

Chapter 3. Growing Pains

Epigraph; *PC*, August 7, 1937.

1. On the Depression's effect on black business, see Walker, *History of Black Business*, 182–83. On the effect on the black film and record industries, see Cripps, *Slow Fade to Black*, 251, 323–39; Walker, *History of Black Business*, 320; William Barlow, *Voice Over: The Making of Black Radio* (Philadelphia, 1999), 25; Nelson George, *The Death of Rhythm & Blues* (New York, 1988), 10–11.

2. *PT*, December 3, 1936.

3. *CD*, September 11 ("Many"), 1937; *PT*, August 17, 1939; *BAA*, June 25 (Gholston), 1932; February 5 (Hardwick), 19 (Gardner), 1938. While financial data from professional black baseball in the late 1930s are generally impressionistic at best, extant records reveal that the Newark Eagles of the NNL grossed $35,135.17 in 1936 and 1937, with expenses of $48,299.55 for a total loss of $13,164.38 over the two seasons. In comparison, Hilldale's 1929 financial records indicate that the team grossed about $29,000 for the entire season. Team attendance figures, while similarly sketchy, reveal that the Pittsburgh Crawfords drew 69,229 fans for baseball games at Greenlee Field in 1932 and the Newark Eagles drew 32,646 fans over 15 dates at Ruppert Stadium in 1939. See Overmyer, *Effa Manley*, 108, 117; 1929 Hilldale Ledger, CTC; *PC*, April 15, 1933.

4. *PC*, June 10, 1933; April 28, 1934; May 9, 1936; April 22 ("I see"), 1939; *BAA*, May 9, 1936; August 12 (Lundy), 1939, cited in Jim Reisler, *Black Writers/Black Baseball: An Anthology of Articles from Black Sportswriters Who Covered the Negro*

Leagues (Jefferson, N.C., 1994), 17; *CD*, May 9, 1936; *PT*, February 22, 1934; January 16 (Harris), 1936; February 24 (Manley), March 3 ("many"), 1938; *NYA*, August 31, 1935; Sterling Brown, "The Negro in American Culture," Carnegie-Myrdal Study, *The Negro in America*, Section I—Sports, roll 1, 110; *PI*, March 15 (Cockrell), 1936; April 11 ("twenty"), 1937.

5. Joseph Pierce, *Negro Business and Business Education: Their Present and Prospective Development* (New York, 1947), 31–32; James Weldon Johnson, *Negro Americans, What Now?* (New York, 1935), 77; *PT*, September 17, 1936; September 14 (Simmons), 1939; *PC*, January 18 (Posey), 1936; April 22 ("give"), June 3 (Smith), 1939; *PI*, May 16 ("$300,000"), June 6, 1937. By 1938, H. B. Webber and Oliver Brown claimed that the two organizations spent over half million per year on "overhead, salaries, publicity, the finest of uniforms, and transportation." See H. B. Webber and Oliver Brown, "Play Ball!" *Crisis* (May 1938): 136–37, 146.

6. *PC*, March 14 ("salvation"), 1936; May 15 ("Negro"), September 11 ("any"), 1937; Cum Posey to Effa Manley, June 2, 1939 ("every club"), NEP; *PT*, August 20 ("every owner"), October 15 ("before"), 1936.

7. *PC*, August 14 ("does not"), September 18 (Greenlee), 1937; *PT*, February 3, 1938; July 29, 1944 ("one of the"); *NYAN*, February 5, 1938; *BAA*, February 5 ("an equal"), 1938; Ferdinand Q. Morton file, Harvard University Archives. Morton continued as a civil service commissioner in New York, retiring in 1948 and dying a year later on November 8, 1949 at age sixty-seven.

8. *BAA*, July 23, 1932; February 5 (Tom Wilson), April 2, 1938; *PC*, April 17, 1937; March 12, 1938; *NYAN*, February 5, March 12, 1938; unsigned account of January 28, 1938 league meeting (owners' statement), NEP; Leffler, "Boom and Bust," 171–86. As early as 1927, William H. Jones noted that "perhaps in few other cities of its size . . . does baseball hold such an insignificant place among colored people as it does in Washington. No prominent Negro teams exist." See Jones, *Recreation and Amusement Among Negroes in Washington, D.C.* (1927; reprint Westport, Conn., 1970), 29.

9. *PT*, March 10, April 7, 1938; *PI*, March 13, 1938; *BAA*, March 12, 1938; March 11, 1939; *PC*, February 26, March 5, May 7, 1938; February 4, 1939; *NYAN*, March 12, 1938; *Brown American* (February–March 1937); *WT*, November 2, December 10, 1935; R. R. Jackson to Cum Posey, May 17, 1939, NEP. The Buffalo Athletics (or Aces), an associate franchise, also joined the league in 1938 but made little impact.

10. *PT*, February 10, 24 (Manley), March 17 ("grade-A"), April 28, May 5, 1938; *NYAN*, February 5, March 10, 1938; June 15, 1940; *PC*, March 5 ("the league"), 19 ("nominal"), April 16, 23 ("say"), 30, May 7, 21 ("played when"), 28, October 29 ("not paid"), 1938; *PI*, March 6 ("blackballed"), May 8, 1938; *BAA*, February 5 ("if we"), 26 ("if they"), April 30, 1938; *CD*, May 9 ("no regrets"), 1936; William Marshall interview with Effa Manley, October 19, 1977, COHP.

11. *BAA*, February 5 ("not eased"), July 16 (Posey), August 6, 13 ("the majority"), 1938; July 29 (Taylor), 1939; *PT*, March 10, June 2 ("many"), 9, July 14, 21 (Harris), August 4, September 15 ("with some"), 1938; Effa or Abe Manley to John Clark, July 22, 1938, Abe or Effa Manley to W. B. Baker, February 14, 1939, NEP; *CD*, March 4, 1939; *PC*, June 25, August 20, September 10, 24, 1938; *PI*, August 7, 14, 28, October 2, 1938; February 12, 1939; Overmyer, *Effa Manley*, 108; Neil A. Wynn, *The Afro-American and the Second World War*, rev. edition (New York, 1993), 39; Leuchtenberg, *Franklin Roosevelt*, 243–51; McElvaine, *Great Depression*, 297–300; Rust, *"Get That Nigger off the Field!"* 55; *NYAN*, July 2, 1938; March 11, 1950; Steven A. Riess, *City Games: The Evolution of American Urban Society and the Rise of Sports* (Urbana, Ill., 1989), 148. In 1939, Joseph Baker of the *Brown American* claimed that blacks

had "hit even a lower low than had been the 1929 case" during 1938. In Philadelphia, a sample of 6,952 black males during the summer of 1938 revealed an unemployment rate of over 50 percent. See *Brown American* (October 1939); *Monthly Labor Review* (October 1939): 838–40.

12. *PC*, October 29 ("in bad"), December 10 ("lowest ebb"), 1938; *BAA*, February 5 ("colored baseball"/"there is"/"there's money"), March 26 ("chronic"/"no millionaire"/"it doesn't"), September 10 ("the owners"), 1938; *PI*, October 2 (Davis), 1938; *CD*, June 25 (Young), 1938.

13. *PC*, June 5 ("petted"), August 14, 1937; June 4 ("fans"), 25, August 6, 20 (Smith), December 10, 17, 1938; January 21, February 4, 25, May 13, June 24, July 22, 1939; November 9 ("successful"), December 28, 1940; *CD*, August 6, December 10, 1938; February 4, 1939; Posey to Abe Manley, December 19, 1940, NEP; Holway, *Black Diamonds*, 80 (Benson); *BAA*, July 23, 1938; *NYT*, June 20, 1939; April 19, 1974; Ruck, *Sandlot Seasons*, 165–69; *NYAN*, January 28, 1938. Local conditions also cut into profits. In 1936, Cum Posey claimed that Pittsburgh was the only city with a federal, state, and city tax on Sunday games. By 1936, Sunday games were rarely scheduled at Greenlee Field. See *PC*, January 25, June 13, 1936; *CD*, May 8, 1937; *PT*, April 16, 1936; interview with Charles Greenlee, June 18, 1980, BSIP.

14. Gus Greenlee to Cum Posey, March 9, 1939, Eddie Gottlieb to all league owners, April 4, 1939 ("has exhausted"), Eddie Gottlieb to Effa Manley, April 7 ("we would"), 1939, Cum Posey to Abe Manley, March 16, 1940, NEP; *PC*, April 8 ("violated"), 1939; *PT*, April 13 (Harris), 1939; *CD*, June 22, 1940. Several letters in the Newark Eagles papers reveal Greenlee's shaky financial status in 1939. The Horace Partridge Company, for example, complained to league officials that while Greenlee had given them two checks, both had been "returned by the bank as 'no funds.'" See Horace Partridge Company to Abe Manley, March 14, 1939, NEP.

15. Prentice Mills, "Southern Stars: Dixie's Contributions to the Negro Leagues," *Black Ball News*, 1992; *PC*, July 29, 1933, December 6, 1941; November 13 ("rough"), 1943; May 24, 1947; *CD*, May 24, 1947; *BAA*, July 22, 1933; February 25, March 11 (Lacy), 1939; May 24, 1947; Tom Wilson to Abe Manley, December 15, 1941, NEP; Leffler, "Boom and Bust," 172; Bill Glauber, "Elite Giants: The Pride of Baltimore Baseball History," *Baltimore Sun*, April 29, 1990; Holway, *Voices* (Manley), 322.

16. Cumberland Posey to Effa Manley, April 14, 1939 (Posey quotes), NEP; *KCC*, March 31, April 7, 1939.

17. Cumberland Posey to Effa Manley, April 19, 1939 ("there is no"), NEP; *NYT*, August 14, 20 ("the most"), 23, September 13, 1938; February 26, May 17, 1939; October 15, 1940; March 27, 1957; Stolberg, *Fighting Organized Crime*, 231, 232 ("without"); *PI*, September 11, 1938; May 21, 1939; *PT*, November 4, 1937; September 8 ("there may"), 1938; April 27, 1939; *PC*, May 13, June 10, 1939; *NYAN*, August 20, October 15, 1938; *CD*, March 4 (Monroe), 1939; *BAA*, April 27 ("would"), 1940. Hines was released on parole in 1944.

18. Effa Manley to R. R. Jackson, April 28, 1939 ("most"); Effa Manley to Rufus Jackson, April 29, 1939; Abe Manley to Hank Rigney, May 6, 1939 ("root"); Hank Rigney to Abe Manley, May 6, 1939 ("why"); R. R. Jackson to Cum Posey, May 17, 1939 ("failed"); Henry J. Rigney to league owners, June 14, 1939; minutes of June 20, 1939 interleague meeting, NEP; *PI*, June 11, 1939; *PC*, April 22, May 6, June 17, July 1, 1939.

19. Ed Gottlieb to Effa Manley, July 13, 1939 ("damn"); Hank Rigney to Abe Manley, July 5, 1939 ("promptly"); S. H. Posey to Abe Manley, August 1 ("if the

west"), 1939; minutes of joint session, February 24, 1940, NEP; *PC*, August 5, 19, 1939; *PT*, December 14, 1939; *CD*, December 16, 1939.

20. Abe Manley to NNL league owners, May 10, 1939, account of 1939 league meeting; Cum Posey to Effa Manley, September 8, 1939, Statement of East-West Game, 1939, Ed Gottlieb to Effa Manley, July 5, 1939, NEP; *PC*, February 4, June 3, 1939; January 13, February 10, 17, 24, 1940; *CD*, August 19 (Monroe), December 16, 1939; *PT*, October 5 ("cleanly"), 1939; February 15, 1940; *PI*, June 18 ("a sort"), October 11, 1939; *NYT*, May 28, June 5, July 3, 24, August 14, 28, September 25, 1939; *BAA*, August 12 (Harris), 1939 (cited in Reisler, *Black Writers/Black Baseball*, 16); September 9, 1939; *NYAN*, November 4, 1939; *NYA*, September 23, 1939. Fay Young claimed that Yankee Stadium charged $3,000 per rental in 1938. See *CD*, August 27, 1938.

21. McElvaine, *Great Depression*, 306–7; *PEB*, December 16, 1939; *NYT*, November 5, 1939; *PINQ*, June 26, 1939; Richard C. Crepeau, *Baseball: America's Diamond Mind, 1919–1941* (Orlando, Fla., 1980), 183; SOMP, 960–63; Peter S. Craig, "Organized Baseball—An Industry Study of a $100 Million Spectator Sport" (B.A. thesis, Oberlin College, 1950), table xviii; *PC*, January 6 (Posey), 1940; *CD*, May 20 (Young), 1939.

22. *PC*, January 16 ("rapidly"), September 25, 1937; *PT*, September 23 ("the proper"), 1937; March 10 ("sonorous"), 1938; March 11, 1944 ("like her"); September 14 ("at first"), 1946; Overmyer, *Effa Manley*, 16; Donn Rogosin, "Queen of the Negro Leagues," *Sportscape* (Summer 1981): 17–19; Cheryl Lynn Greenberg, *"Or Does It Explode?" Black Harlem in the Great Depression* (New York, 1991), 5, 214; Holway, *Voices*, 315 (Irvin); Holway, *Black Diamonds*, 65 (Giles), 162 (Davis). As early as 1935, Randy Dixon considered Effa Manley the "real power behind the throne." See *PI*, August 4, 1935.

23. *CD*, October 21 (Monroe), 1939, J. B. Greer to Abe Manley, December 2, 1939, Ed Gottlieb to Effa Manley, December 4, 1939, NEP. On Hastie, see Philip McGuire, *He, Too, Spoke for Democracy* (Westport, Conn., 1988); Gilbert Ware, *William Hastie: Grace Under Pressure* (New York, 1984); Greenberg, *"Or Does It Explode?"* 163; Leslie H. Fishel, Jr., "The Negro in the New Deal Era," in Bernard Sternsher, ed., *The Negro in Depression and War* (Chicago, 1969), 7–28; Harvard Sitkoff, *A New Deal for Blacks: The Emergence of Civil Rights as a National Issue* (New York, 1978), 221; Beverly Smith, "The First Negro Governor," *SEP*, April 17, 1948; *NYT*, April 15, 1976. Hastie apparently had some interest in sports, participating in track and also tennis. See Ware, *William Hastie*, 3–30.

24. *CD*, December 16 (Young), 1939; William Hastie to Effa Manley, February 1, 1940, NEP. On the attempt to draft Hastie as commissioner, see Effa Manley to William Hastie, September 7, 1939, Abe Manley to James Semler, November 25, 1939, NEP; *PT*, December 14, 1939; *BAA*, April 27, 1940; *CD*, February 24, 1940. During World War II, Hastie served as civilian aide to Secretary of War Henry Stimson but the War Department's continued resistance to integration prompted his resignation in 1943. In 1946, Hastie became the governor of the Virgin Islands, followed by an appointment three years later as a federal judge of the U.S. Court of Appeals for the Third Circuit in Philadelphia. See A. Russell Buchanan, *Black Americans in World War II* (Santa Barbara, Calif., 1977), 70, 94; *PAA*, October 22, 1949; Smith, "The First Negro Governor"; Ware, *William Hastie*, 220–40.

25. *MC*, January 26, 1946; *NYAN*, February 10, 24, 1940; August 21, 1943; October 1, 1977; *BAA*, February 10, 1940; *CD*, February 10 ("we are"), 24, 1940; *PT*, February 15 ("where she"), 22, 1940; *NYT*, September 23, 1977; *PC*, November 16 ("none"), 1940; *PI*, February 11, 1940; *New Jersey Herald News*, February 10 [?],

1940, in Manley scrapbooks, BHOFL; Overmyer, *Effa Manley*, 138–39 ("handker-chief"), 140–41. On the attempts to lease Ebbets Field, see Abe Manley to J. A. Robert Quinn, July 5, 1939, Abe Manley to Larry MacPhail, August 29, 1939, Larry MacPhail to Abe Manley, August 30, 1939, Abe Manley to Larry MacPhail, November 7, 1939, Brooklyn Dodgers to Abe Manley, November 15, 1939, Effa Manley to John Collins, July 2, 1940, NEP.

26. *BAA*, March 2 ("secretive"), 1940; *CD*, February 10 ("broke"), 1940; *PC*, February 17 (Posey), 1940.

27. *PC*, February 17 ("the sole"), March 2, 16 ("opinions"), 1940; *CD*, February 24 (Young), March 2, 1940; *BAA*, February 10 (Carter), March 2, 1940; *PT*, February 29, March 14, 1940; *PI*, March 3, 1940; *NYAN*, March 2, 1940. Carter's own experi-ence as a part-time booking agent in the Washington area likely shaped his attitude toward the controversy. On Carter's booking practices, see Art Carter to Mr. J. H. Byers in ACP, box 170-4, folder 8.

28. Effa Manley to Cum Posey, March 1 ("not done"), 1940, NEP; *BAA*, April 27 ("there is"/"some white"), 1940.

29. Richard Carey to State Department, May 8, 1940, minutes of joint meeting of NNL and NAL, February 24, 1940, NEP; *PT*, February 29, March 14 (Harris), May 16, 23, August 1, 1940; *PI*, April 14, June 2, July 28 (Roberts), 1940; *PC*, February 10, May 4, 18 (Washington), June 1 (Posey), August 24 (Gibson/Smith), 1940; *CD*, March 2, 1940. Black journalists, often underpaid, were equally willing to switch em-ployers at the slightest promise of more money. Randy Dixon, for example, worked for three different newspapers between 1933 and 1938. See *PI*, February 9, 1941.

30. Effa Manley to Randy Dixon, April 15, 1940, Effa (?) Manley to E. B. Eynon, February 8, 1941, NEP; *PC*, April 27, June 15, 29, September 7, November 16, De-cember 28, 1940; April 5, 1941; *PI*, April 28, May 18, August 11, 25, September 29, 1940; *BAA*, April 27, August 24, 1940; *PT*, April 4, May 30, June 27, August 1, 29, September 5, 1940; *CD*, December 17, 1938; April 1, October 28, 1939; Richard Donovan, "The Fabulous Satchel Paige," *Collier's Magazine*, May 30, June 6, June 13, 1953; *NYAN*, May 6, 1939; June 15, 1940; press release on Satchel Paige (1942?) in ACP, box 170-18, folder 2; Frazier Robinson with Paul Bauer, *Catching Dreams: My Life in the Negro Baseball Leagues* (Syracuse, N.Y., 1999), 21–22; *KCC*, June 16, 23, October 6, 1939; June 14, September 27, 1940.

31. Rogosin, "Queen of the Negro Leagues," 18 ("I didn't"); Irvin with Riley, *Nice Guys Finish First*, 44; *PC*, June 1, 15 ("Paige is my"), 29, 1940; Effa Manley to Tom Wilson and B. B. [*sic*] Martin, June 2 ("Negroes who"), 1940, NEP; *PT*, June 27, September 12, 1940; *PI*, June 30, 1940; *BAA*, June 29, 1940; *NYAN*, June 29, 1940.

32. Hazel Wigden to Effa Manley, June 22, 1940, NEP; *CD*, July 6 ("damn"/"con-sensus"), August 3 ("excitement"), 1940; "Satchelfoots," *Time*, June 3, 1940, 44; Ted Shane, "Chocolate Rube Waddell," *SEP*, July 27, 1940. As early as 1935, Al Monroe had suggested that "there is little doubt but that Satchel Paige is the Babe Ruth of Race baseball." Reflecting Paige's growing appeal, a 1936 advertisement in the *Tribune* for an upcoming date with the Crawfords at Parkside Field emphasized that "Satchell [*sic*] Paige will positively pitch this game." See *CD*, April 13, 1935; *PT*, May 28, 1936.

33. Mike Iannarella to Effa Manley, May 13 (?), 1940, Gottlieb to Effa Manley, July 31, 1940 ("we are"), NEP; *PAA*, September 7, 1940; *PC*, June 8 (Dixon), 1940; *BAA*, July 27 (Campbell), 1940; *PT*, August 8 (Harris), 1940.

34. *CD*, August 3 ("Chicago fans"), 10, September 14 ("which we"), 1940; Janu-ary 4, 1941; *PT*, January 2, 1941. By 1948, the American Giants' former home at 39th and Wentworth had become the site of a housing project. See *CD*, February 21, 1948.

35. *PT*, August 8 ("the League"), 22; December 26, 1940; Effa Manley to Jerry Kessler, July 22 ("must cut"), 1940; unsigned letter to John Boschen, August 21, 1940, NEP; Overmyer, *Effa Manley*, 109–11; *PC*, October 19, 1940; *NYAN*, December 21, 1940; March 8, 1941. Although Overmyer claims that Simon was no longer involved with the Eagles after 1945, a 1947 reference suggests his possible later participation. See *Our World* (September 1947).

36. *PC*, March 8 ("signs"), 1941; Overmyer, *Effa Manley*, 92 (Biot), 271.

37. *PC*, April 27 (Smith), 1940; *BAA*, August 6, 1938; July 15, 22, 1939; May 18, 1940; *PT*, August 10, 1939; unsigned letter to John McDonald, November 15, 1939, NEP; *CD*, March 23 (Gant), 1940. Rob Ruck's otherwise excellent *Sandlot Seasons* occasionally overstates the importance of Pittsburgh, particularly his characterization of the city as the "center of black professional baseball from the late 1920s until its demise." In July 1939, Grays owner Rufus Jackson disclosed the team's plans to relocate to Washington because of weak local support. While the Grays continued to play occasional home games in Pittsburgh, Washington would prove a far more profitable venue for the team during the 1940s. See *PC*, July 8, 1939; March 6, 1943; Ruck, *Sandlot Seasons*, 5, 173; *PV*, January 13, May 19, 1945.

38. *PC*, November 9 (Posey), 1940; *PI*, January 19 (Bolden), 1941; *PT*, August 8 (Harris), 1940.

Chapter 4. A New Beginning

Epigraph: *PC*, August 23, 1941.

1. *PT*, August 1 (Dunn), 1940; May 29, December 20, 1941; April 18 (Lee), 1942; *PI*, January 5, 1941; *BAA*, March 29, 1941; Lee Finkle, *Forum for Protest: The Black Press During World War II* (Rutherford, N.J., 1975), 93–105.

2. *BAA*, March 29, 1941; *PT*, November 21, 1940; July 3, August 21, October 4, 1941; January 31, April 25, 1942; Franklin and Moss, *From Slavery to Freedom*, 436–37; Allen M. Winkler, *Home Front U.S.A.: America During World War II* (Arlington Heights, Ill., 1986), 61–63; Charles S. Johnson and Associates, *To Stem This Tide: A Survey of Racial Tension Areas in the United States* (1943; reprint New York, 1969), 18; Finkle, *Forum for Protest*, 93–105; Robert C. Weaver, *Negro Labor, a National Problem* (New York, 1946), 20–21; Merl Reed, *Seedtime for the Modern Civil Rights Movement: The President's Committee on Fair Employment Practice, 1941–1946* (Baton Rouge, La., 1991).

3. Drake and Cayton, *Black Metropolis*, 9; Karen Tucker Anderson, "Last Hired, First Fired: Black Women Workers During World War II," *Journal of American History* (June 1982): 84; Richard Polenberg, *War and Society: The United States, 1941–1945* (Philadelphia, 1972), 123; Merl E. Reed, "Black Workers, Defense Industries, and Federal Agencies in Pennsylvania, 1941–1945," in *African Americans in Pennsylvania: Shifting Historical Perspectives*, ed. Joe William Trotter, Jr. and Eric Ledell Smith (University Park, Pa., 1997), 363–87; Robert C. Weaver, *The Negro Ghetto* (1948; reprint New York, 1967), 78; Franklin and Moss, *From Slavery to Freedom*, 449–50; Allan M. Winkler, *Home Front U.S.A.: America During World War II*, 2nd ed. (Wheeling, W.Va., 2000), 67.

4. Myrdal, *American Dilemma*, 804 (Bunche); *PT*, January 12 (Perdue), 1939.

5. Sitkoff, *New Deal for Blacks*, 242, 323; Buchanan, *Black Americans in World War II*, 116; Robert A. Hill, *The FBI's RACON: Racial Conditions in America During World War II* (Boston, 1995), 29–30, 77, 407; State Temporary Commission on the Conditions of the Urban Colored Population, *Final Report of the Pennsylvania State Temporary Commission on the Conditions of the Colored Population to the General*

Assembly of the State of Pennsylvania, 1943, 179; Claude A. Barnett, "The Role of the Press, Radio, and Motion Picture and Negro Morale," *Journal of Negro Education* 12, 3 (Summer 1943): 488; *PT*, July 17, 1941; March 21, April 4, 25, May 30, June 6, 13 ("unnecessary"), July 25, 1942; March 13, 1943 ("the slow"); March 17, 1945; January 31, 1948; April 26, 1955; Clara A. Hardin, *The Negroes of Philadelphia: The Cultural Adjustment of a Minority Group* (Fayetteville, Pa., 1945), 139; *PI*, July 20, 1941; May 10, July 19, 1942; March 11, April 28, May 26, 1945; *BAA*, September 8, 1945; *PV*, September 15, 1945; Reed, "Black Workers," 368–75.

6. *PT*, January 24 (Fauset), May 2, October 10, December 19, 1942; February 13, March 13 ("it may be"), December 11, 1943; January 27, February 3, 1945; *PI*, January 25, April 19, August 2, 23, 1942; July 23 ("intermixing"), 1944; *PC*, August 15, 1942; *BAA*, January 2, 1943; Maryann Lovelace, "Facing Change in Wartime Philadelphia: The Story of the Philadelphia USO," *Pennsylvania Magazine of History and Biography* (July 1999): 143–75.

7. *BAA*, January 11, 1941; *PT*, January 23 ("skunk"), 1941; Cum Posey to Abe Manley, December 9 ("very doubtful"), 26 ("see little"), 1940, Effa Manley to Cum Posey, December 16, 1940, NEP; Wynn, *The Afro-American and the Second World War*, 40; *Business Week*, January 18, 1941, 22–26.

8. *PC*, January 11, 1941; February 14, 1942; *PT*, January 16, 1941; *BAA*, January 11, 1941; NNL Treasurer's report for 1941 season, Cum Posey to Abe Manley, December 9 ("more players"), 1940, NEP.

9. Effa Manley to Cum Posey, December 16 ("not blame"), 1940; Effa Manley to J. B. Martin, November 25 ("an effort"), 1940, NEP.

10. Cum Posey to Abe Manley, December 26 ("otherwise"), 1940, NEP; *PC*, January 18 ("we cannot"), February 8, March 8, August 16, 1941; *PT*, March 6 (Harris), 1941; *PI*, April 6, 1941; *CD*, February 22, March 1, 1941; *BAA*, March 8, 1941.

11. *Homestead Grays Baseball Club vs. Joshua Gibson*, Court of Common Pleas of Allegheny County, Pennsylvania, No. 3496, April 1941 (Marshall quote); *PT*, April 10, 1941; Effa Manley to Cum Posey, March 15, 1941, Cum Posey to Effa Manley, March 20 ("hated"), 1941, NEP; *PC*, March 22, April 12, October 25, November 15, 1941. In the Lajoie case, the Pennsylvania Supreme Court rejected the claim that his baseball contract was "lacking in mutuality" and eventually granted an injunction to the Philadelphia Phillies preventing him from jumping to the Philadelphia Athletics of the then outlaw American League. On the Lajoie case, see Seymour, *Baseball—The Early Years*, 314–15; Craig, *Organized Baseball*, 132–33.

12. *BAA*, April 15 (Lacy), 1941; *PI*, April 6, 20, 1941; *PC*, April 5, October 25, 1941.

13. *PC*, April 5 (Harris), 1941; *PT*, August 7 (Gay), 1941.

14. *PI*, February 7, 1943; *BAA*, July 21, 1946; Riley, *Biographical Encyclopedia*, 408, 881; Effa Manley to Essex County Draft Board #13, May 5, 1942, Effa Manley to Essex County Local Draft Board, May 15, 1942, Effa Manley to J. B. Martin, August 21, 1942, NEP; *PT*, April 10, 1941; September 12, 1942; June 16, 1945; *PC*, August 1, 8, 1942; *NYAN*, February 2, 1963.

15. Robert Hartgrove to Juan E. Richer, July 22, 1942 ("it is patent"); Robert Hartgrove to Effa Manley, August 13, 1942 ("some definite"), William Smathers to Robert Hartgrove, August 19, 1942, Robert Hartgrove to William Smathers, August 21, 1942 ("the very"); NEP.

16. Robert C. Weaver, "Racial Employment Trends in National Defense," *Phylon* 3, 1 (1942): 22–30; *PAA*, April 29, 1944; *PT*, July 3, 1941; *PC*, June 28, July 12, August 2, 9, 16, 1941; *DT*, July 12, 1941.

17. *PC*, March 5 (Paige), 1938; May 17, June 28, August 16, 30, September 6

("likable"), 1941; *PT*, May 15, July 24, August 14, 1941; *PI*, May 11, 18, 1941; Ed Gottlieb to Effa Manley, May 8 ("would help"), 16, 19, July 20, 21 ("very cheap"), 1941, financial statement for July 20, 1941 doubleheader at Yankee Stadium, Effa Manley to See Posey, August 1, 1941 (Manley quote), NEP; "Satchel Paige, Negro Ballplayer, Is One of Best Pitchers in Game," *Life*, June 2, 1941; *CD*, May 24, 1941; *PINQ*, July 17 ("will definitely"), 1941.

18. *NYAN*, August 9, 1941.

19. *PT*, July 20, 1933; July 26, August 9, 1934; *PC*, August 18, 1934; *PINQ*, May 18, 1934; July 26, September 14, 1935; June 18, 1936; *PEB*, June 13, 26, 1933; August 2, 1934; Fleming, *Dizziest Season*, 194; *BAA*, March 31, 1934; Lawrence S. Katz, *Baseball in 1939: The Watershed Season of the National Pastime* (Jefferson, N.C., 1995), 122; *PR*, September 24, 1939.

20. *PI*, June 21, 1936; *PT*, March 29, April 5, 12, 1934; August 13, 1936; July 18, December 5, 1940; June 4, 1949; June 17, 1952; *BAA*, March 31, 1934. As late as 1952, a Zulu Giants baseball team continued to operate. On clowning in the early days of black baseball, see Lanctot, *Fair Dealing*, 31, 42–43, 245–46.

21. *BAA*, May 16, 1936; August 9, 1952; *CD*, May 9, 1936; *PI*, February 28, 1937; Holway, *Black Diamonds*, 95, 139–40; Rogosin, *Invisible Men*, 141–47; "Baseball's Comedy Kings," *Ebony*, September 1959; *PT*, February 25, 1937; Leonard with Riley, *Buck Leonard*, 139–40. By 1943, Pollock had assumed virtual control of the team after Pierce's withdrawal in 1939 and Hunter Campbell's death in 1942. See Johnnie Pierce to Abe Manley, December 24, 1939, NEP; *CD*, December 19, 1942.

22. *PC*, May 16, 1942. The Clowns, for example, featured King Tut, a performer whose antics included shooting "mythical craps all over the diamond and in the stands." See *KCC*, July 26, 1946. Similarly, the Harlem Globetrotters basketball team entertained fans by "shooting craps and playing cards during a game": Stanley Frank, "Crossroads Champs," *Collier's*, February 8, 1941, 49.

23. *PC*, June 28, 1941; May 30, 1942. Veteran black player Frazier Robinson claimed that "most of us didn't think too much of their clowning." See Robinson with Bauer, *Catching Dreams*, 105.

24. *PC*, July 5, 1941 ("capitalizing"); April 4, 1942 ("swell"); *Indianapolis Recorder*, October 5, 1940 (Pollock), cited in Debono, *Indianapolis ABCs*, 120.

25. *PC*, May 4, 1940; April 5, June 28, September 6, 1941; *PI*, July 6, August 24, 1941; *CD*, June 8, August 10, 1940; March 29, June 14 (Young), 1941; *PT*, May 27, 1937; September 5, 1940; March 6, 1941; *NYAN*, August 31, 1940; April 26, 1941; Syd Pollock to Effa Manley, March 28, 1941 ("we've"), NEP.

26. *PINQ*, May 20, August 16, 1941; January 13, 1942; *PR*, August 12, 1941; *PT*, June 5, September 6, 1941; *PI*, June 8, August 3, 10, 1941; Effa Manley to Cum Posey, October 13, 1941; Vernon Green to Abe Manley, June 9, 1941, NEP; Overmyer, *Effa Manley*, 107; *PC*, August 2, 1941; Wilmington Blue Rocks "Comparative Statements of Profit & Loss—December 31, 1941–1940," PP, box 5; SOMP, 1599–1600. Blue Rocks games at Wilmington drew 100,520 fans in 1941.

27. *BAA*, July 26 (Manley), August 9, 16, 1941; June 13, 1942; *PC*, July 12, August 9, 23, 30, September 6, 20, October 25 ("one of our"), 1941; *MC*, December 8, 1945; February 22, 1947; Wynn, *The Afro-American and the Second World War*, 61; *DT*, August 9, 1941; Seward ("See") Posey to Effa Manley, August 5, 1941 ("the largest"), NEP; *CD*, October 18, 1941; June 27, 1942; *Detroit Free Press*, September 15, 1941 in ACP, box 170-20, folder 1.

28. *PC*, March 27, June 5, 1937 ("as many"); February 24 ("came to"), November 9, 1940; Lanctot, *Fair Dealing*, 220; Ed Gottlieb to Effa Manley, September 27, 1939; William Leuschner to Effa Manley, October 25, 1939, NEP. White booking agents

were also influential in other aspects of black entertainment. See *PAA*, August 1, September 19, 1942; *Our World* (September 1953); *Variety*, June 17, 1942.

29. *PC*, February 24 ("experienced"/"to keep"), November 9 ("low blow"/"they have"), 1940; October 31, 1942 ("awful fix"); Ed Gottlieb to Effa Manley, September 27, 1939; William Leuschner to Effa Manley, October 25, 1939, Effa Manley to Rufus Jackson, April 29, 1939 ("does not"), NEP. Effa Manley claimed that because of her booking agent disputes, the Eagles "were idle an awful lot. We were idle half the time. We played mostly weekends, occasionally a night game in the middle of the week." See Holway, *Voices*, 321; Manley to John Clark, July 22, 1938, NEP.

30. Effa Manley to Rufus Jackson, October 9, 1939; Effa Manley to William Leuschner, July 22, 1941 ("it is"). See Posey to Effa Manley, July 29, 1941 (Posey quote), NEP; *BAA*, June 15 (Carter), 1940.

31. *NYT*, March 16, 1966; Abe Saperstein file, Naismith Memorial Basketball Hall of Fame; *CD*, September 16, 1933; August 10, 1940 (Young); May 15, 1948; Robert Peterson, *Cages to Jump Shots* (New York, 1990), 105–7; *PT*, April 18, 1935; July 11, 1950; *PC*, September 15, 1934; March 2, 1940; August 23, 1941 (Posey); minutes of June 20, 1939 meeting, NEP; *NYAN*, October 17, 1942; August 5, 1950; Stephen Fox, *Big Leagues* (Lincoln, Neb., 1998), 331–33; *SN*, February 8, 1950; Frank, "Crossroads Champs," *Collier's*, February 8, 1941; Randy Roberts and James S. Olson, *Winning Is the Only Thing: Sports in America Since 1945* (Baltimore, 1989), 31. Nelson George claims that Saperstein referred to his athletes as "children" and "had, if not a racist, then a profoundly paternalistic, condescending view of African-Americans." See Nelson George, *Elevating the Game: Black Men and Basketball* (New York, 1992), 45.

32. See Posey to Effa Manley, August 30 ("show"), 1941, Effa Manley to See Posey, August 1 ("we are"), 25 ("it wasn't"), 1941, Cum Posey to Effa Manley, November 17 ("Ed is"), 1941, Cum Posey to Abe and Effa Manley, December 4, 1941, NEP; *BAA*, August 30, 1941 (Rea).

33. See Posey to Effa Manley, August 30 ("white are"), 1941; Effa Manley to See Posey, August 1 ("these Jews"), 1941; Lem Graves, Jr. to Ed Harris, August 21, 1941, NEP; *Norfolk Journal and Guide*, February 26 ("Hebrew menace"), 1921. Subtle allusions to "Jewish gentleman" and "Hebrew booking agent" further reflected the objections of black sportswriters. See *BAA*, June 15, 1946; June 25, 1949; *PC*, November 23, 1946; *PT*, January 30, 1936.

34. *PT*, August 7 ("increasing"), 1943; August 19 ("destruction"), 1944.

35. Steven Riess, "Tough Jews: The Jewish American Boxing Experience, 1890–1950," in *Sports and the American Jew*, ed. Riess (Syracuse, N.Y., 1998), 92; Joe W. Trotter, Jr., "African Americans, Jews, and the City: Perspectives from the Industrial Era, 1900–1950," in *African Americans and Jews in the Twentieth Century: Studies in Convergence and Conflict*, ed. V. P. Franklin et al. (Columbia, Mo., 1998), 193–207; Stephen Norwood and Harold Brackman, "Going to Bat for Jackie Robinson: The Jewish Role in Breaking Baseball's Color Line," *Journal of Sport History* 26, 1 (Spring 1999): 134; *NYT*, September 3, 1964; June 8, 1969; Maurice Zolotow, "Harlem's Great White Father," *SEP*, September 27, 1941, 37, 40, 64, 66, 68; Chandler Owen, "Are Negroes Anti-Semitic?" *Negro Digest* (March 1943): 43–46; Paul Denis, "The Negro in Show Business," *Negro Digest* (February 1943): 34–39. The significance of Jews in black popular culture has also been acknowledged by black author Gerald Early, who cited the examples of George and Ira Gershwin (*Porgy and Bess*), Mike Jacobs, and Benny Goodman, the first major bandleader to integrate.

36. *PT*, March 25, 1944 (Posey); *SN*, July 14, 1962; *Kansas City Star*, July 3, 1962 in TBC, box 1, Thomas Y. Baird, obituary, 1962; Paige, *Maybe I'll Pitch Forever*, 138 (Paige quote); Holway, *Voices*, 182, 246, 287; Holway, *Blackball Stars*, 320; *PC*,

November 16, 1940; June 9, 1945; *PI*, March 15, 1952. By 1948, Jesse Owens was also linked with Saperstein, who had reportedly established a mail order sporting goods firm for him to operate. See *NYAN*, August 14, 1948.

37. Manley to Hank Rigney, May 6, 1939 ("truly honest"), NEP; Holway, *Blackball Stars*, 321–22 (Leonard); *PV*, February 28, 1942 (Bostic).

Chapter 5. An Industry Transformed

Epigraph: *PC*, December 16, 1944.

1. James A. Percoco, "Baseball and World War II: A Study of the Landis-Roosevelt Correspondence," *OAH Magazine of History* (Summer 1992): 60 ("I honestly"); *BAA*, June 7, 1941 (Carter); May 9, 1942; *Washington Post*, January 17, 1942 ("night games") in Dean Sullivan, comp. and ed., *Middle Innings: A Documentary History of Baseball, 1900–1948* (Lincoln, Neb., 1998), 182; Overmyer, *Effa Manley*, 172–79; Goldstein, *Spartan Seasons*, 124–29; *PINQ*, May 19, 1942; *NYT*, December 4, 1942; March 1, 1943; *PV*, August 28, 1943; Frank Graham, Jr., "When Baseball Went to War," World War II file, Baseball Hall of Fame Library; Stanley Frank, "The Diamond Dimout," *Negro Digest* (July 1943): 17–18; Art Carter, "Negro Baseball Players Star for Uncle Sam," *Negro Baseball Pictorial Yearbook*, 1945, 22–23, in ACP, box 170-17, folder 10; Ed Gottlieb to Art Carter, May 11, 1945, ACP, box 170-16, folder 6; *SN*, May 7, 28, June 18, July 30, 1942, Francis Matthews to Effa Manley, late May 1942, NEP. In November 1942, Fay Young claimed that "other than perhaps three or four teams in the two leagues, most of the owners can't pay the ball player what he can make in a defense plant." See *CD*, November 14, 1942.

2. *PI*, April 22, 1942; May 30, 1943; April 16, 1944; *PC*, March 14, 1942; January 23, February 20, May 1, 1943; Effa Manley to John Davis, July 8, 1942, NEP; John B. Holway, "The Kid Who Taught Satchel Paige a Lesson," *Baseball Research Journal* 16 (1987): 42; *NYAN*, August 7, 1943; *PV*, June 12, 1943; *BAA*, May 9, 1942 ("if business").

3. *BAA*, February 21, 1942; *PI*, March 1, 8, 1942; *CD*, March 21, 1942; April 17, 1943; *NYAN*, February 21, 1942; *PV*, February 21, 1942.

4. *PT*, August 17, 1939 (Harris); February 28, 1942; Ed Bolden to John Clark, December 17, 1941 ("stanchest"), EBP, box 186-1, folder 7; Effa Manley to John Clark, December 15, 1941, Cum Posey to Abe and Effa Manley, December 4, 1941 ("not anxious"), Gus Greenlee to Abe Manley, February 21, 1942 (Greenlee), NEP; *PC*, November 22, 1941 ("with all"); February 28, March 7, 1942; *PI*, February 22, March 8, 1942.

5. Effa Manley to S. H. Posey, August 1, 1941 ("please"); Effa Manley to Joseph Rainey, December 23, 1941, January 26, 1942 ("we need"/"going to"), Cum Posey to Effa Manley, November 22, 1942 ("proved consistent"), NEP.

6. Gus Greenlee to Abe Manley, February 21, 1942 ("there are"/"would rather"), Syd Pollock to Effa Manley, February 26 (Pollock quotes), 28, 1942, Effa Manley to Art Carter, March 4, 1942 ("Abe felt"), NEP; *NYAN*, February 21, 1942; *PC*, February 28, 1942; *PI*, March 1, 1942.

7. *PC*, November 9, 1940; February 28, March 7, June 20, October 31, November 21, 1942; *PI*, March 22, April 15, 1942; *BAA*, February 21, March 14, June 27, 1942; *PT*, February 28, 1942; *CD*, March 14 (Young), 1942; Ed Gottlieb to Effa Manley, December 4, 1939 ("our League"); minutes of June 10, 1942 joint session of NNL and NAL, NEP; Murray, *Negro Handbook 1944*, 19; Rogosin, *Invisible Men*, 44–45; *NYAN*, February 21, 1942.

8. Financial statement, 1942 East-West game, NEP; financial statement, 1943 East-West game, ACP, box 170-17, folder 17.

9. Cum Posey to Effa Manley, January 11, 1943 ("biggest"), NEP; *CD*, April 6, 1929; January 31, March 14, April 11, 1931; December 16, 1939; October 25 (Young), 1941; November 30, 1946; May 2, 1953; *PC*, December 17, 1938; November 9, 1940; February 2, November 30, 1946; April 26, 1952; *Memphis Commercial Appeal*, October 1, 1992, July 12, 1994; *NYAN*, December 12, 1936; March 14, 1942; *PI*, January 14, 1940; *BAA*, July 6, 1935; Richard Bardolph, *The Negro Vanguard* (1959; reprint Westport, Conn., 1971), 149–50; Grantham, *Political Status of the Negro*, 498–99; George W. Lee, *Beale Street, Where the Blues Began* (New York, 1934), 168–70; W. S. Martin to Tom Baird, January 4, 1950, TBC, box 2, corr. Matty Brescia, 1949–1953; Kurt McBee, "The Memphis Red Sox Stadium: A Social Institution in Memphis' African American Community," *West Tennessee Historical Society Papers* (1995): 149–64. A fourth brother, Dr. A. T. Martin (1886–1975), was not actively involved in baseball. All four Martin brothers received professional degrees from Meharry. See *Memphis Times Scimitar*, November 15, 1975, in A. T. Martin clipping file, Memphis Shelby County Public Library.

10. "MEMORANDUM REGARDING POLICE PERSECUTION OF DR. J. B. MARTIN OF MEMPHIS, TENNESSEE, BECAUSE OF POLITICAL ACTIVITIES IN 1940 PRESIDENTIAL ELECTION," Church family files, box 7, folder 1, Mississippi Valley Collection, University of Memphis; *CD*, December 7, 1940; January 6, 1945; November 30, 1946; August 7, 1948; January 13, 1951; September 3, 1955; J. B. Martin to Tom Baird, March 2, 1960, TBC, box 2, correspondence J. B. Martin, 1949–1960; *Memphis Commercial Appeal*, October 1, 1992; *PC*, November 30, December 14, 1940; November 30, 1946; *Ebony*, April 1949; *BAA*, January 13, 1951; Christopher Silver and John V. Moeser, *The Separate City: Black Communities in the Urban South* (Lexington, Ky., 1995), 48–50; David M. Tucker, *Memphis Since Crump: Bossism, Blacks, and Civic Reformers, 1948–1968* (Knoxville, Tenn., 1980), 17–18; *Memphis Times Scimitar*, April 15, 1942, in J. B. Martin clipping file, Memphis Shelby County Public Library; *Jet*, October 17, 1963; *KCC*, December 20, 1940; David M. Tucker, *Lieutenant Lee of Beale Street* (Nashville, Tenn., 1971), 127–29. In 1943, Martin attempted to return to Memphis for a baseball game but was promptly arrested by local authorities. See Robert Church to James R. Wright, October 26, 1943, Church family files, box 7, folder 27.

11. *CD*, May 17, August 16 ("how any"), November 1, 1941; August 7 ("nothing goes"), 1954; *PC*, November 13, 1943 (Posey). Despite their family ties, the Martin brothers often squabbled over a number of league-related issues, including the ownership of the Memphis team. In 1949, Martin claimed that, while each of the three brothers had originally owned a third of the club, he had given his share to W. S. and B. B. See Tom Baird to Matty Brescia, December 24, 1949; W. S. Martin to Tom Baird, January 4, 1950, TBC, box 2, correspondence, Matty Brescia, 1949–1953; Tom Baird to J. B. Martin, March 10, 1955; Tom Baird to B. B. Martin (undated, 1955?), TBC, box 2, correspondence, J. B. Martin, 1949–1960; Schedule Meeting, February 7–8, 1949, TBC, box 2, minutes, NAL meetings, 1943–1952.

12. Paige, *Maybe I'll Pitch Forever*, 159 (Paige quote); *CD*, May 23, 30, June 6, 13 (Young), August 22, November 14, 1942; July 24, 1943; *BAA*, June 6, 13, 27, August 22, September 5, 1942; July 24, 1943; August 12, 1944; *PINQ*, May 25, June 5 (Landis), 1942; Holway, *Voices*, 172; *DW*, May 20, 25, 26, June 2, 26, 1942; *PT*, June 6, 27, August 8, 1942; April 24, 1943; *PC*, June 20, 27, August 1, 1942; March 6, 1943; *PI*, September 20, 1942; Weaver, *Negro Labor*, 137; *PV*, August 8, 1942; *DT*, June 20, 1942; financial statement, 1942 East-West game, NEP; *SOMP*, 1618. A July 21,

1942, date at Forbes Field featuring the Grays and Monarchs drew 11,500 fans, a new attendance record in Pittsburgh for a game involving two black teams.

13. *PC*, October 31, 1942 ("best financial"); March 27, 1943 ("over a"); James A. Maxwell and Margaret N. Balcom, "Gasoline Rationing in the United States, I," *Quarterly Journal of Economics* (August 1946): 561–87; *NYT*, May 22, 23, December 1, 1942; *BAA*, March 7, 1942; *PINQ*, September 13, 1942; April 20, 1943; Goldstein, *Spartan Seasons*, 99–115; *CD*, December 12, 1942; Richard Lingeman, *Don't You Know There's a War On? The American Home Front, 1941–1945* (New York, 1970), 238–40; *Business Week*, September 19, 1942; Kenesaw Landis to Joseph Eastman, December 8, 1942 ("will do"), Office of the Director, Railway Transport Department, 1942–1946, RG 219.

14. *PC*, February 6 ("drop"), 27 (Clark), 1943; H. F. McCarthy to J. B. Martin, December 15, 1942 ("requests"); J. B. Martin to Joseph Eastman, March 2, 1943, folder 47877; Records from Highway Transport Department, 1942–1946, RG 219; *BAA*, January 23, April 10, 1943; Maxwell and Balcom, "Gasoline Rationing in the United States, I," 569–73; Marty Weintraub to Effa Manley, 1943 (Weintraub quote), NEP; *NYT*, March 2, 1943; Overmyer, *Effa Manley*, 169–71; *PI*, April 4, 1943; Dixon and Hannigan, *Negro Baseball Leagues*, 207 (Pollock).

15. Cum Posey to "Sir," March 7, 1943 ("very"/"WE"), NEP. Some observers believed that black baseball needed to demonstrate a more direct contribution to the war effort, comparable to the white major leagues' numerous benefits for servicemen's relief agencies and to Joe Louis, who donated his winnings from two 1942 fights. The NNL and NAL, however, were unable to coordinate a specific charity promotion with the exception of a jointly sponsored all-star game on August 18, 1942, at Municipal Stadium in Cleveland, which drew 10,791 fans. Although the wealthy J. B. Martin purchased thousands of dollars in war bonds, several sportswriters felt that black baseball as an enterprise should have given more generously and earmarked at least part of the East-West profits to charity. On benefits during the war, see Ernest Wright to Effa Manley, August 29, 1942, NEP; *CD*, August 29, 1942; October 30, 1943; January 6, 1945; Goldstein, *Spartan Seasons*, 64–68; Capeci and Wilkerson, "Multifarious Hero," 5–25; *PI*, August 20, 1944; *PC*, July 10, 24, August 28, December 18, 1943; February 26, 1944; *BAA*, June 4, 1949; *MC*, August 14, 1943; *PT*, December 2, 1944; *NYAN*, June 13, 1942; *PV*, June 13, 1942.

16. J. B. Martin to Joseph Eastman, March 12, 1943 (folder 47877), Edward Bolden to C. W. Posey, March 10, 1943 (Bolden quote), Effa Manley to Cum Posey, March 8, 1943, Thos. T. Wilson to Cum Posey, March 11, 1943, Allen Johnson to Cum Posey, March 11, 1943, Alex Pompez to Cum Posey, March 10, 1943, Rufus Jackson to Cum Posey (undated), (folder 50062), Records from Highway Transport Department, 1942–1946, RG 219.

17. Cum Posey to ODT, March 13, 1943, NEP.

18. Cum Posey to Mr. [H. F.] McCarthy, late March 1943, folder 50062, Records from Highway Transport Department, 1942–1946, RG 219.

19. Joseph Eastman to C. W. Posey, March 29, 1943 (telegram, Joseph Eastman to Cum Posey, April 6, 1943 (folder 50062), Harry Truman to Mr. Edward Roberts (memorandum), April 27, 1943, Edward Roberts to Harry Truman, April 29, 1943, Joseph Eastman to Arthur Capper, April 27, 1943 (folder 48956), Charles Phillips to Guy Richardson, April 2, 1943, Edward Roberts to Effa Manley, April 6, 1943, J. B. Martin to Joseph Eastman, April 9, 1943 (folder 47877), Records from Highway Transport Department, 1942–1946; RG 219; *CD*, March 20, April 3, 1943; *PI*, April 11, 1943; *PT*, March 13, 20, 1943; *BAA*, April 10, May 1, 1943; *KCC*, April 9, 16, May 7, 1943; *MC*, April 3 ("practically"), 1943.

20. *BAA*, May 1, 1943 ("denied"); C. A. Franklin to Joseph Eastman, April 24, 1943 ("you do") (folder 48956), Records from Highway Transport Department, 1942–1946, RG 219; *MC*, April 10, 1943 ("there is"); *PC*, June 27, July 4, 1942; March 13, 1943; *CD*, April 10 (Young), 1943. The policy particularly affected black musical groups, who typically played briefer engagements than their white counterparts and encountered major difficulties securing accommodations in the South. Following attempts by the NAACP to modify the ODT's policy on charter buses, government officials in late 1942 allocated five buses to allow limited Southern tours, only to rescind the order in January 1943. See Buses for Colored Orchestras, 1942 file in NAACP, Part 15: Segregation and Discrimination, Complaints and Responses, 1940–1955, Series B: General Office Files, reel 3; *PV*, June 6, 27, September 12, 1942; *PAA*, June 27, July 11, August 1, 1942; *Variety*, May 20, 27, June 17, 24, October 7, 1942; *KCC*, January 29, 1943.

21. Effa Manley to James Semler, May 22, 1943 ("not so"), NEP; *PC*, March 13, April 24 ("ridiculous"), June 5, 1943 ("paid"); Samuel Weiss to Joseph Eastman, March 3, 1943, Samuel Weiss to Guy A. Richardson, March 25, 1943, Cum Posey to Joseph Eastman, May 15, 1943 ("compelled") (folder 50062), Records from Highway Transport Department, 1942–1946, RG 219; *BAA*, April 10, 17, 1943; *CD*, April 17, 1943; Goldstein, *Spartan Seasons*, 41; *NYT*, January 18, 1945; *PINQ*, April 14, 1943; *PR*, March 3, 1943. Despite the NAACP's active involvement in the earlier attempt to modify the ODT's policy on charter buses for black musical groups, the organization apparently made only limited attempts to assist the NNL and NAL. Whether this was due to a lack of vigilance by the two leagues or the NAACP's preference to distance itself from an organization that included a number of underworld figures is unknown. Walter White, however, did contact Edward Roberts in late March 1943, suggesting that the ODT require the leagues to submit their schedules in advance to determine actual travel distances. Two years later, Roberts claimed that the eventual exemptions granted the NNL and NAL "were worked out by this Office in cooperation with Secretary Walter White . . . after conferences with the presidents of the two baseball leagues," although the actual role of White remains somewhat unclear. See Walter White to Edward Roberts (telegram), March 29, 1943 (folder 47877), Edward Roberts to Walter George, March 3, 1945 (folder 48910), Records from Highway Transport Department, 1942–1946, RG 219.

22. Edward Roberts to Cum Posey, May 24 ("the gasoline"), 1943 (folder 50062), Joseph Eastman to J. B. Martin, June 25 (Eastman), 1943, Guy Richardson to J. B. Martin, February 26, 1944, Guy Richardson to William Hueston, February 26, 1944, P. N. Simmons to All Regional Directors, April 5, 1945 (folder 47877), Edward Roberts to Alex Pompez, July 12, 1943 ("entirely") (folder 48957), Records from Highway Transport Department, 1942–1946, RG 219; Cum Posey to owners, July 15, 1943 ("we could"), NEP.

23. Edward Roberts to R. B. Jackson, March 22, 1945 ("long-established") (folder 48910), J. M. Johnson to Senator Harry Byrd, July 17, 1944 (Johnson) (folder 48955), Records from Highway Transport Department, 1942–1946, RG 219; Cum Posey to "Member," March 23, 1945 (Posey quote), NEP. The ODT's allocation of buses for black musical groups was underpublicized for similar reasons. See handwritten notation by Walter White (at bottom of John Hammond to E. A. Robert[s], September 28, 1942) in Buses for Colored Orchestras, 1942, NAACP papers.

24. Harry Gormley to J. B. Martin, August 12, 1944 (folder 47877), Ray Doan to Congressman Thomas Martin, March 9, 1945, Thomas Martin to J. Monroe Johnson, May 9, 1945, J. M. Johnson to Thomas Martin, May 16, 1945 (folder 50182), Records from Highway Transport Department, RG 219; minutes of March 5–6, 1945 schedule

meeting ("use"), TBC, box 2, minutes, NAL meetings 1943–1952. As late as July 1945, the ODT refused to grant permission for the use of buses in the north. See J. B. Martin to Edward Roberts, June 29, 1945; Charles F. Warden to J. B. Martin, July 13, 1945 (folder 47877), Records from Highway Transport Department, RG 219.

25. Albert A. Blum, *Drafted or Deferred: Practices Past and Present* (Ann Arbor, Mich.,1967), 184–86; *CD*, February 13, 1943; Polenberg, *War and Society*, 21; *SN*, January 14, February 11, March 25, 1943; George Q. Flynn, "Selective Service and American Blacks During World War II," *Journal of Negro History* (Winter 1984): 14–25; *BAA*, January 23, 30, March 27, 1943; September 14, 1946; *PT*, January 16, 1943; *PC*, February 20, 27, 1943; Goldstein, *Spartan Seasons*, 187; Sullivan, *The Minors*, 165; *NYT*, February 24, September 4, 1943; *PINQ*, June 20, November 30, 1943; National Association of Professional Baseball Leagues, *The Story of Minor League Baseball* (Columbus, Oh., 1953), 45–50; Holway, "Kid Who Taught Satchel Paige a Lesson," 42; *PV*, June 12, 1943; Effa Manley to Ed Bolden, March 4, 1944, NEP; *Newark Sunday Call*, March 14, 1943, in Manley scrapbook, BHOFL; Stanley Woodward, "Absentee—For 15 Rounds," *Negro Digest* (July 1943): 31–32; Stan Grosshandler, "1943—The Nadir," *Coffin Corner* 15 (1993).

26. Effa Manley to Art Carter, February 2 ("solution"), 1943, NEP; Holway, *Voices*, 180 (Radcliffe), 126 (Bell); Ed Gottlieb to Art Carter, May 11, 1945, ACP, box 170-16, folder 6; *PI*, January 24 ("almost"), 31, April 18, May 9, June 6, 1943; *PC*, January 30, May 1, 1943; *PT*, August 7, 21, 1943.

27. *PC*, May 1 ("a simple"), 1943; *BAA*, May 1 ("confine"), 8 (Carter), 1943; *CD*, May 8, 1943; *PI*, May 9, 1943.

28. *PC*, May 1 ("the East"/"sphinx"), June 12 ("the best"/"it is"), July 3, 1943; minutes of June 1, 1943, NNL meeting ("necessary"), minutes of joint session of June 1, 1943, NEP; *PI*, June 6, 13, July 4, 25, 1943; September 17, 1944; *CD*, June 12 ("we are"), 1943. The Grays and Buckeyes eventually negotiated agreements allowing their retention of Bell and Smith.

29. Holway, *Black Diamonds*, 100 (Leonard); *PC*, January 30, 1943 (Martin); minutes of June 1, 1943, joint session, NEP. On the Clowns' performers and comedy routines, see *PT*, April 8, 1944; July 7, 1945; April 9, 1949; May 6, 1950; March 17, May 22, 1951; *PI*, May 14, 1949; Rogosin, *Invisible Men*, 141–43; Ted Shane, "'Peanuts' Nyasses and the World's Wildest Ball Team," *Liberty*, September 19, 1942, 53–54.

30. *PI*, April 18, July 4, 1943; January 16, 1944; *CD*, April 17, 1943; *NYAN*, April 17, 1943; *PC*, May 8 (Greenlee), July 3, September 4, 1943; January 15, 1944.

31. *BAA*, August 29, 1942; July 24, August 14, 1943; J. B. Martin to Effa Manley, February 8, 1944 ("all made"), statement for 1943 East-West game, NEP; *CD*, August 7, 1943; handwritten statement of Monarchs profits, 1942–1946, TBC, box 15, financial records, miscellaneous, 1944–1960; *PC*, December 18 (Smith), 1943; *PT*, October 3, 1942; July 3, August 14, September 4 (Burley), 18, 1943; *PI*, May 16 (Coleman), 1943; *PINQ*, September 30, 1942; June 22, 1943; *NYT*, September 30, 1942; *PAA*, June 26, 1943.

32. *PT*, June 26 ("a free"), 1943; *PC*, March 27 ("one Negro"), 1943.

33. *PT*, May 16, 23, 1929; July 6, 1933; *BAA*, June 26, 1926; *PC*, December 20, 1924; December 31, 1932; May 13, 1933; August 4, 1934; Gerald Early, "Baseball and African American Life," in *Baseball: An Illustrated History*, ed. Geoffrey Ward and Ken Burns (New York, 1994), 415; *CD*, August 4, 1934; March 14, 1942.

34. *PT*, September 9 (Hawkins), 1937; October 16, 1943; *PC*, July 30, 1938; January 11, 1941; Abe Manley to league members, May 10, 1939, Cum Posey to owners (summary of recent NNL meeting), 1939, Effa Manley to Chester Washington, May 26, 1939 ("all wrong"), Cum Posey to Effa Manley, June 2, 1939 ("positively"), Cum

Posey to Abe Manley, December 19, 1940, Abe Manley to Lem Graves, May 25, 1942, Cum Posey to Effa Manley, November 22, 1942 ("a shame"), NEP; *NYAN*, September 30, 1944.

35. *PC*, November 6, 1943; January 15, 1944; *CD*, December 25, 1943; Wendell Smith to Effa Manley, December 22, 1943, prospectus for statistics, Effa Manley to Wendell Smith, February 7 ("the thing"), 1944, NEP; minutes of NAL meeting, December 19, 1943, TBC, box 2, minutes, NAL meetings, 1943–1952. According to one account, some owners welcomed the compilation of accurate statistics, believing "there should be records available when the majors come asking for information on Negro players." See *PV*, January 15, 1944.

36. *PI*, January 16, March 12, 1944; *PC*, March 11, 1944; *PT*, March 18 (Burley), 25, 1944; J. B. Martin to Effa Manley, (April?) 1944 ("the colored"), NEP; minutes of NAL meeting, March 5, 1944, TBC, box 2, minutes, NAL meetings, 1943–1952. Although sportswriters consistently pined for another Rube Foster to rescue black baseball from its difficulties, Foster himself had been unable to solve the essential problems of black baseball and had been criticized for his sometimes dictatorial and self-serving policies during his tenure as president of the first NNL. His reputation, however, continued to grow, and by 1944 Cum Posey observed that some of the stories "written and told concerning Foster are so fantastic that we sometimes marvel at the imagination of the narrators." Black newspaper references to Foster are numerous during the 1930s and 1940s, but see *PT*, February 19, July 1, 1944; *PC*, April 2, 1932; February 17, 1940; *NYAN*, October 9, 1943; *BAA*, February 5, 1938; *CD*, January 14, 1933.

37. *PT*, September 15, 1938; *SN*, March 11, 1972 (Leonard quote); *BAA*, May 21, 1949; *NYAN*, September 30, 1944; Effa Manley to Al Monroe [*sic*] Elias, September 24, 1946 ("still not"), NEP; Thomas Baird to J. B. Martin, September 17, 1954 (Baird), TBC, box 2, correspondence, J. B. Martin, 1949–1960. Unfortunately, league statistics remained unreliable and inaccessible into the 1950s despite the growing interest of Organized Baseball teams in acquiring black players. Recognizing the Monarchs' potential difficulty in providing the Dallas Eagles of the Texas League with requested data on Othello Renfroe, Matty Brescia suggested that Tom Baird "muster together a record of some kind . . . just make it up from memory." See Matty Brescia to Tom Baird, March 2, 1952, box 2, correspondence, Matty Brescia, 1949–1953, minutes of the schedule meeting, June 14, 1951, TBC, box 2, minutes, NAL meetings, 1943–1952.

38. Lanctot, *Fair Dealing*, 120–21, 140, 261–62; See Posey to Effa Manley, July 29, 1941 ("let any"), NEP; *PI*, August 29, September 26, October 3, 1937; *PC*, September 4, 18, 25, October 9, 1937; *PT*, September 16, 23, 30, 1937; October 23 ("glorified"), 1943; September 23 ("three-ring"), 1944.

39. *BAA*, October 9, 1943; September 16, 1944; *CD*, September 25, 1937; October 23, 30, 1943; September 9, November 4, December 2, 1944; *PC*, September 26, 1942; September 2, 9, 16, 1944; *PT*, October 23, November 13, 1943; September 16 (Martin/Wilson quotes), 1944; September 29, 1945 (Garrett); *PI*, September 10, 1944; minutes of NAL meeting, December 19, 1943, TBC, box 2, minutes, NAL meetings, 1943–1952.

40. P. E. Schwahm of State Headquarters for Selective Service to Emanuel Millman, Esquire, April 3, 1943 ("no action"), NEP; *PC*, February 20, July 17, 24 ("cussing"), 1943; February 26 ("the players"), March 18, May 6 (Wells), 1944; *BAA*, July 24, 1943; *CD*, November 4, 1944; Holway, *Voices*, 267; *PT*, April 15, 1944; Roy Campanella, *It's Good to be Alive* (Boston, 1959), 95; *SN*, April 22, 1943; March 9, 1944; C. W. Posey to "Sir," May 16, 1944, BHOFL. Mexican offers to top players continued to rise in subsequent years. In 1946, See Posey of the Grays disclosed that Mexican

representatives had offered $6,000 to $7,000 contracts to Sam Bankhead and Buck Leonard. See Seward Posey to Effa Manley, March 28, 1946, NEP.

41. *PC*, February 20, 1943; March 18, December 16, 1944; *BAA*, July 24, 1943; *PI*, January 16, March 12, June 25, 1944; *PT*, March 25, June 24, July 1, 22, 29, 1944; *NYAN*, April 17, 1943; May 20, July 22, 1944. Within a year, Saperstein once again took part in the promotion of the East-West game. According to Fay Young, Saperstein was not a franchise owner but received 30 percent of the Barons' net profits for booking the team's non-league games. The remainder of the team's income was shared by Tom Hayes (50 percent) and manager Winfield Welch (20 percent). See financial statement of July 29, 1945 East-West game, TBC, box 2, financial records, Negro East West Game, 1943–1953; *CCP*, July 29, 1944.

42. J. B. Martin to Effa Manley, May 29, 1944 ("very satisfactory"), NEP; Tom Baird to J. B. Martin, March 7, 1952 ("control"), TBC, box 2, correspondence, J. B. Martin, 1949–1960; minutes of June 13, 1944 meeting, TBC, box 2, minutes, NAL meetings, 1943–1952; *PT*, August 7, 1943; March 4, June 24, July 29, 1944 (Burley); *PC*, October 11, 1941; July 3, 1943, July 29, 1944 (Smith); *PI*, June 25, 1944; *CCP*, December 23, 1944.

43. *PT*, July 1, August 5 ("rid"/"conditions"), 26, September 2, 9, December 16, 23, 1944; *MC*, July 8, August 26 (Cowans), 1944; May 5, August 18, 1945; *CD*, August 26, November 4, 1944; February 17, 1945; *NYAN*, September 2, 1944; *PI*, August 26, September 3, 17, 1944; *PV*, December 16, 23, 1944; January 13 (Bostic), 1945.

44. Weaver, *Negro Labor*, 86; Wynn, *Afro-American and the Second World War*, 55; Louis Coleridge Kesselman, *The Social Politics of FEPC* (Chapel Hill, N.C., 1948), 227; *Final Report of the Pennsylvania State Temporary Commission*, xxxiv; *PT*, November 11, 1944; January 6, 1945 (Moses); *PI*, September 21, 1946; *PC*, September 9, December 9, 1944; *NYAN*, December 30, 1944; handwritten statement of Monarchs' profits, 1942–1946, TBC, box 15, financial records, miscellaneous, 1944–1960.

45. Effa Manley to Cum Posey, December 16, 1940, Alex Pompez to Effa Manley, April 21, 1941, Effa Manley to See Posey, August 1, 1941, James Semler to "Member," April 11, 1943, Effa Manley to Ed Gottlieb, July 3, 1944, NEP; *PI*, April 18, 1943; January 16, 1944; *BAA*, April 17, 1943; *CD*, April 17, 1943; *PC*, May 29, 1943; Overmyer, *Effa Manley*, 271; *PT*, July 3, 31, 1943; August 26 ("disgrace"), September 16 ("Semler"), 1944; *PV*, October 17, 1942; July 10, 1943; January 15, May 6, 1944.

46. *BAA*, April 6, 1940; June 17, 1944; May 19, 1945; Abe Manley to J. A. Robert Quinn, July 5, 1939, Abe Manley to Larry MacPhail, November 7, 1939, Cum Posey to Abe Manley, December 19, 1940, Effa Manley to John Collins, July 2, 1940 ("Dexter"), Effa Manley to See Posey, August 25, 1941, NEP; *PT*, May 20, June 10, July 1, 1944; *PI*, April 28, 1940; *PC*, December 23, 1944; *NYAN*, April 24, 1948; McKay, *Harlem*, 135. Notably, Gottlieb was apparently reluctant to rent the Polo Grounds for a May 30, 1943, date until "hearing from Mr. [Ed] Barrow of the Yankees that it would be O.K. with him." See Ed Gottlieb to Effa Manley, May 10, 1943, NEP.

47. *MC*, June 17, July 8, August 12, 1944; May 3, 1945; *CCP*, July 25, 1942; *CD*, July 22, 1944; *BAA*, April 1, September 9 (Lacy), 1944; Pietrusza, *Lights On!* 143; Bruce, *Kansas City Monarchs*, 154; Benson, *Ballparks of North America*, 191; minutes of March 5–6, 1945 schedule meeting, TBC, box 2, minutes, NAL meetings 1943–1952; J. G. Taylor Spink, *Baseball Guide and Record Book—1945* (St. Louis, 1945), 129; *PC*, June 27, 1942; J. B. Martin to Effa Manley, February 8, 1944 (Martin quote), NEP. The NNL's potential loss of night games at National League parks in 1944 prompted Cum Posey to contact Ford Frick and other officials in hopes of overturning the policy. See C. W. Posey to "Sir," May 16, 1944, BHOFL.

48. *CD*, May 17, August 16, 1941; March 21, 1942; December 25, 1943; January 8, 1944; Abe Manley to Tom Wilson, May 16, 1939; Cum Posey to Effa Manley, November 22, 1942; J. B. Martin to Effa Manley, February 8, 1944, NEP; *CCP*, April 17, 1948; *NYAN*, December 30, 1944; *PV*, September 23, 1944; Gerald R. Curtis, "Factors That Affect the Attendance of a Major League Baseball Club" (M.B.A. thesis, University of Pennsylvania, 1951), 116; Syd Pollock to Art Carter, June 20, 1945, ACP, box 170-16, folder 12; *PT*, June 10, July 1, 22, 29, August 12, September 2, 23 (Wilson), October 7, 1944; *MC*, March 11, 1944; *PC*, December 23, 1944.

49. *PC*, January 13 ("skeptical"), 1940; October 30 ("there are"), 1943; *PT*, July 15 ("if a"), 29, 1944; Cum Posey to Abe Manley, October 25, 1942 ("pick"); Cum Posey to Effa Manley, November 22, 1942, Abe or Effa Manley to John H. Harden, November 24, 1944 ("if we"), Syd Pollock to Effa Manley, December 28, 1944 ("it may"), NEP.

50. *PC*, October 9 ("if Negro"), December 18 ("perhaps"), 1943; December 23 ("to prove"), 1944; January 20 ("you can't"), 1945; *PT*, December 23, 1944.

Chapter 6. Life Inside a Changing Industry

Epigraph: Lloyd Lewis, "Dusky Hercules," *Chicago Daily News*, August 2, 8, 1944, reprinted in *Best Sport Stories of 1944*, ed. Irving T. March and Edward Ehre (New York, 1945), 68–69.

1. *PT*, April 27 ("high-class"), 1946; *PC*, April 2 (Gibson), May 14 (Smith), 1938.

2. See Posey to Effa Manley, July 17, 1941 ("the players"), NEP; *BAA*, February 8, 29, August 8, 1924; September 4, 11, 1926; June 24, 1950; *PC*, January 28, 1933 (Fuller); January 6, 1940 (Posey); June 5, 1943; Holway, *Voices*, 55 (Malarcher); *PI*, May 31, June 14, 1936; *PT*, August 1, 29, 1940; July 17, 1941 (Harris); *NYAN*, June 17, 1950; Willie Mays with Lou Sahadi, *Say Hey: The Autobiography of Willie Mays* (New York, 1988), 42; interview with Larry Kimbrough, July 22, 1998. In white Organized Baseball, major league and upper-level minor league teams traveled by train, although class B, C, and D clubs usually relied on buses. See *SN*, June 18, 1947; W. G. Bramham to Col. J. Munroe Johnson, February 23, 1945, Office of the Director, Railway Transport Department, 1942–1946, RG 219.

3. *PT*, September 15, 1932; June 24, 1937; June 13, 1940; September 12, 1942, September 23, 1944; *PC*, June 26, 1937; Alvin Harlow, "Unrecognized Stars," *Esquire*, September 1938; *BAA*, September 14, 1946; *NYAN*, January 17, 1942 (McDuffie). The Grays traveled 30,000 miles in 1937 during the course of a 179-game season. See *NYA*, October 23, 1937.

4. Brent P. Kelley, *Voices from the Negro Leagues* (Jefferson, N.C., 1998), 159 (Glenn); interview with Wilmer Harris, March 31, 2000 (Harris); *PI*, August 18, 1935; July 18, 1937; August 6, 1939; *PINQ*, April 24, 1938; May 4, 1939; May 11, 1941; *PT*, July 22, August 12, 26, 1937; July 21, 1938.

5. Woods brothers to Ed Bolden, October 31, 1941, EBP, box 186-1, folder 15; budget sheets, 1949, TBC, box 10; William Maguire to Abraham Manley, March 1, 1939, Effa Manley to Mrs. Elliott of Attucks Hotel, June 4, 1942, NEP; *NYAN*, May 3, 1941; February 21, 1942; John A. Saunders, *100 Years After Emancipation: History of the Philadelphia Negro, 1867 to 1963* (Philadelphia, 1964), 145; interview with Mahlon Duckett, July 2, 1998 (Duckett quote); *PT*, July 19, 1934 ("about the worst"); Marshall interview with Manley, October 19, 1977, COHP (Manley quote); Robinson, *Catching Dreams*, 131 ("we had"). On black hotels and accommodations for black teams, see budget sheets, 1948; budget sheets, 1949, TBC, boxes 9 and 10; *PT*, August 8, 1950; *BAA*, January 11, 1941; Kelley, *Voices*, 178, Honig, *Baseball When the Grass*

Was Real, 174; Walker, *History of Black Business*, 430; Bardolph, *Negro Vanguard*, 328, Robinson, *Catching Dreams*, 131–32; Robert H. Kinzer and Edward Sagarin, *The Negro in American Business: The Conflict Between Separatism and Integration*, 189; Effa Manley to Syd Pollock, June 27, 1945, NEP; *NYAN*, October 15, 1949.

6. *PC*, July 25, 1936 ("I think"); *NYAN*, March 12, 1938; *BAA*, July 26, 1941; Theodore Rosengarten, "Reading the Hops: Recollections of Lorenzo Piper Davis and the Negro Baseball League," *Southern Exposure* (Summer/Fall 1977): 71; Marshall interview with Manley, October 19, 1977; *PINQ*, June 2, 1936; Koppett, *Koppett's Concise History of Major League Baseball*, 193; Harlow, "Unrecognized Stars"; *PI*, September 4, 1938; August 3, 1941; *PT*, September 2, 1937; Effa Manley to Willie Wells, February 6, 1942, NEP. In 1945, player limits for class A-1, A, and B minor league teams ranged from 16 to 18. By 1946, the NNL allowed each team to carry 20 players. See W. G. Bramham to Col. J. Munroe Johnson, February 23, 1945, Office of the Director, Railway Transport Department, 1942–1946, RG 219; *PAA*, June 29, 1946.

7. Tygiel, *Baseball's Great Experiment*, 20 ("no sooner"); Cum Posey to ODT, March 13, 1943, NEP; *BAA*, April 13, 1935; March 7, 1936; *PC*, April 8, 1939; April 19, 1941; *PT*, March 5, 1936; May 16, 1940; April 13, 1946; Overmyer, *Effa Manley*, 121.

8. Bunny Downs to Ed Bolden, August 22, 1941, Ed Bolden to Norwood White, September 12, 1941 ("I would"), McKenzie Wilkins, II to Oscar Charleston, May 28, 1951 ("I am"), Ed Bolden to E. E. Forbes, June 24, 1942 ("could beat"), E. E. Forbes to Ed Bolden, July 5, 1942 ("going better"), Ed Bolden to E. E. Forbes, July 8, 1942 ("pay expenses"), EBP, box 186-1, folders 7, 9, 15; *PI*, October 15 (Buchanan), 1944.

9. Wilmer Fields, *My Life in the Negro Leagues: An Autobiography* (Westport, Conn., 1992), 6 ("picked"); interview with Larry Kimbrough, July 22, 1998; *PI*, August 13, 1939 (Coleman).

10. *PC*, September 8, 1934; May 16, 1936; February 3, 1937; January 23, 1943; *PI*, July 14, 1935; July 31, 1938; August 27, 1939; June 2, 1940; Overmyer, *Effa Manley*, 85; *PT*, November 5, December 3, 1936; January 28, February 25, March 4, April 15, May 20, June 3, 10 ("most of"), July 15, 1937; March 3, 10, 1945; minutes of June 20, 1946, NNL meeting, NEP; Bauer, *Catching Dreams*, 117; Peterson, *Only the Ball Was White*, 120; Sports editor to L. Z. Plummer, March 28, 1940, ACP, box 170-16, folder 12; *BAA*, July 3, 1937.

11. *BAA*, July 29, 1939; Overmyer, *Effa Manley*, 85 ("go and"); *PT*, July 23, 1936; July 20, 1939; August 28, November 20 (Wilson), December 11, 1943; Webster McDonald to Abe Manley, November 21, 1943, NEP.

12. *PI*, August 11, 1935 (Bolden); Historical Society of Pennsylvania, *Proceedings from Philadelphia's Baseball History: Symposium Held on February 24, 1990* (Philadelphia, 1990), 62 (Benson); interview with Mahlon Duckett, July 2, 1998. Young players often experienced similar hurdles in white Organized Baseball. See Honig, *Baseball When the Grass Was Real*, 137.

13. Interview with Wilmer Harris, March 31, 2000 ("managers"); Proceedings from *Philadelphia's Baseball History*, 62 (Benson); *PT*, June 26, 1943; June 3, 1944; June 30, 1945; January 24, 1948; July 3 (Davis), 1951; *PC*, August 31, 1935; Tygiel, *Baseball's Great Experiment*, 20; *PI*, December 6 (Doby), 1947. In 1946, Roy Campanella observed that "in the Negro Leagues they play 'muscle' baseball. In organized baseball they play 'head' baseball." See *PV*, April 20, 1946.

14. Clipping from *BAA* (August 16, 1941?); (Salsinger), courtesy of Dick Clark, SABR Negro Leagues Committee; *BAA*, October 13, 1945; John Lardner, "Recollec-

tions of Old Satch," *Newsweek*, September 30, 1946; *PT*, June 21, 1934; June 17, 1937; June 8, 1939; August 28, 1943, July 15, 1944; Harlow, "Unrecognized Stars."

15. Drake and Cayton, *Black Metropolis*, 122 ("tendency"); *New York Daily News*, February 10, 1933 ("comical"); *WT*, August 3, 1935 (Lacy); Irvin, *Nice Guys Finish First*, 79 ("stronger"); minutes, June 13, 1944, NAL meeting, TBC, box 2, minutes, NAL meetings, 1943–1952; *PT*, February 23, 1939 ("rounding"). Even some black promoters perpetuated the belief that black players would not fit into the more structured world of Organized Baseball. John Williams, for example, argued that integration would force Satchel Paige and others to curb their colorful behavior, noting that "speed, daring and mirth are the God-given characteristics of Negro ball players who play the game for the fun there is in it." Williams's role in the lucrative Briggs Stadium promotions of the early 1940s, however, likely shaped his attitude toward integration. See *MC*, May 19, 1945.

16. *PC*, September 19 ("it has"), 1936; S. H. Posey (?) to Effa Manley, August 16, 1945 ("a lot"); Hazel M. Wigden to Effa Manley, June 22, 1940, NEP.

17. *BAA*, August 27, 1955 (Pompez); *PAA*, May 29, 1948 (Lyle). For assessments of the caliber of play in black professional baseball, see Harlow, "Unrecognized Stars"; *PC*, May 3, 1947; *CD*, May 13, 1950; Marshall interview with Irvin, May 12, 1977, COHP; Tygiel, *Baseball's Great Experiment* (1983 ed.), 20; Rust, *"Get That Nigger off the Field!"* 54; Jack Marshall file, BHOFL. Former major leaguer Marv Owen illustrated the difference between the high minors and majors, explaining that in the Pacific Coast League, "you might face two good pitchers in four games. In the big leagues, you face a good pitcher every day." See Bak, *Cobb Would Have Caught It*, 226.

18. 1929 Hilldale ledger, minutes of Hilldale Corporation Meeting, March 31, 1932, CTC; *CD*, November 24, 1923; *BAA*, August 28, 1926; *PT*, January 16, 1926; January 15, 22, 1927; *PC*, January 30, February 20, March 19, June 11, 1932; November 7, 1942; *SOMP*, 1366–68.

19. "Percentage Games," 1932, box 1, CTC; *PC*, March 5, 1932; December 9, 1933; March 28, 1936; June 4, 1938; April 27, 1940; February 8, July 26, 1941; *BAA*, January 28, March 4, May 13, 1933; April 30, 1938; Henry J. Rigney to league owners, June 14, 1939, Abe Manley to Rev. C. C. Weathers, July 19, 1940, Theodore Alexander to Abe Manley, January 6, 1941, NEP; *CD*, December 18, 1937; *SN*, July 18, 1951; *PI*, April 11, 1937; April 17, 1938; August 27, 1939; *NYAN*, March 1, 15, June 14, 1933; *Brown American* (Fall/Winter 1942); Kelley, *Voices*, 37–40; *PT*, July 4, 1940; Burton W. Perreti, *The Creation of Jazz: Music, Race, and Culture in Urban America* (Urbana, Ill., 1992), 169; *SOMP*, 349, 1377–81. In contrast, Dizzy Dean received $3,000 in 1932, his first full season in the major leagues. See Gregory, *Diz*, 80.

20. Fields, *My Life in the Negro Leagues*, 32 ("it was"); *PC*, April 22, 1939 (Davis); *NYAN*, January 17, 1942 (McDuffie); Echevarría, *Pride of Havana*, 254; *CCP*, October 26, 1946; *CD*, November 4, 1933. Winter baseball in Los Angeles also provided employment for black players and an opportunity to compete against top white stars.

21. *CD*, August 6 (Greenlee), October 15, 1938 ("go on"); Harlow, "Unrecognized Stars"; *PC*, May 7, 1938; James Bankes, "The Magnificent Pittsburgh Crawfords," in *The Ol' Ball Game: A Collection of Baseball Characters and Moments Worth Remembering* (Harrisburg, Pa., 1990), 44–52; Leonard, *Buck Leonard*, 47; *PT*, January 14, 1937; April 14, May 19, June 9, 1938; August 1, 1940; *PI*, September 1, 1935; July 26, 1936; September 11, 1938; August 4, 1940; July 26, 1942; *BAA*, July 15, 1933 (Gibson); April 23, 1938; July 27, 1940; Kelley, *The Negro Leagues Revisited*, 52; "Ed. Bolden's Philadelphia Stars . . . Personnel"—1942, in ACP, box 170-19; Seymour, *People's Game*, 253.

22. *Brown American* (June 1936): 9, 22; July 1936, 5; *PT*, December 1, 22, 1932;

Myrdal, *American Dilemma*, 365; Drake and Cayton, *Black Metropolis*, 513; Hylan G. Lewis, "The Negro Business, Professional, and White Collar Worker," *Journal of Negro Education* (July 1939): 437; *CD*, June 25, 1938; Rogosin, *Invisible Men*, 66; *BAA*, December 29, 1934 (Gholston). In 1936, four of every five Americans earned less than $2,000 annually. See Baker, *Jesse Owens*, 138.

23. *PC*, March 27, 1943; July 21, 1945; *BAA*, April 29, 1944; August 18, 1945; Leonard, *Buck Leonard*, 149; Holway, *Voices*, 267; *CD*, November 4, 1944; J. B. Martin to Effa Manley, January 19, 1944 ("players"); 1941 and 1943 player contracts, NEP; *SOMP*, 1383; Cum Posey to Joseph Eastman, May 15, 1943 (folder 50062), Records from Highway Transport Department, 1942–1946, RG 219. By May 1943, the Grays paid over $5,500 in monthly salaries. The best paid players in black baseball, however, barely matched the major league minimum salary of $5,000 (established in 1946). The files of the Philadelphia Phillies provide a detailed look at earnings for major leaguers in the late 1940s. In 1947, at least eight Phillies earned over $10,000, led by pitcher Dutch Leonard at $14,500. A year later, the club's highest paid players included Harry Walker, who received $21,250 after winning the National League batting title in 1947, Eddie Miller ($17,500), and Leonard ($17,000). By 1950, the Phillies invested $315,279 on player salaries, topped by Del Ennis at $27,000, an increase of $14,000 since 1948. On the Phillies' salaries, see "Philadelphia National League Club and Its Wholly Owned Subsidiaries—Controller's Report upon Operations for the Year Ended October 31, 1947," 48 (PP); "Treasurer's Report—1948," 59, "Treasurer's Report—1950," 63, PP, box 4, financial.

24. *CD*, November 4, 1944; June 12, 1948; *SN*, June 18, 1947; October 20, 1948; January 18, July 19, 1950; July 18, 1951; *PC*, February 19, 1949; *Our World* (May 1952); Effa Manley to John Collins, July 1, 1946 ("we must"), 1946 contracts, NEP; financial records—payroll and insurance, 1948, TBC, boxes 9 and 10; *PT*, July 2, 1946; March 9, 1948; *PI*, May 20, 1950; Leonard, *Buck Leonard*, 37; Kelley, *Voices*, 37–40; *BAA*, September 9, 1944; Frank Menke, *The New Encyclopedia of Sports* (New York, 1947), 167; *SOMP*, 1387–88.

25. Fields, *My Life in the Negro Leagues*, 24 ("contract"); Maxwell Manning to Effa Manley, March 4, 1941 (Manning quote); player contracts 1940 and 1941, NEP.

26. *NYAN*, August 9, 1941 (Burley); *CCP*, May 5, 1934 (Finger); *PI*, October 19, 1946; "Philadelphians," *Our World* (September 1953); interview with Stanley Glenn, February 16, 2000.

27. *PV*, May 6, 1944 (Russell); Ed Bolden to Raymond Pace Alexander, April 19, 1942; J. B. Deans to Ed Bolden, May 5, 1942, Eustace Gay to Ed Bolden, 1942, Herbert Millen to Ed Bolden, May 4, 1942, R. R. Wright to Ed Bolden, May 4, 1942, Ed Bolden to Bob Montgomery, March 21, 1942 ("outstanding"), EBP, box 186-1, folders 7–8, 10–11, 14–15; *PT*, May 7, 1936; May 9, 1940; *PI*, May 14, 1939.

28. *PC*, April 2, 1938; July 21, 1945 (Smith); *NYAN*, March 5, December 31, 1930; Bruce, *Kansas City Monarchs*, 45; *BAA*, August 4, 1922; July 14, 1934 ("plenty"); *PT*, April 17, 1930; August 14, 1941; *WT*, June 9, 1923; *PC*, June 5, 1937; John Holway notes, courtesy of John Holway; "Josh the Basher," *Time*, July 19, 1943, 75–76; *CD*, September 18, 1937; *PV*, July 21, 1945; *NYA*, September 23, 1939; Wilson, "They Could Make the Big Leagues," 305 (Wilson); Holway, *Voices*, 320 ("just a"); Effa Manley to Eddie Gottlieb, April 5, 1939, NEP; Overmyer, *Effa Manley*, 116; Rust, *"Get That Nigger off the Field!"* 56 (Gottlieb).

29. *PC*, May 17, 1941; *PT*, May 15, 1941; "Satchel Paige, Negro Ballplayer, Is One of Best Pitchers in Game," *Life*, June 2, 1941; Dan Parker, "The World of Sports," in *While You Were Gone: A Report on Wartime Life in the United States*, ed. Jack Goodman (New York, 1946), 301; *NYAN*, June 7, 1941 (Burley); August 22, 1942; June

12, 1943 ("freer"); interview with Stanley Glenn, February 16, 2000; interview with Mahlon Duckett, July 2, 1998; Lewis, "Dusky Hercules," *Chicago Daily News*, August 2, 8, 1944, in *Best Sport Stories of 1944*, ed. March and Ehre, 68–73; *BAA*, August 12, 1944.

30. *PT*, May 20, 1944 (Moses); July 28, 1945; April 18, 1950 (Gay); *CD*, May 17, 1947; *PC*, January 23, 1943; August 11, 1945; *PV*, July 21, 1945; *CCP*, May 17, 1947 ("it is really"); *NYAN*, July 11, 1942. After attending an NNL promotion at the Polo Grounds in 1945, white sportswriter Dan Parker alluded to the heavy alcohol consumption, noting that "there was more fancy guzzling on this occasion than I've ever seen at a baseball game." See *New York Daily Mirror*, May 25, 1945, in ACP, box 170-19.

31. *PT*, February 19, 1949 (Moses); *NYAN*, July 11, 1942; September 1 ("like cats"), 15 ("never can"), 1945; *CD*, July 14, 1945; May 17, 1947 (Young); *PINQ*, August 22–23, 1949; *BAA*, August 1, 1942; *MC*, July 7, 1945; February 22, 1947 (Cowans); Rust, *"Get That Nigger off the Field!"* 4; Crepeau, *Baseball*, 47.

32. *CD*, August 22, 1942 (Young); April 26, 1947 (White); *PT*, April 8, 1944; *KCC*, May 9, 1947 ("sit in"); *PV*, June 19, 1943 (Bostic); March 22, 1947 ("family"); Drake and Cayton, *Black Metropolis*, 710; *NYAN*, September 1, 1945 (Burley); March 11, 1950; Anderson, *This Was Harlem*, 343.

33. *NYAN*, July 11, 1942; May 6, 1944; September 1, 1945; *PV*, June 19, 1943; *KCC*, July 20, 1945; *PT*, July 28, 1945; *CD*, July 14, 1945; April 26, 1947 (White); Effa Manley to John Keenan, September 27, 1945 ("others"), NEP.

34. On umpiring during the 1920s and early 1930s in black baseball, see Lanctot, *Fair Dealing*, 9, 41–43, 85, 107–8, 131–33, 161, 215–17.

35. *PC*, June 24, 1933; April 14, 21, 1934; February 2, 1935 ("do away"); January 25, February 15, March 14, 21, 1936; August 7, 1937; March 19, 1938; *CCP*, April 21, 1934; *BAA*, March 16, 1935; April 20, 1940; March 8, 1941; *CD*, January 4, 1936; March 27, 1937; *PT*, January 17, 1935; March 25, 1937; February 23, 1939; September 25, 1943; August 26, 1944; 1942 NNL treasurer's report, minutes of June 1, 1943, NNL meeting, March 12, 1946 NNL meeting, NEP. Some lower-level minor leagues employed a form of the home umpire system. See *SN*, March 20, 1930.

36. Lanctot, *Fair Dealing*, 196–201; *BAA*, May 26, 1934 ("when"); September 25, 1948; June 4, 1949; *PC*, August 20, 1932 ("many"); July 29 ("get men"), August 5, 1933; June 9, August 11, 1934; June 27, 1936; *PI*, June 21, 1947; *PT*, June 30, 1945; *CD*, May 25, 1940; *CCP*, October 4, 1947; Effa Manley to Peter Strauch, April 7, 1945, NEP; *NYAN*, October 27, 1945. As late as 1939, Fay Young observed that "it seems to be a tough job to get our athletes to abide by honest decisions given by those of their own race." See *CD*, June 10, 1939.

37. *CD*, February 22 (Taylor), 1936; *BAA*, June 11 (Clark), 1932; May 14 (Lyle), 1949; *PT*, August 26, 1944; *PI*, August 27, 1944; Leonard, *Buck Leonard*, 94.

38. *PT*, July 23 ("delays"), 1936; *PC*, July 25 ("to drag"), 1936; *CD*, July 9 ("it takes"), 1938; Lanctot, *Fair Dealing*, 85, 107–8, 133, 145–46, 194, 257.

39. *NYAN*, May 12 ("the fans"), 1934; *PT*, August 2, 1934; January 17, 1935; July 9 ("why don't"), 23 (Harris), 1936; July 28 (Blueitt), 1938; *BAA*, June 9, 1934; June 8, 1935; *PC*, July 28, 1934; April 24, 1937; *CD*, July 21, 1934; *PI*, February 3, 1935; *NYA*, February 2, June 1, 1935.

40. *PI*, May 23, June 13, July 11, 18, 25, August 1, 1937; July 3, 17, 1938; *PT*, June 17, July 15, 29, 1937; July 14 ("severely"), 1938; February 23, 1939; *PC*, June 12 (Posey), 19 (Greenlee), 1937; June 25, July 9, 1938; January 14, February 25, 1939; *BAA*, July 16, 1938; summary of NNL meeting, 1939, NEP.

41. Hank Rigney to Abe Manley, July 5 ("called"), 1939, NEP; *CD*, July 15

("now"), 29, 1939; December 22, 1945; Edwin Bancroft Henderson, *The Negro in Sports* (Washington, D.C., 1939), 285; Holway, *Black Diamonds*, 15; *BAA*, August 28, 1943; *MC*, March 2, 1946; *CCP*, June 30, 1945; February 1, 1947; *NYAN*, May 27, 1939; March 9 (Burley), 1940. December 14, 1946; Chalk, *Black College Sport*, 67; *PT*, May 25, 1933; Kelley, *Voices*, 41; *PINQ*, July 20, 1939; September 17, 1940; August 6, 1941; August 7, 1946; *NYA*, June 1, 1935; July 11, 1936; Crepeau, *Baseball*, 38.

42. Robinson, *Catching Dreams*, 163 ("carried on"); Ed Gottlieb to Effa Manley, April 4, 1939, Wendell Smith to Effa Manley, May 19, 1944 ("few"), NEP; Holway, *Voices*, 82–84; Irvin, *Nice Guys Finish First*, 57 (Irvin quote); *PC*, January 16, 1932; December 11, 1943 (Posey); *PV*, January 23, 1943; Holway, *Blackball Stars*, 300; Lanctot, *Fair Dealing*, 47, 230, 246; Rich Westcott, *Philadelphia's Old Ballparks* (Philadelphia, 1996), 60; *BAA*, June 16, 1945; *PI*, August 11, 1935.

43. Jimmy Hill player contract, 1940, NEP; *PC*, September 11, 1937; February 5, 1938; June 29, 1940; July 18, 1942; *PT*, June 13, 27, August 29, 1940; *PI*, May 26, 1935; June 16, 23, September 8, 22, 1940; *NYAN*, June 29, 1940; *CCP*, June 30, 1945; *CD*, June 30, 1945; *KCC*, September 25, 1936.

44. Effa Manley to Tom Wilson, June 8, 1943 ("beat up"), Cum Posey to all own-ers, July 15, 1943 ("tendency"), NEP; *CD*, July 3 (Young), 1943; *PT*, June 6, 1940; July 15, August 5, 1944; June 16, July 14, 1945; *PC*, May 26, 1934; February 25, 1939; July 1, 8, 15, 1944; August 3, 10, 1946; *PI*, July 23, 30, 1944; June 16, 23, 30, July 14, 1945; *BAA*, June 15, 1940; June 30, 1945; *NYAN*, July 14, 1945.

45. *PC*, May 30, 1942; June 30, July 7 ("when"), 28, August 4, 1945; *BAA*, July 14 ("escaped"), August 18, 1945; *CCP*, July 21, August 18 ("jived"), 1945; *PV*, June 9, 1945; *MC*, July 7, August 4, 1945; *PT*, July 14, 28, August 4, 18, 1945; *CD*, June 23, 30 ("will kill"), July 7, 14, 1945; May 7, 1947.

46. *PC*, August 11 ("is there"), 1945; *PT*, September 8 (Wilson), 1945.

47. *PI*, June 7, 1947; *PT*, February 23, 1939; May 11, 1946; Cum Posey to Effa Manley, June 12, 1939, summary of 1939 NNL meeting, minutes of May 6, 1946 NNL meeting, NEP; *KCC*, July 5, 1946; Irvin, *Nice Guys Finish First*, 72; 1928, 1929, 1932 Hilldale Ledgers, CTC; *Norfolk Journal and Guide*, May 18, 1946; *NYA*, August 8, 1936.

48. *NYAN*, September 9 ("we"), 1944; October 27, 1945; *PT*, April 21, May 5, 12, 19, 1945; *PI*, May 5, 12, 1945; Fred McCrary to Effa Manley, May 10, 1945 ("Dicta-tor"); Effa Manley to Peter Strauch, July 25, 1945, minutes of March 12, 1946 NNL meeting, John Craig to Abe Manley, July 30, 1946, NEP; *SN*, August 14, 28, 1946. Lower-level minor leagues (class C and D) were more likely to contend with violence toward officials, although umpires in higher classifications were not always spared. In 1946, an American Association manager assaulted umpire Forrest "Frosty" Peters, prompting his subsequent resignation. As Peters explained, "when an umpire gets socked and they fine the guy only $100 and five days, it's an open invitation for every-body in the league to start punching you around." See *SN*, July 24, 1946.

49. Seymour, *People's Game*, 225–26, 260; *CD*, January 3, 1920; *PT*, June 12, December 18, 1920; December 13, 1924; February 14, 1948 ("they"); Lanctot, *Fair Dealing*, 155–56; *PI*, October 27, 1945; Tygiel, *Baseball's Great Experiment*, 87; Ov-ermyer, *Effa Manley*, 228; *NYA*, February 5, 1949 (Campanella); Jackie Robinson, "What's Wrong with Negro Baseball," *Ebony*, June 1948 ("all"). The reserve clause was fully incorporated into professional baseball contracts by 1887. See Seymour, *Baseball: The Early Years*, 104–15.

50. *PT*, August 15, 1940; April 10 (Harris), 1941; *NYAN*, March 9 (Burley), 1940; Pepper Martin, National League Player's Contract, 1934, courtesy SABR Research

434 ◆ Notes to Pages 185–189

Exchange; *PI*, August 18, September 8, 1940; October 6, 1945; *PC*, August 24, 1940; *BAA*, January 21, 1928; *Philadelphia North American*, July 9, August 14, 1922; Kelley, *Negro Leagues Revisited*, 20. Injured minor league players were entitled to only two weeks salary. See *SOMP*, 205, 583.

51. *BAA*, July 18, 1942; *PT*, June 29, July 6, August 3, 10, 17, 1939; May 30, 1940; March 25 ("how"), July 1, 22, September 2, 1944; September 15, 1945; *PI*, April 7, 1945; *PC*, March 13 (Posey), 1937; July 15, 1944; Effa Manley to Leon Ruffin, March 4, 1939 ("unless"); Abe Manley to Rufus Jackson and Cum Posey, May 5, 1939 ("ridiculous"), NEP; Henry McHenry to Ed Bolden, October 9, 1941, box 186-1, folder 11, EBP.

52. *PV*, August 28, 1943; "Josh the Basher," *Time*, July 19, 1943; *NYAN*, September 13, 1941; July 20, 1946; *BAA*, January 19, 1935; April 3, 1937; July 2, September 10, 1938; October 4, 1941; Clark and Lester, *Negro Leagues Book*, 161; *PC*, September 21, 28, 1935; June 25, 1938; July 22, 1939; November 16, 1940; February 28, 1942; Effa Manley, "Negro Baseball Isn't Dead!" *Our World* (August 1948): 26–28; *PT*, September 13, 1934; September 5, 1935; September 8, 1938; June 26 ("clubs"), 1943; *CD*, September 9, 1939, cited in Reisler, *Black Writers/Black Baseball*, 59; *NYA*, May 16, 1936; Wendell Smith to Effa Manley, May 19, 1944 ("one"), NEP.

53. *PI*, July 26, 1942; *PC*, July 18, 1936; July 16, August 20, 1938; November 4, 1939; February 26, 1944; *PT*, August 20, 1936; April 27, 1939 ("one of"); July 17, 1943; Effa Manley to James Semler, August 22, 1938 ("you have"), Effa Manley to Frank Spair, March 20, 1941 ("the problem"), Effa Manley to Tom Wilson, June 8, 1943, NEP; *NYAN*, September 13 (Burley), 1941.

54. *BAA*, March 28, 1936; August 13, 1938; March 14, 1942; March 27 ("silly"), 1943; *PC*, July 25, 1936; February 17, 1940; February 26 ("positively"), 1944; Rufus Jackson to "Sirs," August 31, 1942, Ed Gottlieb to Effa Manley, August 24, 1943, Ed Gottlieb to all NNL teams, May 3, 1944, NEP; *PI*, September 7, 1941; July 26, 1942; *PT* July 25, 1942; August 28, 1943; September 9, 1944 ("writers"); *MC*, December 1, 1945 ("circuses").

55. Final NNL standings, 1942, 1944, 1945, NEP; *PT*, September 12, 1942; July 10, September 11, 1943; July 15, September 2, 9, 1944; September 15, 1945; *CD*, December 19, 1942; *NYAN*, September 15, 1945; *PI*, February 16 (Winston), 1952. The Homestead Grays' 1943 season provides a typical example of the schedules in black professional baseball. Between April 18 and September 12, the team played 122 games: 67 against NNL teams, 25 against NAL opponents, and 30 against white semipros or non-league clubs. Fewer than half (33) of the 67 games against league teams counted in the final standings. See "Record of Games Played by Homestead Grays 1943 Season," ACP, box 170-18.

56. *PC*, July 21, 1934; July 6, November 30, 1935; August 22, November 7, 1936; August 15, November 21, 1942; August 15, 1944 ("baseball"); *PT*, August 20, 1936; "Agreement Between the Negro American and the Negro National Leagues," June 20, 1939, financial statement, "Tenth Annual East-West Baseball Classic, Sunday, August 16, 1942," NEP; *NYAN*, June 9, 1945 (Semler).

57. Financial statement, August 18, 1946, East-West game, TBC, box 2, financial records, Negro East West Game, 1943–1953; *PC*, March 2, 1940; August 9 (Dixon), September 6, 1941; September 5, 1942; January 2, June 12, 1943; July 29, August 5 (Martin), 1944; *PT*, July 29, August 26, 1944; *NYAN*, August 24, 1946; *BAA*, August 24, 1935 ("they are"); August 12 (Paige quote), September 9, 1944; financial statement, "Tenth Annual East-West Baseball Classic, Sunday, August 16, 1942," NEP; *PI*, August 25, 1935; *CD*, August 5, 12 (Young), 1944; *CCP*, August 19, 1944; Lewis, "Dusky Hercules"; *PV*, August 12, 1944.

58. "Received from Negro National League ($200.00)—Two Hundred Dollars, in payment of salary for Sunday, August 13 . . . Chicago East West game," NEP; *BAA*, August 19 ("we're"), September 9, 1944; August 24, 1946 (Pompez); *CD*, August 19, 1944; *PC*, August 19, 1944; *PT*, August 26, 1944; *PI*, September 3, 17, 1944; Leonard, *Buck Leonard*, 167; financial statement, East-West game, August 13, 1944, ACP, box 170-17, folder 17.

59. *BAA*, August 22 (Carter), 1942; *CD*, August 22, 1942; *PT*, July 17, 1941 (Harris); October 16 ("abandon"), 1943; July 15 ("I know"), 1944; Cum Posey to Effa Manley, January 11, 1943 ("juggling"), NEP.

60. *NYAN*, August 22, 29, 1942; September 23, 1944; October 11 ("don't"), 18 ("our"), 1947; September 10 ("personal"), 1949; *PC*, June 10, 1933; May 19, 1934; August 31, 1935; *PT*, February 22, 1934; May 6, 1950; *KCC*, May 10, July 26, August 23, 1946; February 20, 1948; June 24, August 19, 1949; Overmyer, *Effa Manley*, 60–61; *PI*, January 13, 1951; *BAA*, June 4, 1949; *CCP*, August 11, 1934; Bruce, *Kansas City Monarchs*, 45–47; *CD*, May 31, 1941; Thomas Baird to J. B. Martin, November 1, 1955, TBC, box 2, correspondence, J. B. Martin, 1949–1960.

61. *PC*, February 25 (Posey), 1933; *KCC*, March 7 (Johnson), 1952. Known radio broadcasts before 1945 involving black teams include the 1935 East-West game on KQU, a Black Yankees/Brooklyn Bushwicks game at Dexter Park on WBYN in 1941, and several Homestead Grays games in Washington on WWDC in 1942. See Barlow, *Voice Over*, 56–57, 95; *PC*, August 17, 1935; *BAA*, August 8, 1942; *NYAN*, September 20, 1941; *CD*, September 19, 1942; *PV*, August 1, 1942; Robert Donelson to Art Carter, August 10, 1942, ACP, box 170-5, folder 8.

62. Lem Graves to Effa Manley, April 10, 1942 (Graves), NEP; *Philadelphia North American*, July 7, 1912; *PT*, January 30, 1925; *BAA*, June 30, 1922; Hogan, *Black National News Service*, 72–73; *PC*, June 23, 1934; *CCP*, June 16, 1934.

63. Cum Posey to Effa Manley, March 10, 1939 ("send me"); Abe Manley to Thos. T. Wilson, May 16, 1939, NEP; *NYAN*, September 7, 1940; August 6, 1949; *PT*, June 13, 1940; *PC*, May 1, 1948; *PI*, May 22, 1948; *PV*, October 17, 1942; August 12, 1944; Tom Baird to Matty Brescia, June 9, 1953, TBC, box 2, correspondence, Matty Brescia, 1949–1953.

64. *PI*, August 14 (Barnes), 1938; May 24, 1942; *PC*, May 14, 1932; February 29 ("continued"), 1936; February 17, 1940; Cum Posey to Effa Manley, June 6, 1939 ("bawled"), NEP; *CD*, March 24, July 7, 1945; minutes of NAL meeting, March 5, 1944, TBC, minutes, NAL meetings, 1943–1952, box 2; *PT*, October 30, 1943; *BAA*, September 25 (Lacy), 1948. Organized Baseball officials were equally likely to retaliate against perceived criticism. Dan Parker claimed Larry MacPhail complained to editors about unfriendly journalists and "more than one writer has been barred from traveling with the Dodgers for writing stuff that didn't please him." See Dan Parker, "Barnum of Dem Bums," *Liberty*, June 13, 1942, 25–26.

65. Financial statement, July 29, 1945 East-West game, TBC, box 2, financial records, Negro East West Game, 1943–1953; minutes, NAL meeting, February 7–8, 1950, TBC, box 2, minutes, NAL meetings, 1943–1952; Effa Manley to Ed Gottlieb, May 23, 1939, Cum Posey to Effa Manley, November 17, 1941 ("follow"), Effa Manley to J. B. Martin, March 25, 1944; financial statements, 1939, 1942 East-West games, Effa Manley to Vernon Green, January 25, 1946 ("how"), NEP; *CD*, February 24, 1940; *PC*, January 11, 1936; December 17, 1938; Overmyer, *Effa Manley*, 113; Nick Wilson, *Voices from the Pastime* (Jefferson, N.C., 2000), 176; *PT*, January 30, 1936; ACP, box 170-16, folders 1, 12; *SOMP*, 1034–35. In an example of the practice, a promoter in 1952 urged Monarchs' owner Tom Baird to send $10 to a writer on the *Dallas Morning News*, although cautiously noted that "we MUST protect the guy—you

know that." See Matty Brescia to Tom Baird, March 27, 1952, TBC, box 2, correspondence, Matty Brescia, 1949–1953.

66. *PT*, January 30, 1936; July 14, 1938; January 6, 1945; *PC*, December 21, 1935; January 18, February 1, 1936; February 3, 1940; June 12, 1943; *BAA*, August 7, 1943; January 15, June 17, December 23, 1944; *CCP*, December 23, 1944; *NYA*, September 15, 1934; February 1, May 16, 1936; John H. Johnson to Carl Murphy, February 18, 1948, ACP, box 170-16, folder 7; *CD*, June 10, 1939; August 7, 1943; *PV*, May 9, 1942 (Bostic); September 28, 1946.

67. *BAA*, July 18, September 9, 1939; February 26, 1949 ("the colored"); *PT*, February 14 (Harris), 1935; September 23, 1937; May 19, 1938; May 16, August 29, 1940; February 28, 1942; April 1, 1944; Harlow, "Unrecognized Stars"; *PC*, June 5, 1937; February 17, 1940; March 14, June 27, 1942; January 9, 1943; *CCP*, August 11, 1934; *PINQ*, July 15, 1936; *NYAN*, August 10, 1935; September 14, 1940; February 21, 1942; Overmyer, *Effa Manley*, 109–13; *PI*, May 30, 1937; June 21, 1947; June 19, 1948; *CD*, May 25, July 27, 1940; *NYA*, May 16, 1936; Effa Manley to Jerry Kessler, February 25, 1944 ("a very"), Effa Manley to Sam Lacy, December 22, 1944 ("try"), NEP; *PV*, September 12 (Bostic), 1942; *Norfolk Journal and Guide*, May 25, 1946 ("very poor"); Cum Posey to Art Carter, February 16, 1943, Curtis Leak to Art Carter, July 23, 1946, ACP, box 170-16, folders 12, 8. Class differences may have contributed to the difficulties between owners and sportswriters. In contrast to the shady background common among league officials, a number of journalists were college graduates, including Rollo Wilson (Temple, University of Pittsburgh), Joe Bostic (Morgan), Wendell Smith (West Virginia State), Al Dunmore (Hampton), Ed Harris (Temple), Doc Young (Hampton), and Bill Gibson (Ohio State). See *Our World* (January 1952); *Detroit Free Press*, February 2, 1989; *PINQ*, August 16, 1993; William Matney, ed., *Who's Who Among Black Americans* (Northbrook, Ill., 1976), 699; G. James Fleming and Christian Burckel, eds., *Who's Who in Colored America—1950* (Yonkers-on-Hudson, N.Y., 1950), 209.

68. *CCP*, June 16 ("gate"), 1934; December 7, 1946; *CD*, May 22 (Young), 1948; October 27, 1951; *BAA*, November 20, 1954; *PT*, December 15, 1956; *NYAN*, May 13, 1939 ("glibly"); Brown, "Negro in American Culture," 110.

69. *PV*, August 28, 1943 (Leak); "Comparative Statements of Profit & Loss—December 31, 1941–42" (Wilmington Blue Rocks), box 5, "The Philadelphia National League Club and Its Wholly Owned Subsidiaries—Treasurer's Report upon Operations for the Year Ended October 31, 1948," 54–55, 126, PP, box 4; Hilldale ledgers, 1926–27, CTC; *PT*, August 3, 1918; April 12, 19, 1924; June 16, 1932; June 29, July 27, August 24, 1933; May 6, 1937; May 28, 1946; May 20, June 13, 1950; *PC*, March 19, May 14, 1932; May 9, 1936; January 16, 1937; *PAA*, June 22, 1940; *KCC*, May 21, 1937; June 10, 1938; May 3, 1946; *CCP*, February 23, 1946; financial statement, Philadelphia Stars vs. Newark Eagles at Ruppert Stadium, May 14, 1939; Homestead vs. Newark at Ruppert Stadium, May 9, 1943, NEP; *PINQ*, July 7, 1933. Between 1933 and 1943, major league ticket prices generally ranged from 55 cents to $1.65. By 1950, fans in Philadelphia paid admission prices of 75 cents to $2.50 at Shibe Park. See Craig, "Organized Baseball," table ix, 209–10.

70. *PT*, March 28, 1942; Lanctot, *Fair Dealing*, 231; 1942 Newark attendance figures based on author's compilations from financial statements in NEP; Overmyer, *Effa Manley*, 107, 117; *BAA*, June 4, 1932; May 13, 1933; April 3, 1937; Hilldale ledgers, 1923–1932, CTC; *PC*, December 27, 1924; July 8, 29, 1933; *CD*, April 4, 1936; *CCP*, December 21, 1946; Cum Posey to owners (summary of recent NNL meeting), 1939, Ed Gottlieb to Effa Manley, August 4, 1940, Abe Saperstein to William Leuschner, July 6, 1945, NEP; *NYAN*, December 1, 1934; contract for Kansas City-

Homestead at Griffith Stadium, June 25–26, 1944, TBC, box 5, game contracts, 1944–
1961. In the early 1920s, visiting teams in the NNL and ECL received 40 percent of
the gross.

71. Hilldale ledgers, 1923–1932; Hilldale Club Inc. to Edw. Gottlieb, July 25, 1932,
CTC; "Supporting Item 11a—Deductions" (1936), Ed Gottlieb to Effa Manley, May
10, 1939, Effa Manley to Joe Mingin, April 6, 1939, financial statement, Stars vs.
Newark Eagles at Ruppert Stadium, August 13, 1939, A. B. Karam to Effa Manley,
May 26, 1941, Paddy Moruke to Abe Manley, July 14, 1941. See Posey to Effa Manley,
July 29, 1941, NEP; *PC*, November 17, 1934; "Monarch Ball Club"—"Profit & Loss
and Financial Statement Dec. 31, 1946," TBC, box 15, financial records, miscellane-
ous, 1944–1960; *PT*, December 3, 1936; January 27, 1938; *PR*, September 24, 1939
(Gottlieb).

72. NNL treasurer's report, 1942, NEP; *PV*, August 28, 1943; budget sheets, bills
paid on the road and office, 1951, TBC, box 13; "Monarch Ball Club"—"Profit & Loss
and Financial Statement Dec. 31, 1946," handwritten statement of receipts, expenses,
and profits of Kansas City Monarchs, 1942–1946, TBC, box 15, financial records,
miscellaneous, 1944–1960; *PC*, February 18, 1933; May 15, 1937; January 14, 1939;
March 27, 1943; July 21, 1945; Ed Bolden to Artie Lee, April 23, 1942, EBP, box
186-1, folder 13; *PI*, August 1, 1943; June 28, 1947; *PT*, December 3, 1936; July 25,
1942; July 31, 1943; November 11, 1944; July 30, 1946; *PAA*, September 26, 1942;
Overmyer, *Effa Manley*, 108; 1918 Hilldale expenses, CTC; *BAA*, March 26 (Semler),
1938; February 15, 1947; *SN*, October 20, 1948; *NYAN*, June 15, 1940.

73. *PC*, January 7, 1933; November 23 ("racket"), 1935; August 23, 1941; September 29, 1945; *PI*, June 25, 1944; June 7, 1947; *CD*, July 7, 1945; May 8, 1948;
September 3, 1955; *MC*, March 11, 18, 1944; December 8, 1945; Overmyer, *Effa
Manley*, 107; financial statement, 1939 East-West game, letter to Brooklyn Dodgers,
June 24, 1940, minutes of joint session of NNL and NAL, June 10, 1942, Effa Manley
to James Semler, May 22, 1943, Ed Gottlieb to Effa Manley, June 5, 1943, financial
statement, September 9, 1943, North-South Game at Griffith Stadium, Abe Saperstein
to William Leuschner, July 6, 1945, minutes of February 21, 1946 NNL meeting;
NEP; financial records, gate receipts, Kansas City, 1948, TBC, box 9; *PT*, August 14,
1941; July 1, 1944; February 1, 1949; *CCP*, July 29, 1944; January 10, 1948; financial
statement, May 23, 1946, Black Yankees-Homestead Grays at Griffith Stadium, ACP,
box 170-16, folder 16; financial statement, July 24, 1950, Shibe Park, EBP, box 186-
1, folder 26; *BAA*, June 20 ("it makes"), 1942. At major league facilities, black players
from both teams typically used only the visitor's locker room and dugout, yet as Wilmer Harris noted, "there was so much room in those that you couldn't imagine why
they had to have so much room." Minor league parks in the South, however, were
known to restrict access to black players and fans. See interview with Wilmer Harris,
March 31, 2000; interview with Mahlon Duckett, July 2, 1998; *CD*, June 12, 1948;
Leonard, *Buck Leonard*, 83; Robinson with Bauer, *Catching Dreams*, 118; Brent Kelly,
Nap Gulley, "Well-Traveled Gulley Pitched and Played Outfield," *SCD*, March 5,
1999; Tim Cary: "Slidin' and Ridin': At Home and on the Road with the 1948 Birmingham Black Barons," *Alabama Heritage* (Fall 1986).

74. *PINQ*, May 2, 3, 1903; William Bender Wilson, *History of the Pennsylvania
Railroad Department of the Young Men's Christian Association of Philadelphia* (Philadelphia, 1911), 2023; Matthew T. Robinson, Jr., "A Requiem for Black Baseball,"
Philadelphia Magazine, May 1967, 130–35 ("if you"); *PI*, May 19, 1935; June 18,
1939; September 1, 1945; February 7, 1948; *PT*, May 16, 1935; February 15, 1940;
January 2, 1941; October 9, 1943; February 5, May 6, 20, 1944; March 17, April 7,
1945; *PC*, February 10, 1934; December 26, 1936; February 17, 1940; Edgar Wil-

liams, "When Baseball Was a Matter of Black and White," *Today Magazine, Philadelphia Inquirer*, August 9, 1981; Holway, *Black Diamonds*, 79; Leonard, *Buck Leonard*, 168; interview with Wilmer Harris, March 31, 2000.

75. *BAA*, August 12, 1939 (cited in Reisler, *Black Writers/Black Baseball*, 17, Lundy); August 28, 1943 ("there is"); *PC*, January 7, 1933; January 22, 1938 (Posey).

76. Ross Forman, "Don Newcombe Makes Pitch for HOF," *SCD*, June 3, 1994 (Newcombe); interview with Mahlon Duckett, July 2, 1998 ("taught"); interview with Stanley Glenn, February 16, 2000 ("to travel"); Rich Marazzi, "Mays Wasn't First Fielder to Employ Basket Catch," *SCD*, May 14, 1999, 71 (Benson).

Chapter 7. On the Outside Looking In

Epigraph: *PT*, July 21, 1938.

1. Larry Gerlach, "Baseball's Other 'Great Experiment': Eddie Klep and the Integration of the Negro Leagues," *Journal of Sport History* 25, 3 (Fall 1998): 453–81; Heaphy, "Growth and Decline," 13. Despite the apparent color bar, a handful of black players appeared in Organized Baseball between 1906 and 1916 including Dick Brookins (Wisconsin State League and Western Canada League in 1906–1910) and Bill Thompson (Bellows Falls, Vermont, in the Twin State League in 1911). Meanwhile, Jimmy Claxton, who was part black but "passed" as a Native American, pitched briefly for the Oakland Oaks of the Pacific Coast League in 1916. See Bill Weiss & Marshall Wright, "TOP 100 TEAMS—Team #84—1946 MONTREAL ROYALS," www.minorleaguebaseball.com/pagetemplate/1content_anni_anni_hdr.asp?pageid=969 (accessed November 9, 2001); Riley, *Biographical Encyclopedia*, 177.

2. On the relationship between black and white baseball from 1900 to 1930, see Lanctot, *Fair Dealing*, 164–86. The 1934 major league player contract of John "Pepper" Martin of the St. Louis Cardinals clearly prohibits participation in any postseason game "in which more than two other players of the Club participate." National League president John Heydler also alluded to this rule in a letter to a promoter interested in arranging a game between the Chicago Cubs and a black all-star team. See 1934 contract of Pepper Martin, courtesy SABR Research Exchange; John Heydler to E. B. Jourdain, August 2, 1934, BHOFL.

3. *BAA*, March 25, 1933 (Taylor); August 15 ("dozens"), 1942; John Altavilla, "Schoolboy's Day—Hartford Native Left His Mark in the Negro Leagues," *Hartford Courant*, April 15, 1997; Holway, "Kid Who Taught Satchel Paige a Lesson," 37; *PT*, August 16, 1934; *PC*, March 30, 1935; *NYA*, March 23, 1935; *NYT*, August 23, 1933 (Veeck). Though limited, opportunities for black players to compete against white professionals in postseason games continued during the 1930s and early 1940s, particularly in non-major league cities, including Baltimore, Kansas City, and smaller midwestern towns. The Los Angeles Winter League also featured teams stocked with black and white professional players. Spring training games in Cuba and Puerto Rico provided another chance for black professional players to play major leaguers, although American blacks were often not allowed to play. See *CD*, September 24, 1932; *PT*, September 26, 1935; October 14, 1937; *PI*, October 27, 1935; October 29, 1939; *NYAN*, March 11, 1939; March 22, October 18, 1941; October 30, 1943; October 21, 1944; April 17, 1947; *PC*, March 21, 1936; March 6, 1937; *PC*, April 12, 1941; *PV*, April 8, 1944.

4. *NYT*, August 23, 24, 1933; December 19, 1939; June 25, 1969; Crepeau, *Baseball*, 169; *CD*, February 25, 1933; *SN*, November 5, 1931; Oliver Pilat, *Pegler, Angry Man of the Press* (Westport, Conn., 1973), 102–6; *New York Daily News*, February 1,

1933, cited in *PC*, February 18, 1933 ("another"); *PT*, February 9, 1933 (Broun); Richard O'Connor, *Heywood Broun: A Biography* (New York, 1975). Ironically, Broun and Pegler, philosophically apart on most issues, particularly organized labor, both favored the integration of Organized Baseball.

5. *New York Daily News*, February 8 ("amazed"), 10, 1933; *CD*, March 18, 1933; *NYAN*, March 29, 1933 ("would be"); November 3, 1934 ("misguided"). By 1942, the *Amsterdam News* noted that few New York dailies employed blacks beyond a menial capacity and suggested that black journalists "are being discriminated against just as cruelly as Negro ball players, by the same daily newspapers which yell loud and long for justice for the Negro." See *NYAN*, August 8, 1942; *PV*, April 14, 1945.

6. *BAA*, February 25 (Gibson), 1933; *PC*, February 25, March 11, 1933; September 15, 1934; Hogan, *Black, National News Service*, 90; John Heydler to *Pittsburgh Courier* (telegram), February 20, 1933 ("beyond"), BHOFL; *PT*, March 2, 9 (Comiskey), 1933; January 11, August 30, September 13, 1934; *CD*, October 28, November 4, December 16, 23, 1933. As late as 1946, an unwritten law continued to bar blacks from Big Ten basketball. See John Gunther, *Inside U.S.A.—50th Anniversary Edition* (New York, 1997), 285.

7. "6/17/35 decision re E. C. Pitts," Landis era papers, BHOFL; Joseph Overfield, "Product of Sing Sing Won Public's Support," *Baseball Research Journal* 14 (1985): 19–22; David Pietrusza, "Alabama Pitts," *Oldtyme Baseball News* 6, 4, courtesy of SABR Research Exchange; *PINQ*, June 7, September 10, 1935; *CD*, July 6 (Kountze), 1935; June 14, 1941; *PT*, July 4, 1935; J. G. Taylor Spink, *Judge Landis and Twenty-Five Years of Baseball* (New York, 1947), 219–25; Seymour, *People's Game*, 415–18; David Pietrusza, *Judge and Jury: The Life and Times of Judge Kenesaw Mountain Landis* (South Bend, Ind., 1998), 375–77; *BAA*, June 29 ("it's now"/Spicely), 1935.

8. Curt Riess, "May the Best White Man Win," *Esquire*, September 1941; *PT*, August 6, 20 (Davis), 1936; December 28, 1939; May 23 ("solved"), 1940; *PI*, June 19, 1938; *BAA*, October 20, 1945; *CD*, August 29, 1936; April 17, 1937; *PC*, March 4, 1933; February 12 ("makes"), 1938; William Simons, "Jackie Robinson and the American Mind: Journalistic Perceptions of the Reintegration of Baseball," *Journal of Sport History* 12, 1 (Spring 1985): 51; Hy Turkin, "Foul Bawl!" *Negro Digest* (February 1945): 35–36; *NYAN*, July 21 (Dougherty), 1934.

9. *BAA*, June 8 (Ruark), 1940; Bjarkman, *Baseball With a Latin Beat*, 389–95; Echevarría, *Pride of Havana*, 255; Bob Considine, "Ivory from Cuba," *Collier's*, August 3, 1940, 19, 24 ("rather"); *PT*, June 6, August 8, 1940; October 7, 1944; April 27, 1948; Rogosin, *Invisible Men*, 159.

10. *CD*, July 22 ("more than"), 1939; September 18, 1948 ("adulation"); *PV*, September 1, 1945 ("every"); Katz, *Baseball in 1939* (Jefferson, N.C., 1995), 111–12; *NYT*, January 18, 1952; February 3, 1953; Benjamin G. Rader, *Baseball: A History of America's Game* (Urbana, Ill., 1992), 137; Pietrusza, *Lights On!* 105, 135–37; *PT*, August 6, 1936; *SOMP*, 790; *Washington Post*, April 7, 1939 cited in *PC*, April 15, 1939 (Povich); Tygiel, *Baseball's Great Experiment*, 34 (Frick); Mark Gallagher, *The Yankee Encyclopedia* (Urbana, Ill., 1996), 286–90; William Marshall, *Baseball's Pivotal Era, 1945–1951* (Lexington, Ky., 1999), 191; Anna Rothe, ed., *Current Biography—1948* (New York, 1948), 138–39. In 1941, blacks comprised 7 percent of the 22,000 workers employed by Briggs. The Briggs plant, despite initial reluctance, also hired a sizable number of African American women during World War II. See Anderson, "Last Hired, First Fired," 88; Weaver, *Negro Labor*, 64; Hill, *FBI's RACON*, 123. By 1944, the Crosley corporation faced increasing pressure for refusing to hire blacks. See Reed, *Seedtime*, 217–18.

11. Spink, *Judge Landis*; Pietrusza, *Judge and Jury*, 3–208; Seymour, *Baseball:*

The Golden Age, 311–23, 367, 368 ("grandstand"), 369–71; Henry F. Pringle, "Portrait of a Bench Warmer," *Harper's Monthly*, April 1927 ("few"); *Current Biography* (undated photocopy from SABR); Ron Fimrite, "His Own Biggest Fan," *Sports Illustrated*, 76–80 (undated photocopy from SABR); Edgar Brands, "The Life Story of Kenesaw Mountain Landis," in *Baseball Guide and Record Book—1945*, J. G. Taylor Spink (St. Louis, 1945), 103–8; Jerome Holtzman, *The Commissioners: Baseball's Midlife Crisis* (New York, 1998), 19–24; Theodore Roosevelt to Charles Joseph Bonaparte, September 6, 1907, in *The Letters of Theodore Roosevelt*, vol. 5, *The Big Stick, 1905–1907*, ed. Elting E. Morison (Cambridge, Mass., 1952), 784–85 ("the face"); Robert Smith, *Baseball in the Afternoon: Tales from a Bygone Era* (New York, 1993), 213–17; Rader, *Baseball*, 109; Craig, *Organized Baseball*, 144–46.

12. *SOMP*, 26–27, 476 ("conduct"), 687 (O'Connor), 745, 1080, 1263; Seymour, *Baseball: The Golden Age*, 422 ("a symbol"); *BAA*, May 14 ("eminently"), 1927; *PC*, September 8 ("keenly"), 1934; June 12 (Martin), 1943, December 2, 1944; minutes of joint session, June 1, 1943, J. B. Martin to Effa Manley, January 19, February 8, September 23, 1944, NEP; *PT*, October 3 (Kountze), 1942; Paul Green, "Happy Chandler: He Opened the Door for Jackie Robinson," *SCD*, November 25, 1983 (Chandler); William Wallace, "The Judge and I" in *The Ol' Ball Game*, 79 ("do any"). Several sources suggest that E. Lee Keyser, a midwestern promoter and pioneer in night baseball, discussed the possibility of using black players in the Western League during the mid-1930s. Landis reportedly offered no opposition but remained concerned about the reaction of players, owners, and fans. See *NYA*, September 12, 1936; *PC*, May 6, 1950; press release about Satchel Paige, 1942 (?), ACP, box 170-18, folder 2.

13. *PT*, September 9 (Hawkins), 1937; August 17, September 14 (Simmons), 1939; *BAA*, March 25 (Taylor), 1933; August 29 (Stewart), 1936; August 12, 1939, cited in Reisler, *Black Writers/Black Baseball*, 17; *NYAN*, May 15, 1937.

14. Wiggins, "1936 Olympic Games," 61–79; *CD*, May 8, 1937; Harlow, "Unrecognized Stars"; Baker, *Jesse Owens*, 71–106; *NYT*, August 15 (Slaughter), 1936; *New York Daily News*, July 23, 1936, reprinted in *PT*, July 30, 1936; Kelly E. Rusinack, "Baseball on the Radical Agenda: The *Daily Worker* and *Sunday Worker* Journalistic Campaign to Desegregate Major League Baseball, 1933–1947," in *Jackie Robinson: Race, Sports, and the American Dream*, ed. Joseph Dorinson and Joram Warmund (New York, 1998), 75–85; *NYAN*, July 25, 1942; "Negro Players in Major League Baseball," *Crisis* (April 1937): 112, 120; *PI*, February 20, 1938; *BAA*, April 15, July 18, 1939; *PC*, February 11, 1939; Wilson Record, *The Negro and the Communist Party* (Chapel Hill, N.C., 1951), 120–53; Martin B. Duberman, *Paul Robeson* (New York, 1988), 247; Naison, *Communists in Harlem*, 213; Sitkoff, *New Deal for Blacks*, 146–67; Drake and Cayton, *Black Metropolis*, 86.

15. *PI*, August 30, 1936; *CD*, August 29, 1936 ("sociological"); *PC*, February 25, 1939 ("big leagues"); Ford Frick to K. M. Landis, August 4, 1936 ("the whole"), BHOFL; *New York Daily News*, July 23, 1936, reprinted in *PT*, July 30, 1936 ("silliest"/"they are"/"how would"); "Negro Players in Major League Baseball," *Crisis* (April 1937) (Kinley).

16. *CD*, May 8, 1937; October 1, 1938; *BAA*, October 16, 1937; April 2, 1938; *NYAN*, January 23, December 11, 1937; Sam Lacy with Moses J. Newson, *Fighting for Fairness* (Centreville, Md., 1998), 14–27; Larry Whiteside, "It's Lacy's Honor," *Boston Globe*, July 26, 1998, C1; *WT*, October 12 ("what's going"), November 22, 1935; December 1937 ("which never") in ACP, box 170-19, folder 17.

17. *NYAN*, January 15, 1938; *BAA*, April 22, 1933; June 1, 1940; *CD*, June 18, 1921; June 25, 1938 (Griffith); *PI*, April 9, 1939; May 19, 1945; August 16, 1947;

September 24, 1949; August 25, 1951; *PC*, February 4, 1933; March 18, July 22, 1944; *PT*, August 4, 1932; *WT*, July 21, 1923; September 5, 1925; June 29, 1935; Bjarkman, *Baseball with a Latin Beat*, 121; Leonard, *Buck Leonard*, 141; Jules Tygiel, *Past Time: Baseball as History* (New York, 2000), 44–47; Brad Mitchell Snyder, "They Took Back Griffith Stadium—The Homestead Grays in Washington, D.C. During the 1940s" (Senior Honors Thesis, Duke University, 1994), 2–6.

18. *PC*, February 12 ("heartily"), 19 (Posey), 1938; October 28, 1939; August 29, 1942; *PT*, December 21, 1939; *NYT*, January 17, 1972; Steven Riess, ed., *Sports and the American Jew* (Syracuse, N.Y., 1998), 13; *PI*, January 28, 1950; *BAA*, February 12 (Hardwick), 1938. In a 1950 interview, Benswanger claimed that he had attempted to purchase Josh Gibson several times, only to be rejected by Posey, who felt "such a movement would wreck the Negro leagues. He was not against seeing Gibson or any of the other boys make the grade, but as an official he had to protect his own and league rights." See *SN*, January 11, 1950.

19. *PT*, August 4, 18, 1938; *PC*, August 6, 1938. Ironically, one researcher has suggested that Powell never worked for the Dayton police force and was actually employed as a security guard for a local G.M. plant. See Alvin "Jake" Powell file, BHOFL.

20. *PINQ*, July 31, 1938 (Landis); *NYAN*, August 6 ("there's"/"white"), 20 ("regard"), 1938; *CD*, August 6, 1938; *PC*, August 6 ("slip"), 20, 1938; *PT*, August 11, 1938; *BAA*, August 6 ("would never"), 1938. The *Sporting News* also blamed the radio station, claiming that Powell was "the victim of circumstances, which should not be held against him by the fans. Other players, in other instances, might offend other groups." The American League subsequently prohibited similarly unscripted interviews. See *SN*, August 4, 18, 1938.

21. *CD*, September 17 (Monroe), 1938; March 25, April 8, 1939; *PC*, August 20, 27, 1938; January 14 (Smith), May 6, 1939; *NYAN*, August 20, 1938; February 4 ("he is"), 11 ("why keep"), 1939; *BAA*, August 20, 27, September 17, 1938; December 14, 1940; *PINQ*, August 17, 1938; *NYT*, August 13 ("sustained"), 1938; November 5, 1948; *SN*, August 18, November 10, 17, 1948; Lanctot, *Fair Dealing*, 170–71; Joel Zoss and John Bowman, *Diamonds in the Rough: The Untold Story of Baseball* (Chicago, 1996), 154. Despite Pegler's positive attitude toward baseball integration, his attacks on the black press during World War II would engender considerable controversy. See Finkle, *Forum for Protest*, 65–67.

22. *NYAN*, April 22 (Burley), 1939; David Wiggins, "Wendell Smith, The Pittsburgh Courier-Journal and the Campaign to Include Blacks in Organized Baseball, 1933–1945," *Journal of Sport History* 10, 2 (Summer 1983): 5–29; Michael Marsh, "A Closer Look at Wendell Smith," unpublished paper, courtesy of Negro League Committee, SABR; *PC*, July 15 (McKechnie), 22 (Terry), 29, August 5, 12, 19 (Blades), 26 (Stengel), September 2 (Traynor), 1939; *PT*, October 9, 16, 1920.

23. *PC*, August 5, 12, November 4, 11, 1939; *Daily Worker*, January 31, 1954 (Schomburg Center Clipping File); *PI*, August 27, 1939; *CD*, July 22 (Young), 29, 1939; *NYAN*, October 7 (McCarthy), December 16, 1939; Ross Forman, "Memories Abundant at NLBPA Card Show," undated photocopy, SABR Research Collection (Rust). White players continued to provide cautious or noncommittal responses when questioned about the issue. In 1942, Walter White of the NAACP contacted Dick Bartell of the New York Giants to obtain his "advice . . . about the most effective way of furthering the campaign now so much in the press towards getting Negro ball players . . . into the Big Leagues." Bartell, however, was apparently reluctant to become involved and offered little insight or assistance. See Walter White to Dick Bartell, August 4, 1942, Dick Bartell to Walter White, August 7, 1942, in NAACP papers, Negroes in Sports, 1942–1952.

24. *PAA*, August 19 (Bolden), 1939; *PT*, August 10, December 14, 21, 1939; *BAA*, July 15, 1939; August 1 (Roberts), 1942; June 4 (Griffith), 1949; *NYAN*, August 5, December 9, 1939; September 12, 1942 (Burley); *PC*, August 5 (Posey), 1939; *CD*, December 9, 1939; *PI*, December 17, 1939. Jules Tygiel has also suggested that the "success of the Communists in forcing the issue before the American public far outweighed the negative ramifications of their sponsorship." See Tygiel, *Baseball's Great Experiment* (1997 ed.), 37.

25. *PT*, August 17 ("futile"), 31 (Vann) 1939; May 23 (Harris), 1940; *BAA*, June 28, 1941 (Rea); *NYT*, May 18, 1941.

26. *New York World-Telegram*, September 7, 1934, cited in Gregory, *Dizziest Season*, 238–40 (Daniel); Lacy, *Fighting for Fairness*, 32; Ted Shane, "Chocolate Rube Waddell," *SEP*, July 27, 1940; Brown, "Negro in American Culture," 117; *PT*, August 15, 1940 (Harris); July 11, August 15, 1942; August 26, 1944; Riley, *Biographical Encyclopedia*, 215; *SN*, July 16, 1942.

27. Shane, " 'Peanuts' Nyasses," 53–54; *PC*, June 6, 1953; *BAA*, August 19, 1939; Herb Graffis, "How Dim-Brained Can a Star Be?" *Esquire*, February 1938; Frederic Cople Jaher, "White America Views Jack Johnson, Joe Louis, and Muhammad Ali," in *Sport in America: New Historical Perspectives*, ed. Donald Spivey (Westport, Conn., 1985), 163 ("jungle").

28. *PC*, August 10 ("these"), 1940; February 7 (Posey), 1942; Harlow, "Unrecognized Stars"; *NYT*, November 19, 1963.

29. Riess, "May the Best White Man Win."

30. *PT*, October 6, 13, 1932; April 6, 1933 ("Harlem"); May 7, 1936 ("groups"); April 21, 1938; Myrdal, *An American Dilemma*, 915; E. Franklin Frazier, *Negro Youth at the Crossways, Their Personality Development in the Middle States*, 289; McKay, *Harlem*, 96; *PV*, November 27, 1943. Comparison to whites often provided a convenient frame of reference to characterize black skills. Pitcher Slim Jones, for instance, was described as the "dusky counterpart of Lefty Grove, both in size and speed," while Terris McDuffie earned the title of the "Sepia Dizzy Dean." The phenomenon was hardly limited to sports, as advertisements during the early 1930s promoted black entertainers as the "Colored Kate Smith" and "Colored Bing Crosby." See *PT*, July 27, 1933; June 14, July 5, 1934; July 29, 1937.

31. *PT*, April 16 (St. Clair), 1936; June 3 (Carrington), 1937; Lanctot, *Fair Dealing*, 183–84; *PC*, May 14, 1938; *NYAN*, August 13 (Bourne), 1938; February 25, 1939; *CD*, September 18 (Simmons), 1937; June 25 ("the young"), 1938; July 22 ("as long"), 1939; October 18, 1941; Art Carter to Clark Griffith, ACP, box 170-7, folder 5; Brown, "Negro in American Culture," 110 ("during"). Segregated seating arrangements in Organized Baseball parks were hardly limited to the deep south. At Sportsman's Park in St. Louis, black fans were restricted to pavilion and bleacher seats until 1944, although a 1947 article alludes to continued segregation. Minor league facilities in Baltimore and Kansas City also maintained segregated seating at times during the 1930s and 1940s. See Benson, *Ballparks of North America*, 191; *MC*, April 10, 1943; *PC*, June 26, 1937; *PI*, February 14, 1953; *PT*, February 23, 1933; October 11, 1934; May 13, 1944; *CD*, September 23, 1939; *BAA*, April 22, 1933; James Bready, *Baseball in Baltimore: The First 100 Years* (Baltimore, 1998), 214; *PV*, May 16, 1942; *KCC*, July 29, 1938; *Time*, September 22, 1947, 70; *Sport*, April 1957.

32. Barbara Dianne Savage, *Broadcasting Freedom: Radio, War and the Politics of Race, 1938–48* (Chapel Hill, N.C., 1999), 63–104, 280; Cripps, *Slow Fade to Black*, 349, 376; *NYAN*, June 15, 1940; January 31 (Burley), 1942; May 19 (Adams), August 25, 1945; *PT*, July 3, 1943; J. Fred MacDonald, *Don't Touch That Dial! Radio Programming in American Life, 1920–1960* (Chicago, 1979), 327–70; Myrdal, *American*

Dilemma, 852 ("Negro"), 988; Patrick S. Washburn, *A Question of Sedition: The Federal Government's Investigation of the Black Press During World War II* (New York, 1986), 62–182; Wynn, *Afro-American and the Second World War*, 81–87; Clayton R. Koppes and Gregory D. Black, "Blacks, Loyalty, and Motion-Picture Propaganda in World War II," *Journal of American History* (September 1986): 383–406; John T. McManus and Louis Kronenberger, "Motion Pictures, the Theater, and Race Relations," *Annals of the American Academy of Political and Social Science* (March 1946): 152–58; Denis, "Negro in Show Business"; *NYT*, April 11 ("basketball"), 1942; *Louisville Courier-Journal*, April 12, 1942, cited in *DW*, April 20, 1942; Hill, *FBI's RACON*, 244–46; Lauren Rebecca Sklaroff, "Constructing G.I. Joe Louis: Cultural Solutions to the 'Negro Problem' During World War II," *Journal of American History* (December 2002).

33. A. S. (Doc) Young, "The Black Sportswriter," *Ebony*, October 1970 ("refused"); *DW*, March 23, 1942; William Hageman, "Chicago's 55-Year-Old Secret: Jackie Robinson's Tryout with the White Sox," *Chicago Tribune*, March 26, 1997; *PC*, March 16, 1940; March 1, 1941; March 21, 28, 1942; Clark and Lester, *Negro Leagues Book*, 326; *PI*, April 22 (Dykes), 1942; November 4, 1950.

34. *DW*, March 23, May 6 (Rodney), 16, June 6 (Sheil), 11, 18, 24 ("there is"), 1942; *PT*, July 25 ("I have"), 1942; *BAA*, July 25, 1942; *CD*, July 25, 1942; *PM*, July 17, 1942; *PC*, August 5, 1939.

35. *PM*, July 17, 1942 ("sick"); *BAA*, July 25 (Carter), 1942; *CD*, July 25 ("same"), August 1 ("what keeps"), 1942; *PR*, July 30, 1942.

36. *PI*, July 19 ("all wet"), 26 (Gallagher), 1942; E. G. Barrow to William T. Andrews, August 14, 1942 ("using"); Walter White to William T. Andrews, August 27, 1942 ("arrogance") in NAACP papers, Negroes in Sports, 1942–1952; *BAA*, July 25 (Griffith), 1942. Ironically, several sources suggest that Griffith informally spoke to Buck Leonard and Josh Gibson of the Grays about joining the Washington Senators. Fearful of destroying his relationship with the Grays, Griffith failed to take any further action. While various accounts date the incident between 1938 and 1943, 1942 appears most likely, as Dan Burley specifically noted Griffith's interest in purchasing Gibson. See *NYAN*, July 11, 1942; Leonard, *Buck Leonard*, 99; Bankes, *Pittsburgh Crawfords*, 53; *Boston Globe*, March 29, 1997; Holway, *Voices*, 252; *DW*, July 13, 1942.

37. *Newark Evening News*, July 30, 1942, in Joseph Thomas Moore, *Pride Against Prejudice: The Biography of Larry Doby* (Westport, Conn., 1988), 22 ("unwritten"); *PM*, July 29, 1942; L. S. MacPhail to Rev. Raymond J. Campion, July 28, 1942 ("any") in NAACP papers, part 15, Segregation and Discrimination, Complaints and Responses, 1940–1955, Series A, Legal file, Negroes in Sports, 1942–1952, reel 9; *SN*, August 6, 1942 cited in *NYAN*, August 15, 1942 ("agitators").

38. *BAA*, July 25, August 1 ("there still"), September 5, 1942; *CD*, August 1 ("colored men"), 29, 1942; *PT*, August 1, 1942; *PI*, August 2, 23, 1942; *PC*, August 1, 15, 29, 1942; April 28, 1945; *PINQ*, July 26–28, 1942; *PR*, July 29, 1942; *NYT*, July 29, August 21, 1942; *DW*, October 25, 1951, in Schomburg Center Clipping File; Campanella, *It's Good to Be Alive*, 99–100; *NYAN*, August 29, September 12, 1942 (Burley). Cummiskey confirmed that Smith asked for his help in selecting black players, despite his own admission that he had not had the "opportunity to see some of the great Negro stars of today in action." See *PM*, July 28, 1942.

39. *CCP*, August 15, September 12 (Bradley), 1942; *PI*, September 6, 1942; *NYT*, September 2, 1942.

40. *PINQ*, November 8, 1932; February 5, 1933; *PR*, June 9, 1940; J. Roy Stockton, "Them Phillies or, How to Make Failure Pay," *SEP*, October 4, 1941; Rich Westcott

and Frank Bilovsky, *The New Phillies Encyclopedia* (Philadelphia, 1993), 476; Gerald Nugent file, BHOFL; *PC*, March 4, 1933; August 1, 1942; Kevin Kerrane, *Dollar Sign on the Muscle* (New York, 1984), 249; *BAA*, July 25, August 1 ("just the"), 1942; *PI*, August 2, 1942; October 10, 1943; June 24, 1950; *PT*, July 25, 1942; *PM*, July 20, 28, 1942; *DW*, July 16, 1942. In his autobiography, Campanella erroneously claimed the Philadelphia incident occurred in 1945. See Campanella, *It's Good to be Alive*, 98–100.

41. David J. Jordan, Larry R. Gerlach, and John P. Rossi, "Bill Veeck and the 1943 Sale of the Phillies: A Baseball Myth Exploded," *National Pastime* (1998); *Current Biography* ("Bill Veeck"), undated clipping, courtesy of SABR Research Collection; *PEB*, February 9, 1943; *PINQ*, November 12–13, 1942; Richard Orodenker, ed., *The Phillies Reader* (Philadelphia, 1996), 53–55; William Marshall interview with Bill Veeck, February 23, 1977 ("if they"), COHP; Tygiel, *Baseball's Great Experiment*, 41; Roger Kahn, *A Season in the Sun* (New York, 1977), 130. While Jordan, Gerlach, and Rossi argue that Veeck "did not work with Abe Saperstein and others to stock any team with Negro Leagues stars," there is scattered evidence to suggest his involvement with Saperstein and Fay Young (whom Veeck erroneously confused with another black sportswriter, A. S. "Doc" Young, in his own account of the incident). In 1949, Fay Young reported on a Chicago Urban League banquet where Veeck announced that while he was in Milwaukee several years earlier, he had spoken with Young "for several hours about integrating Negroes in major league baseball. At that time I was planning to buy the Philadelphia Nationals." Five years later, an Associated Negro Press story quoted Saperstein, who described Veeck's planned purchase of the Phillies and use of black players. See *CD*, February 26, 1949; *PT*, August 14, 1954; *PI*, August 14, 1954.

42. *CCP*, August 15, September 12, 1942; *PI*, September 6, December 13, 1942; *NYT*, September 2, December 4, 1942; *NYAN*, September 19, December 12, 1942; December 11 ("we know"), 1943; January 15, 1944; *CD*, September 26, October 10, December 12, 1942; *PT*, December 11, 1943; August 4, 1945; *PV*, September 19 ("should have"), October 3, 1942; Catherine Freeland telegram to Walter White, September 9, 1942, in NAACP papers, Negroes in Sports, 1942–1952; *BAA*, December 12, 1942; *PINQ*, September 24, 1942.

43. *PC*, September 4 ("positive"), December 18 ("just"), 1937; August 1, 1942 ("belated"/"have had"); *PT*, August 1 (Burley), 1935; August 10, 1939; Webber and Brown, "Play Ball!"; *BAA*, February 5, 1938; June 29, 1940; *New York Post*, August 8, 1935, in Schomburg Center Clipping File; *NYAN*, June 15 (Manley), 1940.

44. *CD*, August 8 (Martin/Semler), 1942; *PI*, August 9 (Wilkinson), 1942; *CCP*, August 8, 1942 (Hayes); undated news clipping, September 1942 (Manley), NEP; *PC*, January 23 (Smith), 1943; *PT*, September 16, 1944 (Burley); L. S. MacPhail to Rev. Raymond J. Campion, July 28, 1942, in NAACP papers; *PV*, July 11, 1942 (Bostic).

45. *CD*, August 8, 1942; *BAA*, July 25, 1942; *NYAN*, June 15, 1940 (Manley); *PC*, February 18, April 1, 1933; September 8, 1934; January 29, 1938; September 9, 1939; *PI*, March 20, 1938; Ferdinand Morton to Ford Frick, July 14, 1936, BHOFL; *PT*, March 24, 1938 ("the owners").

46. *PT*, August 10, 1939; *PAA*, August 19, 1939; *BAA*, August 12, 1939 cited in Reisler, *Black Writers/Black Baseball*, 16–17 (Wilson/Harris/Snow); *PC*, September 9, 1939 ("it is"); *NYAN*, June 15, 1940 ("it'd be"); *PI*, June 23, 1940 (Barnes). Stephen Fox, for example, has argued that "for most whites, Paige epitomized black baseball. His image—so gifted on the field, so ungovernable off it—did not appeal to the moguls of white baseball. Paige confirmed what they already wanted to believe about black ball players. In the end he probably retarded big-league integration." See Fox, *Big Leagues*, 336.

47. *SN*, August 13, 1942 ("it wouldn't"); *CD*, August 15, 1942; *PI*, August 16, 1942; Bill Bryson, "Fabulous Flinger," *Esquire*, July 1943; *NYAN*, August 15, 1942; January 23, 1943 (Bostic); *CCP*, August 15, 1942 (Fuster); *BAA*, August 22, 1942 (Carter). As feared, Paige's statement ultimately bolstered the arguments of integration opponents and contributed to a distorted perception of salaries in black baseball. Red Sox general manager Eddie Collins, for example, subsequently claimed that no blacks wanted to play in the major leagues as "they were doing better financially in their own leagues." In 1945, Commissioner A. B. Chandler claimed that "many Negro baseball players make more money in their own leagues than major league players do," echoed by H. G. Salsinger of the *Detroit News*, who asserted that black players "would gain nothing financially" thorough integration and "can do much better for themselves playing in Negro leagues." See *PT*, May 12, 1945; *PC*, December 16, 1944; Arnold Rampersad, *Jackie Robinson: A Biography* (New York, 1997), 119; *NYT*, February 18, 1948; *MC*, May 19, 1945; *Boston Globe*, April 29, 1959.

48. *BAA*, June 23 (Paige), 1945; unidentified clipping from Washington newspaper, August 14, 1942 (Lacy) in ACP, box 170-20, folder 1; *DW*, June 29, 1942 (McDuffie); *NYAN*, June 13, 1942 (Griffith).

49. Goldstein, *Spartan Seasons*, 35 (Frick); *BAA*, December 26, 1942 ("would like"); *PC*, December 5, 26 ("men in"), 1942; March 20, 27, May 15, 1943; *CD*, May 15 (Cohen), June 5, 1943; *PT*, December 12, 1942; May 15, June 5, 1943; Young, "Black Sportswriter"; *PI*, April 25, June 6, 1943; Berlage, *Women in Baseball*, 135–46. In his autobiography, Patterson claimed that Wrigley "listened without an outward show of irritation. He knew the value of the perspective I had outlined—perhaps he saw a pennant or two in the offing. Yet he was afraid to commit himself." The two men reportedly met for a second time (probably in early 1943), this time with Clarence "Pants" Rowland of the Angels present. According to Patterson, "there was talk of Jackie Robinson being acquired by the Angels, but that was not what we wanted," as the goal was major league integration. See Patterson, *Man Who Cried Genocide*, 143–44.

50. Roy Wilkins to Sam Lacy, November 24, 1943; Roy Wilkins to Kenesaw Mountain Landis, November 24, 1943, NAACP papers, Negroes in Sports, 1942–1952; *BAA*, January 8, 1944; *PI*, December 5, 1943; Goldstein, *Spartan Seasons*, 102–15; *KCC*, December 16, 1938; *PT*, December 4, 1943 (Landis). Although Wilkins claimed that the NAACP "has been interested in this question for many years and has felt that the inclusion of competent Negro players on the major league teams . . . would do much to strengthen the American democratic way of life," the involvement of the organization in the integration fight of the 1930s and 1940s was generally minimal. Walter White, however, did contact the owner of the New York Giants (football) in 1938, hoping to interest the team in black college players.

51. *PT*, December 11 (Harridge/Landis), 1943; *PI*, December 12, 1943; *PC*, December 11 (Lewis), 1943; *BAA*, December 11, 1943; *CD*, December 11 (Sengstacke), 1943; *NYAN*, December 11, 1943; Duberman, *Paul Robeson*, 283; Paul Robeson, "Two Strikes on Jim Crow," *Spotlite*, January 1944 (Robeson), Schomburg Center Clipping File. Some accounts of the meeting suggest that Father Raymond Campion and Adam Clayton Powell, the publisher of the *PV*, were also present. William L. Patterson, a friend of Robeson, later provided a possible explanation for Robeson's presence. Patterson reportedly wrote to Landis and in the name of Robeson and Earl Dickerson, a black Chicago politician, arranged a meeting. According to Patterson, Robeson and Landis eventually met privately, although there is little evidence to support this beyond Patterson's account. See Patterson, *Man Who Cried Genocide*, 142–45.

52. *PT*, April 1 (Wilson), 1944; *BAA*, January 8, 1944 (Lacy); *NYAN*, December 11, 1943; David Falkner, *Great Time Coming: The Life of Jackie Robinson, from Baseball to Birmingham* (New York, 1995), 99–100; *PV*, December 11, 1943; March 4, 1944. In the aftermath of the meeting, Lacy confided to Roy Wilkins that he had "*absolutely*" no part in the surprising and totally unexpected turn taken by the major baseball leagues project in New York." In a likely reference to the involvement of John Sengstacke, Lacy complained that the "whole affair was taken out of my hands by persons who have it in their power to do so" and "developed into a vehicle for the advancement of another's *personal* ambitions." Within weeks, Lacy left the *Defender* to rejoin the *Afro*. See Sam Lacy to Roy Wilkins, December 8, 1943, NAACP papers, Negroes in Sports, 1942–1952.

53. *New York Post*, December 4, 1943 (Frank), in Schomburg Center Clipping File; *PT*, December 11 (Wilson), 1943. While already under FBI surveillance by 1943 for his involvement in radical causes, Robeson still enjoyed considerable prestige among blacks and liberal whites and would receive the Spingarn Medal in 1945 from the NAACP. See Duberman, *Paul Robeson*, 254–95.

54. *PT*, December 18 ("from my"), 1943; January 8 ("if the"), December 9 ("the proposition"), 1944; *PI*, January 2, 1944 ("we should"); *NYAN*, December 11 ("we are built"), 1943.

55. *PT*, March 25, 1944 (Posey).

56. *PC*, July 26, 1941 ("Negro baseball"); June 27, 1942 ("the letters"); *BAA*, January 8 ("to reassure"), 15, 1944; *PI*, January 16, 1944 (Coleman).

57. Dan W. Dodson, "The Integration of Negroes in Baseball," *Journal of Educational Sociology* (October 1954): 73–82; *PT*, April 24, 1943; May 20, 1944; *PC*, April 18, 1942; October 2, 1943; February 19, December 23, 1944; May 26, 1945; December 21, 1946; *PI*, April 28, 1940; October 6, 1945; *BAA*, May 29, June 5, 1943; February 26, 1944; May 19, September 22, 1945; Bill Cooper interview with Calvin Griffith, April 22, 1977, COHP; *SN*, March 11, 1972; Holway, *Voices*, 261. Brooklyn's black population, however, grew steadily and by 1940 exceeded 100,000. See *PV*, April 18, 1942; Dominic Capeci, Jr., *The Harlem Riot of 1943* (Philadelphia, 1977), 32.

58. *Philadelphia North American*, September 6, 1919; *PI*, October 20, 1935; October 4, 1942, January 23, July 2, 1944; July 14, October 6, December 15, 1945; *PT*, July 5, 26, August 23, 1934; August 15, September 5, October 10, 17, 1935; July 3, August 14, September 18, 1943; June 10, July 22, August 12, September 2, October 7, 1944; *PINQ*, October 17, 1934; Lanctot, *Fair Dealing*, 14, 112; *PC*, December 16 (Mack), 1944.

59. John R. Williams to Ed Gottlieb and Abe and Effa Manley, July 24, 1945, NEP; *CD*, March 4, 1933; March 6, 1943; *PC*, July 26, 1941; May 30, August 1, December 26, 1942; *PT*, June 6, 1942; *CCP*, February 1, 1947. Because of the relatively small black population in New England, Boston's major league parks were rarely used by black teams, although Fenway Park was rented more frequently during the war years. See *PT*, September 19, 1942; July 1, 1944; April 28, 1945; *BC*, May 29, June 26, July 3, August 7, September 4, 1943; May 13, June 10, 24, July 8, August 19, 1944; July 7, 1945.

60. *NYAN*, May 27 (Thomas), 1944; *PT*, December 9, 23, 1944; *PC*, December 2, 1944.

Chapter 8. Breakthrough and Setback

Epigraph: Cum Posey to Thomas Wilson, November 1945 in James Hendrix, *I Remember Tom* (Nashville, Tenn., 1983), 9.

1. J. M. Johnson to Will Harridge, February 26, 1945, Office of the Director, Railway Transport Department, 1942–1946, RG 219; *NYT*, December 24, 25, 1944; January 5, 18; February 22, 23, March 22, 1945; Goldstein, *Spartan Seasons*, 138, 200–208; *MC*, March 3, 1945; John W. Jeffries, *Wartime America: The World War II Home Front* (Chicago, 1996), 22–23; *PT*, January 6, 13, 1945; Marshall, *Baseball's Pivotal Era*, 16; Graham, "When Baseball Went to War"; Blum, *Drafted or Deferred*, 192–95.

2. *PT*, January 13 ("most"), 1945; Lingeman, *Don't You Know There's a War On?* 319; Goldstein, *Spartan Seasons*, 208; *PI*, April 7, 1945; *NYHT*, April 4, 6, May 13, 1945; *SN*, March 29, 1945; William J. Hayes, District Manager, to P. N. Simmons, Regional Director, March 21, 1945 ("these"); V. T. Corbett, Assistant Director, Passenger Section, Railway Transport Department to J. B. Martin and Thomas T. Wilson, March 26, 1945 ("transportation"); J. B. Martin to V. T. Corbett, April 5, 1945 ("ninety-eight"), Office of the Director, Railway Transport Department, 1942–1946, RG 219.

3. *PT*, January 27, February 3, 17, March 24, April 14 (Wilson), 1945; *BAA*, January 20, February 3, March 24, 1945; *PC*, March 24, 1945; Leonard Levin, "Baseball in 1945—The Pits," *Providence Journal*, February 1995 (courtesy SABR Research Exchange); *PINQ*, April 8, 1945; Julia Baxter, "New York State Bars Economic Jim Crow," *Crisis* (April 1945): 98–99; *NYT*, March 13, 1945; February 25, 1962.

4. Hill, *FBI's RACON*, 429 ("very helpful"); *PV*, February 10, March 24, 31, April 14, 1945; *PT*, April 14, 1945; *PI*, February 4, 1945; *BAA*, February 3, 1945; Duberman, *Paul Robeson*, 330; *NYAN*, May 27, 1944; May 11, 1968; *PC*, April 18, 1937; Harvey Frommer, *Rickey and Robinson: The Men Who Broke Baseball's Color Barrier* (New York, 1982), 100 ("those were"). While the *People's Voice* was not communist-sponsored, the involvement of Max Yergan, the head of the Negro National Congress, and Doxey Wilkerson, a future *Daily Worker* journalist, contributed to the newspaper's reputation as friendly to radical causes. By late 1946, Adam Clayton Powell resigned his editorial position, citing the mounting communist influence in the operation of the paper. See Ottley, *"New World A-Comin'"*, 275; Duberman, *Paul Robeson*, 330; Record, *Negro and the Communist Party*, 197; Roland Wolseley, *The Black Press, USA*, 2nd ed. (Ames, Iowa, 1990), 84; *PV*, February 13, 1943; December 27, 1947; *NYT*, April 13, 1975.

5. *NYT*, April 8 ("professional"), 1945; *PT*, April 14, 21, 1945; *PI*, April 14, 1945; Tygiel, *Baseball's Great Experiment*, 45–46; *PV*, April 14, 1945; *PC*, April 14, 1945; *BAA*, March 17, April 14, 1945; *PR*, April 8, 1945; *SN*, April 12, 1945; *NYAN*, February 17, 1945; *NYHT*, April 7 (Laney), 8, 1945; *PM*, April 8, 1945; Branch Rickey to Mel Jones, May 2 [4?], 1945 ("several"), BRP, box 15, Correspondence, Thomas Melville "Mel" Jones, 1942–63. The actual ages of Thomas and McDuffie remain elusive. In 1937, Cum Posey reported that McDuffie was born on July 22, 1910, but a press release in 1942 provided a birth year of 1907. McDuffie's obituary in May 1968 lists his age as sixty-two, making him thirty-nine at the time of the Bear Mountain tryout. The Social Security Death Index (www.ancestry.com) identifies his birth year as 1902. For Thomas, contemporary accounts suggest a birth date of March 22, 1907 or 1908, although a June 1945 article lists his age as thirty-nine. His date of death is unknown. See *PC*, April 18, 1937; *NYAN*, May 11, 1968; *CD*, March 1, 1941; *PI*, June 30, 1945; ACP, box 170-19.

6. *BAA*, July 22 ("generally"), 1944; *PT*, April 14 ("belligerent"), 1945; *PI*, June 30, 1945; *PV*, May 12 ("goody"), June 23 ("great"), 1945. As early as 1935, Sam Lacy touted Thomas as a major league prospect, yet noted that his "temperament is rotten and his batting worse." Three years later, a fan complained to Abe Manley that

McDuffie "put too much emphasis on his socializing. His arrogant way on the ball field was disgusting to the fans and I dare say had a bad effect on the players." See *WT*, August 3, 1935; Dr. W. W. Wolfe to A. Manley, August 20, 1938, NEP.

7. Robert Rice, "Profiles—Thoughts on Baseball II," *New Yorker*, June 3, 1950, 30–45; Seymour, *Baseball: The Golden Age*, 410–22; Sullivan, *Minors*, 94–99; Frommer, *Rickey and Robinson*, 36–45; Kerrane, *Dollar Sign*, 57–69; Charles Dexter, "Brooklyn's Sturdy Branch," *Collier's*, September 15, 1945; J. Roy Stockton, "A Brain Comes to Brooklyn," *SEP*, February 13, 1943; Bob Smizik, *The Pittsburgh Pirates: An Illustrated History* (New York, 1990), 81 (Kiner).

8. Riess, *Sports and the American Jew*, 40–41; Fox, *Big Leagues*, 337–39; *SN*, November 1, 1945; Joseph Dorinson and Joram Warmund, eds., *Jackie Robinson: Race, Sports, and the American Dream* (Armonk, N.Y., 1998), 93, 99; Arthur Mann, *The Jackie Robinson Story* (New York, 1963), 7–14; *NYT*, October 25, 1945; Red Barber and Robert Creamer, *Rhubarb in the Catbird Seat* (Lincoln, Neb., 1997), 266–68; *CD*, February 28, 1948; Davis J. Walsh, "Mahatma Explains Stand on Lip, PG Shift, Robbie, Raj," *New York Journal American*, November 1955, in AMP, box 10, Clippings, 1925–1961; Capeci, *Harlem Riot of 1943*, 31; Branch Rickey to J. G. Stahlman, January 23, 1950 ("I did"), BRP, box 27, correspondence "S" miscellaneous, January–July 1950; *NYAN*, August 4, 1945 (Burley). Ironically, Powers and Rickey, ostensibly both pro-integration, became bitter enemies during the 1940s, particularly after Powers dubbed Rickey "El Cheapo" because of his supposed frugality in managing the affairs of the Brooklyn Dodgers. By 1946, Powers's continuous criticism of Rickey prompted the team to produce a lengthy report, "The Case Against Jimmy Powers," apparently intended for press release (see Brooklyn Baseball Club, "The Case Against Jimmy Powers," BRP, box 34, Baseball File, Brooklyn Dodgers, James Powers, 1942–1946). Arthur Mann, however, subsequently claimed that Rickey rejected publicizing a potentially damaging letter written by Powers and reflecting "un-American" attitudes, probably anti-Semitism, as the Rickey papers contain a copy of a 1942 letter from Powers referring to his dislike of "certain crackpot politicians and Jews." See Jimmy Powers to "Gene," May 22, 1942, BRP, box 34, Baseball File, Brooklyn Dodgers, James Powers, 1942–1946; AMP, Notes and Fragments, box 11; Arthur Mann, *Branch Rickey: American in Action* (Boston, 1957), 239–40; Tygiel, *Baseball's Great Experiment*, 50–51.

9. Norwood and Brackman, "Going to Bat for Jackie Robinson," 124–25 ("alleged"); Isadore Muchnick file, Harvard University Archives; *PI*, March 18, May 12 ("unless") 1945; *PT*, March 31, 1945; *Boston Globe*, April 29, 1959; March 28, 1997; *BAA*, March 17, 1945; *CD*, March 24, 1945; *NYT*, March 13, 24, 1945; *PC*, April 14, June 9, 1945; May 31, 1952; Rampersad, *Jackie Robinson*, 119; *BC*, March 17, 31, 1945. Numerous accounts have erroneously suggested that Muchnick (1908–1963) was motivated by the changing racial composition of his district, but Norwood and Brackman have demonstrated that there is little basis to this claim, apparently originated by Wendell Smith. Muchnick later served on the Boston school committee and unsuccessfully sought the Democratic nomination for a congressional seat in 1952.

10. Jackie Robinson as told to Alfred Duckett, *I Never Had It Made* (1972; reprint Hopewell, New Jersey, 1995), 29 ("not"); *PC*, April 21, 28, 1945; May 3, 1952; *Boston Guardian*, April 21, 1945; *PT*, April 21, 1945; *Boston Globe*, April 29, 1959; March 28, 1997; *BAA*, April 28, 1945; Falkner, *Great Time Coming*, 102; Rampersad, *Jackie Robinson*, 119–20; *PINQ*, April 17, 1945; Brent Kelly, "Marvin Williams," *SCD*, February 19, 1999; *NYAN*, January 20, 1945; *SN*, November 23, 1949; Rich Marazzi, "Sam Jethroe—His Chance at the Majors Came Far Too Late; Now He Must

Fight to Get Even a Tiny Pension," *Sports Collectors Digest*, November 11, 1994 ("had the").

11. *PI*, May 12, 1945 (Posey); *PC*, May 12, 1945 (Paige); *CD*, December 25, 1943; April 14, 1945 (Young); *NYAN*, January 8, 1944; *PM*, April 8, 1945; *CCP*, May 19, 1945 (Hayes); *PT*, May 5, 1945 (Bolden). In 1939, the *Amsterdam News* reported that New York Cubans infielder Arturo Rodriguez rejected an offer from the Chattanooga Lookouts of the Southern Association. Evidence suggests, however, that this player is actually Hector Rodriguez, who eventually appeared in the major leagues in 1952 with the Chicago White Sox. See *NYAN*, June 10, 1939; Riley, *Biographical Encyclopedia*, 676.

12. *BAA*, April 28, May 5, June 16, 1945; February 28 (Lacy), 1948; Sam Lacy to Edward Collins, March 3, 1945, Edward T. Collins to Sam Lacy, April 11, 1945, Will Harridge to Eddie Collins, April 16, 1945, Will Harridge to L. M. O'Connor, April 16, 1945, L. M. O'Connor to Ford Frick and Will Harridge, April 30, 1945, L. M. O'Connor to Sam Lacy, April 30, 1945, Sam Lacy to Ford Frick, May 4, 1945, BHOFL; Tygiel, *Baseball's Great Experiment*, 42; Lacy, *Fighting for Fairness*, 47; Marshall, *Baseball's Pivotal Era*, 14; L. S. MacPhail to F. H. LaGuardia, August 22 (?), 1945, Municipal Archives, Office of the Mayor (Fiorello LaGuardia), Baseball 1945, July–August file. Myles Paige, a black New York judge, was also named to the committee as a consultant.

13. *NYT*, October 2, 1975; *SN*, February 19, 26, 1931; February 23, 1933; October 15, 1947; Robert W. Creamer, *Baseball in '41: A Celebration of the Best Baseball Season Ever* (New York, 1991), 34–54; Pietrusza, *Lights On!* 102–4; Lee MacPhail, *My Nine Innings: An Autobiography of 50 Years in Baseball* (Westport, Conn., 1989), 3–16; Rothe, *Current Biography—1945*, 375–78; G. Richard McKelvey, *The Mac-Phails: Baseball's First Family of the Front Office* (Jefferson, N.C., 2000), 2–19; Robert Lewis Taylor, "Profiles—Borough Defender—I," *New Yorker*, July 12, 1941, 20–21; Taylor, "Profiles—Borough Defender—II," *New Yorker*, July 19, 1941, 20–22; Larry MacPhail file, BHOFL; William Marshall interview with Red Smith, November 13, 1979 ("way ahead"), COHP; Barber and Creamer, *Rhubarb in the Catbird Seat*, 197–98; *PINQ*, August 10, 1938; Tygiel, *Past Time*, 96–107.

14. MacPhail, *My Nine Innings*, 15 ("not"); Frommer, *Rickey and Robinson*, 104 ("the profit"); *SN*, May 7, 1942; February 1, March 22, May 3, 1945; October 12, 1949; *BAA*, May 5, 1945; February 28, 1948; Newson, *Fighting for Fairness*, 57; Harold Parrott, *The Lords of Baseball* (New York, 1976), 190; Sammons, *Beyond the Ring*, 76; *NYT*, August 13–17, 1926; September 2, 1944; *PINQ*, April 23, 1950; H. Viscount Nelson, "The Philadelphia NAACP: Race Versus Class Consciousness During the Thirties," *Journal of Black Studies* 5, 3 (March 1975): 255–76; *PT*, June 26, 1941; May 5, 1945; William Marshall interview with Fred Saigh, May 16, 1978, COHP; *NYAN*, February 17, 1945; Albert Chandler with Vance H. Trimble, *Heroes, Plain Folks, and Skunks: The Life and Times of Happy Chandler—An Autobiography* (Chicago, 1987), 180; James B. Roberts and Alexander Skutt, *The Boxing Register: International Boxing Hall of Fame Record Book* (Ithaca, N.Y., 1999), 179; Marshall, *Baseball's Pivotal Era*, 17–22.

15. *BAA*, May 5 (Lacy), 1945; *SN*, May 3 ("efforts"), 1945; Potomacus, "Chandler of Kentucky," *New Republic*, October 11, 1943, 479–80; Milton Gross, "The Truth About Happy Chandler," *Sport*, April 1949, 53–62; *Time*, May 31, 1943, 17–18; Gunther, *Inside U.S.A.*, 648–50; "Albert B. Chandler" in *Current Biography—1943*, ed. Maxine Block(New York, 1944), 117–21; *Current Biography—1956*, 106–8 (Chandler), courtesy of SABR Research Exchange; Chandler, *Heroes, Plain Folks, and Skunks*; *CCP*, May 5, 1945; James R. Devine, "The Past as Moral Guide to the Present:

The Parallel Between Martin Luther King, Jr.'s Elements of a Nonviolent Civil Rights Campaign and Jackie Robinson's Entry onto the Brooklyn Dodgers," *Villanova Sports and Entertainment Law Journal* 3, 2 (1996): 523; *PI*, May 12, 1945; *PC*, May 5, 1945; Marshall, *Baseball's Pivotal Era*, 24–27; Walter Hixson, "The 1938 Kentucky Senate Election: Alben W. Barkley, 'Happy' Chandler, and The New Deal," *Register of the Kentucky Historical Society* 80, 3 (Summer 1982): 309–29; *NYAN*, August 20, 1955; Vincent X. Flaherty, "The Life Story of Albert B. 'Happy' Chandler," in *Baseball Guide and Record Book—1946*, ed. J. G. Taylor Spink (St. Louis, 1946), 111–29; *PM*, April 27, 1945; Happy Chandler file, BHOFL. In 1942, Chandler voted against cloture during discussions of the Pepper Anti-Poll Tax bill. Two years later, Chandler voted in support of a bill to "lay aside consideration of poll tax question," but did not vote on a measure to eliminate appropriations for the FEPC. See Goodman, *While You Were Gone*, 578–89; *PV*, November 28, 1942; *PAA*, November 28, 1942.

16. *CD*, May 12 ("barring"/"tolerant"), 1945; *MC*, May 12, 1945; *PINQ*, May 4, 1945 ("Negro"); *CCP*, May 5, 1945 (Williams). Chandler resigned his Senate seat in fall 1945.

17. Minutes, December 15, 1944, NAL meeting, TBC, box 2, minutes, NAL meetings 1943–1952; *PT*, January 6, 1945; *CD*, January 6, 1945; *MC*, July 8, December 30, 1944; *PV*, March 24, 1945; *PC*, January 6 ("we do"), 1945; *PI*, February 18 ("merely"), 1945; *NYAN*, October 5 (Burley), 1946. The *Chicago Defender* reported that Wendell Smith was the league's original secretary but relinquished the position after rumored pressure from Grays officials. See *CD*, January 6, February 17, 1945.

18. J. G. Shackelford to Walter White, May 29, 1945, folder 48910; Records from Highway Transport Department, 1942–1946, RG 219; *CD*, December 25, 1943; July 29, 1944; *MC*, March 11, 1944; *PC*, April 28, 1945; *PI*, March 19, 1944; March 18, 1945; *PT*, March 14, 1940; February 28, 1942. Atlanta and St. Louis withdrew prior to the start of the season. By June, the USL consisted of franchises in Toledo, Pittsburgh, Brooklyn, Detroit, Philadelphia, and Chicago. See *PI*, June 9, 1945.

19. *NYAN*, March 31 ("booking"), 1945; *BAA*, June 2 (Lacy), 1945; J. G. Shackelford to Walter White, May 29, 1945, folder 48910; Records from Highway Transport Department, 1942–1946, RG 219; *CCP*, January 13, May 19, 1945; May 25, 1946; *SN*, May 3, 1945; *MC*, May 19, 1945; *PI*, January 28, February 18 (Shackelford), May 12, 1945; *Joseph Hall v. Branch Rickey*, United States District Court for the Southern District of New York, Civ. 43–514, 1947 (National Archives—Northeast Region, New York); *PT*, January 6 ("we want"), 13, February 24, 1945. During 1944, Mazzer and Hall had been involved in independent baseball as owners of the Camden-based Cuban Yanks. See *PT*, June 24, 1944; *PI*, June 18, 25, 1944.

20. Shackelford to White, May 29, 1945, folder 48910, Records from Highway Transport Department, RG 219; *CD*, March 10, 1945; *PT*, January 6 ("has two"), 13, February 24, March 3, May 19 ("when you"), 1945; *NYAN*, March 10, 31, 1945.

21. *NYT*, April 7, May 8, 1945; October 1, 1947; *MC*, May 26, 1945; *PT*, May 12, 1945; *BAA*, May 19 ("leagues"), 1945; October 11, 1947; *NYAN*, May 12, 1945; *Hall v. Rickey*; Memorandum to Harry Walsh, November 29, 1947, BRP, box 33, Baseball File Brooklyn Dodgers—general 1946–1947; *NYHT*, April 7, May 8, 1945; Jules Tygiel ed., *The Jackie Robinson Reader* (New York, 1997), 74–75 ("poorest"); William Marshall interview with Effa Manley, COHP. The placement of "black" or "brown" before team names already used by well-established white clubs increasingly annoyed a number of observers, including Rollo Wilson, who questioned whether it was a "tacit admission of racial inferiority." One *Tribune* reader complained, "I never heard of any ball club calling itself the 'White Hilldale,' the 'White Lincoln Giants,' the 'White Pittsburgh Crawfords,' etc." To Eustace Gay, the practice was ultimately "a sign of pure

LAZINESS on the part of men with money to invest, but with no sense of originality, and who take the line of least resistance." On the naming problems of black teams, see *PT*, May 25, 1933; October 2, 9, 1943; February 24, June 9, 1945; May 21, 1946; *BAA*, July 10, 1943.

22. *PT*, May 12 (Gottlieb), 19 ("it was"/"most"), 1945; *PI*, April 7 (Coleman), 1945; *BAA*, May 19 (Lacy), 1945; July 14 ("we don't"), 1945; *CD*, May 26, 1945; *PAA*, May 12 ("I only"), 1945.

23. William Marshall interview with Effa Manley; Holway, *Voices*, 324; *BAA*, May 26 (Griffith/Rickey), 1945; September 11, 1948; *MC*, May 26 (Cowans), July 7, 1945; *PT*, February 10, June 2, 16, July 7, September 15, November 17, 1945; *CCP*, May 12, 1945 (Greenlee); *PC*, June 2, 1945; *PI*, July 7, 1945; *NYAN*, May 11, 1946. By July, Rickey acknowledged the failure of the Brooklyn Brown Dodgers, noting "the man who owned the franchise and operated the club, Joe Hall, has no idea of promotional work and they did not draw at all." See Branch Rickey to Mel Jones, July 1, 1945, BRP, box 15, Correspondence, Thomas Melville "Mel" Jones, 1942–1963.

24. *BAA*, May 19 (Lacy), 1945; *PT*, June 16 ("Branch Rickey controlled"), 1945; *Hall v. Branch Rickey* ("take over"). Late in his life, Rickey distorted his role in the USL, not only claiming that "we organized that racket colored league" but also labeling the Brooklyn Brown Dodgers a "mythical team." See Jackie Robinson with Charles Dexter, *Baseball Has Done It* (Philadelphia, 1964), 42.

25. See Memorandum to Harry Walsh [most likely Henry J. Walsh, Jr., a member of Walter O'Malley's law firm], November 29, 1947, BRP, box 33, Baseball File Brooklyn Dodgers—general 1946–1947.

26. Mann, *Jackie Robinson Story*, 19–20; Rogosin, *Invisible Men*, 208–9 (Veeck); *Hall v. Rickey* ("was anxious"). Rickey's continued involvement in the USL beyond 1945 somewhat invalidates Mann's interpretation. Dodger scouts may have not been fully aware of their mission, as Clyde Sukeforth claimed that up until August 1945 he believed he was scouting black players for the Brooklyn Brown Dodgers. See "MEMORANDUM OF CONVERSATION BETWEEN MR. RICKEY AND MR. SUKEFORTH, MONDAY, JANUARY 16, 1950," AMP, box 4. Rickey himself asserted, "I was able to scout the negro player throughout the world with the understanding that he was being scouted for the Brooklyn Brown Dodgers, which was a franchised member of the negro league. Well, that was true, and I did scout them for that purpose, but it enabled me to carry out my plan without any of my own scouts knowing it, feeling that they were scouting for the Brooklyn Dodgers." See BRP, box 58, Interviews—Davis J. Walsh [1955].

27. Minutes of March 23, 1945 meeting ("we will"), BRP, box 33, Baseball File Brooklyn Dodgers—Board of Directors Minutes of Meetings 1945–1947; Marshall interview with Effa Manley, October 19, 1977 ("had in"), BRP, box 58, Interviews—Davis J. Walsh [1955] ("the best"). While Wendell Smith claimed that Rickey offered the use of Ebbets Field rent-free until the league began to prosper, Rickey himself admitted that his agreement with Hall "provided for a percentage participation in receipts." See *PC*, July 19, 1952; Memorandum to Harry Walsh, November 29, 1947, BRP.

28. Minutes of the June 12–13, 1945 schedule meeting, TBC, box 2, minutes, NAL meetings 1943–1952; *PC*, December 16, 1944; *PI*, February 11, 1945; *BAA*, December 9, 23, 1944; *PV*, January 6, 1945.

29. File of Robert Reed Church, Jr., Oberlin College Archives; *PC*, April 23, 1932; *KCC*, December 20, 1940; April 25, 1952; Tucker, *Memphis Since Crump*, 18–20; *PC*, April 26, 1952; Bardolph, *Negro Vanguard* (1959; reprint Westport, Conn., 1971), 149–50; *Memphis Commercial Appeal*, October 1, 1992; Silver and Moeser, *Separate*

City, 48–50; Grantham, *Political Status of the Negro*, 498–99; Kesselman, *Social Politics of FEPC*, 216; Lee, *Beale Street*, 250–86; Tucker, *Lieutenant Lee of Beale Street*, 68–126.

30. G. James Fleming and Christian E. Burckel, eds., *Who's Who in Colored America*, 7th ed. (Yonkers-on-Hudson, N.Y., 1950), 276; Bardolph, *Negro Vanguard*, 197–98; *PT*, May 18, 1933; Lanctot, *Fair Dealing*, 154–55; *WT*, August 27, 1935.

31. Cum Posey to Effa Manley, November 17, 1941 ("aggressiveness"), November 22, 1942 ("personal"); Cum Posey to Effa and Abe Manley, December 4, 1941, Effa Manley to Wm. Hueston, June 24, 1944, minutes of joint session, June 12, 1945 ("willing"), NEP; William Hueston to Guy A. Richardson, February 7, 19, 1944, Guy Richardson to William Hueston, February 26, 1944, folder 47877, Records from Highway Transport Department, 1942–1946, RG 219; *PT*, January 27, November 10, 1945; *CD*, September 11, 1954.

32. Minutes of joint session, June 12, 1945, NEP; *PT*, June 23, 1945; *CD*, September 11, 1954; *SN*, May 3, 1945; *BAA*, June 16, 30, July 14, August 11, November 3, 1945; February 28, 1948; June 25, 1949; Newson, *Fighting for Fairness*, 57.

33. *CD*, June 2 (Young), 1945; *PT*, May 26, June 9, 23, 30, July 14, August 4, September 1, 15, December 29, 1945; *PI*, June 30, July 7, 14, August 11, September 8, 29, October 6, December 15, 1945; September 21, 1946; *PC*, July 21, August 4, 1945; undated clipping, BHOFL; Effa Manley to Mrs. Elliott, August 21, 1945 ("drawing"), John R. Williams to Eddie Gottlieb, Effa and Abe Manley, July 24, 1945, Effa Manley to Rufus Jackson, May 15, 1945, financial statement, September 9, 1945 at Briggs Stadium, NEP; *MC*, September 15, 1945; *NYAN*, September 22, 1945; Bruce, *Kansas City Monarchs*, 159; financial statement, July 29, 1945, East-West game, TBC, box 2, financial records, Negro East West Game, 1943–1953; handwritten statement of Monarchs profits, 1942–1946, TBC, box 15, financial records, miscellaneous, 1944–1960; financial statement, July 29, 1945, East-West game, ACP, box 170-17, folder 17; *PV*, June 2, 1945.

34. Ed Bolden to Abe Manley, June 29, July 6, 1945, NEP; *PI*, June 30, July 7, 14, August 11, September 8, 29, October 6, December 15, 1945; *PT*, May 26, June 9, 23, 30 (Bolden), July 14, August 4, 25 (Wilson), September 1, 15, 1945; *Wilmington Journal Every Evening*, May 31, June 13, 1945; *Wilmington Morning News*, June 24, July 10, July 25, August 12, 14, 19, 25, 30, September 2, 9, 23, 28, 1945; "The Philadelphia National League Club and Its Wholly Owned Subsidiaries—Treasurer's Report upon Operations for the Year Ended October 31, 1952," 112, PP, box 4, financial.

35. Eddie Collins to William Harridge, April 11, 1945 ("issue"), BHOFL; Larry MacPhail to A. B. Chandler, April 27, 1945 ("Rickey"), cited in Tygiel, *Baseball's Great Experiment*, 42; Moore, *Pride Against Prejudice*, 30 ("Rickey"); Branch Rickey to Mel Jones, May 2[4?], 1945 ("organize"), BRP, box 15, correspondence, Thomas Melville "Mel" Jones, 1942–1963; *PC*, May 12 ("will never"), 1945.

36. *NYA*, November 20, 1948; *NYAN*, June 30, 1945; Duberman, *Paul Robeson*, 426; *MC*, August 18, 1945; *NYT*, April 19, May 2, 1945; *PT*, October 6, 1945; *PI*, April 28, 1945; *PV*, August 11, 18, 1945; *NYHT*, April 18, 27, 1945; Henry Turner to Walter White, August 22, 1945, NAACP papers, Negroes in Sports, 1942–1952; Polenberg, *War and Society*, 106–7; *BAA*, April 28, May 5, 1945; *CD*, April 28, 1945; *PM*, April 8, 22, 1945; Dodson, "Integration of Negroes in Baseball," 73–82; flyer for "End Jim Crow in Baseball Day," Municipal Archives, Office of the Mayor (Fiorello LaGuardia), Baseball 1945, July–August file; *PC*, April 28 ("the matter"), 1945.

37. Edgar Feeley to Fiorello LaGuardia, August 9 (?), 1945, Fiorello LaGuardia to Ben Goldstein, August 14, 1945 ("if it"), Ben Goldstein to Fiorello LaGuardia, August

17, 1945, Municipal Archives, Office of the Mayor (Fiorello LaGuardia), Baseball 1945, July–August file; Ben Goldstein to "Friend," July 26, August 6, 1945, NAACP papers, Negroes in Sports, 1942–1952; Dodson, "Integration of Negroes in Baseball"; *BAA*, August 18, 25, 1945; March 20, 1948; *NYT*, August 12, 1945; *PT*, August 18, September 8, 1945; *NYAN*, August 25, 1945; *PV*, August 18, 25, 1945; William Manners, *Patience, and Fortitude: Fiorello LaGuardia* (New York, 1976), 266; Capeci, *Harlem Riot of 1943*, 165–67.

38. *NYAN*, August 25 (Burley), 1945; *PT*, August 25 (Wilson), September 8, 1945; *PV*, August 18, 1945. Ten years earlier, Sam Lacy had objected to Robinson's association with Joe Louis, explaining that "Robinson belongs to the minstrel world. Louis is a part of our athletic life, a life we are anxious to raise from the slough of burnt-cork performance." Thomas Cripps has noted that between the wars, "famous blacks such as Robinson never stepped from their public roles of smiling entertainers." Rather than actively protest against the color line, Robinson was an avid Yankee fan, functioning as an unofficial mascot, and even danced in the dugout during games. See *WT*, October 19, 1935 (Lacy); Cripps, *Slow Fade to Black*, 99; *PC*, March 25, 1933; Fox, *Big Leagues*, 123.

39. *NYAN*, September 22, 1945 (MacPhail statement); *SN*, October 4, 1945; *BAA*, September 29 (Lacy), 1945; Mann, *Jackie Robinson Story*, 116. Lacy's comments originally appeared in "Will Our Boys Make Big League Grade," *Negro Baseball Pictorial Year Book* (1945), 9 in ACP, box 170-17, folder 10.

40. *NYAN*, October 20, 1945; *PT*, October 6, 13, 20, 1945; Effa Manley to John Collins, September 5, 12, 1945, Effa Manley to Vernon Green, October 20, 1945 (Manley), NEP; *CCP*, October 13, 1945; *KCC*, October 12, 1945.

41. *PT*, February 29, 1940; October 13 ("the shrewd"), 1945; Mann, *Jackie Robinson Story*, 33–126; *PC*, September 8, 1945; January 4, 1947; March 5, 1949; May 10, 1952; *PI*, October 27, 1945; *CD*, September 1, 1945; *PEB*, August 21, 1949.

42. *SN*, April 14, 1997 (Mathis); Ron Fimrite, "Sam Lacy: Black Crusader," *Sports Illustrated*, October 29, 1990 (Lacy); *PC*, March 30, 1940; Rampersad, *Jackie Robinson*, 55–89; *CD*, May 23, 1942; Young, "Black Sportswriter"; *Daily Worker*, January 31, 1954, in Schomburg Center Clipping File; Clark and Lester, *Negro Leagues Book*, 251; *KCC*, May 4, 1945; *BC*, August 25, 1945; June 1945 clipping, BHOFL ("as the one"). Several former players have suggested that integration occurred because of a desire to boost attendance by attracting black fans. Yet the financial motivation was probably minimal, as major league baseball set a new attendance record in 1945, drawing 10,950,000 fans (including a National League-best 1,059,000 in Brooklyn), and anticipated continued gains in the postwar period. Moreover, Organized Baseball had relatively little need to solicit black attendance, since a number of owners were already profiting through rentals to black baseball, and, as noted in Chapter 7, most officials feared the impact of an increased black presence on existing white patronage.

43. *NYT*, October 25 ("the Negro"), 1945; February 21 ("our league"), 1948; *BAA*, March 6 ("worked"), 1948. While some observers have interpreted Rickey's "racket" reference as a criticism of the underworld background of several black baseball officials, Arthur Mann claimed the statement actually alluded to the "monopolistic game-booking enterprise" within the leagues. In any event, Organized Baseball was not without its share of individuals with questionable backgrounds. Minor league head William Bramham, for example, complained that the lower circuits were "infested with punks, petty chiselers, and racketeers." At the major league level, Landis banned Phillies owner William Cox in 1943 for wagering on his own team, although the usually moralistic Rickey dismissed the offense as minimal. Wary of similar problems, Landis's successor Happy Chandler warned of the presence of "known gamblers in the club

houses" and alluded to reports that gamblers owned some stock in major league teams. Chandler also objected to Yankee part-owner Del Webb's connections with a Las Vegas casino and rumored dishonest dealings with the government during World War II. Meanwhile, Lou Perini, who became part-owner of the Boston Braves in 1943, had been fined for income tax evasion several years earlier, while Fred Saigh, owner of the St. Louis Cardinals in the late 1940s and early 1950s, was later imprisoned for the same offense. See Mann, *Branch Rickey*, 218; William Marshall interview with Fred Saigh, May 16, 1978, Red Smith, November 13, 1979, Bill Cooper interview with Calvin Griffith, April 22, 1977, COHP; Chandler, *Heroes, Plain Folks, and Skunks*, 198–99; Koppett, *Koppett's Concise History of Major League Baseball*, 238; Marshall, *Baseball's Pivotal Era*, 194–204; *SN*, April 30, 1952; Branch Rickey to Fiorello LaGuardia, February 19, 1945, BRP, box 17, correspondence—"L" miscellaneous 1943–1946; William D. Cox to Branch Rickey, December 20, 1943, BRP, box 7, correspondence—"C" miscellaneous 1943; *SOMP*, 284–85.

44. J. B. Martin to Effa Manley, August 23, 1945 ("we would"), NEP; Irvin, *Nice Guys Finish First*, 116; Marshall interview with Effa Manley, October 19, 1977; *NYT*, October 26 ("we have"), 1945; *PC*, November 3 ("something"), 1945; *KCC*, October 26 ("we are"), 1945; *CD*, March 6 ("owes"), 1948; *PI*, February 5 ("was not"), 1949. As late as 1948, the Monarchs still hoped to receive compensation for Robinson. A contract establishing Tom Baird as the sole owner of the franchise stipulated that Wilkinson would receive half of the future sale price (above $500) of any player on the 1947 roster and half "of any money received for the assignment and transfer of the player, Jackie Robinson." See Contract, February 5, 1948, sale of Kansas City Monarchs, TBC, box 1, folder 2.

45. *NYAN*, November 10 ("contracts"), 17 (Burley), 1945; *PEB*, October 25 ("there is"), 1945; *PINQ*, October 25 ("signed a"), 1945; *MC*, December 22 (Gottlieb), 1945; *PC*, December 1, 1945; *PR*, October 26, 1945; John Phillips, *The Mexican Jumping Beans* (Perry, Ga., 1997), 18. Although Organized Baseball typically considered players appearing on semiprofessional or independent teams as free agents, regardless of their contractual status, at least some officials rejected such a view. In 1930, Commissioner Landis reportedly "scolded owners who tampered with players under contract to a semi-pro, or any other team, and gave the impression that he will uphold their claims." Independent owners, however, typically had little recourse, although some believed civil lawsuits would validate their legal control over players. See *SN*, February 27, 1930.

46. *PEB*, October 25 ("several"), 1945; J. B. Martin to Effa Manley, October 29, 1945 ("I believe"), November 1945 press release (Martin), NEP; *PI*, November 4, 1945. Political pressure in New York forced Rickey to abandon his original plan to announce the signing of a group of black players, rather than simply Robinson. See Thorn John and Jules Tygiel, "Jackie Robinson's Signing: The Real, Untold Story," *National Pastime: A Review of Baseball History* 10 (1990): 7–12; Tygiel, *Jackie Robinson Reader*, 81. The Dodgers, however, secretly signed Don Newcombe, John Wright, and Roy Campanella to preliminary agreements in October. See Brooklyn Baseball Club, "The Case Against Jimmy Powers," BRP; Donald Newcombe to Robert Finch, August 5, 1946, BRP, box 21, correspondence—"N" miscellaneous, 1945–1949; *PV*, April 20, 1946.

47. The letter to Chandler appeared in the November 17, 1945, editions of the *Philadelphia Tribune, Baltimore Afro-American*, and *Pittsburgh Courier*. An earlier draft written by Posey is in the Newark Eagles papers.

48. *PT*, November 17 (Griffith), December 22, 1945; *NYT*, November 14, 1945; *PC*, February 2, 1946; *CD*, December 8 (Wilson), 1945; Cum Posey to Thomas Wil-

son, November 1945 in Hendrix, *I Remember Tom*, 9 (Posey); *NYAN*, November 17, 1945.

49. Minutes of joint meeting, December 12–13, 1945, TBC, box 2, meeting minutes, NAL 1943–1952; "Resolution," undated (late 1945–early 1946?) ("respect"); Effa Manley to Art Carter, February 25, 1946; NNL meeting minutes, March 12, 1946, NEP; *PI*, December 29, 1945; January 26, 1946; *PT*, December 22, 1945; March 23, 1946; *PC*, December 22, 1945; January 5, February 2, 16, March 23, 1946; Matney, *Who's Who Among Black Americans*, 101; *Negro Baseball Pictorial Yearbook*, in ACP, box 170-17, folder 10; Curtis Leak to Art Carter, April 3, 1946, ACP, box 170-16, folder 8; *CCP*, December 22 ("it is"), 1945.

50. *PC*, February 2 ("honest"), March 2, 1946; Cum Posey to Effa Manley, January 10, 1946 ("we were"), Effa Manley to Cum Posey, January 12, 1946 ("the fact"), minutes of NNL meetings, February 20–21, 1946, NEP; Effa Manley to Art Carter, February 23, 1946 ("we could"), ACP, box 170-16, folder 9. On Battle, see *NYAN*, August 13, 1966; *Our World* (October 1953); "The Reminiscences of Samuel J. Battle," February 1960, Oral History Collection of Columbia University; *NYA*, January 12, 1935; *NYAN*, August 30, 1941; January 19, 1946; *Who's Who in Colored America—1950*, 24.

51. Minutes of NNL meetings, February 20–21, 1946, NEP; *PI*, January 26, 1946; *PT*, January 26, February 16, 1946; *CD*, January 26, 1946; *NYT*, January 21 ("the Negro"), 23 ("no mention"), 1946; *SN*, January 24, 1946; *PC*, March 2, 1946; *Dallas Morning News*, January 21, 1946 ("put their").

52. C. W. Posey to "Sir," May 16, 1944 ("he and"), BHOFL; *NYAN*, March 9 ("farce"), 1946; *CD*, November 10 ("greatest"), 1945.

53. *BAA*, January 26 ("colored baseball"), March 30 ("pulling"), 1946; *PC*, January 26 ("few"), March 23 ("as long"), 1946; Effa Manley to Vernon Green, January 25, 1946 ("this seems"), minutes of joint session, June 19, 1946, NEP; *PT*, November 17, 1945; *SN*, January 31 (editorial), 1946; *PV*, March 2 (Hurt), 1946. Too often, self-help was an inadequate response to the difficulties faced by black institutions. A study of the underfunded Bureau of Colored Children in Philadelphia in the early 1940s illustrated the dilemma. While clearly deficient in several key areas, the organization was "not in a position to lift itself by its own boot-straps, and cannot hope to secure additional State funds until it has improved its services, and cannot improve its services without additional funds." See *Final Report of the Pennsylvania State Temporary Commission*, 320.

54. Dick Lundy to Abe and Effa Manley, November 2, 1945 (Lundy), Effa Manley to Monte Irvin, February 9, 1946 ("a good"), NEP; *PC*, January 8, 1944; February 9, 16 ("any time"), 1946; Riley, *Biographical Encyclopedia*, 883–84; *PT*, February 16, 1946; *BAA*, September 15, 1945; February 9 (Posey), 1946; Kelley, *Voices*, 137; *NYT*, January 30, 1946; *NYAN*, April 26, 1946; *SN*, February 7, 1946; John Wright to Branch Rickey, July 20, 1946, BRP, box 33, Baseball File, Brooklyn Dodgers—general 1946–1947. There is evidence to suggest Rickey's general reluctance to contend with black baseball contracts, at least initially. In a December 1945 letter to Rickey, Wendell Smith recommended Kenny Washington, an accomplished football player and former teammate of Jackie Robinson at UCLA, who was "free to be signed without encountering contract technicalities with the Negro Leagues." Two months later, Buster Haywood claimed that he had been approached by Dodger scouts whose interest apparently waned after discovering that he was under contract to the Indianapolis Clowns. See Wendell Smith to Branch Rickey, December 19, 1945, Wendell Smith papers, correspondence folder; *PV*, February 9, 1946.

55. Roy Campanella to Branch Rickey, August 6, 1946 ("although"), AMP, box 1,

1947 January 29–1948 March 10 folder; *PT*, April 13, 1946; *NYT*, April 5, 1946; Effa Manley to Biz Mackey, January 19, 1946, Effa Manley to Abe Manley, April 5, 1946 ("we have"), NEP; Donald Newcombe to Robert Finch, August 5, 1946 ("I was"), BRP, box 21, correspondence—"N" miscellaneous, 1945–1949; *CD*, December 8, 1945.

56. *PT*, November 17, 1945; *CD*, December 8 ("owed"), 1945; Effa Manley to Cum Posey, January 12, 1946 ("one of"), NEP. When first approached by Dodger officials, Roy Campanella believed he was being recruited for the USL rather than Organized Baseball. Meanwhile, Don Newcombe's initial agreement with the Dodgers reportedly stipulated that he would play "for the Brooklyn Brown Dodgers or any other club the Brooklyn organization might designate." See Campanella, *It's Good to Be Alive*, 106–7; Harold Rosenthal, "He Made the Difference for the Dodgers," *SEP*, April 8, 1950, 155.

57. Minutes of NNL meeting, February 21, 1946 ("morally"), Gus Greenlee to Effa Manley, February 23 ("such a"), March 1 ("it seems"), 1946, NEP; *BAA*, March 2, 1946.

58. Minutes of NNL meeting, March 12, 1946 ("obtained"), NEP; *PT*, May 21, June 4, July 20, 1946; *PC*, April 27, June 1, 1946; February 1, 1947; *PI*, June 22, July 13, 20, August 3, 10, 1946; *NYAN*, July 13, August 3, 1946; Ruck, *Sandlot Seasons*, 70, 76; *PV*, July 13, August 10, 1946; *SN*, August 21, September 18, 1946. On the Robinson barnstorming trip, see Charles H. Matthews to Thurgood Marshall, July 17, 1947, William Nunn to Thurgood Marshall, July 31, 1947, Ira Lewis to Walter White, September 30, 1947, Thurgood Marshall to Jay Rosenfeld, November 6, 1947, in Papers of the NAACP, part 15, Segregation and Discrimination, Complaints and Responses, 1940–1955, Series B: General Office file, Robinson, Jackie, 1945–1955, reel 14; Mann, *Jackie Robinson Story*, 158–59.

59. *PT*, January 8, July 15, 1952; Ruck, *Sandlot Seasons*, 182; *PAA*, July 20, 1946; *CD*, September 1 (Young), 1951; *PC*, July 19, 1952; *SN*, July 23, 1952.

60. *PINQ*, May 15 ("no howls"), 1946; *PT*, May 4, 18, June 15, 1946; Tygiel, *Baseball's Great Experiment*, 127; Mann, *Jackie Robinson Story*, 133; *PI*, November 30, 1946; *PR*, May 15, 1946; Brooklyn Baseball Club, "The Case Against Jimmy Powers," BRP; Ed Bolden to Branch Rickey, April 26, 1946 ("we are"), AMP, box 1, 1901 May 8–1946 December 27 folder; *NYAN*, September 8, 1945; *PAA*, September 29, 1945; Leonard, *Buck Leonard*, 190–91 ("the kind"). The Dodgers' delay in offering Partlow a contract for 1946 probably led to his decision to sign with the Stars. While some accounts have suggested that Partlow was thirty-six at the time of his signing, the Social Security Death Index (www.ancestry.com) identifies his date of birth as June 8, 1911. Other sources list his year of birth as 1912. See Roy Partlow to Branch Rickey, August 12, 1946, AMP, box 1, 1947 January 29–1948 March 10 folder; Tygiel, *Baseball's Great Experiment*, 127; *PINQ*, April 22, 1987; 1942 Homestead Grays press release in ACP, box 170-18, folder 18.

61. "Monarch Ball Club"—"Profit & Loss and Financial Statement Dec. 31, 1946," TBC, box 15, financial records, miscellaneous, 1944–1960; *PT*, May 14, June 4, 18, September 7, 17, 21, 1946; *PINQ*, July 2, 9, 1946; *BAA*, May 11, 1946; January 24, September 11, 1948; *PC*, December 21, 1946; *MC*, December 14, 1946; *PI*, May 18, August 10, 17, 1946; *CD*, June 1, 1946; Buck O'Neil with Steve Wulf and David Conrads, *I Was Right on Time: My Journey frm the Negro Leagues to the Majors* (New York, 1996), 174; Manley, "Negro Baseball Isn't Dead!" 26–28; *SN*, January 5, 1949. For Monarchs attendance figures, see *KCC*, May 17, 24, 31, June 21, 28, July 5, 26, August 16, 23, September 6, 13, 20, 27, 1946.

62. Jerry N. Jordan, *The Long Range Effect of Television and Other Factors on*

Sports Attendance (Washington, D.C., 1950), 25 ("tremendous"); Collie Small, "The Terrible-Tempered Mr. Chapman," *SEP*, April 5, 1947; *PINQ*, June 30, September 15, 1946; Spink, *Baseball Guide and Record Book—1946*, 138; *PC*, January 4, 1947; Thomas G. Smith, "Outside the Pale: The Exclusion of Blacks from the National Football League, 1934–1946," *Journal of Sport History* 15, 3 (Winter 1988): 255–81; Menke, *New Encyclopedia of Sports*, 40, 168; Ross, *Outside the Lines*, 37–100; Roy Wilkins to Walter White, November 13, 1946, Papers of the NAACP, part 15, Segregation and Discrimination, Complaints and Responses, 1940–1955, Series A, Legal file, Negroes in Sports, 1942–1952, reel 9; *Business Week*, December 7, 1946; "Sports Have Big Revival," *Life*, July 1, 1946, 19–23. The AAFC merged with the NFL after the 1949 season.

63. Clark and Lester, *Negro Leagues Book*, 272, 327–28, 335; Robinson, *I Never Had It Made*, 44; *PT*, March 9, June 26, July 20, September 10, 1946; Tygiel, *Baseball's Great Experiment*, 126; Dodson, "Integration of Negroes in Baseball," 78; Merl Kleinknecht, "Integration of Baseball After World War II," *Baseball Research Journal* (1983): 100–106; *SN*, June 12, 1946; *BAA*, April 27, July 20 ("a terrible"), August 17, 1946; *PC*, April 27, July 20, August 3, 1946; Tygiel, *Jackie Robinson Reader*, 129–33; *BC*, May 11, 1946; Marshall interview with Manley ("started"); Holway, *Voices*, 324; *MC*, April 27, 1946; *PI*, June 8, August 3, 1946. During 1946, a sixth black player, Manny McIntyre, appeared in 30 games in the class C Border League with the Sherbrooke (Quebec) Canadians, a club not affiliated with any major league franchise.

64. *PT*, March 2, 30, April 13, 27, May 21, 25, 1946; *PC*, March 23, April 6, July 6, 1946; *CD*, January 26, November 23, 1946; *Pittsburgh Sun-Telegraph*, March 29, 1946 in ACP, box 170-19, folder 19; *NYAN*, December 29, 1945; June 29, September 14 ("New York"), 1946; *CCP*, March 23, April 13, June 8, 1946; Jay Feldman, "He Was Out of His League," *Sports Illustrated*, June 8, 1987; *PI*, April 20, 1946; Gerlach, "Baseball's Other 'Great Experiment'"; *SN*, June 5, 19, August 28, 1946. Despite its apparent success, the publicity bureau headed by Art Carter lasted only a single season, and by 1947, Rick Hurt complained that the NNL was now "muddling along with a jack-of-all-trades secretary who is good at typing business letters but fails completely otherwise." See *PV*, September 6, 1947.

65. Effa Manley to Eddie Gottlieb, April 16, 1946 ("I think"); Curtis Leak to Effa Manley, August 2, 1946, Louis Carroll to Curtis Leak, August 5, 1946, report of September 26, 1946 meeting with Louis F. Carroll ("special"), NEP; *NYAN*, October 5, 1946; Overmyer, *Effa Manley*, 224; *NYT*, October 26, 1971. According to Dan Parker, Manley eventually confronted Rickey, who was in attendance at an NNL doubleheader on July 4 at Yankee Stadium. After expressing her hope that Rickey was "not going to grab any more of our players," Manley warned the Brooklyn official that they "could make trouble for you" regarding the uncompensated signing of Don Newcombe. See *SN*, July 17, 1946.

66. *NYT*, August 27–29, 1946; *PINQ*, August 28, 1946; Paul M. Gregory, *The Baseball Player: An Economic Study* (Washington, D.C., 1956), 194; Tygiel, *Baseball's Great Experiment*, 83; Turner, *When the Boys Came Back*, 139–40; Marshall, *Baseball's Pivotal Era*, 74–78; *SOMP*, 474–75, 489–92, 1062–64; Tygiel, *Jackie Robinson Reader*, 131 ("the employment"), 133 ("could conceivably"). MacPhail's 1945 statement appears in *NYAN*, September 22, 1945 and *SN*, October 4, 1945. For section E of the 1946 report, see Tygiel, *Jackie Robinson Reader*, 129–33. The complete unedited document ("REPORT OF MAJOR LEAGUE STEERING COMMITTEE FOR SUBMISSION TO THE NATIONAL AND AMERICAN LEAGUES AT THEIR MEETINGS IN CHICAGO") is reproduced in *SOMP*, 474–88.

67. Marshall, *Baseball's Pivotal Era*, 79–80, 134–35; *SN*, February 25 (Wrigley/"I suppose"), 1948; October 24, 1951; *SOMP*, 472–515; *PC*, February 28 ("deny"), 1948; *PT*, February 21, 1948; *BAA*, February 28, 1948; *CD*, February 28, 1948; *NYT*, February 18 (Bradley), 1948; *PEB*, February 17, 18, 20 (Pollock), 1948; Tygiel, *Baseball's Great Experiment*, 81; Mann, *Jackie Robinson Story*, 134. Happy Chandler subsequently distorted the contents and context of the 1946 report to magnify his own role in the integration of Organized Baseball. According to Chandler (a "frightfully unreliable source" according to Roger Kahn), major league owners voted 15-1 against integration at a January 1947 meeting in New York. Rickey then sought the assistance of Chandler, who agreed to support the transfer of Robinson's contract to the Brooklyn Dodgers. For Chandler's version, see A. B. (Happy) Chandler with John Underwood, "How I Jumped from Clean Politics into Dirty Baseball," *Sports Illustrated*, April 26, 1971, 73–86; Chandler, *Heroes, Plain Folks, and Skunks*, 226–29; Falkner, *Great Time Coming*, 147; Jeffrey Marx, "Happy's Vote of Confidence," *Sports Heritage*, 1990 (SABR Research Exchange); Green, "Happy Chandler"; Zoss and Bowman, *Diamonds in the Rough*, 144; Holtzman, *Commissioners*, 69–71. While Chandler spent the final decades of his life perpetuating this account and berating "several smart alecks who tried to give Rickey all the credit," there is little if any evidence to support his interpretation of events. Bill Veeck offered a more sensible assessment of Chandler's modest contribution toward integration, noting that he "certainly could have opposed it. And he certainly could have made it more difficult." See Tygiel, *Baseball's Great Experiment*, 81–82; Roger Kahn, *The Era: 1947–1957, When the Yankees, the Giants, and the Dodgers Ruled the World* (New York, 1993), 53; Marshall interview with Veeck, February 23, 1977; Red Smith, November 13, 1979.

68. For MacPhail's response, see *PEB*, February 21, 1948. Nine years later, MacPhail continued to insist that Rickey "jumped the gun. Instead of going along with a broad scheme to subsidize the Negro leagues and take them into Organized ball, he raided the leagues and grabbed their best players." See *SN*, October 30, 1957. During 1946, ongoing media criticism of Rickey's "raids" prompted the Dodgers to solicit letters from all five players asserting their free agency status at the time of their signing. Three years later, a comment from Yankees general manager George Weiss linking the Dodgers' success to the raiding of black baseball elicited a similar reply from Rickey, claiming he could "show legal documents in the case of every Negro player on our roster." See Brooklyn Baseball Club, "Case Against Jimmy Powers"; Jackie Robinson to Branch Rickey, July 13, 1946, John Wright to Branch Rickey, July 20, 1946, Donald Newcombe to Robert Finch, August 5, 1946, BRP; Roy Campanella to Branch Rickey, August 6, 1946, Roy Partlow to Branch Rickey, August 12, 1946, AMP; *SN*, November 2, 1949.

69. *PEB*, February 18, 21 (Smith), 1948. Branch Rickey to Joe Cummiskey, March 31, 1948 ("a year"), BRP, box 7, correspondence/"C" miscellaneous 1947–1948; *NYT*, February 19, 1948 ("other people"/"other reasons"); *SN*, February 25 ("assigned"), 1948. Radio networks and advertising agencies also used a similar economic argument to rationalize their limited roles for blacks. J. Fred McDonald has noted that "sponsors were reluctant to finance all-black or racially mixed programs if white listeners, the bulk of the audience and the potential customers for the sponsor's product, would be alienated." See MacDonald, *Don't Touch That Dial!* 357.

Chapter 9. Integration and the Changing Postwar World

Epigraph: *KCC*, July 18, 1947
1. Peter J. Kellogg, "Civil Rights Consciousness in the 1940s," *Historian* (Novem-

ber 1979): 18–41; Franklin and Moss, *From Slavery to Freedom*, 461–65; George Brown Tindall and David E. Shi, *America: A Narrative History*, 5th ed., vol. 2 (New York, 1999), 1401; August Meier and Elliott Rudwick, *From Plantation to Ghetto*, 3rd ed. (New York, 1976), 306; Drake and Cayton, *Black Metropolis*, 819. Although attempts to create a permanent national FEPC failed, several states and communities established similar agencies in the postwar years. See *PI*, May 9, 1953; *PT*, November 15, 1955.

2. Douglas Massey and Nancy Denton, *American Apartheid: Segregation and the Making of the Underclass* (Cambridge, Mass., 1993), 46–77; John F. Bauman, *Public Housing, Race, and Renewal: Urban Planning in Philadelphia, 1920–1974* (Philadelphia, 1987), 84–86; Chester Rapkin and William Grigsby, *The Demand for Housing in Racially Mixed Areas* (Berkeley, Calif., 1960), 4; Franklin, *Education of Black Philadelphia*, 184–85; *PT*, May 31, 1952 ("whenever"); February 11, 1956; Kenneth Kusmer, "African Americans in the City Since World War II: From the Industrial to the Post-Industrial Era." *Journal of Urban History* 21, 4 (May 1995): 458–504.

3. Reed, *Seedtime*, 350; Kusmer, "African Americans in the City," 466–68; *BAA*, September 8, 1945; February 21, 1948; Franklin, *Education of Black Philadelphia*, 174, 186 ("still"); *PT*, August 18, 25, 1945; August 24, 1946; November 6, 1954 ("our first"); April 26, 1955 ("you'll"); Philip Scranton and Walter Licht, *Work Sights: Industrial Philadelphia, 1890–1950* (Philadelphia, 1986), 244; G. Gordon Brown, *Law Administration and Negro-White Relations in Philadelphia: A Study in Race Relations* (Philadelphia, 1947), 48; Franklin and Moss, *From Slavery to Freedom*, 463–72; *PI*, January 1, 1949; Weaver, *Negro Labor*, 267.

4. George S. Schuyler, "Jim Crow in the North," *American Mercury* (June 1949): 663–70 ("the Negro"); Kusmer, "African Americans in the City," 463–65; *NYT*, July 11, 1951.

5. Kinzer and Sagarin, *The Negro in American Business*, 93, 108 ("extremely"); *PT*, May 7, June 29, 1946; June 30, 1953; August 13, 1954; April 26, 1955; E. Franklin Frazier, "Human, All Too Human," *Survey Graphic* (January 1947): 75; Myrdal, *American Dilemma*, 310; Hardin, *Negroes of Philadelphia*, 141–42.

6. Pierce, *Negro Business*, 219 ("dilemma"); Kinzer and Sagarin, *Negro in American Business*, 11 ("antagonism"); E. Franklin Frazier, *Black Bourgeoisie* (1957; reprint New York, 1997), 171 ("the employment").

7. *PT*, December 1, 1945; October 18, November 22, 29, 1947; March 6, 1948; January 3, 1952; November 28, 1953; September 14, 1954; February 26, 1955; November 22, 1960; Peterson, *Cages to Jump Shots*, 152–70.

8. *PI*, July 19, 1947; October 13, 1951; *PT*, February 3 ("one of"), 1945; September 17, 1949; December 21, 1954; *PAA*, March 25, 1950; Fimrite, "Sam Lacy"; *PC*, October 8, 1949; July 11, 1953; *CD*, September 24, 1949; *BAA*, January 7 (Lacy), 1947; May 1, 22, 1948; September 24, 1949; November 17, 1951; January 29, 1955; Lacy, *Fighting for Freedom*, 5–9; Smith papers, box 1, folder 1, informational folder.

9. *CD*, September 24 (Young), 1949; Vishnu Oak, *The Negro's Adventures in General Business* (1949; reprint Westport, Conn., 1970), 120; *PT*, June 26 ("one of"), December 28, 1954; *PI*, January 20, 1951; October 10, 1953; Jessie Parkhurst Guzman, ed., *Negro Year Book: A Review of Events Affecting Negro Life* (Tuskegee, Ala., 1952), 35; *BAA*, December 16, 1950.

10. *PT*, March 13 ("many"/"to create"), 1943; April 27, 1946; May 18 ("how some"), 1948; June 20, 1953; *PAA*, September 19 (Hyder), 1942.

11. Gamble, *Making a Place for Ourselves*, 182 ("shifted"); David McBride, *Integrating the City of Medicine: Blacks in Philadelphia Health Care, 1910–1965* (Philadelphia, 1989), 150–90; Elliott Rudwick, "A Brief History of Mercy-Douglass Hospital

in Philadelphia," *Journal of Negro Education* 20, 1 (Winter 1951) (Rudwick); *PT*, November 3, 1945; July 13 (Gay), 1946; January 27, March 13, April 20, 1948; June 23, 1951; July 19, 1952; January 20, September 22, 1953; March 27, June 26, 1954; *PAA*, April 2, 1949; *PINQ*, December 9, 1982; *BAA*, February 26, 1949 ("misuse"). By 1951, the national branch of the NAACP refused to sanction the construction of a separate black unit at a municipal hospital in Memphis, arguing that "civil rights should prevail over practicalities." See Gamble, *Making a Place for Ourselves*, 188.

12. Minutes, NAL meeting, February 24, 1947, TBC, box 2, minutes, NAL, 1943–1952; W. S. Martin to Tom Baird, January 4, 1950, TBC, box 2, correspondence Matty Brescia, 1949–1953; *CD*, January 4, March 8, 15, 1947; *CCP*, April 19, 1947; *PI*, March 15, 1947; *PC*, January 4, 1947.

13. *NYAN*, January 4, 11, 1947; February 7, 1948; September 10, 1949; *PI*, January 4, 11, 25, 1947; *BAA*, January 11, 1947; *PC*, November 2, 1946; January 11, 1947; *PV*, July 13, 1946. In 1942, Cum Posey privately suggested that "Semler will do anything if money is shoved him." See Cum Posey to Abe Manley, October 25, 1942, NEP.

14. John H. Johnson file, Columbia University Archives and Athletic Department; *NYT*, August 23, 1945; May 25, 1995; *BAA*, March 15 ("the Negro"), 1947; May 14, 1949; *MC*, December 1 ("definite"), 1945; Mann, *Jackie Robinson Story*, 137; Overmyer, *Effa Manley*, 16, 151; Greenberg, *"Or Does It Explode?"*, 118–25; Naison, *Communists in Harlem*, 117–19, 232, 237; Capeci, *Harlem Riot of 1943*, 165–67; *NYA*, May 25, 1935; *PC*, January 11, July 19, 1947; *PV*, February 1 (Manley), 1947; John H. Johnson to Effa Manley, April 25, 1941; Effa Manley to J. B. Martin, October 26, 1945, NEP.

15. *NYAN*, January 11 (Burley), 18, March 15, 29, April 26, 1947; *PC*, December 23, 1944; January 11, July 19, 1947; *BAA*, January 11, March 15, 1947; October 2, 1948; May 14, 1949; *PV*, February 1, March 22, 1947; *MC*, January 11 (Cowans), 1947; William Leuschner to Effa Manley, March 21, 1945, NEP; *CD*, March 15, 1947; *PI*, March 15, 1947. Despite confiding to Effa Manley that "Semler and I are going to try to develop the Yankees into an attraction where they will really mean something," Leuschner was equally unsuccessful in transforming the fortunes of the franchise, which finished last in 1945 and 1946.

16. *PC*, January 11 (Smith), May 24, 1947; *BAA*, May 24, 1947; June 4, 1949; *CD*, May 24, 1947; *NYAN*, May 24, 1947; Robinson, *Catching Dreams*, 113; Kelley, *Voices*, 30; Campanella, *It's Good to Be Alive*, 76, 122; Rust, *"Get That Nigger off the Field!"*, 126–28; *NYA*, February 5, 1949; *PI*, March 8, 1947; John Johnson to Ford Frick, May 1, 1947, Ford Frick to John Johnson, May 16, 1947, BHOFL.

17. *PI*, January 20, March 8, 15, June 21, 1947; *NYAN*, May 10, 31, June 14, 21, July 12, August 9, 1947; January 3, 1948; *KCC*, June 20, July 6, 1947; *CCP*, October 13, 1945; May 10, 1947; *PINQ*, May 8, 1947; *SN*, June 4, November 5, 1947; *PC*, October 4, 1947; *BAA*, September 6, 1947; *PV*, June 24, 1944; September 6, 1947; Billy Yancey to Effa Manley, June 14, 1944, NEP.

18. Tygiel, *Baseball's Great Experiment*, 162; Frommer, *Rickey and Robinson*, 124–25; Mann, *Jackie Robinson Story*, 160–65; *CD*, April 19 (Young), 26 (White), 1947; *PC*, April 19, 1947. In 1955, Rickey acknowledged that the potential response of black fans was the "biggest problem that confronted me initially . . . and the one I dreaded the most." See BRP, box 58, interviews, Davis J. Walsh.

19. *NYAN*, April 19 (Brown), 1947; Tygiel, *Baseball's Great Experiment*, 163 ("efforts"); Robinson, *I Never Had It Made*, xxi ("they"); *CCP*, May 17, 1947. Karen Anderson, for example, notes that the National Council of Negro Women organized "Keep Your Job" campaigns during World War II "encouraging conformity to white-

middle-class specifications regarding dress, behavior, and attitudes." Meanwhile, the *Tribune* ran a syndicated cartoon feature, "Do's and Don'ts," offering suggestions on behavior, while the *Courier* and *Defender* also spearheaded similar campaigns. As Cayton and Drake explained, "because the upper class and upper middle class control the press, the schools, and the pulpits of larger churches, they are in a position to bombard the lower class with their conceptions of 'success,' 'correct behavior,' and 'morality'— which are in general the ideals of the white middle-class." See Anderson, "Last Hired, First Fired," 94; *PT*, September 9, 1944; June 26, 1954; Maurice R. Davie, *Negroes in American Society* (New York, 1949), 203; Drake and Cayton, *Black Metropolis*, 710; Wallace Lee, "Are Negroes Guilty of Misconduct in Public Places?" *Negro Digest* (September 1943): 60.

20. *SN*, April 23, 1947; August 18, 1948; *KCC*, May 16, October 17, 1947; *NYAN*, July 12, 1947; *PC*, June 14, 1947; *PV*, April 19, 1947; Holway, *Voices*, 294 (Smith); minutes of joint meeting, June 10, 1947 (Hayes), TBC, box 2, minutes, NAL meetings, 1943–1952; *CCP*, May 12 ("has made"), November 10 ("few people"), 1945.

21. *CD*, June 21, 1947; *PI*, June 21 (Coleman), September 17, 1947; *PC*, June 21, 1947; Dan Dodson to Branch Rickey, May 14, 1947 (Dodson), Branch Rickey to Dan Dodson, May 22, 1947, BRP, correspondence, box 9, "D" miscellaneous 1947–1948. A handwritten notation at the bottom of the letter reads: "if this thing could come later—post season if possible I would be glad to clear for it."

22. Moore, *Pride Against Prejudice*, 39; *PC*, June 21, August 16, 1947; *CD*, July 14, 1951; *CCP*, July 27, 1946; May 24, 1947; May 15, 1948; *PI*, July 26, 1947; J. Ronald Oakley, *Baseball's Last Golden Age, 1946–60* (Jefferson, N.C., 1994), 72; A. S. "Doc" Young, *Great Negro Baseball Stars and How They Made the Major Leagues* (New York, 1953), 52–53. The Dodgers were reportedly interested in purchasing Doby as early as November 1946. See *PV*, November 16, December 7, 1946; *PI*, November 30, 1946.

23. Moore, *Pride Against Prejudice*, 41; *SN*, July 16 (Veeck/editorial), 1947; October 20, 1948; *PI*, July 12, 1947 ("liberal"); September 18, 1948; *PC*, July 12, 1947; December 27, 1952; A. S. "Doc" Young, *Negro Firsts in Sports* (Chicago, 1963), 158. *Newark Evening News*, August 31, 1948 in ACP, box 170-19, folder 16.

24. *SN*, July 30 (Veeck), August 13, 1947; Jim McConnell, "Baseball's Dark Past," *Grandstand Baseball Annual*, vol. 14; *NYAN*, July 26 (Baird), 1947; August 23, 1947; Marshall, *Baseball's Pivotal Era*, 146–47; *KCC*, August 15, September 19, 1947; *PI*, July 26, August 9, 16, 30, 1947; *PC*, July 26, 1947; *PINQ*, August 2–4, 1947; *CD*, April 10, 1948; *PT*, August 30, 1952; Oakley, *Baseball's Last Golden Age*, 61. The Browns also signed a third player, former Indianapolis Clown Charlie Harmon, who reported to Gloversville of the Class C Canadian-American League and later played major league baseball in the 1950s. In addition, Piper Davis of the Birmingham Black Barons was placed on a 30-day option to allow the Browns to evaluate and potentially sign him. Davis, however, reportedly rejected the Browns' offer to play minor league baseball because of an anticipated reduction in pay. On Davis and Harmon, see *KCC*, August 15, 1947; *NYAN*, September 6, 1947; *SN*, August 13, 1947; Kelley, *Voices*, 226–30; Riley, *Biographical Encyclopedia*, 218, 356; Tygiel, *Baseball's Great Experiment*, 222; July 18, 1947 clipping in ACP, box 170-19, folder 17; typewritten note (late 1948–early 1949), Race and Ethnicity: Integration file, BHOFL.

25. *SN*, July 2, 16, August 6, 1947; *PI*, July 12, August 2, 16, 30, September 27, 1947; July 17, 1948; *PT*, November 22, December 30, 1947; *PC*, September 6, 1947; *NYT*, March 16, 1947; B. B. Martin to Branch Rickey, BRP, box 5, correspondence "B" miscellaneous 1947–1948; Kleinknecht, "Integration of Baseball"; Riley, *Biographical Encyclopedia*, 567, 641; Zoss and Bowman, *Diamonds in the Rough*, 170.

26. *PT*, October 14, 1947; August 13 (Rhodes), 1949. *PI*, October 11, 1947; *PV*, October 11, 1947; Ron Powers, *Supertube: The Rise of Television Sports* (New York, 1984), 61; *NYAN*, October 11 (Burley), 1947; Thomas Cripps, *Making Movies Black: The Hollywood Manager from World War II to the Civil Rights Era* (New York, 1993), 144 (Cripps).

27. *KCC*, May 9, 1947; *BAA*, May 10, 1947; January 24, September 11, 1948; *PI*, April 5, 19, 26, May 10, 24, June 21, July 26, August 2, 9, 16, 23, 1947; *PC*, August 2, 1947; *NYAN*, October 11, 1947; September 10 (Forbes), 1949; *CCP*, October 4, 11, 1947; *SN*, January 5, 1949; *PT*, January 20, 1948; *PV*, October 18, 1947; *PINQ*, May 20, 27, June 17, 24, July 8, 22, August 8, 19, 27, 30, September 9, 25, 1947; *PAA*, July 12, 1947.

28. *NYAN*, April 26 (Burley), July 12, 1947; *PC*, May 31 (Roberts), August 9, September 20, October 4, 1947; *PI*, June 7, August 9, 1947; *PV*, March 8, October 18, 1947.

29. *CCP*, July 26 (Jackson), 1947; *NYAN*, April 26, October 11 (Burley), 1947; Alex Pompez memo to "all owners and managers of Major League baseball teams," 1947 ("to get"), ACP, box 170-16, folder 12; *PI*, November 29 (Coleman), 1947.

Chapter 10. "The Golden Era Has Passed"

Epigraph: *NYAN*, February 7, 1948.
1. Roland Wolseley, *The Black Press, USA*, 2nd ed. (Ames, Iowa, 1990), 80–81; Vishnu V. Oak, *The Negro Newspaper* (1948; reprint Westport, Conn., 1976), 68; *NYAN*, January 3 (Burley), 1948; *PI*, November 29, 1947; John H. Johnson to Carl Murphy, February 18, 1948, ACP, box 170-16, folder 7.

2. *NYAN*, October 11, 1947; January 24, 1948; *CCP*, May 8, July 31 ("never"), September 11 ("must be"), 1948; Lester Rodney clipping (probably from *Daily Worker*, April 28, 1947) in ACP, box 170-20, folder 2; *CD*, April 10 (Martin), 1948.

3. *NYAN*, May 3, August 9 ("wise"), 1947; February 28 (Semler), 1948; *BAA*, September 6, 1947; *PI*, June 7, 1947; *PT*, January 24, 1948; August 8 (White), 1950; *CCP*, January 10 (Young), 1948. By the late 1940s, J. B. Martin was probably the most affluent NAL official, reportedly worth more than $250,000. See "The Ten Richest Negroes in America," *Ebony*, April 1949.

4. *NYAN*, January 3 ("represents"), February 14, July 24, 1948; April 9, 1949; Tom Baird to Lee MacPhail, January 10, 1949 ("we have"), BHOFL; *BAA*, July 5 (Lacy), 1947; *PT*, June 15, 29, 1948; April 5, 1949; *CD*, July 10, 1948; *KCC*, September 30, 1949; *PI*, June 5, 1948. Yankee officials apparently regarded Semler as partly to blame for the declining attendance. In a note from late 1948 or early 1949, an anonymous Yankee official (probably George Weiss) observed that "they put the pressure on Yankee Stadium about two years ago to let Semler . . . promote the games in there. I am sure you know what has happened since the stadium was taken from Gottlieb and given to Semler. Semler is out of baseball, owes plenty of bills etc., but the pressure was put on the officials of the stadium and everybody lost money because Semler wasn't big enough for the job and this may have been a big factor in the failure of the Negro National League." See typewritten note (late 1948–early 1949), Race and Ethnicity: Integration file, BHOFL; email from Robert Burk, January 18, 2002.

5. *NYAN*, October 9 ("there seems"), 1943; February 7 ("because"), April 3 (Davis), 1948; *CCP*, May 8 ("the Negro"), June 12 ("when the"), 1948; *PI*, July 19 (Coleman), 1947.

6. *NYAN*, September 27, 1947; *SN*, January 14 (Chandler), April 14, 1948; *PT*, January 20, 1948; *CD*, March 6 ("satisfactory"), 1948; April 1, 1950; Riley, *Biograph-*

ical Encyclopedia, 666; *PC*, January 24 ("slipshod"), 1948. Although some owners remained careless in their handling of contracts, Tom Baird of the Monarchs claimed that he sent his players a contract "every spring by registered mail with return receipt they have to sign to get same." See Tom Baird to John Mullen, May 26, 1952, TBC, box 4, correspondence Boston Braves, 1949–1953.

7. *SN*, April 23 ("it is up"), 1947; August 4, November 3, 1948; October 26, 1949; January 11, 1950; *KCC*, January 25 (Johnson), 1946; *SOMP*, 209. The continuation of black baseball continued to offer some value to major league teams reluctant to integrate. In 1949, Monarchs owner Tom Baird confided to Yankee farm director Lee MacPhail that "no doubt the Negros have been putting the pressure on the big leagues to hire the Negro players and perhaps they will go stronger since the Negro National League folded up . . . as long as we can continue it will help keep these pressure groups off you fellows." See Baird to MacPhail, January 10, 1949, BHOFL.

8. *PT*, March 2 (Trautman), 6 ("we know"), June 28, 1948; *BAA*, January 31, March 6 ("we cannot"), May 22, 1948; *NYT*, February 24, 26, 1948; January 15 ("well within"), 1949; *NYAN*, February 28 ("new white"), March 6, 1948; *PI*, February 28 ("no status"), 1948. Two years earlier, Organized Baseball had granted a probationary membership to the Mexican National League, a short-lived rival to Pasquel's organization, yet apparently lacked any real motivation to reach a similar agreement with the NNL and NAL. While affiliation remained elusive for the NNL and NAL, several foreign leagues ultimately became part of Organized Baseball. In 1947, the Cuban Winter League was accepted by the NAPBL as an unclassified affiliate and was later joined by similar organizations in Panama, Venezuela, and Puerto Rico. The Mexican summer league was admitted as a class AA organization in 1955. See *PINQ*, May 13, July 12, 1947; *SN*, July 30, 1947; National Association of Professional Baseball Leagues, *Story of Minor League Baseball*, 56; Echevarría, *Pride of Havana*, 47–48, 306; Oleksak, *Béisbol*, 155; *SOMP*, 233–39; Phillips, *Mexican Jumping Beans*, 14.

9. *NYAN*, October 11 (Burley), 1947; January 24, February 28 (Semler), April 3 (Davis), 1948; *PC*, January 10 (Smith), 1948; *PT*, January 6, February 1, 1948; *BAA*, February 14, August 28, 1948; *CD*, June 12, 1948; *SN*, October 20, 1948. The monthly salaries of the Kansas City Monarchs in 1948 ranged from $275 for rookie Gene Baker to $600 for former major leaguers Willard Brown and Hank Thompson. See TBC, box 9, financial records, payroll and insurance, 1948.

10. *PT*, February 3 ("devoted"), 1948; *BAA*, March 6 ("should be"), May 22 ("gave colored"), 1948; John H. Johnson to Carl Murphy, February 18, 1948, ACP, box 170-16, folder 7; *PC*, May 15, 1948; *CD*, September 18, 1948.

11. *NYAN*, January 3 ("Every Hit"), 1948; *PT*, June 5, 1948, January 28, April 1, May 13, 23, 1950; *CD*, September 24 ("his rise"), 1949. For examples of Robinson or Dodger products for sale, see *PT*, November 4, 1947; April 20, 1948; *BW*, July 8, 1949; *Color*, September 1949; *Our World* (May 1950). In 1947, the *Tribune* offered a free copy of *Baseball's Beloved Bums*, a book about the Dodgers, to readers who purchased a year's subscription.

12. *NYAN*, October 11, 1947; January 3, April 24, May 8, 22, 1948; August 13, September 10, 1949; *PT*, May 18, 1948; *KCC*, May 21, August 27 (Johnson), 1948; *CCP*, June 12, 1948; *CD*, June 12, 1948; financial statement, Monarchs at Comiskey Park, June 11, July 16, 1948; Monarchs at Cleveland, June 13, 1948, TBC, box 9, financial records, gate receipts, 1948; Tom Baird to Lee MacPhail, June 20, 1950, TBC, box 4, correspondence, New York Yankees, 1949–1953; *PC*, September 4 ("this is"), 1948. By 1950, Brooklyn's already extensive radio exposure was broadened by the creation of a second "Dodger Network," broadcasting recreated games in the South and other regions. See Tygiel, *Past Time*, 153.

13. *SN*, June 2, October 20 (Manley), November 10, 24 (Shaughnessy), December 8, 1948; "The Philadelphia National League Club and Its Wholly Owned Subsidiaries—Treasurer's Report upon Operations for the Year Ended October 31, 1948," 122, PP, box 4, financial; Drake and Cayton, *Black Metropolis*, 606; Michael Kammen, *American Culture, American Tastes: Social Change and the 20th Century* (New York, 1999), 85; Research Company of America, *The New Philadelphia Story* (Baltimore, 1946), 75; E. Franklin Frazier, "Research and Amusement Among American Negroes," in *The Negro in America*, Carnegie Mellon Study, Schomburg Collection, roll 4, July 15, 1940, 107–8; *CCP*, May 15, June 5, September 25, 1948. As early as June 1947, Joe Bostic claimed that an upcoming NNL promotion at Ebbets Field would be televised. It is likely, however, that the appearances of black baseball teams on television in the late 1940s and early 1950s were largely limited to the Cleveland experiment of 1948, a Birmingham promotion in 1949, an NAL game at Pelican Stadium in New Orleans in 1950, and exhibition games with the Brooklyn Bushwicks at Dexter Park in 1950. See *CD*, May 13, 1950; *NYAN*, June 21, 1947; May 27, 1950; *PC*, May 6, 1950; *PT*, May 16, 1950; *BAA*, May 22, August 14, 1948; *BW*, July 5, 1949.

14. *Memphis World*, April 20, 1948, in Peter Marshall Ostenby, "Other Games; Other Glory: The Memphis Red Sox and the Trauma of Integration, 1948–1955" (M.A. thesis, University of North Carolina at Chapel Hill, 1989), 42 (Black); *CD*, July 30 (Young), 1949; *BAA*, April 10, June 12, 1948; *PC*, April 24, October 16, 1948; *PI*, October 16, 1948; June 25 ("if the"), 1949; *PT*, June 15 (Perry), 1948.

15. *PT*, March 2 ("colored baseball"), June 15 ("joke"), 1948; January 8 ("comparable"), 1949; *PC*, March 27 (Bankhead), September 18 (Smith), 1948; March 5, 1949; *NYA*, February 5 (Campanella), 1949.

16. *PT*, February 14 ("Negro baseball"), 1948; Robinson, "What's Wrong with Negro Baseball." Late in his life, Robinson continued to display a negative attitude toward black professional baseball, exemplified by references to "Jim Crow teams" and "humiliating segregation" in the Negro Leagues. See Robinson, *I Never Had It Made*, 23, 36; Robinson, *Baseball Has Done It*, 38.

17. Jack Sher, "Jackie Robinson—The Great Experiment," *Sport*, October 1948, 95 ("really"); *BAA*, August 8, 1942 (Roberts); May 29 (Manley), 1948; *PT*, May 18, 1948 (Perry); *CD*, June 5 ("a little"), 1948; May 7 ("practically"), 1949; Effa Manley, "Negro Baseball Isn't Dead!" *Our World* (August 1948): 26–28. Manley won praise from fellow owner Ernest Wright, who viewed "Jackie's lambasting" as "a shock and a possible moment of anger to any member of our race but more so to us who were touched so directly by it." See Ernest Wright to Effie Manley, May 29, 1948, in Manley scrapbook, BHOFL.

18. *PT*, June 1 (Browne), 29, 1948; *PI*, June 19, September 4, 18, 1948; *SN*, January 5, 1949; *BAA*, September 11, December 11, 1948; *PC*, December 11, 1948; Overmyer, *Effa Manley*, 240; *NYAN*, September 11 (Bostic), 1948.

19. *PC*, February 14, May 22, September 4, 1948; January 8, 1955; *PI*, February 7, April 17, July 17, 31, August 7, 14, September 4, 11, 1948; *PAA*, May 29, 1948 (Brower); *Wilmington Morning News*, December 19, 1947; *NYAN*, September 18, 1948; *PT*, June 15, 1948; *PINQ*, August 3, 10, 17, 24, 1948; financial statement, September 8, 1948, Shibe Park, Baird collection, box 9, financial records, gate receipts, 1948.

20. *NYAN*, July 17, 1948; *NYA*, September 24, 1948; *PT*, April 24, June 26, 29, 1948; Riley, *Biographical Encyclopedia*, 427, 719; *PI*, September 4, 1948; *CD*, September 4, 1948; February 21, 1953; *CCP*, March 4, 1950; Kleinknecht, "Integration of Baseball," 100–106; Contract, February 5, 1948, sale of Kansas City Monarchs, TBC, box 1, folder 2; Rudie Schaffer to J. L. Wilkinson, July 10, 1948, TBC, box 4,

correspondence Cleveland Indians, 1948–1953; *SN*, July 14, August 25, 1948; *KCC*, February 20, April 16, May 28, August 27, 1948; *PINQ*, August 25, 1948; Paige, *Maybe I'll Pitch Forever*, 195.

21. *SN*, March 17, 1948 (Stoneham). By July 1948, fifteen black players were in Organized Baseball, appearing in the American, National, International, Pacific Coast, Eastern, New England, Colonial, Sunset, and Mid-Atlantic leagues. At least eleven had previously spent time in the NAL or NNL. See *PI*, July 17, 1948.

22. *CD*, May 15, September 4, 1948; February 21, 1953; *PI*, September 18, 1948; *PT*, April 27, May 8, June 12, 1948; *BAA*, December 11, 1948; June 25, 1949; *MC*, January 12, 1946; *NYAN*, June 26, 1948; Wendell Smith to Branch Rickey, July 5, 1949, Smith papers, BHOFL; *CCP*, May 15 ("a complete"/"Brer Abe"), 1948. By 1952, Tom Baird noted that "Abe has several clubs running to him for players." See Baird to J. B. Martin, March 7, 1952, TBC, box 2, correspondence J. B. Martin, 1949–1960.

23. *BAA*, September 4, 11 (Jackson), 1948; November 5, 1955; *CD*, December 11, 1948; Effa Manley to Seward Posey, August 1, 1941; Cum Posey to Abe Manley, October 25, 1942, NEP; *PT*, April 26, 1949; May 10, July 30, 1955; *NYAN*, December 3, 1955; J. B. Martin to Albert Chandler, March 12, 1949, in *SOMP*, 1548–49.

24. *PC*, September 11 (Saunders), 1948; *PI*, September 18, November 13, 1948; Marshall interview with Effa Manley, October 19, 1977; *SN*, December 31, 1947; May 19, June 2, October 20, November 17, 1948; Overmyer, *Effa Manley*, 236–40; *CD*, September 18 ("Negro fans"/"inferiority"), 1948; July 30, 1949; *NYT*, November 10 ("the gullibility"), 12, 1948; January 15, 20, December 7, 1949; June 26, 1951; Philip J. Lowry, *Green Cathedrals* (Boston, 1992), 186; Dan Daniel, "TV Must Go—Or Baseball Will!" *Baseball Magazine*, November 1952; *BAA*, June 25 (Lacy), 1949.

25. *PC*, November 16 (Posey), 1940; September 18 (Smith), November 13, 1948; March 5 ("Mrs. Manley"), 1949. Manley, for example, had earlier exhorted blacks to "develop some race consciousness and stop ramming themselves down white people's throats. Integration will follow naturally when you are qualified." See *CD*, June 12, 1948.

26. Tom Baird to J. B. Martin, December 24, 1949; W. S. Martin to Tom Baird, January 4, 1950, TBC, box 2, correspondence Matty Brescia, 1949–1953; minutes of NAL meeting, November 30, 1948, TBC, box 2, minutes, NAL meetings 1943–1952; 1948 ledger, profit and loss statement, TBC, box 16, financial records, 1948–1951; TBC, box 9, financial records, gate receipts, 1948; *NYA*, September 24, 1948; February 5, 1949; *PI*, September 18, December 4, 1948; April 23, 1949; *PC*, November 27, 1948; February 10, 1951; Overmyer, *Effa Manley*, 241; *BAA*, September 11, November 27, December 11, 1948; January 29, March 5, 1949; *CD*, November 27, December 11 (Young), 1948; March 19, 1949; *CCP*, December 4, 1948; *BW*, September 2, 1949.

27. *CCP*, December 4, 1948; *PT*, January 8, 22, February 1 (White), 15, March 5, 22, 1949; *PI*, September 25, 1948; February 19, April 23 ("he did not"), 1949; *BAA*, January 31, February 14, September 25 (Lacy), December 11, 1948; January 15, February 19, March 12, 1949; *PC*, November 13, 1948; *SN*, August 25, October 20 (Manley), 1948; *NYA*, July 30 (Burley), 1949; *NYT*, October 29, 1947; September 21, October 30, December 25, 1948; *NYAN*, January 3, 24, 1948; *PAA*, January 31, 1948; minutes of joint session, November 29, 1948; NAL meeting, November 30, 1948, TBC, box 2, minutes, NAL meetings 1943–1952; *KCC*, February 18, 1949; J. B. Martin to A. B. Chandler, March 12, 1949, *SOMP*, 1548–49; "See" [Posey] to Art Carter, December 12, 1948 ("to protect"), ACP, box 170-9, folder 13. Chandler eventually lifted the ban on the major league Mexican jumpers on June 5, 1949. See *PINQ*, June 6, 1949.

28. Minutes of schedule meeting, February 7–8, 1949, TBC, box 2, minutes, NAL meetings 1943–1952; *BAA*, January 15, March 5 (Posey), 12, 19, 1949; *CD*, December 25, 1948; *PC*, March 5, 12, 1949; *PT*, March 5, 1949; Vernon Green to Art Carter, January 22, 1949, ACP, box 170-16, folder 6; *NYA*, March 26 (Burley), 1949; Ernest Wright to Effa Manley, June 25, 1942 (Wright), NEP.

29. "Negro Ball Clubs Hope to Make Comeback This Season," *Ebony*, May 1949 (J. B. Martin); *CD*, April 23, 1949 (Green, B. B. Martin, Gottlieb, and Hayes statements); *BW*, April 8 ("thousands"), 1949.

30. *CD*, May 7 (Young), 1949; *KCC*, May 27, June 3, 1949; *PT*, May 24, July 2, 1949; *PC*, June 4, July 9, 1949; *BAA*, May 21 (Green), June 4, August 27 (Overbea), 1949; TBC, box 10, gate receipts, KC, 1949.

31. *BAA*, September 3, 1949; *PT*, May 7, 1949; *NYAN*, August 6 (Bostic), 1949; *SN*, April 27, 1949; *PI*, June 25, July 9, 1949; financial statement, July 3–4, 1949 at Comiskey Park, TBC, box 10, financial records, gate receipts, 1949.

32. *CD*, April 23, June 11 (Young), August 27, 1949; *CCP*, August 26 (Fuster), 1950; *PT*, February 1, 5, March 12, April 12, June 14, 1949; May 27, 1950; *BAA*, May 6, 1950; *NYA*, July 9, 1949; *NYAN*, February 5, 1949; Dan Parker, "How Democratic Is Sport?" *Sport*, September 1949 ("I suppose"); Tom Baird to Jack Sheehan, March 18, 1949 ("he was"), TBC, box 4, correspondence, Chicago Cubs, 1949–1957. Perhaps sensing the reluctance among baseball officials, Baird also emphasized the light skin color of Richardson and other promising Monarch players. See Baird to Sheehan, March 3, 1949, TBC, box 4, correspondence, Chicago Cubs, 1949–1957.

33. *NYAN*, February 5, 1949; *PT*, February 5, 15, March 1, 1949; *CD*, November 6, 1948; *NYA*, November 6, 1948; *BAA*, March 5 (Posey), April 2, May 14, 1949; Abe Saperstein to Tom Hayes, July 28, 1949, Thomas Hayes Collection, Memphis Shelby County Public Library and Information Center; Lee MacPhail to Tom Baird, February 25, 1949, TBC, box 4, correspondence, New York Yankees, 1949–1953; *PC*, February 19, 1949; *SN*, February 23, May 25, 1949; 5/13/49 Decision No. 26, Office of the Commissioner, BHOFL; J. B. Martin to A. B. Chandler, May 23, 1949 in *SOMP*, 1549. An unsigned document at the BHOFL, presumably written by a Yankee official shortly prior to the signing of Wilson, provides a fascinating unguarded view of the organization's attitude toward black players and black baseball. While admitting that Wilson and Piper Davis were "both good ball players," the author asserts that "there isn't an outstanding Negro player that anybody could recommend to step into the big league and hold down a regular job. The better players in Negro baseball are past the age for the big leagues." In a discussion of the ongoing agitation for integration, the report alludes to "how these committees apply the pressure on the big leagues to hire one or perhaps two players. If you hire one or two, then they will want you to hire another one. There will be no compromise with them and they are mostly bluff." Historian Robert Burk has identified the author as Yankee general manager George Weiss. See typewritten note (late 1948–early 1949), Race and Ethnicity: Integration file, BHOFL; email from Robert Burk, January 18, 2002.

34. *BAA*, February 19 (Lacy), May 14, 1949; *CD*, February 19 (Young), 1949; 5/13/49 Decision No. 26, Office of the Commissioner; *PT*, May 14, 1949; A. B. Chandler to J. B. Martin, June 9, 1949 in *SOMP*, 1550; Marshall interview with Veeck, February 23, 1977 ("silly"); MacPhail, *My Nine Innings*, 49 ("soured").

35. *PC*, March 5, 1949; August 12, 1950; *PT*, March 5, May 14, 1949; J. B. Martin to A. B. Chandler, May 23 ("a man"/"you promised"), June 7, 1949; A. B. Chandler to J. B. Martin, June 9, 1949 (Chandler), in *SOMP*, 1549–1550; *PI*, May 28, 1949; *CD*, June 4, 1949; *BAA*, March 26, 1949; Riley, *Biographical Encyclopedia*, 829.

36. *NYT*, January 12, 29, 1949; *PT*, January 15, 18, 1949; *PI*, January 1, 22, 1949; *BAA*, March 9, 1946, January 22, 1949; *NYA*, February 5, 1949; Irvin with Riley, *Nice Guys Finish First*, 120–23; Rust, *"Get That Nigger off the Field!"*, 112; *CD*, February 5, 1949; *PC*, January 22, 1949.

37. Charles Feeney to Tom Baird, January 31, 1949; James Gallagher to Tom Baird, June 10, 1949, Eddie Gottlieb to Tom Baird, March 1, 1949, March 11, 1949 sheet on Ford Smith sale, TBC, box 4, correspondence about other player sales, 1949–1953; Tom Baird to Lee MacPhail, February 11, 1949, Lee MacPhail to Tom Baird, February 25, 1949, TBC, box 4, correspondence New York Yankees, 1949–1953; *NYA*, August 13, 1949; *PT*, February 1, 26, June 14, 18, August 2, 1949; *CD*, March 5, August 27, October 8, 1949; Thomas Hayes Collection, Memphis Shelby County Public Library and Information Center, Memphis; *BAA*, June 25, 1949; Rust, *"Get That Nigger off the Field!"*, 112; Holway, *Voices*, 325; *CCP*, December 10, 1949; January 14, 1950; Milton Gross, "Will the Yankees Hire a Negro Player?" *Our Sports* (July 1953): 9–10, 58–59, in AMP, box 4.

38. Wendell Smith to Branch Rickey, June 3, 1948, July 5 ("desperate"), 1949, Smith papers, BHOFL; Michael Marsh, "A Closer Look at Wendell Smith," unpublished paper, courtesy of SABR Negro Leagues Committee; *NYA*, July 30, August 6, 1949; *CD*, April 23, August 27, 1949; *PT*, June 18, 21, 1949; September 9, 1950; *BAA*, March 26, 1949; *NYAN*, April 9, 1949; National Association of Professional Baseball Leagues, *Story of Minor League Baseball*, 38; Riley, *Biographical Encyclopedia*, 784; *SCD*, September 27, 1991; November 11, 1994; "Treasurer's Report, 1948," 21, 67, PP, box 4; working agreement, Philadelphia Phillies and Toronto Maple Leafs, August 15, 1949, PP, box 7; Robert W. Smith, "The Business Side of Major League Baseball" (senior thesis, Princeton University, 1948), 42; *PI*, August 27 (Overbea), 1949; Rogosin, "Queen of the Negro Leagues," 19 (Manley). During 1948, several major league teams paid bonuses as high as $75,000 for young players. Anthony Pascal and Leonard Rapping later suggested that the "mounting bonus costs" contributed to the increasing pursuit of black players, typically "available for modest bonuses or none at all." See Anthony H. Pascal and Leonard A. Rapping, *Racial Discrimination in Organized Baseball* (Santa Monica, Calif., 1970), 27; J. G. Taylor Spink, comp., *Baseball Guide and Record Book—1949* (St. Louis, 1949), 92.

39. Wendell Smith to Branch Rickey, July 5, 1949, Smith papers; *CD*, June 11, October 8, 1949; *KCC*, June 17, 1949; *BW*, September 2, 1949; January 3, 1950; *CCP*, July 23, 30, August 27, 1949; Tom Baird to Matty Brescia, December 24, 1949 ("better off"), January 9, 1950 ("white elephant"), TBC, box 2, correspondence Matty Brescia, 1949–1953; *NYA*, July 22, 1950; *PT*, July 19, 1949; February 18, 28, 1950; *CD*, January 21, 1950.

40. *PC*, February 18 (Smith), 1950; *SN*, April 19 (Harding), May 10 (O'Neil), 1950; *PT*, September 9 (Overbea), 1950; *NYAN*, April 23 (Garlington), 1949; *CD*, May 13, 1950 (Young).

41. *BAA*, January 14, 28, 1950; *NYAN*, August 27 (Farrell), 1949; April 22, 1950; Wendell Smith to Branch Rickey, July 5, 1949, Smith papers; *PT*, February 11, 18, 28, May 2, 1950; *CD*, March 31, 1937; January 9, December 25, 1943; December 3, 1949; *MC*, December 22, 1945.

42. *CD*, April 23, 1949; *PT*, April 22, August 8 ("constantly"), September 9, 1950; *BAA*, August 13, 1949; *PC*, December 16 (Martin), 1950. Martin later claimed that the commissioner "did a very good job. . . . He tried in every way to help our league, and he kept his word about giving the boys a fair deal." On Chandler's relationship with Martin and the NAL, see *SN*, February 23, 1949; 5/13/49 Decision No. 26, Office of the Commissioner, National BHOFL; *BAA*, December 23, 1950 (Martin); *PT*, Janu-

ary 2, 1951; *CD*, December 30, 1950; Albert Chandler to J. B. Martin, June 9, 1949, in *SOMP*, 1550.

43. Tom Baird to Von Price, June 12, 1950, George Trautman to Tom Baird, April 5, 1951 ("no power"/"your conception"), TBC, box 5, correspondence about Roy Williams and Leonard Hunt, 1950–1953; Tom Baird to R. P. Brown, February 1, 1952, TBC, box 4, correspondence Capilano Baseball Club, Vancouver, 1951–1952, George Trautman to Earl Sheely, February 8, 1952 ("it is not sufficient"), George Trautman to Tom Baird, March 5, 1952 ("it is not the function"), TBC, box 5, correspondence about Herbert Souell, 1952; Tom Baird to J. B. Martin, February 22, 1952 ("the least"), TBC, box 2, correspondence J. B. Martin, 1949–1960; *SOMP*, 225–26, 241–43. Hunt and Williams were eventually released and returned to the Monarchs. In a similar case in 1951 involving Butch McCord of the New Orleans Eagles who jumped to Paris of the Mississippi-Ohio Valley League, Trautman ultimately sided with NAL officials, compelling the club to purchase McCord's release for $1,000. See B. B. Martin to Clinton McCord, March 15, 1951, C. Dutch Hoffman to J. B. Martin, June 14, 1951, J. B. Martin to George Trautman, June 18, 1951, George Trautman to Hillman Lyons, July 11, 1951, J. B. Martin to George Trautman, July 30, 1951 in *SOMP*, 1296–1301.

44. *PT*, January 15, 1949; February 21, 1950; *PC*, April 16, 1949; *SN*, August 6, 1947; April 19 (King), 1950; *CD*, April 23, 1949; Bruce Adelson, *Brushing Back Jim Crow* (Charlottesville, Va., 1999), 121; *BW*, February 1, April 12, 1949; *PI*, February 4, 1950. By 1950, Branch Rickey noted that he had to "split the squad enroute North in order to accommodate requests for exhibition games specifying the appearance of Negro players." See Rickey to J. G. Stahlman, January 23, 1950, BRP, correspondence, "S" miscellaneous—January–July 1950.

45. *KCC*, October 17 (Johnson), 1947; *CCP*, October 2, 1943; January 14 (Fuster), 1950; *PT*, June 12, 1948; April 23, May 21, September 10, 1949; *NYAN*, April 9, May 14, August 27 (Silvera), 1949; *PINQ*, May 31, 1949; *PI*, July 13, 1946; July 5, August 9, 1947; May 8, 1948; April 9 ("interracial flavor"), 1949; *BAA*, July 29, 1950; Effa Manley to Ed Gottlieb, April 16, 1946, NEP. During World War II, interracial clubs became somewhat more common in the North. Concurrently, several industrial sponsors, including Disston Saw of Philadelphia and Alcoa of Cleveland, also began to relax the racial policies of their athletic teams. Mixed teams were still far from universally accepted, as an interracial nine from Battle Creek, Michigan, was barred from the National Amateur Baseball Federation tournament in 1946. See *PT*, September 7, 1946.

46. *PT*, March 5, 1949; July 4, August 12, September 9, 1950; *NYT*, June 30 (Martin), July 10, August 8, 1950; *CD*, June 17, July 1, 8, 15, 22, 29 (Young), 1950; *PI*, July 8, 15, August 12, 1950; *PC*, June 17, 1950; *CCP*, July 8 (Fuster), 1950; *SN*, July 26, 1950; *NYAN*, July 15, 1950; *BW*, August 15, 1950; financial statement, Monarchs-American Giants at Comiskey Park, July 16, 1950, TBC, box 11, league gate receipts, 1950.

47. Jordan, *Long Range Effect of Television*, 55; *PC*, June 17, July 8, December 16 (Smith), 1950; *PT*, June 17, July 25, August 1, 12, October 3, 17, December 30, 1950; *BAA*, July 22, August 19, September 9, December 23, 1950; *CD*, June 17, July 15, 1950; *NYT*, July 16, 1950; *SN*, November 29, 1950; *PI*, August 5, 1950; minutes of NAL meeting, February 7–8, 1950, TBC, box 2, minutes, NAL meetings 1943–1952; J. B. Martin to Tom Baird, September 15, 1950, TBC, box 5, miscellaneous correspondence, 1948–1962; February 8, 1950, check to Cleveland Buckeyes, $400 loan, TBC, box 17, canceled checks, 1943–1961; Clinton McCord to B. B. Martin, 1951, in *SOMP*, 1294. Not surprisingly, several veteran players drifted to Mexico in 1950, while others

found opportunities in the highly competitive Provincial League, a formerly independent Canadian organization that had recently joined Organized Baseball as a class C circuit, and the "outlaw" Manitoba-North Dakota ("Man-Dak") League.

48. Financial statements, May 14–15, 1950, Blues Stadium, May 28, 1950, Yankee Stadium, TBC, box 11, league gate receipts, 1950; Stars' May 1950 schedule, EBP, box 186-1, folder 26; *PT*, July 25, 1950.

49. Leffler, "Boom and Bust," 182; *BAA*, May 29, 1948; January 15 (Green), 1949; May 13, June 3, 24, August 19, October 14, 1950; March 24, April 14, May 5, 1951; *PI*, July 29, 1950; *PC*, December 16, 1950; *PT*, June 24, 1950; *BW*, May 31, 1949; *KCC*, May 11, 1951; Kelley, *Negro Leagues Revisited*, 86; *Baltimore Sun*, March 6, 1949 in ACP, box 170-19, folder 18; *Baltimore Sun*, July 24, 1994 (Powell).

50. *CD*, January 7 (Martin), May 6, 1950; *PI*, May 20, June 10, September 16, 1950; *BAA*, June 24, 1950; *NYAN*, August 12, 1950; *PT*, August 11, 1953; *KCC*, September 29 ("a natural"), 1950; April 11, 1952. As late as 1953, Fritz Pollard noted that when integrated teams appeared in St. Louis, "Negroes charter buses from Georgia, Alabama and points south to get a look at 'their boys.'"

51. *SN*, February 9 ("nobody"), 1949; August 9, 1950; Al Hirshberg, "Boston Needs a Negro Big-Leaguer," *Our Sports* (July 1953): 11–12, 64–65, in AMP, box 4; *PT*, May 27, June 17, July 15, 29, August 5, 8, 19, September 2, 1950; *PI*, August 20, 1949; June 10, 1950; Tygiel, *Baseball's Great Experiment*, 263; *BAA*, April 1, 1950; *CD*, June 5, 1948; August 12, 1950; Al White, "Five Years Later: Negroes in Big League Baseball," *Our World* (October 1950).

52. Tom Baird to Jack Sheehan, March 8, 1950, TBC, box 4, correspondence Chicago Cubs, 1949–1957; Harry Jenkins to Tom Baird, July 3, 1950, Tom Baird to Harry Jenkins, August 1, 1950, TBC, box 4, correspondence Boston Braves, 1949–1953; Lee MacPhail to Tom Baird, July 24, 1950, TBC, box 4, correspondence New York Yankees, 1949–1953; "KC Monarch Baseball Club Comparative Profit & Loss Statement for Calendar Years 1950 & 1951," TBC, box 18, folder 1; 1949 ledger, TBC, box 16, financial records, 1948–1951; *SN*, July 26, August 9, 1950; *PI*, April 22, July 8, 29, August 19, September 16, 23, December 30, 1950; *BAA*, April 22, 1950; February 7, 1953; *PT*, July 29, October 3, December 30, 1950; *CD*, July 29, December 23, 1950; *SOMP*, 646 (O'Connor).

53. *CD*, August 20 (Hayes), 1949; Willie Mays as told to Charles Einstein, *Willie Mays: My Life In and Out of Baseball* (New York, 1966), 28–31 (Montague); Mays, *Say Hey*, 45–50; Bill Klink, "Our Friend Willie," in *The Ol' Ball Game*, 126–33; *PI*, September 1, 8, 1951; *SN*, July 5, 1950; August 15, 1951; Hayes papers; *CD*, July 8, 1950; *Wilmington Journal Every Evening*, July 5, 1950; *BW*, June 23, 1950. Although several accounts suggest that Mays received $6,000 and the Barons $9,000, the Hayes papers record the sale price as $10,000. It is possible, however, that the Barons paid Mays an additional $1,000 as a portion of the sale price.

54. *CD*, April 1 ("don't"), 1950; February 10, 1951; *SN*, July 26 (Daniel), 1950; *PC*, December 30, 1950; February 10, 1951; *PI*, August 26, October 7, 1950; *PT*, August 12, December 30, 1950; W. S. Martin to Tom Baird, January 4, 1950, TBC, box 2, correspondence Matty Brescia, 1949–1953.

55. Tom Baird to J. B. Martin, March 7, 1952 ("the quieter"), TBC, box 2, correspondence J. B. Martin, 1949–1960; *SOMP*, 1087; *PT*, August 13, 1949; May 30, July 29, September 9 (Burley), 1950; March 17, 1951; *SN*, August 10, 24, 1949; July 26, October 4, 1950; *PI*, December 9, 1950; *CD*, July 23, 1949; *NYAN*, July 23, 1949; Rosengarten, "Reading the Hops," 78; *CCP*, April 8, 1950; *BW*, March 6, 1951. Viewed within the context of the late 1940s and early 1950s, the sums paid by Organized Baseball may not be exceptionally low. During 1946 and 1947, for example, the

Phillies purchased Dutch Leonard from the Washington Senators for $10,000, Buster Adams from the St. Louis Cardinals for $20,000, and Ken Heintzelman from the Pirates for $15,000, although the acquisitions of Howie Schultz from Brooklyn and Jack Albright from Boston cost the team $52,500 and $35,000 respectively. During the following three years, the Phillies bought major leaguers Russ Meyer, Nick Strincevich, Ken Trinkle, and Dick Whitman, all for $12,500 or less, although the team paid $18,500 to acquire Jimmy Bloodworth from the Cincinnati Reds. Prices for upper-level minor leaguers appearing with clubs unaffiliated with the Phillies ranged from $2,500 (with a balance of $12,500 to be paid if the player was retained) for Al Flair of New Orleans (Southern Association) to $25,000 for pitcher Homer Spragins of Memphis (Southern Association). The Phillies also drafted veteran pitcher Milo Candini from the Pacific Coast League in 1949, paying the standard price of $10,000. See "Treasurer's Report, 1948," 21; "Treasurer's Report—1949," 21, PP, box 4, financial; "Controller's Report—1947," 16, PP.

56. Benjamin Rader, *In Its Own Image: How Television Has Transformed Sports* (New York, 1984), 59; Benjamin Rader, *American Sports: From the Age of Folk Games to the Age of Televised Sports*, 3rd ed. (Upper Saddle River, N.J., 1996), 241; Ruck, *Sandlot Seasons*, 203; *Wilmington Journal Every Evening*, July 21, 1950 ("lucky"); *NYAN*, July 15, 1950; *SN*, October 3, 1951; *PI*, September 3, 1949; June 17, 1950; *PT*, July 9, 1949; *PINQ*, July 14, 1987.

57. Francis Wallace, "Are the Major Leagues Strangling Baseball?" *Collier's*, March 10, 1951, 65; Ruck, *Sandlot Seasons*, 195–97; Rader, *Baseball*, 161; *NYT*, June 26, 1951; *SN*, March 8, 1950; *PEB*, May 1, 1949; Jordan, *Long Range Effect of Television*, 10–17; Fredric Miller, Morris Vogel, and Allen Davis, *Philadelphia Stories: A Photographic History, 1920–1960* (Philadelphia, 1988), 281; Koppett, *Koppett's Concise History of Major League Baseball*, 235; Rader, *In Its Own Image*, 33–52; *Time*, February 13, 1950, 44. A 1950 National League report discussed radio's effect on minor league baseball, warning that the "granting of unlimited broadcasting rights in minor league towns, except during the actual hours a minor league home game was being played" had resulted in "saturation." According to the report, it was "not unusual for two or three major league ball games to be broadcast in a . . . town within a 24-hour period," effectively destroying interest in the local minor league team's game. Meanwhile, although minor league clubs were theoretically able to block major league broadcasts competing against its home games, public pressure (often fostered by the radio stations) typically forced them to yield. See NATIONAL LEAGUE TREASURER'S REPORT NOVEMBER 1, 1950—CONFIDENTIAL BUSINESS, PP, box 7.

58. *SN*, May 19, June 2, November 24, 1948; April 20, August 3, September 14, November 30, 1949; January 25 (Cronin), 1950; Spink, *Baseball Guide and Record Book—1950*, 90; Wallace, "Are the Major Leagues Strangling Baseball?" 18; *PEB*, February 19, May 1, 1949; Westcott and Bilovsky, *New Phillies Encyclopedia*, 797; *PINQ*, September 27, 30, 1947; *NYT*, December 7, 1949; June 26, 1951; February 3, 1953; September 18, 1955; National Association of Professional Baseball Leagues, *Story of Minor League Baseball*, 73–74; Jordan, *Long Range Effect of Television*, 58–59, 109–12; *PDN*, May 2, 1947; "The Philadelphia National League Club . . . Treasurer's Report upon Operations for the Year Ended October 31, 1949," 126, PP, box 4, financial. The Phillies sold their television rights for $10,000 in 1947, increasing to $25,000 a year later. By 1951, combined television and radio revenue for the Phillies totaled $240,089, a nearly 300 percent increase since 1947. See "Treasurer's Report, 1948," 54–55, "Treasurer's Report, 1950," 55, "Treasurer's Report, 1953," 14, PP, box 4, financial.

59. *PEB*, May 1, 1949; *SN*, December 8, 1948; *PAA*, December 4, 1948; May 20,

1950; December 6, 1952; Oakley, *Baseball's Last Golden Age*, 323; *NYAN*, August 13, 1949; December 4, 1954; *BW*, June 14, 1949; Curtis, "Factors That Affect the Attendance of a Major League Baseball Club," 79; *CD*, February 18 (Young), 1950. According to the *Amsterdam News*, 375,000 blacks owned television sets in the New York area by 1954.

60. *NYT*, July 16, 1950; *SN*, July 24, September 6, 1950; *PEB*, September 27, 1950; *Wilmington Morning News*, June 19, 1950; *Wilmington Journal Every Evening*, July 20, 1950; Spink, *Baseball Guide and Record Book—1951*, 261; "Treasurer's Report, 1950," 73, PP, box 4, financial; Randy Roberts and Olson, *Winning Is the Only Thing*, 109–10; Patrick Hannigan, *The Detroit Tigers Club and Community, 1945–1995* (Toronto, 1997), 13–19; Oakley, *Baseball's Last Golden Age*, 189–94; James Edward Miller, *The Baseball Business: Pursuing Pennants and Profits in Baltimore* (Chapel Hill, N.C., 1990), 5–9; Rader, *Baseball*, 174–76; Andrew S. Zimbalist, *Baseball and Billions: A Probing Look Inside the Big Business of Our National Pastime* (New York, 1992), 110; Rader, *In Its Own Image*, 33–52; Curtis, "Factors That Affect the Attendance of a Major League Baseball Club," 25, 28, 38–40, 57; *SOMP*, 1629. The Wilmington Blue Rocks provide a typical example of the fate of many minor league clubs in the postwar era. After averaging 2,428 fans per date and turning a profit of $30,913.23 in 1947, the team's attendance began to decline, falling to 1,016 per date in 1949 and 785 in 1950. Despite fielding competitive teams, the Blue Rocks lost $69,844.73 in 1948, $27,627.77 in 1949, $25,005.75 in 1950, and $158,850.82 in 1951. For the Blue Rocks' financial records, see "Treasurer's Report, 1948," 121–22, 125–32; "Treasurer's Report 1949," 125–26; "Treasurer's Report 1950," 73, 136, "Treasurer's Report 1951," 114; "Treasurer's Report 1952," 112; PP, box 4, financial.

61. Wallace, "Are the Major Leagues Strangling Baseball?" 66 ("major-league"); Kammen, *American Culture*, 170–71; *SN*, October 25 (Dewitt), 1950; *Wilmington Journal Every Evening*, June 21, 1950 (Carpenter). The growing number of major league games played at night likely also cut into the appeal of minor league and semi-professional baseball. In the American League, night games rose from 35 in 1941 to 204 by 1950, nearly one third of the schedule. See Pietrusza, *Lights On!*, 193; Curtis, "Factors That Affect the Attendance of a Major League Baseball Club," 31; *SOMP*, 137.

62. *BAA*, June 24 (Lyle), 1950; *CCP*, January 10 (Young), 1948; *PT*, July 3, 1943 ("pay to").

Chapter 11. The End of a Business

Epigraph: *PT*, February 8, 1955.

1. *CD*, July 15 (Young), 1950; *PC*, May 5 (Smith), 1951; *BAA*, August 27 (Overbea), 1949; *PT*, July 29 (Martin), 1952.

2. *NYAN*, April 28, 1951; undated clipping, *Pittsburgh Courier Magazine* (Webster), EBP, box 186-1, folder 41. Ironically, the phenomenal postwar growth of urban black communities theoretically presented entrepreneurs with unprecedented opportunities to build successful race businesses. Fueled by the mechanization of southern agriculture and the lure of northern jobs, a heavy migration of southern blacks to northern and western cities continued through the 1950s and into the late 1960s. Despite the massive influx of newcomers, black economic development generally remained stalled. In 1973, only 26 of the top 100 black corporations recorded sales over $5 million. See Kusmer, "African Americans in the City," 460–68; Meier and Rudwick, *From Plantation to Ghetto*, 327–28.

3. *PT*, April 20, 1948; November 5 (Rhodes), 1949; Gamble, *Making a Place for Ourselves*, 188.

4. *KCC*, February 25 ("there is"), 1949; *BAA*, October 27, 1951; *PC*, September 8, 1951; *CD*, September 4 (Young), 1954; Wolseley, *Black Press, USA*, x ("integration"); *PI*, February 12 (Winston), 1955; *PT*, May 27 (Martin), 1952. Black players debuted in the NBA during the 1950–1951 season. In football, only three teams were without black players by the end of the 1953 season. See Peterson, *Cages to Jump Shots*, 170–72; Ross, *Outside the Lines*, 131–34.

5. Oakley, *Baseball's Last Golden Age*, 81, 164, 189–94; *SN*, December 5, 1951; November 26, December 3, 1952; Spink, *Baseball Guide—1953*, 221; Spink, *Baseball Guide—1950*, 184; Jordan, *Long Range Effect of Television*, 32, 50, 109–12; *PEB*, February 7, 1953; *NYT*, September 4, 18, 1955; Rader, *In Its Own Image*, 33–54; *Business Week*, December 5, 1953; August 14, 1954; Gregory, *Baseball Player*, 84; Roberts and Olson, *Winning Is the Only Thing*, 97, 109–10; Miller, *Baseball Business*, 5–9; Hannigan, *Detroit Tigers Club*, 18; Rader, *Baseball*, 174–76; Grantland Rice, "Is Baseball Afraid of Television?" *Sport*, April 1951, 12–13, 90. The All American Girls' Baseball League, an organization that never integrated, disbanded in September 1954, victimized by similar postwar trends. See Berlage, *Women in Baseball*, 158–77.

6. *SN*, December 24 (Gottlieb), 1952; August 7, October 23 (MacPhail), 1957; *KCC*, March 7, 1952; June 12 (Johnson), 1953; *NYT*, June 26, 1951; September 18 ("when people"), 1955; *PEB*, June 8, 1951; *BAA*, November 15, 1952; William Johnson, "TV Made It All a New Game," *Sports Illustrated*, December 22, 1969; Roberts and Olson, *Winning Is the Only Thing*, 99; Oakley, *Baseball's Last Golden Age*, 281; *PINQ*, May 9, 1952; *CD*, December 16, 1950; *Business Week*, January 27, 1951, 49–52; Hannigan, *Detroit Tigers Club*, 17; Ruck, *Sandlot Seasons*, 199; *NYAN*, March 8, 1952; *PDN*, August 24, 1949; *Our World* (November 1952); (May 1955); Tygiel, *Past Time*, 152; *PC*, November 22 (Smith), 1952.

7. *KCC*, September 17 ("the owners"), 1948; July 11, 1952; July 31, 1953; *CD*, June 9, 1951; February 21 (Cowans), 1953; August 7, 1954; *SN*, March 12, June 25, 1952; *BAA*, August 25, 1951; *PI*, August 4, 1951; *BW*, May 30, 1952; Hillman Lyons to George Trautman, June 19, 1951 in *SOMP*, 1296; Robinson with Dexter, *Baseball Has Done It*, 153; *PT*, July 3 (Davis), 1951; Harris interview ("average sandlot"), March 31, 2000.

8. *PT*, May 26, 1951; February 7, April 11, May 19, July 18, 1953; July 21, 1956; Adelson, *Brushing Back Jim Crow*, 36–242; *Our World* (August 1951); *BAA*, June 25, 1955; *BW*, April 15, 1952; *KCC*, June 27, October 17 (Henry), 1952; May 1, 1953; *PI*, September 19, 1953; Kenneth Fenster, "Notice on Nat Peeples," *Baseball Research Journal* 27 (1998): 94; Tom Baird to J. B. Martin, November 1, 1955 ("he didn't"), TBC, box 2, correspondence, J. B. Martin, 1949–1960. By 1961, the laws banning interracial sports in Birmingham and Louisiana had been declared unconstitutional.

9. *PT*, April 8 ("comedy"), 1944; May 6, July 11 (White), 1950; July 22 ("Boogie"), December 8, 1952; July 18, 1953; *CD*, March 29 (Young), 1947. On King Tut, Spec Bebop, and other featured performers for the Clowns, see *PT*, September 17, 1946; May 17, 1952; July 11, 1953; *BAA*, August 9, 1952; *NYAN*, August 2, 1952; *KCC*, May 21, 1948.

10. *BW*, May 19 (Jackson), 1950; *CCP*, March 6 (Young), 1948; *BAA*, April 4 (Lacy), 1953; *NYAN*, December 18 (Bostic), 1954; Peterson, *Cages to Jump Shots*, 101; *PT*, July 11, August 15, 1950; November 18, 1952; October 10, 1953; May 8, 1954. Renaissance owner Robert Douglas, for example, often received letters from promoters requesting whether his players "could sing or dance."

11. *KCC*, March 10 ("there is"), 1950; Tom Baird to Oscar Rico, February 23,

1953 ("just"), Oscar Rico to Tom Baird, February 27, 1953 ("Cuban"), TBC, box 3, correspondence and information about Cuban Giants, 1953; *PI*, January 13, 1951; *PT*, January 27, February 17, 1951; *BAA*, August 4, 1951; Alex Pompez file, BHOFL; Ostenby, "Other Games; Other Glory," 58, 66. Pompez died in 1974 at the age of eighty-three.

12. Minutes of the Schedule Meeting of the NAL, June 22–23, 1949, TBC, box 2, minutes, NAL meetings 1943–1952; *PT*, September 10, 1949; August 1, 15, 1950; May 26, 1951; *PI*, July 22, 1950; *PC*, August 1, 1951; *BAA*, June 2, 1951; Holway, *Blackball Stars*, 326 (Posey).

13. *BAA*, July 14, 21, September 8, 1951; *PT*, January 13, 1951; April 29, May 20, 1952; May 8, 1954; *PI*, January 13, April 7, May 12, 1951; *PC*, January 13, September 8, 1951; *CD*, January 13, 1951; May 24, 1952; February 21, April 18, September 19, 1953; August 7, 1954; August 13, 1955; *PINQ*, July 6, 1951; *SN*, November 23, 1949; *MC*, January 12, 1946; *PAA*, March 29, 1952; Tom Baird to J. B. Martin, March 7, 1952 ("keep on"), TBC, box 2, correspondence J. B. Martin, 1949–1960; minutes of NAL schedule meeting, February 13–14, 1951, TBC, box 2, minutes, NAL 1943–1952; Bill Nunn to Branch Rickey, May 15, 1951, BRP, correspondence file, box 23, "N miscellaneous."

14. *PI*, May 5 ("not"), 1951; January 5, 1952; *PC*, January 6, 1951; January 12, 1952; *PT*, January 9 ("a club"), February 17, June 30, 1951; *BAA*, January 13, March 24 ("we haven't"/Powell), April 14, May 5, 1951; B. B. Martin to Clinton McCord, Jr., January 29, 1951 in *SOMP*, 1293; B. B. Martin to Tom Baird, April 4, 1951, TBC, box 18, correspondence and stationery; minutes of schedule meeting, June 14, 1951, TBC, box 2, minutes, NAL meetings, 1943–1952; Kelley, *Negro Leagues Revisited*, 87.

15. *BW*, January 15 (Hayes), 1952; *KCC*, July 20, August 3, 1951; *PT*, July 3, September 8, 1951; *CD*, August 4, September 8, 1951; September 19, 1953; *PC*, March 3, 1951; *SN*, July 4, October 24, 1951; *PI*, July 28, August 4, 1951; *PEB*, July 8, 1951; Tom Baird to Bob Howsam, February 27, 1951, TBC, box 4, correspondence Denver Bears, 1950–1952; balance sheet, May 7, 1951, TBC, box 16, financial records, 1948–1951; W. C. MacPhail to Tom Baird, October 18, 1951, TBC, box 4, correspondence about other player sales, 1949–1953; financial statement, May 6, 9, 25, 1951, Kansas City at Memphis, TBC, box 13, gate receipts, 1951; "KC Monarch Baseball Club Comparative Profit & Loss Statement For Calendar Years 1950 & 1951," TBC, box 18, folder 1.

16. *SN*, July 25, September 5, 1951; February 20, 1952; *PT*, July 14, 17, 1951; *PI*, July 21, 1951; *PC*, May 24, 1952; *CD*, September 8, 1951; Tom Baird to R. P. Brown, December 31, 1951 ("they all"), TBC, box 4, correspondence Capilano Baseball Club, Vancouver, 1951–1952. By May 1952, the Browns had 22 black players in their organization, more than any other major league franchise. Continued poor attendance in St. Louis, however, forced Veeck to sell the team, which relocated to Baltimore prior to the 1954 season. See Spink, *Official Baseball Guide 1954*, 98–100.

17. *PT*, February 19, 23, May 6 ("make a"), July 19, 1952; June 9, 1953; minutes of the schedule meeting, February 6, 1952, TBC, box 2, minutes, NAL meetings, 1943–1952; *SN*, February 20, 1952; *CD*, February 16, 1952; Riley, *Biographical Encyclopedia*, 107–8; *BW*, January 15, February 5, March 25, 1952; *KCC*, May 11, July 13, 1951; February 22, 1952; *PI*, July 7, 1951; July 26, 1952; *NYAN*, August 2 ("quality of play"), 1952; May 16 ("Jim-crow"), 1953. Each team received $253.95 for its participation in the July 26 doubleheader. The four teams drew 2,207 fans in Baltimore on July 27 and 3,811 in Washington two days later. See financial statements, July 26, 1952, Yankee Stadium, July 27, 1952, Baltimore, July 29, 1952, Griffith Stadium, TBC, box 14, gate receipts, 1952.

18. *PAA*, March 15, April 5, December 6, 1952; *PT*, March 1, May 27, June 3, 7, 10, July 22, 1952; *SN*, March 26, June 25, 1952; Henry Aaron with Lonnie Wheeler, *I Had a Hammer* (New York, 1991), 31–38; January 7, 1952 statement of sale of Eddie Locke, Tom Baird to R. P. Brown, February 20, 1952, TBC, box 4, correspondence Capilano Baseball Club, Vancouver, 1951–1952.

19. *BAA*, September 27 ("jim crow has"), 1952; *SN*, December 10 ("our old"/"the tide"), 1952; financial statement, Monarchs-Clowns at Briggs Stadium, August 10, 1952, TBC, box 14, gate receipts, 1952; *PT*, August 19, 1952; *PC*, November 29, 1952; *PAA*, April 5, 1952; *KCC*, April 11, May 23, 1952.

20. *PT*, March 22, April 12, May 31, June 3, 28, July 15, 22, 26, 29, August 26, September 16, 1952; January 6, April 11, 1953; *PINQ*, July 29, 1952; financial statements, Shibe Park promotion, July 28, 1952, Monarchs-Stars at Galveston (June 23), Austin (June 24), Fort Worth (June 25), Dallas (June 26), TBC, box 14, gate receipts, 1952; interview with Wilmer Harris, March 31, 2000 (Harris quotes); *KCC*, July 11, 1952.

21. Tygiel, *Baseball's Great Experiment*, 291; *Philadelphia Daily News*, August 1, September 17, 1952; *PEB*, September 18, 1952; *PINQ*, September 18, 1952; *PT*, September 20, 1952; April 11, 1953; *Washington Post*, October 24, 1993; R. R. M. Carpenter, Jr. to Charles Shorter, June 22, 1956 in Case No. 7-6-1406 (55) *June D. Tuber v. Philad. National League Club*, City of Philadelphia, Department of Records, City Archives, RG 148, Commission on Human Relations; contract card, Theodore Washington, BHOFL; *PI*, October 31 (Rosenthal), 1953.

22. *BAA*, March 20, 1948; April 1, 1950; *PI*, February 11, 1950; Kerrane, *Dollar Sign*, 106; Hannigan, *Detroit Tigers Club*, 85; Leonard Shapiro, "Fewer Blacks Participate in Baseball," *Washington Post*, July 7, 1991, A1, A12; Tim Cohane, "A Branch Grows in Brooklyn," *Look*, March 19, 1946, 72; *PT*, August 26 ("saturation"), 1950; Harry Jenkins to Thomas Baird, March 9, 1951, cited in Dixon and Hannigan, *Negro Baseball Leagues*, 306 (Jenkins); "Round Table Discussion: The Negro in American Sport," *Negro History Bulletin* (November 1960): 28–29 (Doby) (published originally in *Sport*, March 1960). Branch Rickey later claimed that "five of the directors thought we had too many." See "Branch Rickey Discusses the Negro in Baseball Today," *Ebony*, May 1957.

23. *PINQ*, April 26, May 15, 1952; *PC*, May 24, 1952; *PT*, June 10, 1952; March 14 ("it's been"), 28, April 11 ("if it were"), November 17, 1953; July 27, 1954; *CD*, February 28, July 18, September 19, 1953; *SN*, December 24, 1952; *PEB*, December 17, 1952; January 31, 1960. Gottlieb eventually sold the Philadelphia Warriors in 1962, yet remained active in professional basketball as a schedule-maker for the NBA until his death in 1979.

24. *PT*, February 24 ("this is no"), May 26 ("very much"), 30 ("until I"), June 30, July 11 ("what I have"), 21, August 11, September 8, 26, 1953; March 9, 1954; "Lady Ball Player," *Ebony*, July 1953; *Our World*, July 1953; *PC*, July 9, 1949; July 8, 1950; June 6, July 11, August 15, 1953; *PI*, February 28, June 6, 1953; Barbara Gregorich, *Women at Play: The Story of Women in Baseball*, 169–76; financial statement, Clowns-Monarchs at Blues Stadium, May 24, 1953, Briggs Stadium, June 21, 1953, Comiskey Park, July 4, 1953, Forbes Field, August 4, 1953; TBC, box 15, total gate receipts, 1953; budget sheets, 1953; *PINQ*, June 22–24, 1952; *CD*, June 6, July 18, 1953; *KCC*, May 22, 29, 1953; *BAA*, March 27, 1954.

25. *CD*, August 28 ("she plays"/Young), 1954; *PC*, June 20 (Smith), July 11, 1953; *BAA*, July 25, 1953; O'Neil, *I Was Right on Time*, 194–95; Gregorich, *Women at Play*, 174 ("mostly"); *PT*, March 27 (Overbea), 1954. As part of the league's greater emphasis on entertainment during 1953, the Black Barons signed a harmonica player to tour

with the team and also traveled with a pair of acrobats. Not surprisingly, former owner J. L. Wilkinson viewed the organization as a "joke." See *CD*, April 4, 1953; January 23, 1954; *BAA*, July 24, 1954; *KCC*, June 12, 1953.

26. *CD*, November 7 (Pompez), 1953; January 13, March 6, 1954; January 22, 1955; *PC*, February 13, March 20, July 24, 1954; January 8, 1955; *PT*, September 22, 1953; July 27, 1954; *BAA*, March 27, 1954; June 25, 1955; *PI*, May 22 ("virtually"), June 25 ("startling"), 1954. After receiving a reported $12,000 contract with the Clowns in 1953, Stone signed with the Monarchs in 1954 for only $400 per month and the possibility of a $200 bonus if the team profited. See contract of Toni Stone, 1954, TBC, box 6, player contracts, 1954.

27. *BAA*, July 24 (Kimbro), 1954. Not surprisingly, both Bridgeforth and fellow NAL owner Ted Rasberry were reportedly involved in the illegal numbers. Meanwhile, Rasberry may have also dabbled in the drug trade. A 1960 letter to Tom Baird alludes to the "Feds" looking for Rasberry as a "Heorin [*sic*] peddler . . . you thought he was in the dope racket, you sure had him pegged right." See Tom Brice to Baird, July 23, 1960, TBC, box 5, miscellaneous correspondence, 1948–1962; Riley, *Biographical Encyclopedia*, 107–8; Holway, *Black Diamonds*, 102.

28. Tom Baird to Oscar Rico, January 20, 1955, TBC, box 3, correspondence about Cuban Giants, 1954; Tom Baird to J. B. Martin, March 9, 1955, box 2, correspondence J. B. Martin, 1949–1960, TBC; "Profit & Loss Statement for the period: April 1 thru Dec. 31, 1954 KC Monarchs Baseball Club, Inc.," TBC, box 15, financial records, miscellaneous, 1944–1960; *PT*, January 25, February 8, May 24, 1955; September 18, 1956; "Baseball's Comedy Kings," *Ebony*, September 1959; *CD*, April 16, 1960; Debono, *Indianapolis ABCs*, 123; *PI*, February 12, 1955; *SN*, December 7, 1968; Richard Ian Kimball, "Beyond the 'Great Experiment': Integrated Baseball Comes to Indianapolis," *Journal of Sport History* 26, 1 (Spring 1999): 156; Ed Hamman to Art Carter, February 22, 1965, ACP, box 170-16, folder 6. The Globetrotters continue to operate successfully today and are now under African American ownership.

29. *PT*, March 19, July 19, 30, 1955; *PI*, May 14, June 11, July 23, 1955; *CD*, March 12, 1955; *PC*, February 5, August 6, 1955; Tom Baird to J. B. Martin, June 3, 1955, TBC, box 2, correspondence, J. B. Martin, 1949–1960.

30. Tom Baird to Oscar Rico, May 21, 1955 ("cut our"), TBC, box 3, correspondence about Cuban Giants, 1954; Tom Baird to Emanuel Celler, June 17, 1955, TBC, box 18, correspondence and stationery; *Kansas City News-Press*, July 12, 1955, in TBC, box 18, clippings; Tom Baird to J. B. Martin, June 9, July 2 ("we are chumps"), October 26 ("the people"), November 1 ("same old"), 1955, J. B. Martin to Tom Baird, November 3, 1955 ("if we fold"), TBC, box 2, correspondence, J. B. Martin, 1949–1960; amended tax return, TBC, box 15, financial records, taxes, 1956; *CD*, August 27 (Pollock/"for everything"), 1955; August 22 ("the attendance"), 1959; *SN*, February 8, 29, 1956; August 7, 1957; Dixon and Hannigan, *Negro Baseball Leagues*, 323–29; Lyle Wilson, "The Last Negro League Baseball Game," www.geocities.com/Colosseum/Field/1538/negro.html; Kelley, *Negro Leagues Revisited*, 367 (Webb); Bruce, *Kansas City Monarchs*, 126; *Jet*, June 16, 1960, October 17, 1963; *NYT*, July 31, 1960. The exact date of the NAL's collapse is uncertain, although I was unable to locate any mentions of the league after an October 1963 article in *Jet*. Despite the collapse of the NAL, individual black teams, most notably the Clowns, continued to operate independently. The Kansas City Monarchs disbanded after the 1964 season.

31. *PC*, May 27, 1950; Wendell Smith, "The Most Prejudiced Teams in Baseball," *Ebony*, May 1953 ("competent"); *Sport*, September 1950, 100 ("there are"); *MC*, April 28, 1951 (Evans); *NYT*, January 18, 1952; *PT*, April 12, 1952; August 29,

1953, *PINQ*, August 27, 1953; Hannigan, *Detroit Tigers* Club, 58–59; *PC*, August 29, September 5, 1953; Bak, *Cobb Would Have Caught It*, 105.

32. *PT*, January 6, September 5, 1953; December 18, 1954; June 19, 1956; July 15, 1958; *PI*, January 3, 1953; *BAA*, October 24, 1953; *CCP*, May 22, 1948; *SN*, December 24, 1952; Tygiel, *Baseball's Great Experiment*, 263, 330; Young, *Negro Firsts in Sports*, 222; Al Hirshberg, "Boston Needs a Negro Big-Leaguer," *Our Sports* (July 1953): 11–12 (Cronin), 64–65 in AMP, box 4; Curtis, "Factors That Affect the Attendance of a Major League Baseball Club," 41–42; *Jet*, July 17, 1958.

33. *PT*, August 18 (Collins), 1953; June 26, 1956; April 16, May 7, 1957; June 28, 1958; February 17, 1959; March 10, 13, 1962; Personal Contact Record, June Tuber, July 11, 1955 ("we don't"), Case No. 7-6-1406 (55). *Tuber v. Philad. National League Club*; "Report of Investigation" in Case No. 8-1-1739 (58) *Mahlon H. Duckett v. Philad. National League Club*, City of Philadelphia, Department of Records, City Archives, RG 148, Commission on Human Relations; *PINQ*, September 18, 1952; Chris Threston, "With All Deliberate Speed—The Slow Progress of the Integration of Philadelphia Baseball" (M.A. Thesis, Rutgers University, 1998).

34. *BAA*, September 24 (Lacy), 1949; April 21, December 8, 1951; February 23, 1952; January 31, April 11, October 24, 1953; September 11, 1954; November 19, 1955; *PC*, May 20, 1950; February 23, 1952; April 11, 1953; *PT*, December 4, 1951; April 12, May 27, June 17, 21, September 23, 1952; February 24, March 14, April 28, June 6, 27, 1953; *PI*, December 8, 1951; March 29, 1952; October 17, 1953; March 27, 1954; Smith, "Most Prejudiced Teams in Baseball"; *SN*, July 4, November 28, 1951; February 27, July 23, 1952; Spink, *Baseball Guide, 1953*, 99; *Negro History Bulletin* (February 1955); Collie Small, "Baseball's Improbable Imports," *SEP*, August 2, 1952; *Our World* (April 1953).

35. Gross, "Will the Yankees Hire a Negro Player?" 9–10, 58–59; *PT*, August 12, 29, October 17, 21, 24, 1950; October 9, 20, 1951; March 18, 1952; *BAA*, May 17, 1952; *NYAN*, April 24, 1954.

36. *PT*, April 29, December 2 ("it seems"), 9 (McCorry), 1952; February 14, 1953; Kahn, *Era*, 189; *BAA*, October 24, 1953; Gross, "Will the Yankees Hire a Negro Player?" 9–10 ("hire Negro"/Gross), 59; *PC*, December 13 (Smith), 1952; *NYT*, December 18 ("I have"), 1952.

37. "End of an Era for Negroes in Baseball," *Ebony*, June 1961; Drake and Cayton, *Black Metropolis*, 802–3. A subsequent study revealed that of the 984 American-born players who appeared in the major leagues between 1959 and 1963 and for whom biographical data were available, 11 percent were black. See "The Development of Major League Baseball Players in the United States 1959–1963," in PP, box 1, Player Development.

38. Jean Barth Toll and Mildred S. Gilliam, *Invisible Philadelphia: Community Through Voluntary Organizations* (Philadelphia, 1995), 775; Walker, *History of Black Business in America*, 254; Weems, *Black Business in the Black Metropolis*, 103–5; Leonard Broom and Norval D. Glenn, *Transformation of the Negro American* (New York, 1967), 140; Meier and Rudwick, *From Plantation to Ghetto*, 328; *NYAN*, November 7, 1953, January 30, February 6, 1954; Gamble, *Making a Place for Ourselves*, xi; Foley, "Negro Businessman," 106–44; *PINQ*, December 10, 1984; Andrea K. Walker, "Black-Owned Banks Struggle Against Times," *Baltimore Sun*, June 29, 2003. A recent attempt to establish a black-controlled bank in Philadelphia illustrates the continuing difficulties for black businesses. Founded in 1992 and half-funded by blacks, United Bank has been unable even to corner the African American market share after Philadelphia's larger financial institutions began to cater to inner-city customers later in the decade. On United, see Joseph N. DiStefano and Jennifer Lin,

"What Happened to Emma Chappell's Dream?" *Philadelphia Inquirer Magazine*, January 21, 2001, 16–21, 24.

39. Kenneth B. Clark, *Dark Ghetto: Dilemmas of Social Power*, 2nd ed. (1965; reprint Middletown, Conn., 1989), 177 (Clark); "A Victim of Negro Progress," *Newsweek*, August 26, 1963; Walker, *History of Black Business in America*, 353; Wolseley, *Black Press*, xvii, 80–81, 105, 350–51; *PINQ*, October 30, 1985; January 19, 1994; Maxwell Brooks, *The Negro Press Re-Examined: Political Content of Leading Negro Newspapers* (Boston, 1959), 105; Hogan, *Black National News Service*, 236; Henry Drewry and Humphrey Doermann in collaboration with Susan H. Anderson, *Stand and Prosper: Private Black Colleges and Their Students* (Princeton, N.J., 2001), 160–225. The two major black news agencies, the ANP and NNPA, also ceased operation by the late 1960s.

40. Harvard Sitkoff, *The Struggle for Black Equality, 1954–1980* (New York, 1992), 211–16; Arna Bontemps and Jack Conroy, *Anyplace But Here* (New York, 1968), 230; Foley, "Negro Businessman," 107; Gamble, *Making a Place for Ourselves*, 195; *SN*, April 14 (Johnson), 1997; *PINQ*, May 11, 1993 (Woods). Historian Diane Delores Tucker, for example, suggests that black musicians in Philadelphia gained little from the creation of an integrated union in 1971 and ultimately surrendered their "autonomy and identity" in the process. See Diane Delores Tucker, "Organizing and Improvising: A History of Philadelphia's Black Musicians' Protective Union Local 274, American Federation of Musicians" (Ph.D. thesis, Temple University, 1993), 298.

41. Frazier, "Human, All Too Human," 75 ("it is the"). In May 1952, Wendell Smith claimed there were at least 104 black players in Organized Baseball. By the end of the season, Doc Young placed the number at over 150. See *PC*, May 24, 1952; Young, *Great Negro Baseball Stars*, 222-25; John A. Harvey, "The Role of American Negroes in Organized Baseball" (Ed.D. thesis, Teachers College, Columbia University, 1960), 37.

42. *NYT*, September 12 (Ruck), 1988; Early, "Baseball and African American Life," 413 ("like a"); interview with Tom Johnson, June 23, 1998 ("the black"); Ruck, *Sandlot Seasons*, 206; Kusmer, "African Americans in the City," 460–68; John Hadley Strange, "Blacks and Philadelphia Politics, 1963–1966," in *Black Politics in Philadelphia*, ed. Miriam Ershkowitz and Joseph Zikmund, II (New York, 1973), 128; Franklin, *Education of Black Philadelphia*, 184–85; Foley, "Negro Businessman," 121; Robin Fields, "Census Fuels Debate over Integration," *Los Angeles Times*, June 24, 2001; Janny Scott, "Races Still Tend to Live Apart in New York, Census Shows," *NYT*, March 23, 2001; Massey and Denton, *American Apartheid*, 222–23. No black managed in the major leagues until the Cleveland Indians hired Frank Robinson prior to the 1975 season. Meanwhile, no black has gained complete control of a major professional baseball or football team, although a few African Americans have served as part-owners. In 2002, Robert L. Johnson, founder of Black Entertainment Television, was awarded an expansion franchise in Charlotte and became the first black owner in the NBA. See Walker, *History of Black Business in America*, 355; Kenneth Shropshire, *In Black and White: Race and Sports in America* (New York, 1996), 2–3, 178–79; *Philadelphia Inquirer*, December 19, 2002.

43. Leonard Shapiro, "Fewer Blacks Participate in Baseball," *Washington Post*, July 7, 1991, A1, A12; Brent Staples, "Where Are the Black Fans," *New York Times Magazine*, May 17, 1987; Daniel Cattau, "Baseball Strikes Out with Black Fans," *Chicago Reporter*, April 1991; Zoss and Bowman, *Diamonds in the Rough*, 192; Paul Domowitch, "The Seats Blacks Rarely Sit In," *PDN*, December 5, 1989; *SN*, February 19, 1977; June 22, 1978; Kelley, *Negro Leagues Revisited*, 145.

44. Tom Verducci, "Blackout," *Sports Illustrated*, July 7, 2003, 56–58, 61–62, 64

(Robinson), 66; *PT*, September 10, 1936; Early, "Baseball and African American Life," 416–17; Kuklick, *To Every Thing a Season*, 143–68; Gerald Early, "No Other Life," *Pennsylvania Gazette*, March–April 2001, 44–52; Domowitch, "The Seats Blacks Rarely Sit In"; *PINQ*, July 7, October 19, 1993, July 12, August 6, 2003 (Selig); *Philadelphia Daily News*, January 11, 1990; O'Neil, *I Was Right on Time*, 234; interview with Mahlon Duckett, July 2, 1998 (Duckett).

45. *NYA*, August 6 (Burley), 1949; Charles Hardy, "Race and Opportunity: Black Philadelphia During the Era of the Great Migration, 1916–1930" (Ph.D. thesis, Temple University, 1989), 368 (Hardy); Michael Lomax, "Black Baseball, Black Community, Black Entrepreneurs: History of the Negro National and Eastern Colored Leagues, 1880–1930" (Ph.D. thesis, Ohio State University, 1996), 329, cited in Jim Goldfarb, "Harlem's Team: The New York Lincoln Giants," seminar paper, Columbia University, 2000, 44; *CD*, August 7 (Young), 1954; interview with Tom Johnson, June 23, 1998 ("in the absence").

Index

Echevarría, Roberto González, 213
Edwards, Chick, 207
Elias Bureau, 142, 295
Elks, 272
Ellington, Duke, 132, 163
Elson, Bob, 221
End Jim Crow in Baseball Committee, 275, 276
Escalera, Nino, 389
Esquire, 228, 229
Estalella, Roberto, 213
Estrada, Oscar, 258
Estrellas Orientales, 62
Ethiopian Clowns, 107–10, 114, 121, 127–28, 137–38, 150, 151, 227, 228, 343, 356, 368, 370, 371, 374, 376–78, 381–84, 386, 455, 472, 475
Evans, Billy, 387

Fair Employment Practices Committee (FEPC), 97–98, 229, 231, 237, 250, 254, 262, 353, 450, 459
Farley, James, 262
Farrell, Dave, 279
Farrell, George, 351
Farrell, Jack, 35
Farm system, 158, 159
Fauset, Arthur Huff, 99, 115
Federal League, 215
Feller, Bob, 127
Fenway Park, 257, 446
Fernandez, Humberto "Chico," 389
Ferrell, Leroy, 356
Fields, Wilmer, 158, 163, 165
Fillmore, Joe, 368
Financial status of black baseball, 38, 49, 58, 66–68, 71, 72, 75, 84, 90, 93, 106, 110, 111, 116, 122, 126, 128, 139, 140, 147, 151–52, 156, 166, 173, 186, 188, 196, 199, 201–2, 237, 274, 287, 292, 293, 310, 317, 322, 328, 334, 338, 340, 348, 349, 353, 355, 357, 359, 366, 372, 374, 375, 378, 381–83, 386, 395, 396, 405, 412; expenses, 198–201; financial policies, 24, 198, 200, 437
Finger, Bill, 43, 167, 195
Florida International League, 369
Forbes, E. E., 158
Forbes Field, 12, 19, 52, 144, 146, 150, 168–69, 220, 235, 264, 303, 382, 423

Forbes, Frank, 101, 174, 176, 190, 307, 309, 317
Ford, Jim, 179
Forkins, Marty, 15
Foster, Andrew "Rube," 5, 9, 15, 14, 17, 19, 23, 58–59, 77, 79, 124, 142, 162, 173, 264, 426
Foster, Willie, 23
Four-team doubleheaders, 38, 50, 185
Frank, Jacob, 102
Frank, Stanley, 246
Franklin, C. A., 131–32
Frazier, E. Franklin, 302, 312, 393
Freedom's People, 231
Frick, Ford, 74, 212, 214, 218, 239, 240, 243, 281, 284–86, 310, 347, 427
Fuller, Jimmy, 154
Fuster, John, 241, 344, 353, 354

Gaines, Willie, 378, 379
Gale, Moe, 116
Gallagher, James, 234
Gamble, Vanessa, 305
Gant, Eddie, 94
Gardner, Chappy, 68
Garlington, S. W., 350, 364
Garner, Horace, 356
Garrett, Leonard, 143
Garrett, William, 148
Gasoline rationing, 128–29
Gay, Eustace, 103, 170, 304, 305, 450
Georgia State League 369
Gholston, Bert, 16, 19, 36–37, 68, 164, 175, 179
Gibson, Bill, 17, 18, 21, 27, 164, 210, 436
Gibson, Josh, 12, 61, 63, 65, 90, 91, 102, 127, 141, 144, 153, 163, 165, 167, 169, 177, 183, 192, 208, 220, 227, 234, 235, 237, 283, 310, 411, 441, 443
Gibson, Josh, Jr., 335
Giles, George, 86
Gilliam, Jim, 356
Glaser, Joe, 116
Glenn, Stanley, 155, 167, 202, 357, 368
Goodson, M. E., 15
Gottlieb, Eddie 9, 25, 28, 30–33, 35, 37, 58–59, 78, 83, 84, 87–90, 93, 100–102, 105, 106, 111, 112, 114–16, 120–22, 129, 139, 140, 144, 145, 148,